QUITE MAD

D0873015

MACHETE
Joy Castro, Series Editor

QUITE MAD

AN AMERICAN
PHARMA MEMOIR

Sarah Fawn Montgomery

MAD CREEK BOOKS, AN IMPRINT OF
THE OHIO STATE UNIVERSITY PRESS
COLUMBUS

Copyright © 2018 by The Ohio State University.
All rights reserved.
Mad Creek Books, an imprint of The Ohio State University Press.

Library of Congress Cataloging-in-Publication Data
Names: Montgomery, Sarah Fawn, author.
Title: Quite mad : an American pharma memoir / Sarah Fawn Montgomery.
Other titles: Machete.
Description: Columbus : Mad Creek Books, an imprint of The Ohio State
    University Press, [2018] | Series: Machete | Includes bibliographical
    references.
Identifiers: LCCN 2018009254 | ISBN 9780814254868 (pbk. ; alk. paper)
    | ISBN 0814254861 (pbk. ; alk. paper)
Subjects: LCSH: Mental illness—Treatment—United States—History. |
    Women—Mental health—United States. | Montgomery, Sarah Fawn—
    Mental health.
Classification: LCC RC443 .M66 2018 | DDC 362.196/8900973—dc23
LC record available at https://lccn.loc.gov/2018009254

Cover design by Amanda Weiss
Text design by Juliet Williams
Type set in Adobe Sabon LT Std

♾ The paper used in this publication meets the minimum requirements of
the American National Standard for Information Sciences—Permanence of
Paper for Printed Library Materials. ANSI Z39.48-1992.

For Brady,
who has created such a life
with me I sometimes believe it
the dreamy hallucination of our
strange, wonderful brains.

CONTENTS

ACKNOWLEDGMENTS

Grateful acknowledgment is made to the journals in which portions of this book first appeared: *The Normal School* and *The Rumpus*.

First, thank you to my parents, Karen and William Montgomery, whom I love more than all the fences and miles between us. I have always had many words—you remember the stories I told long into the night while sitting in your laps—but no matter how I try, I struggle to write how dear and how sweet you are to me. Still I try. These words, all my words, are for you.

Thank you to my siblings, Dale, Natalie, Candy, Casey, Cameron, Bailey, and Victoria, for sharing your lives and stories with our family and giving me permission to do the same in these pages. Our bond is forged through tears and years rather than bestowed by the convenience of blood. I am grateful for our mosaic brood.

To the fierce women I come from—grandmothers, aunts, cousins, sister-in-law—who are beautiful, not broken, and who have crafted a narrative I am proud will have me, even as I desire more and better for each of us. I admire your imperfection and contradiction in a world that so often denies these to women. You have made me a storyteller.

To Barbara and Chuck Wilbur, strangers who decided to love me before I was born and adopted me as their granddaughter. To be your friend and family for my entire life has taught me what it is to love unconditionally.

To the women that sustain me: Darcie Maffioli, Amanda Smith, Annie Bierman, and Natalie Montgomery. Thank you for listening, for laughter, and for the years of your fierce friendship.

To California State University–Fresno MFA and University of Nebraska–Lincoln PhD colleagues who kept me honest on the page, motivated me to work, and shared many a family-style meal and cocktail toast over the years. Cheers to you—especially Robert Lipscomb, Nick White, Mitch Hobza, Dan Froid, SJ Sindu, Jennifer Dean, Laura Dimmit, Nicole Green, Zachary Beare, Marianne Kunkel, and Hali Sofala, all of whom are wonderful professionals, but more important, wonderful people.

Education has always been a safe haven, and I thank the many teachers who have influenced both my writing and my sanity. To MFA mentors—Steven Church and Connie and John Hales—who gave their time, their encouragement, and their feedback as I was figuring out that I wanted to write, and still offer wisdom no matter how many years have passed since graduation. To PhD mentors Stacey Waite and Jonis Agee, who read early drafts of this book, Ted Kooser, who made me believe I could write poetry, and Kwame Dawes and the *Prairie Schooner* team, who make loving and sharing literature a way of life.

Thank you especially to Joy Castro, who mentors me as a writer, academic, and woman moving fearlessly in the world. The care and critique you gave my work shaped much more than this book, and there is no better home for this memoir than in the book series you edit to champion for others.

A heartfelt thank you to Kristen Elias Rowley and The Ohio State University Press team for making this story about the abstract reality of living with mental illness a tangible book I can hold in my hands and share with others.

And gratitude to the countless health care providers who have cared for my brain and body—medicine is a difficult art, and so many nurses, doctors, psychologists, and massage therapists make it their life's work to heal. I am grateful—so many patients are grateful—for your work.

Finally, to my small family. To Carson, Katinka, and Harvey, the companions with whom I am my most authentic self. Your devotion helps me navigate frightening times and sweetens the best.

And to Brady—a man of math and science and computer code, and the one I trust to read each draft. To you, of course and always.

PROLOGUE

I'm on my knees again, like I was an hour ago and the hour before that. Like I've been each day for the past few months since I first arrived here. *Here* is a large brick building in the middle of a college campus, in the middle of America. *Here* is where I am teaching and earning a PhD. *Here* makes people widen their eyes, impressed by the "Dr." they will eventually include before my name, but mostly by the way my job doesn't have nine-to-five hours or summers.

Here is also the third stall of a bathroom on the third floor where I run several times a day to throw up, shaking and sweating, my head spinning with thoughts of cancer or brain disease, thoughts that an asteroid is heading towards Earth, or that my cat was right when she looked at me funny this morning, stretched her paws, and told me today was the day I would die.

If I hear someone come in—esteemed professor of this, distinguished writer of that—I pause. I try to think really hard, to focus, to hold what little breath I have and bear down on my teeth and tense every muscle in my body. I pull myself in stiff like a reed. It's not that I don't want them to know I'm here—it's that if I don't hold taut and still, all dread and dead, eyes and mouth pinched shut, I won't be able to stop heaving and gasping. I won't be able to function as I should, won't be able to go about my day smiling and nodding. I won't be able to keep pretending.

The truth: I'm throwing up because this is what I do lately when I hear students outside, their voices interrupting one another, or planes overhead, sirens racing through the intersection, the professor in his office next to mine eating lunch, pop of lid, crunch of can, ringing telephone. This is what I do lately when I see the news—floods and famines, chemicals and cancers, children murdering their parents, parents murdering their children, all interrupted by celebrity gossip and lifestyle reports. Lately I throw up every time I leave the house. Sometimes I feel so sick I think the planes are going to bomb somewhere, think the sirens are racing for me like I don't know what's wrong yet, think the news reports are broadcasting warnings from the future. I think the neighbors I can hear fighting through the walls of my apartment might fire a gun and that the bullet might arc directly down into my skull, blazing across my sight with a white hot light. Fear tingles in my limbs like a premonition.

I have generalized anxiety disorder, which means I live a socially stigmatized existence ruled by chronic fear and worry, my stress over lack of sleep or bills or work twisting itself in my psyche until it manifests as constant distress, irritability, restlessness, catastrophic paranoia, and strange delusions.

Sometimes I have panic attacks, feelings of terror that come on suddenly, peaking within a few minutes, but whose symptoms—palpations and chest pain some liken to a heart attack, trembling and sweating, the feeling of being smothered or choked, nausea, lightheadedness, numbness and tingling, chills and hot flashes, the fear of losing control, the sense of impeding death, a detachment from reality and my body—last several hours and leave me with the lingering fear of having another attack, a worry that often brings on several more.

I was twenty-two the first time I had a panic attack. One night I took two ibuprofen and quickly became convinced I'd swallowed a handful. A burn enveloped my body, I lost my breath, my limbs went dead, and even though I felt trapped in the chaos, I also seemed to be floating above the scene, disconnected from the moment, powerless to stop whatever was seeping through me, building speed until it surged. I grew hysterical, pacing the house, hyperventilating and sweating, eventually cowering in a cold shower. Afraid to sleep after the attack, I spent much of the night retching and crying, gnarled fingers clutching at my unreliable heart. The attacks continued the next day and in the weeks after, building in frequency until I began experiencing them each night, waking up in a cold sweat unable to breathe, crying out as I clawed at my chest.

Ever since, I've had attacks that stem from mundane things—driving by a car accident causes catastrophic thoughts of my own mortality, a thunderstorm brings about thoughts of electrocution's fantastic fireworks making my body fluorescent, unusually sore muscles leads to thoughts of cancer creeping through my body like a blush. Coming up the stairs and finding myself out of breath triggers a fear that I'm having an attack, and my body follows suit. It's mostly miserable, irritatingly irrational, entirely inexplicable.

I'm afraid of dying a lot these days, so I retreat to bathrooms, bathtubs, the floor, trying to make the world disappear by focusing on the toilet, the shower stall, a bit of fuzz on the carpet. It's like I think that focusing intensely on some small detail will help me forget my fear of future destruction. But then again, focusing on tiny details—a cough, a bump on my shin I'd never noticed before—is how the madness starts in the first place.

These are the details I focus on now, here in the third stall of a bathroom on the third floor, in a building in the center of a college campus in the center of America: two graffiti messages and a picture etched into the stall's thick paint. Right next to the toilet is the phrase, *Every day is a gift,* and a little further down, tucked into the back corner of the stall, *He's watching. He knows. He's on your side,* and a drawing of the symbol for the female gender, a large circle atop a tiny cross. The symbol looks like a heavy head weighing down a tiny body. The letters are jagged, like whoever carved them into the stall's peach lacquer struggled to leave the mark, like the message took time, effort. Like the effort broke the pen.

As I lean over again to heave, averting my eyes from my pitiful reflection in the water of the toilet, I focus on the messages, trying hard not to wince at the idea of a gift, trying not to think about the fact that sometimes I know someone is watching, that he is a stalker or a murderer, or worse, that he is God telling me who will die, when, and how. He expects me to save them but gives no direction, so I try not to imagine what will happen when I am sent to eternal damnation for my failings.

Because I am prone to paranoia, reading messages into the simplest things, I'm convinced these etchings are meant for me. On good days they are glimmers of hope. They are painted secrets, a beautiful Lascaux. Of course, if every day of throwing up, dizziness and blurred vision, trembling hands and staggered heart is a gift, I'm not sure I want even one more. I've had nearly a year of these days. Much of the past year has been a waiting game—waiting for another panic attack to subside, waiting for the class I'm teaching to start, for the class I'm taking to finish, waiting for the day or the world to end so I can sleep and forget the overwhelming fear. I'm waiting for a doctor to understand this thing in my head, waiting for a medication to start working so I can be fixed. I'm waiting to find a medication that won't make me sicker.

My nausea and my dizziness and my scattered thoughts are some of the side effects from my medication—one designed to balance fear and coerce happiness, but that makes it so I don't feel like the same person anymore. Doctors have explained this to me many times. My brain is unstable, so I need medication. I need to take medication every day. I need to take medication for the rest of my life. They don't say it will take years of my trial, their error to find a medication that does not injure me. They don't say that many of the pills will make me feel even more unbalanced or that some will send me spiraling when I stop swallowing them. They don't say that some will leave me unconscious, as though my life is better spent asleep, that some will make my hair fall out, that some will leave me unable to orgasm, some will permanently change my vision, some will ignite a burning rage that leaves me clutching a butcher knife as I shout at my lover. Even though I am not in chains or an insulin coma, even though this is the 2000s and I am not lobotomized or Valium-comatose like a 1950s housewife, I am still wrong, dangerous, still not to be trusted. And I am not alone—the National Institute of Mental Health reports that 18.1 percent or 42 million Americans live with anxiety disorders, the largest prevalence of mental illness in the country (followed next by 6.9 percent or 16 million Americans with major depression). Though we are promised relief by contemporary medicine, we are still waiting—waiting for evidence, waiting for answers, waiting for proof that we in America have come a long way in our understanding of mental illness and our ability to control and cure the unstable.

The waiting game will continue for many years, as I bounce from medication to medication, searching for something that will make this madness fade, something that won't injure my body so much, something that will let me off my knees. No matter the drug, I will retreat to the same stall— anxiety is, after all, an illness of control—the meaning of the messages changing depending upon the chemical lens over my life. I'll read and reread these messages, even after a janitor tries to scrub the scratches out, leaving a cloudy mess blurring and distorting the phrases. Still I'll know the words are there under the tangle—the way he has tried to hide the mess, distract from what he cannot fix. I will know what they are saying to me, will see through the surface to what lies beneath. I won't tell anyone, of course, what I see, what I know. I'm crazy, after all. Who would believe me? Who would care about a tiny detail, a fixation, a message to a mad woman?

I finish throwing up and wipe my mouth. *He's watching. He knows.* I lean my forehead against the cool metal of the bathroom stall. *He's on your side.* I breathe slowly. One. Two. Three. *Every day is a gift.* I'm still shaking, still seeing flashes of darkness and decay out of the corners of my eyes. *Every day.* I open the door and head downstairs to teach a class to bright-eyed university students—a class, ironically enough, on critical thinking. Logic.

PART I

CHAPTER 1

THE INFLUENCE OF INTERVENTION

I am twenty-two the first time someone says, "I think you need medication." It is spring in California and I'm home from graduate school visiting my parents, their backyard filled with daffodils and the scent of overgrown lilacs. At the edge of the yard sits a multiroom shop that my father crafted using spare scraps of wood and limited time off from work. On one side my father keeps his motorcycle and every tool imaginable for building and fixing. In the middle is a storage room filled with boxes of discarded toys and too many holiday decorations, and a spare bedroom and bathroom for when visitors overflow out of the house. On the other side is a TV lounge full of hand-me-down recliners, a used pool table, and a bar. This is where my parents have parties and escape summer heat that climbs well past 100 degrees. My parents also come here to escape my seven siblings.

"Sissy," my father begins from his place behind the bar, closing the window curtains. This makes the wood-paneled room even darker, and though I can spy bits of sunlight and green grass around the curtains, hear my siblings laugh outside, I know this is serious. "You're stressed lately," he says, looking into his glass, then across the bar at my mother. My father rarely gets involved in the day-to-day activities of his children, but sets the tone for serious discussions with his no-nonsense frown. A construction man for over thirty years, he is used to ordering grown men around dangerous sites, and he brings this severity to family discussions.

"What Daddy means," my mother steps in, rattling the ice in her glass and turning in her bar stool to face me, hunched over and quiet in mine, "is that like the rest of the family, you're going to need medication."

What my mother means is that she and my father have taken the same medication—Celexa—for many years and they anticipate I'll need to do the same. The reason for this, however, is unclear. In his sixties, my father was initially prescribed Celexa for headaches but found the drug helped with the stress he secretly harbored, stress that kept him up each night worrying over how to provide for his growing family, how to endure the long commute and long hours of his construction job, how to convince his tired body and brain to labor through each day when he had been feeling so poorly lately. A few months later, doctors discovered pituitary tumors that altered the endocrine gland responsible for secreting hormones that create stability in the body. After several surgeries removed the tumors, my father remained on Celexa, growing sullen and short-tempered. "Daddy needs to take his happy pills," my siblings joke when he grows angry, angrier by the laughter, and while we don't understand what the pills do inside his large, muscled, work-weary body, we do notice when he stops taking them, as he does sometimes when the bottle runs out and he forgets to pick up a refill, or when he grows tired of doctors insisting he will always need the little white pills.

I know even less about why my mother takes the drug. Her orange bottle sits on top of her medicine cabinet, out of sight from my younger siblings, who are no match for my mother's six-foot-one stature, and probably don't realize she takes anything at all to enhance her mood or calm her nerves. Years after the intervention, I will ask my mother why she takes pills and she'll admit she has had panic attacks for several decades, moments where she gets overwhelmed by work and life—"It always happens at the end of the week," she laughs, as though the body shutting down is a sign of a job well done. When I press her for a timeline, she admits that she began taking Celexa shortly after adopting twins, though she is quick to say that the difficult transition period had nothing do with the prescription. Now though, I am hardly aware she takes the pills. Like my young siblings, I've barely noticed them on top of her medicine cabinet. They seem as natural and innocent as her toothbrush.

My older brother, too, has taken a similar medication since his suicide attempt at sixteen. I was an infant when he loaded our father's gun and shot himself clean through the abdomen, leaving my young parents confused and financially avalanched by the hospital bill. A thick keloid, puffy across his stomach, is the only reminder—my mother told me the story once when I was curious about the scar, but my father has never spoken about it to me. My other siblings do not know and my brother has never acknowledged it, as though it's some long-forgotten memory, a secret moment of madness.

My grandmother was also prescribed antidepressants prior to her death, doctors giving her samples of Zoloft to combat the natural fatigue and lethargy of old age. The medication, doctors assured, would perk up her remaining years, even though well into her eighties, battling a failing heart and lung cancer, this hardly seemed natural. Unlike my parents and brother, my grandmother took the pills until the samples ran out, then shrugged and said she never noticed a difference and she was perky enough thank you very much.

I'm not sure if my parents have planned or rehearsed our conversation. I do know, however, that while medication seems unnecessary, the way my parents are speaking to me—in hushed tones, worry stretched tight across their faces—is unusual. With eight children, my parents rarely have one-on-one time with anyone. Consoling ill children seldom happens, dwelling on pain a waste of energy, sickness a burden for individuals to bear. This kind of attention is usually reserved for punishing poor behavior.

Sixteen years older than me, my half-brother, Dale, was born when my father was seventeen, and seems closer to my father's age than to the rest of the children, so I am often referred to as the oldest child. As such, I have been raised to obey rules, follow directions, and succeed. Much of the stress my parents are referring to now comes as I wait to hear back about PhD applications. As both a high school and college senior I was able to choose among all of the colleges I applied to, many with full scholarships. After graduating with my bachelor's degree early, I've moved through a master's degree just as quickly and am now looking towards doctoral programs across the country, waiting to see if I will make my parents proud.

Neither of my parents went to college and much of my life has been built on the notion that higher education is essential to move beyond our working-class identity. Living fifteen minutes outside the nearest town, I commuted several towns away to a school where kids turned up their noses at my thrift-store clothes and announced that my daddy was their construction man, building fences around their tennis courts and horse stables, so covered in dirt and cement from his work that he couldn't come inside the house to use the bathroom. Why did I live so far away, they asked, in a town full of immigrants? Did I speak Spanish like the men my father worked with? Why wasn't I allowed to go to movies? Did I really not have money for an after-school soda?

The pressure increased as my family grew. When I was seven, my mother gave birth to my sister, Natalie, and a few years later my parents decided to adopt—a decision that over the years added five more children to our family.

The first adoption happened when I was in middle school, my parents moving two-year-old twins into our small house.

Both had experienced severe abuse, the social worker said, which made them aggressive and cold. Years later, when I was in college, my parents added two more to our family, two- and three-year-old boys from even more abusive backgrounds with a range of other health challenges, including asthma, ADHD, OCD, and Tourette's. When I was in graduate school, my parents adopted a fifteen-year-old girl who was emancipated from her family and undergoing intense legal battles. Each time my parents added to our family, the lengthy adoption process and the kids' difficulties reinforced my need to behave, to succeed. "We need you to listen," my parents chorused. "They've had a hard time. There's no reason for you to act up."

Now I twist silently on the bar stool, embarrassed I've let them down. They shouldn't have to worry about me. As my mother tells me she is concerned, that I seem worn out from long hours, something outside hits the window and my father goes to see what the trouble is, his mouth firm beneath his mustache. My younger siblings have been known to break limbs and start small fires, and even the teenagers can't be left alone too long without breaking toilets and refrigerators, without getting caught vandalizing or suspended from school. Interruptions like these are not uncommon around here.

"You're too thin," my mother adds, looking at me. "You need to remember to eat." This is something I've heard before. As a five-foot-ten college undergraduate, I dropped dangerously close to 100 pounds, and my parents saw my hollow smile and counted the vertebrae in my rigid spine when I came home weekends, completing my work and helping my siblings with their homework instead of going to parties with my peers, who skipped class to tan at the beach.

"Do you have a hard time sleeping at night?" my father asks when he returns, disaster averted outside. "Do you think about all the things you have to do?" I don't struggle to sleep, instead find it a welcome luxury each night, but I do make a lengthy list each morning of the things I need to accomplish, focusing on this list throughout the day, making my way through the hours and my life by making my way through the tasks. This is something most of my coworkers do, I explain to my parents, something that allows for productivity and performance. The university I attend and where I teach hands out "To Do" notepads at the start of each academic year.

"Do you have an upset stomach?" my parents continue. "Do you feel overworked?"

The truth is that I don't feel the way they are describing. I feel like I always do. I feel tired but motivated. I feel overwhelmed but capable. I feel stretched thin, but isn't that the point? I feel stressful but successful, except for when I feel like a failure. I change my mind about this daily. This doesn't seem out of the ordinary, though. This feels like how I am, how my coworkers are, how anyone with a successful job in the United States feels. I tell them this, but they insist to me again and again they are worried, that there is something wrong with me, that I need to seriously consider medication.

My biological family members aren't the only ones medicated. Each of my adopted siblings has or will take various medications for mood and personality, their mental illnesses the result of poor parenting, violence, and instability. Discarded from foster home to foster home, my brother Bailey's arm was snapped in half when he was two, and his brother Cameron's spine is scarred where their biological father put out the smoldering ash of his cigarettes. Infant and toddler assaults they don't remember show up in their night terrors and the ways they play—stringing up action figures and dolls as though to hang them, trying to kill small animals, saying "God wants them to die," with knowing smiles at two and three years old. It is expected they will suffer—social workers warned us.

But I'm not adopted. I don't share this abuse record or these scars. The way my parents talk about my internalizing stress and hyper-focusing, it seems as though I am responsible for my issues. It seems as though I am to blame.

"You have anxiety," my parents insist, looking worried, but also as though they knew they would need to give this speech. "You need to go to a doctor."

At first I protest, confident in my ability to persuade—I medaled in state speech and debate competitions, I teach persuasive writing at a respected university. I speak slowly and clearly. I make eye contact and use body language. I provide specific points of refutation, examples to illustrate my main points, appropriate analysis to explain the connections. They wait for me to finish speaking, raising their eyebrows and shaking their heads. This kind of conversation is new to me—I can think of many times my parents have sat down like this with my siblings, but I don't remember any of these conversations directed towards me. I feel embarrassed and ashamed, like I've done something wrong. I stare through the curtains at those brief flashes of green, the sounds of my siblings' shrieks backdropping my parents' warnings, and wish I'd stayed at my apartment to finish some work, instead of following my parents' suggestion I make the long drive home to relax.

It seems I am on a projected course to collide with medication. Everyone in my family is medicated. Nearly everyone I know takes or has taken antidepressants. Much of America takes psychopharmaceuticals—one in six; white Americans twice as likely to take medications and take them long term.[1] The contradiction in what my parents are saying—on the one hand, this is expected, one the other hand, something is very wrong—is American. Obsessed with mental health, America labels mental illness both imaginary and epidemic.

What strikes me, years later, is the way both my parents and I refused to acknowledge any middle ground. As far as I was concerned, I was fine, my behavior nothing to be questioned or corrected. I didn't feel wrong and balked at the suggestion I might not be myself. And as far as they were concerned, there was something terribly amiss. I had changed, they insisted. I was different, a new person sitting in front of them. Neither party could admit that maybe it was more complicated, that maybe I'd always been a bit anxious, that the shift wasn't sudden, but built over time, certain traits amplified by circumstance until I became a caricature—my anxious tendencies oversimplified and exaggerated so they became the most prominent feature in the picture. No matter how I tried to explain that I was being myself, that I wasn't unhappy, my parents insisted I was wrong, that whatever it was I was thinking or feeling was false. This was the first time I heard mention of the binary between me and my illness. It would not be the last.

The binary that exists in our understanding of mental illness is one that pits the self against the disorder, the individual against their own body and mind, as though those who suffer from anxiety or depression or OCD are not themselves, as though the disorder has taken over their spirit, as though the self has been split. "Bipolar" suggests this rift, as does the word "schizophrenia," whose Greek etymology means "to split" mental functions, but whose mental state and symptoms have nothing to do with splitting. While encouraged to take medication in order to "get back to normal," individuals feel normal already, their fears or sadness, their highs and hallucinations a part of their lived and emotional experience, their reality. An accusation of abnormality feels instead like an accusation against inherent selfness.

"You have anxiety," my parents repeat, opening the curtains to signal our conversation has come to an end and I am to follow directions. "You need to take care of this or else it is going to get worse."

Weeks later, my parents' predictions come true.

CHAPTER 2

THE SICK ROLE

*A*fter I was labeled anxious, I was unable to exist any other way. Medical institutions have incredible transformative power over patients: a patient is renamed after diagnosis, their experience redefined by the new label. Now, many years later, my family still refers to me by way of my illness. "You seem anxious," they say when I greet them after months or years apart. Or, "You look better." I now live on the East Coast, my husband and I and our tiny family as happy as we could have ever hoped, and still those who know I have anxiety view me as always on the verge of collapse, forever anxious no matter how I laugh with my toes in the sea, breathe content at my family sleeping late in Sunday sun. I cannot escape diagnosis or remove anxiety as the lens through which others view my life.

First described in Talcott Parsons's 1951 *The Social System*, the "sick role" requires patients to participate in particular social scripts, enacting the social roles associated with their illnesses. Traditional social roles are undermined by the limitations of the disease, but also by the expectations associated with being a patient. For example, if someone has the flu, they are allowed to forego normal responsibilities and expected to stay home from work until they are well. If someone has anxiety, they are allowed to focus their efforts on relaxing. Both are expected to succeed. The sick role requires me to present myself as patient over person.

These scripts are appealing to patients because they release them from ordinary social obligations—I could put off studying to relax, my parents urged, I could cancel classes to get more sleep—but they are dangerous in the ways they control and limit bodily and human experience. *A sick person shouldn't do that,* goes traditional wisdom, which insists "good" patients seek medical treatment and comply with all orders. When I was initially diagnosed, the sick role seemed a relief, but much of what I was expected to do—lie down alone during a panic attack, keep quiet about paranoia so as not to indulge it, not disturb others with my worries—was behavior modification enforced by the healthy world in order to ensure their own comfort.

Patients are free from blame so long as they comply with what is expected. But if a person with the flu does not stay home, he is blamed for not taking better care of himself and exposing others to the illness. If a person ordered by her parents to relax does not slow down from her steady work routine, she is blamed when she breaks down. While patients might not be at fault for having the illness, they are responsible for getting better.

I did not get better.

We take for granted that people know how to be sick, but it is learned behavior. We teach children how to be sick from an early age: no school, plenty of TV, and Gatorade or ginger ale because a spoonful of sugar makes the medicine go down. We believe someone with the flu should stay home from work because we have been taught not to compromise others, much as we have been taught that people who are obese should implement exercise routines, diabetics should not eat sweets, those with lung cancer should stop smoking, and those with stress-related illnesses should do whatever it takes to just calm down and stop bothering everyone else with their worry. These orders require patients with stress-related illnesses to amend their regular roles, implying that which is deeply ingrained is somehow unnatural, suggesting patients themselves are somehow wrong.

The sick role is complicated further by self-fulfilling prophecy. Tell a cancer patient her cancer is curable and she is more likely to improve. Give the same patient a different prognosis—her cancer is terminal and she only has a few weeks to live—and there is a far greater likelihood that her health will deteriorate. Tell a patient his depression is temporary and it likely will be, but tell the same patient his depression is chronic and it often becomes so. Symptoms are amplified by cultural expectations and personal beliefs, ideas about the cause and course of an illness influencing the shape it takes. The ways we talk about illness impact patients, the care they receive, and what we believe to be true about the illnesses themselves. While my parents were certain I had anxiety or worried I would develop it, it was their insistence something was wrong with me that amplified my fear and my belief in the illness's power.

This is not to say that the simple act of my parents suggesting I had anxiety caused me to develop it, but there was certainly a change in my behavior and the way I thought about my mental health in the weeks that followed. During the intervention, I know my parents are wrong. After I return home, however, I can't forget what they said. I begin to lie awake at night thinking about my father's questions— *Do you have a hard time sleeping?* I think about my parents' questions about stomachaches, fixating on my stomach in the process. When I worry about a deadline, I hear them ask—*Do you feel overworked?* The self-scrutiny is exhausting, and I sense they might be right. Weeks pass this way, and while spending so much time thinking about these symptoms doesn't suddenly make them appear, my mental gauge shifts. I question myself. I doubt.

Prior to the intervention I'd had one panic attack, but after I begin to panic every few days, then daily, then several times a day. My early panic was not performative—it would take me years to learn to lecture in front of thirty students while enduring an attack, to smile to strangers at parties while my heart raced, to sit through a flight gasping for breath quietly enough so as not to attract attention.

During that first panic attack I was at my partner, Brady's, house, a year into our relationship. We'd been dating long-distance, Brady driving several hours from the city where we'd been friends in college to the city where I was attending graduate school. A large, laid-back man who spent his days in cargo shorts and flip-flops, his hair gelled into a tragic fauxhawk, Brady was my opposite in nearly every way. While I'd graduated early, fussing over assignments and taking careful notes, Brady stretched his undergraduate experience past its expiration date, completing assignments in the early morning hours before classes or skipping them to go to the beach. While I planned ahead, made careful lists, consulted rules, Brady liked to wing it, laughing as he repeated his mantra, "It is what it is." I was a stingy lover, careful with my heart—I said "I love you" after five years together—but Brady doted on me, showering me with affection and persistence, insisting, despite my protests, he accompany me when I moved out of state to pursue my PhD.

I first panicked while watching the pilot episode of a television show whose opening five minutes feature soldiers taking cover from spaceship gunfire while twangy cowboy music plays in the background. There is little overt violence and no established tension, mostly sci-fi nostalgia and camp. Still, within minutes I felt something descend on me like a terrible cloud. The darkness swept with speed, sucking oxygen from the room. Despite the ocean breeze coming from the open windows, I broke out in a sweat. My limbs twitched, my mouth pursed without permission. I sat up on the edge of the couch. I tried to hold still. When I couldn't, I left to pace in Brady's room, closing the door gently behind me.

My heart staggered and I struggled to breathe. The weight of existing was too much, so I cried out and flapped my hands like wings to try and fly from this body and moment. I moaned and flailed and the world went dark. Brady checked on me moments later, but it felt like forever, and by then I was alternating between curling into a comma to pause the clause and darting around his room to exclaim the pain. I whimpered, I wailed. I tore the clothes from my body because the fabric was suffocating and a weapon. I crouched in the shower, afraid and embarrassed to be acting so feral, what with Brady's roommate in the living room.

When I dried off and dressed again I stretched a smile over my face and opened the door. "I don't know what happened," I laughed, trying to brush off my discomfort. "I didn't feel well for a minute." We restarted the show and as the music began to swell again, so did the fear. (This happened each time I tried to watch the show throughout the next decade, each viewing triggering an attack, anxiety a learned response after all, one that hardwires into the brain and body.)

That night I struggled to feel safe in my skeleton. Brady stayed awake with me as I monitored my heart, my breathing, my body, my brain. I called my mother, who confirmed it was a panic attack, mentioning casually that she'd had them before telling me, "Don't get hysterical." Despite their reassurance, existing was unbearable—non-anxious people underestimate what it takes to simply be, to rest in the cage of your body. The tremendous effort ease requires.

I did not have another panic attack during the following months, but after my parents press me, panic becomes routine. It is as if they have triggered the "on" button. Things change entirely. I can't sleep. I do have a stomachache. Even though I love my work, I start to feel strained. I grow exhausted from staying up all night, develop aches from holding my stomach muscles tense, can't read for pleasure anymore without thinking that perhaps I should relax some other way. My parents seem pleased when I admit they are right.

I go further than they expect, though. I catastrophize. Convinced I have cancer, I feel a lump in my breast so roughly I leave bruises. I think my increasing headaches aneurisms. I become afraid pesticides linger on my vegetables and I retch at the metallic taste, unable to eat. My limbs become strangers, for though I am paying closer attention to their movement than ever before, their motions feel strange and unnatural. I am out of sync, out of rhythm, lurching and hobbling, jarred, erratic. I am broken. I perch on the edge of terror most of the time, unable to catch my breath or settle into my skin, pulsing electric like I've been frightened or injured, helpless and humming, thanks to that rush of adrenaline that comes when we avoid disaster.

I begin to see things. One day my kitten predicts my demise by looking at me and yawning. Another day she winks as if to let me know my sister will die in a car wreck on the side of a dusty highway, sun glinting off twisted metal and shattered glass.

I become afraid to drive. One rainy day Brady and I head out for lunch, but I know we are going to skid through an intersection and collide in a fiery crash. I watch this play out through the window and in this moment I realize I can predict the future. (This superhuman quality will follow me for years. I will see cancer before it strikes, know a friend will die prematurely and hold that truth close to myself. I will hear God speak to me, know in my gut and heart that he exists and is going to punish us. I will see disaster on a colossal level—galaxies spinning uncontrolled, solar flares gone awry. I will believe the 2012 apocalypse true, my life a countdown to the disaster when Planet X, kept quiet through government conspiracy, makes its way from behind the sun. I will want to shout and tell people what I see, but know they won't listen, will think me some muttering madwoman, like the homeless women on the corner Brady drives by in the rain, never noticing that their cardboard signs warn of the very things I see.)

The storm is in full force when we arrive at the restaurant and I feel dizzy and sick and afraid to eat. I roll broccoli around on my plate with a chopstick and watch out the window. I am hot and sticky but afraid to press my forehead against the cool glass—the rain splats as though it's aiming fast and sharp for my face. Later that night, we watch the animated movie Brady has rented to cheer me up, a movie where a misunderstood penguin leaves the isolation of Antarctica to surf in a sunny Hawaiian community. I can barely get through the film, thinking of drowning, flinching each time the animated camera descends underwater. When Brady goes into the kitchen to cut up some fruit, all I can focus on is the blade's gleaming edge.

I leave the living room and the movie, the dancing birds and celebrity voices, and lie down in the darkness of my bedroom. Even though I have moved farther from the kitchen and the knife in Brady's hands, the thoughts come with me, hovering over my head. I imagine Brady stabbing me over and over. I see my own hands on the knife and worry that while cooking my hands will turn against me. I end the night diving like the cartoon penguins to hide in my bedsheets.

Soon I am having panic attacks every night, waking up from sleep choking for breath in the dark, bolting out of bed to pace the house with my hand over my heart, my body fighting me even in sleep. The attacks increase in frequency and duration, something not uncommon with mental illness. Anxiety attacks, depressive periods, bipolar swings, and schizophrenic episodes are a learned response—the more patients have, the more likely they are to increase over a lifetime, getting more frequent and more severe. Studies that induce seizures in animals show that eventually seizures become automatic, animals seizing even when the stimulation is removed. Our bodies are the same—my body is learning to panic.

Shopping for groceries becomes unbearable because people palm fruit after coughing and I cannot put my hand in bins of poison apples. I can't eat them either; meals become a bargaining. I have difficulty going up or down stairs because my ankles bend like elastic and I tumble over myself. If I go outside, germs glint in sunlight.

I am finishing my master's thesis when my hands go numb, tingling and fuzzy so that it is difficult to grip, touch, exert enough pressure for a keyboard. The feeling moves past my wrists, to my elbows, currents running electric along the lengths of my limbs. Friends who don't know I am terrified and delusional insist my tingling hands are carpal tunnel from hunching over a keyboard, so I start wearing a brace, my hands aching from what I pretend is too much typing, but is actually adrenaline racing through my body. I carry my arm around like a broken wing, my brace signaling to those who see me that I have a physical illness—a real, visible illness—but signaling to my increasingly worried family that it's all in my head. When my feet go numb, the dead ache creeping to my knees, I struggle to walk, a stitched-together Frankenstein from a dozen rotting parts.

At my worst I am a fearful, shaking wreck. I do not want to leave the house. When I manage to leave I only make it a few blocks away before throwing up on the side of the road. One of my favorite writers is coming to campus and I've been asked to introduce him, but I throw up each time I practice. Then I begin to black out, crumpling into the floor and a field of stars. I decline at the last minute; the shame I feel is very heavy.

I am afraid of my muscles and bones and I avoid moving my body. I spend long, lonely hours in the bathtub. Hot water helps with the tingling and the soreness from trying not to move. Underwater I feel all right, enclosed in my water bubble so nothing can harm me. I pass my days like this, eventually only able to bathe because water from the shower pounding on my head is too much.

CHAPTER 3

NATURE OR NURTURE

I was a fearful child. You surely guessed as much. Sleeping alone in my room, I'd dream fire sparking bright behind my closed lids, cloying smoke pressing down on my small bed. Half sleeping, half awake, I'd watch flames crowd the dark house, snaking up the hallway separating me from my parents' room across the hall. I'd choke and cry out, sobbing for my parents to come and save me. Taking turns, they'd try to soothe me back to sleep, brushing my hair from my face, resting a steady hand on my chest, my heart in their palm. I tried to reason with them, to tell them what my elementary school fire drill had said about house fires and electric blankets, wall heaters and carelessness. They acquiesced as long as they could—I do not fault them for growing tired—but eventually grew frustrated, irritated at my imagination, turning their backs and off the lights.

I would lie awake as long as I could, the glow from my mother's reading lamp casting a path towards my door, before tiptoeing to their room several times each night to ask if I could sleep on the floor, where the lamplight swept over my face and I could hear the rustle of my mother's book pages. I slept in my parents' room so often I can still see the pattern on their mattress—a winged staff circled by serpents. I would trace the image with my fingers and then my eyes after my mother told me to hold still, and eventually drift to sleep, dreaming sometimes of angels, but mostly of serpents.

I slept in their room each weekend and holidays, nestled in my bed on the floor, secure under the weight of my sleeping bag, surrounded by stuffed animals and books. When my baby sister Natalie was old enough she joined the ritual, the two of us uniting in protest if our parents so much as hinted that we sleep in our own rooms. But eventually they announced I was too old and Natalie carried on without me.

This was around the time girls at school organized weekend sleepovers with shimmying and shrieking until late into the night. I hated these—the crowds, the compulsion to talk terribly about the girls who weren't invited, to try and hoist one another up by our fingertips, the smallest, lightest girls rewarded, while tall girls like me held our breath and prayed to be light as a feather. Still, I did not want to be left out. I usually made it through pizza dinners and cake if it was someone's birthday, through movies and makeovers, truth or dare, though I was always afraid someone would ask me to break the rules, which I wouldn't.

Sometime between when we crawled into our sleeping bags and when the whispering stopped is when the panic set in. I couldn't stand the sound of so much breathing, the way it came from all directions, rhythms overlapping and out of sync. The sounds stifled me with discordance and I'd lie awake alone. Eventually the panic about not being able to sleep would turn into resolve to stay awake and I'd fixate on electronics lights, the sound of water in the pipes, the whir of the air conditioner, anything to keep me awake. I don't remember what I thought might happen if I fell asleep, but each time I'd crescendo to a panic, then creep into the rooms of parents, sniffling and ashamed, asking them to please call my parents. Often they'd refuse, try to cajole me into staying a bit longer, promising pancakes in the morning, more soda even, if I'd let them go back to sleep. Many times my fear angered them. Stubborn as I was, I balked at their authority, demanding through my tears they contact my parents, who lived thirty minutes away in the zip code we could afford. Eventually, they'd acquiesce, sighing at me for the inconvenience and letting me call my parents, who would sigh too, but nonetheless rise in the dark to come retrieve me. I felt better as soon as I knew they were on their way, chattering at disgruntled host parents until my parents arrived, waving gleefully at the other children forced to remain until morning. On the way home my parents would sometimes stop for Denny's, nestling me in the booth between them as the sun came up over my smiley face pancakes.

Perhaps my fear had the volume turned up or seemed abnormal to the parents of outgoing children made fearless by social class, but looking back, there seems to be no reason for alarm. My shyness was as much a part of me as my love of reading or desire to be a ballerina despite a contentious relationship with rhythm. I only felt shame over my caution when others pointed it out. Though taxing to others, what harm was there in letting me go for pizza and cake and then bringing me home before the sleepover? Calling attention to my feelings and insisting me different seemed like poking a bruise, watching it spread, and then wondering why.

Recently a friend voiced concern because her child's preschool pulled her aside to say her son was "too particular" about toys. "They think he might have OCD," she said, and I recognized the impact of intervention, the doubt skirting her face. At what point did we begin to pathologize play? When did imagination become suspect? What is most enviable about innocence is its individuality—children say whatever comes to mind, free, for at least a few years, from the self-consciousness brought on by social norms—yet our search for abnormality increases along with mental illness rates for children and prescribing patterns for everything from hyperactivity to shyness. "I have issues with depression," she admitted. "But what if it's the way we're raising him?"

The question of whether mental illness derives from the nature of a person or the nurture (or lack thereof) they receive from their environment is hardly a new one. Alfred, Lord Tennyson described his family's legacy of insanity as "black blood"—his father had a long history of mental instability, several brothers were confined to asylums, and each of the eleven children who reached adulthood suffered from at least one mental breakdown during the course of their lives. The specter of mental illness plagued Tennyson for much of his life, a mental anguish as real as the perceived threat. I can trace anxiety through the women in my family tree, branches tangled with apprehension, just as I can trace alcoholism through the men, a sad desperation clutching at their throats. I've grown accustomed to my anxiety by now, but the fear of alcoholism looms large—as I've aged, alcohol leads more frequently to heaviness in my heart, a pervasive sorrow I know generations of my family have felt before.

My biological sister Natalie and I have a running joke that no matter how many miles separate us—currently over 3,000—we will end up with the same haircut, same soft slouchy sweater, same penchant for music, for cream tea and pad thai. Our tastes and talents run parallel despite the distance in a way that illustrates the bond of blood. Our mental health is the same—we suffer the same strange fears, though Natalie, by way of her younger sister status, has my brain to lead the way. I'm able to warn her about what is coming—fear of cancer-causing deodorant, for example—years ahead of time. Our anxiety, in these moments, is genetic, coursing through our veins as much as our taste for old films or feline friends.

But mental health may not be purely genetic; it may also be environmental. The way a being is nurtured during early childhood can have a great impact later in life. During the

1950s and '60s, Harry Harlow conducted a series of now-famous experiments during which he separated infant rhesus monkeys from their mothers to see how they would psychologically respond. Infant monkeys were raised with surrogate mothers made either of heavy wire mesh or foam rubber and soft terry cloth. Infants clung to soft mothers, even when wire mothers provided nourishment or heat, running to cloth mothers when frightening objects were placed in the cage, and curling up next to them even when there was no present danger. Infants with cloth mothers were more likely to explore, take risks, and play, while those whose only option was cold wire mothers were timid and anxious.

Some infant monkeys were raised without contact altogether, kept in isolation for a period of months up to a year. As adults, monkeys who had been isolated during childhood compulsively clutched themselves, rocking back and forth. They huddled in corners and hunched in fear around "normal" monkeys. They were afraid and agitated, unable to form attachments, or sexually bond. Female monkeys who had been isolated were unable to care for their offspring, refusing to comfort, protect, or nurse their infants, even smashing their infants onto the floor.

The theory of attachment suggests that children who do not have a nurturing environment—physical necessities like food, safety, and warmth, along with emotional ones like love and acceptance—exhibit long-term psychological impacts. Monkeys separated from their mothers in infancy had permanently increased levels of the stress hormone cortisol and grew up with physiologically different brains. Even monkeys raised with cloth mothers for longer periods of time had more difficult social interactions later on, timid, shy, and easily bullied. Monkeys raised in isolation exhibited visible fear, compulsive behavior, violence, and self-harm. Those kept in isolation for the longest were unable to recover.

The studies, however questionable in their animal ethics, also concluded there is a critical period of childhood during which maternal deprivation is most essential—infants deprived during this time could not reverse the emotional damage no matter the treatment.[2]

I was especially afraid to be without my mother; in her absence, loneliness led to terror. When I accompanied her to the preschool where she worked, I refused to stay outside with the other children when she went inside to lay out the nap beds. I'd grow agitated as the sun climbed overhead, asking my mother how soon until she needed to go inside. And though the other teachers tried to hold me at their sides, scolding me for "not being a big girl" and then shaming me by asking, "Why won't you stay with me? Don't you like me?" I'd sneak away as soon as they turned the other way, running across the seemingly endless lawn and inside to my mother, who let me help her, smiling and sighing at my big, needy love.

But this grew tiresome. In middle school I was so shy I could not leave the car when my mother dropped me off early in order to get to work on time. I was so lonely sitting on the bench in the morning mist waiting for other students to arrive that my fear grew into paranoia. I felt the pointed headlights of each minivan spotlighting my awkward height, flat chest, the unruly teeth my parents could not afford to wrangle into braces. Twisting with shame from the imagined inspection, my stomach would lurch, my shoulders aching from trying to slouch into disappearance. Eventually I refused to leave the car and my mother shouted at me, exasperated by my fear.

"What's wrong with you?" she'd ask. "This is ridiculous."

"I don't want to. I can't," I'd plead, offering little more because I knew what she really meant was that *I* was ridiculous.

Her frustration grew exponentially after we adopted the twins the spring of my first year in middle school. "I don't have time for this," she'd sigh, pursing her lips at me.

"Even the twins don't do this and look at what they've been through," she'd offer as proof, shaking her head at my disobedience. Sometimes she slammed her hand on the back of my seat, her disapproval ricocheting. "You're doing this on purpose."

Still, I would wait until a friend came to chaperone me from the car.

When acceptance letters arrived from each of the universities to which I applied during my senior year of high school, I was overwhelmed by choice. Driving the length of California to visit the schools, my stomach tangled the farther we ventured away from home. We hadn't thought to book any tours, hesitated, even, to enter the sprawling buildings with their golden plaques. That I might gain access seemed a separation from my family, and in the weeks leading up to my decision I cried and cried, seeking solace in my mother's lap.

Though I'd received generous scholarships to most schools, I ultimately decided to go to a university forty-five minutes away, the only school from which I'd neglected to pursue scholarships, so sure I had been that I was leaving. The day my parents dropped me off, unpacked my belongings into the dorm room, remarking on how it was just like kids going to college in the movies, I swooned with heartsickness and begged them to take me back home for one more night. We returned the next morning, and as I watched them leave it felt like I was abandoning them. Natalie and the twins were fastened neatly in the van and my parents filled the rest of the seats with new children the following year.

I do not mean to suggest my parents are cruel. If anything, they are too kind. My parents have adopted four children from a foster care system that struggles to find homes for abused children and sibling groups. They have adopted a homeless emancipated teen. They've housed foster children, children who have been thrown out by their parents, children whose parents need an evening, a weekend, a week to themselves.

They've also housed adults in need. The daughter of an old friend and her young child lived with us for six months when I was in high school. My father's homeless coworker lived with us for a year when I was in college. While I was working on my PhD, a mother and her three children moved in for six months shortly after her divorce. My mother's alcoholic brother has lived off and on with my parents for the last several years.

My mother also runs a home daycare for low-income families and charges a minimal rate, sometimes forgoing tuition altogether if a family can't pay. She watches children extra hours and on the weekends. She lets the children spend the night free of charge. She provides meals, makes baby blankets and quilts, sends home birthday and Christmas gifts. She lets parents skip payments, delay payments. Sometimes parents stop bringing their children altogether, leaving her without months of earned income.

My parents do not have money, but that does not stop them from giving money to others—friends, strangers they see on the news, workers at gas stations or grocery stores. A recurring memory: my mother panicked at the grocery store register that her card will be declined, then giving a Christmas bonus to the gas station attendant who rings up her Diet Cokes. When I was growing up we ran out of food, toilet paper, toothpaste, sheets, and towels. As children we learned to hoard snacks and toiletries in our rooms, to be first in line to load our plates at dinner because there never seemed to be enough for us all. Even now, when I return to visit, I bring my own soap and shampoo, towel and snacks.

Transparent in their desire to be needed, my parents talk openly about their kindness, referring to their donations in a way that makes me blush. They lead with tales of their selflessness, asking adoration of others with such earnestness I am both embarrassed and saddened. They seem so desperate to be needed I doubt they will ever be satisfied. What is most upsetting is that I hardly know them outside of their deeds. We struggle to talk about anything but daycare children or families in need. Sometimes I wonder if my parents feel a sense of purpose or identity beyond the selfless narrative they have crafted.

I hear one of two things when people learn about my family. "Your parents must be saints" or "Your parents sound crazy."

Their sacrifice has not been without consequence. The upheaval of so many adoptions and houseguests and day-care children is etched on their lined faces and worn bodies. They struggle to pay their bills. They do not have health insurance or retirement savings. And despite their earnestness, their kindness is abused. My parents surround themselves with people in need and the power dynamic cannot stand once the need is met. People leave my parents' lives as quickly as they enter. As a result, my parents have fewer and fewer friends—people grow tired of the constant chaos, old friends and coworkers pulling away, and family members, who admit they can't remember the names of all the children, can't keep up with the constant rotation of bodies.

Even the siblings have withdrawn. My older brother Dale decreased his visits after my parents adopted Cameron and Bailey and long before Victoria arrived. When he does return he speaks mostly to my parents, tunes out his younger siblings, some of whom are thirty years younger. My brother Casey left as soon as he turned eighteen and never looked back. No one knows his phone number or address and he goes six months or more without contacting anyone. The choice is between fight and flight. Those who have stayed—Candy and Natalie, or Cameron and Bailey, who are still in school—must fight for survival. They are consumed by my parents' charity, either live at home or are called in to help several times a week, unable to form fully independent lives, unhappy with our fractured family despite their loyalty.

Ultimately, I chose flight, moving first to the Midwest for graduate school and then to the East Coast for work. The physical distance gives me the emotional space I need to breathe. This is not to say it is easy. Recently I spoke with my mother, whom I miss terribly and long for so deeply that even now, writing this, I am tearful and aching. I was trying to tell her how much I hate being away, about the guilt and the sorrow, and as she often does with difficult emotions, she brushed it aside by saying that one of her daycare parents, born the same year as me, is named Sarah too, so now she has another Sarah. I know she meant that she misses me and that taking care of this young mother is a comfort to her. At least this is what I hope.

My parents' sacrifice has had deep consequences for their children. Despite being from five different sets of parents, all eight of us suffer mental health struggles. We each have anxiety, depression, OCD, attachment disorder, PTSD. It is difficult, of course, to know the cause, for so many have abuse in their backgrounds, but while we do not share genetics, we do share environment. Our familial anxiety is nature and nurture, a blend of genetics and triggering circumstance.

My parents, too, are a product of their environments. They were raised in fractured families held together by the thin veneer of the American Dream. Their parents were married, had the required three children, and provided economically better than the generation before. But the marriages were unhappy, full of addiction and the loneliness and violence that accompany it, and as children my parents clung to their siblings for survival in such a way that when the siblings reached adulthood they each ran as far away as they could to escape. Fight or flight. Members of the families hardly speak now, a generation shattered across the country like broken glass. The reason my parents have devoted their lives to giving themselves to others is that like me, they are desperate, needy for a kind of love that can never be satisfied.

"Missing someone who is loved and longed for is the key to an understanding of anxiety," wrote Sigmund Freud, and like Harlow's monkeys, my siblings, my parents, and I are desperate to cling to something. Anxiety is a fear of the future—what hurts might happen, what pain could be possible—caused by fears from the past. Anxiety occurs when a seed of fear grows wild, and while it may look irrational to those who do not understand how fears of asteroids relate to childhood, you can trace the vines back to the root. Our do-gooder family grew unchecked, until the real threat of more children, more houseguests, less resources, less control manifested as unreal panic.

Anxiety writes itself on both the brain and body, physical symptoms making manifest emotional distress. I was also a sickly child, but my predisposition to illness increased with time. I had chronic ear infections from an early age, the side of my face hot and throbbing, pulsing with the sound of my heartbeat. Sometimes my eardrums would rupture, leaving my pillow wet with infection, once, conveniently, at middle school sleepover camp, just as my best friend announced she wanted to be best friends with the girls in her cabin. I caught colds and flus easily, my immune system weakened by my mother's constant exposure to germs at the preschool where she worked. I broke my arm while playing tag, suffered frequent stomachaches, got sore muscles from walking too fast, bruised, it seemed, from the wind.

I did not like to hurt, but I learned that illness captured my parents' attention. My mother would tuck me into a sickbed on the couch and bring me cups of tea. She would slow down long enough to watch a movie with me. My father would come home and hold a hand to my forehead, the smell of sawdust mixed with sweat a comfort. Long before so many bodies made illness a burden, illness provided an escape from everyday routine, enforced quiet and calm. Illness made me the center of the universe, my parents orbiting around each symptom.

As Y2K and high school approached, I was quietly convinced the world would end (a lasting preoccupation). Instead of celebrating the New Year as I usually did with friends, nachos, and an MTV countdown, I retreated to my sick couch with a terrible flu. My parents put Natalie and the twins, newly adopted, to bed and stayed up with me long into the night, as I went feverishly in and out of sleep, waking to find the world and my parents as I'd always remembered. The flu disappeared as fast as it had developed.

When my parents finally saved the money for braces, an ordeal that required two surgeries and many years, I relished the ache. It meant my mother took time from her job to drive me to appointments, these drives our only time alone. After, she would buy me a cold milkshake and let me escape the twins to watch TV in my parents' bedroom, like I had as a child before all the adoptions began. Hurting increased her attention, seemed in some ways a strange requisite for her love. After all, my parents seemed to love those who suffered most.

During senior year of high school I broke out with Henoch–Schönlein purpura, raised areas of bleeding under the skin that covered the lengths of my legs and arms. The hemorrhages were deep scarlet and purple against my pale skin, and crusted into thick, half-inch scabs that oozed and prevented me from wearing pants or long sleeves. I do not remember being afraid, though mildly ashamed when the doctor sent my mother out of the room to inquire if I was sexually active. I did not understand and hung my head, whispering that I'd secretly kissed a boy all the previous summer before he moved away to college. The rash, it turned out, was the result of being sick for several months over the winter, a persistent flu about which I never consulted a doctor. With my illness—perhaps their negligence—made visible, my parents doted on me with the kind of attention I craved going into graduation.

Whether nature or nurture or a combination, anxiety is conditioned. Our bodies and brains learn to turn fear into physical symptoms. Eventually it is an automatic response, as hardwired as our heartbeat. I never made up an illness for attention as a child—I was, indeed, sick—but now it seems clear that illness accompanied periods of great stress. Bronchitis my first semester in the dorms. Walking pneumonia my first semester of my MFA program. Mono my first semester of my PhD program. I've had over fifty urinary tract infections and dozens of sinus infections. Fungal and bacterial infections once fought for space in my body for eighteen months. I had oral thrush for a year. I've had chronic migraines for the last fifteen years, a condition my father and sister Natalie share, and I slip into the comfort of darkness with an ice pack a few times a week. While the pain of a migraine is terrible—the knot at the base of the spine, the aura that blurs my vision, the sensitivity to light and sound, the strange smells I get before one begins—crawling into my sickbed is a soothing comfort.

Anxiety also accompanies feelings of neglect in my life. As an adult, my anxiety flares most during times of loneliness—winter or summer breaks, when I do not teach and am left on my own for weeks at a time, during holidays when I long for my family, even during joyous occasions like when I publish a book, receive an award, adopt a pet, and cannot tell my mother because, as she reminds me hastily on the phone before quickly hanging up to comfort a crying child, "No time."

I do not recall if I had panic attacks as a child, but when I think back to this time I am overwhelmed by the adoptions, Candy and Casey, Cameron and Bailey, Victoria, the foster children whose name and faces I cannot recall, though I can feel the weight of their bodies as my parents place them in my lap, can hear my mother on repeat, clicking, clicking like a metronome, "No time, no time," a phrase that lines up with my blinking and breathing and makes me twitch and choke, suffocating, too many bodies taking up air in the house, none left for me.

CHAPTER 4

AN AMERICAN DIAGNOSIS

*A*fter weeks, maybe months of anxiety, I admit something is wrong. It is my twenty-third birthday. Or it is the day before, or the day after. It might be the following week. Forgive my error, but incorrect is the best way I know to tell this story. Chronology is disjointed. My anxiety has altered recollection to an impressionist painting where images defy conventional lines.

I am visiting my family, my parents' suggestion hanging in the air like a ghost, the way it has since they brought it to life. I am watching a movie with my mother and two of my sisters in the living room, while Brady and my father barbeque in the backyard, my younger brothers biking circles around them.

About an hour into the film, I recognize what is becoming a familiar surge in adrenaline, the staccato breath, the rolling eyes, muscles tensing and tingling, and though my hands—one still wrapped in a brace—and feet have been numb for weeks by now, I grow frantic and hysterical. My mother follows me as I pace the house; my sisters watch silent in fear.

I can no longer control my body. I fall to the floor. I can't form words. I can't do anything. Embarrassed and confused, further panicked, I shriek and the noise swells and soon the living room fills with the sound of my wailing.

We pause the movie and my mother and Brady rush me to a Saturday urgent care where a doctor feels my spine, which hurts, and my hands and feet, which also hurt, and then my hurting head and jaw. They run urine and blood tests and X-rays, which I want to protest because the radiation is going to burn the core of me, is going to light me up electric for them to see, leave me seething with poison, the very marrow of me rotten.

"We're not sure what this is," the physician says at last, shrugging his white-coated shoulders. "You should probably see a doctor about this. It may be stress-related."

I return home, where my sisters are hiding in their rooms, unsure what has happened to their straight-A sibling. The television is still on, the freeze-frame showing a young woman with thick bangs and sad eyes staring lonely into the camera. I think it would be nice to be her, someone who is sad but doesn't ruin a Saturday afternoon, like I ruined today or the night before when friends and family arrived for the surprise party my mother arranged to cheer me up. I felt bombarded and trapped like a bug under glass, so much attention on me, my arm brace, how thin I've grown. I have little recollection of this night—so much of this time gone, matte black in my memory—but in photos I am hunched like a pale question, afraid, even as I smile, that the celebration candles will set me ablaze.

On Monday I creep to another doctor, a family friend who has agreed to see me on short notice and without health insurance. I explain my weakened limbs, my churning stomach, my shortness of breath, blurred vision, stiff neck, clenched jaw. I explain that I see bright flashes of light like exploding stars, and lines across my sight like wriggling worms under a microscope. I explain that most nights I wake up from a dead sleep vomiting. I admit that I am afraid to go out, afraid I'll faint in public, afraid people will look in my eyes and see through the circle of color to my brain scuttling about inside. I can't calm my mind, I can't get my ideas off of repeat, I can't focus. "I have work to do," I offer, as though hard workers are the only ones who deserve relief.

Before I finish explaining my symptoms, afraid to describe what I've seen in my strangest of paranoias, what mundane fear I've worked over in my mind until gargantuan, the doctor begins to ask me questions: Am I constantly tense, worried, or on edge? Does my anxiety interfere with work, school, or family responsibilities? Am I plagued by fears I know are irrational, but can't shake? Do I believe that something bad will happen if certain things aren't done a certain way? Do I avoid everyday situations or activities because they cause anxiety? Do I experience sudden, unexpected attacks of heart-pounding panic? Do I feel like danger and catastrophe are around every corner?

"You have anxiety," he says with a confident smile when I answer yes to nearly every one of his questions, averting my eyes around the office to read the names of various drugs stamped across the tissues, the hand sanitizer, the clock. He offers this diagnosis as though it solves my problems.

According to the *Diagnostic and Statistical Manual of Mental Disorders (DSM)*—a guide published by the American Psychiatric Association and used by clinicians, researchers, psychiatric drug regulation agencies, health insurance companies, pharmaceutical companies, the legal system, and policy makers—an anxiety diagnosis can be made if a patient has at least six months of "excessive anxiety and worry" about a variety of events and situations. "Excessive" is vaguely defined as "more than would be expected for a particular situation or event." (Who is doing the expecting is unclear.) Other symptoms include struggling to regain control, relax, or cope with the worry in a way that causes "clinically significant distress" or problems functioning in daily life. ("Excessive" and "clinically significant" are up to physicians to determine.) Finally, in order to receive a diagnosis, patients must have three or more of the following symptoms for most days over a period of months: feeling wound-up, tense, or restless; easily becoming fatigued or worn out; concentration problems; irritability; significant tension in muscles; difficulty with sleep.

The *DSM* lists six major types of anxiety disorders, each with its own distinct symptoms. Generalized anxiety disorder features the symptoms I've described. Obsessive compulsive disorder is characterized by unwanted thoughts or behaviors that seem impossible to stop or control. Those with panic disorder experience repeated, unexpected panic attacks and the fear of experiencing another. Those with phobias experience irrational fears of anything from animals to insects, heights to thunder, driving to public transportation. Social anxiety disorder is a debilitating fear of being humiliated in public or being seen negatively by others, a fear that may lead sufferers to avoid social situations entirely. Finally, post-traumatic stress disorder occurs after a traumatic or life-threatening event, flashbacks and nightmares leaving sufferers in the midst of what feels like a continuous panic attack, startling easily, withdrawing, and avoiding situations that remind them of the event.

Anxiety disorders have been revised along with the *DSM*. Referred to as the "Bible" of mental health, the *DSM* is a complicated text, a strange combination of social values and scientific evidence, political influence and insurance red tape. Though the primary function of the *DSM* is to categorize mental illnesses, it is most often used for insurance purposes—to be reimbursed, physicians and psychiatrists must provide *DSM* codes. As Scott Stossel points out in *My Age of Anxiety*, "Only in 1980—after new drugs designed to treat anxiety had been developed and brought to the market—were the anxiety disorders finally introduced into the third edition. . . . In an important sense, the treatment predated the diagnosis—that is, the discovery of antianxiety drugs drove the creation of anxiety as a diagnostic term."[3] Beyond that, however, the *DSM* outlines acceptable behavior and attitudes about a range of human emotions and activities, including anger, sadness, joy, anxiety, sexual desire and activity, eating, and sleeping. Above all, the manual outlines how we should live. Revised seven times since it was first published in 1952, the *DSM* and the number of mental illnesses have grown—what began as a 150-page text now stretches to nearly 1,000 pages.

The *DSM* reflects—and also has the power to influence—our cultural understandings of mental illness. Homesickness, for example, was once considered a legitimate psychological disorder, with English, French, Spanish, and German medical papers reporting on the disease. Coined "nostalgia" in 1688 to describe the symptoms felt by Swiss mercenaries—fever, fainting, stomach pain, and death—the label quickly gained popularity as a way to account for what many immigrants felt during a time of great migration. Despite the fact that nostalgia began to lose credibility as an actual illness in the eighteenth century when doctors tried, unsuccessfully, to trace the disease back to a nostalgic bone in the body, Civil War army doctors often discharged soldiers who displayed signs of homesickness for fear the illness would prove fatal. Cases of nostalgia were documented by the U.S. military until well into the twentieth century, when it began to be considered a normal form of psychopathology, a way to express our attachment to home.

More recently, shyness has fallen into fashion as a mental disorder, though it was once considered an acceptable human trait. Added to the *DSM* in 1980, social phobia, which was rarely discussed prior, became an epidemic by the mid-1990s. In 1993, *Psychology Today* announced that "social phobia" was the "disorder of the decade," a stern warning about something previously considered harmless—normal, even—and a trait valued in many Eastern cultures. Psychologist Barry Wolfe, PhD, of the National Institute of Mental Health, labeled social phobia "one of the worst neglected disorders of our time."[4] In a time of booming economic growth, shyness seemed counter to American productivity, an insidious illness that made sufferers quiet and meek, traits dangerous to an individualist culture that values confidence, entrepreneurship, and self-promotion. Today even common stage fright is classified as a social phobia, treatable with a range of drugs.

When the doctor gives me his diagnosis—tells me what I have and am—I feel the salty taste of shame at the back of my throat, but swallow it down so that I don't feel anything at all. Months later I will feel relieved, glad there is a reason for the way I am thinking and acting. I will feel justified: I have an illness to blame for the ways I am different. The illness will become a scapegoat of sorts, a way to distance myself from the things I do that others don't quite understand, the things that I can't quite accept. After several years, I will feel frustrated by the diagnosis, which follows me forever on medical charts, making its way through life with me, casting a shadow over the ways others view me and the way I view myself. Eventually, though, I will claim this diagnosis as my own—an identity that links me with other anxious folks, our habits and predilections a welcome recognition. We see one another. The way I feel about the diagnosis will be endlessly contradictory—relief, regret, resistance, recognition—but initially, sitting in the doctor's office, hearing it fall nonchalantly from his lips, I feel too much. So I force myself to feel nothing. The diagnosis lingers in the air and then evaporates. I hardly blink.

(I learn to do the same as my diagnosis changes over the years, depending upon my symptoms, of course, but also upon the age and gender of the physician with whom I am speaking, upon my age, my job, my marital status, upon my location in the country or where I am treated—an emergency room versus a university health center versus a therapist's office, for example. While I am initially diagnosed as suffering generalized anxiety disorder, I will eventually also be diagnosed with obsessive compulsive disorder and post-traumatic stress disorder, as though my mental state were a kaleidoscope of illnesses, shifting with each view, making new shapes and colors, my hand always responsible for the movement and madness.)

After his diagnosis, the doctor asks me to catalogue my full list of symptoms. I want to ask how long he's got.

Depression is often described as an absence—of feeling, energy, appetite—but anxiety is an overwhelming presence, with a long list of symptoms that varies from patient to patient, darting around consensus. Anxiety affects the entire body, each muscle, each organ molded by the disorder. Physical symptoms include back pain that shows up as stiffness and tension, as pressure or soreness or spasms, sometimes making your muscles immobile; blushing or paleness; body aches that feel as though your entire body has been beaten by invisible fists; body jolts or zaps, shaking or tremors, your body moving without you; body temperature changes that leave you cold and shivering or hot and sweating; breathing changes that make your breath so staggered you have to remind yourself to inhale and exhale, make you yawn and cough as you run out of breath, then taste metal and ammonia and burp from swallowing too much air; burning skin that feels itchy or prickly, as though your frightened limbs are forever waking up or going to sleep or some unseen bug has whispered its wriggling antennae across you; chest pain and tightness; choking; exhaustion as though your body has taken all it can and is giving up; clumsiness, your hands unable to hold onto the simplest of objects, your limbs refusing to perform tasks gracefully; difficulty speaking, in finding words and coordinating your lips and tongue, soft palate and cheeks, your jaw clicking and grating, your tongue swollen or itchy so you slur your speech, unable to form your mouth around what it is you want to say; dizziness as though your world is spinning, lightheadedness, your skull a balloon drifting off the spine on a string; ear pain and tickling like there is a pebble you can't get out or a bug working its way into the canal, blocking you from hearing at all or making sounds that aren't there; excess energy despite the fatigue, too much to sit still; falling sensations, you dropping or sinking even when you are on steady ground; feeling faint; feeling "wrong"; flu-like symptoms so you always feel ill and everyone insists you are imagining it and why are you doing that and what's wrong with you; increased allergies so that foods and most medications make you sick, make others believe you are making up your sensitivity; frequent urination; hair loss or thinning; heart palpitations as the muscle skitters, sputters, races, and comes to a grinding halt, disorienting you from inside; head pain that burns, itches, feels numb, feels tight, the skin stretched shining across your skull, tension headaches and frequent migraines; increased or persistent infection; nausea and vomiting; night sweats; numbness; rib cage tightness and pressure, like you're bound and suffocating; sensitive skin that leaves you blotchy and scaly, covered in rashes from sunblock, welts from the adhesive on Band-Aids; sex drive changes; shooting or stabbing pains so severe you feel as though your body is rebelling, as though someone has come up behind you and stabbed you clean in the gut, your body bleeding and bruising around the blade; vision changes that make your eyes itch and burn, sensitive to light, spots dotting your vision, lights flashing when you close your eyes, your depth perception shot, things scurrying in the corner of your sight. These are just some of the symptoms I've experienced with frequency for the last decade, though my body and brain like to surprise me and new ones appear from time to time.

While the physical symptoms are awful, endless and contradictory—you are hot and cold, your eyes dry and watery—the emotional symptoms consume you more. The physical symptoms make madness tangible, but you are too embarrassed to tell people what you fear, obsess over, what thoughts intrude, control. You are embarrassed to admit you can't tolerate uncertainty, that you need to know what is going to happen, when and where it will be, that you crave the future, want to roll it around in your mouth like a marble. You are afraid to admit that things feel unreal and you are the only one that sees the truth—that death is near, doom on the horizon, that the front door, an artery in your brain, the sun could explode at any minute. That one minute you feel as though your brain is in a fog and you don't know how to cope, and another minute you feel a strange sense of déjà vu, like you've done this all before. That even though you have no memory, you are always playing the same reel again and again—thoughts of decay, destruction, thoughts that people think you are strange, that you are trapped in a room with no way out, that you will make a fool of yourself, faint or throw up in public, that you will fold up like sad origami. That you believe if you worry now, worry tomorrow, worry forever, bad things won't happen. That if only you'd started worrying sooner, they never would. That this mind chatter consumes you as you try to make your way through your day, feeling trapped in your own head, in your own way, sleep only a slight relief, for when you finally drift off after hours, you have bizarre dreams, hear things that jolt you upright in bed, feel worse when you wake, because now you have to face that what everyone has been saying is coming true—you are losing your mind.

I don't say this all to the doctor—he doesn't seem to want or need to know. The entire conversation only takes ten minutes before we're talking drugs. I've come to the doctor with a name brand in mind—Celexa. I know this drug because this is the medication my parents take and because like most Americans, I've seen ads on television and in magazines, know people who take Prozac or Paxil, Lexapro or Zoloft, drugs with millions of prescriptions filled each year.

Americans are sold two narratives about mental health along with these name-brand drugs. First, there is the story about the dangerous mental patient, the one who is unstable and moody. These patients are bipolar or schizophrenic or everlastingly sad, and they are frightening. These are the patients blamed for shooting up schools, organizing mass murders and cults. They are at fault for their violent actions, and ultimately their illnesses, the narrative goes. "If only they'd sought treatment earlier," newscasters report each time, while we, the rest of the mentally ill world—those who do not commit violent acts, wait for the backlash. The second story is about sufferers who are ill because they are American, because they work hard clawing at bootstraps, and the struggle leaves them weary. These sufferers are not blamed. What is interesting, though, is that despite these two seemingly disparate narratives, the solution remains the same—patients must be medicated. No matter nature or nurture or which of these additional categories I belong to, medicines like Celexa are what I must take if I am to be well, normal again.

The stories we tell about mental illness label it both chronic and curable because to talk of disease without cure is problematic for a country concerned with triumph. Gone are the days of straightjackets and insulin comas that leave patients dazed and almost dead. Now, a simple pill can make me—can make us—well. We can all be normal. Better, even. Our approach to mental illness is purely American, for while we cower from its specter, stigmatize it with silence, we also claim to know what it is and how to combat it. As a weapon we brandish a single narrative arc—patient is ill, seeks help from the sane, finds pill and is cured, suddenly saved from the solipsism of illness, a productive member of society once more.

But as much as they shun mental illness, Americans also claim it. In *Darkness Visible,* his classic 1990 memoir about depression, William Styron writes, "As assertively democratic as a Norman Rockwell poster, it strikes indiscriminately at all ages, races, creeds and classes, though women are at considerably higher risk than men."[5] The National Institute of Mental Health (NIMH) currently reports that one in five adult Americans experience mental illness in a given year, one in twenty-five living with a severe mental illness. Similarly, NIMH reports that one in five American children are mentally ill, half of chronic mental illnesses beginning by fourteen, three-quarters by twenty-five. Mental illness in America is as diverse as the country itself, though as with so many things, we fixate on the straight, white, cis experience, treatment limited for those who don't fit this narrow sliver of the American pie. (NIMH reports that African Americans and Hispanic Americans use mental health services at a rate of half that of white Americans, Asian Americans at a rate of one-third, and that LGBTQ individuals are twice as likely to have mental health problems as their straight counterparts, LGBTQ youth two to three times more likely to commit suicide. Multicultural communities are less likely to have health insurance or access to treatment, and are therefore less likely to receive treatment, and those who do receive treatment are more likely to experience higher stigma, poorer quality of care, culturally insensitive health care systems, bias and discrimination, and language barriers.) Though patients are stigmatized as they make their ways through daily life, American rhetoric insists mental illness is as much a part of the American experience as hot dogs and baseball, fashion and film. It is not difficult to find discussions of mental illness alongside ads for footwear and articles about the latest health craze—newspapers and online articles, news stations and Oprah report on this growing epidemic daily. Recently, *Vogue* ran an article about Prozac's impact on sexuality along with photos of the latest seasonal trends.

Popular rhetoric also identifies mental illnesses—depression and anxiety in particular—as contemporary afflictions. Some evolutionists argue that anxiety was once useful for hunter-gatherer human societies who needed the emotions to survive and thrive, but we've now outgrown the need for quick fight-or-flight responses. Today many blame mental illness on alienation from other people, broken communities and family structures. We blame the pace and race of our lives, the increase in technology, the impacts of globalization and mass media. We blame the decline of religion. We blame social and political corruption. We blame overcrowding and urbanization. We blame history.

But mental illness is not a recent development or fascination. The Greek god Dionysius, son of Zeus and a mortal mother, was believed mad, and his followers demonstrated their devotion by inciting wild ecstasies, his illness spreading to those who associated with him. Though a myth, other traits associated with Dionysius—uninhibited and unrestrained sexuality, drunkenness, uncontrolled passion, ecstasy and bestial violence—have been associated with the mentally ill ever since, along with the idea that mental illness can be spread or caught.

As early as the second century AD, physicians noted that for some people despondency preceded mania and the two tended to cycle. In the Dark and Middle Ages, what is now considered depression was seen as a manifestation of God's disfavor, sufferers afflicted for their sins, an early example of patient blaming.[6] Like pharmacists today, Hippocrates believed depression was an illness of the brain that could be cured by oral remedies.[7] Cauliflower, basil, ginger, and honey were all used as treatments, red meat and black bile accused as depression's cause. Beginning in the Middle Ages, laxatives were given to the mentally ill, the colon believed to store toxins and thus madness. Patients were starved, bled, purged, made to swallow plants that depress heart rate, fed drugs to induce nausea and pain, the rationale being that patients would focus on pain rather than delusion, and would fear physicians, thus remembering their place and power.

The word "melancholia" first appeared in the English language as early as the year 1303, "depression" first used in 1660 and making its way into common usage in the mid-nineteenth century.[8] Melancholy became fashionable in the late 1800s, much of the Romantic Age characterized by brooding. The Byronic hero—moody, temperamental, emotional, and mysterious—dominated literature, fashioned after Lord Byron, who is said to have suffered bipolar disorder, the trope leading to contemporary visions of the tortured artist, the world-weary bad boy with a soft side. Images of troubled artists and movie stars who produce great works despite their pains continue to dominate contemporary culture, glamorizing illness, everyday folks bearing the burden of stigma. Perhaps what is contemporary is that mental illness diagnoses have shifted with the times, the list of potential maladies increasing exponentially, the rising rates indicative of our fascination with pathology.

Though the doctor has already diagnosed me, he is required to perform a physical examination. He doesn't talk while he does this, so I'm left to wonder what's happening. This will not be the first time I'm examined without eye contact, my body an artifact, and given only bits of information, left to piece together the narrative.

"I'm going to have you take off your shirt," my family-friend-doctor instructs, and I have flashbacks to babysitting for his children, folding his undergarments and bathing his babies. Mortified, I remove my shirt and he moves his fingertips cross my chest. "Fascinating!" he cries, with a look of discovery. "You have pectus excavatum," he says to my chest. My concave chest, he explains, looking at me finally, is diagnostically interesting. While I've always been self-conscious about my small chest and poor posture, this statement solidifies my abnormality. It seems there is a diagnosis for everything.

After giving me a diagnosis I wasn't looking for, the doctor scribbles "Celexa" on his notepad. This is the drug I asked for, one quickly gaining popularity. The year before, it ranked seventeenth in the top psychiatry prescriptions for the year, but shot to number two the following year. According to IMS health, an independent organization founded in 1954 to track global prescribing patterns, and the largest vendor of U.S. prescription prescribing data, processing more than 40 billion transactions each year, 37,728,000 prescriptions were written for Celexa in 2011, up 36 percent from 2009. The most recent data available shows that in 2013, Celexa ranked third, but a total of 39,445,000 prescriptions were written that year, a 5 percent increase despite dropping a slot in rank.[9]

Created in 1989, Celexa has FDA approval to treat major depression, though off-label it is prescribed for anxiety, panic disorder, obsessive compulsive disorder, premature ejaculation, migraines, hot flashes, post-stroke pathological crying, body dysmorphic disorder, and premenstrual dysmorphic disorder (a severe form of premenstrual syndrome, which was added to the list of mental disorders in the *DSM* in 1994).

Assuring me Celexa is the solution, the doctor writes instructions with a flourish of his Celexa-emblazoned pen, telling me the drug will take six to eight weeks to take effect. He hustles me out of the room into the noisy lobby. A man's oxygen tank sounds and the air conditioning unit rumbles to life. Phones ring while music bounces up and down the hallways. A fax buzzes at the same time my phone vibrates in my purse, jangling my keys. I think I will faint and rush outside, gasping upwards for breath, unable to see in the bright sun.

CHAPTER 5

PATIENT HISTORY

In the decade since diagnosis, I have come to understand my anxiety as a round antagonist with complex moods and mannerisms. As such, the brevity of my initial doctor's appointment strikes me as odd—the story arc was limited to symptoms, diagnosis, and cure, with little room to develop characters or build rising tension. Dénouement without climax.

Here is what my doctor did not ask: He did not ask about my lifestyle. He did not ask how much I worked (long graduate student days). He did not ask how much I played (weekends of college binge drinking). He did not ask how much I slept (enough when there was time, less when there wasn't). He did not ask about my diet (cheap meals on a student budget). He did not ask if I consumed caffeine (I subsisted on a steady drip, ending only when the tunnel vision got bad enough to impact my productivity). He did not ask about exercise (my last was mandated high school PE, the only class I did not ace).

Nor did he ask about my personal life. He did not know Brady graduated and moved into my small apartment, both of us living on my graduate student stipend as we prepared to move across the country. He did not know that prior to Brady I'd had a series of terrible relationships, one that left me unwilling to eat, another that made me afraid. Though he knew my grandmother had recently passed away, he did not know my only remaining grandparent was in hospice.

In fact, he did not inquire much into my family history at all beyond confirming that my parents both took Celexa. If he had asked about my family history, he may have linked the sudden upheavals—five adoptions and several foster children in ten years—to my developing anxiety, for the stress, conflicting emotions, and sense of unreality I felt as a child are not unlike a panic attack. Trauma, we know, results in repetition, and though my childhood was nowhere near what my siblings and so many in the foster care system experience, it was lonely, confusing, tumultuous, and the symptoms of my anxiety—which increases when I am too close to my family—are a kind of echo. The way we treat children determines the way they see themselves in the world; I learned early on that children are expendable.

I was thirteen the first time my parents announced they were planning to adopt. I loved my older brother Dale, who, sixteen years my elder, visited in ragged jeans and rock T-shirts, and let me play his electric guitar and bother his friends. And I loved my sister Natalie, who, seven years my junior, was an agreeable friend who held my hand while I led our playtime. Initially, I was excited at the prospect of a new little sister to join our games, but social workers quickly urged my parents to adopt a sibling pair. Sibling pairs, especially those labeled "high risk" by a crowded system ill equipped to care for abused children, are difficult to place, and social workers move quickly if they think there is a home available. My parents, eager for more children after my mother's long struggle to get pregnant with Natalie, barely hesitated before agreeing to meet a twin boy and girl.

We met the two-year-olds at McDonald's, where we ate on special occasions. Natalie and I shared fries and sipped small sodas in a booth at the back, far from where my parents and the social worker had "grownup talk." The twins shrieked and ran from booth to booth, hitting one another, throwing napkins, and leaving salt and pepper trails behind them. My parents had instructed Natalie and I not to leave our booth, but the social worker admonished, "Why didn't you look after them?" when one twin hit the other hard in the face with a pepper shaker, leaving the beginning of a bruise. We didn't even know their names yet. When we got in the car to leave, my parents asked what we thought. I told them the twins were naughty. "Please don't do this," I pleaded.

The twins moved in a few days later. Casey did not speak, cried often, and binged at every meal. When we lifted him from his high chair, we'd find food stuffed underneath him, in his pockets, down his diaper. We had to pry loose the food clutched in his hands. Sometimes he left food in his mouth to spit out and hide under his tiny bed. His twin, Candy, ran from room to room screaming. She'd smile charmingly, then bite you. She'd giggle, then slap you full in the face. The morning after they arrived, I sat on the couch playing a game, stomach-sick by the sudden change. When I refused to share my game with Candy, who reached into my lap to pull pieces from my hands, my parents scolded me. "She's had a rough life," they said in unison. "It's your job to be nice." Candy threw game pieces, crunched them beneath her feet, hit me surprisingly hard. "Be patient," my parents called after me as I closed the door to my room.

Each weekend my parents traveled hours away to attend adoption classes or take the twins to visit the biological mother who had willingly surrendered them to social services. Sometimes she came, sometimes, like the biological father they never met, she never showed, my parents waiting hours just in case (this was required until the adoption was legal). I watched seven-year-old Natalie, both of us suddenly allowed to stay home alone. I took my abrupt maturity seriously, cooking our meals, washing the dishes, and cleaning the house, hoping to surprise my parents upon their return. I scrubbed the walls and baseboards. I made the beds, smoothing the blankets, surveying them from all angles for a stray wrinkle. I organized the toys and tried to fix what the twins had broken because my parents couldn't afford to replace things. I felt lonely lately and didn't want Natalie to feel the same, so I turned cleaning into a game, giving her small tasks and rewarding her with a French braid when we finished.

In the afternoons when Natalie napped, the house was silent as a curse. Each noise echoed off the walls and down the hall; I noticed my heartbeat for the first time. We had no cable, no computer, and I was not allowed to play outside alone. Instead I sat quietly while Natalie slept, rereading each of the books on my shelves. When there was nothing left to read, I began staring at the walls, trying to find shapes in the plaster. If I stared long enough, my vision began to swim. I began to see things.

My parents did not own cell phones and I was not allowed to answer the telephone when I was home alone, so I was never sure how long they'd be gone. Hours slipped by, slowly, slowly, like wax from a candle. Saturday melted away. My parents returned at night, my mother opening the door slowly, a child cradled in her arms, my father behind her, a child in his. The twins were sleepy and hungry and irritable from all the time in the car. If they'd seen their birth mother, they were tearful, anxious, and angry. My mother rushed to make a dinner before bed, and I set the table, staying quiet because I knew she was tired. I waited for her to notice that I'd dusted the house, done laundry, made her bed. At first she was pleased, but soon I was expected to clean while she was away. I stopped expecting praise. I stopped expecting a response at all.

I missed my parents. I missed my mother reading to me each night, curling up next to me in bed while she read *A Wrinkle In Time, A Tree Grows in Brooklyn, Little House on the Prairie,* her voice even and sweet, our bodies touching, her side moving up and down with her breath and the voices she did, safety lulling me to sleep. Now the twins would not

stay in their beds, screamed and laughed and cried out in the
night, and my mother's evenings were spent coaxing them to
sleep. There was no time for stories.

During the week my father woke at four-thirty a.m. to
commute to his construction job, returning at seven p.m.,
and his additional absence on the weekends left a hole in
my heart. He seemed ghostly and unreachable, the twins
now occupying any rare chance in his lap. I longed for time
alone with him and became his shadow. We drove to the
dump early in the mornings, bouncing along back roads. We
talked while I held his tape measure, handed him nails and
bolts, the smell of his sweat and sawdust a comfort I craved.
Sometimes he let me watch him lift weights in our garage
late in the evening, as long as I did not interrupt his counting. This is when I learned the importance of silence, how to
become invisible even when you are there.

Social workers came in and out of our home, inspect-
ing our lives. Medicine, chemicals, anything dangerous was
locked up. My mother's crochet hooks and needlepoint. My
father's tools. We hid my Easy Bake oven, my rock polisher,
the metal shovel I used in my sandbox, the one that matched
my father's. We installed locks on the cabinets so that despite
my new responsibilities, I became a child again. We turned
down the hot water heater to prevent burns, water in my
parents' house forever lukewarm or cold from too much
use. We installed a gate around the wall heater my father
and I once stood in front of early in the mornings, his arms
around me as the sun rose.

The transition was painful. I hurt in ways that confused
me. This was compounded by the fact that so many adults
told me it was wrong to pout, wrong to be angry, wrong
not to love these children, smile, be a good person. If what
I was feeling was wrong, then it couldn't be real. Confusion
became second nature. I watched Casey crawl under his bed
to cry each night, Candy calling out "Mommy?" to strangers on the street, and I could not bear to think about them
living anywhere else. At the same time, I hated when Casey

crawled into my bed in the middle of the night or when strangers thought Candy was my child, *tsssking* under their breath and wondering aloud why we weren't the same color. I felt sad, angry, indignant, and ashamed of myself for feeling this way. Eventually, I wasn't sure what I felt at all. (Years later, a therapist gave me a "feelings wheel" because when she asked, "How does that make you feel?" about something as benign as a grocery list, the words I listed weren't emotions.) Above all, that anyone could treat others so terribly—social workers spoke of hunger, bruises, molestation—made me afraid.

I cannot tell you more, reader, because I don't remember, though perhaps there is something in the not-remembering. The immediate years following the adoption are full of black spaces, as though things have been redacted. I know that I babysat frequently—before and after school, weekends, summers. Candy stole and lied and had difficulty making friends. Casey argued with teachers and fought students until he was expelled from the preschool where my mother worked and later from the wealthy district Natalie and I had attended since kindergarten, the increased scrutiny over our address nearly revoking our interdistrict transfers as well.

My parents broached another adoption a few years after adopting the twins. When Natalie and I protested, our parents asked, "Don't you love the twins? Where would they be if we hadn't adopted them?" This silenced us, for we were horrid and selfish if we wished ill on children without a home. When my father's pituitary tumor was discovered, my parents put the idea on hold, future adoptions a threat throughout my high school years, made real by frequent calls from social services and occasional foster children, like two rough and tumble brothers who added to our family's developing multiculturalism and punched you when you touched them, their voices permanently hoarse from shouting. I distracted myself by working hard in AP classes, on the school newspaper, in Girl Scouts and various clubs, winning state awards with the Mock Trial team and marching band, tutoring after school and babysitting to save up for college. If I was good, I believed, my parents would not need to adopt. If I worked hard, I might be enough. Still, despite my feverish efforts, I worried I wasn't.

During my second year of college, my parents adopted again. Since I was no longer a minor, I had to be fingerprinted and have a background check in order to stay at the house when I came home. To expedite the process, however, my parents and social workers found a loophole based around the fact that I didn't live at home full time (although I was hopelessly homesick and came home each Friday through Sunday). In order to avoid the paperwork, I would now be considered a visitor.

Social workers interviewed each family member. Quiet Natalie, now fourteen, had grown even shyer, refusing to talk to most people and relying on my mother or me to translate for the world. She cried when the social worker tried to speak with her, and though interviews were supposed to be one-on-one, she refused to meet social workers unless I was present.

When the social worker asked how I felt about adoption, I said it wasn't right for our family—my parents were strained by their five children already, their stress levels high from the twins' frequent troubles, my father only a few years removed from his health scare, my mother's stress (which I now recognize as anxiety) transforming her, making her shake and sob, lock herself in the bathroom or leave to go on long drives alone. As only a pretentious college student could do, I spouted statistics, sprinkling my protest with true tales of the twins. When the social worker asked how my previous experiences might be altering my feelings, I asked how her paycheck might be altering hers. When she insisted our family was a good contender for adoption, I pointed out she'd never adopted or done any type of foster care, just preliminary paperwork, which I'd looked at and noticed was grammatically incorrect. When she tried to relate with me, saying she'd graduated from the college I was attending, I asked her what year, noting she'd graduated only a few years ahead of my projected graduation date.

As they had before, social services only called my parents about sibling groups—three children, four—pleading, "We know you want just one, but no one else will take them." Sure enough, two boys, ages two and three, arrived after being shuffled from home to home for several months, a dozen other potential families changing their minds after just a few days. "It's not that they're difficult," social workers reassured when mentioning the "extremely high risk" label on the boys' case file. "They haven't found the right fit. If anyone can do it, it's you."

On move-in day two-year-old Bailey cursed and hit the twins, who begged to send him back, and three-year-old Cameron hit the dog, spitting on us when we untangled fur from his fingers. Natalie retreated to her room to hide and I scowled, forced to skip college classes to meet my new brothers. Bailey clung to me (I was his mother's age) and I groaned when he squatted in front of me to poop, grunting and hitting himself in the face. My parents stared straight at me and said in near unison, "If you can't be nice, you can leave."

The adjustment was harder the second time. The boys had asthma, allergies, ADHD, dermatitis, scabies, eczema, delayed speech, severe stutters, eventually OCD and Tourette's. They also both had attachment disorder, which meant they were controlling and argumentative, defying rules just to get caught. They lied straight to your face, making eye contact as they tried to manipulate you, but refusing to meet your gaze if you pulled them into your arms. Affection them stiffen and sometimes they'd choke themselves after a hug, wrap their chubby hands around their throats until they were breathless and blue to show you what happened if you dared to love them. Attachment disorder also meant they were hyperactive, aggressive, impulsive. They liked to break things—the armrests in the family van, the walls of any room, the toilet, one another's bones. They did not show remorse for lying or stealing or hurting others, for wrapping a plastic bag around the cat's head or dragging the family dog about the house by her tail.

The boys would always be dangerous, social workers warned, requiring my parents to sign a liability form saying they understood the children posed a threat to themselves and others, might cause injury or set fires, might commit suicide. Attachment disorder meant the boys would not form healthy relationships, social workers reported. Still, it was our responsibility to try.

I came home each weekend from college to get to know my new brothers. I read to them, then realized that they'd colored on my shoes when I wasn't looking. I played cars with them, then found money missing from my purse. I cooked for them, then had the food thrown at my back when I turned.

No matter how hard I tried, I couldn't escape feeling uncomfortable around my new brothers. Everything they did seemed tinged with sex and violence. If I was lonely in my house before, now I grew afraid. Three-year-old Cameron masturbated freely, cursing and spitting and hitting while touching himself. Two-year-old Bailey never spoke, but crawled into corners and punched himself hard in the face, laughing when we rushed to his side. Their preoccupation with fire and blood, weapons and evil was the most frightening. They only paused their evening play when the news reported car crashes or shootings, and as they aged, they collected nails and bullet casings, frequently referred to bringing weapons to school, to killing their friends, to suicide.

If my first years with the twins are blurry, then the first years with the boys—the years just before my anxiety diagnosis—are gone entirely. I do not remember when we legally adopted them. I do know that Bailey had night terrors and chronically wet the bed, peeing on the stairs, furniture, and toys. Cameron stole from siblings, classmates, and teachers. The boys set a small fire in my parents' room, but we never found any matches. (Years later, they would be expelled from one school after another for punching elementary school kids, threatening to bring weapons to school, talking about bombs, organizing fight clubs that left bodies bursting onto concrete.) The twins acted up in response; Natalie was nearly mute and developed a chronic migraine that lasted more than a year. Dale visited so infrequently he did not know names. Aunts, uncles, grandparents couldn't keep up either. The preschool job my mother found after quitting her old one following Casey's expulsion would not look after the boys, so she quit again. She quit the next too, opening a home daycare and priding herself on looking after problem children other daycares would not accept. Working from home gave her time to retrieve children in an endless rotation of suspensions.

I graduated college a year early and moved hours away to begin graduate school. I lived alone in a cheap area in dangerous city, and though I was often lonely and afraid, I was not homesick. I was relieved. One month after I moved away, my parents adopted again.

This time it was a fifteen-year-old we already knew—my mother had been Victoria's preschool teacher, I'd babysat her, and my father had done construction for her wealthy parents, building fences around multiple pools, their tennis court, their putting green. Her father died of a heart attack while the two were on vacation in New Zealand, and Victoria bounced between her estranged mother and family friends for several months. Meanwhile, my mother learned of this and reconnected with the family, spending hours on the phone with Victoria's mother, contacting Victoria through MySpace, and insisting Natalie and I reach out, though we hadn't spoken to Victoria since she was a toddler.

Soon Victoria was staying at our house every few weekends, perched stiff on the edge of the living room sofa as she answered my parents' questions, sleeping in Natalie's bed, while my sister slept in a sleeping bag on the floor. Though my parents did not broach adoption, I knew well enough by now that their intentions were always permanent. Hours and cities away, my opinion hardly registered.

Still, I hoped to be kind. Sometimes Victoria was there when I visited, opening the door for me like she did for daycare parents. She would look at me suspiciously when I arrived and I'd have to explain that this was my home. Eventually I realized it wasn't.

Victoria must have felt strange. Her town, with its swimming pools and stables and the Rolls Royce in her drive, replaced with our town, dirty farms and mended fences, tiny shops with hand-painted signs in Spanish, homes with broken bottles and rusty machines in the yard. Each time she arrived, climbed out of our family van, she seemed surprised by how far we commuted to work and school. "You drive all this way every day?" she'd ask my mother in between sending a text message and adjusting her headphones, staring at the train tracks that lined the fields. "I can't believe you don't have air conditioning," she'd sigh, shaking her head. "You don't have a treadmill? I don't want to run in the ghetto."

"I don't think it's a good idea," I said over the phone when my mother suggested Victoria move in permanently. The boys had moved in eighteen months before, and after thirty-five years with the same company my father had been laid off. "She's different," I said, trying to be polite, feeling guilty anyway, knowing this argument wouldn't hold up with our already mismatched family. "What about her age?" I added, for my parents had never adopted a child over the age of two or three. Plus, Victoria was legally emancipated from her birth mother, the two embroiled in a bitter legal battle over her father's sprawling estate, stocks, and bank accounts. Would, could, my parents legally adopt her? How long would she stay? What if she wanted to leave?

"It's awkward at school. It feels weird. I don't think she wants to live with us," Natalie whispered when my parents weren't around. Natalie didn't mind feeling strange, she insisted. When my sister told me this, I felt myself tense, felt the way I felt at thirteen when we adopted the twins, then again in college when the boys arrived. The tightness at the back of my throat, the heat of my body, the desire to hold myself still because the world moved too fast.

My doctor did not inquire into this family history. He did not suggest upbringing has any relationship to mental health. He did not suggest lifestyle or current events or past trauma had any relationship to mental health. He did not consider causal connections, if conscientious overachievers are prone to anxiety because of our need to control things, or whether the need for precision, for order and success, is fueled by our anxiety. He did not suggest therapy or diet or meditation or any other treatment. He never suggested changing the way I live. In fact, he never required me to come in for a follow-up appointment.

Because my parents insisted it was the nice thing to do, I invited Victoria to move into my childhood bedroom. I called her my sister.

CHAPTER 6

MY VOICE
FOR THEIR DRUGS

*C*elexa will take a month to build up in my system. "You might not feel any better," the doctor warned. "But you must keep taking it." In the meantime I can't concentrate, can't remember what happened last year or last month, can't remember last night. My memory leaves like water through a sieve. I clutch at strands of my narrative as it unravels.

I wake each morning to see if I feel different, a fine-tuned vigilance to my body's rhythms and moods that removes me from the rush of the world. The focus illness has stolen from my work makes me feel unproductive, un-American, unreal. I live in a strange in-between, not really sick since I have promise of a cure, but not really well, either. In the book *Illness as Narrative,* which explores the stories we tell about wellness and health, and the ways our society interprets the tales patients tell, Ann Jurecic explains, "To live in prognosis is to be in limbo between health and illness without a clear life narrative."[10] I feel that way, suspended between the way I was and the way I've become, staring across a tightrope at how I could be if the drugs work. If I can just be patient. I hope life will go on quickly without me, for every day, every conversation, every significant event—publications, acceptance into PhD programs, my MFA graduation—becomes something more to endure.

For example, on the way home from an anniversary trip with Brady, we stop at a chain fast-food place in a small California town. I order my usual sandwich, and it tastes good, the way it always tastes. I finish and am immediately aware something is wrong. I've been poisoned. Something evil lurked in my food. I didn't taste it, but it was there. No, not poison—someone put cocaine in my sandwich.

The world speeds up until it is fast and angry around me and I hyperventilate as I twist in my seat, hoping that if I match speed with the world, move fast enough, I won't die. Brady tries to calm me down with logic. "Your brain's been doing this lately, so don't you think it might be anxiety?" "What are the odds this would happen?" When reassurances don't work, he plays my game: "Even if the cooks were drug users or dealers, why would someone waste cocaine on a drive-thru customer? Why wouldn't they keep it for themselves or sell it?"

I have an answer for each question. It was an accident: the cocaine slipped from the bag in their pocket into my sandwich while they were assembling. It was intentional: the cook was so full of malice he wanted me to suffer, or he wanted to expand his clientele and was getting people hooked on drugs as he worked, hoping to later recruit them as customers, and yes, yes he made enough money dealing drugs but wanted to work at the fast-food joint to keep his cover. Brady volleys back and forth with me for a while until we are both exhausted.

My hysteria lasts well into the evening, as we wind our way through the dark, me trembling when we pull into our garage at two a.m., slouched low in my seat, trying to hide.

The people I can't hide from: Brady, my parents, a few close friends, my siblings. We are all waiting for the medicine to work, but things will get worse before they get better. I spiral down and down, building up speed until the world is a blur around me. I know I look unreasonable and inconstant. I know I am frightening them. So I try to explain.

At first I insist that what I feel is normal. "My hands and feet have gone to sleep and they won't wake up," I say, watching doubt skirt their faces as the days pass. "My tongue is swollen twice its size," I cry, holding my mouth open for them to see.

When they don't believe me I insist that I have the right to be frightened. "It's like I have a thousand acupuncture needles trapped in my skin," I press. "There's an electric current running through my fingers, pulsating out of my toes." Soon I grow frustrated and shout, "I can't move my mouth because my tongue is growing each day and the place where it meets my throat is a stone and I need to speak to you so badly that it is beginning to taste like salt."

I try to justify myself, the things I feel and fear. I want to describe them, to name them in a way that others can understand and thereby accept. If they cannot comprehend my pain, they will never believe it. Because "it hurts" or "it burns" or "it stings" falls short, I turn to figurative language. Yet the more detail I include, the more listeners wrinkle their noses or widen their eyes. The more I explain, the more incredulous they become.

Perhaps this is because we cannot accurately describe our pain, because pain exists beyond narrative. In *The Body in Pain: The Making and Unmaking of the World*, Elaine Scarry reasons that pain is inexpressible by language, for "whatever pain achieves, it achieves in part through its unshareablility, and it ensures this unshareability through its resistance to language."[11] It is this inability to accurately describe our pain to others, and their inability to understand our suffering, that makes pain so powerful, so frightening, so injurious.

We cannot describe our pain to others because pain separates our realities. For those suffering, there is no existence beyond pain—it frames the world. Those not in pain have an alternate reality, separated from the sufferer by way of the body. Sufferers cannot articulate their truths and those without pain cannot begin to comprehend. What exists for those in pain is unreal to those without it. As Scarry explains:

> For the person in pain, so incontestably and unnegotiably present is it that "having pain" may come to be thought of as the most vibrant example of what it is to "have certainty," while for the other person it is so elusive that "hearing about pain" may exist as the primary model of what it is "to have doubt." Thus pain comes unshareably into our midst as at once that which cannot be denied and that which cannot be confirmed.[12]

I feel this rift between our worlds each time I try to explain my pain to a family member. I called my mother the first time I experienced a panic attack, trying to catch my breath, certain my heart was giving out. "I can't breathe," I cried, closing my eyes to steady myself, to convince myself I still existed. "My heart is beating too fast and it's unsteady. It feels like there's a pressure on it. Am I having a heart attack?" I asked again and again. And I screamed and screamed and then whimpered like a child. Yet no matter how I tried to explain, tried to dutifully list each symptom, my mother could not understand. At last she offered, "I think it's a panic attack. Just calm down." Brady could not understand either, though he'd watched me pace the house afraid, looked so worried yet refused to call an ambulance.

As the attacks increased in frequency, I could see my family and friends would not believe my descriptions. This was real, this was true—I was certain. This was doubtful—they knew. They lived in a separate world, one without the veil of fear, without electricity running through their limbs or uncertainty overtaking their mouths, growing in the damp and dark so that soon they could not control their tongue, could not speak their stories. They did not live in a reality where the body was unreliable, plagued by aches and phantom pains, where limbs and muscles moved on their own as if haunted. Other symptoms—I constantly shivered, I saw the world moving before me as if under water, I could not stop the tremor in my hand or the blotches and strange bruises that appeared on my skin without warning.

Scarry differentiates between language's ability to share physical and emotional anguish. She argues that while emotional suffering can be described with language—many have written about heartbreak or loss—physical pain cannot. While I could describe the shame and frustration, it was difficult to describe the physical sensation of eternal fear, of perpetual panic. I could list the symptoms, report what parts of the body hurt, but "hurt" is a vague term, one a listener understands abstractly, applies to a blister or broken finger. And if describing the physical symptoms was difficult, it was even harder to describe the mental pain, which was both in my brain but also resonated through my body. I was inarticulate, grasping at metaphors.

These are the metaphors I used: Waiting for the medication to work was like waiting for a too-large meal to digest or the hurt of a failed love to fade. The feeling of dread in my stomach was that catch-a-breath moment when you come around a corner and rush into a stranger, or a group of people jump out to yell "Surprise!" My hands and feet felt like wrapping a thread around your finger and flicking the blue knuckle and nail, realizing that part of you is dead, or the pruning that happens to your fingers and toes after too long in the tub. Waking up like coming out of anesthesia, thrumming and blurred, the dull ache of what's been stitched together, each moment moving closer to the hurt. Shortness of breath like the time I blew up too many balloons, like falling into the deep end of a pool as a child, like running in the humid South, like breathing through gauze, through purple velvet, like eating too much shortbread or chewing on a cotton ball. When the immediacy of fear was gone, when the physical and mental sensations faded momentarily, I was left with this language, these visceral descriptions that so perfectly captured how I felt, yet remained distant from the experience, forever unreal.

Because I could not say what I meant, or mean what I said, because I could not form the words around the feeling, or sound out the sensation, I grew tearful, frustrated, a moody child. Family and friends coddled my temper, talking to me without expecting an intelligible answer, doing things for me as though I could not do them for myself, for they viewed me as helpless, my cries and moans those of a child. "Physical pain does not simply resist language but actively destroys it," Scarry insists, "bringing about an immediate reversion to a state anterior to language, the sounds and cries a human being makes before language is learned."[13] The larger implications are deeply political, for if a sufferer cannot express herself, she cannot interact with the world. To have language is to have power, voice a way of knowing and being, a form of agency and control. To be unable to explain your pain is to lose everything.

Adding to this loss is the doubt and skepticism the well place upon the ill and their attempts at narrative. "Surely it doesn't hurt that badly," they insist. "You don't look sick." Already struggling to describe the indescribable, the ill are further unmade by the suspicion and disbelief of the well. Recovering from a leg injury, neurologist and writer Oliver Sacks was shocked to find his experience summed up in his medical chart as an "uneventful recovery." Yet for him, the experience was anything but uneventful. "What damned utter nonsense," he writes. "Recovery . . . was a 'pilgrimage,' a journey in which one moved, if one moved, stage by stage, or by stations. Every stage, every station, was a completely new advent, requiring a new start, a new birth or beginning. One had to begin, to be born, again and again. Recovery was an exercise in nothing short of birth."[14]

Like Sacks's, my language was seen as dramatic and overblown, and as the weeks went by, listeners took on the placid look of someone not really listening. Eventually this look was replaced by a look of fear. Not for me. Fear of me. So I revised. "My hands are still numb, but the doctor said it's temporary." "Right now I can't talk because my tongue is covered in fur, but the medicine should help." I adopted the language of my physician, who had brushed aside my symptoms to focus on diagnosis and prescription. Pain became secondary, Celexa taking the lead. He hadn't seemed concerned with the sensory details or the rising tension, so this was the narrative I repeated. A hero without the villain. A climax and conclusion without the characterization. And though it felt incomplete, the narrative of treatment is an easy pill to swallow and being understood was what I wanted most.

Many patients have to revise their narratives if they want to be heard. After being diagnosed with depression, Lauren Slater, a psychologist and writer, found that her words ceased to hold power and authority. As a psychologist she could construct narratives about illness, but as a patient she was no longer recognized as an authority—physicians would not accept her poetic descriptions of depression. In order to be taken seriously by doctors, Slater eventually adopted the tone and style she heard around her, asking in her memoir, *Prozac Diary,* "Why can't I manage a simple story? Why is my voice—all my voices—so lost?"[15]

K. Steslow, a bioethicist who was briefly institutionalized, shares a similar experience, writing, "Everything I said or did was taken to be a product of my illness and categorized accordingly. There was a clear and distinct vocabulary being used to talk about my experience, and that vocabulary was not mine." The only choice she had was to modify, to adapt. "I felt that I had traded my voice for their drugs," she says of her language after treatment.[16]

This "common" language comes at a cost, for to invalidate a patient's language, their way of knowing and being in the world, is to remove one of the core features of being human—

the power of communication, the agency of narrative. As physicians, Sacks, Slater, and Steslow no doubt used language to diagnose patients, but when they became the patients, their language was somehow insufficient. Their descriptions of pain were met with disbelief and their physicians found their narratives inconsistent. They were accused of constructing, when all reality is a construct, each story we tell—a memoir, a medical chart, even the facts of an illness—constructed from what we experience, what we find, what we think we know.

I am accused of constructing as well. No matter how hard I try to explain the short- and long-term effects of anxiety to others, the reality of the experience often eludes us both. Listeners are left skeptical and I am left speechless, because I cannot make the words right, cannot make the listener—even you—understand. Pain destroys language for patients, destroying patients as well. Emily Dickinson argues against the ability of the writer to express pain through language, writing, "Pain has an element of blank; / It cannot recollect / When it began, or if there were / A day when it was not. / It has no future but itself."¹⁷ Pain is the focus of her poem. Dickinson is not even present. She is gone completely.

And so am I. As I wait for the drugs to take effect, I want to tell Brady, my family, my physician that the pain feels like pressure but also like weightlessness. I want to say I am alert to every nerve, but also numb. I want to say I can't breathe, yet am gasping all the time. I want to say I am cold, but am covered in sweat. No one would believe me. I keep quiet, but the metaphors continue. My brain is full of bubbles, bobbing gently against my skull, so that I feel asleep and walk through the day in a daze. At night they pop with such violence that each burst seems a gunshot.

This language is accurate. These stories are true. But listeners do not live here. They cannot know this. They find it—they find me—unreal. They fill the abstraction with easier subjects—patient, diagnosis, cure. They craft easier narratives. The story I am allowed? Celexa.

Know this. There are ropes around my feet, holding me down, and when I bend to untie them they are vines that grow and grow and take root even deeper. And then they are serpents that wind their ways back through time. There is a salamander in my throat, his black body slimy with regret, his claws piercing my words.

PART II

CHAPTER 7

A FEMALE MALADY

"There's nothing wrong with taking medication indefinitely," the doctor explained during that first appointment. The suggestion that my anxiety might be permanent hovered in the air between us until he brushed it aside by asking, "If medication makes you feel better, what's the harm?" His question didn't require an answer, but I wanted to say, "If I need medication indefinitely, the word is 'chronic,' not 'cured.'"

Perhaps because he forgot, but I suspect because I was protesting, the doctor took back the prescription sheet and scrawled a secondary precaution across the bottom. Despite his optimism about Celexa, he said, I would have continued—perhaps increased—anxiety while it took effect, and might need additional medication, even after. "Take these as needed," he explained, prescribing plentiful refills before tapping his branded pen with finality. "Xanax" was written in cursive, one letter linked to the next, the arms of each X reaching out to find something else on which to chain.

I'd heard of Xanax before, conversations with those who take the drug falling squarely into two camps: hushed necessity or unashamed amusement. Those required to take the drug are reluctant to admit they need it, while recreationalists herald it as a good time. Created in 1981, Xanax hit the market as one of the first drugs to treat anxiety disorders as the disorders were being added to the *DSM-III,* fortuitous timing that led to their immediate and continued popularity. Xanax has consistently ranked as the number one psychiatric medication for years. The year prior to my prescription, 44,029,000 perceptions were written, an increase of 29 percent from the last report; the following year, 47,792,000 prescriptions were written, an increase of 9 percent. The most recent data shows that in 2013, 48,465,000 prescriptions were written, an increase of 1 percent.[1] In 2010, *Forbes* reported that doctors wrote more than one Xanax prescription every second.[2]

The pills rest like pinpricks in my palm. "Take one the moment you start to feel anxious," the doctor had encouraged, but I feel anxious all of the time, so I hoard the pills away while I wait for The Big One, the attack that will send me over the edge.

When The Big One finally arrives, I swallow a quarter milligram pinprick and it drains the fear from my body, along with every other emotion. The doctor promised Xanax would "take the edge off," but it knocks me out completely, sending me into a deep, limp sleep that leaves me hollow when I wake. I'm afraid to take more pills after this, afraid of how quickly they consume my body, make me dull and numb, incapable of remaining conscious, let alone functioning.

I'm also afraid of the drug's gendered narrative. "I need a Xanax in this champagne," laughs a friend who works as a nurse each time my girlfriends get together, the rest of the women laughing in agreement while kicking off their heels and stretching their cramped, carefully pedicured toes. "She took a Xanax and slipped into a bubble bath," a chick flick narrates. "My mom was always popping Xanax," a colleague says, shaking his head.

I've seen similar advertisements on television and in countless women's magazines—O *Magazine,* for example, had three advertisements for antidepressants in last month's issue. You've seen the ads too: A woman sits in the center of the visual frame, hair disheveled, face free of makeup, eyes downcast. She wears dark colors, her clothes soft and sloppy. No jewelry. Sometimes she stares out the window at her family playing in the sunshine. Her husband, young son, and daughter ride bikes, toss a Frisbee, play in the sprinklers as their golden retriever runs alongside. The woman remains indoors in darkness. Sometimes in the frame behind her, the house is visible—cluttered, unorganized, her kitchen a mess. The image presents a clear narrative—crazy women ignore womanly hygiene, wifely duty, motherly roles, and domestic space.

If the ad is on television, a voice (often male) explains the science. Something has broken down in the woman's body; a chemical imbalance is responsible for the chaos. Her feelings of hopelessness, hours of crying, lack of appetite, loss of sleep, her destructive thoughts can all be attributed to serotonin, norepinephrine, dopamine, those delicate chemicals that dance through the brain and body. The advertisement offer large logos and solutions, however: Prozac, Paxil, Zoloft, Cymbalta, Celexa, and newer drugs like Abilify and Effexor, whose very names suggests they will enable women—perhaps even improve them—to do their duties once more.

Pristiq has one such advertisement. Since 2008, when Pristiq came on the market, the company has run a series of print and commercial ads that depict depressed patients as windup dolls slowed to a stop because of their illness. When medicated, however, the dolls are fixed, reenergized and productive, suddenly able to perform their usual duties. The use of a windup doll demonstrates what we have come to believe about mental illness—that it's caused by malfunction easily located and corrected. In the ads, dolls simply take a pill that winds them up properly.

More problematic, however, is the fact that nearly all of the dolls are women, as though only women need to be medicated, or worse still, as though mental illness is a woman's disease. When "wound down," the dolls each wear the same outfit—a drab, ill-fitting taupe shirt, a shapeless blue skirt, and black house slippers. Their hair hangs limply about their expressionless faces. Each woman is unattractive, unfashionable, and lifeless by way of her appearance. But we see what she could be if only she were medicated: The "cured" woman wears bright, form-fitting clothes and socializes, suddenly popular, as though mental illness makes one unlovable. She performs womanly tasks like hosting parties and cooking for her family. She walks in the park with the kids and the dog. She is also suddenly superhuman—hiking without losing breath, doing acrobatic yoga, bending and posing as the face of calm control. Robotics is success.

These advertisements can be found in women's magazines, health and fitness magazines, and many times per week on television, but they only made their ways into mainstream marketing in 1997, when the Food and Drug Administration relaxed regulations on pharmaceutical ads.[3] While the ads themselves are fairly new, their premise is not—they continue a centuries-old narrative about women and mental illness, the fairer sex unable to cope with their womanly duties or social pressures and thus confined to the fainting couch. Medicine has long treated women's bodies as if they are perpetually ill, as if menstruation, pregnancy, and menopause are chronic disorders in need of medical treatment rather than natural processes, as if women's sexuality is something in need of monitoring, as if women are, at their core, unhinged.

The story of the sickly woman dates back to Eden, crazy Eve ruining Paradise for everyone with her weakness and instability. A child in need of supervision, Eve and her faulty body and gender—hunger, impulsiveness, irrationality—are the heart of all our troubles. Hippocrates, whose oath to "do no harm" physicians still obey, and his followers added to this narrative, writing of women's "perpetual infirmities." His treatises argued that women's physical and mental differences could all be traced to their "wandering womb," that temperamental organ that rules women's bodies, usurping their energies and mental faculties, making them susceptible to physical and mental illnesses. Aretaeus of Cappadocia, a first-century CE Greek physician, called the womb "an animal within an animal," as though women are infested and ruled by a wild creature.

Greek physicians ordered women to engage in frequent intercourse to keep the womb occupied, and suggested women become pregnant as often as possible to redirect the womb's energies into something productive. Another cure for the wandering womb involved applying enjoyable or malodorous fragrances to the vagina to move the womb into proper position, for it was believed the womb, like women, enjoyed pleasant smells. Roman physician, surgeon, and philosopher Galen of Pergamon theorized madness was caused by menstruation, arguing that when menstrual blood or the mixing of male and female "seed" built up in the womb, it caused a kind of suffocation, creating noxious vapors with the corrosive power to corrupt other organs.[4]

Depictions of "madwomen" throughout history reveal the growing belief that along with the female body, the female mind is inherently ill. Margery Kempe, an Orthodox Catholic Christian who lived from the late 1300s to mid-1400s, experienced spiritual visions after the birth of her first child, and devoted herself to a holy life, weeping for forgiveness, wearing a hair shirt, pursuing a chaste marriage. Though male mysticism was common during the Middle Ages, Kempe was viewed as inordinately strange, a mother and wife forsaking her duties to descend into madness. (Had Xanax existed, Kempe would no doubt have received a prescription, the *DSM* dazzled by her symptoms.) Despite her "madness" and illiteracy, Kempe managed to write her spiritual autobiography using various scribes in the early 1430s. Her legacy of madness, however, rivals her religious devotion and scholarly accomplishment as the first English autobiographer and one of the first women writers.

Joan of Arc, who lived from 1412 to 1431, helped lead France to victory during the Hundred Years War because voices and visions instructed her to, beginning when she was thirteen. After taking a vow of chastity and refusing an arranged marriage, she gathered a following and convinced a beleaguered Charles VII (whose father, Charles VI, was known as "Charles the Mad") to let her take charge of the French army for a relief mission, one that lifted the siege after only nine days. Though she was able to curry political favor because of her passion in a time of despair and a long-standing prophecy that a virgin would lead France to victory, she was ultimately punished for her refusal of gender roles—captured by the English and tried for heresy, the short hair and male armor she wore in battle (and later as protection against rape in prison) used as evidence of "cross-dressing." Later canonized, Joan of Arc was burned at the stake at nineteen.

Joanna of Castile's political legacy of the early 1500s is also tied to mental illness, her nickname—"Joanna the Mad"—ensuring diagnosis defines her. Following her husband's sudden death shortly after being crowned king (many believe he was poisoned by his father-in-law), Joanna attempted to rule alone. The country fell into disorder with the assistance of her father, who then confined Joanna to a nunnery after she refused to transfer her power to him, a confinement accompanied by sudden rumors of her madness. Though she inherited the kingdom back after her father's death, Joanna remained imprisoned until her death, her son continuing the family's usurping tradition. Forbidden any visitors, Joanna degenerated—convinced the nuns wanted to kill her, she experienced difficulty eating, sleeping, and maintaining personal hygiene. Some historians argue Joanna suffered from inherited depression or schizophrenia, for her grandmother suffered similarly (after she too was exiled following the death of her husband).

The Salem witch trials of the late 1600s also demonstrate the desire to control female behavior through diagnosis. Influenced by Puritan beliefs, political tension, and bickering between community members, seventeenth-century colonialists quickly transformed their supernatural beliefs about the devil and sin into an ongoing trial by fire fueled by mob mentality and the targeting of women—of the nineteen executed, fourteen were women. Accused of carrying out the devil's tasks (difficult to prove since all one had to do was flail and shout as evidence of hexes), women who did not attend church, those who did not conform to popular beliefs about modesty and female performance, poor and homeless women, and women with angry husbands were assumed guilty. So was any woman who questioned the proceedings. The youngest accused was between four and six when she was taken into custody for several months, her imprisonment, not surprisingly, leading to temporary insanity. Constructed by a vastly male majority as a way to point blame in a time of political and social unrest, women's bodies and brains became scapegoats for unhappiness, unrest, and unmitigated power.

Passionate women, powerful women, problematic women, the story goes, are mad. Madness seems a label for undesirable character traits as much as a label for symptoms. Because silencing and policing of women's behavior can cause mental and physical responses—the sick role, self-fulfilling prophecy—perhaps instead of asking if women are inherently mad, we ought to ask if the world is imbalanced. Why does the world we've created for women lead to their madness? Consider this: Paris, 1825. Doctors testified that if a woman insists she is not mad, her denial was absolute proof of her insanity.[5]

However frustrating and painful my experience with mental illness has been, the narrative has been carefully crafted for middle-class, straight, white women like me. Studies about mental health and access to resources are systematically denied to minority communities, and medical training and practice often overlook the needs, desires, and circumstances of mentally ill people of color, the LGBTQ community, and the working poor. Mental illness impacts people regardless of identity, but the stigma surrounding mental illness in these communities is markedly different. This, too, is not new.

In the mid-nineteenth century, attitudes towards women's health divided along lines of class and race. Affluent, white Victorian women were considered inherently fragile and weak, prone to illness, while working-class women of color were viewed as robust and capable of bearing the great burdens the wealthy hoisted upon them. This biological explanation reinforced classist, racist attitudes—working-class women of color were ordered to work in the very conditions that made people sick, while health spas and specialists, routine rest and frequent doctor visits became an expected part of wealthy white women's lifestyles. (To see how this continues today, look no further than the latest wellness fads—expensive yoga classes, juice cleanses, colonics, IV infusions—that target mostly white women with disposable income.) According to *Complaints and Disorders,* Barbara Ehrenreich's and Deirdre English's classic study of medical sexism in the nineteenth and twentieth centuries, this thinking "fostered a morbid cult of hypochondria," creating a "cult of female invalidism" that reinforced the notion that the female body was inherently ill.[6] With femaleness *itself* the culprit, this rationale prevented women from acting in any other way.

The nineteenth-century medical industry also continued to link illness to women's sexuality. Puberty was blamed for creating chaos in the female body, while menstruation was deemed an illness during which women should rest, avoiding physical and mental activities like socializing, reading, even walking. The theory that a woman's uterus and ovaries controlled her body persisted, medical professionals of the time arguing reproductive organs caused everything from headaches and sore throats to bad posture and stomachaches. They also led to insanity.

As such, women's sexuality was deemed dangerous. Leeches were applied to breasts and vulvas, and beginning in the early 1860s, physicians began to conduct gynecological surgeries to remove the clitoris as a cure for sexual arousal, and ovaries to combat a host of ills. Thousands of oophorectomies were conducted from 1860 to 1890, Ben Barker-Benfield, a scholar in the history of sexuality, reporting that doctors passed ovaries "around at medical Society meetings on plates like trophies." These treatments may seem far removed from contemporary medicine, but the last clitorectomy was performed in the United States as recently as 1948—on a child of five years old, as a cure for masturbation, which was believed to cause uterine disease and tuberculous. Oophorectomy still accompanies hysterectomies today.[7]

At the same time suspicion circulated around women's sexuality, some Victorian physicians treated madness with genital massage, for they found the resulting "paroxysms" calmed nervous women. Paroxysms were considered therapeutic, rather than orgasmic, however, because women were not believed to be sexual and therefore incapable of orgasm. That sexually repressed Victorian women sought out doctor assistance again and again was seen only as proof of medical genius. The electric vibrator was invented by an industrious English physician in 1880—more than a decade before the electric iron or vacuum cleaner—to answer the call of physicians suffering from chronic hand fatigue from all that strenuous work. Had physicians instructed patients to engage in healthy sexual activity, everyone may have been healthier.

Conflicting information, maddening treatment—it is no wonder affluent women in the nineteenth century suffered en masse from hysteria (originating from the Greek word for "uterus"), which took many forms: nervousness, faintness, insomnia, muscle spasm, shortness of breath, irritability, loss of appetite, decreased or increased sexual desire, loss of voice or screaming, laughing or crying. Because any female behavior could be deemed troublesome, there is still debate over whether women experienced these symptoms as a conscious response to the social conditions of the time, or if they were subconscious revolts. Whatever the cause, doctors found this illness a drastic departure from the delicate illnesses expected of women and adjusted their treatment accordingly.

Developed by American physician and writer Silas Weir Mitchell, "the rest cure" intensified the leisure ill women had been prescribed before. Mitchell believed femininity caused mental illness, explaining in *Doctor and Patient,* "The woman's desire to be on a level of competition with man and to assume his duties is, I am sure, making mischief." His cure ordered women permanently to bed—submission now prescription—isolating them from family and friends, from reading, writing, painting, or any other movement that required the use of limbs for months or years at a time. Patients were silenced, interacting only with nurses, who treated them as children, bathing and feeding them fatty foods to increase their energy levels. Mitchell believed women responded to the cure, because, as he explained in 1888, "With all her weakness, her unstable emotionality, her tendency to morally warp when long nervously ill, she is then far easier to deal with, far more amenable to reason, far more sure to be comfortable as a patient, than the man who is relatively in a like position."[8] Mitchell's treatment for nervous men, on the other hand, including patients Theodore Roosevelt and Walt Whitman, was quite the contrary. He allowed men to choose between rest or his "West cure," which involved rugged adventure—horse riding, cattle roping, hunting, socialization with other men—all of which would invigorate the male body and mind.[9]

(I witness the same medicalizing of gender each time I raise my voice in anger or do not meet my smile quota for the day, fail to labor over my appearance or express the expected enthusiasm for weddings and babies. If I voice frustration, I need to relax. If I shout, I must be anxious. If I do not wear makeup, I look "sick." If I do not delight in selecting linens and bows for a wedding, or smelling melted candy bars in diapers at a baby shower, I'm letting my illness stop me from living a full life. I have been called hysterical for my political opinions or my response to being followed on the street late at night. But what seems crazy is how often the label of mental illness is used to monitor my behavior. When I do experience a panic attack, I am told to abandon work and rest, the familiar, lilting sound of patriarchy dripping from each syllable.)

Of course, patients worsened under the rest cure. In the classic short story "The Yellow Wallpaper," Charlotte Perkins Gilman fictionalizes her experience with Mitchell's cure, which began in the spring of 1887 after she suffered depression following the birth of her daughter. Diagnosed with hysteria, Gilman was told by Mitchell to "live as domestic a life as possible. Have your child with you all the time . . . Lie down an hour after each meal. Have but two hours' intellectual life a day. And never touch pen, brush, or pencil as long as you live."[10] In the story, an unnamed woman—readers only learn her diagnosis—is ordered to spend her days in a room covered in yellow wallpaper and quickly degenerates as a result, eventually ripping down the wallpaper to free the woman she begins to see trapped inside. The story's conclusion is both victorious and devastating—a woman freed by descending into the very madness of which she was accused.

Winifred Howells's ten-year rest cure treatment was not fictional. Treated with no effect during her mid-teens for psychological problems thought to stem from emotion and the intellectual strain of schoolwork, she was sent to Mitchell in 1888, who labeled her a hypochondriac and continued the ineffective treatment. She died of cardiac arrest weeks later, most likely from the strain force-feeding put on her bedridden body and weakened heart. Still, Mitchell maintained little patience for patients, insisting women be removed from their homes and "the whole daily drama of the sick-room, with its little selfishnesses and its craving for sympathy and indulgence,"[11] for "when they are bidden to stay in bed a month, and neither to read, write, nor sew, and to have one nurse—who is not a relative—then rest becomes for some women a rather bitter medicine, and they are glad enough to accept the order to rise and go about."[12]

The rest cure also utilized electroconvulsive therapy, which scientists began experimenting with in 1870, by placing electrodes in dogs' mouths. Despite the fact that more than half of the dogs died from cardiac arrest, scientists pursued the line of inquiry all the way to a slaughterhouse, where Italian scientist Ugo Cerletti watched pigs take electric volts to the head and decided this method might be suitable for humans.[13] By 1940, electroshock therapy was practiced in U.S. hospitals, physicians noting that with the treatment patients' psychotic symptoms declined along with their cognitive function. Still, removing psychosis, delusion, and paranoia was deemed a success—when patients' families began to notice and protest, the procedures were performed without consent.[14]

Meanwhile, physicians were also exploring drug treatments. When faced with the alternatives, it is not surprising women preferred drugs that could knock them clean out. Developed in the early 1950s, diazepam (also known as Valium) is a benzodiazepine whose effects are sedative and hypnotic, antianxiety and anticonvulsant. Benzos are considered useful in treating anxiety, insomnia, agitation, seizures, and muscle spasms, and for use in medical procedures. In addition, they are often prescribed for alcohol, opiate, and other benzodiazepine withdrawals. If this seems counterintuitive, it is. Considered safe and effective for short-term use, benzos can cause tolerance, dependency, and severe withdrawal symptoms if used over the long term. Nevertheless, Valium is prescribed for long-term use and was the most commonly prescribed medication in the world when it was first marketed in the 1960s. By 1974, Valium became the first drug to exceed what would today be $1 billion dollars in sales.[15] The most successful drug in pharmaceutical history until Prozac, the Valium craze faded in the early 1980s, but millions of Valium prescriptions a year continue to be written in the United States.[16]

The shift to drug treatment was swift—who doesn't seek the taste of tranquility?—and by 1971, one in five American women and one in thirteen American men were using minor tranquilizers. Two million Americans were addicted to diazepam during the 1970s—four times the number of heroin addicts—and it is estimated that up to 18 percent of all American physicians regularly took tranquilizers.[17] By 1980, physicians were writing 10 million prescriptions a year for antidepressants.[18] Eventually there were more than a thousand kinds of benzodiazepines, including the Xanax prescribed to me.[19]

When I received the prescription my family joked, "Sissy needs a Xanax," like it was merely a matter of choosing one from plenty—Ambien, Lunesta, Librium, Klonopin, Atavan, Restoral. "Take one the moment you start to feel anxious," the doctor encouraged, which seemed counterintuitive to what I'd heard all my life—what so many girls and women have heard—about the dangers of roofies, also a benzo.

Though vaginal perfume and leeches are behind us, women's rates of mental illness and dependence on doctors have increased. Women are now twice as likely as men to suffer from depression and anxiety, have disorders occur earlier than men, and are more likely to have multiple mental health disorders during their lifetime. NIMH reports that women utilize mental health services like antidepressants far more than men. Women and mental illness—the established narrative insists—go together, women more likely to have their experience medicalized through diagnosis and treatment.

Examining medical practices reveals the social values placed on female bodies and the ways we continue to blame gender. What is considered "normal" shifts with time, age, gender, race, sexuality, socioeconomic class, and location.

What we deem illness is always changing, the symptoms, diagnosis, and treatments fairly subjective. What remains constant, however, is that blame rests with the female body. What remains is the potential for financial gain, for there is profit to be made when someone is in need of treatment, and the cult of hypochondria and popular narratives of frailty and cure create financial interest.

A peek inside women's magazines reveals our current attitudes towards women's health, everything from worry or laugh lines to collagen, vaginal dryness to vaginal reconstruction presented as ailments with ready-made cures. Women are warned of the dangers of high blood pressure and obesity, depression and vaginal pH disruption, all of which impact the cultural work women are expected to perform with their bodies. Alongside these ills are new aesthetic ailments—sagging breasts, lumpy noses, stomachs scarred from childbirth—and the surgical cures that will offer visual remedy.

"You look awful," my family says when I am fretful and sick. "Take a Xanax."

I take Xanax three times—twice when Brady insists, frightened by my wailing and the way I clutch at my throat, and once when a migraine shadows my sight and makes me feel as though my spine is being crushed. Each time I submit to the blackout.

Time marches forward and I move with Brady from California to Nebraska to begin work on my PhD. If my symptoms have lifted I can't tell—everyone says I'm better than I was, but still not well enough—so I carry the bottle of Xanax with me religiously. I check my purse, afraid someone will know I have the bottle with me while also petrified it will slip out and I'll be left to my own devices. Sometimes I cradle the bottle in my hand and roll it around like a worry stone. Eventually the paper label wears smooth.

When Brady and I drive to Nebraska, making our way across our map, I think about how people prefer me asleep. How they'd rather X me out. "You look awful. Just take one." "You're hysterical. Just take one." This becomes a refrain. But even obeying doesn't seem to solve the problem—the specter of anxiety hovering over me when I drift off creeps in when I sleep, looming closer than ever when I wake.

I hope that when we begin somewhere new, I will also be new. I cradle the bottle as I stare out the window. The mountains flatten out to the plains, each highway chained to the next. I clasp my hands around the drugs like prayer.

CHAPTER 8

LEARNED BEHAVIOR

We narrate our lives in terms of time—how long something lasted, when something began or ended. In doing so, we downplay the importance of place and position—the spaces where things occur, the spaces we are expected to fill, the spaces we are denied. The space of my life changes when I move to the Great Plains with Brady, for though Nebraska is wide and open, the margins of my life narrow, the walls of what is considered sane pressing in on me until I see myself as bulky, clumsy, on display. I spend more time in my new home, trapped in solipsistic contemplation of each pain and ache, space becoming so tiny I forget how good using the body can feel, forget the way I used to run or sprawl out. I am too busy trying to disappear.

When you are anxious you are confined to the space illness allows. The occupation is suffocating. Anxiety is compressed, dense, and claustrophobic, a million things packed in a tight mind. And it reduced even further on the Great Plains, the looming expanse pressing down on anxiety's frantic nature until it reverberates. The first women settlers here went mad: lured by the promise of a lush utopia, they arrived to find isolation, barren earth whipped away by merciless wind.

In *The Bell Jar*, Sylvia Plath describes the space of Ester's depression as "very still and empty, the way the eye of a tornado must feel, moving dully along in the middle of the surrounding hullabaloo."[20] If depression is the eye of a tornado, anxiety is where the storm tethers down, a fear funneling up and out for miles, growing wild and frenzied overhead.

Several years after I arrive in Nebraska, I teach *The Bell Jar* in a women's literature class for college juniors and seniors who are surprised to hear about the history of women's madness.

"I designed this course around the long-standing notion that women are 'mad,'" I begin carefully on the first day, worried my students will know I've planned the course because I have a personal interest in the subject, have had anxiety several years by now. I continue, "Because a student last semester came to my office to talk about a paper and while doing so told me, 'All women are a little crazy,' and I wanted to explore that common misconception."

(I don't say anything more about the student, that his fiancé had recently left him and he called her "that bitch" and "that slut" when he talked with his classmates, or that he wrote war stories with all-male casts and enough explosives to blow up whatever was haunting him from his own military experience, or that he wrote opinion pieces for the university's newspaper about the danger of feminism and why women shouldn't be allowed to wear leggings. I didn't say that he stretched his legs wide in my office and said he rarely takes classes from women "because they're all a little crazy." Or that I chose silence, smiling because I knew what would happen if I did anything else.

Resist, talk back and face male anger, incredulity. Couch your opposition and face the same. Give an unexpected grade—a D, a C, a B, the letter doesn't matter—and be asked to explain yourself. Hear students say, "*Everything Is an*

Argument isn't a book title—it's my ex-wife" or "The girls in my group were bossy, that's why I couldn't help." Overhear a student say, "She wishes I raped her." Have male students shout at you, stand over you and point their fingers in your face, refuse to leave your office until the male professor next door intervenes. Have students write papers defending the multiple rape allegations against their fraternity house or about why the U.S. women's soccer team shouldn't be paid as much as the men's because "women's muscles, like their brains, are smaller," or about how women wouldn't get raped so much if they would date nice guys. Have students write, "I didn't really care about the course material, but she's hot" on your course evaluations. The first class you taught? The first assignment? A student wrote a paper detailing why you should date him, then crossed his arms and argued at the back of the class for the rest of the semester when you ignored him. He took a class with you the following semester.

When the student looked me in the eye and said all women were crazy, I felt angry. Then the anger turned to fear. I blamed anxiety for making me too weak to prevent this, for being too afraid to react after it occurred. Anxiety, I'd been told time and again, made me irrational and emotional. *It's all in your head.* Now, with a decade of teaching and anxiety under my waist-cinching belt, I recognize that I was not angry and afraid because of my madness. It was because of my gender.)

I watch students that semester—mostly women—applaud writers like Virginia Woolf, whose "Angel in the House" they compare to their mothers and grandmothers and times long before their own. They are sympathetic to Pecola, the little black girl who descends into madness after being raped by her father and blamed by her town in Toni Morrison's *The Bluest Eye.* They repeat, "Your silence will not protect you," after Audre Lorde. They ask how they can "Dive Into Wreck" like Adrienne Rich. We read Jennifer Finney Boylan and other trans writers, and when we watch *Boys Don't Cry* and they learn Brandon Teena was murdered not far from our Nebraska city, they organize a campus film night. They tackle complex texts, hold one another accountable. They are kind to themselves and other women.

But in *The Bell Jar* Ester Greenwood is privileged, they insist, lives a glamorous lifestyle and is therefore undeserving of the tornado around her. And Edna, the protagonist from Kate Chopin's *The Awakening,* is crazy. Really crazy. She's wealthy, she's white, she's suffered no abuse. She may be unhappy with the gender roles available to her, but the students question Edna's decision to commit suicide, find it an act of selfishness or cowardice, the ultimate seal of insanity. They feel sorry for the narrator from Charlotte Perkins Gilman's "The Yellow Wallpaper," but refer to Gilman as "crazy" all semester even though I assure them the work is fiction and Gilman never hallucinated to the extent her narrator does.

Similarly, they do not sympathize with Marya Hornbacher's book *Wasted,* which details her experiences with anorexia, bulimia, and bipolar disorder. They dislike Elizabeth Wurtzel intensely when they read *Prozac Nation,* which chronicles her depression in high school and college with a ferocity for which many students are unprepared. They accuse her of being too angry, are frustrated that she "relapses" so many times and can't "get it together." They ask, "How can she be so depressed when nothing bad ever happened to her?" Writers accepted to prestigious universities, earning simultaneous A's and asylum stays have no reason to suffer.

My students believe that Hornbacher and Wurtzel, middle-class white women who published books in their twenties, did not suffer enough to warrant illness, are too successful to be mentally ill. They champion a cause-and-effect version of mental illness wherein something terrible—trauma, physical and sexual abuse, racism, homophobia, extreme poverty, the curse of genetics—leads to madness. I wonder if this is a way to protect themselves—the majority of my students are not unlike the women they critique. They do like the 2001 movie adaptation of *Prozac Nation,* however, which stars the beautifully tragic Christina Ricci. Ricci is dark and artsy, her bitterness contrasted by her porcelain skin and sad eyes, and students find the film gritty, the kind of film with raw images and an indie soundtrack that leaves viewers tastefully angsty by the final credits. They don't like Wurtzel, but they do like Hollywood, and this film, they insist, redeems the book.

Before and after class I hear female students say, "The guy on the third floor won't leave me alone" or "We have to go dancing in a group" or "My friend was raped over the weekend." Some bring their younger siblings to class when the elementary schools are closed, or take time off to care for ailing parents, or use their allotted absences to have the baby they've been hiding all semester. Some cry in my office or the hallway before class because they've been raped and want to apologize if they seem "out of sorts." I read their papers about depression, anxiety, OCD, eating disorders, bipolar disorder, but most are too afraid to voice their experiences in class.

Women's silence is learned. Since childhood I've been taught that working-class women—women like my grandmothers, my mother, me—need to be tough and resilient. There is no time, no space for weakness, for emotion, for the indulgence of madness.

My father's mother, Ginny, was only five-foot-one, but as the oldest of seven Oklahoma children, born when her mother was fifteen, she had to help raise her siblings, even helped to raise her mama, some said, the two more like sisters than anything. I picture her, tiny thing struggling to balance babies that aren't even hers on her hips, watching funnels form in the panhandle.

By the time Ginny married my grandfather, six-foot-nine with an even larger temper, she was already adept at making do, and took in laundry to help with the expense of raising their four boys. If she felt any regret over her marriage, any postpartum grief after one of her twin sons died in infancy, she never showed it, set her mouth in a flat line like the horizon she'd grown up with and her gaze on the laundry as her sons tumbled around the house and her stormy husband raged. She smoothed wrinkles and made clean folds for years as they fought, swallowing down the bitterness of her life until one day she found a lump, a hard mound the size of a cantaloupe in her stomach.

Ginny never spoke of the mass. She said talking about it gave it power, made it prophecy. When she finally went to the doctor he named what she'd feared, and while diagnosis is not what killed her body, the stigma killed her spirit, made her so afraid that for once she shrunk to her size, seemed so unlike the sharp-tongued woman whose stories made her larger and stronger for much of her life, words bone-sharp and raging from a ragged jaw on a sagged porch.

My great aunts, her sisters, are much the same: Oklahoma women patched in scraps, yellow calloused fingers dangling chained cigarettes, spirals whipping quick-time around their tornado mouths on slow afternoons. They speak of broken bikes, dirty dogs, rusted cans. They are worn down from a man, or another baby, or a small town. They grimace when they down hot beer, hips cocked, eyes squinting at the sun. They shoo away flies crowded around their sweaty faces, spit out words like clotted blood or something on fire. Like gunmetal. These are the women I come from.

My mother's mother, Glenna, was fierce as well, though I called her Poopsie, a soft, doting name. Hers is a story of turmoil, of violence—if anyone earned madness, she did, but she shrugged away antidepressants in old age, chaotic fears and feelings routine by then. Married to an alcoholic for over fifty years, she laughed when they danced and flinched when he raised a voice or a hand. She never spoke of this to me—the grandfather I knew slipped me secret butterscotch candies—so I learned of his whiskey temper only after he died, always in whispered flashes, fragments rather than in full. Learning the truth explained why she seemed so happy after his death. As a child, I thought my grandmother was relieved not to have to care for my grandfather any longer—helping his heavy body into a wheelchair, wiping food from his mouth, cleaning up his incontinence for six years after his stroke—but now I think the reason she whistled with the radio and delighted in sweets, her once-lithe body growing plump, was because she was finally free.

Poopsie showed little hurt or fear for herself, but worried endlessly over her children and grandchildren. She warned me against the unpredictability of men when I went away to college, and scolded me when I called, asking how late I walked around campus at night, why I wanted to move to a dangerous city for graduate school. Because I did not yet know about my grandfather or what the world could do to a woman, I thought her paranoid. Anxious.

Poopsie's death was slow and painful. She endured until she didn't. When doctors found lung cancer, my grandmother, a smoker for over seventy years, never asked for another cigarette, her only vice besides my grandfather. The cancer disappeared with radiation and medication, and though the tissue-thin skin on her arms was marbled black from blood draws and IVs, my grandmother never admitted pain, only said her feet were cold every once in a while or complained she'd broken a nail too short. One night she pulled on her housecoat and slippers before she dialed 911 and collapsed to the floor because she refused to bother my parents, who lived a half-mile away. She died for a moment and was revived, spending a long final week in the hospital, shooing us all away with manicured fingers, her hands tied down to keep her from removing the breathing tube. Spare the children, keep it inside. She taught this to my mother, who taught it to me.

My mother rarely shows pain, despite limping when she walks, one leg shorter than the other, her six-foot-one frame tilted, her feet marked with arthritis and bone spurs, structures that make visible how she hurts. Her fingers quilt scraps into something beautiful despite being stiff with arthritis. She aches and hurts—this I know from the expression she makes when she bends to pick up a child, thinking no one sees her wince, or the way she sighs alone as she makes dinner after a twelve-hour workday. Pain is not an option for my mother, nor is illness—my mother does not take sick days, even when she is feverish or throwing up. She recently put off surgery to replace a torn rotator cuff for over a year, learning to pick her daycare children up with one arm. "I don't want to let the parents down," she says when I plead with her to get some rest. Pain is not an option for my mother, who rarely speaks about her violent childhood or the violence that shadows the lives of her children.

When I look at my mother, I see her age, her strain, and her worry written in the lines on her face. My mother does not go to the doctor for illness or prevention. Like many working-class families, we've never had much for health insurance. The only prescription I've known her to take is Celexa, which she has taken in secret each day for years. Silence, like madness, runs rampant in our family.

This is the legacy of women I come from—a legacy tied to gender, to class, to male violence and the threat thereof, poor women with too many children and not enough food and too much hurting and hating, women too afraid to say anything of their pain or their terror. Women so worried, so afraid, their bodies and minds react. Women bound by silence not to speak of the things that dart around their brains late at night, instead letting them settle in dark corners, where they lurk for a lifetime.

I think about carrying on and keeping quiet in my new home. I know I have burdened my family with my illness for over half a year. Here I will be different. Here I will burden only myself. Swallow it down. Spare the children. I think about carrying on and keeping quiet as I set up house in Nebraska and prepare to begin my new degree and new teaching job, a life so unlike those of manual labor the women I come from live. Over the last few months, Celexa has eased my shaking hands and loosened the tangle in my throat, but I still see disaster, fear apocalypse. I still carry the bottle of Xanax with me like a nervous housewife.

And I act the role: I fret over my new home. I purchase dozens of paint samples for each room, painting patches of color on the walls, moving from angle to angle as I try to decide which version of off-white makes the bedroom look most peaceful. I worry I will choose wrong. I worry I'm taking too long to decide. Then I worry about worrying. Something scurries across my sight. I swallow seawater and blood. The world vibrates painfully around me.

I must carry on. I must keep quiet. I put up curtain rods and ironed curtains. I buy new linens for the bed, for the bathrooms. I hang and rehang paintings. I buy a dozen potted plants, organize the kitchen, the bookshelves. I make pitchers of fresh sun tea each day, cook dinner each night. I work so intensely to make this space one that is bearable that I make myself sick. It is still summer, but when school begins in the fall I'll do the same. In Nebraska I am a Celexa doll: I wind myself up. I smile.

CHAPTER 9

THE WORLD WE'VE MADE FOR WOMEN

We seem to have made a world for women where it is easier to blame their sanity than their circumstance. It is easier to point to a part of women's bodies—uterus and ovaries, serotonin and cortisol—than to point to a world that faults them. It is easier to believe women broken than bruised.

One in four women take antidepressants, according to a study of prescription claims data from 2001 to 2010, and women are twice as likely compared to men to take anti-anxiety medication.[21] In 2017, the National Center for Health Statistics announced that the suicide rate for girls between fifteen and nineteen reached a forty-year high, doubling between 2007 and 2015.[22]

Another one-in-four statistic: in 2015, the Association of American Universities found that one in four women experience sexual assault while on college campuses.[23] As is always the case when discussing definitions of sexual assault, the data was contested by some, but previous reports indicated that one in five women will be sexually assaulted in college, and the Rape, Abuse and Incest National Network (RAINN) reports that one out of every six American women have been the victim of an attempted or completed rape in her lifetime.

On the RAINN website, there is a countdown with a reminder that "every 98 seconds, another person experiences sexual assault." The webpage is filled with symbols of bodies and as the timer progresses, the bodies change colors to indicate when they have been raped. The infographic looks strikingly similar to those I've seen about the rise in mental illness in America, particularly for young people.

A few years ago I started keeping track of how many of my students disclosed their rape, either in office hours or in their writing. "I will not let it define me," wrote a woman who took several antidepressants. "I'm not a victim," wrote another who described her bulimia in a different paper. "*The Handmaid's Tale* is a science fiction novel that brings to light many of the issues facing women in the 1980s," wrote a student who was raped during the semester our class was reading the book and withdrew from the university mid-semester. Several students had panic attacks in class. Many more wiped away tears when we read about violence against women. Nearly each semester a student disappears for a few days. When they come to my office, the apology always comes first. Then the story: Walking alone late at night, at a fraternity party, in the dorms, after a football game. An acquaintance, a friend, a partner, a student athlete. They remove emotion from the narrative. They focus instead on what they must do to catch up.

"I'm sorry," I began when I told my therapist about my rape. I'd been coming to her for a year, seeking anxiety treatment for five. No one had ever asked if I'd experienced trauma or abuse. No one had ever pointed to an external source of my fear. Anxiety was all in my head; something inside was broken.

I believed this. I worked too hard. I was not good at relaxing. I was hysterical. When I finally told my therapist about my rape it was because I felt guilty, like my secret prevented her from doing her job. It took me longer to apologize than to tell the story. When I did, the story came back in flashes, full of blank spaces. The rest was blurred, circular and contradictory. It is no wonder my life was the same.

It is my final year of college. My parents adopted Cameron and Bailey the year before and my mother has informed me she's learned of a young girl, Victoria, stranded in another country. I hear the familiar flicker of goodwill in her voice. I am not welcome at the house if I can't be nice, so I begin spending weekends in my apartment with books.

Because I am a good girl, I am nearly twenty-one before I taste alcohol, but when I try it, I like the way alcohol dissolves my shy awkwardness. Suddenly strangers are friends—now I see why my classmates seem to always know each other.

On a Thursday my roommate's boyfriend breaks up with her, which makes me glad, because he sometimes stares at me when he comes to the house to pick her up, looking me up and down while he waits for her to finish getting ready. She wants to go out for drinks to forget him. This sounds fun until he asks to tag along "as friends." He insists on driving us in his flashy car, the one he parks wherever he feels—"With a car this nice you can make your own spot," he says without laughing. Premonition tingles in my limbs, but I brush it aside as paranoia.

At the bar, I shout to my roommate over the music and watch her swallow drink after drink. I toast with drinks of my own, because this is what girlfriends do. We "wooooo" with the rest of the women in the bar each time the DJ tells us. I feel silly if I think about it too much.

I sit on one side of her, her ex on the other, whispering in her ear while he reaches his hand around her to stroke my hair. When she goes to the bathroom he slides up close to me, whispering how sexy I am into the side of my neck. His breath is hot and sour and I go clammy. The women "wooooo" again as his hand snakes its way to my lower back.

My roommate returns drunk and sad, and the air between them is sharp, but soon he is distracted by the sequins on her top and he dances with her until the bar closes. I long to go home, but know not to walk alone late at night. I ease the tension with my drink, wincing at the sting of the lemons I suck to pass the time.

I hold my roommate's hand on the way home. I pretend to comfort her, but I'm secretly afraid, for her ex has had too much to drink and he drives too fast, sharp turns pushing me against the sides of the car, my roommate shouting at him to slow down, which only seems to urge him on. When we finally arrive at our apartment, I need help getting her up the stairs, and he sits in the living room while I close her bedroom door and take off her shirt. Sequins sparkle on the floor. She holds my shoulders as I help her out of her skirt and tuck her into bed. She wants him to stay. She insists they need to talk. I escape to my room and don't lock the door in case she needs me in the middle of the night.

I do not remember how long I slept or if I slept at all. Forgive me, reader. The memory is blurred. Except for the places where it is sharp.

Suddenly he sits on the edge of my bed. He says he is worried he hurt my roommate's heart. I yawn and murmur, "Yes, I think you did and maybe you shouldn't come here anymore," sleepy from the drinks and the late hour. I will feel the same years later, when I take the muscle relaxers doctors eventually prescribe for my body that cannot find comfort.

I bear the burden of his heavy body. I try to talk him out of it, try to push him off, try to escape as he slides his hands and then his body over mine, but he goes fast and hungry.

I cry when he won't listen. I want to call out to my roommate, but she is so sad. I cry quietly instead, so much so that after a while he places his hand over my wet mouth.

My head is mixed up, my emotions too. I'm present but I'm gone. I panic. I doubt.

I manage to push him off, untangle myself from the sheets and his limbs, and crawl to the end of the bed, but he yanks me back by the hair, pulling at my neck. It is a series of knots for days after. For years. I hold still as he puts hands across my eyes, his fingers in my mouth, as he lifts my legs like a puppeteer. He wraps his hands around my neck, tightening until things go black. My memory stops here.

I skip class the next day. When I hear my roommate talking to him on the telephone, I sneak out, drive home, play with my new brothers, and then feign illness in the dark of my bedroom for the weekend. Natalie reads at the foot of my bed while I hide in the sheets.

I drive back late Sunday night and wake early Monday morning to find a note on my car, parked beneath my window. He says things went too far—unlike me, he isn't the kind of person to sleep with someone right away—but he wants to see where things go. He knows I like books so he makes a metaphor about cake—he tasted the frosting the other night, but now he wants to eat the whole piece. "Isn't that clever?" he asks.

When my roommate is gone at the afternoon class they share, he knocks on the door. I am afraid he might tell her. Afraid he might tell my friends. They know him too. He knocks and knocks. "I know you're in there," he coos. Then he says it louder. I'm afraid the neighbors will hear. I worry that if people know it will become real. My parents can't find out because I am the oldest and I should know better. So I let him in. After that he doesn't ask for permission—I find him waiting in my bedroom days later, the window open, the ripped screen blowing in the wind.

I pretend romance. I worry what my roommate will think, but I'd rather be a man stealer than a slut. We go on dates. I talk about him like a high school crush. Sometimes I even convince myself—one night I go to a party at his house and watch a young girl straddle his lap in front of me, feel a twisted surge of jealousy, though I never like when he fucks me, hate that he listens to baseball games or old political speeches while he does, pausing his thrusting to listen more closely, lectures me about politics while he's on top of me. I hate the way he chokes me each time he comes, the framed picture of Ronald Reagan he keeps next to his bed the last thing I see before blacking out.

I can't escape. When I avoid his phone calls, he shows up at my house and threatens to expose our relationship unless I leave with him. After months I spit out that I don't care, that everyone probably knows by now. I slam the door in his face. He begins to follow me when I walk home after school. He drives slowly behind me, my phone vibrating in my schoolbag. He inches his bumper closer to me, calling out the window at my back. If anyone passing by notices, he calls out brightly, "I really messed up with my girlfriend," and they laugh before driving away, another college couple fighting in the rearview mirror.

I'm afraid of his car and the anger in his voice, so I always end up in the passenger seat. We drive out past the city limits, his hand heavy on my knee. Later, in the campground or the park or at the beach, he slaps me, chokes me, tears me inside, the trees or the stars the last things I see, the sound of waves and his heavy breathing echoing in my ears. When I wake, I am blooming: pink palm prints, purple bruises, red in the toilet.

I remember this: his sweat tasted like moss, he smelled of ocean caves. He once threatened to leave me at a campground if I didn't climb on top of him, threatened to pull me out of the car and leave me there with no cell service. At the beach, he showed me a cave carved out of the side of a hill by the water's force. He made me walk inside and then refused to let me out when the tide came in, laughing at my terror, my fear of the rising water. When I remember him, it is mostly darkness, because that is how most of our encounters were—he used to tap softly on my window in the night and then text me that he would break the glass, smiling as I read the words. He kidnapped me in a parking lot one night, refused to take me home and instead drove me far out into the country, where he made me pull down my pants on the side of the road, the lone car that passed convinced, no doubt, we were lovers on the hood of his car. The same thing happened the night he drove me to an affluent neighborhood near our university. I was on all fours, his hands around my neck from behind, as passing cars rushed through the stop sign directly above us. I threw up afterward and felt guilty for soiling the grass in such a nice neighborhood.

I learned new ways to be in my body and brain. His hands around my throat soon seemed an embrace, the bruises across my back a sign of affection, the grit in my palms after he pushed me to the ground a map.

When I arrived at the house he shared with several room-mates he would hide, bursting from a closet or grabbing me from behind and cupping his hand over my mouth, twist-ing my arms behind me, laughing, "You're cute when you're scared." One day I couldn't find him, but each time I walked to my car to leave, he called my phone. "I see you trying to leave. You can't go yet," he whispered. Back in the house, I heard noises, the walls creaking and pounding. I wasn't sure they were real. I thought I was going crazy. At last I texted to say I was leaving, but when I opened the front door, he jumped down to block my path. He'd been on the roof all along.

Another time I sat in his kitchen watching him prepare a steak, pounding it tender with a meat cleaver, blood seep-ing from the sides. He brought up that first night, laughing, cleaver in hand—"You know I've done this before. To lots of girls."

I became an expert at explaining. I blamed his late-night visits on drunken friends, my long absences on library study-ing. At first I said he had an unrequited crush. "I don't want to hurt his feelings," I insisted, ashamed. Months later, when friends who'd met and disliked him pointed to his arrogance and anger, I said I was having fun, wasn't looking for some-thing serious. It's easy to rewrite a narrative that doesn't suit you.

Surely someone knew. The friend who watched me jump each time my phone rang, the one I bribed to come to lunch with us, to ice cream, to the beach. Natalie, who was staying with me when he arrived unannounced and threatened to expose me if we didn't go to a nearby strawberry festival. At the festival he moved orange cones out of his way so he could drive up the blocked road, and when the police stopped him, Natalie and I afraid we'd be in trouble, they chuckled and said, "I remember college," asking about his sports car, and giving him a warning. "I can't believe you let me be around that creep," Natalie hissed then. She still says it now.

Surely the group of girls he saw me with at the donut shop one morning—"She lets me stick it anywhere," he said, jamming his finger through the hole in my donut—suspected. Or his roommate who drove me home the night he yelled at me to come to bed. The roommate must have seen something in my face, must have heard me crying through the wall they shared so many afternoons, heard the slaps, my gasps for breath. I wanted to finish the movie we were watching with the roommate and his girlfriend, kind, copresidents of the Christian club on campus. She stayed behind while her boyfriend drove me home, both of us ignoring our phones flashing over and over, the honking and flashing lights behind, the flashy car trying to run us into the shoulder. When we finally escaped, the roommate pulled to the side of the road and attempted to kiss me. "Don't you think you owe me?"

It lasted six months—throughout my final semester of college and well into the summer. My memories of graduation are memories of him, for I'd barely slept the night before, refusing to see him at three a.m. for a "quick fuck" because I had to be up early for the ceremony. He pounded on my window for so long I finally crawled into bed with my roommate. He called me repeatedly throughout the ceremony the next day and I whispered, "Please let me hang up," because it was rude to talk during the commencement speech and I worried my parents would see me on the phone during such an important occasion.

I last saw him at the end of summer. I was looking after Cameron and Bailey at my parents' house, sweating in the heat and growing tense as he threatened to drive to my small town and find my car. I needed to protect my brothers, so I agreed to meet him that evening. When we met, he told me get into his car, whistling "Take Me Out to the Ballgame" as we drove, turning to smile at me in the passenger seat as he sang, "I don't care if I never get back."

When we got to the baseball park, he dragged me into a bathroom behind the dugout and pushed my face to the ground. There was a grate on the floor so janitors could hose down the room and I focused on it while I waited for him to finish. I focused only on the drain—the shape, the size, each detail—until the room and the sound and the feel of him, and eventually my own body became secondary. I did not see the dirty tile floor or his hands on either side of my face. There was only the drain. I did not feel him slapping my ass or gripping my neck. The drain. I not feel frightened. I did not feel anything. Drain. I focused so much that when he'd finished and stood up, I remained on the floor a long time.

(I still do this, with anxiety. In times of stress, I focus on some small detail—a lump in my neck, a bump on my bone, a crooked tooth—so intently the rest of the world disappears. Only now my body is present. As are my emotions. Everything is amplified and each hurt is a hundred times worse, my body making up for lost time.)

I was numb afterward, as we walked back to the car, and I suppose this is why I felt brave enough to run away after six months and up a hill. I watched him from afar, frustrated, turn his back to leave me stranded. At the top of the hill, I lay down. I made myself tight and rigid. I pulled myself in stiff like a reed. And then I rolled down the other side of the hill and away from him. He shouted and cursed me for acting silly, for laughing though he was always telling me to smile. He threatened me, but I held my breath and body so still it was like I wasn't even alive. Down I went, spiraling too fast to catch.

After the summer ended, I moved away to graduate school and lived alone in a new city. I stopped answering his phone calls—the ones that came dozens of times each day and all throughout the night. I was afraid he would find me, so I kept my curtains and blinds shut tight. I spent a lot of time alone in the dark—I was too afraid to make friends.

After I moved away to graduate school, my mother visited me in the city where I tried to forget about him, where I tried to get lost. She spent her visit talking about Victoria, who'd moved in permanently. I needed to come home and visit more often, my mother said. I needed to get to know Victoria. I needed to be a good sister, a good person.

One night I sat on my kitchen counter, my mother on the couch in the living room, a distance between us so wide we had to raise our voices to speak to one another. Suddenly the story burst out. I spit it out like salt and lead. "I'm sorry," I repeated over and over.

My mother rose from the couch, rushed over and cried out, nearly shouted, "Sweetie, why didn't you tell me? Why didn't you tell me? I'm your mom."

I stopped, humiliated and stomach sick. I looked down at my feet swinging frantic over the counter, my hands clutching at the counter's edge. I balanced my feet on the trash can, watched it wobble under the pressure.

"That was stupid," said my mother.

Later, I admitted what happened to Natalie, because she had been lying for Victoria, who snuck out at night to get drunk by the beach, who woke up and didn't know where she had been. "You should tell Mom," I pleaded. I was ashamed to tell Natalie what had happened to me and when I was done, she shuddered and said, "I wish you hadn't told me that. Don't talk about it again." When I broke this promise she said, "You know that was your fault, don't you?"

This is the world we've made for women. One where it is easier to blame sanity than circumstance, easier to believe women broken than bruised. Most of the women in my family—grandmother, aunts, cousins, my mother, I suspect, though she does not speak of it—have been raped.

There are four sisters in my family. We've all been raped.

It is the final days of summer. I meet with a group of teach-ers, writers, and scholars to swim. These women come from many states and several countries. We gather at the deep end of the pool because college boys occupy the center, drinking beer and splashing.

We talk about the books we are reading and writing, and our travels and teaching in the upcoming semester. And then we talk about rape. Of six women, five have been raped. No one calls it that, of course, each using euphemisms and the kind of vague language we warn our students against. We tell our stories with smooth faces. Our narration is practiced. Though no one apologizes, we tell our stories without emo-tion. We raise our voices to hear one another over beer pong and country music. Over all the laughter.

Later in the day, I leave the water to take a picture of the women taking up such a small space in the deep end. They pose and smile. They hold themselves perfectly still. From my angle I can see them treading water, legs and arms thrashing below the surface, fighting to stay afloat.

CHAPTER 10

EDITING

In Nebraska I try to be new. I take classes for my PhD and learn to keep my hands under the desk so my colleagues can't see them tremble, to keep nodding and saying, "That *is* problematic," while my vision jolts like an old TV, goes static and then comes back into focus, a giant spider crawling across the scene. I teach classes and lecture in the midst of panic attacks, sweating from the effort of holding it together, listening to variations of "The dog ate my homework" after class. I throw up between each class, one hand holding back my long hair, another holding onto my cell phone so that I am not late to wherever it is I have to run to next. My Xanax bottle rattles when I rush down the halls.

Sometimes I slip, like when I get a migraine, the aura taking over my sight on one side, white and pulsing. I can't keep my eyes open in front of my office mate and I slump into a chair, trying to get relief from the knot forming at the base of my spine. I can't drive and must ask her for a ride. I play this on repeat for as long as I know her. My new colleagues go out for dinner, for drinks, for cigars. They invite me along, but my evenings are reserved for massaging my limbs back to life or screaming when I wake up from a dream that the Yellowstone caldera has exploded and I'm downing in ash. I don't say this, of course, so soon I've got a reputation for being stuck-up.

Before bed I swallow Celexa like I'm supposed to—it's been six, seven, eight months now. I've come to view medication as the hall monitor for my out-of-control fear—a fear I still don't understand because no one, myself included, has thought to question what makes me so afraid. The drug is guardian, authority, savior, but if I feel more in control than before—I can leave the house, after all—it's mostly because I've had so much practice. I've learned how to live when you're convinced you're dying. I look weak, but the amount of energy I spend simply getting through my life is superhuman.

Each morning I talk to my mother on the phone and despite the time difference and the early time I've risen, she's always up before me, already working. She tells me about my siblings—Cameron's asthma attack, Bailey's worsening OCD, Casey kicked out of high school, Victoria applying for college. She tells me about her upcoming day—her day-care hours begin at six a.m. and ends after six p.m., and she will have a total of sixteen children at the house. I try not to burden her with my anxiety.

One burden: A few months after I arrive in Nebraska, I go to urgent care on a Saturday for pain that begins much like the dozens of urinary tract infections I've had before, but then worsens until I can hardly stand. After several hours in the waiting room, a physician lets me pee in a cup, and because there's blood in my urine, she sends me to the emergency room across the street for a CAT scan. Blood-work there can get expensive, so she draws it first.

The ER doctor insists he can't use the bloodwork, and after repeating it, conducts a full pelvic exam first. I lie on the bed, stripped to the waist, as he finds nothing, but says I will also need an ultrasound. I ask to use the restroom first since I've had a lot of water to help flush what I assumed was a UTI. "It's not a problem," he says, calling in a nurse to insert a catheter, though I really want to use the restroom I can see from my bed.

The nurse brings in a medical student and asks if the student can insert the catheter. I am afraid to say no. I'm afraid to say anything for fear that once they find out I have anxiety, they'll dismiss my complaint entirely, as people with psychiatric illnesses have higher rates of ER use than the general population when compared to a national sample.

One in eight emergency room visits involve mental health and/or substance use, a 15 percent increase between 2007 and 2011. Visits related to depression, anxiety, and stress reactions rose 55.5 percent during that period, while those for psychoses or bipolar disorder rose 52 percent.[24] I wonder what the staff will think of my pain if they find out I am mentally unstable. Will they label me a part of the growing number of anxious Americans rushing for help, wasting time and money when they should take a nap or try some yoga?

My pain is real, but I'm learning Americans like to rank suffering, and mine does not qualify. I let the student insert the catheter, a process that takes fifteen minutes and pinches—"That's normal, honey," the nurse coos beside me. When the student is finished, the nurse inspects the results and sees the student has inserted the catheter into my vagina instead of my urethra, so we must start again. I want to say smugly, "I told you it pinched." I don't.

Eventually, I'm rolled through the hallways, past several restrooms, to the ultrasound room. The technician heaves a sigh of inconvenience and tells me he needs to find a female nurse to sit in the room since law requires a female witness. He does an abdominal ultrasound, then adds another procedure, inserting a thick wand inside me. The wand moves in and out, roving around while the technician stares at his screen for results. I don't think he ever looks at me. There's nothing to report, so he sends me for the CAT scan I've been asking for since I arrived hours earlier.

After the CAT scan, a new physician joins the doctor to report the results. "Nothing there," the two men say, arms crossed over their white coats as they stare at me in bed. I haven't been allowed to get dressed. Urine drips through the catheter.

It may be a twisted ovary, they add, though this would have been revealed via the ultrasound and CAT scan, both of which said nothing of the sort. "These things cause anxiety in a lot of women," the older doctor says, walking over to the bed to rest his hands on the bars

"You need to consult with an OB/GYN," the younger doctor recommends, adding, as he leaves the room, "Tylenol should help. Like with menstrual cramps." I wait a while for the nurse to remove the catheter so I can dress, still doubled over. I apologize for wasting their time. I leave angry, angrier still when the $1,500 bill arrives months later, despite the decent health insurance my university provides.

"Well, that was an expensive lesson," my mother laughs. "It's mind over matter," adds my father, who does not believe mental illness is real. "Yuppie disease," he jokes, and I wonder what he thinks of chronic fatigue, fibromyalgia, Lyme. What would he think of the fatigue women who have had hysterectomies report? This fatigue lasts longer than pain, and women often feel embarrassed to report it, for though some doctors suggest iron supplements in case of postoperative anemia, many label it depression and anxiety, suggest, like my father, it is "all in your head."

When my pain subsides after a week, I wonder if it was my hormones. I wonder if it was all in my mind.

You must doubt me too, reader.

My hair begins to fall out during my first Nebraska autumn, but no one believes me. I lose it slowly at first, strands wrapped around my fingers in the shower, but eventually it comes out in clumps. "This isn't normal," I tell Brady, leading him into the bathroom to point at the tangle clogging the drain. "I have to empty the plug two or three times during every shower," I offer, trying to convince him something is wrong.

"It's probably stress," Brady reassures when I brush my hair to show him, the brush dragging strand after strand out from my scalp. He repeats this for weeks, but soon he can't ignore that our white kitchen floor is littered each time I make a meal, or that I leave hair on the pillow each morning.

My family and the few friends I've told insist I'm paranoid. "I can't tell a difference," they say over the phone when I send them photos. It's all in my head, they insist, but *if* my hair were falling out—"Which it's not," they add—my stress is the culprit.

Since my diagnosis, my illness is always at fault. I don't have the flu; I'm queasy because I'm anxious. I don't have a cough; my throat is tight because I'm anxious. I don't have a migraine; my head hurts because I'm anxious. Anxiety sufferers are more likely to develop physical illnesses and more likely to have severe symptoms. They also have a greater risk of death when they become ill and shorter life spans. Yet a pattern of doubt and blame shadows the health care they receive. The healthy world often considers infection or pulled muscles anxious phantoms, and even when physicians confirm strep throat or a sprain, my anxiety remains at fault, stress the bringer of each ill, everything somehow my fault.

Weeks pass. My hairline recedes, my widow's peak disappearing, bald patches forming at my temples. "See?" I cry, victorious, pointing to my pale scalp through my dark hair. "I told you," I shout, triumphant, clutching strands of hair in my clenched fist, gleeful for physical proof.

But no one believes me when I point to Celexa as the reason for my hair loss. And I can't convince them why it matters—*If medication makes you feel better, what's the harm?* Losing my hair without consent is terrifying, and that my sisters and girlfriends do not believe me even as they, too, fret over the cultural work of appearance is maddening.

My hair reached down my back for most of my childhood, long enough I needed help with washing and brushing. When I was finally allowed to choose my own hairstyle in middle school, I chose a short bob, something I saw beautiful grown women wearing on television. But I missed the curtain of hair to hide my braces and acne and the burden of my height behind and began growing it back as quickly as I'd cut it.

When I reached college, my waist-length hair was bleach blond, and when my first boyfriend left me for another girl, I copied women in the movies, dying it glossy black and cutting it short and jagged around my jaw. The cut made me feel new, grown up and desirable for the first time. Strangers approached me on the Internet, waiters scrawled phone numbers onto the check, and a man once followed me around a grocery store, asking for my number in the checkout aisle. "You've got sexy hair," he said as I wheeled my cart away.

My new hair was a bit like a costume, but I felt, finally, pretty. As time passed, few people remembered the girl who hid behind her hair, too shy to get out of the car when her mother dropped her off at middle school. Brady met someone self-assured in college. "My sassy girl," he whispered in my ear when he asked me to date him, insisting he would take care of me, though he didn't know how accurate this would prove.

I had short hair for several years, but the desire to hide returned with my increasing anxiety and I began growing my hair long again.

"There is no link between Celexa and hair loss," the doctor says when I finally book an appointment. "This is most likely caused by stress."

I tell my new Nebraska doctor that I've researched Celexa and quite a few patients report hair loss. The National Center for Biotechnology Information provides access to biomedical information, including articles about the hair loss associated with Celexa and similar drugs. Medical literature remains calm about the effect—which occurs primarily in women—listing efficacy and statistical significance, labeling the chance of alopecia "rare," but frantic patients flood forums online to report how the drug leads to intense hair fall. A friend's husband quit taking Celexa when he experienced irreversible hair loss.

The doctor tells me not to worry. Then he suggests I switch medications.

It is not uncommon for new patients to switch medications—more than 80 percent of depressed patients are responsive to some medication, but only 50 percent are responsive to their first medication.[25] Finding the right medication is akin to dating—the search holds hope and promise, yet is often awkward and embarrassing, the body waiting for release, experiencing disappointment instead.

The doctor deliberates, his gaze buried deep inside my medical chart. He asks me questions without looking at me, translating my answers into medical jargon, my life and illness distilled into brief, easily identifiable notes for him or the next doctor. Medicine is, after all, an act of narrative and translation—patients tell doctors their stories and physicians translate these tales to create narratives of recovery and resolution, prescribing medications and treatments that will offer a happy ending. The stories involved in medicine offer conflict, the climax of diagnosis, the dénouement of treatment.

While patients experience illness within the larger story of their lives, physicians value abstract lists of symptoms and diagnostic materials. Much of a patient's story is edited by doctors, who choose what is relevant, what is included in charts and records, what is written onto a patient's paper existence. Doctors learn in medical school to request bits of information, to extract from patients' lives only what is essential, to pare down the rest so only the basic, most essential is available for doctors to quickly glance at in a rushed appointment. Physicians learn to edit.

I stare out the window while I wait. Outside, the trees are burnt orange and yellow, like a blazing fire. The leaves fall slowly, but when the wind picks up, entire branches go bare.

"I'm going to recommend Lexapro to you, uh . . ." The doctor can't seem to remember my name and keeps referring to his chart as though I am a character in a play and there are stage directions, dialogue next to our names. Indeed, there is a script we are to follow, one where he tells me what will cure me and I follow suit. "We'll switch you to Lexapro to see if Celexa was causing the hair loss," he says before adding, "Though I doubt that's the case."

When I question his choice of drug—Celexa and Lexapro are from the same parent company and share a similar molecular structure—he sighs. "Are you saying you want to go off medication altogether?" he asks, eyebrows raised.

Both Celexa and Lexapro are selective serotonin reuptake inhibitors (SSRIs) that inhibit cells from the absorption, or "reuptake," of serotonin, thereby increasing serotonin levels that exist outside of cells. Both are prescribed primarily for depression, but can also be prescribed for anxiety disorders, and more recently for chronic pain, which is why SSRIs are the most commonly prescribed medications in the country.

The first SSRI to hit the market was Prozac, in December of 1987, and while the drug is now a household name when it comes to depression, dug company Eli Lilly stopped development seven times because of unconvincing drug results.[26] Prozac was initially marketed for weight loss and made no mention of antidepressant qualities, but marketing strategies shifted, so that Prozac became known as an antidepressant with the added benefit of weight loss (a far cry from other mental illness medications that cause severe weight gain).[27] In 1988, a year after the FDA approved Prozac, Americans filled 2,469,000 prescriptions, and within five years, Prozac had been prescribed for 8 million people.[28] This popularity directly influenced prescribing patterns, for while only a quarter of all psychiatric patients received prescriptions during office visits in 1975, one half of patients received prescriptions by 1990.[29]

By 1994, Prozac was a celebrity, the number two best-selling drug in the world, featured on the covers of magazines like a fresh-faced model. *Newsweek* reported, "Prozac has attained the familiarity of Kleenex and the social status of spring water."[30] In addition to providing relief, the drug also gained a reputation of providing euphoria to those taking it, and patients began to seek out Prozac in order to make them feel "better" than well, sometimes regardless of whether or not they suffered from depression. Dubbed "cosmetic psychopharmacology" by Dr. Peter Kramer in his pivotal text, *Listening to Prozac,* Prozac and other SSRIs began to be prescribed to patients to increase energy, confidence, and traits needed to make them feel more "socially attractive."[31]

Now Prozac is prescribed for everything from depression to severe PMS to what would have previously been considered routine shyness. In 2007, Eli Lilly, the maker of Prozac, released Reconcile, a drug chemically identical to Prozac, but in a chewable, beef-flavored version for dogs. This release coincided with a Lilly-funded study claiming that 17 percent of all dogs suffer from separation anxiety and could benefit from the drug.[32]

Other SSRIs quickly came to market following the success of Prozac, and antidepressants are some of the top most prescribed medications in the United States. The appeal of SSRIs like Prozac, Celexa, and Lexapro is their ability to target specific neurotransmitters. SSRIs were the first class of psychotropic drugs to locate a specific target and create a molecule to affect it, the illusion of precision and efficiency reassuring to both patients and physicians, so much so that the process by which SSRIs work became known as "rational drug design," the name implying control and reason in the face of madness.

When I hesitate about Lexapro and its similarities to Celexa, the doctor rattles off other options like Zoloft or Cymbalta. I try to explain I'm not opposed to medication, merely opposed to adverse reactions, many of which are linked to SSRIs. The doctor seems irritated, as though I'm one of *those* patients, the ones who spend too much time on WedMD and similar websites, hunching in front of their computers late at night, diagnosing themselves while eating ice cream, alternately checking their email and hyperventilating. As much as I hate to admit it, I am.

I leave his office still unconvinced, but like a good patient I fill an expensive prescription for Lexapro. The difference between the generic Celexa and name-brand Lexapro is the cost of a thirty-minute massage, and I can't help but wonder if that might be more effective.

The bottle of Lexapro sits unopened on my bedside table. My doubt, Brady says, my mother says, my friends say, is a sign that my anxiety is worsening. Stubbornness is a symptom. Clearly I need this new medication. More medication. I believe them, and while I don't switch to Lexapro, I continue to take Celexa each night, my hair coming out in handfuls.

At the doctor's recommendation, I purchase Rogaine from a local drugstore, embarrassed when I make eye contact with an older balding man in the aisle. Rogaine smells and makes my hair stiff and crunchy, strands drying together in spikes. I can't wash the product off, so I brush through the knots each day, pulling out more hair. Using Rogaine makes me feel unfeminine and unattractive, and even though I purchased the pink and purple "for women" bottle—the same medication, ounce for ounce increased 40 percent in price for women—the label warns that some women experience increased hair growth on their arms, chest, and upper lip.[33] Soon I'm scanning my upper lip along with my hairline.

When I'm not searching for a developing mustache, I take classes for my PhD and instruct students about logic and critical thinking as I feel completely out of my mind, convinced that an angry student, disgruntled over a grade or something I wrote on a paper, is going to pull out a gun and shoot me, panicking about the way I fell over my words in front of my colleagues because my tongue is so swollen and soft. My office is covered with hair, as are my clothes. A colleague who thinks she's helpful picks hair off of my clothes like I don't realize the hair is there. I do. I've just given up.

CHAPTER 11

MOLECULAR MYTHS

I decide to stop taking medication.

The symptoms of withdrawal are immediate. I feel like I have a flu that won't pass—I'm inexplicably tired, my muscles sore and achy, my head heavy and full of hurt, my throat and lymph nodes swollen.

The reason physicians warn against discontinuing medications is because while doing so can cause mental health setbacks, it also causes antidepressant discontinuation syndrome. Symptoms include nausea and vomiting, dizziness and difficulty balancing, fatigue and anxiety, headache, nightmares, loss of coordination, and muscle spasms. The reason previously medicated patients feel relief after starting a new drug has as much to do with alleviating withdrawal symptoms as a drug's efficacy.

More frightening, deliberately altering brain chemistry (for this is what happens when patients start or stop medication) can cause mental disturbances in patients—studies reveal increased cycles and durations of depressive, manic, and anxious episodes of patients taking psychotropic drugs. Many depressed patients struggle to find the best medication to effectively treat their symptoms, but cycling on and off drugs actually increases the chances their depression will become chronic by 10 percent.[34] Altering brain chemistry creates patterns of upheaval that can remain permanent, so even if patients find medications they are responsive to, their brains are marked by the search.

I do not realize this is withdrawal, however. I think it is punishment for noncompliance, and I nurse blame for several aching weeks before slinking in for a second opinion.

My new doctor, Terry, has a friendly face with deep laugh lines and a teased halo of hair that belongs in '80s fashion magazines. We've never met, but she knows my name without glancing at my chart, and she extends her hand to shake mine, introducing herself by her first name. She gives me the raised eyebrow of warning I've come to expect about my low weight—at five-foot-ten I hover around 120 pounds, lower with heightened anxiety—but she looks me in the eye when she does this, so that's an improvement. She spins in her chair to face me and asks where I am from, what I do at the university, what I like to watch on TV. The conversation is natural, going in different directions until soon I know little details about her family and hobbies.

"I have anxiety," I say when we finally discuss the reason for my visit. "I took Celexa for six months, but my hair started falling out so I stopped taking it," I admit, waiting to be scolded. I tell her I feel run down and awful, but that I know it's probably all in my head. I tell her about the other doctor and Lexapro.

Terry feels my neck and takes my temperature. She talks to me while conducting a general exam, her words and cool hands a comfort. It's been a long time since I felt like more than just a body.

"You need medication," Terry tells me matter-of-factly. "Your anxiety is not going to cure itself. It may be temporary, but it most likely won't be." She repeats the narrative which by now I have memorized—neurotransmitters are naturally occurring, but there is something wrong with the way my body produces them, and I need SSRIs to restore my system's balance.

You are probably familiar with the biomedical model of medicine, which reduces the body to a series of chemical processes and biological mechanisms. Much like a machine, various parts—the liver, the kidney, the heart—each do their assigned jobs to keep the device going. By imagining the body a machine and ourselves the mechanics, illnesses are easily attributed to a faulty part and become something we can fix. This sense of control and comfort may be the reason this model has been used by physicians since the mid-nineteenth century.

Mental illnesses, previously mystifying, become a broken bit in the body, a rationale that rids of us blame, reassuring us illness is not our fault, merely some mechanism not working properly. But while this model succeeds in ridding individuals (perhaps society) of blame, it simultaneously implies the brain and body are damaged—by insisting that people can be "fixed" via medication, it suggests they are broken. Categorizing disease this way actually decreases the power of the patient, with scientific theory—rather than patient perspective—accepted as powerful, often political, sanctioned word. While providing a better quality of life for patients is at the heart of medicine, it is dangerous to tell patients they are deficient—this model allows biology to become destiny, a strange curse whereby people are assumed guilty because of their birth and blood, societal factors, trauma, and emotion overlooked to focus instead on brain structures and neurotransmitters. This model may be, in part, responsible for increasing the stigma that the mentally ill are weak, dangerous, unstable, and untrustworthy.

The biomedical model has pointed to low serotonin, a neurotransmitter first isolated in 1948, as a faulty cog for many years. George Ashcroft, a leader in serotonin research, suggested mental illness is linked to serotonin deficiency in the late 1950s. The one transmitter/one disease theory quickly took hold, for it provided a sense of order and control where none had existed before, and it fueled the development of antidepressants like SSRIs, which promised to restore serotonin balance.

But the narrative began to fall apart, and by 1970, Ashcroft had publicly given up on his serotonin-depression connection. In 1969, Malcolm Bowers at Yale University first explored whether depressed patients had lower levels of serotonin metabolites in their cerebrospinal fluid, and his studies found little difference between patients who were depressed and those who were not. In 1974, Bowers reported that depressed patients who had not been exposed to antidepressants had perfectly normal serotonin levels. By the 1980s, the National Institute of Mental Health reported that depressed patients had a variety of serotonin levels, even when patients were taking SSRIs.[35]

We continue to rely on this model, though there is no current scientific consensus that depression is linked to serotonin deficiency or that SSRIs help restore balance of this neurotransmitter. The American Psychiatric Press *Textbook of Clinical Psychiatry* states that "additional experience does not confirm this hypothesis."[36] More problematic is that the biomedical model is contested by many scholars in mental health, research indicating that while depression, for example, is considered a brain disorder, there is not as much evidence to support this theory as pharmaceutical companies would suggest. So why do so many report feeling better on these medications? How did these medications gain popularity?

The first reason is the placebo effect, which occurs when a patient's condition improves, though not necessarily because of a specific treatment. Used during drug treatments, placebos determine if patients respond to a specific treatment or to the idea of being treated. (The converse can also be true: the nocebo effect creates adverse side effects in patients who believe medication is harmful, even if it is not.) Studies in the late 1980s revealed that 74 percent of surveyed patients reported feeling much better while taking antidepressants, but a later study conducted by Irving Kirsch, a leading researcher on the placebo effect, SSRIs, and expectancy found that 75 percent of an antidepressant's effect could have been obtained merely by taking the placebo.[37] The placebo effect may also be amplified when placebos produce physical side effects, thereby convincing patients they are receiving the drug.

The second reason stems from the way these medications have been positioned in popular discourse—as wonder cures. Many early studies on SSRIs were written by ghostwriters hired by drug companies, and some scholars took hundreds of thousands of dollars—some report millions—to hide or disguise negative data.[38] In 1961, one writer reported making $17,000—more than a year's salary—for a magazine article that manipulated ideas about antidepressants.[39] Not much has changed—in a 1999 article in the *Journal of the American Medical Association,* sociologist Edward O. Laumann warned, "Everyone is at risk of sexual dysfunction, sooner or later," a frightening suggestion, until it was revealed that Laumann was a paid consultant to Pfizer, the maker of Viagra.[40]

Drug companies also infiltrated medical journals though advertising. In 1950, the American Medical Association received only $2.6 million from drug company advertisements in their journal, but a decade later received up to $10 million.[41] Not surprisingly, with this increased profit came decreased regulation—a 1959 review of six major medical journals found that 89 percent of the ads provided no information about the drugs' side effects.[42]

(When Irving Kirsch began researching the placebo effect, he examined previous published and unpublished studies of antidepressants and found the placebo effect accounted for more than the 74 percent he initially determined. The effects were up to 82 percent—in other words, four-fifths of the benefits patients felt may have been obtained by swallowing *any* pill. Kirsch discovered what many already suspected—

that pharmaceutical companies exaggerated the benefits of antidepressants by manipulating information the public received.[43] A separate study submitted to the FDA reported that while five of ten test subjects given SSRIs improved over a couple of weeks on a depression scale, four of ten patients taking a fake pill also improved, meaning only one in ten test subjects showed a positive response that could be attributed to SSRIs.)[44]

We have also relied on the neurotransmitter theory for so long because it is comforting. It is comforting to believe we can heal the body and brain by simply locating the faulty part. It is comforting to believe we have control. Yet though we can increase serotonin's availability to the brain and body, this does not mean the increase improves depression or anxiety. People with higher levels of certain neurotransmitters are no happier, nor do depressed or anxious people always have lower levels of these same chemicals.

And though people may experience a pleasant placebo effect, SSRIs can impact our brains and bodies in dramatic ways. SSRIs can reduce synaptic connections (the way our bodies transmit information) to the brain, alter the thalamus (responsible for relaying sensory signals), impair the hippocampus (responsible for moving information from short-term to long-term memory, as well as for spatial memory), and create abnormalities in the frontal lobe (the part of the brain responsible for our long-term memory and our ability to choose right from wrong).[45]

Myths develop when cultures try to explain the unexplainable, and we've created myths about madness, where it comes from, who gets to decide what it is, and our abilities to cure it. Myths rely on gods or superheroes as saviors. Myths create awe and establish models of behavior. Our current neuromythology is no different—it rationalizes what eludes us, granting superhero strength to current treatments, and asking society to stand in awe of medical authority. Contemporary narratives suggest SSRIs are the solution to frightening illnesses, yet despite these narratives, we live in an age of chronic mental illness.

"It can happen," Terry admits when I ask about Celexa and hair loss. Psychopharmaceuticals cause so many side effects that even high-speed recitation during commercials can't report them in full, and anxious people are more likely to report side effects. On the other hand, anxious people are also more likely to somaticize, their worry manifesting as physical symptoms.

Terry suggests I try another SSRI, Zoloft. ("The drugs are essentially the same," she scoffs at Lexapro. "Save your money," she insists about Rogaine.)

She also considers putting me on a serotonin-norepineph-rine reuptake inhibitor, or SNRI, which acts on both serotonin and norepinephrine, another neurotransmitter believed to impact mental health. SNRIs are prescribed for everything from depression and anxiety, to arthritis and chronic back pain, to fibromyalgia and weight loss. Terry compares SNRIs to a cup of coffee or a brisk walk, saying they offer "a boost." "We'll try them if SSRIs don't work," she smiles.

I fill a prescription for Zoloft, and carry it home in a paper bag. Terry has reassured me millions of people take Zoloft—the year before, it ranked number four, a total 19,500,000 U.S. prescriptions were written, and the following year rose to number three, prescriptions increasing to a total of 37,208,000. The latest data from 2013 shows that it remains highly prescribed, ranking at number two, prescriptions up 11 percent for a total of 41,416,000.[46] Later that night I share news of my latest prescription with Brady over dinner. We spear lettuce and juicy tomatoes with our forks, the pulp running between the tines. Brady is optimistic about this prescription—"Maybe this one will work"—as he searches for a crouton, the crunch finality.

It doesn't look that noticeable, becomes my mantra as I wait for the Celexa to leave, for Zoloft to take effect, for my hair to regrow. I go to classes, teach classes, take care of my home. At least I can stop searching for signs of a mustache. I fill in the bald patches with eye shadow and use expensive shampoos and take vitamins I can't afford on my graduate school budget. I feel as if I'm going backwards—appearance-obsessed like a middle-schooler.

The leaves I watched out the window during my first visit have long since fallen to the ground, making branches barren and sharp-looking. Dangerous. Fall gives way to winter and soon Nebraska is covered in rounded snow drifts. Another mantra as I make my way through the ice and flurry: *It's only hair.* But when I return home over Christmas break friends and family whisper, "You look terrible."

I begin the New Year in Nebraska on my knees in the third stall of the bathroom on the third floor. Sometimes I run into another professor, whom I chat pleasantly with at the sink, hoping she'll leave so I can get back to my cold sweat. I run into the chair of my committee, and stumble through an answer to her "How are you?" feeling foolish and sick, catching a glimpse of myself in the mirror, wide-eyed and panicked, my teeth bared back in a skeletal smile. When I wash my hands, I leave hair in the sink.

Sometimes I can't see straight and it's hard to make out the words etched into the paint. *Every day is a gift.* When a janitor eventually scrubs the graffiti, the images blur, the symbol for femaleness bleeding through scratches in the paint, right next to what now looks like *Every day is a girl.*

PART III

CHAPTER 12

BITTER PILLS

*C*hristopher Pittman looks baby-faced in photos, wide-eyed under thick brows, soft and always a little confused, as though he isn't quite sure how it happened. He was just a child, so perhaps he played with action figures or Matchbox cars moments before he loaded the shotgun.

Christopher Pittman was twelve when he threatened suicide and ran away from the Florida home where he lived with his father alone and his father's second and third wives. His grandparents, whom he had lived with off and on for much of his life, had recently moved to South Carolina, and the estranged mother who left him as an infant had reestablished contact and then cut it off abruptly. When authorities found the boy with the deep sadness behind his eyes, they deemed him mentally unstable and sent him to a facility for runaway children. He was placed in a psychiatric hospital for six days, medicated for depression, and upon release he went to South Carolina to live with his grandparents.

Though Christopher Pittman swallowed Paxil in the psychiatric ward, his new doctor in South Carolina did not have any samples and gave the boy Zoloft instead, despite the fact that the medication is not recommended for children under eighteen. The results were immediate—Pittman described a burning sensation, and he acted, according to his sister, "manic." His father visited that Thanksgiving and noted his son seemed "more upbeat," but later said, "Now I look back at it, it was almost like an adrenaline rush. He was shaking his hands and feet like he was nervous."[1] When Christopher Pittman complained, the doctor doubled his dose.

Two days later, on November 28, 2001, Christopher Pittman choked a student on the school bus and got into an argument with the piano player at his church. That evening, his grandfather said it might be better if the boy went back to Florida. Then he disciplined the boy and sent him to bed. In the middle of the night, Christopher Pittman took his grandfather's shotgun—the one his Pop-Pop taught him to use while his Nana made suppers—walked into his grandparents' bedroom where they lay sleeping, and shot them. He set fire to the house and he drove away in his grandparents' SUV, bringing along $33, guns, and his golden retriever.

The murders sparked national controversy, for a while Pittman initially insisted a strange man shot his grandparents and kidnapped him, he ultimately confessed, admitting his grandparents deserved their fate. Many speculated this was another act in Pittman's long, troubled history, but others pointed to Zoloft. Pfizer, the maker of Zoloft, insists there is no link between the drug and violence in children, yet early FDA reports suggest otherwise. And despite the frequency with which physicians prescribe Zoloft and other antidepressants to minors, Zoloft is not approved to treat depression in children. Known side effects for children on Zoloft include paranoia, hallucinations, delusions, aggression, and manias accompanying high doses.

Doubling the dose of a young boy in the midst of such personal chaos, a young boy already experiencing intense side effects, seems irresponsible and inhumane. I imagine Christopher Pittman lying awake the night of the murders,

staring at the glow-in-the-dark stars on his ceiling and wondering what was going on inside his body and brain. I imagine him wrestling thoughts, trying to determine where they
were coming from—if they were the result of medication or
something flickering up from inside of him.

When Christopher Pittman went to trial on January 31
of 2005, he was tried as an adult.

His aunt testified that she talked to him five days before
he shot her parents and that he reported being unhappy on
the medication. She noted how rapidly he spoke, like he
couldn't stop or slow down, like he was out of control—
"I'm burning under my skin and I can't put it out," he'd said.
A psychiatrist for the defense pointed to Zoloft as the culprit
behind the burning. Patients, he said, "feel like they're going
to jump out of their skin. They often say their skin is burning." This psychomotor restlessness, or akathisia, is often a
precursor to violence.

Pittman's sister added, "He'd be sitting there fidget-
ing with his hands all the time. He was constantly up and
down. He was crazy." She pointed to Zoloft as responsible for changing her quiet, shy brother, noting that shortly
after beginning the drug her brother became restless, that he
would speak, lose track of himself, then dart to an unrelated
subject. "You couldn't get him to shut up," she testified.[2]

Pittman's defense attorneys requested Pfizer turn over
sealed confidential documents that link Zoloft to acts of
suicide and violence. (Similarly, during the 1999 trial that
pitted Brynn Hartmann's grieving family against Pfizer after
Brynn, who was taking Zoloft, shot her celebrity husband,
Phil Hartman, before committing suicide, attorneys pointed
to an article written by Pfizer scientists noting akathisia in
users even though drug inserts did not list it as a possible
side effect. During the trial Pfizer insisted, "There's no scientific or medical evidence that Zoloft causes violent or suicidal behavior.")[3] The FDA encourages doctors and parents
to watch for agitation and aggression in children, warning
that the medications can lead to increases in suicidal behav-

ior, but they are increasingly less vocal about linking the drugs to violence, and Pfizer continues to insist there is no evidence linking their drug to violence.

Prosecutors during Christopher Pittman's trial called the focus on Zoloft a "smoke screen," insisting the boy's actions showed premeditation. Sixteen days after the trial began, and after less than one day of jury deliberation, Christopher Pittman was convicted on two counts of murder and sentenced to thirty years in prison. His appeals were denied.

Aggression has been linked to these kinds of drugs for years—a 1990 study found that 50 percent of all fights on psychiatric wards were linked to the side effects of Haldol, a drug for schizophrenia—and court cases often debate whether to place blame on the patients' insanity or medication.[4] When thirty-eight-year-old David Hari shot and wounded his wife and shot and killed her lover six days after beginning Zoloft, the defendant's mother testified that after beginning Zoloft her son became "restless," "tired," and "more depressed." A psychiatrist for the defense testified that the medical literature on SRRIs indicates they can cause violence and that adverse reactions occur most frequently when the medications are first taken or dosages are changed. He went on to testify that Hari suffered a range of side effects, including akathisia, which is "like an itch that can't be scratched." Hari was sentenced to seventy-three years.[5] When thirty-four-year-old Leslie Demeniuk killed her four-year-old twin sons, defense lawyers blamed her sudden shift from Zoloft to Paxil in the days before the shootings, and the combination of medication and alcohol. Though experts testified she was "involuntarily intoxicated" and "psychotic" as a result of the drugs, she was found guilty of first-degree murder.[6]

I know none of this when I begin taking Zoloft.

I have problems with Zoloft from the start. I lose my appetite and am nauseated for a month, throwing up several times each day, shaky and short of breath. Though serotonin is considered a brain chemical, approximately 90 percent of the body's serotonin is produced in the cells lining the digestive tract, which is why many people who begin taking SSRIs experience upset stomachs at first. After the first several days on Zoloft, my brain begins to feel upset, too, muddled, crowded, like there is something scurrying about inside. I don't tell anyone at first, for I've learned by now people are tired of my panic and paranoia, but the feeling persists and soon I am closing my eyes and wincing, shaking my head from side to side to try and get free of whatever is inside.

"It feels like worms, doesn't it?" Terry asks when I mention my head has been feeling funny. I am amazed by the accuracy of her metaphor, and I imagine fat, juicy worms wriggling in the crevices of my brain, their soft bodies wedging into the darkest corners of memory and imagination. But the metaphor is not original to Terry. Instead, she says, it is the way thousands on Zoloft report the side effect. I'm not the only one feeling something twisting and turning from the inside.

Terry assures me this will pass after a few months and it does. It happens very slowly, like the worms are crawling into tight corners of my brain, lying in wait. The metaphor takes such hold for me that I long to see them leave, wish they would squeeze from my eyes and nose and mouth so I have evidence they are not a permanent infestation. I live in fear they will return. Though the worms do not bother me again, other symptoms develop.

After a month on the medication, my temper grows short. I am irritable, biting. One night I am headed out with Brady. He says something. Or he doesn't say something. Or I am hungry or we are late. I don't remember what he does or what happens that sets me into a rage, but soon I am pacing the house screaming, unable to catch my breath from the fury. I hate him; he is incompetent; he deserves to burn.

I run into the bathroom because I suddenly cannot stand to be near him, am so repulsed I must pace and pace, must not hold still, for if I do the rage will consume us both.

There is a knot in my stomach, a coil of hate so twisted I don't know where it begins or where it ends. I don't know how to remove it. *At last,* I think, *I know where the worms have gone.*

Brady follows me, trying to calm me down because I'm screaming and stumbling over my words, losing track of syntax. My sentences escape before I have formed them. I refuse to meet his eyes in the bathroom mirror, can't stand even to look at myself, and I retreat to the bedroom to punch at the furniture and the walls. Then I squeeze my fists into stones and punch my legs. I feel rage deep in the bone, and when my thighs recoil from the pain I slap myself hard on the head, stunned briefly by the sound, the smack of my palm flat against my skull. I hit myself again and again, the world going black and smooth.

Brady is frightened, crying and apologizing for whatever it is he has done—he doesn't know either. The more he pleads, the more he tries to calm me, to touch me, the louder I scream, trying to escape the arms he reaches out to me. I dart away from him and around the bed where we hold each other each night, grabbing an oversized glass candlestick from the nightstand. I clutch it, violent and wild, and race to the bathroom to smash it in the sink. It shatters, scatters glass over the counter and against the mirror that reflects my maniacal smile. I laugh and laugh.

The anger continues for months, growing in intensity as I snap at each minor irritation. Brady takes the worst of it, an easy outlet for whatever is melting inside of me. When he comes home from his job as a computer programmer, he places his keys and wallet on a ledge inside the door. The clutter jolts my vision, red and clicking, and because it is not right and it hurts and I feel as though each item he deposits weighs me down until I can't breathe I call him a slob, call him lazy. "Are you a moron? Are you trying to make me mad?" I shout. When he stares at me, still wearing his business suit and heavy overcoat, confused by the way I'm leaning heavy and gasping against the wall, I take my hand and clear the ledge, watching his things scatter across the floor. "Do you want me to ruin your stuff?" I call, hearing the cruelty in my voice. "This is what I do when you don't listen." I watch Brady crawl on his knees to pick things up. I am not sorry. I want him to hurt.

I never consider there may be a link between the Zoloft I've recently begun taking and my newfound rage—the one that leaves me burning and churning late at night, that wakes me up each morning with a cold white heat in my stomach, flames that flicker up my throat and out my mouth at the man I love. Family and friends suggest my anger is further evidence of my mental illness. Terry increases my dosage.

When Brady stops responding after several months, I hit him. We are fighting, or rather I am fighting, but he has stopped crying when I tell him he's worthless and threaten to leave him, so in a fit of adrenaline, frustrated he won't match my violent energy, I slap him hard on the arm. It doesn't do much to his 250-pound frame, but it also doesn't provoke the reaction I'm expecting. He never meets my anger or raises his voice. I am left burning up alone.

Soon I clench bloody half-moon slivers into my hands and grit my teeth until they wiggle. My arms and legs are patterned with bruises the shape of my palms. One day I stab a butcher knife into the kitchen countertop, regretting only the fact that I have marred the white surface. Eventually I imagine the gleam of the blade each time I tense—the precision of the point, the reassurance of the handle, violence in my grip.

Brady is endlessly patient, for while I have forgotten how to be a good partner, he has not. He is patient as I curse, tell him I want to leave him, how bad he is at time management, how he needs to lose weight, needs to make more money, needs to spend less money, needs to spend more time with me, needs to leave me alone. He gives me space as I whirl around the house to get rid of the tremendous energy my body seems to have suddenly acquired. If depression is the silent eye of the tornado, Zoloft makes me the storm, restless and aggressive, determined to leave destruction in my path. And when my storm inevitably blows out and I fall to my knees on the floor sobbing, Brady holds me close as I wrap my arms tight around his neck and tell him—even in our embrace—that I hate him.

Patients are frequently unaware of the risks associated with taking various pharmaceuticals, since there are so many and patients react to drugs differently. Physicians do not have the time during office visits to detail each potential side effect, and patients rarely read the informative pamphlets included with their prescriptions. And although side effects that occur in as few as 1 percent of patients must be included in warnings, it takes time for these warnings to find their way to consumers. Negative results almost never see print and so rarely find their ways into mainstream conversation.

A review of seventy-four antidepressant studies found that nearly all of the positive studies (thirty-seven of thirty-eight) were published in professional journals. Yet only three of the thirty-six negative studies were printed. Many of the other thirty-three negative studies remained unpublished. And those that were published were written in a way that emphasized positive benefits different from those the study intended to explore.[7]

We shouldn't be surprised by this, however—there has been evidence that psychopharmaceuticals can make people ill for as long as they have existed. Synthesized in 1950, chlorpromazine—the first drug developed as an antipsychotic—is neurotoxic by design, derived from a chemical used in agricultural insecticides to kill parasitic worms and slime.[8] Though Smith, Kline & French capitalized on the drug that eventually became known as Thorazine, chlorpromazine was actually synthesized in 1950 by French researchers looking for a way to numb the central nervous system. The drug was not initially conceived of as an antipsychotic, but instead as an anesthetic, for in 1951 French surgeons tested chlorpromazine on patients and found that they could operate with almost no anesthesia.[9] When Smith, Kline & French pursued the drug, they, too, had no intention of using it as an antipsychotic, purchasing Thorazine as an anti-vomiting drug, signing a licensing agreement and marketing it as such before they began to conduct drug trials.[10] These trials were limited, Smith, Kline & French spending only $350,000 to develop the drug and administering it to under 150 psychiatric patients before seeking approval by the FDA. The reason for such a limited drug trial? They had administered the drug to over 5,000 animals and assumed it would be safe.[11]

The dangerous side effects of chlorpromazine showed up as soon as patients began treatment—tardive dyskinesia (TD) causes involuntary repetitive body movements like grimacing, lip smacking, tongue protrusion, puckering and pursing of the lips, and rapid eye blinking, as well as symptoms similar to Parkinson's, and a dangerously quick rate of brain inflammation.[12] Yet despite the fact that TD affected up to 40 percent of patients taking chlorpromazine and other antipsychotics in the 1960s, these side effects were not considered common enough to issue a warning.

Often compared to penicillin and its success with infectious disease, chlorpromazine is considered the turning point in psychopharmacology.[13] An immediate success for the way it made patients lethargic and sedated, it led the transition from the rest cure and electroconvulsive therapy to the drug therapies (benzos and SSRIs) of today. By 1970, 19 million people were being written chlorpromazine prescriptions annually, but it wasn't until thirteen years after the first report of TD appeared in medical literature that the FDA finally asked drug companies to update their labels.[14] (Until 1962 pharmaceutical companies were not even required to prove to the FDA that their drugs were effective.)[15] Yet because this information was not disseminated quickly, and many physicians did not understand TD was caused by the medications they were prescribing, many treated patients by upping dosages of the very medications at fault. It is estimated that more than 200 people per day began to suffer from the disorder, and by the 1980s more than 90,000 Americans developed TD each year.[16]

Although TD may be reversed by lowering or discontinuing doses of medications, it can persist months and years after drug withdrawal, and is often irreversible. Neuroleptic malignant syndrome, a life-threatening neurological disorder caused by adverse reactions to antipsychotic drugs, is also estimated to have caused 200,000 deaths in the United States between 1960 and 1980, 80,000 of which could have easily been prevented if doctors had known the dangers of the drugs they were dispensing.[17] Many early neuroleptics also altered dopamine production, producing Parkinson's in patients.[18]

How could this occur when early studies of chlorpromazine revealed the drug altered the brain functions responsible for both motor movement and emotional responses?[19] The answer is careful editing. When Smith, Kline & French hired someone to investigate the effects of the drug in 1953, the investigator largely ignored the Parkinson's symptoms, focusing instead on the benefits of sedation and the ways the drug calmed patients.[20] By 1958, *Fortune* magazine ranked Smith, Kline & French second among American industrial corporations in terms of highest profit of uninvested capital. By this time the company was charging six times what the original inventor of the drug charged in France, making $53 million in 1953 and $347 million by 1970. The company made $116 million in 1970 alone.[21] With rising profits, the rhetoric surrounding chlorpromazine shifted from describing patients as lying listlessly in bed to describing them as miraculously "cured." Indeed, studies echo this change in rhetoric, later studies contradicting early ones. Whereas early studies reported that the drug made patients lethargic and hindered recovery, later studies reported that the drug—unchanged—reduced apathy and made patients energetic and lively.[22] Chlorpromazine was soon heralded as a "chemical lobotomy," capable of producing the desired effects without the hassle of surgery.

The popularity, thus power, of this rhetoric fueled the creation and concealment of chronic illness despite continued studies that suggested the inefficiency of drug treatment. In the early 1960s, studies revealed that schizophrenic patients treated with medications were more likely to be rehospitalized than patients who were not treated with medications. In 1966, the German physician H. P. Hoheisel reported that exposure to antidepressants shortened intervals between depressive episodes. In 1984, the National Institute for Mental Health reported that 71 percent of depressed patients relapsed within eighteen months of drug withdrawal.[23] Other studies revealed that relapse rates increased with drug dosage. Those who weren't treated with drugs? They were less likely to suffer relapses at all.[24]

What strikes me most, these years later, is that while my rage was a clear result of the Zoloft, common misconception insisted the anger was because of my mental illness. I don't know why it took me so long to realize what was happening, why others insisted the anger was because of my anxiety and never questioned if the medication was responsible for the sudden change, and worse still, why Terry never mentioned violence was a possible side effect. I felt so misunderstood, frightened, and embarrassed by my behavior that I longed, at times, to jump in a car in the middle of the night and leave the blaze behind me.

This is not to say that Zoloft does not provide comfort to many, or that medication is ineffective. On the contrary, medications like Zoloft allow millions of people with mental illnesses to live more comfortably, to find relief, to survive. I still suffer from anxiety's strange fears, paranoia and hallucinations less frequent but still familiar. I still take medication daily and credit drugs for my ability to live with less anxiety.

Yet from my vantage point, I am incredibly lucky. Years after I sliced the air between us with a gleaming knife, Brady and I remain strong. It is a miracle I did not hurt either of us more seriously.

Stories like mine are not uncommon. Neither are stories like Christopher Pittman's—those that make us flinch at the human potential for violence. In 1993, seventeen-year-old Victor Brancaccio attacked and killed an eighty-one-year-old woman after she criticized his vulgar rapping, covering her corpse with red spray paint. His attorneys insisted he was "involuntarily intoxicated" because of alcohol and Zoloft, which he had been taking a month prior to the murder.[25] In the days following the 1999 Columbine school shooting that killed twelve students and one teacher, injuring twenty-three others, much of the discussion centered on eighteen-year-old Eric Harris's prescription use, for he had been taking the SSRI Fluvox.[26] James Holmes, the twenty-four-year-old PhD student who opened fire on a movie theater in Aurora, Colorado, in 2012, took Zoloft.

These people were deranged, the familiar narrative goes. Mental illness, perhaps even its drugs, leads to violence, media reports blare, eager to find a reason for so much bloodshed in America.

Believe me: I do not want to suggest that the medications that help so many lead directly to violence. I reference these stories because they are ones that shape cultural attitudes towards mental illness and its treatments. It should go without saying that these acts of violence are not all linked to mental illness and that the drug correlation does not equal causation. But still, media is quick to link mental illness to acts of carnage, enough so that those of us in the mental illness community grow weary of more mass shootings, more reports that imply we are inherently evil, or that the medications that allow us to get through each day are triggers that might be pulled at any moment. We are tired of this narrative. I worry sharing my experiences will contribute to this narrative. No—I do not share my experience here to suggest that violence is linked to mental illness or drugs when it is so often linked to misogyny, privilege, and easy access to guns. Millions of people take drugs like Zoloft without committing violent acts and many who commit violent acts do not take drugs at all.

I share this story because it seems required, because the American fascination with mental illness and violence is one that haunts me, haunts us. The separation between patient and illness, the moment where a person ceases to be and where the illness takes over, captures our cultural imagination. For physical illnesses, the line is clear—he *has* high blood pressure, he *has* diabetes. But when discussing mental illness, the line shifts—a patient *is* his diagnosis, we insist. He *is* bipolar. He *is* anxious. Christopher Pittman, the narrative insisted, *was* crazy. He was evil.

What is the line between patient and prescription, the border where agency and action give way to chemical persuasion, where free will is rerouted by white pinprick pills? How can we critique the drug industry without villainizing it entirely, demonizing what for many makes the difference between life and death? Other countries make distinctions between people and their illnesses, between people and their drugs.

When seventy-four-year-old David John Hawkins murdered his wife of nearly fifty years, Australian courts found Zoloft at fault. Suffering depression since the early 1970s, Hawkins first took Zoloft in 1995 after his daughter died of breast cancer. He reacted poorly to the medication—describing that is made him feel "as if he was walking two feet above the ground"—but was prescribed the drug again in 1999 after his depression worsened. One night Hawkins took his prescribed Zoloft to help him sleep, and later said in an interview with police, "I was that bad that night. I had taken Panadol. I couldn't sleep. I was panicking. I just was, I couldn't, I couldn't, I couldn't function, so I took one (Zoloft tablet) . . . And I went back to bed and waited. It had no effect and I, I don't know, I must have taken more."

Though the normal dose is 50 mg and patients can be gradually increased to 200 mg, Hawkins is reported to have taken 250 mg that night.

The next morning he wrapped his hands around his wife's neck and strangled her to death. "I just went absolutely berserk. I can remember shouting and screaming," he said. ". . . I was berserk, I went absolutely berserk. I have never done it before," Hawkins told police, insisting he saw his own face instead of his wife's. After calling the police, Hawkins attempted to gas himself in his car, but said he thought of the effect it would have on his children and stopped. He pleaded guilty.

During the trial, Judge Barry O'Keefe said, "But for the Zoloft (the Australian and U.S. brand name for Lustral) which he took on the morning of August 1, 1999, it is overwhelmingly probable that Mrs. Hawkins would not have been killed on that morning."[27]

(That same year, a Wyoming jury awarded $6.4 million to the family of sixty-year-old Donald Schell, who killed his wife, daughter, nine-month-old granddaughter, and himself, hours after taking his first two sample tablets of Paxil. He had received the prescription for depression the day prior. During the trial, it was revealed Schnell had taken Prozac years earlier for depression but discontinued use after experiencing agitation and hallucinations. Marking the first time a plaintiff won in a lawsuit claiming antidepressant have caused suicidal or violent behavior, the makers of Paxil, GlaxoSmithKline were ordered to pay the settlement to surviving family members.)[28]

Though Pfizer found the Hawkins ruling "extraordinary," the literature they produce alludes to the potential danger of Zoloft. Pfizer encourages patients to contact doctors if they have thoughts about suicide or dying; attempts to commit suicide; new or worse depression, anxiety, or panic attacks; if they feel agitated, restless, angry, or irritable; act aggressive or violent or on dangerous impulses. Zoloft places this danger directly on patients, writing clearly in their warning that patients "must balance this risk with the clinical need."

The balance between risk and need seems American in nature, perhaps more aptly called risk and profit, variables changing depending on who is writing the story. The National Institute of Mental Health reports that serious mental illness costs the United States $193.2 billion annually, but this statistic says nothing of personal risks, personal cost.

The risk of my anxiety is uncontrolled fear and panic attacks, but the cost was my agency, my self-control, perhaps nearly my life. The risk for a child with mental illness may be that he runs away from home, but the cost of putting him carelessly on one medication and then another was much greater. I am fortunate Zoloft did not cost me my family; Christopher Pittman cannot say the same.

Now I lie in bed, many years removed from Zoloft and the flames it left flickering throughout my body, singeing those who dared get close to me. Brady sleeps, his body stretched along the length of mine. He breathes deep, relaxed and secure next to me. There is warmth where our bodies meet, where he and I have closed the space that once was, the temperature steady and controlled.

I wonder if Christopher Pittman will ever know this warmth, this heat without the burn. I do not know if his actions were motivated by agency, by illness, by drug, but I do know what it is like to be lonely and afraid and to have the world insist you are broken, evil.

There is something instinctual about reaching out to find comfort. I know it is too much to hope Christopher Pittman was trying to reach out when he placed his hands around another child's throat on the school bus. But I hope he was asking for help when he shouted at his grandparents that night, clenched his fists as he tried to explain that he was "burning up." It is hard to think of the before, harder still to think of the after. The moment he loaded the shotgun and aimed.

But I try. I imagine Christopher Pittman as he drives away from his grandparents' home, their bodies blazing inside. He is barely tall enough to see over the dash. He is confused and frightened. Then he reaches his hand over to the golden retriever curled up next to him. He runs a hand along the dog's warm muzzle, smoothing the fur. He keeps his hand there a long while.

I don't deserve your sympathy, reader. Looking back, piecing together brief flashes of scenes I barely remember, my mind as chaotic as it was, I'm an unsympathetic character. An unlikable, unreliable narrator. True, those in pain often lash out. True, if we were to assign blame, it might instead go to Zoloft. But the question is, as it always is with mental illness, how much was illness and how much personality? What do we attribute to agency and what to imbalance? When factoring in medications, the question becomes trifold: where do person, illness, and chemical exist independently of one another, and where do they intersect and overlap?

I look back at myself years later, Zoloft and the rage and much of the anxiety gone, but no matter what I try to attribute to mental illness, what I try to attribute to Zoloft, the fact remains that I was cruel. Terrified, isolated, but cruel.

Illness narrative requires I go on trial, make myself sympathetic, garner favor so readers might understand the way I was, might trust me, believe me now. If I were to do that here, I might bemoan my state, talk about the things I did and how they were not my fault. But they happened. They were. They are.

I am relieved by the distance narrative provides, as I strain memory for truth, untangle the narrative threads of reality from the knot madness made. Narratives have a plot, a methodical arc, rhetorical tools for creating meaning, a narrator to lead the way and suffer the burden of conflict. Narratives promise that despite chaos and upheaval, despite rising tension, there will be resolution. There is something reassuring, both for me—and perhaps for the reader—in the fact that this story has been constructed and arranged to present a greater meaning from the madness. Something comforting in knowing that I am different now, that time and space and maybe medicine have revised me from the way I am on the page—shouting at my lover, seeing strange things from the corners of my eyes, slicing through air with a blade. There is something reassuring in knowing time has passed, that it is afterward now, but in the immediate moment—in real life—there was no reassurance, no greater meaning, only panic and pain, a quick building heat and the fear that it was only a matter of time before I burned it all down.

CHAPTER 13

REBUFFED

One afternoon, after more than a month on Zoloft, I lose the ability to orgasm.

The rage is beginning, and my bedroom ways have remained consistent despite my anxiety (which isn't particularly mood-enhancing). I'd been warned prior to Celexa that SSRIs could lower my libido, but I never had trouble achieving orgasm with Brady, who is a patient and curious lover. None of the partners after my college abuser made me feel safe, but sex with Brady is a delicious kindness. I ask for what I want and need, and welcome the warm, elastic afterward.

Until the day it is denied. It is one of those languid afternoons where the sunlight makes you want to delight in your body, then nap until the evening. Where you feel slick and tingling with the sense of being and needing. I am aroused and Brady is pleasing me and we are smiling and kissing and laughing, losing breath with our purpose and rhythm. We climb like the roller coasters we love to ride, over peaks, up and up, the effort of the wheels against the track, the bodily rattle of the ascent, the anticipation of the view from the apex, and just as the cart is about to plummet—the body suddenly weightless, that slow-motion rush and sweet seep—my body stops. I am deprived of the fall. Anticipation and momentum are replaced by numbness, by nothingness. I feel wrong, disconnected after such a buildup, anesthetized.

We continue, but a few minutes later, the same thing happens. I make up an excuse to stop, pulling on my clothes and retreating to the bathroom where I try deep breathing to calm myself down enough to try again. Brady asks if I'm okay through the door.

I refuse to be the kind of woman who feigns orgasm, so I tell him what has happened, reassuring him it is not his fault. I've had unsuccessful lovers before, sexual encounters with rushed, distracted boys that left me unfulfilled and bored. This is different.

Active, healthy sexuality is difficult enough for women, who must walk the line between virgin and whore, prude and promiscuous. Girls at my elementary school were given scented pads and told to hide our menstruation while the boys received deodorant strong enough to warrant opening the classroom windows. The scent spread across the room while girls shrank in their seats. In middle school biology class I sat across from a boy who licked his braces and lips at me while the teacher talked about sperm, and then pretended to gag when the slide switched to the image of a uterus. My high school boyfriend was a good Christian who liked anal sex and lecturing me about sin. When his sister got pregnant outside of marriage, as their mother had done, I was not allowed over unless the bedroom door was open. "My parents want you to come to church," he said. In college, my friends let strangers finger them on dance floors and found out the men they were seeing were married. Most of my friends then—as now—had never orgasmed, either with a partner or on their own. Add the shared trauma of sexual violence and it is no wonder so many women feel shame talking about their bodies and sexual satisfaction.

Women's sexuality is blamed so often—"She dressed provocatively," "She shouldn't have been drinking," "She lured another woman's husband away," "If she'd had more sex with her husband he never would have left"—I automatically assume my inability to orgasm is my fault. Anxiety is an illness of control, orgasm the willing release of control. Of course I can't accomplish this task: I'm a doll with a broken cog.

For weeks Brady and I make love, each unsuccessful attempt at orgasm making me feel as though I've been slapped. The failures make me retreat to the end of the bed and curl into the fetal position. Sex feels dangerous again.

My rage is starting to build, and Brady thinks maybe he *is* sloppy and lazy and overweight and the other awful things I've been shouting. He thinks I'm not attracted to him.

"It's not that," I say, thinking about how I complained at breakfast because the eggs he cooked me were runny, how I threw them in the trash with an exaggerated sigh. How he ate alone. "There's something wrong with me."

Terry is surprisingly unsurprised when I gather the courage to tell her. "Anorgasmia," she announces, diagnosis rendering even my sexuality inept. "This is fairly common," she adds, though she'd never mentioned it before as a possible side effect.

I've never been embarrassed by my sexuality—I talk freely with my gynecologists, arranged "birth control parties" in college to escort groups of women too nervous to go to clinics alone to get IUDs and condoms, took Natalie to a gynecologist when she became sexually active, encourage girlfriends who have difficulty achieving orgasm to visit adult novelty stores. I like talking about sex. We should have, I think, more sex. But then a chemical harms my sexuality without my consent and Terry warns, "It can last after patients stop taking the medication."

She encourages me to stay on Zoloft while we wait to see if this latest side effect will disappear. If the anorgasmia lasts more than six months—or if I develop other sexual side effects like genital anesthesia—she assures me, we can add Wellbutrin, another antidepressant from a new class of drugs, typically prescribed for atypical depression or to counter SSRI-induced sexual dysfunction.

In the meantime, I'm supposed to have sex with Brady whenever I'm not screaming in his face or throwing dishes at walls, and even though the point is to try and orgasm, I'm not supposed to think about it too much or I could ruin my chances. "Don't overthink," Terry warns, "or you'll get in your own way." If practice with Brady doesn't work, I'll need to take matters into my own hands. "Try it on your own," she suggests, "if it doesn't work with the two of you." No matter the method, though, her advice remains the same: "Relax."

Terry ushers me out of her office with her hand on my shoulder. "At least you'll have fun trying," she jokes, giving me a conspiratorial nod, like she's rooting for my sex life.

I don't have fun. Either I have sex, so uncomfortable in my body I disconnect, floating above the scene, the whole thing so reminiscent of assault I panic. Or I don't have sex at all. My connection with Brady disappears, intimacy fading with each unsuccessful attempt, then months without trying. The tenderness and vulnerability of sex is replaced by shame and isolation.

Not overthinking means not overtalking, and sex is suddenly shrouded in silence. I grow shy, embarrassed first by my body, then by my desire. This feeling is still hard to shake years later.

Prescribing patterns mean women are more likely than men to experience sexual side effects as a result of psychophar-maceuticals. And while erectile dysfunction medications are advertised by presidential candidates and covered by medical insurance, there is little conversation, let alone medical support, for women's sexual dysfunction. Contemporary women's sexuality seems as intertwined with madness as it ever was during Victorian times, sexual satisfaction a fair price to pay for sanity, vibrators still part of the prescription.

If vibrators seem a strange cure for women's madness, consider the others. Archaeologists have unearthed skulls full of small round holes that date back to at least 5000 BC, twelfth-century surgeons drilled into skulls to allow demons to escape, and 1800s surgeons removed parts of patients' brains in order to quell hallucinations and help depression.[29] Lobotomy as we now know it was first conducted in 1935, by a Portuguese neurologist who drilled holes into a patient's skull to gain access to the brain. The first lobotomy in the United States was performed in 1936 on Alice Hood Hammatt, a sixty-three-year-old Kansas housewife, whose excessive emotions, her physicians believed, were a sign of mental illness. By cutting into her brain nerves, they reasoned, they could sever the links leading to all those feelings and help stabilize her—though "flatline" is a more accurate description. Hammatt was "anxiety free" after her surgery, never requiring institutionalization, and though she suffered related convulsions months after her surgery and died of pneumonia five years later, her husband insisted this time was the "happiest" of her life. Lobotomy did not require consent (Allen Ginsburg authorized his mother's lobotomy when he was twenty-one) and rendered patients passive, complacent, and childlike; as such, it was prescribed primarily to women.

Hammatt's "success" helped her physicians, Dr. Walter Freeman and Dr. James W. Watts, and their procedure rise to fame, media touting overwhelming success. In 1937, the *New York Times* reported that lobotomy could help with "tension, apprehension, anxiety, depression, insomnia, suicidal ideas, delusions, hallucinations, crying spells, melancholia, obsessions, panic states, disorientation, psychalgesia (pain of psychic origin), nervous indigestion and hysterical paralysis."[30] In their 1950 book on psychosurgery, Freeman and Watts said their operation helped more than 80 percent of their patients.[31] As with most wonder cures, this public-

ity increased the rate of treatment rapidly; approximately
10,000 mental patients—mostly women—in the United
States were lobotomized between 1950 and 1951, nearly as
many as all during the 1940s.[32] Similar to antidepressants,
the treatment was soon prescribed for a range of disorders,
including women suffering from depression, college graduates suffering neuroses, and troubled children.[33]

In 1946, Freeman introduced transorbital lobotomy in an
attempt to perform lobotomy without drilling into patients'
skulls. Known in popular culture as "ice-pick lobotomy,"
this procedure did not require as many tools or as much
cleanup, and was also quick—Freeman could perform it in
ten minutes. With the help of his increasing notoriety and
this speedy new technique, Freeman went on to perform
about 2,500 lobotomies, once conducting twenty-five lobotomies in a single day. Injecting a little humor and drama into
the operating room, he sometimes inserted picks in both eyes
simultaneously.[34]

What media and medical texts failed to report, however, is
that most patients suffered following surgery, seeming to return
to childhood, becoming lethargic and unresponsive, uninterested in their old activities and focused instead on immediate
needs, much like toddlers. Patients gained weight, had little
motivation, and 25 percent of those who were discharged
adjusted to life as invalids or household pets. Another 25
percent never progressed beyond the initial stages of recovery, and were forced to remain institutionalized.[35] The first
to boast of their success, Freeman and Watts merely alluded
to this in their findings, noting that patients lost a certain
"spark" after surgery, a spark, they promised, that might be
rekindled through additional lobotomies that disconnected
larger sections of the frontal lobe.[36]

Perhaps their most famous patient was Rosemary Kennedy, who at twenty-three underwent a prefrontal lobotomy in 1941. Rosemary was known for heightened emotion
and behavior unbecoming to a lady or political family—she
sometimes snuck out of her convent school—and the physi-

cians recommended a prefrontal lobotomy, but neither they nor her father informed Kennedy. Watts described the surgery thusly: "We went through the top of the head, I think she was awake. She had a mild tranquilizer. I made a surgical incision in the brain through the skull. It was near the front. It was on both sides. We just made a small incision, no more than an inch. We made an estimate on how far to cut based on how she responded."[37] When the young woman became incoherent—reduced to the estimated brain capacity of a two-year-old—unable to speak and incontinent, they stopped. She never recovered.

Kennedy was not the youngest patient. Freeman and Watts also operated on troubled youth whose parents complained of everything from fits to overactive imaginations. In 1950, they operated on eleven children, including a four-year-old. The rationale for treatment, they explained, "has been to smash the world of fantasy in which these children are becoming more and more submerged. It is easier to smash the world of fantasy, to cut down upon the emotional interest the child placed on his inner experiences, than it is to redirect his behavior in the socially acceptable channels."[38] Their success was doubtful—of the eleven children they operated on, two died, three had to be institutionalized, and three others suffered irreversible permanent childhood. Their reports, however, suggested that these first surgeries on children produced "modest results," and they continued to perform lobotomies on young children.[39]

The last surgery Freeman conducted took place in 1967, shortly before he was banned from further operations. Though he had been conducting lobotomies with dubious results for over thirty years, it was only after Freeman performed a third lobotomy on a patient (she died after developing a brain hemorrhage) that he was reprimanded.[40]

More surprising than how long it took Freeman to be criticized is how long it took the United States to discontinue the practice of lobotomies, which lasted until the 1970s. As early as the 1950s, many nations, including Germany and

Japan, began to outlaw lobotomies. The Soviet Union prohibited the procedure in 1950 because it was "contrary to
the principles of humanity." The United States, however,
ever aggressive in their pursuit of treatment for madness—as
with current prescribing patterns, which outnumber those of
countries around the globe—performed more lobotomies on
its citizens than any other country, estimates ranging from
40,000 to 50,000.[41] And despite the fact that many nations
regarded the surgery as nothing more than a means to eutha-
nasia, Egas Moniz, the Portuguese physician who first performed the surgery, was awarded the 1949 Nobel Prize in
medicine and physiology for his work.[42]

The erasure of women's sexuality and consent is crystal-
ized in the eugenics movement, which began in the United
States in the early 1900s and was eventually adopted by Hitler's regime during World War II. In the early 1900s, America housed large numbers of the mentally ill in asylums,
numbers that increased as definitions of "madness" widened to include those with "deviant behavior" or "criminal-
ity" (tied to race, sexuality, and class), addicts, those with
physical disabilities, and the elderly—estimates suggest that
in the 1930s fewer than 50 percent of people in asylums suffered from madness.[43] Widening definitions of insanity led to
costly overcrowding, and many began to argue that immigrants brought madness into the country, the working poor
reproducing so quickly mental illness ran rampant.

The solution to this contamination? Stop the spread of
defective bloodlines. Eugenics advocated for the diminished
reproduction of people with undesirable traits in order to
improve human genes. By regulating who reproduced with
whom—or who reproduced at all—eugenicists argued,
nations could regulate rates of mental illness. By 1914, forty-
four colleges in the United States had introduced eugenics
into their curricula—schools like MIT, Harvard, Columbia,
Cornell, and Brown—and by 1924, more than 9,000 papers
on eugenics had been published, much of the research pointing towards sterilization as a way to control mental illnesses

in the United States. Estimates ranged, some insisting 10 percent of the American population was in need of sterilization,
a long-term estimate that 5.76 million Americans needed to
be sterilized over a span of forty years in order to prevent
mental illness from spreading.[44]

Legislation to control what the mentally ill could do with
their bodies and lives began—in 1896, Connecticut became
the first state to create a law forbidding the insane from having the right to marry, by 1914, more than twenty states
had laws that prohibited their insane from marrying, and
by 1933, the other states had followed. After banning the
mad from marrying, sterilization seemed the next step, and
in 1907, Indiana became the first state to pass a compulsory
sterilization law. Over the next twenty years, thirty state leg-
islatures approved sterilization bills, the definition of what
constituted "insane" expanding—a 1913 Iowa bill insisted
that those who should be sterilized included "criminals, rap-
ists, idiots, feebleminded, and imbecile, lunatics, drunkards,
drug fiends, epileptics, analytics, moral and sexual perverts,
and diseased degenerate persons." From 1907 to 1927, about
8,000 eugenics sterilizations were performed, and by the end
of 1945, 45,127 Americans had been sterilized.[45]

The legal basis for mass sterilization was *Buck v. Bell,* a
1927 Supreme Court case that affirmed the constitutionality
of Virginia's state-enforced sterilization. The case concerned
three generations of women. The first, Emma Buck, was
deemed a "low grade moron" and committed to a state institution after she had a child out of wedlock. That child, Carrie Buck, received the same diagnosis after having her own
child out of wedlock at seventeen, following her rape by her
foster parents' nephew. Though Carrie had reached the sixth
grade, her foster family had her committed for "feeble mind-
edness," their charge of "promiscuity" an attempt to save the
family reputation. Though they assumed care of her infant
child, Vivian Buck, while Carrie joined her mother at the
colony, Vivian, too, was diagnosed as "not quite normal" at
six months—no doubt in an effort to push the legal agenda

to sterilize Carrie. (Vivian was later on the honor roll at her elementary school.)

The superintendent of the state institution, Dr. Albert Sidney Priddy, was hoping to sterilize many women under his custody when he filed a petition to sterilize Carrie Buck. Six months prior, law was passed allowing for state-enforced sterilization for those genetically "unfit," and Priddy hoped to test it in court before proceeding on large levels. He focused his legal efforts on Carrie by claiming she had the mental capacity of a nine-year-old, her mother Emma that of an eight-year-old, and that the family had an inherited history of prostitution and immorality.

The decision to uphold the law authorizing Carrie Buck's sterilization was passed eight to one. Justice Oliver Wendell Holmes explained, "It is better for all the world if, instead of waiting to execute degenerate offspring for crime, or to let them starve for their imbecility, society can prevent those who are manifestly unfit from continuing their kind." He went on to say, "Three generations of imbeciles are enough." In the decade that followed, seven states and Puerto Rico created sterilization statutes, while those with preexisting laws revised theirs to more closely model Virginia's. During those ten years, almost 28,000 Americans were sterilized. The Supreme Court has never officially overturned this finding.[46]

The definition of "troubled" and "troubling" widened along with sterilization rates, science used in order to justify segregation. Labels like "mentally deficient," "feeble brained," or "imbecile" were used to target women, people of color, the poor, and unwed mothers. Between 1929 and 1974, 7,600 people were sterilized in North Carolina: 85 percent were women and girls, 40 percent were minorities, and most were black women. From the 1930s to the 1970s, more than a third of women in the U.S. territory of Puerto Rico were sterilized. At least 25 percent of Native American women using the Indian Health Services were sterilized during the 1970s.[47]

Alexandra Minna Stern, whose work focuses on eugenics and social justice in California, writes:

> Those sterilized in state institutions often were young women pronounced promiscuous; the sons and daughters of Mexican, Italian, and Japanese immigrants, frequently with parents too destitute to care for them; and men and women who transgressed sexual norms. Preliminary statistical analysis demonstrates that during the peak decade of operations from 1935 to 1944 Spanish-surnamed patients were 3.5 times more likely to be sterilized than patients in the general institutional population.

Eugenics soon spread across the Atlantic, and Germany credited the United States when it passed its first sterilization bill. Eugenics was more popular in the United States prior to World War II—Germany's parliament actually defeated a sterilization bill in 1914—and leaders of the German sterilization movement looked to the United States as a model. Some historians suggest Hitler wrote a letter to the founder of the American Eugenics Society thanking him for his contributions and ideas about sterilization, and claiming a eugenics text about sterilization was like a Bible to him.[48] (If this choice of words seems odd, it isn't—we use the word "Bible" to describe the *DSM*, our manual for diagnosis of mental illness.) At the Nuremburg trials, multiple Nazi defendants referred to *Buck v. Bell* as justification for their eugenics programs.[49]

Sterilizations in the United States continued well into the 1950s, the same number of patients sterilized in the 1950s as during the height of popularity in the 1920s.[50] Though outlawed, this practice continues—in the summer of 2013, the Center for Investigative Reporting found that doctors working for the California Department of Corrections and Rehabilitation sterilized 146 female inmates from 2006 to 2010, the majority black and Latina and first-time offenders. All sterilizations were conducted without required state approv-

als and at least three dozen violated informed consent procedures. The physician who conducted the procedures argued it
would save the state money "compared to what you save in
welfare paying for these unwanted children." California law-
makers banned forced sterilization of prisoners in 1979, but
state documents reveal up to an additional 100 women were
sterilized dating back to the late 1990s. Once the nation's
leader in sterilizations, sterilizing about 20,000 men and
women from 1909 to 1964, California seems to still be coerc-
ing and pressuring sterilization upon those locked up—America's prison systems mirror, after all, America's asylums in the
early 1900s.[51]

It might seem strange to think our nation could buy
into these ideas, but the prevailing notion has always been
much as it is today—caring for the mentally ill is costly to a
nation, mental illness contagious, the mentally ill incapable
of caring for themselves or others.

"You wouldn't be a good mother," my mother once told
me. "Because of your mental health."

Sex turns into a chore, my love life a series of hardy attempts
and colossal failures. Brady comforts me as I cry after each
unsuccessful endeavor, and soon our bed is a space for
humiliation and regret.

After months of practice—Brady trying to assure me this
time will be different, trying to persuade me without pressuring me, trying to push us to where we need to go without
pushing me beyond where I am comfortable—I no longer
want him to touch me. I no longer want him to even hold my
hand, no longer want to feel aroused or know he is aroused
either, for the thought of my deficiency, my failure, is unbearable. I no longer feel safe when we make love, instead feel
tense and on edge. I feel out of control and so, so alone.
Sometimes I let Brady pull me close so that he can't see that
I'm crying. Our home is stifling with the tension of unre-
solved anger and unfulfilled desire. We become strangers.

When Brady comes up behind me in the kitchen to rest his hands on my stomach or bury his face in my neck, I flinch. When he pulls me tight to his chest in the middle of the night, I stiffen. When he speaks of his desire, I cringe and blush like a small child. Eventually he stops altogether, and then I worry he no longer loves me.

It seems I'm in a relationship with my anxiety instead. As with lovers, we are attuned to the needs and changing desires of our illnesses. We are forever bound to our history together—we remember the ways our illnesses have wronged us, the things we have done to make them lash out, and we try to soothe and please our illnesses so they don't hurt us again. We hold them close to us, inside of us, until they seem to become a part of us. I spend more time with my anxiety than with Brady. My illness lies closer to me in bed. It is always with me. Brady cannot compete.

Still, Brady remains patient. Perhaps he is patient because he knows this isn't me. Perhaps he is patient because he loves me so much he doesn't recognize the abuse in my words and actions. Perhaps he is, like I screamed in the midst of a rage, foolish and weak. Perhaps he is patient because he hopes this will pass and I will hold him again. But I think the real reason Brady is patient is because he understands.

There is a tendency for people with mood disorders to pair off, to find each other amidst a crowd, and see something of themselves mirrored in the other. To find this comforting. To love this about the other. This phenomena, called assortative mating, is a nonrandom mating pattern where people with similar physical and social traits pair off with one another. While people might draw to one another based on intelligence, religion, or political viewpoints, there is something reassuring and beautiful in those with mental illnesses finding one another, mending or not minding one another's madness. Brady and I found each other long before my anxiety, yet we must have known we were alike. Even though we hadn't shared those bits we believed at the time made us broken, I think they are what drew us together.

The first time Brady came to my house alone, we lay side by side on my bed too nervous to touch, a sliver of space and sunlight between our bodies. There was an unfamiliar intimacy in this moment, for we normally spent time together in groups—even on our first date we were accompanied by a mutual college friend, the three of us miniature golfing and slurping Chinese noodles. As we lay on the bed, the sun filtered through the dark curtains I kept drawn shut, Brady whispered to me that he had a secret. Rolling over to face me, he clasped my hand in both of his, wrinkling his forehead with worry, insisting he had to come clean if we were going to venture forward together. I felt the same way, for while I was not experiencing panic yet, I was afraid to walk alone on my graduate campus at night, afraid to walk the short distance from my car to my front door, afraid to be alone with a man—my reason for our initial double date— afraid, even, to open the curtains. I admitted this while Brady held me and admitted his own secret.

Brady is bipolar, and while I won't share all the details of his diagnosis or treatment, since they are his to tell, I can say this: He was diagnosed in high school and has taken more medications than I have. He has been medicated more than half of his life and will no doubt be medicated for the remainder. Though he takes medication daily, which dulls the edge of his manias and keeps him from plummeting into the dark places he rarely speaks of, there are times when the medications don't work, and there are times when he stops taking them altogether, only to fluctuate rapidly, which frightens me. Brady's bipolar disorder does not cause paranoia, and I've never seen him delusional, but I know he is experiencing manias when he seems scattered, energetic beyond counsel, when he begins to ignore what is going on around him in favor of what is going on in his mind, when he cannot be present in a conversation and spends money lavishly and stays up late into the night to sneak cigarettes and sit alone. When he seems distant and distracted. When he seems to love me less. I've never seen him depressed because he tends more towards manias, but I know once he was irrevocably sad, and there are days when the slightest disappointment sets him into despair, and though he is a grown man with broad shoulders and a big belly and an intense physical strength, he cannot hide this sadness, and seems instead like a small boy whose hopes have been crushed.

If Brady's patience seems unwavering, that's because it is. And though it may not appear so, this patience is something I try to have in return for him when he peaks into a mania or when something tips him into a valley of sadness. Brady's complicated nature makes me long to know him more deeply and intimately. These enigmas are the very things that make him human, forever elusive, and the longer I sit with my own illness, mull it over from so many angles, the more I come to see him as perfectly imperfect. Though books and movies and the world repeat that people with mental illness are a burden undeserving of love, I cannot imagine a partner more understanding or supportive than one who is also mentally ill, one who also sees the world differently, who has learned to live in it differently. This is why my lack of empathy during the time I spent on Zoloft shames me so, why remembering my cruelty pains me. Why thinking of Brady's kindness, and the way he demonstrated so much faith in me, and for so long, in spite of my rage and disconnection, brings me nearly to tears.

The void Zoloft creates rests between Brady and me each night in bed. My hair is still falling out and I am still shouting and throwing things. It has been months since we tried to make love. The distance subdues us. I know Brady is awake because his breathing has not steadied into sleep and he holds still so as not to disturb me. When he is awake Brady knows not to touch me, folds his arms across his chest, clasping his hands and fingers together like a corpse, but during sleep his arm slips into its familiar position around me.

Six months pass and I begin to wonder what I am gaining by taking Zoloft. My old fears do not go away—I still worry about aliens and broken bones and missile strikes—and new fears show up daily. My hair is still falling out, the worms lie in wait, and I am simultaneously trying to hurt my partner and longing for him. I feel more out of my mind than ever before, but everyone—my family, my friends, my physician, medical reports, news stories—insists Zoloft is the answer. The fear and uncertainty, the physical symptoms are all in my head—my problems the result of noncompliance, of willful madness. *Relax,* they chorus. If I give Zoloft a chance, it will work. If I stop complaining, I'll feel better. This is all part of the narrative.

So I swallow this story each night. I stare at the tiny pill in the cupped palm of my hand, my throat tightening. It takes coaxing to unlock my jaw, and even then I struggle to swallow, gasping for breath from the effort. Eventually, I learn to chew a bit of banana, mash it around my mouth and pop the pill in just before I swallow. I trick myself like a sick dog.

CHAPTER 14

DELICATES

The water is just below scalding, the kind of heat that makes hands go red and rough. Combined with detergent, the water causes the skin around my knuckles to crack, a little seep with each movement. But my rhythm remains steady—squeeze, squeeze, rub—washing clothes by hand routine. Soon the heat and the hurt dull, mechanization all that remains.

I'm washing clothes too delicate for machines—silk blouses and lace dresses I wear to work. Today, the washing is a welcome distraction. The balance between my professional and personal life has been difficult lately, balancing my job as a professor with my role as a wife, my email inbox and "To Do" list overflowing, along with my laundry basket. So I shut myself into the laundry room and I make clean that which is dirty. I smooth out the wrinkles. The metaphor here is not difficult.

Then the knock.

My husband speaks without pause before I've even opened the door, his syntax staccato. He looks at the floor, the ceiling, the soapy water. His gaze is distracted; the bubbles burst. He speaks so quickly he loses track of his sentences. He paces while he speaks. My husband has forgotten that we've already talked about his latest fixation—the desire to travel or a video game or a news story. More than a dozen times. For several months.

I tense. I feel the sting in my eyes, a little seep with each movement. I turn back to the washing.

This is not unusual. In the past few months, Brady has disappeared for hours at a time, spent an hour in the bathroom with the shower running but come out dry, driven through stoplights and over curbs. He has acquired bruises and opened up cuts and bled unaware in the night, leaving a poesy-spattered trail on the sheets. He has made a dozen plans for the same time, spent thousands of dollars without recollection, and misplaced objects around our house so that each day is a scavenger hunt. Yesterday he cleaned the carpet and then lifted the steam cleaner above his head in celebration, dumping muddy water all over the floor.

Brady's latest mania is not odd—this has happened several times a year for the decade we have been together—but it is long. He has been cycling longer and more frequently than he used to, and his psychiatrist reminds us that bipolar is accumulative. Cycles increase with time.

It was Brady's mania that first attracted me to him, though I did not know this at the time. I saw a confident, kind man who was easy to talk to, full of big stories about driving too fast along the California coast and crooning to his childhood macaw, a man up for the clichéd adventures of the senior year of college—drinking until you didn't care if you danced poorly, late night beach bonfires, potlucks with too much food and not enough seats. It was easy to become friends, easier still to begin dating a year later. Ours was a spring romance and by summer I was infatuated with the man whose face never creased in worry or anger, and who had endless time, it seemed, to win my favor with long conversations and meandering drives in the sunshine. Summer became electric, unending—this, I later learned, was because Brady quit taking his medication when we began dating, convinced that after many years of being medicated he wanted to know me without drugs, wanted to indulge in the fever pitch of manic infatuation.

Brady's mania returned each summer—studies link sunlight exposure to increased mania—and soon mania was not symptom but season. Summer was energy, love, intensity, the whole world ripe and succulent and shining.

Though I did not recognize Brady's manias for several years, he never hid his diagnosis from me—on our second date he hung his head, loosening his clasp on my hands.

"I have something to tell you," he whispered with a quietness I'd never known from him, his forehead wrinkled for the first time. "If we date you need to know, and I understand if you don't want to move forward."

He needed to come clean, he said, as if his diagnosis were a dirty secret. "I'm bipolar," he announced with finality, adding, "It's difficult to be in a relationship with a bipolar person. My psychiatrist told me more than half of bipolar people end up alone." He said this with such certainty—he has repeated it time and again during our years together—I nearly believed him. And because he was diagnosed as a young teenager, I understood more about his earnestness, his sweetness—how painful to have been told you are unlovable for much of your life.

When I did not leave, he protested, urging, "I don't get depressed, but I do have manias."

Over the years I've only seen him depressed a few times, often after an argument, though sometimes for no reason— "I'm having a mopey day," he'll offer, a soft, sad animal. His manias, however, became more familiar, increasing with excitement—travel, holidays, career advancements, cross-country moves, our wedding and honeymoon—and eventually with time. The cycles are cumulative—the more he cycles, the more frequent they will become. Recently, his psychiatrist explained that untreated, Brady's manias will increase in intensity and speed until he is manic much of the time. "If we don't get this under control," he said sternly, "it will get worse. It will grow unchecked."

Brady has been manic for six months. Six months unable to concentrate on a task, unable to sit still for more than a few minutes. Six months of pacing, jumping up and down from the couch, twitching his leg in bed at night like a metronome. Six months of losing track of his topic mid-sentence, trying to locate his original thought before asking me a question and interrupting my answer. Six months of eating with abandon, rushing through meals so quickly he sometimes chokes, gulping down soda after soda at restaurants until waiters leave several at once, eating so beyond his fill that his stomach swells each night and he moans about the pain, acid snaking up his throat. At night he settles into a deep sleep, the large arm he throws over my body weighing me down.

Trapped is how I sometimes feel, though I try to hide this from my husband. Mania, he explains, feels good. It feels fast and exciting, and watching his zeal and enthusiasm, I imagine him in the midst of an undulating light wave, the rush and blur, heat and pulse. It must feel so very pure. Though bipolar disorder is classified as a mental illness to be monitored and medicated, it is a part of who my husband is, and thus, his mania must also feel so very right.

Still, I feel a sense of obligation when he is manic, when he indulges on caffeine and alcohol, stays up all night and sleeps in all day, spends money lavishly, acts primarily on impulse, consequence be damned. Years ago, during a mania where Brady accumulated several thousand dollars of secret debt, gained forty pounds, and I worried he would lose his job, Brady asked me to oversee his care. "I don't always recognize it," he explained, as he had many times. His yearly manias were beginning to last longer, stretching from July or August into September or October, fading for a few weeks only to resurface during the holidays. We bickered, me frustrated with behavior I still didn't understand, him frustrated by my frustration.

"I need your help," he admitted. "But you have to understand that I'll probably be stubborn and not want to listen. Even if I don't listen at first, keep trying."

In my mid-twenties, I was still learning to look after myself, navigating a PhD program across the country from my family and the storm of my anxiety, and the responsibility of looking after someone else seemed daunting. I did not know where boyish carelessness ended and bipolar disorder began. I did not know what it took for Brady, who had spent the last decade hiding his diagnosis and resisting medical treatment, to ask me for assistance.

After many years together, however, we've reached an agreement—I monitor what he eats and drinks, how much he sleeps, how much he spends, if the bills get paid, if he wears a seatbelt, if he comes home at all, and he trusts that I have his best interest at heart. It is a delicate arrangement. It requires trust, respect, and careful attention—if either of us forgets the arrangement it is easy to get frustrated or resentful. We remain side by side, though it sometimes seems impossible.

It seems impossible to know where the line exists between care and control. Sometimes it seems as if I must control Brady in order to care for him. I wonder when pointing out his manias—as he has asked me to do since he doesn't always recognize or accept them—becomes armchair diagnosis. I wonder when regulating his behavior becomes a means to defining what I deem acceptable rather than what is best for him. This is, after all, how so much of the world determines what we label mental illness. It pains me to point out the places Brady falters when what I want most is to praise his many successes. It seems impossible to be a good partner when I am chastising him. Caregiving requires a careful balance and I feel the tightrope shake with the effort. It seems only a moment before I misstep and fall, zooming towards the ground.

In the laundry room, I realize my hands have tightened too, tense around the fabric, loosening the delicate weave.

My husband talks without looking at me, his eyes on the skies, his hands flying fast around his face. He rushes through a list of activities he'd like to do, before rushing away as abruptly as he appeared. He does not finish his sentence.

I breathe. I wash—squeeze, squeeze, rub.

I met Brady when he arrived uninvited with a friend to my birthday party. He quickly introduced himself to the guests and organized events the next day to extend the celebration. The next time I saw him, he arrived uninvited to a dinner party hours after guests had finished eating, showing up with a laugh and libations and extending the event well into the night. He did the same at each gathering in the months that followed—game nights, beach picnics, afternoons at the park, helping friends move from their college apartments, fixing broken laptops, moving heavy furniture, the tedium of a Wednesday afternoon. Eventually, my friends and I began to invite him. No matter the task or time of night, Brady could be counted on to show up, all grin and fervor. This was, he later admitted, because he was manic much of the time, bursting with untapped energy.

A decade later, Brady is still this way, though the circumstances have changed. Now Brady helps build websites for friends' startup companies, moves friends into their newly purchased homes, helps a friend's father with home repairs, attends and assists with every wedding back home in California, though we lived in Nebraska for seven years, now in Massachusetts. The circumstances have changed, but the mania has not.

I feel depleted from the constant worry, the guilt I feel about whether I am worrying enough or whether I am bordering on resentment. Though he is not ashamed of his bipolar disorder, Brady is also not forthcoming with his diagnosis, which means I must find a way to avoid social activities, excessive stimuli, the demands of family and friends on his time and space when he needs stillness and routine to bring him out of mania. This is difficult because mania makes Brady even more charismatic. His energy is contagious. He is always funny, always confident, and with mania he accepts every invitation, volunteers to drive people to the airport or fix their flat, arranges dinner parties and game nights, and buys rounds of drinks and movie tickets. He is the life of the party he throws all night, a handsome man with broad shoulders and full, laughing belly and deep dimples. Of course others flock to him.

And of course they grow angry when I put a stop to the fun. I've grown the reputation of gatekeeper, cruel nag, and, I fear, mother. Brady relies on me to manage his schedule because he has a hard time saying no even when mania does not make time swirl, but others know me only as the one who refuses them help or fun. I want to tell our friends that building a website means Brady will work forty hours at his corporate programming job, then spend another forty hours a week fixating on engineering this task for a friend, that he will focus so intently on delivering the best he will grow frenzied and distracted, forget to eat, to sleep, will build, unaware, a mania as well. Even seemingly small pleasures take their toll—too many birthdays or holiday parties, too many movies or dinner parties result in mania, as do too many videogames, which Brady's old college friends can play endlessly without episodic mood swings. Brady, likeable as he is, must constantly turn down requests for fun, and because this makes him feel guilty and ashamed, I'm often the one to do it.

I have no doubt that some find us distant or antisocial when we pull away for months at a time, and we've lost friends who require more maintenance than we can offer.

"I haven't seen you in so long. Don't you miss hanging out?"

"It's our first child—don't you want to fly home for the baby shower?"

"It's just a few days. Why won't you help?"

I long to talk openly about the times we are unavailable, to make others understand that Brady cannot sustain such frantic energy all the time. I want to tell our California friends that the week of celebrations leading up to their wedding is so sweet and good that when Brady flies cross country back to me he is glassy-eyed and exhausted and tells me he has not slept since he left. I watch him vibrate with energy; the mania lasts months. I want to say that though we love traveling back to California and seeing our parents spread across the state, my seven siblings, our old friends and their growing families, that the excitement is exhausting, that disruption—even welcome disruption—requires an invitation to mental illness. I want to say that it's hard to celebrate when you know piecing yourself together is waiting at home for you when you return. But Brady's bipolar diagnosis is his to share. I say nothing.

My professional life also suffers as a result of the time I spend overseeing our lives. I am a professor of English, a writer, an editor, but the time I have to devote to these passions is diminished by the work I do for my family—cooking, cleaning, caregiving. Like many women who feel the pressure to choose between family and career, each professional decision—projects, travel, promotion—I make is based in part on how it will impact my husband. It pains me to admit that I sometimes wonder where my career might be without mental illness. We must make a fine pair when we work from home together—Brady programming in his Star Wars shirt and batting me with the lightsaber he keeps at his desk, me with stacks of student papers, fretting over thesis statements. Still, on these days my husband wraps his large hands around my waist, lifts me up to the ceiling and sways us both back and forth like he did on our wedding day.

It changes at night. I begin wheedling Brady to get ready for bed several hours in advance. I ask him to get in the shower, brush his teeth, take his medication. He ignores me for video games, for computer updates, for television, his phone. He ignores me for silence. Sometimes he takes the garbage outside and disappears. During this recent mania he did not shower or shave for several weeks.

Once I convince Brady to get in the shower, I must then plead with him to get out, which can take an hour or more and several hearty pounds on the door. The same goes for putting out his clothes for work, setting his alarm, coming to bed. If I go in to bed first he stays up all night, and then the next night and the next, sitting alone in the dark, glowing with the light of his computer screen. He once went without sleep for several weeks.

When I look at my feet, the tightrope shakes.

Mornings we repeat this routine—I beg Brady to rise, to get dressed, to accomplish the tasks we have set for the day. I alternate between frustration and fear—frustration that he relies on me so much, fear that I won't be able to do what I must, frustration that perhaps I am not empathetic enough, fear that being a good partner, a good wife, requires I give all of myself. I am frustrated with the both of us; I fear our lives will look like this forever.

I've used humor, I've cried, I've shouted. Each has left Brady annoyed and degraded, left me ignored and disrespected. I think of how we were a decade ago, when we were younger, when we ate and slept and made love with abandon, when mania felt like part of falling in love. My husband was impulsive, driving three hours each way to see me each weekend while I completed my master's degree. He was lavish with his attention and frequent gifts—bouquets that made a flower shop of my apartment, dessert with every meal out, a tiny black and white kitten who is now a soft, squishy senior—though I knew he needed to focus on school and his student budget. His compulsive behavior—weekend trips, a move with me across the country—seemed sign of his devotion. And they were. Sometimes I long to go back in time.

One Wednesday night I called him from graduate school to tell him the day had been fittingly long and uneventful and that I missed him terribly and could not wait for Friday evening to arrive so he could hold me again. We talked for an hour, then another, and he offered to drive to see me in the middle of the night—"I don't have difficulty staying awake," he said when I mentioned the late hour. "I could drive back for class early in the morning." More than six hours of driving for only a few moments together seemed illogical and impulsive, and when at last I said, "We should hang up, you practically could have driven here by now," he laughed and said, "I know," and then knocked on my door and held me, whispering, "I love you," before driving home again. Impulsivity is attractive when you are young and believe love requires sacrifice, but it loses its appeal when your partner spends the rent money. Obsession seems romantic until you are not its object.

Sometimes I retreat to a closet and I lie down on the floor and I sob, trying to hide my despair but hoping he might hear, that this might shock him out of his mania and he will pull me close and rock me and breathe into my dark hair. More often than not, he is unaware, and when I return at last, red-faced and sniffling, he does not lift his eyes from whatever consumes him. One manic summer, years ago, when he was working forty hours a week and playing video games another forty, accumulating a secret debt we have only recently paid off, I made several passes naked in front of him, hoping to attract his attention. He did not lift his eyes from the screen, slaughtering a village, carnage marking his path.

Reader, know this: bipolar disorder does not define my husband, but it is an integral part of his identity. I am frustrated by the very thing that brings me joy. Mental illness is a braided part of identity, impossible to tease out. There is not illness and man, symptom and personality. Like a Venn diagram, they merge and shade one another. To wish illness away is to negate the man himself.

At least, that is how I feel about my anxiety, a disorder which for years has left me rattled and afraid, constantly on the edge of regret, my life a sequence of catastrophe and mourning. Ten years after my disorders began, I still have panic attacks, frequent migraines, and phantom pains. I stumble over my tongue and its words. I black out mid-conversation—I am forever losing time. I fluctuate between a heightened sense of awareness, all thrash and gnash, and a numb detachment from reality, the sure ache of that knowledge. Like Brady's, my illness flickers and flares, and sometimes I see meteors crashing through the heavens or spiders scuttling in my periphery or ghosts hazy in the afternoon light. My anxiety is not odd—Brady and I are used to the anxiety that clutches my heart, the way my muscles clench and leave me partially paralyzed—but it is long. I've had over a decade of these symptoms. Just as I have never known Brady apart from his illness, he has never known me without mine. Our understanding of one another is braided and shaded by symptom and diagnosis.

I dunk a new garment in the water and the wrinkles disappear. I lift the shirt up by the collar and it looks like something drowned. I apply friction to vanish a stain—my force wears it down to nothing.

Brady is wearing down too. The language of illness and treatment is its own kind of friction. The language of care implies weakness, neediness, incapability. To be a patient is to be framed as someone in need of supervision, as someone foolish or naïve. As a child. While I have experience with this language by way of gender—medical language is at its heart patriarchal—my husband, whose gender and size grant him the comfort of much of the world, is not experienced in the ways language can wound. That he must be "cured" or "controlled" shames him. The language he would need to adopt in order to share his story with others is precisely why Brady tells no one, despite the fact that we've just begun a years-long process to find new or additional medications to help his increasing manic episodes. (Brady will eventually find an effective medication that evens his mood swings without leaving him numb and lethargic, one that allows for his vitality and energy, but at an even pace. With this medication Brady will become the best version of himself—enthusiastic, responsible, creative, caring—seeming, suddenly, to try to make up for lost time, to apologize for the manic years before, even though he needn't. And he will apologize, too, for how frequently he must see doctors, psychiatrists, for the overwhelming cost of so many appointments, the staggering cost of a medication that could help so many, but that no insurance—a privilege many do not have—seems willing to cover.)

Like my washing, the language surrounding mental illness has become routine. But language matters. Those without anxiety tell me to relax and all will be well. They laugh at the fears they see as strange but I experience as a normal part of daily living. There are few things that make me angrier than when someone blames an unpleasant film or food for "giving me PTSD," or when someone laughs and justifies unwarranted actions by saying, "I'm kind of OCD" or accounts for irresponsible choices by announcing, "I guess I'm a little bipolar." The metaphors associated with bipolar disorder—that a bipolar person is dangerous, an unpredictable Dr. Jekyll/Mr. Hyde—are overused and inaccurate, clumsy figurative language. Worse still is when people say that a manic person has "gone away" or "isn't themselves" anymore, as if the illness takes over and makes them disappear entirely. Brady is as much himself while manic as when he is not.

Though Brady's illness can be frustrating for the both of us, his illness is what I love most about him. My husband is lively, exciting, good-natured. He is quick to laugh and eager to help. He is vibrant. I love his bipolar brain. And Brady's mental illness means that he is understanding of mine. As someone who has watched news stories linking each shooting to madness, heard jokes made about crazy people—most recently at a workplace meeting where a professor said poets hoping to land teaching jobs should "keep their crazy to themselves"—watched the term "anxiety" become a contemporary buzzword tossed around carelessly, I believed myself foolish and unlovable for many years. Loving a mentally ill man has made me realize I am capable and deserving of love.

"I could never be married to someone like that," my closest friend says when I fret over Brady. "I couldn't put up with it."

"Tell him you're not going to deal with it any longer," my mother suggests over the phone.

"Take his credit card."

"Count his pills. Watch him swallow them."

"Just leave if he gets too bad."

The same could easily be said to Brady about me. I have often wondered why relationships are considered conditional when mental illness comes into play. Mental illness strips you naked and isn't this all we can ask of our partners, of ourselves if we are to love? When Brady struggles, my love is fierce and full, and when I am afraid of the world and myself, his care makes me know love concretely. Comments like these reveal how quick the world is to label us broken.

"You aren't going to have kids, are you?" is the other question I've heard time and again, even though I am young and career-driven and have not yet decided. That we could not care for a child when we have done so for one another for many years, dedicated, nurturing, accepting that we cannot control everything while trying to help one another be our best, sometimes makes me laugh. Other times it makes me cry. We do not know if we want children, but it is because we might rather travel or write or experience the solitude so difficult to find in the world these days. If we choose not to have children, it will not be because we are incapable.

I hear my husband moving in the other room, the television flashing to life, his phone beeping the distraction of a dozen tasks and reminders. I track his movements.

It is precisely this thinking, I realize, catching myself red-handed in the steaming water, that is dangerous. What strikes me most about this kind of language is its desire to create ownership and control over the disabled body. To accuse someone of suddenly not being "themselves" implies the power to see the person for who they truly are, as though a mentally ill person does not or cannot know. Or worse, is not "normal," "human," even, while ill. Brady is self-aware, proclaims himself "Manic Man," his superpower the ability to move at the speed of light. Similarly, I know when my anxiety peaks, am so attuned to my mind and body that I register the slightest flicker of fear and recognize discomfort in others. We do not need someone to oversee our illness. We know them better than anyone, more than anything. To assert that a person has "gone away" because of their mental illness implies a kind of omnipotence about the world that a bipolar person, an anxious person, with their limited world-view, is somehow unable—too naïve, too out of control, too sick—to see. This language is coercive, convoluted, cruel.

Still, I seek language to describe Brady to others—to ask not for their patience but for their understanding when he forgets things, when he interrupts them, when he seems distracted. Mostly I wish I could ask others to leave him alone so that he can have the kind of self-care we all require from time to time. I also seek language to describe Brady to himself—to explain why I sometimes feel so alone in our marriage. When I sit down with Brady and fit my small hands into their place between his much larger ones, I long for the language to tell him how frustrated and fearful I am, to explain how the feelings twist and braid themselves into knots in my stomach. The only words I have are flat and stale. They make him cry.

I also seek language to describe myself, to explain to Brady or my friends what I feel and fear, to explain to myself in the darkest of times that what it is I see in the shadows is both real—my feelings are to be validated and honored—but simultaneously not real, for I am safe, I am whole. Our worries are, after all, more about ourselves than about the mentally ill; our fears are illuminated in the way we monitor those who are different. My worries for Brady are, at their core, worries for myself.

Above all, I seek language because I am a lover of words, someone who makes sense of my life and the world through storytelling, and yet it is difficult for me to reflect on Brady without resorting to the very tropes that anger me. Even now, trying to write this all down, to put the being into knowing into writing, I find my words taking ownership of his health, the filter of my perspective shading his story into one where he seems less capable, where his illness seems a burden.

I finish the washing and hang each garment out to dry. I rinse the scum of soap from the sink and wash my red hands. I close the laundry door firmly behind me and I sit beside my husband, who is never my burden, who is capable and charismatic and merely does things I can't put into words.

Some weeks or months later Brady's mania will subside and my anxiety will rise in response, as it often does, our moods, we joke, ebbing and flowing in rhythm with one another's, each of us taking over when the other needs it. I will become shaky and fretful, unable to hold myself steady, unable to breathe, my heart, even, unable to retain the beat it is designed to keep. I will look into the clouds and see death swirling, feel poison in the breeze, taste metal and blood and feces. I will imagine my brain squirming inside my skull, twisting in on itself, purple and stinking with necrosis.

I will keep this to myself as I go about my work, as I've learned to do for so many years—putting this into story will only alarm my colleagues. It would surprise them to learn that behind my blazer and glasses and my armful of papers that I slicked my hair back that day without the help of a mirror, for when I look at my reflection all I see is a ghoul. That I've imagined myself dead for weeks, my consciousness floating above my body. That my heart is a stone. That my throat closed long ago.

But my husband, my caretaker, will pull me close and rock me and breathe into my dark hair. He will hold my hands with their knuckles cracked from washing. I will heave and gasp, rigid with spasm. I will see the future, the past, all sorts of demons. I will see rips in time. There is no cure—my body and brain act the way they want to, and I'm not sure where the illness ends and I begin, a Venn diagram the easiest metaphor—but sitting with him will calm me until I can swallow once more. I will stop gasping for breath, stop choking on my tongue. I will find words. But here, with my husband, there is no need for language.

CHAPTER 15

UNBEARABLE WEIGHT

"Stay away from crazy people on the Internet," my mother warns. After more than six months on Zoloft, I am beginning to doubt the side effects will go away. I want to investigate.

Mental illness presents a struggle over private versus public, the individual versus the institutional. On the one hand, my anxiety is a private illness, one that exists in my unique blood and brain. At the same time, however, my anxiety is public to family and friends, part of a larger institution because I am a statistic, one of millions of people who suffer from mental illness, who buy a medication each year. Still, I am warned away from online support groups and forums. I am told to seek solace in statistics but to shun individuals. The public, institutional nature of mental illness makes it difficult for patients to protest—who will believe someone with an altered sense of reality over scientists, doctors, a successful drug's twenty-year history and impressive revenue? I wonder how many people are accused of causing side effects with their bad attitudes.

When I ask permission to go off Zoloft, I focus on my continued hair loss. I'm too ashamed to admit that I'm still unable to orgasm and Terry's recommendation for this, I know, is adding another drug. We do not discuss my anger, which neither of us has recognized. We do not discuss my continued anxiety. Instead, we focus on my hair loss, my appearance. We run more blood tests to check my thyroid. We reexamine files from a dermatologist who spent ten minutes with me before saying, "It's probably stress. Come see me again if it's falling out in six months."

"Hold on," Terry says suddenly, leaning forward toward her computer. "Let me check something."

The blinds are closed, but I know outside it is green and moist, new growth pushing up through the soil, squirrels and wild rabbits in the fields, a host of birds looking for seed. I've lived in the Midwest nearly a year, and while it seems I am growing older, twisting like a wild root beneath the surface, I am always surprised by the way time marches on, by the way there is growth and renewal despite all I feel and fear.

I look around the room while Terry studies the screen. I shift in my seat, my nervousness accentuated by the crackle of the paper on the examining table. Pamphlets for sexual health line the walls—not a problem, I think, since it's been so long since Brady and I have had satisfying sex. To be honest, I can hardly remember making love. Another memory vanished. I pick long hairs off my top to distract myself. One, two, three. At last Terry says "Aha," and spins in her chair to face me.

"Well," she begins with an optimistic smile. She leans forward to me like a friend. "I've never seen this in a patient before, but a small percentage of people report hair loss with Zoloft." She assures me that my hair loss is still probably stress-related. But my hair didn't start to fall out until I was put on drugs, I want to say. But most of my stress lately is because of drugs, I want to protest. But both Celexa and Zoloft are linked to hair loss, I want to scream. What about the worms, the anorgasmia, my volatility—how can we ignore that?

Instead I smile. I nod.

"Have you been able to achieve orgasm yet?" she asks next, her cheery delivery implying the question is routine. I wince at the implications of the word "achieve," orgasm a task worthy of a gold star, another symptom box to check as we move through the rest of our appointment.

I leave Terry's office with several less-than-desirable options. The first option is to stay on Zoloft and try to adapt. The second is to try a medication selected from the long list she rattles off. One medication is called Effexor, and she laughs and says, "You notice when you take it. Or if you forget. I call it 'Side Effexor.'"

After several weeks of mulling over the decision, I decide to switch over to another class of drugs, rather than the host of SSRIs I've tried before, or the SNRIs Terry suggests. Playing with an additional neurotransmitter when I've had such bad luck before doesn't seem wise.

I am relieved to be going off antidepressants. The drugs I've taken have offered little relief. What has helped most is spending more time with my illness. I now recognize anxiety at its start and feel strangely comforted when I begin to imagine danger—a piece of toast has gone down the wrong tube, punctured my lung, and I am dying; an eyelash is really a splinter burrowing into my eye, and I am dying; some evil thought has combined with karma, and I am dying—because I know it is not real. Understanding and accepting my anxiety seem more valuable than trying in vain to medicate it away.

I am also relieved to be going off of antidepressants because I've never had signs of depression—no fatigue or decreased energy, no feelings of guilt or worthlessness, no sense of hopelessness, no thoughts of self-harm or suicide. A close friend has experienced severe depression for many years. She is young, sharp as a razor, and exceedingly kind. Yet I can see the pain and strain in her face, the lethargy and weight on her body, in her limbs, her gait, the effort she must put into each movement. She dwells, much like I do, but her obsessions have more to do with feelings of worthlessness, of self-loathing, of despair, a sorrow so close to the bone that she feels it in each breath. Depression, it seems, pulls people under the water of their worst failures and greatest losses, suffocating them with shame and the pain of regret. While I don't always like my actions or thoughts, I've always liked myself.

What frightens me most about depression is how likely it may be in my future, for studies indicate anxiety is often a precursor to depression—about half of patients with pure anxiety disorders develop major depression within five years.[52] While others might view anxiety as a perpetual death sentence, the sufferer seeing torture again and again, developing depression is the most frightening thing I can imagine. My greatest fear is going insane—ironic, since most people would argue I'm already there—but though my fears that the world is ending, that some fiery ball is headed straight towards Earth, sending sparks through space as it hurtles towards us, can send me into the fetal position, this is nothing compared to my fear of developing depression.

When I feel comfortable enough to reveal to friends that I have anxiety, they sometimes assume depression, and I clarify my feelings, remind them that I am not sad, that I am panicked, and that there is a difference. I say that I have plenty of energy—nervous, tense energy. I say that I have visions of aliens and that I see a world of ash and smolder, but this is not a world that goes on without me. I am always dying, never dead. There are differences in the ways my depressed friend and I move through the world and need and deserve to be treated, and these differences matter.

Since I began treatment with Terry, she has asked me about sadness and suicidal thoughts during each visit. Depression has followed me like an unwelcome shadow—

a shadow that isn't even mine—no matter how many times I explain the course of my illness. I understand anxiety and depression are sometimes linked and that medication can cause depression, but Terry's insistence has always seemed accusatory. Over and over, I assure her that I am panicked but perky, convinced I am dying but with the zest of a cheerleader. Each time it is true.

Terry tapers me slowly from Zoloft, weaning me like a puppy from its mother, or an addict from her fix. She simultaneously eases me slowly onto my new medication, Buspirone. For months I take various levels of the two medications at the same time. I have to write down what I take, when I take it, how much I take just to remember. The milligrams are always shifting; nothing is permanent.

It is Saturday afternoon and I am lying in bed as sunlight streams through the window. Trees outside are in full bloom, their flamboyant leaves pressing against the glass in all directions. The sun hurts my eyes, though. More than that, it hurts my body, which is so lethargic I've been unable to get out of bed all day. I call Brady into the room to close the curtains. In the dark, things feel right.

It has been several weeks since I began to wean off of Zoloft and ease onto Buspirone, and I'm feeling out of sorts. I feel sad. Irrevocably, uncontrollably sad. I lie in bed, without the strength to raise my head to drink water, let alone stand or walk around. I cry for hours. I mourn. I have decided I'm worthless. My presence is a burden, to me, to Brady, to anyone who has had to put up with my nonsense the last few years. I shouldn't be here, I think, and when I glimpse myself in the bathroom mirror, I don't recognize my face. In fourth grade I realized there was a difference between the body and the mind and I spent hours staring in the mirror wondering what connected spirit to sinew. The longer I stared, the more I was convinced by magic or mystery. Now, the longer I stare, the less convinced I am of anything except our impermanence, the ways the world is disconnected, pierced and pieced together by pain.

When someone is depressed, her neurotransmitters dance in different directions, or they do not dance at all, synaptic function stalling, sputtering, or ceasing altogether. Gene expression alters, and neurons increase or decrease excitability. The frontal cortex is disturbed, along with the circuits that link thalamus and basal ganglia. The amygdala and the hypothalamus are disrupted, and prolactin and cortisol go haywire. Blood flow to the occipital lobes decreases, altering sight perception. Body temperature flatlines.[53] Fatigued from this internal turmoil, a depressed person can't find energy for daily activities. She does not sleep, lying awake for hours, restless without the release the night brings. Or she sleeps away entire mornings and afternoons, unable to wake, her frenzied body soaking up sleep, then moving slow-motion through her waking life as though she were still in slumber. She feels worthless and guilty. Indecisive and unhappy. She cannot muster interest in activity. She cannot find solace. She does not know pleasure. She feels empty. I feel empty.

I feel like I am no longer living. Entire days, then weeks go by during which I don't want to get out of bed, though I do wake and fake my way through the day. I feel flat, without, for a change, the peaks and pivots of my paranoia, without the jagged jolts fear sends though my body. If anxiety makes my body a stranger to me, this new feeling makes me feel as though I don't have a body at all. I am hollow, disembodied. A ghost. I'm not sure I even exist.

I wonder if this feeling is withdrawal, but at the back of my throat this tastes dense and purple, like something too viscous and slow-moving, something too saturated to swallow. This tastes like depression.

I am depressed for a month or so, spring fading into summer without my even realizing. The only times I leave my bed are when I have to put on a blazer and pretend like I care about citing sources when I really just want to think about how awful I am and cry some more. When the school year ends, I fly home to visit California for several weeks. My family last saw me at Christmas, and they gasped at my thin hair and frail body. I'm hoping this time I can smile big to prove I'm okay.

My mother and Natalie meet me at the airport with big hugs, filling the car with chatter as we drive home. No one mentions my health and this is perfect. When I step into the house, Cameron and Bailey have colored a banner for me with a stick figure for each member of our family and Candy has written "Welcome Home Sissy" in big bubble letters. I bubble too, grateful they've missed me.

The next day I cut my waist-length hair into a short bob. The stylist who has cut my hair for the last decade combs her fingers over my scalp, asking why my hair has thinned so much since I left. When I tell her about the medication she is not surprised. "I've seen this before," she says, gathering my long hair into a ponytail and slicing through it with a pair of scissors. The ponytail she hands me is thin and brittle. I wrap it around my fist like a noose.

The haircut makes me lighter. My family and I picnic at the park. We have backyard barbeques. I play hours of Uno with Cameron and Bailey. My sisters and I go out for decadent cakes at an expensive restaurant, laughing when Candy gets so high on sugar she chatters the entire way home and crashes once she sits on the couch. Our entire family goes to the beach and spreads out dozens of towels, even my father in his construction boots helping to bury Cameron and Bailey, sculpting mermaids in the sand above their bodies.

Natalie graduates high school and I am overcome with nostalgia. As an infant, she was my shadow, resting her hand on my arm throughout our play as though I were her anchor. As a preschooler, she delighted when I put loose change on a ceiling fan, turning it on to rain money; she never realized I recycled the change to create the illusion again. In elementary school, she got permission from her teacher to run across the imaginary line separating her school from my middle school so she could give me a hug as I ate lunch with my friends. Though she was too shy to say hello to anyone sitting next to me, she came every day. When I was in high school, Natalie spent long hours in my room, listening to music and helping me reorganize the posters of musicians I kept collaged across every inch of wall space to surround me with familiar faces. When I was in college, she spent nights in my dorm, then my apartment, the two of us playing grownup in a house all to ourselves. Any hurt I've had—braces, a broken heart—Natalie has helped heal, and while she does not understand my anxiety, I hope it is because she is still young.

My family stretches across a long line of seats at her graduation. We whoop and cheer and I don't feel crazy for a moment. That night there's a party with yellow flowers and balloons, a sunny cake. My face hurts from smiling. My heart, too, from swelling. I feel that joy akin to pain, the kind that leaves you clutching your side but grateful for the ache.

But when they think I'm not listening, my parents whisper warnings to my siblings: "Don't do that because Sissy will freak out." My mother rushes about, trying to make me comfortable, apologizing when they run out of toilet paper or towels again, or when Casey jumps into my bed covered in mud because the dryer is broken and there are no other clean sheets. "I know how picky you are," she says. All their effort makes me feel like a burden.

I'm a bug under a microscope, gangly legs and swollen abdomen, struggling against the glass while everyone stares. My siblings talk about me openly, even after I enter the room, switching to words like "she" or "her" to disguise the subject of their ridicule. They glance at each other when I do something they find odd. Because it seems like everyone is already making fun of my "issues," as they call them, I join in, joking about myself and chuckling along with everyone around the dinner table. I laugh extra loudly like everything is fine.

But things are not fine. I am not fine. My mother wakes up at five a.m., and strangers drop off their children at our house before she has finished her morning coffee. By each afternoon, there are dozens of children ranging from infants to teenagers running through the house. There is nowhere to sit; the bathrooms are always full; the trash cans too. When I venture into the living room the children crowd around me and ask, "Who are you?" Victoria is home from college for the summer. Casey's friend has recently lost his mother to a cancer, so he, too, lives at our house. My father's unemployed friend sleeps in the spare room out back. He smells like beer and cigarettes and makes comments about my butt. One night he comments on sixteen-year-old Candy's breasts, and when she stands up for herself, my father hushes her for being rude to an adult. Trying to avoid him brushing against me in the hallway sets me on edge. So many bodies crammed into a small house sets me on edge. Being so on edge sets me further on edge until I wonder where the edge actually is, when I'll go so far I'll finally fall. There is so much clutter: backpacks, hairbrushes, toothbrushes, wet towels, muddy shoes, plates and cups in the sink, dirty diapers, sometimes, on the couch or kitchen counter. There is so much noise: crying, clapping, singing, the doorbell, the phone, the TV, toys. I feel claustrophobic, unable to sit or breathe because I can't find a space. I am out of place, awkward and in the way. I try to be inconspicuous, but the more I try, the more anxious I get. I want to escape, to catch a breath, but I'm staying in the room Cameron and Bailey share, sleeping on the bottom bunk, encircled by toys. Natalie's room is on one side, Victoria's room on the other, and they surround me with music and TV until three a.m., alarms they snooze for hours each morning, hours spent on the telephone each afternoon. Candy's, Casey's, and my parents' rooms are upstairs; I am surrounded.

When we caravan with two cars full of kids the long stretch of miles to Disneyland, I am stretched thin. The car ride is full of shouting and people throwing snacks, siblings refusing to sit next to certain people, burping and sneezing, and the hum of a half dozen iPods and phones. Brady has flown in for the vacation, and I whisper to him, "I want to go home," over and over, though Nebraska doesn't feel like home either. Still, I long for the open space of the Great Plains, the quiet solitude. This trip would probably be too much for anyone—mentally ill or not—unaccustomed to such a hectic lifestyle.

During the six-hour drive, we stop at a beach for lunch and my mother has not packed enough food and it is cold and there are no blankets to sit on and my jaw grates on an angle. Later we get lost looking for the hotel and we drive around for an hour while I sit stiff on the edge of my spine. My sisters are fighting—they will go the entire trip without speaking to one another. Natalie and Victoria pick on Candy and when I tell them to stop, I'm greeted with the sour silence of angry eighteen-year-olds.

That night at dinner my family tells me to order something with nuts in it, laughing because recently my lymph nodes swelled up like a golf ball in my neck and I thought it might be a nut allergy when it was really mono exacerbated by stress. They tell the waitress to ask me about it. With a table of eleven, all talking over one another and laughing, I'm sure everyone in the restaurant can hear. "Shut the fuck up," I hiss, slouching in my seat, scowling so I don't cry. My parents scold me; I am not supposed to curse. Everyone avoids me the rest of the night. This is my fault.

The next day we go to Disneyland. Natalie and Victoria beg to explore on their own. Candy gets in trouble with my father. Casey is uninterested, staring at girls and pretending he isn't walking with our ragtag group. Cameron and Bailey are overtired, whining and crying. This is expected with a large group, but with anxiety, each conflict is overwhelming. I want to correct it all.

On the long car ride home the next day, Natalie says I ruined the vacation. She accuses me of taking Candy's side and being cruel to Victoria. "You're mean," she insists. Because I don't feel mean, and because I am hurt no one can see how hard I've been trying, and because I'm embarrassed that everything I do lately seems to be wrong, and because I am so sad and empty, I show Natalie mean. I shout, spearing insults right into her soft spots, like the fact she didn't apply for financial aid or scholarships, a sore subject for my sister, who has spent her life compared to me by former teachers, and who realized in her senior year that she'd have to stay at home in the chaos, find a job, go to the local community college. I don't really feel disappointed like I say, but I know it will hurt, and as I spit each insult out, I feel better because now I know why the eyes are on me, because now there's a reason for everyone in the car to look at me, because no one needs to whisper anymore. I hurl insults like flame, scorching the car and all my attempts to be normal over the last few weeks.

Natalie, whose temper is not unlike my own on Zoloft, throws her phone hard into my face. It bounces off my temple. I want to cry, but instead I roll down the window and threaten to throw the phone out the moving car, leave it flattened and sparking on the Los Angeles freeway. Natalie shrieks, "How dare you" and calls me "crazy," hurling more items—a water bottle, a flip-flop, magazines. Soon my mother screams at me too—"God bless it" and "You should know better" and "What's wrong with you?" Bailey, only seven, is nearly in tears, his hands stuffed inside Mickey Mouse gloves. This is my fault.

When my mother finally pulls off the freeway, I jump out of the car and drag Brady, who has watched open-mouthed (but perhaps not surprised, given my temper lately), into the car my father is driving behind us, forcing Cameron and Candy to trade places. Natalie and I don't speak when we arrive home, and since she heads to her boyfriend's house immediately, I don't get a chance to say good-bye before I fly back to the Midwest. Candy and Casey tell me Natalie was out of line before leaving to whisper about me in the hallway. They refuse to speak to me for months. I'm ashamed and full of sorrow. "Take care of yourself," my parents order as I board the plane. "Get yourself together."

The plane ascends, patchwork landscape disappearing beneath the cloud cover. I press my forehead against the glass and let the vibration of the engine take over my body. I feel sick and the feeling goes to my stomach and then to my heart and it cowers and flaps its monstrous wings, beating shame throughout my body. The world cowers below.

"I think I'm depressed," I admit when I finally drag myself to Terry's office. I try to make myself look nice so Terry won't know I've been lying around in mismatched pajamas and one sock since I returned from California. She will think I've had depression all along. The stigma shifts, deepening the wound.

I don't make it past that first, dejected sentence before Terry interrupts me, not even inquiring after my symptoms, my feelings, my—

"People going through withdrawals from an antidepressant can sometimes feel as though they are depressed," she says matter-of-factly. "It will pass when your body adjusts. This isn't real depression," she promises, and I wonder why so many insist my anxiety is real when this depression is denied.

There is a half-life for Zoloft, Terry explains, as though the pills I've been swallowing are radioactive. The medication will linger even after I've stopped taking it altogether. Sure, trace elements remain in our bodies—iron and zinc, copper and chromium, essential to our health—but I don't want this chemical lurking around in my system any longer. It's not that the anorgasmia will last another six months after I stop taking Zoloft, the fallout coloring my relationship with Brady years later—even now—or that when the anger dies down, I become frightened it was ever there, afraid it might blaze again, even more hesitant to express anger in a world that prohibits this emotion to women. More than that, the remnants take up a part of me, as though my life is not my own, the months and years that follow a fraction of what they could be, me a fraction of what I should be.

I wait for the drug to leave and wonder if anyone will be waiting for me once it's gone. Chronic illness isolates people, makes them turn inward. When your days and weeks and months and years have been spent charting progress, cataloging symptoms, experimenting with new medications, going to various doctors' and specialists' appointments, your sense of self shrinks. Anxiety is, after all, an illness of ego. After years of worrying about everything from my breathing rate to my skin pallor, much of my life has been spent worrying only about myself, and I find it difficult to maintain close friendships. So much of my time is spent consumed by what I am thinking and feeling I have a hard time living beyond the sphere of myself. I don't want to be around those who are stressed, for their emotional burdens often become my own. When relationships become difficult or painful, I sometimes abandon them entirely. This might seem selfish, but it is not wrong to take the care we need. Plus, healthy people have little patience for hearing about illness, little sympathy for that which they cannot understand. It doesn't take long for your illness to become their burden. For the inevitable, "Can't you talk about something more pleasant? Can't you be more cheerful?" When your life revolves around illness, most of your encounters with others regard your illness as well, until illness seems the tiny, painful center of the world.

Natalie refuses to talk to me for six months. I see her the following Christmas, another stranger at my parents' house.

PART IV

CHAPTER 16

RAPTURE IN MAY

*A*ll summer my anxiety plays out on the Nebraska skies—storms sweep over the Plains, the rain determined, hard and sharp against the walls, shaking the chimney and the windows. Lightning rips the sky into uneven pieces, hitting trees, gashing them to splinters. The storms frighten me because they remind me of myself. I spend hours at the windows looking past my reflection, waiting for Zoloft to leave and Buspirone to build up in my system.

Patented in 1975 and approved by the FDA in 1986 (the year I was born) to treat generalized anxiety disorder, Buspirone acts on certain nerves sensitive to serotonin, and is useful for long-term control of anxiety, as opposed to more fast-acting drugs like Valium or Xanax. This may be why it is prescribed less often than other psychiatric medications, the year I begin taking it, though prescriptions are still up 15 percent from the last reporting, a total of 6,334,000 written, and this number will steadily increase to 8,065,000 (up another 26 percent) by 2013.[1]

Prescribed in place of benzos, whose high risks for patients including drug tolerance, drug dependence, and extreme drug withdrawal symptoms, Buspirone is also prescribed alongside SSRIs to augment treatment and counter sexual side effects.

The drug is time-sensitive—three pills spaced throughout my waking hours, so it seems I'm always swallowing pills. If I take them without food, I get dizzy. If I don't wait long enough after eating, I get dizzy. I can't always take my pills at the required time, however—if I'm teaching a class or at a meeting I can't pause to pull out the bright orange bottle. Medicine is a trade-off, and I must balance cost and gain as I try to determine when to take a pill. If I take one late, my chest tightens, my heart quickens, I feel fuzzy and unsteady and spend my lectures and meetings unsteady, my vision growing dark, sound blurring into a rush. I pray they don't run longer than usual. But I can't take a pill early, either, for then I grow dizzy, unable to see my students, meetings spinning around me like some great kaleidoscope. My life revolves around time like hands on a clock. Lurching forward to keep pace.

The inadequacy of time is why the story I am about to tell is out of place. In my memory this happened after I returned from California, but when I piece together the timeline, it occurred weeks before. This is the story that exists in my memory, so I tell it this way.

In early summer and Brady and I drive to Iowa for his grandmother's funeral. Our relationship is still strained, but we are trying. Buspirone should be working, but like Celexa and Xanax and Zoloft, it has never seemed to work beyond the side effects. I am still nervous and on edge. I am entirely apprehensive about this trip. You see, I've found out I am going to die.

My impending death, it seems, is all anyone can talk about. News of my death fills social media; reports of my death make the nightly news; my death is proclaimed on billboards across the country. Harold Camping, a Christian evangelist with a large following, has announced the Rapture will take place on May 21, 2011, the world ending completely five months later, on October 21, 2011. Most people take his prediction as a grand joke, laughing about the bodies of the saved floating upward and the zombies left behind. Not me. As someone for whom worry is a natural state of being, the prediction is true and imminent.

I'm also preoccupied with apocalypse because I've invested the last bit of hope I had into this new drug. Religiosity for the mentally ill is not uncommon: many see visions or hear voices, become fascinated with narratives of higher power and redemption, pray for cures or seek spiritual guidance. Victorian Americans linked illness to sin, blaming people for their ailments because of their moral failing. Early American asylums were religious institutes. "Have you tried praying?" a colleague once asked about my mental illness. Mental health is as tied to faith as it is to gender, the three linked by the abstraction of purity.

I spend the weeks leading up to the supposed Rapture sick to my stomach (but perhaps that is from the Buspirone), avoiding most media and the cavalier way people talk about the end. They don't seem to understand the severity of apocalypse—worse is that I'm not sure exactly what the Rapture entails. I can count the number of times I've been to church; I associate it with the Werther's Original butterscotch candies my mother fed me to keep me quiet while a stern-faced minister shouted at us for something I wasn't sure we'd done.

The dogmatic children at the conservative school I attended and their parents were similar, reminding me that God, faith, and my soul in my human body were to be feared. God controlled everything—he could lift you up, but if you disobeyed or doubted his power for even a minute, if you failed to fear, he could strike you down.

Though I attended a public school, religion reigned supreme. In elementary school, Christmas pageants and nativity artwork made up the whole of December, and in November we had Thanksgiving picnics on our classroom floors, discussing how wonderful Columbus was for discovering America and bringing faith to the savages. In the spring, each elementary grade dressed as historical figures for History Day, acting out various time periods, each moment in time featuring elaborate backdrops and props donated by parents. No matter the time period—1492 and the ocean blue, cowboys shooting at Native Americans from broomstick horses, the sandbox turned into the gold rush with garden hose rivers and fool's gold—there always seemed to be several crosses present, the greatest moments in American history fueled by faith.

The Fellowship of Christian students was the largest club on our middle school campus, teenage girls flocking to the handsome, flirty teacher who led the group and liked to pick up the girls at recess, wrapping his hands around their waists and spinning them around the blacktop as though they were dancing. "It's like Jack in *Titanic*," the girls would whisper breathlessly afterward, blushing and adjusting their training bras before praying, speaking aloud so all could hear, opening their eyes to glance around the group, staring up at the teacher through half-closed lashes, delighted to find him staring right back. A few years later, our middle school principal left his wife and two children for a child he met at the youth group he counseled.

In high school, students and teachers met by the flagpole to pray before school certain days each month, and during pep rallies and assemblies Christian bands led prayer disguised as school spirit. The largest donors to our wealthy school were religious families, and their names and values permeated each banner and jersey. The Pledge of Allegiance was mandatory and on certain days—September 11, for example, or Fridays—it was accompanied by prayer disguised as a moment of silence, teachers sending those who didn't comply with bowed heads and closed eyes to the principal for their disruption. When a classmate in our small high school killed himself, the entire community turned out for his funeral, where we were treated to a sermon on the sin of suicide, the boy's grieving parents acknowledging to the crowd via microphone that their son would not escape his grief like he'd hoped, and would instead spend eternity tormented by hell demons, never to be reunited with his family and friends, good, God-fearing people who knew better than to depart this world by their own hands. That the boy had been closeted and teased mercilessly by his classmates for his fashion sense and love of Britney Spears was ignored, and his tormentors cried great big tears for his lost soul, holding hands and praying in the halls at school after his death, coming late to class with heaving shoulders instead of homework. "We know why he did this," the reverend said in the final moments of the funeral, the boy's parents nodding sternly, the audience, too. "Don't stray from God's love."

Still, my strongest association with Christianity remains an illustrated children's Bible someone gave me when I was six or seven. I looked at the glossy pictures when I wanted a good scare, which was often, because it gave me a rush and a chill, then the reassurance that I would be safe as long as I behaved—a precursor to anxiety. I didn't understand the stories—a man and two of every animal in one boat, a man swallowed by a whale, a man nailed on a cross—but the illustrations, the fear, were real. I could spy the book spine on our family bookshelf from anywhere in the living or dining room and I used to stare at it when I was supposed to be eating, or when my mother or father carried me to bed each night. I memorized the illustrations: there was the torrential rain and the drowning people waving their arms for help, there was the great whale and its strands of baleen like a dangerous harp, there was the blood dripping from the crown of thorns gracing the kindest man's brow.

The most frightening of all the illustrations, however, was that of a burning Sodom and Gomorrah, women fleeing from danger, running towards safety. I loved this seemingly singular story of women and the illustration of their flowing dresses and hair, flames curling towards their heels. What had they done, I wondered, so bad as to deserve this?

In the drawing, Lot's wife—a woman so wicked she did not deserve a name—ignored the angels' warnings and did not keep moving forward at their command. Instead she turned back to look at her home burning behind her and was transformed into a statue of salt, foolish and bitter.

I think I was drawn to this picture because Lot's wife looked like me—white nightgown and dark hair—and because my greatest fear and most prominent dream as a child was of burning alive in a house fire, my parents and I smothered by flames that licked at the walls and melted our skin. What little I knew of faith—for no one had explained to me anything beyond the fear—was fire and brimstone, lies or stealing or some other wrongdoing punishable by fire and the devil soft-shoeing on my soul for eternity. While my parents' use of religion in our house involved little more than setting up a Nativity scene at Christmastime, I knew enough from the stony-faced preacher and my quick-to-judge classmates and their parents to fear God and myself and the wrongdoings of man, a large, evil group I was associated with by nature, if not by gender, whose sins would bring about my destruction even if I were on my best behavior.

Years later, I am still that little girl peering at photos of suffering sinners—cancer patients or the unemployed, their stories of misfortune littering the nightly news. But now the illustrations move and they are accompanied by a male news anchor's voice-over, authoritative, commanding, the media's best attempt at the voice of God. The voice tells us how to avoid diabetes or depression, bankruptcy or foreclosures. *Live a good life* is always the message. *Follow orders or else you'll be punished.* Nothing has changed.

As the days before the impending Rapture and funeral approach, I spend my time reading headlines, knowing we are all doomed. I have visions of rogue planets crashing into the Earth, the marble of blue and green exploding, sending flames out into space, lighting up the darkness for a brief moment before it—and, more important, I—vanish forever. I see a thousand solar flares billow off the sun, acid rain, gravity giving up. I die a thousand deaths.

Surrounded by an academic institution that values logic and reason, my fear is out of place. My PhD-pursuing peers would most likely scoff at these terrors, offer me theory or philosophy as a counter. "As an atheist I can't believe in evil because I don't believe in good," a dear friend once said, his face stoic as he offered me this latest wisdom. "I am no longer afraid," he added, and though I believed him, I know it could never be true for me. Just before the Rapture, I keep quiet at a barbeque, murmuring, "That's problematic," into my potato salad when what is really problematic is that we are all doomed. I want to throw deviled eggs at everyone's logical, doctoral faces.

The day before the scheduled Rapture is appropriately stormy. I spend most storms cowering by the window, afraid and half in love with the intensity of the dance, the potential for destruction. This storm is no different, the sky glowing a sickly yellow, cicadas screeching, birds flying in erratic patterns, raindrops pelting the window, sliding at garish angles like broken necks down the glass.

Brady and I drive to Iowa that night as the sky grows darker. His grandmother has died and we are attending her funeral. Death is everywhere. I try to convince Brady the Rapture will happen at exactly midnight. He tells me the day has already turned in other parts of the world, so shouldn't we have died already? Since my anxiety makes me the center of the universe, I don't believe him. The world will end when it gets to me. I watch the clock like a fiend as we drive through the empty prairie. Nestled on a rise of farmland is a billboard, a solitary spotlight on the message: "Judgment Day Begins May 21, 2011."

By now, lightning racks the sky, and I am afraid it will strike our moving metal car. Brady drives quickly to shorten the journey and my stress, which makes me afraid we'll be in a wreck. He can't win. Out the window the land is flat and expansive, nowhere to hide. Catastrophizing is exhausting and it is late; soon I'm afraid I'll fall asleep and miss my own death. When the clock signals midnight, I hold my breath. It feels like I don't let it go for the next twenty-four hours.

We pick Brady's older sister up from the airport along the way. She's bipolar as well, and in the midst of a mania. They are both excited about the trip and catching up with family despite the sad occasion, and they talk rapidly, with intense energy, euphoric and lively, moving at a speed I don't comprehend. They interrupt and wave their arms, and Brady puts his foot heavier on the gas pedal and his sister leans her head out the window into the two a.m. air to smoke a cigarette. She doesn't wear a seatbelt and shifts back and forth in the backseat, Brady turning around to speak at her, taking his eyes off the dark road to laugh and laugh. Though we can barely hear each other over the rush of wind from the open windows, Brady's sister leans forward from the backseat to turn up the radio, her hand pulling the back of my chair, tilting me suddenly backward. All at once I am staring out the moon roof, up at the blackness, the million stars waiting to crash down. She tunes rapidly between the radio stations, static and evangelical preaching the only thing available during the middle of the night in rural Iowa. The sounds mix with the wind and her constantly humming cell phone and she and Brady shout above it all. This isn't the apocalypse—but it feels like it.

We arrive at the hotel at four a.m. and sleep three hours before heading to the cemetery as the sun comes up. The ground is damp from rain the night before, our feet sinking with each step. *Zombies,* I think. *Everyone was right.* I stand around the grave with Brady's family, many of whom I am meeting for the first time, and they pray, staring down while I try not to crane my neck upward, searching for a sign. Today is the Rapture: how appropriate I am standing by a pre-dug hole. I wonder, briefly, if I should climb in.

Next we head to church, a building with windows perfect for lightning to pierce, and beamed ceilings perfect to crash down on unsuspecting bodies. I meet aunts and uncles and dozens of elderly friends with glowing white hair who talk about Brady's grandmother's pies. Their laughter bounces overhead, reverberating and pressing down on me like a countdown. No one else seems concerned, but perhaps this is because they all know the words to the hymns. I pretend to move my mouth, but God knows. *He's watching. He cares.* When the Rapture comes, all these elderly Iowans will be lifted up and I'll go to Hell for my ignorance.

When I don't, Brady and his sister take me to a local amusement park they used to visit with their grandparents. The park is tiny, a few rides sitting along the edge of a clear lake, funnel cakes and hot dogs and all the smiling faces making the place a regular Norman Rockwell painting. Brady and his sister want to go on an old wooden roller coaster, but because the rattling wood track will knock loose a brain aneurysm, I wait on a bench in the sun. I shake my head with pity at the crowds—they don't realize there are only a few hours left to live. Three bronze monkey statues sit on the bench, too, hands over their eyes, ears, and mouths. Lucky.

The sky is full of big clouds and when the sun passes behind one I know it is time. The Rapture is here. There is no cloud. Actually, the sun has gone out. I bend my head down to my chest, curl up, and wail. I can't breathe. I am already dead. No one stops to help. Brady and his sister are still on the coaster with a dozen cotton candy kids and even some old folks braver than me. The rattling of the wood and metal sounds like gunfire.

Even though I know the laws of physics, know that if the sun blew out we'd be dead before the darkness reached us, my terror builds until I am having a full-blown attack, afraid to pace like I usually do to get rid of the nervous energy, because now I'm imagining a meteor with a homing device that will target me if I move. I hold still next to the bronze statues, so, so still, waiting for the end of the world. I am a monkey counterpart: I have my hands over my heart.

Like any chronic illness, anxiety alters time, the notion of minutes or days, even a handful of years, suddenly arbitrary. Joy compacts into seconds, while dread lasts forever, the Earth a giant sundial that casts a menacing shadow. I remain dying on the bench even after Brady and his sister return from their ride, even after we leave the park, even after the sun goes down and we meet up with the rest of the family for dinner and reminisce late into the night. I remain dying long after Camping's prediction runs out, long after I return to Nebraska. I am forever on that bench, waiting, waiting, fixed and frozen with fear. Already dead.

Months go by as I take Buspirone and feel no relief. I'm still afraid. After all, the real end of the world, according to Camping, is in October, and if that fails, there is always the 2012 Mayan apocalypse.

CHAPTER 17

OCCAM'S RAZOR

In the fourteenth century, English Franciscan friar William of Ockham theorized that among various competing hypotheses, the hypothesis with the fewest assumptions should be selected. Translated from Latin, Occam's razor reads: "Entities should not be multiplied unnecessarily," meaning if rival theories make the same prediction, the simplest, most elegant theory is likely correct. In other words, the simplest explanation is usually the answer.

To apply the principle to my mental health: either I was dying of cancer and I had carpal tunnel and I could predict the future or I had anxiety. This is comforting, for when I am in the midst of panic, I imagine the friar beside me in his wooly robes. "You know this is anxiety," he says kindly. "That's simplest." Anxiety appears clumsy and awkward, but Occam's razor points to the elegance. The principle shifts the burden of proof.

Doctors apply Occam's razor in diagnostic parsimony, which suggests that when diagnosing a patient, doctors should look for the fewest possible causes that account for symptoms. In other words, a variety of symptoms are probably caused by one illness rather than many. But danger lies in always assuming illness is the culprit.

Another application: After beginning Buspirone my existence has become slanted, shimmering, and gelatinous. I feel vertiginous within an hour of swallowing a pill, sometimes so shaky I have to lie down for an hour or more until the spiraling passes. My vision has also changed. Things are permanently blurry, approaching cars and road signs too hazy to make out from a few feet away. Perhaps I have several disorders that account for the anxiety, dizziness, and vision. Perhaps my anxiety has evolved to create these symptoms. Or, Occam's razor suggests, it's Buspirone.

"Hmm," Terry says, unconvinced when I suggest this possibility. The dizziness is overwhelming, I try to explain, rolling over me in a great wave, leaving me bobbing like a boat on rough water. Terry reminds me that to avoid dizziness I must take my medication with a meal, problematic since I must also take a pill when I go to sleep. She says I should lie down when I get dizzy. She doesn't seem to understand that if I take the pill three times a day, get dizzy three times a day, and alternate between bed and bathroom for the nausea, I won't have much time for living.

"You're overthinking this," she says with a laugh. "You have a tendency to do that, right?" While friendly banter is part of the reason I enjoy Terry's care—she remains the most human and humane physician I've encountered—this feels dismissive. The bottle comes with a large warning that Buspirone will cause dizziness, so how is my imagination at fault?

Then there's the trouble of my blurred vision. I can barely read what I've written on the board when I teach, never mind what the professors write on the board when I'm in their classes. I can't read menus on coffee shop walls or see where to step in crowded restaurants. I feel uncertain when I enter new spaces. Finding my way in the dark is impossible. I squint to focus on the digital clock on the television when I'm a few feet away on the couch. I ask Brady, who is very accommodating now that our relationship is mostly back to normal, to double-check. At first, I'm sometimes wrong. Then I'm mostly wrong.

Terry suggests I wait a month or so to see if these side effects fade. Occam's razor tells her they are caused by my brain scurrying around looking for something new to worry about, catastrophizing whatever comes my way. It is not elegant. But it is easy.

Eventually my vision is Van Gogh's *Starry Night*—things glowing and spiraling, reality melting, and though bipolar disorder colored Van Gogh's world, Buspirone could just as easily have been responsible.

"I'm going to send you to an optometrist," Terry announces during my checkup a few months later. "It might be from the medication," she admits, but says glasses could easily correct the side effect.

The optometrist is a young man who asks me about my PhD and the classes I teach. He was a student at the university I work at, he adds, and he would have loved to have me as a teacher. He tells me I have beautiful eyes when he is inches from my face and says that if I need glasses, it will be hard to find ones that my long lashes don't touch. He smiles a lot. I can feel his breath on my cheek. Once I think I see him wink, but I can't tell because my eyes are dilated, and my vision is wonky, and let's face it, I see things that aren't there all the damn time. I am annoyed by his advances, but also flattered he still finds me attractive even though my short hair is still thinning and I am squinting and everyone thinks I'm crazy.

After the eye exam, the optometrist consults with me about my vision as I try not to panic about my numb eyes. (Clearly, the numbness will last forever.) Yes, he says matter-of-factly, my vision has changed. Yes, I need glasses. And yes, it's possible the Buspirone is at fault.

I'm not thinking about the Franciscan friar, mostly my frozen eyes and the way the optometrist has wheeled his chair even closer, his hand inching towards my knee. I'm angry but not surprised, and the optometrist doesn't seem surprised either.

"You could stop taking the medicine," he says, flashing a smile. "Your vision might correct itself. But it might not. We have no way of knowing," he adds, still smiling as though this isn't a big deal, like he says it all the time and could he have my phone number please. "You may as well stay on the medication if you need it," he says definitively, "and get glasses to correct your vision."

He hands me a prescription and a business card he has inked with a heart. I tuck the prescription into my wallet and toss the card into a trash can outside his office.

In the weeks that follow, Terry orders more lab work, rechecks my thyroid, sends me back to the dermatologist who previously told me to wait it out.

The dermatologist doesn't remember me. Two nurses join us, all three staring at the papers in their hands as opposed to looking at me. The dermatologist ignores me and asks the nurses about my history. "We saw her six months ago?" "Yes, she came in about hair loss." "We sent her home and told her to come back after a few months?" "Yes." "We gave her the appropriate literature?" "I think so." No one mentions Celexa or Zoloft, so I remind them, adding, "Now I take Buspirone."

The dermatologist gives me a pointed look of skepticism over his glasses. "It's probably stress," he diagnoses—again. The nurses nod confirmation. They hand me the same pamphlet on hair loss as before. The pamphlet talks about hair growth, proper hair care, alopecia. It never mentions stress.

"Try Rogaine," he says.

His second recommendation comes in a tiny bottle with a long applicator. "I'm going to give you a sample, because this medication is very expensive," he says like he is giving me a gift. This admission can only mean the topical medication costs a small fortune.

Each day I am to shake the bottle and then apply the product over my entire scalp. This sample is enough for one dose. "It's going to burn," he says, making eye contact for the first time. I wonder if he does this so I can't blame him later for the pain. "You'll want to stop taking it, but you need to keep it up," he finishes. "We won't know if it works for about six months."

"Remember," he says, as I leave, the nurses nodding in unison, "to work on your stress."

Here is the skit each time I see a specialist: I explain what is on my chart, repeat my memorized lines while looking at the wall, the floor, the ceiling, it doesn't really matter because no one is ever looking at me. The nurses take my vitals, commenting on how small my arm is—"Looks like we need the children's cuff"—when they take my blood pressure, asking a question right when they put the thermometer in my mouth. They wave the props around and I follow my cues. I list the vitamins, birth control, and other medications I take. When I get to Buspirone, the drug in question, the nurses look at me quizzically. They ask how it's spelled.

In her classic 1978 text, *Illness as Metaphor,* Susan Sontag describes a kingdom where power and rule are tied to health. "Illness is the night-side of life," she writes, "a more onerous citizenship."[2] Onerus is right. I'm constantly repeating myself and despite my growing file, information gets lost from person to person, a giant game of telephone. Nurses and physicians reintroduce themselves to me as though we've never met. Sometimes they leave me in a room to run a test and forget me, returning an hour later, chuckling about their forgetfulness. Sometimes they contradict one another— themselves—saying the opposite of what they said in a previous visit. The only thing that remains constant is that I am wrong. I have no power here.

Time and anxiety wear on. After a year on Buspirone, I prepare to go to Chicago for a writers' conference, thousands of professionals and enthusiasts coming together for panels and readings, dinners and drinks, endless hours of small talk. Nervous about the conference and the work I have agreed to do there, I feel anxiety slip into my brain like a serpent and glide along the gray matter. I know I'm nervous, but I'm not prepared for what comes next.

I become paralyzed.

One day I wake up unable to move my back. The muscles are numb and phantom and I spend the weekend on the couch, so stiff I must swing my legs in order to gain enough momentum to stand. I walk stiffly. I cannot bend. My mind, clever smooth talker, convinces me this is a sign I won't be well in time for the trip. Brady rubs my muscles, brings me tea and food. He tries reason to will my body back. But nothing works, and by the end of the weekend I have barely moved, slipped into hibernation, my body shutting down, reserving its energy for more important things. Like worry.

Monday morning I shuffle across the snow on the way to work. Brittle ice crunches beneath my feet like breaking bones. I talk to colleagues in the hall when I arrive, answer student questions, attend meetings. I teach courses, hold office hours, grade stacks of papers. I do it in slow-motion, each movement the result of long, silent negotiation. My office-mate, a woman who charges through her life and degree with intensity, her success leaving little time for the failures of friends, asks why I am walking strangely. I tell her my back hurts, open up and say, "Sometimes my body gets sick when I am stressed."

"Take vitamin C," she says, standing up brusquely and walking to the door with ease.

Several days later, I wake frozen from the waist down. I slide myself to the floor, scooting on my behind from my bed to my desk to begin work. Later, I drag myself around the house to the bathroom, the kitchen. My arms ache from the extra responsibility.

For some reason, I'm able to walk at work. I walk cautiously, amazed when my body responds to the concentration. I look like I've been in an accident as I hobble across campus. People stare. Since movement takes longer, I'm constantly coming across colleagues in the hall—during one trip to the copy center I'm stopped five times. I listen to two colleagues complain about spending the weekend grading. I agree to help another with a writing assignment. I discuss a difficult student with another. I stand for twenty minutes in the hallway while my officemate has one of her intense academic meltdowns, which mostly consist of her moaning about PhD work and not being appreciated. "Of course I'll read your book manuscript. Anything I can do to help," I murmur before she rushes away. When I finally make it back to my office I am sweating. I wonder who will help me.

The day of the trip arrives and Brady helps me into the car. When we arrive at the train station where I am meeting the coworkers I am traveling with for the next few days, I will not accept his help. Once I make it onto the train and settle in for the journey, I focus on the passing landscape, hoping I will be able to move when we arrive in Chicago. My officemate spends the trip with her back to the window, hunched over her laptop and stacks of books. She has a pen in her hand, a highlighter in her mouth. Though it is six a.m., she holds a conference call.

Naturally, I don't remember much of the trip, but I do know the numbness lessened the closer I got to Chicago and the future I feared. I was able to stand once we arrived, could walk to our hotel, could even make it to the restroom without scooting along the floor while my traveling companions debated literary theory. I was practiced enough in the performance of health that I got through the conference by smiling and shaking hands and balancing a cocktail in my numb fingertips. I read my work in front of an audience I couldn't see, their heads replaced with demons and flashing orbs, publicized the magazine I worked for as an editor, met editors who had published my work, and chatted with strangers, all while convinced I would be unable to turn around once the task was complete or make my way home again.

Though my paralysis might sound strange—those I've told say, "It must have *seemed* that way, but surely you could move"—symptoms affecting voluntary sensory and motor functions have long been associated with hysteria. During the nineteenth century, patients experienced paralysis, seizures, and blindness, though physicians were unable to find anything medically wrong with them. While Victorian husbands and physicians were doubtful, contemporary brain imaging studies reveal that patients with hysterical paralysis have healthy nerves and muscles, but changes in brain function that prevent movement. Hysteria has not disappeared, merely changed names, the *DSM-III* revising the diagnosis "hysterical neurosis" to "conversion disorder" in 1980. In fact, some estimates suggest that conversion disorder accounts for 1 to 4 percent of all diagnoses in Western hospitals.[3]

My inability to move returns during periods of stress, my body shutting down in response to perceived threats. The summer before my final year of my PhD program, my right knee spasmed and swelled to the point I could not put pressure on it. I went to Terry, to an X-ray technician, to a specialist, to physical therapy three times a week for six months. Then it disappeared.

For a period I fainted. It happened first at the chiropractor, who talked about my increasing back pain while holding up a plastic spine. I made it as far as the reception area before blacking out, other patients leaning forward as I fell. I fainted nearly every time after. For a year or so the sudden heat, the rush of sound, the feeling of falling followed me. I fainted in front of needles. I fainted watching medical movies. I nearly fainted when students cracked their knuckles, but knew enough not to prohibit it, lest I wanted a chorus. Once I fainted while talking to a colleague across the hall. She had accepted a tenure-track position and I knew I'd have to endure the academic job market soon. The sinking began while we were still talking, but I managed to chirp out, "Well, I've got to run, congratulations again. I'll shut the door so you can work," closing her door as the world went black. I came to enough to crawl back to my office, where I sat waiting to recover on the floor in the dark.

For the past few years I've grown accustomed to chronic pain. My neck has a permanent knot on the right side that snakes up and around my ear. My shoulders are raised to accommodate the knots beneath. Sitting is a matter of finding the position that hurts the least. Hot baths, once-a-month massage (which I like because of the way the therapist sighs, "Oh, honey," when she rubs her hands across the length of my spine), and muscle relaxers provide minimal comfort. Doctors tell me to take muscle relaxers once a day, twice a day, three times a day.

Terry says my continued anxiety is because of my low dose. She wants to be more aggressive. She says more is better—the American Big Gulp, supersize fries. Increasing dosages of psychotropic drugs became standard in the 1960s and 1970s, when physicians prescribed thousands of milligrams, sometimes up to ten times what earlier physicians found sufficient.[4] European physicians initially trialed chlorpromazine at 100 milligrams a day, reporting that doses of 300 milligrams produced too many negative side effects, but American psychiatrists gave patients up to 5,000 milligrams a day. Despite evidence that large doses were dangerous, American average daily doses doubled from 1973 to 1985.[5] Recent studies confirm that patients may do better on lower doses.

The friar interjects. "There are too many assumptions," he urges. He reminds me to choose the simplest explanation. I've been told by friends and family, by medical professionals, by pharmaceutical companies, by history that madness is to blame—I am to blame—for most of the ills of my life, but now the friar looks into my eyes and repeats himself. "There are too many assumptions."

The simplest explanation for my continued anxiety when I was not on medication is that I required treatment. The simplest explanation for my continued anxiety despite so many medications is that drug treatment alone is not working. The simplest explanation for my hair loss, my rage, my anorgasmia, my dizziness, my vision is that they are side effects of the chemicals I swallow each day. The simplest explanation for the litany of things others think make me wrong, so wrong, is that perhaps I am not the problem.

I tell Terry I want to wait. I will not increase my dose. I would like to simplify, to be still for a moment without the poking and prodding I've undergone over the last few years. I've tapered on and off enough medications, felt the physical effects of tampering with brain chemistry, the psychological impact of starting over. I'm afraid to undergo the process again.

More than anything, I don't feel like playing God anymore. It seems this is what the "healthy" world has been trying to do, as though the body is something to be interrogated and improved, as though I am clay to be molded. It is not only my physical body under scrutiny, but my thoughts and emotions—my very soul.

To control the body and brain this way, to determine how a person will live, seems fraught with the religious tension I never understood as a child. Just like in church, I am always imperfect, always trying to please, always suffering because of some sin. When I don't respond to suggestions properly, I am shamed, left to repent my way back into grace. When treatments don't work, it is because I do not have enough faith in them. If I doubt, I am punished. I return again and again to these places of modern worship. I give tithing. I hold out my tongue and swallow the reminder of my devotion to that which heals. I look up from the examining table to the one who will save me—he stands cloaked in white, head surrounded by a halo of light.

CHAPTER 18

COMPULSION

When you fill a glass with water, wait eleven seconds before holding your cup under the flow. This frees poison from the pipes. If you forget and time slips to twelve seconds or thirteen, wait until twenty-two seconds. If it happens again, thirty-three.

Set alarms for palindromes. Wake at 6:06, 6:56. Aim for the nearest hour or half hour: the right alarm is 6:26, never 6:36.

Cook by palindrome. Remember, germs—thus death—come from undercooking, so overshoot to the next palindrome. Things might burn. Better safe than sorry.

Symmetry is safe. Even numbers of candles, chairs, cats. Unless the space calls for groupings of three. Pillows, plants, picture frames. These must be in odd numbers. Crave symmetry for security, the reassurance of numbers an antidote to what is wrong with the world.

Aesthetics rule. Notice if angles don't line up. If wood colors or grains don't match. If a painting hangs uneven, a floor dips, the seam shows in the carpet. Leave dirty stores, crowded stores. Visually remove the clutter from a friend's house when you Skype.

Feel most comfortable in your safe, symmetrical home. When you move across the country from Nebraska to Massachusetts, see tiles out of place, discolored planks in the wood floor. See spots in the paint, places where the painters dripped. See gaps in the windows, dirty screens. A closet door sticks and you can't breathe. The ceiling fan lurches and so does your heart. Try to sleep at night and hear the on on on of the air conditioner. The moon shining from its new position makes your shadow the chalk outline of a dead body.

I was diagnosed with obsessive compulsive disorder without being informed.

One afternoon, several years into anxiety treatment, I was at Terry's office for a routine Buspirone checkup.

"You're here about anxiety and OCD," the nurse said, yellow ducks on her scrubs staring blankly at me.

Too surprised to be incredulous, I murmured, "OCD?"

The nurse pointed—"It's here on your chart"—and put a thermometer in my mouth.

I never asked who added the diagnosis—Terry, a prior physician, a specialist, a therapist?—or when it was added. Perhaps I was too surprised. Perhaps I'd never considered comorbidity, or the fact that mental disorders can occur alongside others. Mostly, I think I didn't believe it, figured it another error or miscommunication. I'd never suspected I had OCD. No one had ever suggested I did. And I'd never consulted with a physician.

My youngest brother, Bailey, was diagnosed with OCD as a young child right around the time he learned to tie his shoes, a long process that sometimes lasted an hour as he painstakingly arranged his socks, placed a foot gingerly in one shoe, tested it out with a few steps, then put the next foot in its shoe. He tied the laces slowly, retying them as many as ten times, measuring the length of each tail, the width of the bows. After getting his shoes tied, he'd carefully cuff his socks, each fold the same width, and finally walk around, quickly finding fault and starting over. Though he has since moved on from this fastidious process, he approaches many tasks—washing his hands before dinner or after ice cream, cleaning his room—the same. He is often unable to complete homework because he writes and rewrites the words, trying to perfect the arc of the letter "C," the straight back and contradictory curve of the letter "P." Sometimes he is so concerned with penmanship or producing the correct answer he is unable to write at all. At the movies, he focuses on the dirty screen rather than the film, clenching the arm rests, moving his head from side to side, whispering, near tears, "I don't know if I can watch this."

When the nurse announced I'd been suffering from OCD unbeknownst to myself, I didn't believe her. As with anxiety, I felt the way I always felt. I knew there was no good in protesting, however—arguing further cements madness in the eyes of sane. To prove how not obsessive I was, I tried not to obsess over the fact that I'd been diagnosed without my knowledge or participation. Why hadn't anyone told me? Had I been treated for OCD without my consent? Was OCD the reason Terry wanted me to remain on Buspirone? Or had an OCD diagnosis been added but without proper treatment? I tried not to think about the power of suggestion. The harder I thought about not obsessing, the more obsessive I felt.

Now, years later, my OCD is becoming more extreme. Compulsion enters from the right. It pierces through my eye again and again, reminding me, scolding me, warning me. The rhythm jolts, makes me squint and wince. It's like a record skipping inside. The vinyl scratch signaling the comedic "uh oh" in a movie, only gone terribly wrong. The repetition feels like ragged nails on the chalkboard of my mind, a sickening cue in my temple. It stabs. Lately, when it comes I wince, my eyes at first, then my head, like I'm bracing for an invisible blow.

The tics are increasing. When I try to explain what it feels like to be on repeat, 11, 22, 33, I blink, I grimace, I rock back and forth. Sometimes I get stuck on a word, on a word, and so I snap to try and clear it out of my throat, blink and cough, my speech punctuated, dramatized, but still I'm hinged on that word that word that word that won't come free, get loose, come free and so I snap, dodge the pierce again, and again it reminds me to get off that word that word that word I know clearly but can't manage to get right.

I can't look in the mirror lately, because I am not symmetrical. One ear is higher and my glasses sit cooked, or is it my eyes that don't line up? One cheekbone is wider than the other. One eye bulges. I'm convinced my teeth move—one front tooth dangling a millimeter lower than the other, some suddenly too square, others too round—and I stare and stare, trying to convince myself of what is right, what is real. My lower gums have worn away from my furious brushing. I've learned it's best not to look in the mirror. I don't even know what I looked like on my wedding day.

If I pay attention to my body long enough I realize it's decaying. I am less worried about being unattractive or aging than I am about my body changing without my permission, moving on without me. Nothing is fixed. The only thing permanent is that everything falls apart.

Even language. Tiles surround the fireplace in my living room, crisp white symmetrical squares. I like to watch firelight flicker across them. I like how they are warm in the winter, cool in the summer. Lately, though, I play a game with the tiles and the words on TV. The game is this: When I hear a word I must put each letter into a tile until the word is spaced evenly around the fireplace. I can have empty tiles between letters if this helps the symmetry. It's best to fill all the spaces, but if I can't, then there are rules about how to fill them, how to arrange the words in a manner that doesn't hurt. There are lots of ways to lose points. When I'm play-ing, the rules come sharp, above my right eye, over and over until I know not to fail. Here is one rule: I can't breathe until I finish. I can't stop until it is right. One letter, one space. When I win—and I will win—I get the ability to move onto the next word that catches my fancy. Sometimes I see the tiles when I'm not in the house. I put words from billboards around my imaginary fireplace. Words from airplanes. Words I write on the board in my classroom.

I am putting the words from this book around my imagi-nary fireplace. I am piecing together the story of how I fell apart. There is then and there is now. There is the me that did not believe I was ill, and the me that was ashamed it was true, and now there is the me that would not have my brain any other way. I cannot make the words fit in the squares—leaps in time, missing time, confusion, contradiction. Writing this book makes me jolt, sputter, makes me click click on a turn of phrase, makes me check a transition in the middle of the night, makes me close my eyes right now because it is wrong wrong, but because being wrong wrong may also be right. It is hard to put these words around my fireplace. But I'll get there.

"Obsessive Cat Disorder." "Obsessive Camping Disorder." "I've got PMS, OCD, and ADD. I want to cry and look pretty while I kill people, but I can't focus on that right now, I'm too busy cleaning." "Obsessive Christmas Disorder," read a 2015 holiday sweater at Target. "We apologize for any dis-comfort," Target reps said when they refused to pull the item.

In online quizzes succinctly titled "How OCD are you?" people can rank how much images "bother" them on a scale of one to four, mental illness as simple and humorous as discovering "Which Disney Princess Are You" or "Are You More of a Sweet, Savory, Or In-between Person." Images include alphabet soup letters lined up incorrectly, color-coded M&Ms with one misplaced, dirty hands, someone sneezing without covering their mouth, a dirty living room. The National Institute of Mental Health reports that 2 percent of the American population between eighteen and twenty-nine and 2.3 percent of those thirty to forty-four have OCD, but a large majority would "fail" the quiz based on how little room for variation it allows.

While OCD is on some level the desire for order and control, these representations remove OCD from the spectrum of "normal," when compulsions are often everyday habits with the volume turned up. According to NIMH, what differentiates "normal" ritual and habit from compulsion is when someone

> can't control his or her thoughts or behaviors, even when those thoughts or behaviors are recognized as excessive; spends at least one hour a day on these thoughts or behaviors; doesn't get pleasure when performing the behaviors or rituals, but may feel brief relief from the anxiety the thoughts cause; and experiences significant problems in their daily life due to these thoughts or behaviors.

The definitions of "control," "excessive," "relief," and "significant" are unclear and likely change depending on who is doing the defining.

I find the NIMH criteria conflicting. On the one hand, my OCD can certainly cause me pain. When it is heightened, I am uncomfortable, compelled to perform certain rituals, unsatisfied after. I would argue I have always had an affinity for pleasing aesthetics. I like elements of design and have an appreciation for arrangement—I pursued writing and teaching writing in order to be surrounded by art. I have always been perturbed by germs—I enjoyed cleaning my room as a child and found comfort in that space amidst the mess of my home. I have always had difficulty feeling comfortable when it is too hot, too cold, when the seams of my shirts or socks rub my feet the wrong way. Over time, the volume has increased, which is not surprising, for similarly to anxiety, people who have experienced trauma are at an increased risk for developing OCD, which enhances with time.

Take double-checking, for example. We each double-check those tasks of importance. It might be our phone when waiting to hear back about a promotion, or the sprinkler timer on a new lawn, or the lock on an expensive car. Where you might check an email once to make sure it sent, I check it twice, then again an hour later, then again the next day. I check on a desktop, a laptop, my phone. I check before I go to bed. I check when I wake up. I check the recipient, the subject, the message itself. I want to stop checking, but I can't; this hurts. The only thing that stops me is when something else comes along for me to check.

But on the other hand, certain behaviors that others would call "compulsion," I simply call normal. I do not want to share food or drink with strangers or be around people who are sick, especially when I am prone to getting ill. I carry hand sanitizer to use when I eat or when I travel. I do not particularly enjoy public restrooms or hotels. I Lysol my couch after visitors leave, the bottoms of my shoes when I return home. None of this causes me pain. When people point to my desire for cleanliness as though it is a detriment, I wonder why they care. I don't find my patterns vexing, so who, exactly, is worried about "control" and "relief" in this situation? Who is being "excessive"?

Stereotypical depictions of OCD portray obsessive handwashing and stove checking, neurotic unlovables so fixated on foolish paranoia they are unable to function. In *Scrubs,* Dr. Kevin Casey, surgeon extraordinaire, must touch every person and object before he starts work each morning, and ends his day unable to leave the operating room because his hands aren't clean. In *Friends,* Monica Geller cleans her cleaning products. In *The Big Bang Theory,* Sheldon must sit in the same spots, eat the same meals, and knock three times. He does not follow social cues and imposes elaborate rules on his relationships. These flat caricatures occupy two camps: either the characters are inherently good, their odd quirks deserving of pity, or they are childlike and narcissistic, genius freaks whose brains have gotten the best of them. No matter the character, though, a laugh track accompanies their OCD. When I watch these shows I resent the laughter—why laugh? Nothing these characters do seems out of the ordinary to me—but mostly I resent the way the characters are never afforded a storyline beyond their diagnosis. They exist so the audience can think, "Thank God that's not me."

I would not get rid of my OCD, though at times it vexes me. My love of aesthetics allows me to create beautiful spaces and beautiful words. My awareness of space means I am deeply rooted where I live, know the shaggy dog on the nearby walking trail or the family of geese at the end of the lane, know the temperament of the clouds, and delight in geology. My attention to detail means I notice when others are uncomfortable and care enough to help ease their discomfort. OCD means I see and feel things more fully than others can imagine; I've been moved to tears by beautiful sunsets and delicious meals.

The thing I've loved most in this world was a feral cat someone gave to me in middle school. I adopted him before my siblings. The cat was proud and spiteful, full of the haughty revenge that makes for both a good tomcat and a singing diva. He bit me when he wanted me to pet him longer. He dug his claws into my legs when I tried to stand and he was not ready to get off my lap. He perched on furniture and took careful swipes when I walked near. But he also followed me during panic attacks, first placing a single paw on my arm to let me know he was there, then curling into my lap when he sensed I was steady. He slept under the covers with me each night, his whiskers up my nose, his sour breath wet on my cheek, his off-rhythm purr keeping me awake. He did this for seventeen years until he stubbornly refused to eat and then stubbornly refused to die. When the vet put my old friend to sleep, I had to remove the cat's claws one by one from my leg, so intent he was not to let go of me. In the days following his death, as I was flying across the country for a job interview, preparing to put a smile on my face despite the fact that I'd sink into a deep months-long depression once I returned, I saw my cat on the plane wing, guiding me home. This does not sound crazy. At least, not to me. He was there, perched with the stars, and I felt him and knew he was saying good-bye.

Madness makes me see things—spiders, shattered sky, sometimes ghosts standing in the cemetery—but I am grateful for this moment. Many cultures experience collective visions of deceased family members, natural and spiritual phenomenon, but Americans label this delusion. Ours is a nation intent on medicating madness away; I feel sorry for those who haven't experienced the mystical.

Last month I flew home to California for the first time in two years. A few days before my trip, my mother announced that one of the daycare children had head lice and her arduous task was to inform the parents of other children he might have infected.

"I was so grossed out my head started to itch," she said over the phone, "but then I said to myself, 'Freaking out is what Sissy would do' and I stopped."

That night Brady filled a cup of water for me. He sighed when I reminded him to wait eleven seconds and left the sink running for several minutes while he completed a chore. He did this to point out the ridiculousness of my request. The ridiculousness of me. And when he realized what he'd done, he apologized.

He should. I do not groan when adding the extra pepper he likes on his food or when he folds and refolds his electronics cords. I do not mock my mother's love of ancestry research or refusal to eat avocado. This is how they are.

My quirks are as much a part of me as food preference or sense of humor or anything else. My OCD flares with times of stress (in the last few years I have graduated with my PhD, gotten married, and moved across the country for my first tenure-track job), but mostly it is as innocuous as my eye color. There is nothing inherently wrong with me. What is wrong is how frequently people feel the compulsion to correct my behavior.

Here's what I want to say to anyone who implies there is something wrong with my brain: the only one who has a problem with it is you. In fact, I might repeat this statement. You know, for symmetry.

CHAPTER 19

MORAL TREATMENT

*M*ention the word "asylum," and people imagine padded cells, comatose patients, and movies like *One Flew Over the Cuckoo's Nest.* Yet the first American asylums—established by Quakers in the late 1700s and early 1800s—centered on therapeutic care called "moral treatment." Aimed at happiness, moral treatment focused on talking and esteem rather than illness and symptoms. Founders hoped asylums would provide routine, establish supportive relationships, and build community between patients and staff.[6] Patients were seen as equals in need of sympathy and nurturing, rather than as the diseased in need of lock and key. Care came in many forms: patients spent time reading and painting, taking walks with staff, sharing their histories and hobbies, listening to doctors read to them, and even receiving small gifts. Recovery rates revealed the success of moral treatment: at McLean Hospital, one of the first American asylums, 59 percent of the 732 patients admitted between its opening in 1818 and 1830 were discharged as "recovered," "much improved," or "improved." Similarly, 60 percent of the 1,841 patients admitted at Bloomington asylum in New York between 1821 and 1844 were discharged as either "cured" or "improved."[7]

Early asylums were privately funded, treating affluent patients with the means to pay for treatment, but medical societies quickly sensed the potential for profit and lobbied for the funds to build state asylums. The first public asylum opened in 1833, and the number of mental hospitals in the country increased from eighteen in 1842 to 139 by 1880.[8] Soon after, physicians created the Association of Medical Superintendents of American Institutions for the Insane, which determined asylums must have physicians as their chief executive officers and superintendents, despite the fact that asylums existed before psychiatry and had success with limited physician interaction.[9] Establishing a binary between mental illness as pathological or philosophical, biological or existential, allowed physicians to privilege treatments that required medical authority as opposed to community-based treatments of the past (still evident in today's preference towards psychopharmacology as opposed to cognitive-behavioral therapy).

The population of state asylums quickly escalated—in 1840, only 2,561 mentally ill patients were treated in U.S. hospitals and asylums, but fifty years later, 74,000 patients were confined in state mental hospitals alone.[10] Between 1903 and 1933, the number of patients in psychiatric institutions in the United States more than doubled.[11] Asylums became overcrowded, filthy, and inhospitable—a place to sentence those deemed "rebellious," "unstable," and "dangerous," terms used mostly for minority populations—leading to our images of the cruel Nurse Ratched.

The increase in patients was accompanied by a rapid decrease in recovery rates—by the 1930s, asylums were discharging fewer than 15 percent of their patients annually.[12] That patients could no longer be "cured" was the result of changes in treatment—the advent of chronic watch over personal therapy. But it was also the result of new ways of looking at mental illness—as dangerous, latent, and permanent.

Shortly after the FDA licensed chlorpromazine, America began the process of deinstitutionalization, expelling thousands of patients from mental institutions. The number of patients in state and county mental hospitals in the United States declined from 559,000 in 1955 to 338,000 in 1970. By 1988, the numbers were down to 107,000, a decrease of more than 80 percent in thirty years.[13] The numbers of Americans diagnosed with mental illnesses has continued to increase, but mental illness is now "managed" (a word that implies both taking charge or care, but also dominating and controlling) by chemical, as opposed to physical, institutions, those without access to health care making up a large portion of the homeless population (NIMH reports that 26 percent of homeless adults staying in shelters live with serious mental illness, 20 percent of state prisoners have "a recent history" of a mental health condition, and 70 percent of youth in juvenile justice systems have at least one mental health condition).

Because medication alone does not seem to be working, I decide to seek something like the moral treatment of the past. One day I follow up with a specialist who barely bothers to look at me, much less remember my name, and whose main suggestion is that I relax. I walk outside and sit in my car and cry into my hands and the steering wheel, unconcerned with who might see. I cry because it has been years and no one seems to be helping or to understand and I am tired of being scolded and accused, tired of feeling helpless. I cry until my body lets me know it is time for my afternoon dose of Buspirone. Then I drive home, swallow my pill, and call a therapist.

I've never considered going to therapy because for years I've been told the cause of my anxiety is chemical. How will therapy help with serotonin imbalance? Can talking improve neurotransmitter levels? No physician or specialist has suggested therapy.

I've also delayed therapy because for many, it is the ultimate sign of madness. While America claims the epidemic of mental illness, it shames those who indulge in self-reflection (ironic, considering it also values individualism). To navel-gaze is to coddle; therapy becomes an extension of the perceived weakness of madness.

For working-class people like my father, therapy is a sign of prosperous vanity. Therapy is for those with too much money and too much free time. It's for those who want to pay someone to pay attention to them, to agree with them, to boost their fragile egos. ("Isn't it supposed to be about me?" a friend asked me recently. "I'm paying my therapist to listen, but she keeps trying to give me advice.") The men and women I've grown up around scoff at the thought of paying hundreds of dollars per session, taking an hour or two off during the middle of the day each week to talk about feelings. To my father, who openly rejects that mental illness even exists, this is for the frail. Unlike me, he does not have friends who speak with admiration and something of love for the therapists that have helped them with eating disorders, childhood abuse, gender identity, disability, the death of a parent.

After he was diagnosed as bipolar in high school, Brady briefly went to therapy. "I get why it can help some people, but I wasn't open to it. They didn't tell me anything I didn't already know," he says of his experience. I can imagine Brady—who enjoys arguing for the sake of arguing, who often speaks with an air of knowing when it's clear to most listeners he is only supposing—at fifteen, full of hormonal stubbornness, shrugging and silent when it came to talking about his feelings. When it comes to me, however, Brady is encouraging. "Go into it with an open mind," he says. "If it can help, you should try."

There are several therapists at the office I call, and the office website includes photos of each and descriptions about their educational background and hobbies. Most of the female therapists are young and have recently received their PhDs from the school where I teach. They list motherhood, cooking, baking, and arts and crafts as their primary hobbies. The men in the photos are much older, with deeply lined faces, gray hair, and glasses. They look severe and I can imagine them chastising my behavior, looking with skepticism over their glasses, frowning or clicking their tongues in disproval. They seem like the emergency room doctors who blamed my ovaries. Or my doubtful father. Their activities range from athletics and being outdoors, to reading and watching movies, to travel and learning new languages. There is no mention of parenthood or domestic arts.

The website also lists each therapist's areas of study, which include health and well-being, multiculturalism and diversity issues, eating disorders and body image, anxiety and depression, women's issues, grief, relationships, gender and sexual identity. Not one mentions mental illnesses like bipolar disorder or schizophrenia, nor is there any mention of disability.

I settle on a stern-looking therapist named Gail. Judging by her listed educational history, she is in her late fifties, and unlike many of the female therapists who have only worked at the office for a few years, she has been there more than twenty. She is smiling in her photo and though her smile looks sincere, she also seems serious by nature. Her areas of interest include couples therapy, depression, anxiety, attention deficit disorder, women's issues, trauma, dreams, and spiritual issues. I like that she does not indicate if she has children and that her hobbies do not include baking.

I make a phone call and wait a few days for my appointment. When my family learns that I am going to therapy, my father is disappointed. He never says it to me directly, but through the tangled grapevine that is our family, word gets back to me. Therapy is a waste of time, he believes. It is a waste of money, of which I have very little—even with my employer-provided insurance—since I'm spending it on so many doctors. More important, "It's mind over matter," he insists, even now, years later, growing angry when I protest. "Nope," he counters when I point to my increased happiness, the long history of psychoanalysis, studies done on the benefits of cognitive therapy. Perhaps he imagines therapy akin to spas in the 1800s, where nervous patients spent months bathing and drinking the waters, "nerves" an affliction for only the wealthy. "Nope," he says resolutely when school officials ask my parents to send first Casey, then Cameron, then Bailey to therapy.

My mother has a different reason to decline therapy for her children. She's convinced a therapist will turn us against her parenting. "Don't come back hating me," she says, laughing, but it's apparent she believes this will be true. "Your father said no," she says about my siblings, as though my father is the final decision maker, but then she adds, "I'm not going to let a stranger tell my child what he feels."

My family finds my going to therapy odd, for if anyone should go to therapy, it's my adopted siblings. Candy spends more time on her relationship with food than on her relationships with people, her dependence on eating for comfort revealed in her increasing weight and inability to sustain connection with people. We do not know the name of a single friend. Casey cries and screams, paces the yard muttering to himself when upset, throwing and punching things, sometimes himself. He sobs for hours over small slights, something he's done since two, and still does at nearly eighteen. Cameron and Bailey, who cursed and pantomimed sexual motions when they moved in at two and three, now start fires and try to hurt cats, hurting themselves because they like the feeling of pain. Even Victoria might benefit from therapy to discuss the loss of her father or her manipulative mother, with whom she is engaged in a years-long court battle over inheritance, a mother who has attempted suicide on more than one family birthday or holiday.

But if my parents don't believe in therapy for these histories, they certainly don't believe in it for me. For the responsible oldest child, the soon-to-be PhD, therapy is selfish, unnecessary. It's crazy.

I can see the mottled shapes of patients through the fogged glass of the front door when I arrive at the therapists' office. It will be impossible to hide here like I do in the doctor's office, sitting in the waiting room and hoping others think I have the flu as I perch pleasantly on the edge of my seat and try to smile so no one will know what is careening around my mind. I take a deep breath as I prepare to open the door. This is an important move, I believe—too much intimidation and others will know how nervous I am, but too much force and they might think me aggressive. But no one is looking when I get inside, the other patients focused on their phones or magazines, equally intent on appearing inconspicuous.

My voice shakes as I whisper my name to the receptionist so the others in the waiting room don't hear.

"What?" she asks, leaning forward and looking at me. "I didn't catch that." I repeat myself, wincing at the sound of my voice. Even my name is painful.

The receptionist hands me a clipboard with a large questionnaire, and I retreat to the only available seat, just inside the door. I can barely focus on the questions because I'm afraid someone outside will spy me if the door opens. Across the room, a woman studies her nails. Next to me a man shifts in his seat. Tranquil music floats throughout the office. I try so hard to be quiet, I stop breathing. I realize this when my pulse quickens and I gasp out loud. Embarrassing.

Unlike medical paperwork I've filled out before, which focuses on medications and lengthy details about my insurance provider, this paperwork asks about everything from my daily routine to my feelings about certain topics. I answer questions about diet and exercise. I answer questions about sleep. I answer questions about suicide or suicide attempts in my family. I answer questions about physical and sexual abuse, about drug and alcohol abuse, about pregnancy and abortion. I answer lots of questions about feelings.

When asked to rate my symptoms on a range of scales, I want to point out how severe my suffering is—I'm not here for couple's counseling after all, or grief, which is real and awful, but which is nothing like my delusions of ghosts and

God. I want to be crazy enough to warrant serious attention, so that my father is wrong, those depictions of people lying on sofas in *New Yorker* cartoons, movie scenes where rich women on chaise lounges discuss their affairs are wrong. At the same time, however, I don't want to be too crazy. My pencil hesitates between bubbles.

I feel a similar struggle when people say, "I'm having a panic attack" about running late or work deadlines, or sigh dramatically for emphasis before announcing, "I almost had a panic attack" when telling stories about mundane frights. I have *real* panic attacks, and the brief adrenaline they speak of is not the same. I don't like the appropriation of the word "anxiety" into everyday use, don't appreciate the way what is real and frightening for me is now something people say theatrically, rolling their eyes and waving their hands as they complain about work woes or family frustrations. "I have a real illness," I want to say bitterly, offering up my diagnosis as a bit of ownership. But doing so requires confession.

And while I bristle at the misuse of "anxiety" as a blanket term for stress, I know enough about anxiety to know it takes many forms. While I have frequent panic attacks about imagined extremes, perhaps someone else has panic attacks about work or a discussion with a family member. What's more, it is likely that many people who use the phrase "panic attack" loosely are medicated for the stress of their daily lives. Though they may not experience the same debilitations in the face of fear as I do, they may have received the same diagnosis, may swallow the same pills each day. With so many medicated, our illnesses cannot possibly look and feel the same, despite our same diagnoses.

I fill the paperwork out quickly and hand it to the receptionist. My writing is close to illegible, my answers too brief, but I doubt anyone will mind. I've grown so used to the fact that what I report is misinterpreted, lost, ignored, or rewritten that I don't value my own story much these days. I flip through a magazine, trying to appear unconcerned. A woman sits rigid in her chair, a man wrings his hands. I look down and realize I'm doing the same. At last my name is called and I stand to follow the woman who will change my life. I tower over her.

Although I am nearly a foot taller than Gail, her commanding presence fills her office. She looks like a character from *Harry Potter,* a petite, pixie woman with short, spiky hair. From afar her hair looks like a natural color, but up close it is a range of vibrant purples and oranges. She wears a bright teal pantsuit, covered in beads. It rustles and jangles, announcing her movement, the silk fabric catching the light. She wears pink clogs. Over the years, I will grow accustomed to her strange way of dressing—billowing culottes with bright orange knee socks, a black gown with sneakers, four dozen bangles and a plastic watch clanging along her tiny arms—and grow to find it endearing, brave, spunky. But on this first visit she appears odd.

Gail's office is cozy. In one corner her desk is littered with papers, a webcam perched on the filing cabinet, surveying the room. During this first meeting I wonder if she is recording our session, a question I never ask her, but always ask myself over the years we meet. A sofa faces her chair, a whiteboard on the wall, as though she will lecture and I'll be expected to take notes. One wall is lined with bookshelves, full of textbooks and first-person accounts of madness. Many of the same books are nestled on my own shelves at home.

The corner of her office is filled with dozens of plants. There are two large trees, pots resting on the floor, balanced on the windowsill. There is no order to the arrangement. The growth is wild and unruly. It is beautiful. "Wow, you have a lot of plants," I say nervously. I have dozens at home, but am not sure if I should tell her, in case she thinks I'm trying to butter her up. I've spent time rehearsing what I'm going to say to her so I'll appear calm and controlled. This conversation about plants is off script.

"Yes I do," she says. "So," she continues, when I get settled on the couch, "what brings you in today? Why are you here?"

I start timidly, explaining I have severe anxiety and have tried medications for several years, each without much success. I manage to keep it together the way I rehearsed until I get to the part about why I'm interested in therapy. When I try to explain how hard it is to keep going to doctors, how hard it is to swallow drugs when they cause so many unpleasant effects, how hard it is to try a new one, how much paperwork there is, how much blame, how much money I've spent, how much time I've lost, how angry I get when doctors question me, ask if I'm taking the medication properly, ask if I'm exaggerating my side effects, speak with authority like they know what I'm thinking and feeling, tell me about my choices, my body, my future, I stray further from my script.

I grow angrier and angrier as I speak uninterrupted. And all this time I thought I was sad. I begin to cry and turn my head to avoid looking at Gail. On a table next to the sofa is a box of Kleenex.

I tell Gail about the doctor who prescribed me Lexapro in place of Celexa, about Terry prescribing Zoloft with no mention of the worms or the rage or the anorgasmia, about the dermatologist and his two nodding nurses. I tell Gail about the times my name has been forgotten, the times I've been forgotten in examining rooms. We talk more about my dissatisfaction with my quality of care than my dissatisfaction with my anxiety. I tell Gail I feel like I'm being manipulated each time I go to the doctor, and while I've said this to Brady before, said it to my mother, who tsk-tsked and said, "Let's change the subject to something happier," saying it here and now is refreshing. It's honest.

The first session lasts nearly two hours. I keep glancing at the clock because it feels strange to talk about myself for so long. I've spent so much time trying to deflect attention in order to appear normal that this feels counterproductive. Gail asks about my early childhood, about where I grew up, about what my parents do for a living. She asks about elementary, middle, high school, college. She asks about each of my siblings, trying hard to keep them straight. She asks about my feelings a lot, and I'm surprised to find that I can't really tell her how I feel. In all my doctor's visits, I've never been asked about emotions.

Though it feels as if she is asking about every other part of my life, Gail never inquires about my medications, despite the fact that my dissatisfaction with them is the impetus for my visit. When I mention medication, she directs me back to my feelings. This, I later learn, is part of the difference between physical medicine and psychology. The average consultation in a medical doctor's office lasts roughly ten minutes and often concludes with a prescription (a psychiatry appointment may last forty and conclude the same), whereas a session with a therapist can last an hour or more, clients returning for weeks or months, and never beginning or changing or quitting drugs.

The terminology, too, suggests the philosophical differences between each field. A visit to a doctor or psychiatrist is a "consultation," patients seeking advice or information from an authority. A visit to a psychologist is a "session," the therapist working in conjunction with clients. Even the word "client," as opposed to "patient," suggests the act is communal. Gail asks so many personal questions because psychology views mental illnesses as deep-seated parts of people, identities that can be understood by looking at clients' life stories.

I initially hoped talking to a therapist would result in the right prescription, but I leave knowing this will be a longer process. Gail never once mentions my treatment, instead schedules our next appointment for a week later, and another appointment the following week. She appears eager to see me, a welcome change from my other physicians, who each seem exasperated I'm back in their offices, that I can't take my pills and be happy already. Gail wants to keep close watch on me, even get to know me.

After the session ends, I call my mother, who's asked me to tell her exactly what was discussed. I recount the entire session while my mother murmurs "Mmmhmm" into the phone, holding it away from her ear to talk to my siblings when she thinks I can't hear, putting the phone down to talk to daycare children and their parents. I'm in the middle of a sentence when the phone goes quiet. I hear rustling in the background and my mother chatting to a baby while she changes a diaper. I feel angry my mother is ignoring me, and then guilty for bothering her while she's so busy with work, guiltier still Gail seemed less interested in my parents' philanthropy than in my feelings about our family. I don't tell my mother that Gail asked, "Were the adoptions very difficult on you?" like she wanted me to admit to something. "That sounds interesting, sweetie," my mother says when she picks up the phone again, putting the phone down once, twice, three times more to corral daycare children, eventually, when Cameron makes the family dog a soccer ball, hanging up abruptly. She never calls back.

Over the next few weeks and months, Gail asks a lot about the years leading up to my anxiety. This makes sense, given that she is trying to find what led to my panic, but I find it strange we rarely talk about anxiety itself. I want to talk about getting well and proving that I am normal and does the pulse in my thigh mean I have cancer and does that pinprick of pain on my temple mean I have a tumor. Instead, Gail asks questions about my family, about my feelings towards my siblings, about the ways my family has changed throughout the years.

Sometimes I feel Gail's judgment towards my parents. Sometimes I feel like she is suggesting I am angry with them. I worry she thinks I do not love my family. Up until this moment I've never been happy about the adoptions, but I've learned to keep quiet, learned to smile and nod and agree when people say, "Wow, your parents are amazing." I know to add, "Yes, they are selfless."

I repeat that now. When Gail asks how all the adoptions made me feel, I say things like, "It was pretty crazy at my house, but we worked together." I say, "I didn't like the adoptions at first, but I'm older now, so I know it was the right thing to do." I hope Gail does not see the selfish child who begged her parents not to adopt orphans.

"Those aren't feelings," Gail reminds me. What I do feel is how she is pushing, asking me to explore emotions I'm ashamed to have, emotions I've been told are selfish and cruel, emotions I've learned to ignore. Sometimes I don't answer. I stare out her window to the open sky, then at her empty white-board, my hunched figure reflected in the surface. I stare at my hands in my lap. My fingers are tangled around one another into a tight knot, seemingly impossible to loosen. Holding them this way hurts.

Before I began therapy I never considered there was a link between my chaotic upbringing and my chaotic brain. I never considered that my panic might be the result of a lifetime of panic, that my attempt at control stemmed from a loss of control, that feeling disconnected from my body came from feeling disconnected from my family, or that feeling wrong came from growing up believing this was true. I never thought that the pain that wrote itself on my body was the result of keeping it in so long. Trauma is learned as much as narratives about what makes a good person, a good family, a good girl.

When Gail asks me to recall memories, I am shocked by how much I've lost. I barely remember my childhood, I realize, and though I've always blamed my panic for my memory loss—prolonged anxiety shrinks the hippocampus, the part of brain responsible for memory—I begin to see a pattern in the loss. "Children who have experienced trauma," Gail says gently, "have difficulty remembering."

A few sessions into our work together, Gail says, "Your symptoms sound like PTSD." I exhibit many of the symptoms—a predisposition to frightening thoughts, frequent nightmares and faulty memory, plus a difficulty connecting to others, a reluctance and sometimes inability to allow myself certain feelings—but I bristle at the suggestion. I don't need another diagnosis. Plus, post-traumatic stress disorder seems to have become the catchall diagnosis in recent years, even minor events becoming psychological cataclysms. Gail does not try to persuade me, but she relates PTSD to my family history. It is hard not to think of the cliché of going to therapy and blaming my parents, hard not to feel very Freudian when what once seemed ludicrous now hits my stomach and heart as partially true.

Yet I know there is something more. The weight of familiarity hits when Gail discusses how the body manifests trauma. She returns to this diagnosis again and again, but I wait a year before telling her about my rape. She must have read it in the paperwork I filled out the first day, but she never asked, instead waited for me to make the connection between those six months of terror and hurt, and the terror and hurt I experience again and again years later. I'd never made the connection, my physicians had never asked, and my parents, who both knew, refuse to speak about it. I do not remember what Gail said about my rape that day or in the months and years that followed, but I do remember this: she never said it was my fault.

It has taken me a long time to admit how I feel about my family. That I am sad and angry with my parents. That I miss them, grieve for them. That I feel guilty for creating the physical and emotional distance between us I need in order to protect my mental health. That I want so much to make them proud and know I will hurt them with this story. "I think it's best if I don't read your book," my mother says.

For many years I argued with Gail and myself that my feelings were wrong; I was wrong. My parents still insist this is true. A few years ago, while I was visiting my parents, my father asked how I felt about the adoptions now that I was an adult. When I said that I loved my siblings and would not change anything, but that my feelings about the chaos of our family remained, he laughed and said, "You don't feel that way. Stop." When I protested, he persisted. I was a thirty-year-old doctor, but eventually, he scolded me for arguing and sent me to bed.

As I begin seeing Gail regularly, I worry about my family states away. Each injury or fiasco is reported to me on the phone by my mother every morning. I hear about the simultaneous suspension of both twins for engaging in an after-school fight, about Bailey's referral to the principal for refusing to attend kindergarten detention, about Candy driving her car through the front yard fence, about Casey sneaking out to spend time in a hotel with a known drug dealer, about Victoria's ongoing legal battles. Because I have gone to college, I get phoned for each question or complaint. I am asked to help with Victoria's financial aid and Natalie's classes. Because I am a teacher, I am asked to explain the kids' needs to their teachers and expected to listen when my mother blames teachers for the kids' bad behavior. I am asked to look over the kids' homework, to help them write their essays. When they receive bad grades they sigh, "I thought you were a teacher," as though that should guarantee them a passing grade, when Casey is barely literate at eighteen, can't read a menu without photos of the food, when Bailey can't write a word without erasing it fifteen times. I receive phone calls about the family's lack of health insurance, about their accumulating debt, about my parents' failing health and unwillingness to seek medical attention, about the latest fight my father had with Casey, about Candy getting high. There is always something: Victoria is unable to pay for college; Natalie has dropped out of college; Casey will not graduate high school and is homeless and then his girlfriend is pregnant; Candy does not want to go to college and then she is pregnant; Cameron is stealing from school; Bailey struggles to move from grade to grade. My parents ask if they can list me as the legal guardian on their will, if I will parent the kids if something happens. It takes years to gather the courage to say no and even then they will not accept my decision. My phone rings several times each day, even though I am knee-deep in my own PhD work and teaching. My phone rings before Brady and I have risen in the morning, when we are eating dinner, when we are out to a movie, when we are reading together before bed. The phone rings late into the night when I am sleeping in Brady's arms. No matter the time, I jolt myself from sleep, pull away from him, and reach for my phone in the darkness. I always answer.

CHAPTER 20

TAKING UP SPACE

t wasn't difficult to be silent. My undergraduate college campus was dark when I woke, the stars disappearing one by one. I'd tiptoe to my dorm kitchen, pull a bowl from my designated shelf, and carefully measure oatmeal before adding water and placing it in the microwave. I was an expert at holding still, hunched in front of the microwave, my face yellow with the glow as my meal jerked in pirouette. I held my breath during the countdown, and before zero beeped my consumption, I'd press the button releasing the pressure and my food. I smiled each time at my cleverness—my ability to avoid the signal.

I'd grab my bowl, cupping warmth between my hands like prayer, and scurry back to my room. Alone, I'd chew slowly, move the food around my mouth until the grains went soft with saliva. I'd swallow with intention. Sometimes I'd shake from the effort.

I followed the same routine every morning. Eating my half cup of plain oatmeal—no butter, no sugar, no milk—lasted half an hour. Even though I was hungry when I finished, I did not scrape the bowl. Sometimes I'd leave a bite or two in the bottom to prove I wasn't greedy.

After eating, I'd move from class to class until midday, when I'd return home for lunch. My three roommates were up by then, women who complained about their growing bodies while praising my shrinking one. I wasn't jealous of their burgers, pizzas, Frappuccinos; watching food travel down their throats made me sick with panic.

So I'd retreat to my room, locking the door behind me, and wait to cook until they left the kitchen, the apartment. I'd eat—another half cup of oatmeal spread over many serious bites—until I had enough strength to walk down the hill from our dorm to my afternoon classes.

In the evenings I could barely return, trudging up the gradient into sunlight so bright I felt like I'd pass out. I'd open the door to an icy blast, my roommates forever negotiating the thermostat down—sixty, they said, was best—until I resorted to many layers to keep from shivering. I'd sit in my room and listen to the clock's metronome, counting down until it was acceptable to eat. If I ate too early, I got hungry again before bed and spent the night tossing, my hipbones and spine raw against the thin dorm mattress. If I waited too long, I got lightheaded and fuzzy, my body vibrating from inside.

When the time was right—6:00, a habit I still keep, others laughing at my childish dinnertime—I'd head down the echoing hall to the kitchen. I cooked my only lavish meal of the day loudly. I steamed broccoli and made teriyaki noodles while roommates complained about their weight and searched for ice cream in the freezer. No one knew I'd eaten oatmeal all day—each day for months—and I'd make a mound of food high on my plate. Alone in my room, I'd savor the large portion over an hour. For the first time all day I'd feel full.

The feeling didn't last long, though, and when the rumble and anxiety returned, I'd shower to distract myself. I'd remove all of my clothes and urinate and breathe out for thirty seconds before stepping on the scale my roommates left in our bathroom as inspiration, along with images of women in bathing suits they taped on the mirrors and the fridge. This was the best part of my day—when I saw the results of my dedication—for the number was what mattered, not the way I shrank from size medium to extra small, or the way my period disappeared along with my thighs, my jeans slipping off when I walked. At five-foot-ten, I whittled myself from 131 pounds to 115, but the only number that mattered was 111. A nice, symmetrical number, a good number. One was the number of winners.

Soon I dropped extra pounds like I left extra bites of oatmeal in my bowl—108, 106—to prove I wasn't greedy.

It started my first year of college. I was taking a nutrition class and spent three afternoons a week packed into an auditorium of fifty women, their sorority names emblazoned on the seats of their yoga pants, most on their ways to exercise after class, and eventually to matching degrees in nutrition and the Mrs. degrees they wistfully joked about before springtime proposals began, squeals of delight echoing every Monday.

We spent the semester talking about how the body metabolized food, the workings of the digestive system, and the absorption of nutrients. We discussed the caloric content of different foods, our teacher answering questions about carbohydrates and alcohol, even going so far as to discuss which cocktails had fewer calories. As the semester wore on, winter coats were replaced by short shorts, pizza and chips by carrot sticks and hummus. Collectively, we shrank.

(We shrank literally, too. For the first few weeks a young mother came to class with her infant. She took notes while using her foot to rock the baby's car seat. The baby never cried. During class breaks, the mother breastfed, covering her baby and chest with a blanket before returning to her notes. The first time the class was shocked, gathering in circles to cast disgusted looks. After a few weeks, some grew vocal, asking loudly, "Can't she go somewhere else? Some of us are here to learn." Apparently, breast was not best. Even in nutrition class, eating was suspect, hunger an inconvenience. One day, a few girls pulled the professor out into the hall to protest, their gesticulations visible through the glass door. The mother never returned.)

While the girls in my class knew about healthy food choices, I was alarmed, then ashamed when my textbook labeled the food I'd grown up eating deficient. I'd never considered that my body was somehow inferior, but while my classmates stocked their dorm pantries with organic food and shared advice on smoothie supplements, when I visited my parents, I opened the freezer to find TV dinners and fries, the cupboards full of off-brand Cheez Puffs and Honey O's, processed foods my mother purchased in bulk from the dollar store. These were the same groceries she sent me back to school with each week, food my parents' contribution to the university I attended on scholarships, paying for my tuition, books, and housing from funding I cobbled together from various community groups and tutoring. I often felt lost and amazed I could fool everyone into thinking I belonged, and the desire to adapt my diet proved no different.

I became fixated on healthy eating, my dedication to nutrition fueled by the food diary I had to keep for class. On campus I avoided junk food and the freshman fifteen, and at home I skipped meals altogether to avoid my professor's red pen in the margins—"Frozen food is full of sodium. Review your notes." I thought about food constantly, but refused to give in lest I became overweight like all the women I'd grown up with, women who talked about losing weight while sipping extra-large Diet Cokes, while the men smoked and drank and ate red meat, battled high blood pressure and cancers. When the spring semester ended and I moved home for the summer, I kept up a mental food diary.

I was dating my first serious boyfriend at the time, a shy, funny boy with a big heart and body. Our first year of dating he lost fifty pounds, gaining more confidence in the process until he ditched his glasses for contacts, and began shaving his chest and dreaming of moving to Hollywood to become an actor. He ran three miles a day. He only drank water and Gatorade. He did not eat condiments except for mustard because it was low in calories. He covered everything in pepper because it sped up digestion. He expected me to do the same, not because I was fat, but because, he explained, he needed my support. If we cooked together, we avoided butter and cheese and bread. If we went out to eat, he reminded me that we were eating healthy before we parked the car, sometimes before we got in the car at all. I'd been a vegetarian for years, but he liked to remind me how important protein was for building muscles, like the six-pack he'd begun to develop and tan each afternoon, or the biceps he flexed only from certain angles because he had stretch marks on the inside of his arms. Once a week he would have what he called a "cheat day," where he could eat whatever he wanted and so could I. We ate plates of greasy fries and vats of guacamole and the pizzas his parents ordered every Friday night, boxes piled high on the kitchen counter and left out until the last slice was gone. The bloated pain that followed was a reminder of what happened with overindulgence.

The following fall semester, my roommates, who had never had boyfriends, praised mine and his square jaw. "Does he speak Spanish?" they asked. "Does he have brothers?" When they put a scale in our bathroom and began marking their weight together on a chart on the fridge, weighing in a weekly event leading up to spring break, I, too, began weighing myself each week, then each night. Soon I was stepping on the scale many times throughout the day.

I both feared and longed to be caught, hoping that people—my roommates, my boyfriend, my parents—would be impressed by what I'd achieved. When I returned home, my parents were surprised by my thinness, but blamed my weight on dorm food, college stress, and my vegetarianism. Still, I wanted them to worry, wanted my mother to put down a new child long enough to make me a cup of tea.

It was many years later, during therapy, that I realized my fascination with disappearing coincided with the adoption of Cameron and Bailey. They moved in with my family in January; by mid-February I stopped eating. On Valentine's Day, I slid the half-eaten heart-shaped cake my boyfriend brought me—"Tonight can be cheat day," he whispered—into the dorm trash after he went home. My parents told me not to come home unless I could be supportive of my new brothers, so I stayed in my college apartment eating bowls of plain oatmeal. Eventually I skipped meals altogether because no one noticed anyway.

Fifteen years later, my students are hungry. Students in creative writing and gender studies classes write about their experiences with anorexia, with bulimia, with weight gain, with body dysmorphia. They write about depression, anxiety, and OCD. A student writes about the eating disorder she developed while studying abroad. Her classmate writes about the reappearance of the high school bulimia she thought was gone. Another writes about the weight she gained after her rape. Several write about suicide attempts.

We work hard to cultivate a space where the personal is political, where taking up space with our stories is an act of resistance. I make this space for myself as much as for them. My students' openness is a vulnerability and strength I've only recently discovered, my disordered eating continuing through my undergraduate work and part of graduate school, though I mostly keep this to myself.

One semester I have to travel in and out of state for several weeks. I arrange online activities and substitutes and when the travel is done, I bring pizza and soda to my classes to say thank you for their patience while I was away. The students in one class are primarily women. They take one slice and one soda and a napkin, and they eat delicately, pausing to raise their hands and participate in the class discussion. The class is held in the late afternoon, but more than one woman remarks this is the first thing she's eaten all day.

More than one woman says it is the only thing she will eat all day.

The male students stand together at the end of the line, thanking me and remarking on their hunger. They pile their plates with two slices, three slices, four. They make two trips for sodas. One later stands in the middle of the discussion to saunter up for another soda, commenting on our reading for the day while doing so, the crack of the soda can a humorous addition. The last man in line finishes off the pizza even though several women stand behind him. "We weren't hungry anyway," they say, shuffling back to their seats without taking a soda. They watch their classmates eat. I watch too. I'm relieved there's no pizza left for me.

After class I ask students to take a soda or two for the road. "I don't need all this soda," I laugh, hoping I'm not left with all those full cans and empty calories.

"Are you sure?" they ask. A few male students take sodas for the road. "I should only have one," female students say. "I'm watching my weight."

One student, a shy girl who talks to me, but rarely to her classmates, asks if I'm sure about the extra sodas. "Of course," I say, turning to erase the board. When I turn back around, she's gone. So is the twelve-pack, a bit of sweetness to savor later.

In gender studies courses, we examine the history of the undergarment, from the Victorian corset to the waist trainer students see in their Instagram feeds, and students identify a preoccupation with the failure of the female body. If there is an aspect of womanhood that unites women across time, across race, sexuality, gender identity, ability, class, and age, it is that the female body is faulty. It must be controlled by dedication to diet and exercise, by the rituals of skin and hair care, by the offerings in glossy pages of magazines and in malls across America where mannequins grow ever smaller, my own tiny hand capable of encircling a plastic woman's calf like a shackle.

In the classroom space I share with my students I invite them to confront, resist, and embody the world in ways they see fit. I believe my lectures.

I did not believe I had an eating disorder until years into therapy, and even then I kept the revelation to myself. I was eating more than oatmeal by then, and my anxiety, OCD, and PTSD seemed more pressing. I'd sensed I was on the edge of something painful in college, but it was not until therapy that I recognized the severity. Still, all the women I knew had had an unhealthy relationship to food and it seemed to have passed, so I swallowed it down.

After acknowledging the role hunger occupied in my life, I compensated by eating whatever I pleased. For years I'd refused to keep sugar or honey in my cabinets, refused any beverage with calories, condiments, too, and I swung the opposite direction, eating candy bars whenever I desired, elated that snack food no longer made me want to avoid social gatherings because of the inevitable, "What do you mean you don't eat processed food?"

My weight climbed to 125 pounds, which in my late twenties still seemed slight compared to many of my friends. My favorite weight was 121, a symmetrical palindrome high enough to avoid scrutiny, but low enough that I could slip into the teens again if I ever felt panic. As had been the case with my college roommates, I measured my success in comparison to my friends, though some ran marathons and some were pregnant. We did not compare numbers, but I relished being the smallest person in the room, hearing someone say, "How do you eat all that cake and stay so thin?" Eventually I measured the success of my femininity against colleagues, a strange comparison when they were professors and authors with enviable academic accomplishments. Yet as it always had, accomplishment came back to the body. If I was smaller, thinner, if my clavicle jutted or the bones in my wrists bulged, I felt safe.

I wasn't the only woman doing this. In graduate school, other PhD students learned that one of the feminist scholars had written about her experience with disordered eating. She was a tiny woman made strong by yoga and the compassion she offered students, many of whom were first-time teachers. Students spoke of her with admiration and lusted over her curriculum vitae, but it was inevitable they would eventually blurt out, "Did you know she had an eating disorder?" as if it were a tawdry secret and not the basis for her feminist work. The gossip was vicious, most often proffered by female students who seemed to find their own strength by her perceived weakness.

Since finishing graduate school, my weight has settled back to where it was when I was in high school. I weigh the same—131, though the number is not by design—which makes me proud and also terrifies me. I am fortunate that eating has mostly become a pleasure rather than a fear. I avoid the mirror when I can, and am weighed only by the doctor. Still, there are times the familiar dread creeps up my spine and clamps its jaw at the base of my neck and I know nothing is in my control. When I received my university's prestigious award for distinguished dissertation, I could not eat at the banquet. The same held true for the meals I ate while on campus interviews during my job search. It is hard for me to eat loud foods, messy foods, smelly foods. I do not want people to see me eat, to watch food travel down my throat. When my younger self surfaces, I am reminded that the way I experience myself physically in the world is fraught with issues of power and agency.

My age means that my hips have begun to widen, my waist to soften, and the firmness of my youth is being replaced with the tautness that comes not from age, but from a lifetime of worry. One of my biggest fears remains that I will lose all control and consume, consume, my body growing expansive. It is strange I should fear this because I think I might delight in taking up space, in being satisfied for once. It is strange I should fear this because my body has never felt as though it were my own. I sometimes wish I still had the vigilance I had in college. When my body seems beyond my control, as though it will change without me, my breasts and butt, even my smile drooping with age, the control of my youth is intoxicating. I do not say this in order to praise the pain I put myself through or to glorify a cult of thinness, but to point out how naïve I was to think that my body might be my own, that I had any say in the way I viewed it.

My students know culture is responsible for how we perceive our bodies, and they point to the magazines and television shows that make them feel inferior. This is not new. A thin body, nineteenth-century literature taught us, is a lovely body, often, too, a wealthy body, a white body, a (mostly) able body. To be delicate to the point of frailty was—still is—to be beautiful, desirable. To be thin is to be in need of protection, something I hear Brady say when he wraps his large hands around my ribcage and whispers, "I love that you're small and I can wrap my hands around you. I love to feel your ribcage." And while I know that he means that this complements his 250-pound frame and seems a counterpart to his own insecurities about weight, I can't help but focus on the word "cage" in the sentence. Something catches in my throat and I gasp for air, worried that one day I might not be so easily encircled, that my ankle has never been small enough to shackle.

What I know of the female body, its strain and size and stature, I've learned from the women in my family. My father's side is all boys, his five-foot-one mother a tiny, tender thing whose sharp tongue and sass make her legend by way of contrast with her size. On my mother's side the legacy of the female body is one of transformation, each woman a slim beauty until marriage and children hang unhappiness around their hips. Each woman, family myth goes, gains a hundred pounds from the time she was last happy. Her last signs of happiness only exist in photos, and the warning that "women in our family are fat women" feels like a life sentence. I can't recall when I first started scanning my own photos for signs of desperation and extra pounds.

I learned early on that for women in my family, eating is sometimes a comfort and always a curse. Food punctuates the run-on of their lives—a rare steak the exclamation mark of success, a trip through the drive-thru a period at the end of a tough day. My memories of these women involve baking or preparing meals, and eventually, when the family scattered apart, infrequent visits marked by loud conversations afterward about "how fat" everyone had grown. Criticizing a woman's weight was a family event. Family whispers about weight are a refrain as much as "I love you."

The men in my family escape scrutiny by occupation as much as by gender, for they are each construction men, building fences and airplanes, laying cement and constructing cabinets while their wives pulse out children and scrap together working-wage suppers.

My own husband is a large man, raised by a woman who spent much of her time away, leaving him frozen dinners and money for pizza. Brady grew up associating binge eating with independence, the feeling of fullness an antidote to loneliness. We make a strange pair—his desire for the heaviness of a full stomach, the ache of overeating, my desire for the lightness of an empty one, the ache of hollowness.

Though Brady has been on medication for his cholesterol since he was fifteen, now takes medication for high blood pressure, and doctors tell him he needs to lose at least fifty pounds, he rarely feels shame about his body. He is strong and sturdy, and while this is the result of weight rather than muscle, his barrel chest and big thighs outsize those of most men he encounters. His size is physically intimidating, overtly masculine, and he balances size with the humor he has learned accompanies men whose bellies roll over their waistbands. When he sits, Brady spreads his legs wide, and he stretches his arms along the back of seats as though he is claiming the world. He walks in easy, sprawling steps, eyes focused on his destination, unaware when others—often women—scurry from his path.

Writing this now, I am shocked by how devoted I was—perhaps remain—to my desire to be the smallest, how intently I believed it could be achieved. I have not been as devoted to any other dream as I have been to disappearing. I do not know why I believe(d) becoming invisible would allow me to be seen. I was a girl so desperately hungry that comfort was running my hands across the lengths of my bones, the sharpness a reminder of my task. And I am woman who sometimes still feels this way and cannot understand why and so grows sad, angry, and confused, all those things along with "fat" magazines and mothers tell us are not ladylike.

My college roommates sighed about their weight while cooking and banished food to the garbage to prevent themselves from eating. One set an early morning alarm she hoped would wake her into becoming a runner—it announced her failure in ten-minute intervals for hours each morning as she hit the snooze button. Eventually, she'd pull herself from bed and use lipstick to scrawl slogans on the bathroom mirror: "Sore or sorry. You pick."

When I look up these women after many years of silence, I find professional clues they are aerospace engineers and computer programmers like they'd hoped to become when they were still the only young women in classrooms full of men. But their personal social media tells a different story— the women are absent altogether, replaced by photos of food and diet tip aphorisms. "Learn to work through the pain. Then push harder." "Nothing tastes as good as being fit feels." "Don't listen to your inner fatty. She's a bitch. She misses bread." "Once you see results, it becomes an addiction."

The women in my family also grow absent as they grow larger. It is as if the space their bodies occupy denies them the right to also take up space with their stories. They rarely talk about themselves beyond their children. I'd like to ask my mother, my aunts, my grandmothers what nourishes them. I'd like to ask what satiates. It's as if any dream disappeared as they sipped Diet Coke after Diet Coke, their only bit of sweetness, afternoons stretching long and silent into the evening's darkness.

I write the stories of my body to prevent my erasure. I want my words to take up the space I've denied my body, the space my body has been denied. Here is one of those stories: Once I did not eat for two weeks because a boy left me. My first boyfriend left me one August for another girl, a tiny thing who sang in the church choir and blew him afterwards and wanted to be a movie star too. I'd been giving up pounds since February, reached 111, the number of winners, but I lost. And because he did not want my body anymore, neither did I.

I stopped eating altogether. I subsisted on the tea my mother left by my bedside because I was too sad and weak to walk. The tea was thick with sugar and honey because my mother was afraid and it was the only comfort she could pass along to me. I shrank to 100 pounds and I stank of rot because my body feasted on itself. I didn't leave my bed, woke each morning sobbing because I'd been abandoned, pushed aside for someone newer, someone better. My siblings took a backseat to my sadness. My father grew angry that my ex-boyfriend impacted my health and didn't even realize it. My mother fretted and said if I dropped to double digits, she would take me to the hospital.

I'd practiced disappearing for years, but this is the story of when I learned disappearing could be an act of devotion—to the boy who left me for another girl, a tiny five-foot thing whose body was so small he could wrap a hand around her ankle.

Not all my stories of hunger are tied to romance. Sometimes I wanted to be small because I longed for my mother, whose many children took her away from me. Other times because the world seemed to be moving too fast. Then I hungered for the control starvation afforded, the way my body became a landscape I could rule. Injury reminded me of my power.

When I tell these stories, listeners furrow their brows. They laugh nervously or change the subject. Even when I'm fighting to be seen, disappearing seems the only option. A preferable story about consumption and the body? My husband's tale of the time he ate a dozen chocolate pudding cups in under two minutes, the middle school gymnasium chanting his name. Listeners laugh and laugh at the precocious boy eating with abandon, all the world his to taste.

These are our stories, though Brady tells his more readily. Brady keeps clothing in different sizes for when his weight fluctuates. I have a shirt from the fifth grade that washes me in relief as it slips easily over my shoulders. Each of Brady's white shirts is stained from the food he spills in his haste to eat, while I have dresses for occasions during which I could not eat. Brady makes a plate for me ahead of time when we host dinner parties, storing it in the fridge until I can eat alone. We requested plates of food be sent home with us after our wedding so Brady could eat his fill again and I might be able to nibble something at all. The caterer forgot and I didn't eat all day, floated on champagne like a weightless pink cupcake. Brady dieted for six months to button his coat and my dress was taken in because I had no appetite leading up to the wedding. "You're so thin," everyone congratulated. "You look like the perfect bride."

I wonder what it feels like to occupy space without shame. We tell women they cannot take up space to such an extent that women, en masse, feel they don't deserve certain spaces, or space at all. We confine women to the silent eye of the tornado; the curled fetal space of an anxiety attack; the compulsive space of trauma. Perhaps women fixate on the house—the most relaxing shade of white, the symmetry of fireplace tiles—because it is the only space they command.

Inhabiting space via the body, women are told, is our failure. Craving smallness is our repentance. We store our shame in the very vessel from which it is provided. I've spent so much of my life concerned with how much space I occupy—not only physical space, but emotional and mental space—that disappearance seems reward. I've tried to become as diminutive as I feel and now my shoulders curve in on themselves until my neck and back are stiff with knots. I look like one part of a parenthesis, hunched over onto myself—now I understand that the stooped backs of old women are not the result of age, but rather a lifetime of feeling small. The body eventually follows suit.

I am forever being told to stand up straight—this comes as frequently as I'm told to smile—and how I wish I would. I hurt from hunching. Erasure is not easy.

CHAPTER 21

TURNING AROUND

"I need to tell you something," Gail announces at the end of one of our sessions.

I've returned from a trip to visit my family, the dynamic chaotic as ever. I am agitated and twitchy, on high alert and in need of quiet. The anxiety will last for weeks. I'm eager for the calm Gail provides.

"I'm retiring," she says.

I flatline. Breathless. Heavy.

"It's unexpected. My mother is ill," Gail apologizes. "We only have time for a few more sessions."

I want to weep—for her ninety-nine-year-old mother, for Gail, mostly for myself. I'm embarrassed to admit to Gail how much she means to me. I'm embarrassed to admit this to myself. When did I get so attached to a therapist?

As I drive away from her office the world spins. I sob. I call Brady and tell him I'm devastated because Gail has become my friend. I will miss her. Then I get to the heart of it—"I don't think I can do it alone."

I've gone to therapy once a week, then once a month, for four years. Gail remembers our last session and the dozens before. Gail remembers my current problems and asks about my future plans. Gail remembers how my present fits into my past. Above all, Gail remembers my name.

She listens to the mundane—financial planning, a burdensome department committee, my officemate's penchant for piling her books on my desk—but she is also one of the first people I tell about my milestones. Gail is there when I jump through the various hoops of my PhD, when I publish a little book of poems, when I travel to Boston and New Orleans and fall in love with these spaces and how free they make me feel. I tell Gail how after five years together, Brady is manic and wearing on my patience, and suddenly I laugh and say, "You crazy man—I love you," delighted to find that I mean it not in spite of his madness but because of it, more so because I have not said "I love you" since I was twenty, convinced that saying this leads to vulnerability, to boyfriends leaving and cruel men. Gail is the first to see me after Brady proposes and though she is never one to comment on clothing or hair—thank goodness—she clasps her hands to her heart and smiles for me, for Brady, for the little family we are making. (After she retires I imagine sharing with her stories about graduating with my PhD and getting married a week later, or flying to Europe to honeymoon with Brady, both of us pinching ourselves as we tumble in and out of museums. And Gail is there in spirit when I publish another little book of poems and another, when this book about my anxious life is accepted for publication, and I land a tenure-track job and move to Boston, an exercise in luck and serendipity that leaves Brady and I wide-eyed at the ways our life has become so sweet.)

Gail also sees me during difficult times. She sees me when I'm convinced I have breast cancer, or think a disgruntled old boyfriend is lurking around the parking lot trying to shoot me, or as the 2012 Apocalypse approaches and the world doesn't end (again). Gail is stern and serious—she does not coddle—as she encourages me to be more forceful with bossy coworkers who abuse my kindness, tells me it's okay if I don't lend my siblings money, insists I have every right to tell my parents no when they suggest Casey move in with me so I can help him graduate high school. Gail never says that I should be ashamed of what I fear, want, need. I feel respected. I feel loved. And I learn that I deserve this. We all do.

Over time, I become more self-assured. I am aware of my choices instead of controlled by what I feel is expected of me. I tell my siblings that I am too busy to help with their essays, tell my mother that I do not want to hear about calls from social services, tell my officemate that I cannot read her dissertation for a third time. I explain to Brady how the burden of domestic labor makes me feel, and he takes on much of the cleaning and cooking.

Brady and I adopt new a technique towards our mental illness: we laugh. We laugh all the time. When I take a pill and get dizzy, he sings, "You spin me right 'round, baby, right 'round." I croon Carole King back to him because feeling the earth move under my feet is applicable, but so are fears of the sky tumbling down. When we eat sandwiches, we look first for cocaine. I am tired of thinking about hair and cut mine into a pixie, shaved close at the neck. I refer to myself as Rapunzel. When I finally orgasm, we high-five.

I don't mean that madness is something to laugh about, rather, that it is human and there is no reason to hide what so many feel. Fear and pain are as natural as joy and pride, and while we've been conditioned to hide these things, to value strength over weakness, to label anything else failure, there is value in the things that challenge us. I have learned more in my life from what we label failure than I have from what we label success. I don't welcome these moments—I'd still prefer not to have anxiety attacks or hallucinations—but I don't run from them either. I take what comes and I laugh. And this, believe me, is a whole lot less frightening.

The anxiety does not go away entirely, but when I do experience fear and delusion, I don't fault myself. When the shadow passes, I try not to dwell in shame. When it is time to take a pill, I no longer hide the bottle. I no longer resist medication—Buspirone, I accept, helps me. I am fortunate I have found something that does. I no longer feel shame for taking medication. Someday I might like to find another medication, for I've seen Brady aided beyond what we thought possible with the help of new medications. If I see someone I know in the therapist's office, I say hello. I begin to write about mental illness and teach courses on the literature of women's madness, on illness and disability in literature. I do not hide that this work is informed by my own experience. My anxiety is always with me, but where I used to think of it as an evil that lurked from the shadows to frighten me before retreating to the darkness once more, I've come to think of it as an old friend, someone who knows me intimately but with whom I bicker from time to time.

None of this comes easily—talk therapy is not what we see on TV, housewives lounging on couches, wealthy businessmen sharing their stressors after a long day. Talk therapy requires work—after all, it affects the shape of our brains. It requires mental work—sifting through the past and present to make connections. It requires emotional work—confronting those things that have hurt us, or, more difficult, those things about ourselves we dislike, those secrets that make us ashamed. It is physical work—like a job, it requires your presence and many hours. Making therapy an important part of my life is a necessity and a kindness, but above all it is a privilege—I am lucky to have health insurance and access to health care, luckier still that it covers mental health care, which is increasingly under attack by medical reform.

You've probably heard this definition of insanity: doing the same thing over and over and expecting different results. Therapy, however, taught me mental illness is a deliciously complicated way of knowing and being, an intricate resistance.

Gail never provided me with concrete "yes" or "no" answers, "good" or "bad" interpretations, or any of the other oversimplified binaries we rely on to govern the world. She never labeled things "clinical" or "normal," never even provided a definition of anxiety. Instead, she taught me first to tolerate, and then to embrace ambiguity. As I discussed the same story with Gail a dozen times, telling it from multiple points of view, with differing points of rising tension, imagining many resolutions, I learned there is no set narrative. That's what therapy offers—choice, agency, the knowledge that nothing is permanent. Where contradiction was frowned upon by people who could not tolerate my inability to be "cured," therapy rewards complexity. It broadens the definition of normal. It does not fix all, however, or even many, of the problems in our lives. It does not make everything clear. In fact, therapy sometimes confuses. But this, I've learned, is all right. Therapy allows us to be messy and imperfect (and anxious), reminding us that people are endlessly complicated, a lesson that is undeniably healing.

I like when I am reminded that life is difficult, that while I am anxious, I am also human and allowed—perhaps expected—to feel certain ways. Sometimes I blame things on anxiety, wondering out loud why my brain insists on thinking this way. "Have you ever stopped to think," I imagine Gail suggesting calmly, "that it's normal to feel nervous if you've never done this before?" Or, "Why should you feel happy about this situation? What's wrong with vocalizing your frustration?" When I'm not feeling well, I imagine Gail saying, "Perhaps you're actually ill," encouraging me to go to the doctor, where it is revealed I have an ear infection or strep throat. In these moments I am not overly nervous, or refusing to be happy, not an obsessive worrier. I am not someone ruled by anxiety—I just am.

Yes, my fears are often exaggerated, but they stem from the real hurts of any human. While I certainly replay moments in my head more times than most, the fears of looking foolish in front of others or getting hurt are basic ones. So, too, is the fear that our loved ones will leave us, though mine manifests itself in perfectionism. The fear I feel most often is the most common fear of all—the fear of death—and while my paranoia about cancer or asteroids or even God might seem unexpected, fears of impermanence, of leaving too soon, of wanting something beyond this life are not. Much of America has been conditioned to leave emotion behind in order to forge ahead. We label vulnerability as weakness and weakness as illness, yet it is often emotion—weakness, failure, vulnerability, and a certain kind of questioning—that leads to invention and discovery.

The difference between the narrative patients construct in therapy and the one their medical histories tell is the active subject. In a medical history, my illness is the subject, I am secondary. In therapy, I am the subject. For the first time since I've been diagnosed, my body, my illness, my sanity are not the center of my narrative. Neither are drugs, which I've come to see differently. Just as I am neither hero nor villain, nor my parents who have tried their best, neither are drugs. For as many stories of adverse reactions, there are stories of success. Drugs have helped me after all.

It is true that the life stories we create in talk therapy are collaborations between client and therapist—I could not have understood my life in this way without Gail—but they are also collaborations between various versions of ourselves, various ways we have lived and existed. We create alternate versions of ourselves—the stories that have happened, the stories we thought we must tell, the stories we still hope to write. They are dynamic and changing, stories that seek accuracy, but also stories that amend.

Narrative medicine asks we consider how illness fits into our life story, the ways we can use our stories to understand pain and healing. Sitting in Gail's office, now here at my desk, writing the narrative I wanted to tell all along—the one I never had enough time to share in brief doctors' visits—I realize narrative has saved me. Some have suggested that psychoanalysis failed to thrive because the needs it was designed for—community, confrontation of past, emotion, even story-telling—are no longer considered necessary or important in our own time.[14] Yet isn't this a part of humanity? Connection, history, the need to write ourselves?

Writers seeking to share their illness are burdened by the attitudes that dominate contemporary thinking about mental illness. I must reconcile my experience with what society has told me, try to portray my stories and experiences as "sane" when I have been diagnosed otherwise. You, reader, want to see me cured, want to know I am writing from beyond those frantic moments, writing from a place where I have reconciled this, where I have found a way to live through this.

To tell you the story of my mental illness honestly would be to put it on the page as I see it in my mind. To tell you this story accurately would be to leave you wondering how you got here, to leave you with moments or entire years gone, memory erased by the trauma of long-term anxiety. To tell you this story truthfully would be to rely on silence, long pauses, white space. To write this story would be to leave words out of sentences entirely, to render through syntax the times I've tried to speak but nerves or adrenaline have left me stuttering. Short, choppy sentences to demonstrate how it felt. How disrupted. Fragmented. To write this story would require a narrator that is unreliable, that shape-shifts and changes, and sometimes becomes the antagonist. To write this narrative as it actually happened means that the narrative must falter, must be ambiguous. It must even confuse.

Modern medicine demands we find some way to cure this narrative. Society requires resolution. The reader wants closure. And so my narrative, too, if it is to satisfy, demands I find a way to write this linearly, to tell you, reader, how it started, to tell you about my diagnosis and the course of my treatment, and to leave you hopeful. If therapy appears to have resolved everything, it is only because I have constructed it that way. Though I feel better most of the time, I don't feel better all of the time—and while my illness has been painful and confusing, I would not cure it away. Many narratives of mental illness privilege prescription over patient, cure the ultimate success—but no, my narrative can't, my narrative won't do that.

I spent my last session with Gail watching the clock, waiting for resolution or finality. I tried to appear hopeful and hardworking because I didn't want to worry Gail or myself. "I know you'll be fine. You've learned a lot," Gail said as our time together drew to a close, her face stoic as always. "But I'll think about you," she added. "I'll wonder how you're doing."

As I stood to leave, feeling all the sadness in the world, Gail held out her arms to me. In all our years together, we'd never touched, never come close, her support always offered from a professional distance. But in this moment she knew what I needed.

This is what I carry most from my time with Gail. A single hug, a brief, passing moment, but one that resonates with me still, reminds me when I am frightened or alone that I am worthy of care and nurturing. I wish these things for Brady on the days when he slips into sadness. I wish them for students who twist and turn and sometimes cry in my office. For the thousands in online forums, isolated and despairing.

After Gail retired, I spent months feeling lost. Anxiety overwhelmed me. Then the sadness faded. And so did the anxiety. I miss Gail, but I don't need her. I've tucked away all sorts of strategies and sayings. Even when I am anxious, I feel purposeful as I make my way through the world. For the first time in a long time, I know that everything will be all right.

People who find out about my disorders are often surprised. Several years after coming to Nebraska, a colleague came across an essay I'd published about my anxiety. Sitting with other coworkers at dinner one night, he leaned across the table and said with an astonished laugh, "You seem so normal. I never would have known." He repeated this several other times—in the hallways, a department banquet—always amazed at how "together" I was, as though I should be a cowering mass. Over time, my concern over what others think about my illness has lessened. I do not worry what will happen if future employers find out, or what those who know me, but nothing of my illness, might think when they read this book. Where I was once concerned with hiding my illness from people, now I find that the line between illness and identity blurs. I quite like the ambiguity.

I have been told I am crazy, been warned against myself, for a growing portion of my life, yet what for others defines me as abnormal are the qualities I value most. I would not be without anxiety, without OCD, without PTSD because they have changed the way I see the world. I feel, I think, I am, richer, fuller, and more human because of them. I have been created by my illnesses, but at the same time illness has made me a creator. I have become a storyteller because of my illnesses, have stories to tell because of them, and there is something good and beautiful in that.

Once, when I lived in Nebraska, severe weather passed over the Plains, several states on tornado watch for nearly twenty-four hours. When I dressed for the day, I threw on jeans and a T-shirt emblazoned with the university logo. Immediately I realized that by wearing the shirt, with the state's name so clearly written, I had tempted fate and thus the storm to come my way. When a tornado came, my clothing selection would be to blame. I thought briefly of wearing something else, but it was too late, one arm was already in the sleeve and to take the shirt off would not only be ridiculously too late, but might actually incite the fates further.

I must have looked entirely foolish, standing partly topless in my bedroom, one arm in, one arm out of my shirt in some strange dance, my cats staring up at me. But instead of thinking their stare was God frowning at me, warning me to stop playing around because tornadoes are serious, because the Moore, Oklahoma, tornado had occurred the day before, because dammit wearing a shirt with a state's name brazenly across the chest was too much, I laughed. I thought—as I've learned to do—*This is anxiety, this is you, this is fine, this is funny.* And then I put on the shirt and went about my day—worrying only slightly.

The point is this: the anxiety might not change, but the way I view it can. I still have stress and worry that lead to strange visions of death and decay, but everyone has these, the stress and worry, at least. I can shame and blame myself for not getting these thoughts "under control," or I can accept that my brain does this, that I respond to real stresses and worries in a more imaginative and visceral way. I no longer lust for a life without mental illness—I think it would be rather dull. After being told for so long that there is something wrong with me, that I shouldn't see certain things or think certain ways, I've come to realize that there are days I will look out the window and barely notice the clouds, and there will be days when I'll look out the window and be moved to tears by the clouds, and there will be some days when I'll look out the window and see pictures and messages in the clouds, something that was acceptable when I was a child, but somehow becomes madness when I am an adult.

My anxiety appears most when I am silenced. It vocalizes my anger and frustration for me. By forcing me to slow down enough to care for myself, it reminds me to be kind to myself when the world is not. My OCD provides me control in a world that does not like women to have power. My PTSD is a reminder that I must tell the stories of what has happened to me and share the stories—an entire history—of women made mad. Our illnesses, our stories, will not be ignored.

Family, friends, physicians insisted I look forward. Don't dwell in the past, they maintained, ushering me from room to room, specialist to specialist, drug to drug, always moving forward. Don't question, don't doubt. Don't allow madness to take over reason—you've seen how that fire consumes. Don't look back at the burning city.

When the friar William of Ockham sat with me, he revealed there were too many assumptions. Assumptions are those things we take for granted to be true without proof or questioning.

All women are a little crazy. Assumptions can mean arrogance. *Don't question our authority.* Assumption can even mean taking possession of or power from. *It's your fault.* Yes, there were too many assumptions.

But assumption can also be an act of acceptance. So accept this: I am Lot's wife, white gown, dark hair. Everyone around me commands silence, commands I keep faith, follow instruction. The city is burning behind me, bright and hot against my back, flames licking at my heels, yet no one wants to discover what began the blaze.

Looking back, turning to the past to understand the present, is at the heart of therapy, which asks people to examine their cities in relationship to themselves. Talk therapy asks we look back to learn from the flame, or further back still, to before the fire.

The truth: I turn around. And after I transform, I am glittering.

CHAPTER 22

IS SATISFIED ENOUGH?

*I*n my final year under her care, Terry presented me with two options. The first was a new medication, even though I'd long since accepted Buspirone and therapy. "You could be better than fine, better than good," Terry insisted. When I shrugged, repeating that I was satisfied, she asked, "Is satisfied enough?"

Terry's insistence is indicative of the way we've pathologized human emotion and behavior, narrowed our definition of normal. While diagnosis frees us from blame with scientific, medical proof that we have a "real" illness, it has also become the tool we use to try and achieve perfection, when perhaps it is our own outrageous expectations and desire for control we should be examining. We pathologize what is normal, narrowing our definition of acceptable behavior and collecting lists of symptoms so that soon most behavior can be seen as symptomatic.

We need only look at the history of the *DSM* to see where our interrogation of "normal" began. Published in 1952, the first *DSM* was slim in size and created in a single year. Its popularity—along with inaccuracies—led to a revision, and the

DSM-II, a 150-page spiral-bound notebook, priced at $3.50, was published in 1968. As with the first volume, this popular edition contained inaccuracies, and revisions began quickly, including more types of mental illnesses, along with more inclusive lists of symptoms. When the *DSM-III* was published in February of 1980, it was a staggering 500 pages, and sold for more than ten times the price of its predecessor. The *DSM-III-R* (not to be confused with the *DSM-IV*, which was already scheduled for publication) was published in May of 1987 and followed the inclination towards expansion—it contained hundreds of changes to illnesses and symptoms, added dozens of new ones, and reached nearly 900 pages. Published in May of 1994, the *DSM-III-R* brought in $18 million in the first ten months. The *DSM-IV* appeared in 2000, shortly followed by the *DSM-IV-TR* revision.[15]

The latest edition, the *DSM-V*, published in May of 2013, is even more expansive. At a cost of over $100, the text reaches nearly 1,000 pages and adds new illnesses like disruptive mood dysregulation disorder (which many argue is a way to diagnose childhood temper tantrums), cannabis withdrawal, caffeine withdrawal, binge eating disorder, and central sleep apnea. The text also revises previously included illnesses to suggest increased medication as treatment. Bereavement-associated depression following the loss of a loved one, for example, was included in previous *DSMs*, but earlier editions warned against diagnosing mourners for at least eight weeks following a death. The *DSM-V* suggests mourners be prescribed antidepressants after as little as two weeks. Many worry the *DSM-V*'s altered timelines will further increase the reliance on pharmaceutical treatments, and that the creation of new diseases "treatable" by previously existing drugs are opportunity for drug companies to profit, for in order to be reimbursed for insurance claims, mental health professionals must list both the psychiatric diagnostic label and the appropriate code number found in the *DSM*.[16]

While various editions of the *DSM* have succeeded in providing a language for health care professionals to speak about mental illness, they have also widened the net of mental illness, capturing many decidedly human behaviors as symptoms—the *DSM* lists frustration and anger, difficulty concentrating and restlessness, increased appetite or weight gain, losing one's temper, being easily fatigued, muscle tension, being arrogant, or lacking empathy as symptoms of various mental illnesses. Countless studies have shown that those without disorders still meet the criteria, yet reliance on the manual persists.[17] A series of studies conducted in the early 1970s by Stanford University psychology professor David Rosenhan revealed the difficulty of diagnosing mental illness using these criteria. In one study, he and several "normal" people went to various mental hospitals describing fake symptoms, and were quickly admitted. Once admitted, they began acting as they normally did, but were still considered mentally ill, receiving over 2,000 pills, though other patients saw that the imposters really were sane. In another study, Rosenhan warned hospitals he would be sending imposters to try to gain entry, and after dozens were accused of faking illnesses, he revealed there were no imposters at all. Another study found that 80 percent of the schizophrenic patients admitted to a Manhattan hospital never exhibited the symptoms necessary to support the diagnosis. A final study found that 69 percent of American psychiatrists diagnosed someone as schizophrenic versus only 2 percent of British psychiatrists.[18]

Though the *DSM* presents a scientific, didactic tone, each edition revises existing diagnostic categories as mental illnesses like "homosexuality" go in and out of fashion (this was not removed until 1987). The descriptions and criteria for anxiety-based mental disorders have been changed three times since they were added the *DSM* in 1979, though early editions conducted no new studies despite changing and adding diagnostic categories.[19] Until 1980—nearly 140 years after the American Psychiatric Association (APA) was founded and twenty-eight years after the *DSM* was first published—the *DSM* provided no formal definition of what constitutes a mental disorder.[20] Michael First, one of the developers of the *DSM-IV*, explained that the *DSM* "provides a nice, neat way of feeling you have control over mental disorders," even though this control is "an illusion."[21] This is why a few weeks before the 2013 publication of the *DSM-V*, the National Institute of Mental Health announced its plan to move away from the manual, Thomas Insel, the director of NIMH explaining:

> The strength of each of the editions of *DSM* has been "reliability"—each edition has ensured that clinicians use the same terms in the same ways. The weakness is its lack of validity. . . . Indeed, symptom-based diagnosis, once common in other areas of medicine, has been largely replaced in the past half century as we have understood that symptoms alone rarely indicate the best choice of treatment.[22]

Recently, control has shifted to the public—the APA's website for the *DSM* now provides a suggestion box for anyone to provide feedback, submitting suggestions about existing disorders or new ones, as though we are all a part of the diagnostic process. Like the comments sections of online news outlets, where people with no knowledge or expertise are granted equal access to a public forum and public influence, the *DSM* is now open to suggestions. Now anyone can judge and categorize human behavior, shaping our understanding of "normal" and determining what is acceptable by popular demand.

"What do you think?" Terry finished, holding her prescription pad in her hand. "Would you like to try and improve?"

In the decade since my anxiety diagnosis, many of my siblings' mental health has worsened. While not related by blood, our family seems to be connected by madness.

Some years ago Natalie began experiencing anxiety much like my own. It started as panic attacks, Natalie calling me on the phone while she gasped for breath and pleaded for help. The calls grew more frequent as other symptoms developed, trembling and stomachaches, migraines and palpitations. Along with blood, Natalie and I share similar physical features and tastes—no matter how much time has passed, it is inevitable that when I step off a plane she will greet me, hunched over in an identical outfit and haircut, and order the same thing at lunch. It makes sense we share the same fears, our brains and bodies react the same. It is both reassuring—I'm not the only one—and heartbreaking. I wonder if her anxiety is self-fulfilling prophecy, for we've spent our entire lives compared to each other. While we joke about the fact that she is a few years behind me when it comes to her growing love of red wine and stinky cheese, it is not so funny when it comes to madness.

My parents approach Natalie's anxiety much the same as mine, blaming hormones and the responsibility of being in her early twenties for her worsening mental health. They said it was the result of poor decision making when it came to jobs and apartments and boys. My father, who still doesn't believe in anxiety, blamed dramatics. My mother tried to distract with snacks and chirpy talk about our siblings. Eventually she ignored it altogether—when my sister calls, panicked, I also hear sorrow and anger in her voice. "I tried calling Mom," she cries. "But she was too busy to deal with me. She hung up." The air between my parents and my sister—who has become the responsible one now that I am so far away, called upon to fix each catastrophe—is heavy with the unacknowledged. "I'm sorry I let it happen, Sissy," Natalie apologized when she finally told me she was raped, something my parents kept hidden despite her increasing anxiety. "You tried to warn me."

For the past several years Natalie has dated a man who for a long time did not believe in mental illness, who held a beer in his hands and paternalistically declared, "There is no such thing as anxiety," blaming her vegetarianism, her low weight, her sensitivity when she began to panic. She complained too much, he said. She was too emotional. When she had a panic attack, he insisted it was not real. When Natalie got sick, her boyfriend said she should take vitamins. When fears clouded her vision, he brushed her aside. I don't know which was her heaviest burden—trying to live with her pain or trying to convince someone her pain exists. I imagined him a Victorian husband, leading his wife by the hand to S. Weir Mitchell. "I don't know what to do with her," he said, leaving her to the rest cure. I have not seen him in several years, but she says he's better now; the rest of the world is not. I imagine the doctors who blamed my tilted ovary. "Try some Midol." I imagine, even, the men in my family who've brushed aside their wives, their children's fear as preposterous. "I will not discuss it," my father says of therapy before turning in his chair to face the football game. I saw my sister stiffen when her boyfriend said these things, watched her worry over what he thought of her, bend under the weight of his expectation. In some lights, she looked like the stick figure in the bathroom where I hid so many years ago, the graffiti symbol for the female gender, a large circle atop a tiny cross. A heavy head weighing down a tiny body.

Our adopted siblings have experienced similar changes in their mental health. Though they had different environments during the first years of their lives, we've shared the same environment since, no doubt impacting the ways we respond to stress. Casey was prescribed various medications throughout middle and high school to target his inability to focus in class, his anger, his attitude—the objective changed every so often, though doctors' insistence Casey remain medicated did not. I was never quite sure what teachers and my parents believed was wrong with my brother, besides the fact that he was a brown boy in a white school and his jovial backtalk was considered aggressive rather than clever like that of the boys who tossed blond bowl cuts out of their faces. My brother's buzzed head, baggy jeans, and growing build made him a perceived threat, and no one had patience for a boy who struggled to read, to add, to write his name small enough to fit the dotted lines.

Physicians changed Casey's medications frequently, and my busy parents forgot to pick up refills or check that he was consistently taking the medication. "We were good for a few months, but not the last few weeks," my mother would report. Casey took a dozen antidepressants, antianxiety medications, and ADHD medications over the course of five or six years, growing detached and sullen. "He's increasingly angry," reported teachers. When I came home I watched Casey protest the medications, which made him gain thirty pounds in six months, his former athleticism replaced by an awkwardness that showed in every movement. "They make me feel crazy," he sobbed. "There's nothing wrong with me." Crying was not okay for sixteen-year-old boys, so my mother scolded him and my father shouted. More than once they cornered him as he tried to storm out of the house, forcing him to swallow whatever medication he was taking at the time before letting him free. Casey and my parents fought the last years he lived at home, first about medications and doctors' appointments, then about school and his failing grades, eventually about everything from the way he slept and spoke to the chains he wore around his neck, one with a jeweled cross inspired by the church Casey dutifully attended, but too flashy, too "urban," apparently, for his high school's taste.

My brother did not graduate. He struggled in public high school, teachers and the principal calling nearly every day because he smirked, talked to girls during history, tried to speak Spanish, and walked too jauntily, like "gang culture," teachers said pointedly. He was pretending to be stupid, they insisted, but my brother can still barely read. When the school threatened to send him to continuation school, my parents enrolled Casey in online high school. At first, it was meant to be a second chance, but eventually it became a punishment. He spent long hours alone on the computer, which was old and unreliable, the Internet frequently failing. He was in trouble most of the time and my parents called him away from his studies to help with the daycare, make lunches, take out the garbage, fold laundry, to mow the lawn as punishment. The online program required parental guidance, but my mother often forgot. When it became clear my brother would not graduate high school, she swore she'd complete his work but never managed. My father said Casey could not live at home if he did not graduate. My parents and Casey barely spoke the last six months he lived at home, passing each other like strangers. Casey moved out after his eighteenth birthday.

Casey is much like my father—he does not speak of what goes on inside, ignores the emotional world for the physical one—so he threw himself into construction work, using the body as a means to escape the brain. I watched him grow quiet, retreating into himself, a shadow of the vibrant boy I once knew, the mischievous glint in his eyes replaced by a look of worry and distraction. When he visited, he was uncomfortable and out of place, wandering from room to room, unable to hold a conversation with my parents or siblings. Often he sat in silence, shifting in his chair, chewing his nails. He looked like I felt at home. When he spoke, he winced, looking out of the corners of his eyes for judgment, a distracting wisecrack or joke ready at the tip of his tongue. He referred to himself as a dropout, mimicking the language my parents used, his teachers used, the rest of the world used. I could see myself in those moments, making jokes about my anxiety.

Much of Casey's behavior seemed performance, a young man acting out what the world expects of him. I want to know why the world had so little patience or understanding for a boy who had difficulties in school when they knew his mother used drugs during much of her pregnancy. Why they faulted him for the anger and not his childhood abuse, for how else should a child feel when his mother beats him, fails to feed him, leaves him and his twin in front of a social services office, but keeps her other children? Why they pathologized the frustration he felt over being labeled wrong, dangerous, stupid, eventually even his sadness when he sobbed alone at night, his wails audible over a thumping bass line.

Casey rarely returns. He does not come home for holidays or vacations, though he recently announced he will be a father and has minimally resurfaced. Still, we do not know his phone number or where he lives. He is like a ghost. I haven't talked to my brother in several years, but I like to imagine his distance is a kind of protection like the one I've made for myself. I like to think he's satisfied.

His twin, Candy, spent much of high school sullen and anxious. The last sister living at home, many of the domestic burdens—cleaning, cooking, watching after Cameron and Bailey—fell to her, and she accused my parents of adopting her for slave labor, insisting she would have been better off if her birth mother, dead from a seizure most likely linked to overdose, had kept her. She withdrew, stiffening at anyone's touch. She would not join us for family events. She would not answer my calls or texts and barely talked to me when I visited. "When I graduate, I'm going to leave," she used to say pensively, as though she couldn't wait to get away. "I can't wait to find my real family." For a time she carried around a photo album from her first foster family, the one she lived with for a period of months. "I could have stayed with them if you hadn't taken me away," she'd say wistfully. "I bet they miss me." We kept hidden the fact that the foster family had willingly returned the twins to social services, had run into my mother and I once but declined our phone number.

During her last year of high school, Candy located her biological brothers, who were my age and lived a few towns over. They knew she lived locally, but had never looked her up. She arranged a meet-up and my mother emailed me photos of the reunited family standing in our backyard. Candy beamed. A few months later, her brothers stood her up at her eighteenth birthday party, then again at her high school graduation. Eventually, she stopped calling and started to have panic attacks. The first few were visible, her gasping for breath in the middle of a crowded family vacation, but eventually, she kept them to herself.

Candy recently had a baby. She lives with my parents, who do not want her to move out and take this newest child away. Candy is the happiest she has ever been, holding her daughter—her family—close to her heart. She is open, free, content. She feels, finally, as though she has a purpose, claiming—much like our mother and father—her role and identity as a parent. She is a wonderful mother. I hope her daughter finds the world so many women have been denied.

Cameron and Bailey seem to be following in Casey's footsteps, or at least that's what teachers, physicians, and my parents say as the boys struggle with school, authority, the pressure of so much scrutiny. They, too, have taken a dozen medications each for ADHD, OCD, Tourette's. Diagnosed with ADHD and OCD as a young child, Bailey took several medications to treat the symptoms, nothing seemed to change his penchant for arguing, his desire to be correct. Bailey has always had difficulty talking to others, for he constantly corrects those he speaks with, delights in pointing out the mistakes of others, cannot move forward in conversation or activity if a detail is not to his liking. And when he is confronted about his argumentative tone or forced to move on despite something he does not agree with, he resorts to sarcasm, muttering cruel threats under his breath, calling others stupid or threatening to break things because he is so frustrated. He often cries to end arguments.

Much of my brother's behavior could be explained by examining his position as the youngest child in a ragtag group, the child least likely to have a leadership role, least likely to be heard or acknowledged. Much of his behavior might be childhood obstinacy. This is not to say that my brother does not face real difficulties—I see the strain in his movements, the anxiety and pain when others do not understand his perspective—but not everything he does is symptomatic. Still, our parents, Bailey's teachers and physicians, insist every utterance and decision stems from the obsessive compulsive area of his brain.

Bailey was nine when he began taking Zoloft.

The doctor recommended a low dose—the same dose I took at twice his size. I reminded my mother of this, trying not to sound accusatory. My mother doesn't agree when I try to explain that being part of the working poor doesn't mean my family doesn't have the right to health care, to honest physicians, and effective treatment. There is a growing divide between us, my parents on one side, not quite understanding their crazy daughter, who grows more liberal with each degree, who critiques the medical industry, when she will only ever be a doctor of letters.

"What's going to happen to him?" my mother asked, remembering me shouting at Natalie, punching Brady when I was so angry. She remembered my sobbing over the phone, her so far away and powerless. I admitted I didn't know. All I knew is what happened to me, and I am biased and burdened because of this. I told her about the worms, about the anger, about the anorgasmia, about feeling out of control. I told her it was the worst time of my life.

I urged my mother to take Bailey to therapy so he could talk, something he rarely did, clamping his mouth shut, staring wide, refusing to tell anyone how he felt, instead muttering under his breath and hiding in his bedroom when he got frustrated, smashing his lamp or breaking his favorite toy. "He's the youngest, Mom," I said quietly. "He doesn't get a lot of one-on-one time, and lately he has been saying that no one likes him. Therapy could give him some ways to manage his feelings. Plus, it would be nice for him to have something all his own," I added, knowing that the younger boys didn't have hobbies or extracurricular activities through which to express themselves because the daycare kept my parents busy twelve hours a day. The boys helped out with the daycare after school, muttering a familiar phrase, "But it's my house."

"The doctor says we need to begin medication as soon as possible," my mother sighed. "He needs it." I pictured my mother, her out-of-date glasses taped together in the middle, the hair she never cuts because haircuts are expensive, her one pair of jeans and holey sneakers. Though my mother doesn't go to the doctor, the state provides her adopted children health care. She sits with her child in her lap and doctors say the child is broken. She will try anything to fix him.

I told my mother children on antidepressants can experience side effects like depression, apathy, mood swings, crying, anxiety, hostility, mania, paranoia, hallucinations, even increased obsessive-compulsive symptoms. Others include drowsiness, appetite loss, lethargy, insomnia, headaches, abdominal pain, motor abnormalities, facial and vocal tics, jaw clenching, skin problems, liver disorders, weight loss, growth suppression, hypertension, and sudden cardiac death.[23] I told her the United States overprescribes to children—the year Prozac came to the market, one in 250 children under nineteen years old in the United States took an antidepressant, but between 1988 and 1994 the percentage of children who were medicated tripled, and by 2000, one in every forty children under nineteen years of age in the United States was taking an antidepressant.[24] I told her this is not as common in other parts of the world—in 2007, the Centers for Disease Control reported that one in every twenty-three American children ages four to seventeen years old is medicated for mental illnesses, and children in the United States consume three times the quantity of stimulants consumed by the rest of the world's children combined.[25] I reminded her the number of mentally ill children has increased thirty-five-fold in the last twenty years.[26]

Above all, I remind her that Bailey's early childhood was full of bruises and broken bones, shouting and sexual abuse. He was homeless, without food at two. It is no wonder he experiences anxiety, desires control, feels misunderstood.

After six months on Zoloft, Bailey became a shadow. "He's withdrawn," my mother whispered over the phone. "He's distracted and anxious. He hasn't gotten better."

One day, Bailey threatened to kill a classmate. He was incredulous when he got in trouble—the classmate was teasing him, after all. As punishment, Bailey was suspended for several days, then had to sit in the principal's office for several more, missing a school trip. His punishment lasted weeks, school officials trying to shame him into remorse. My parents were called to a meeting where no one questioned Zoloft. They suggested therapy. My parents refused.

The final solution? Adding another medication. Bailey's doctor began augmenting his treatment with other drugs until he became so unlike himself my mother switched doctors entirely. The new doctor weaned Bailey off of everything and began the process again. They are still searching. My parents do what they think is best; still, from the outside it seems easier to medicate children than to listen to them.

Cameron, too, has tried several medications in the last few years. He was expelled last year for participating in a fight club at his high school, a dozen boys beating the shit out of one another because they like the way causing pain makes them feel alive, like the rush that comes from making someone hurt. "I'm raping this game," Cameron says with pride when he plays video games. He now attends the same online high school as Casey, using the same out-of-date computer, interrupted by chores, daycare children, and Candy's crying infant. It is only his first year of high school, but it already appears as though he won't graduate. Recently my parents caught him sneaking his girlfriend in the house to spend the night and have grounded him for the summer. On his fifteenth birthday, he rose early to join my parents in the living room before the daycare children began to arrive. "Why are you up?" they asked, forgetting the date.

I don't fault my parents. They have devoted themselves to a lifetime of service, to the notion that being a parent is the most powerful identity someone can claim. They have done this because they, too, were punished and ignored. They also feel unloved. I wish my father, my mother could know love from their abusive, absent parents, the same love they have been trying to provide to others all these years. I miss them often, long for them in a way that aches, and I believe this is how they must have felt their entire lives.

My parents take the antidepressants they've swallowed for much of my life, and they have begun, in the last few years, drinking heavily, but I don't think they are satisfied. Their children who have moved out rarely return home, while those who live in the house rarely speak to them. Nor do we eight siblings speak to one another much, though when we do there is an urgency, a grasping at one another for connection and care. When we gather, we sit close, piled on the couch or one another's laps, awkwardly hugging at first, clutching each other after a few days, staying up long into the night because we fear there is not enough time, juggling our schedules so we might all be together, a strange dream because we were never raised under the same roof at the same time. We are desperate for one another in a way that is needy, hungry, but only recently have some of us felt brave enough to say, "I love you." I hunger for Natalie, for Candy and Casey, those siblings I grew up with and without whom I feel incomplete. I regret that I did not get the chance to know Cameron and Bailey this way. I long to know my brother Dale, who seems so like me in so many ways, yet who left, as did I, when the family soil began shifting beneath him too quickly. I long, too, to know Victoria, who is thriving and kind and full of hope, and who reaches across the country to tell me she misses me, a sister I am ashamed to admit I did not think possible, and am so happy will have me. I want to sit with my sisters—each of us fierce feminists with sharp tongues and tempers, who will not tolerate a world telling us our gender is deficient—and marvel at our power. My siblings are fast and funny, sweet and so different than their adoption records would have the world believe, yet it is hard to escape a narrative that has been written for you—perhaps this is the reason we remain so isolated. Our visits are short-lived and far between; months, then years go by without contact. The narrative of family togetherness my parents tried to craft for so long is now the story of a fractured family. Nurture or nature, the debate goes.

Terry's second suggestion was to wean myself off Buspirone. "What's the harm in trying?" she asked.

Doctors had long positioned my mental illnesses as chronic, so I was unsure why this option was presented. (While United States citizens with mental illnesses have access to health care and other advantages of developed nations, their recovery rates are lower than those of people living in developing nations. The World Health Organization [WHO] found that in the past twenty-five years, outcomes for people in the United States with mental illness have steadily worsened, now no better than they were in the first decades of the twentieth century.[27] Living in a developed nation was a "strong predictor" that patients would never fully recover, the only link between the developing nations in the study being that doctors did not prescribe large doses of medication, or keep patients on them for long amounts of time. Their patients recovered with the help of family and community ties.)[28] Terry never reconciled her suggestion with earlier discussions about my serotonin levels. Had my serotonin levels suddenly been restored? Wouldn't they change once I quit medication? Or had I learned to live peacefully enough that I could manage alone?

In *The Noonday Demon,* his remarkable book on depression, Andrew Solomon writes, "It is fashionable at the moment to explore the ways the pharmaceutical industry is one that takes advantage of the sick. My experience has been that the people in the industry are both capitalists and idealists—people keen on profit but also optimistic that their work may benefit the world."[29] Despite my frustration with my experience and the history of exploitation of the mentally ill, it is not individuals who are insidious. It is difficult to write about pharmaceutical companies without bias. I am biased because the drugs I take are part of a tradition of drugs whose manufacturers have profited at the expense of others. I am biased because I have looked with hope towards things that made me sick. It is hard to write without bias towards a medical industry that has been the culprit when society insisted my faulty brain was to blame.

At the same time, however, it is difficult to write without bias towards drugs that in many ways have aided me. I have been eased from the darkest corners of my mind, if not by the medications themselves then by the promise and hope they offered. I have been relieved of uncertainty through diagnosis and the act of filling a prescription. It is difficult to write without bias towards drugs that have freed me of many of the symptoms associated with my illness.

I don't mind when anxiety, PTSD, and OCD return because I have reframed the way I look at my disorders—my story is not one of brief illness and recovery, not one of doctor wisdom and patient success. Medicine is an act of storytelling, diagnosis the ultimate narrative—naming something and thereby creating it. As with any narrative, certain stories are privileged, others silenced or rewritten. This narrative ends an argument I had no hopes to win—one of person versus diagnosis, patient versus prescription. This narrative is one that asks us to rethink mental illness and treatment. It asks us to reconsider the stories we tell about what constitutes madness, how we are able to live, how we are treated, and most important, how we feel about ourselves.

Much of the trouble, it seems, comes from the way we oversimplify things into categories, distill them down until we can easily digest them. Binaries between sane and insane have long existed, binaries which invalidate the lived experiences of those suffering and allow others to rewrite and dominate. Our current health care system creates new categories, however, when it medicalizes the body in ways that remove agency from the ill (perhaps also the well and "normal") and even from physicians. Patients have long turned to physicians for answers concerning their health, thereby putting their bodies and experiences in someone else's control, but the advent of pharmaceuticals removes control from physicians too, turning it over to corporations selective about revealing information. As frustrated as I was with my health care, my doctors were not at fault. More frightening is the way even corporations have little control, the real source of power left to chemical components, those cures contained in plastic-coated capsules FDA policies deem "safe" and "effective."

With so many medications with the power to alter nature, the very stuff of humanity, the definition of health in U.S. society is changing. We demand to be healthy and insist we have the right to health, when the body is in constant flux. Health, like illness, is somewhat of a construct. Overmedicalizing means we diagnose and treat even the most natural and mundane of bodily responses. We seek cures for aches and ailments previously considered expected parts of life, label things disorders at an alarming rate. We value physicians and prescriptions and blame patients for their performances and recovery, judging their choices and actions rather than examining our distorted views of what it means to be healthy and our unrealistic expectations about the power of medicine. The danger in this, of course, is that we are constantly seeking perfection, and we interrogate our bodies and minds so frequently that we become strangers to ourselves.

This is not to say I didn't and don't require medication for my anxiety disorder, or that all medication is dangerous or unnecessary. I remain on medication and bristle when people suggest taking medication is a weakness. What I mean, rather, is that knowing the body and the mind requires faith in both. When patients and doctors invalidate patient knowledge or experience, there is loss. Had I valued my experience more, not doubted what I knew to be true, had my friends and family not insisted my lived experience was determined by my diagnosis, not redefined me by my illness, and had my physicians validated the stories I came in to their offices to share, not silenced some away, rewritten and revised others in the form of medical charts, sucked the very marrow from them, perhaps this narrative would be different.

Sometimes people, surprised to find I still take medication three times a day, ask, "You're doing so well—why don't you quit?" Brady, who continues to thrive in part because of the new medication he takes for his increasing episodes of mania, encourages me to go off of medication, though he will take drugs indefinitely. I used to consider this option. Perhaps one day I will consider it again. I realize there are contradictions in this choice, in this narrative. I like this agency. Much of my understanding of my illness and myself has been about contradiction. Above all, about acceptance.

In the meantime, I am less critical of my thoughts and emotions. I still have panic attacks, but I am able to prevent them from reaching full force with breathing techniques and I do not blame myself when they occur. I take care of my body with good food and exercise and sleep and the occasional massage. I try to avoid caffeine and alcohol, but I don't deprive myself. I guard my time against pushy people, undesirable social or work events, my own need for perfection. I allow myself to be angry when the world demonstrates how little it respects women. I do not force myself to smile. I protect my heart by limiting who has access to it and loving fully—my husband, my friends, my imperfect family, pleasing words and spaces, solitude, forgiveness.

Tonight I lie in bed with Brady, resting my hand on his chest, his heart in my palm. I relish this time together, secure under the weight of our blankets, our two cats curled around us. In the dark, shadows play across my vision like sparks and smoke. It could be madness; it could be stars reflecting off the water outside. Soft colors swirl together, ethereal and unreal. I swoon, beauty making me breathless.

EPILOGUE

On October 9, 2016, my mother, Natalie, and I curled ourselves onto my couch to watch the second presidential debate between Hillary Clinton and Donald Trump. We hadn't seen one another in several years, and the opportunity to sit together and watch the woman we knew would be our next president stand her ground against a man who had nothing but contempt for women was something we did not take lightly. My mother delighted in how political her daughters had become, asking us questions and breathing a sigh of relief she was not with my father, who had referred to Clinton as "that bitch" since she made an off-the-cuff remark in the 1990s that she would not use her time as First Lady to bake cookies.

Now, in my living room, my mother, sister, and I toasted with the champagne we'd purchased for the occasion, two generations of women who had been told to be quiet, smile, and diet, looking to the television and the future, each of us loud and unapologetic as we cheered our hero and booed the man emblematic of our frustrations.

The political was personal. Two days prior we awoke to released audio of him saying, "I moved on her like a bitch. . . . You know, I'm automatically attracted to beautiful—I just start kissing them. It's like a magnet. Just kiss. I don't even wait. And when you're a star, they let you do it. You can do anything. . . . Grab 'em by the pussy. You can do anything." We did not speak of my rape, Natalie's rape, the rapes of my other sisters and other women in our family, but the importance of this debate, this election was palpable. The audio, we were certain, indicated Clinton's victory over a pompous, bombastic man spewing ignorance and hate, while she used decades of service and experience to navigate towards the inevitable.

In the opening moments, moderator Anderson Cooper said, "We received a lot of questions online, Mr. Trump, about the tape that was released on Friday, as you can imagine. You called what you said locker room banter. You described kissing women without consent, grabbing their genitals. That is sexual assault. You bragged that you have sexually assaulted women. Do you understand that?" And while the moment was unprecedented, as we would hear time and again during his tenure, the response was not. I'd heard it before, as had my sister, my mother, so many women who have been called "slut" and "bitch," who have been groped on dance floors, harassed at work, catcalled on the street.

"I don't think you understood what was—this was locker room talk. I'm not proud of it. I apologize to my family. I apologize to the American people. Certainly I'm not proud of it. But this is locker room talk . . . And we should get on to much more important things and much bigger things . . . I have great respect for women. Nobody has more respect for women than I do."

"You know I've done this before. To lots of girls," I remembered. "She wishes I would rape her," I heard. "Women wouldn't get raped so much if they would date nice guys," I heard. "I'm sorry I let it happen, Sissy," I remembered, Natalie beside me. "You tried to warn me."

We sat transfixed that evening, giddy and outraged as he interrupted and protested like a petulant child, threw insults and incorrect statements around with the casualty of a man who has been allowed to speak his whole life. I'd seen this man—loud, aggressive, and inarticulate—in my family, in my classroom, on the street. My father, uncles, and male family friends spend dull hours lecturing me about things I already know or correcting things I've said that they don't find agreeable. Male friends outside of academia give me their opinions on teaching and lecture me on the evils of feminism. Male students interrupt female classmates or dominate class discussions when it is clear they haven't done the reading. Yes, I'd seen this man my whole life.

More disturbing than his rhetoric, however, his stern face and wagging finger, was the way he stalked Clinton onstage, circling her like a predator. When Clinton walked to the edge of the stage to talk to audience members, he came close behind her, loomed like the men women fear on the streets late at night, the ones who grope us on crowded subway platforms, rub their hands across our breasts, then grab our wrists when we react. His movements implied violence rather than power—at one point, he gripped the back of a chair until his knuckles turned white. I knew that look, like there was something he wanted to strangle. He tightened his grip as she spoke, closed his eyes and leaned his pelvis in towards the chair, trying to fuck away his frustration.

As the debate wore on, he sprawled across the stage, taking up more and more space, extending his time, waving his hands and rolling his eyes when things did not suit him. On the couch, my mother, sister, and I sat hunched, legs crossed, taking up as little space as possible, holding our breaths and ourselves still while we watched. We waited to see if the country would allow us to spread out.

We valued Clinton not because she was a woman, but because she was articulate and firm, powerful and kind. Above all because she was imperfect, something we'd long been taught is unacceptable for women. We valued this moment because Clinton had endured the shame women have been taught to crumble beneath—constantly corrected, blamed for her husband's infidelity, criticized for her hair, her makeup, her clothing, told to smile more, to laugh less, accused of being too strong, too sickly, shamed for following ambition rather than accepting the docile role of grandmother. She was untrustworthy, the news reported. She was unstable. The fixation on her wrongness by way of her woman-ness—nasty woman—was familiar.

I taught an early class the morning after he won. Students, many who had voted for the first time, sat stunned. Several women emailed to say they were too sick to attend. "I'm sorry," they wrote. A male student turned to the women in his group, the students of color and apologized. "This is going to be hardest on you," he said. In the following days, hateful chalk messages proclaiming victory appeared on campus.

Men I thought friends gloated on social media. "We grabbed that voting ballot by the pussy," said one. "Women need to stop crying because we aren't going to pay for their abortions and birth control anymore," wrote another. "Crybaby bitches. Grow the fuck up." A third posted news stories: "Woman Creates False Rape Story Because She Was 'distraught over the election'" and "Hillary Sexually Assaulted Me." At home, Casey, who was targeted by the proposed border wall, said he would never vote for Clinton. My father forbid anyone from talking poorly about the new president, banning what he called "hysteria."

I took comfort in those who shared my outrage, but what began as solace quickly turned to accusation. "He's crazy," "What a whacko," "He's mentally ill and should be removed from office," rang out daily. That the nation was frightened, in danger, and full of animosity because of mental illness cut me to the core. Madness was not the same as privilege or prejudice, ignorance or narcissism, misogyny or xenophobia, or any of the hundred hatreds unsubstantiated diagnoses sought to symptomize. And though I saw the administration as a kind of lunacy, the armchair diagnosing made me sick. The campaign reminded me how much the world hates women, but the transition revealed how much the world hates the mentally ill.

That unanswered male privilege and aggression thwarted the professional desires of a highly qualified woman was echoed in the job search I undertook that fall and winter. I assumed academia free of many prejudices, but interviewing for various tenured positions around the country revealed that sexism and ableism—particularly for a woman presenting herself as a scholar of madness—run rampant. All but one of my interviews asked illegal questions like was I married, did I have children, did I want children? During one campus interview, a professor raised his hand to say that he had never heard of the "disability community" I spoke of and did not believe one existed. Later, when he took me to lunch, he chided me for not knowing the poets he had been classmates with forty years earlier, then invited me to taste his half-eaten burger, reaching his hand into my plate to take a portion of what was mine. A professor asked if I was a writer because it was cheaper than therapy. One asked if I was medicated. A graduate student asked how I could be a professor when I was mentally ill. "You're different than your writing sounds," said another student, laughing because I'd apparently seemed unhinged on the page. During an evening meal, a professor asked me to list all the medications I'd taken. "I couldn't live like that," he said as though my madness were some pitiable reason to quit living. "I took antidepressants for a few weeks after my divorce," his colleague admitted. "But I couldn't keep doing it." During a conference I attended later, I saw a member of one of the hiring committees at a bar. He pulled me close under the guise of hearing me better, and whispered, "I voted for you" into my neck, his hand at my waist.

Throughout the collective anxiety following the election, I tried to remind myself of my privilege. I was a cisgender, straight, white woman, whose disability is easily invisible. I knew little of the fear working-class people like my parents felt over potentially losing their health insurance, that Muslim students felt when their parents were unable to reenter the country, that LGBTQ students who came to my office to say that strangers had thrown beer bottles at them during their walks home felt, that female students who had been raped that semester—one losing her virginity to her rapist days before the election—felt over the fear of losing access to birth control, abortion, and mental health services. In a triggered nation, my madness became a kind of privilege—I had practice navigating anxiety, I could cope with the daily drama, the endless news cycle of catastrophe.

Still, my back knotted into oblivion. My shoulders grew gnarled and knots lined my spine. I had a permanent tension headache that no hot shower, ice pack, or drug could shake. I could feel the vertebrae bulging in my neck, one in my mid-back. I could see a muscle snaking around my neck. I could not exist comfortably in my body; I was in chronic pain. The year before, I'd been prescribed muscle relaxers to take when anxiety wrote itself like this on my body. I'd taken a few during particularly bad muscle spasms, but now my doctor and the massage therapist I saw once a month urged me to take one every night.

I did. Each day I drank cup after cup of tea to propel me through teaching and writing and the endless travel to different schools in different states, twisting my twisted body into a small plane seat and counting the seconds until I could step into the airport and stretch under televisions reporting the latest news disaster. Each night I swallowed a pill that sent me into a deep, emotionless sleep, waking dull the next morning to repeat the process. Because the drugs knocked me out for many hours and I taught in the morning and had to be prepared for long interview days, I took them early in the evenings, spending what little free time I had comatose, unable to lift my limbs from the couch, to think clearly, to speak. Day after day, I was a doll, a mannequin. Brady cooked each meal and rubbed my sore body while we watched the news report how the world had changed, even though for many it felt like the same old hate.

Months passed, my neck and back unchanged. I looked forward to the way drugs numbed the pain. I grew frightened that I would rather be asleep than awake. In the meantime, more students were raped, several could not finish the semester because of depression and anxiety, some cried in class, some had panic attacks, some brought notes from doctors and counselors.

Together, we witnessed a nation go mad because it would not accept a woman.

NOTES

NOTES TO PART I

1. Moore and Mattison, pages 274–75.
2. McLeod.
3. Page 10.
4. *PT* Staff.
5. Page 35.
6. Solomon, page 85.
7. Solomon, page 285.
8. Solomon, page 285.
9. Grohol.
10. Jurecic, page 21.
11. Page 4.
12. Page 4.
13. Page 4.
14. Page 132.
15. Page 91.
16. Page 30.
17. Dickinson, pages 323–24.

NOTES TO PART II

1. Grohol.
2. Herper.
3. Metzl, page 80.

4. All quotes from this paragraph and the paragraph above are from Simon.
5. Appignanesi, page 76.
6. Page 49.
7. All quotes from this paragraph are from Ehrenreich and English, pages 77–79.
8. Ehrenreich and English, page 52.
9. Stiles.
10. Gilman, page 96.
11. *Fat and Blood*, page 37.
12. *Fat and Blood*, page 43.
13. Whitaker, *Mad in America*, pages 97–99.
14. Whitaker, *Mad in America*, pages 97–99, 104–5.
15. Stossel, page 194.
16. Shorter, page 319.
17. Whitaker, *Anatomy*, pages 130–31; Stossel, page 194.
18. Porter, pages 205–6.
19. Shorter, page 317.
20. Page 3.
21. Bindley.
22. Scutti.
23. Pérez-Peña.
24. Weiss.
25. Solomon, page 60.
26. Stossel, page 209.
27. Shorter, page 23.
28. Mukherjee; Porter, page 206.
29. Shorter, page 319.
30. Shorter, page 324; Fitzpatrick.
31. Page xvi.
32. Braitmen.
33. MacMillan.
34. Solomon, page 57.
35. Whitaker, *Anatomy*, pages 72–73.
36. Watters, page 235.
37. Mukherjee.
38. Watters, page 234.
39. Whitaker, *Mad in America*, page 150.
40. Szaz, page 40.
41. Whitaker, *Mad in America*, page 149.
42. Whitaker, *Anatomy*, page 57.
43. Mukherjee.
44. Watters, pages 238–39.
45. Watters, page 170.
46. Grohol.

NOTES TO PART III

1. Waters.
2. Polk.
3. Waters.
4. Whitaker, *Mad in America*, page 188.
5. *The People of the State of Illinois v. David Hari.*
6. Waters.
7. Watters, page 238.
8. Whitaker, *Mad in America*, page 203.
9. Whitaker, *Mad in America*, page 143.
10. Shorter, page 253.
11. Whitaker, *Anatomy*, page 58.
12. Whitaker, *Mad in America*, page 146.
13. Shorter, page 255.
14. Whitaker, *Mad in America*, page 241.
15. Whitaker, *Anatomy*, page 94.
16. Whitaker, *Mad in America*, pages 206–7.
17. Whitaker, *Mad in America*, pages 206–8.
18. Whitaker, *Mad in America*, page 163.
19. Whitaker, *Anatomy*, page 49.
20. Whitaker, *Mad in America*, page 155.
21. Whitaker, *Mad in America*, page 155.
22. Whitaker, *Mad in America*, page 107.
23. Whitaker, *Anatomy*, pages 150, 157–58.
24. Whitaker, *Mad in America*, pages 181–82.
25. Testa.
26. Achenbach and Russakoff.
27. Boseley.
28. Waters; Hilts.
29. Porter, page 10; Whitaker, *Mad in America*, page 111.
30. Whitaker, *Mad in America*, page 117.
31. Whitaker, *Mad in America*, pages 121–24.
32. Whitaker, *Mad in America*, page 142.
33. Whitaker, *Mad in America*, page 132.
34. Tartakovsky.
35. Whitaker, *Mad in America*, pages 123–24.
36. Whitaker, *Mad in America*, page 127.
37. Kessler, page 243.
38. Whitaker, *Mad in America*, pages 135–36.
39. Whitaker, *Mad in America*, pages 135–36.
40. Tartakovsky.
41. Tartakovsky.
42. Whitaker, *Mad in America*, page 138.
43. Whitaker, *Mad in America*, page 68.

44. Whitaker, *Mad in America*, page 49.
45. All quotes from this paragraph are from Whitaker, *Mad in America*, pages 56–60.
46. Wolfe.
47. Nittle.
48. Whitaker, *Mad in America*, pages 63–65.
49. Wolfe.
50. Whitaker, *Mad in America*, page 142.
51. Johnson; Stern.
52. Solomon, page 65.
53. Solomon, page 5.

NOTES TO PART IV

1. Grohol.
2. Page 3.
3. Kinetz.
4. Whitaker, *Mad in America*, page 176.
5. Whitaker, *Mad in America*, pages 208–9.
6. Shorter, page 18.
7. Whitaker, *Mad in America*, page 27.
8. Whitaker, *Mad in America*, page 34.
9. Whitaker, *Mad in America*, page 29.
10. Whitaker, *Mad in America*, page 34.
11. Shorter, page 190.
12. Whitaker, *Mad in America*, page 84.
13. Shorter, page 280.
14. Shorter, page 146.
15. Kutchins and Kirk, pages 40–45.
16. Kutchins and Kirk, page 12.
17. Kutchins and Kirk, page 181.
18. Whitaker, *Mad in America*, pages 169–70.
19. Kutchins and Kirk, pages 46–47.
20. Kutchins and Kirk, page 29.
21. Kutchins and Kirk, page 260.
22. Insel.
23. Whitaker, *Anatomy*, page 28.
24. Whitaker, *Anatomy*, page 229.
25. Whitaker, *Anatomy*, page 220.
26. Whitaker, *Anatomy*, page 8.
27. Whitaker, *Anatomy*, pages xiii, xip.
28. Whitaker, *Anatomy*, page 220.
29. Page 13.

REFERENCES

Achenback, Joel and Dale Russakoff. "Teen Shooter's Life Paints Antisocial Portrait." *The Washington Post*, April 29, 1999. http://www.washingtonpost.com/wp-srv/national/daily/april99/antisocial04299.htm.

American Psychological Association. *Diagnostic and Statistical Manual of Mental Disorders.* 5th ed. American Psychological Association, 2013.

Appignanesi, Lisa. *Mad, Bad, and Sad: Women and the Mind Doctors.* W. W. Norton, 2008.

Bindley, Katherine. "Women and Prescription Drugs: One in Four Takes Mental Health Meds." *Huffington Post*, Nov. 16, 2011, http://www.huffingtonpost.com/2011/11/16/women-and-prescription-drug-use_n_1098023.html.

Boseley, Sarah. "Prozac Class Drug Blamed for Killing." *The Guardian*, May 25, 2001, https://www.theguardian.com/uk/2001/may/26/sarahboseley.

Braitmen, Laurel. "Do Our Pets Need Prozac? Are We Making Them Feel Better, or Ourselves?" *Salon*, June 21, 2014, http://www.salon.com/2014/06/21/do_our_pets_need_prozac_are_we_making_them_feel_better_or_ourselves/.

Dickinson, Emily. "Pain Has an Element of Blank." *The Complete Poems of Emily Dickinson*, edited by Thomas H. Johnson, Little, Brown and Company, 1960, pp. 323–24.

Ehrenreich, Barbara, and Deirdre English. *Complaints and Disorders: The Sexual Politics of Sickness.* 1973. The Feminist Press, 2011.

Fitzpatrick, Laura. "A Brief History of Antidepressants." *Time*, Jan. 7, 2010, http://content.time.com/time/health/article/0,8599,1952143,00.html.

Freud, Sigmund. *Inhibitions, Symptoms, and Anxiety.* Norton, 1990.

Gilman, Charlotte Perkins. *The Living of Charlotte Perkins Gilman: An Autobiography.* 1935. Arno Press, 1972.

Grohol, John M. "Top 25 Psychiatric Medication Prescriptions for 2009." *Psych Central,* https://psychcentral.com/lib/top-25-psychiatric-prescriptions-for-2009/.

———. "Top 25 Psychiatric Medication Prescriptions for 2011." *Psych Central,* https://psychcentral.com/lib/top-25-psychiatric-medication-prescriptions-for-2011/.

———. "Top 25 Psychiatric Medication Prescriptions for 2013." *Psych Central,* https://psychcentral.com/lib/top-25-psychiatric-medication-prescriptions-for-2013/.

Herper, Matthew. "America's Most Popular Mind Medicines." *Forbes,* Sep. 17, 2010, https://www.forbes.com/2010/09/16/prozac-xanax-valium-business-healthcare-psychiatric-drugs.html.

Hilts, Philip J. "Jury Awards $6.4 Million In Killings Tied to Drugs." *The New York Times,* June 8, 2001, http://www.nytimes.com/2001/06/08/us/jury-awards-6.4-million-in-killings-tied-to-drug.html.

Insel, Thomas. "Director's Blog: Transforming Diagnosis." National Institute of Mental Health, April 29, 2013, https://www.nimh.nih.gov/about/directors/thomas-insel/blog/2013/transforming-diagnosis.shtml.

Johnson, Corey G. "Female Inmates Sterilized in California Prisons Without Approval." The Center for Investigative Reporting, July 7, 2013, https://www.nbcbayarea.com/news/california/Female-Inmates-Sterilized-in-California-Prisons-Without-Approval-214634341.html.

Jurecic, Ann. *Illness as Narrative.* University of Pittsburg Press, 2012.

Kinetz, Erika. "Is Hysteria Real? Brain Images Say Yes." *The New York Times,* Sep. 26, 2006, http://www.nytimes.com/2006/09/26/science/26hysteria.html.

Kessler, Ronald. *Sins of the Father: Joseph P. Kennedy and the Dynasty He Founded.* St. Martin's Press, 1996.

Kramer, Peter D. *Listening to Prozac: A Psychiatrist Explores Antidepressant Drugs and the Remaking of the Self.* Penguin, 1993.

Kutchins, Herb, and Stuart Kirk. *Making Us Crazy: DSM: The Psychiatric Bible and the Creation of Mental Disorders.* The Free Press, 1997.

MacMillan, Amanda. "A Popular Hair Loss Drug Costs 40% More for Women Than Men." *Time,* Jun 9, 2017, http://time.com/4811985/rogaine-women-hair-loss-men/.

McLeod, Saul. "Attachment Theory." *Psychology Today,* 2009, https://www.simplypsychology.org/attachment.html.

Metzl, Jonathan M. "Selling Sanity Through Gender: The Psychodynamics Of Psychotropic Advertising." *Journal Of Medical Humanities* 24.1/2 (2003): 79–103.

Mitchell, Silas Weir. *Doctor and Patient.* 3rd ed., J. B. Lippincott, 1901, http://www.gutenberg.org/ebooks/15004.

———. *Fat and Blood and How to Make Them.* 6th ed. J. B. Lippincott, 1891, http://www.gutenberg.org/files/16230/16230-h/16230-h.htm.

Moore, Thomas J., and Donald R. Mattison. "Adult Utilization of Psychiatric Drugs and Differences by Sex, Age, and Race." *JAMA Internal Medicine* 177.2 (2017): 274–75. doi:10.1001/jamainternmed.2016.7507.

Mukherjee, Siddhartha. "Post-Prozac Nation: The Science and History of Treating Depression." *The New York Times,* April 19, 2012, http://www.nytimes.com/2012/04/22/magazine/the-science-and-history-of-treating-depression.html.

National Institute of Mental Health. National Institutes of Health, 2017, https://www.nimh.nih.gov/index.shtml.

Nittle, Nadra Kareem. "The U.S. Government's Role in Sterilizing Women of Color." *ThoughtCo,* Oct. 31, 2016, https://www.thoughtco.com/u-s-governments-role-sterilizing-women-of-color-2834600.

Pérez-Peña, Richard. "1 in 4 Women Experience Sex Assault on Campus." *The New York Times,* Sep. 21, 2015, https://www.nytimes.com/2015/09/22/us/a-third-of-college-women-experience-unwanted-sexual-contact-study-finds.html.

Plath, Sylvia. *The Bell Jar.* 1971. Harper Perennial, 1999.

Polk, Jim. "Kin Testify in Teen's Zoloft Defense Trial." *CNN,* Feb. 7, 2005, http://www.cnn.com/2005/LAW/02/07/zoloft.trial/.

Porter, Roy. *Madness: A Brief History.* Oxford University Press, 2002.

PT Staff. "Disorder of the Decade: What Happens When the Mere Thought of Talking to a Stranger is Terrifying?" *Psychology Today,* July 1, 1993, https://www.psychologytoday.com/articles/199307/disorder-the-decade.

The Rape, Abuse & Incest National Network. RAINN, 2017, https://www.rainn.org/.

Sacks, Oliver. *A Leg to Stand On.* Touchstone, 1984.

Scarry, Elaine. *The Body in Pain: The Making and Unmaking of the World.* 1985. Oxford University Press, 1987.

Scutti, Susan. "Suicide Rate Hit 40-Year Peak Among Older Teen Girls in 2015." *CNN,* Aug. 3, 2017, http://www.cnn.com/2017/08/03/health/teen-suicide-cdc-study-bn/index.html.

Shorter, Edward. *The History of Psychiatry: From the Era of the Asylum to the Age of Prozac.* Wiley, 1998.

Simon, Matt. "Fantastically Wrong: The Theory of the Wandering Womb That Drove Women to Madness." *Wired,* May 7, 2014, https://www.wired.com/2014/05/fantastically-wrong-wandering-womb/.

Slater, Lauren. *Prozac Diary.* Random House, 1998.

Solomon, Andrew. *The Noonday Demon: An Atlas of Depression.* Scribner, 2002.

Sontag, Susan. *Illness as Metaphor.* 1978. Farrar, Straus, Giroux, 1988.

Stern, Alexandra Minna. "That Time the United States Sterilized 60,000 of Its Citizens." *Huffington Post,* Jan. 7, 2016, http://www.huffingtonpost.com/entry/sterilization-united-states_us_568f35f2e4b0c8beacf68713.

Steslow, K. "Metaphors in Our Mouths: The Silencing of the Psychiatric Patient." *Hastings Center Report* 40.4 (2010): 30–33.

Stiles, Anne. "The Rest Cure, 1873–1925." *BRANCH: Britain, Representation and Nineteenth-Century History.* Ed. Dino Franco Felluga. Extension of *Romanticism and Victorianism on the Net,* http://www.branchcollective.org/?ps_articles=anne-stiles-the-rest-cure-1873-1925.

Stossel, Scott. *My Age of Anxiety: Fear, Hope, Dread, and the Search for Peace of Mind.* Knopf, 2014.

Styron, William. *Darkness Visible: A Memoir of Madness.* Random House, 1990.

Szaz, Thomas. *Pharmacracy: Medicine and Politics in America.* Praeger, 2001.

Tartakovsky, Margarita. "The Surprising History of the Lobotomy." *PsychCentral,* March 21, 2011, https://psychcentral.com/blog/archives/2011/03/21/the-surprising-history-of-the-lobotomy/.

Testa, Karen. "Man Convicted of Widow's Slaying Gets New Trial, Fashionable Defense." *Los Angeles Times,* Oct. 11, 1998, http://articles.latimes.com/1998/oct/11/news/mn-31350.

The People of the State of Illinois v. David Hari. Illinois Courts, 2002, http://www.illinoiscourts.gov/opinions/appellatecourt/2005/4thdistrict/january/html/4030130.htm.

Waters, Rob. "My Antidepressant Made Me Do It!" *Salon,* July 19, 1999, http://www.salon.com/1999/07/19/zoloft/.

———. "Prosecuting for Pharma." *Mother Jones*, Nov./Dec. 2004, http://www.motherjones.com/politics/2004/11/prosecuting-pharma/.

Watters, Ethan. *Crazy Like Us: The Globalization of the American Psyche.* Free Press, 2010.

Weiss, Audrey J., Marguerite L. Barrett, Kevin C. Heslin, and Carol Stocks. "Trends in Emergency Department Visits Involving Mental and Substance Use Disorders, 2006–2013." *Healthcare Cost and Utilization Project,* Dec. 2016, https://www.hcup-us.ahrq.gov/reports/statbriefs/sb216-Mental-Substance-Use-Disorder-ED-Visit-Trends.jsp?utm_source=AHRQ&utm_medium=EN1&utm_term=&utm_content=1&utm_campaign=AHRQ_EN1_10_2017.

Whitaker, Robert. *Anatomy of an Epidemic: Magic Bullets, Psychiatric Drugs, and the Astonishing Rise of Mental Illness in America.* Broadway, 2010.

———. *Mad in America: Bad Science, Bad Medicine, and the Enduring Mistreatment of the Mentally Ill.* Perseus Publishing, 2002.

Wolfe, Brendan. "*Buck v. Bell* (1927)." *Encyclopedia Virginia.* Virginia Foundation for the Humanities, Nov. 4, 2015, https://www.encyclopediavirginia.org/Buck_v_Bell_1927#start_entry.

MACHETE
Joy Castro, Series Editor

This series showcases fresh stories, innovative forms, and books that break new aesthetic ground in nonfiction—memoir, personal and lyric essay, literary journalism, cultural meditations, short shorts, hybrid essays, graphic pieces, and more—from authors whose writing has historically been marginalized, ignored, and passed over. The series is explicitly interested in not only ethnic and racial diversity, but also gender and sexual diversity, neurodiversity, physical diversity, religious diversity, cultural diversity, and diversity in all of its manifestations. The machete enables path-clearing; it hacks new trails and carves out new directions. The Machete series celebrates and shepherds unique new voices into publication, providing a platform for writers whose work intervenes in dangerous ways.

Quite Mad: An American Pharma Memoir
SARAH FAWN MONTGOMERY

Apocalypse, Darling
BARRIE JEAN BORICH

FRANCE

ON

BACKROADS

THE MOTORIST'S GUIDE TO THE FRENCH COUNTRYSIDE

THE MOTORIST'S GUIDE TO THE FRENCH COUNTRYSIDE

HUNTER
PUBLISHING, INC.

This revised and updated edition published 1997 by Hunter Publishing Inc.
300 Raritan Center Parkway,
Edison,
NJ 08818
Tel. (908) 225 1900
Fax (908) 417 0482

Conceived, edited and designed by Duncan Petersen Publishing Ltd.
54, Milson Road, London W14 0LB

© Duncan Petersen Publishing Ltd, 1986, 1993, 1997
© Tours text, individual contributors as listed 1986, 1993, 1997
© Maps, Institut Géographique National (French Official Survey)
authorization number 701036
107 rue la Boëtie. 75008 Paris

Printed and bound in Slovenia by DELO – Tiskarna d.o.o., Ljubljana
ISBN 1–55650–775–5

All rights reserved. No part of this publication may be reproduced, stored in
a retrieval system or transmitted in any form, or by any means, electronic,
mechanical, photocopying, recording or otherwise without prior consent of
the publishers and copyright owners.
  All routes described in this book are undertaken at the individual's own
risk. The publisher and copyright owners accept no responsibility for any
consequences arising out of use of this book, including misinterpretation of
the maps and directions.

■ Information on opening and closing times, and telephone numbers,
was correct at time of publication, but those who run hotels, restaurants
and tourist attractions are sometimes obliged to change times at short
notice. If your enjoyment of a day out is going to depend on seeing, or
eating at a certain place, it makes sense to check beforehand that you
will gain admission.

■ Many of the roads used for tours in this book are country lanes in the
true sense: they have zero visibility at corners, they are too narrow for
oncoming cars to pass, and they include hairpin bends and precarious
mountain roads with sheer drops. Please drive with due care and
attention, and at suitable speeds.

■ Many of the roads used for tours in this book are in upland areas.
During winter, they could be closed by snow. Consult a motoring
organization or local tourist office if in doubt.

The authors

Every kilometre of *France on Backroads* was not only planned, and written, but driven by a team of dedicated Francophile travel writers:

Ile de France, Alsace, the three Loire tours, and the Jura and Burgundy tours are by **Leslie and Adrian Gardiner.** Leslie Gardiner first visited France in a minesweeper and came to know the small harbours of the Channel and Biscay coasts intimately. Later, as a travel writer and correspondent of the *Guardian* and *The Times*, he undertook many motoring, walking and boating tours of the hinterland when writing about French life and leisure in his books on Western European travel and transport. His son Adrian has lived and worked in the Loire and Pyrenees regions and makes annual visits to other parts of the country.

Dordogne: Périgord Blanc, both the Auvergne tours, Gorges du Tarn, Northern Ardèche, both Pyrenees tours, The *Bastides* of Gascony, Lower Rhône and Provence are by **Peter Graham,** who has lived in France since 1962. He contributes articles on food, wine and travel to *The Sunday Times* magazine, the *Guardian* and *The International Herald Tribune.* He was a major contributor to the *American Express/Mitchell Beazley Pocket Guide to Paris* and wrote *The International Herald Tribune Guide to Business Travel and Entertainment.*

The Brittany and Normandy tours (except for Rouen and the Seine Valley) are by **Stephen Brough,** editorial director of the *Economist Business Traveller's Guides* and formerly Deputy Editor of *Holiday Which.*

Dordogne: Vineyards, Rivers and *Bastides*, Languedoc and Côte d'Azur are by **Fiona Duncan,** author, travel writer and editor of the *American Express/Mitchell Beazley Pocket Guides* to *Paris* and the *South of France.*

The two Alps tours are by **Christopher Gill,** formerly editor of *Holiday Which* and co-editor of *The Good Bath Guide.*

Normandy: Rouen and the Seine Valley is by **Anthony Abrahams,** Oxford doctor and childrens' author, and by **Joy Abrahams**; Eastern Picardy is by **John Farndon,** journalist and writer on an encyclopaedic range of subjects.

Contents

The tours are arranged in a north-south sequence, beginning in Picardy, north of Paris, and ending with the south-eastern corner of the Pyrenees. Where several tours fall within the same region, for example Normandy, Brittany, the Auvergne or the Dordogne, these are grouped together, even if it means deviating temporarily from the north-south sequence.

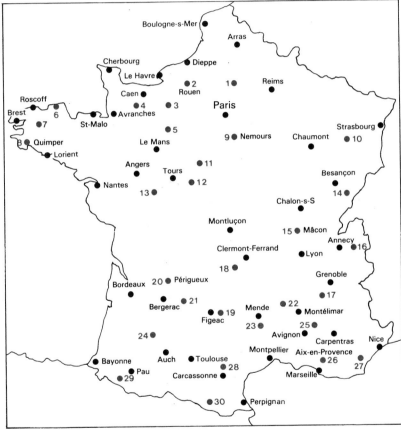

Contents

Touring with *France on Backroads*

Meandering on sleepy French country roads from restaurant to shady café, stopping here and there to take in a dignified château, a charming old village, or simply pausing to admire the view: for many, life has few greater pleasures, and this book is made for them. But it is also very much a book for those who have not yet discovered the unequalled delights of the French countryside, indeed for anyone with a day or two to spare in France and the urge to explore.

Whichever the case, you will get most pleasure from *France on Backroads* if you read these two pages.

The routes

The figure-8s are designed to be driven in either two days or one. But you will enjoy the tours most if you drive them in two, or more, days. On every tour there is so much to see and enjoy that it would be a shame, unless you are short of time, to take them any faster.

Even taking them at this pace, you are not intended to stop at every point of interest described, merely the ones that interest you. Regard the routes as frameworks for exploration, not as exercises to be undertaken exactly as the manual instructs. It is far more important to enjoy them, at whatever pace suits you, and indeed to modify the routes according to your needs, than to complete them in a given space of time.

There are, however, occasions when one finds oneself in a locality with limited time, and the desire to see at least something of it. With an average length of about 160 km, all the figure-8s can be driven inside a day, and approaching a tour in this way is perfectly viable, and, in its way, an interesting undertaking. You won't be able to make many stops, but because the two loops making up a figure-8 are usually devised to take in contrasting landscapes, driving them gives an excellent overall feel for an area.

The tours are in 30 locations all round France (see map on page 6). The locations are chosen for a combination of qualities: interesting backroads; beautiful landscape, seen to advantage on country roads; interesting towns and villages; strong local identity, including, naturally, cuisine and wine; and, sometimes, major tourist attractions. Several of the tours take in important sights where you will temporarily be forced to forget the peace of the backwaters through which you have just driven; don't be disheartened - the crowds are soon left behind once more. By contrast, some of the tours are located in the vicinity of major tourist destinations but don't actually take them in, usually because this would compromise the route, and in any case the place in question is best tackled on a special visit.

The roads

France on Backroads is about country roads, warts and all: expect some terrible surfaces. In upland areas, be prepared to creep through terrifying hair-pin bends, and to edge past unprotected verges, wheels centimetres from the void. In some country areas, be ready for blind corners, slow farm vehicles and poor signposting.

The maps The routes are featured on the Institut Géographique National's *Serie Rouge* maps: general-purpose motoring maps at a scale of 1:250,000.

The IGN is the French official survey, and its cartography is the product of meticulous surveys - accurate measurement of the ground combined with aerial photograph. The result is a precision product from which all other mapping of France ultimately derives. The 1:250,000 maps used in *France on Backroads* carry, moreover, plenty of helpful extra information for the tourist and road user. The scale allows road bends as close as 250 metres apart to show up; and the 'white' roads, with no coloured infill, are a faithful representation of the network of country lanes. However, in common with all other maps at this scale, not every single minor road is featured (the tours occasionally use short stretches of unmarked road - see below under **Route Directions**) and the names of some small settlements are omitted.

Road numbers In recent years, many of the 'D' (Département) and 'N' (National) designation of French roads have been changed. In some localities, the signposts do not yet reflect the change. Thus map, and what you read on signposts, may differ. In practice this is not as confusing as it sounds; and in the interests of consistency, the text uses the version given on the map. Some place name spellings also differ on the map and on the ground; once again, the text follows the IGN version. And remember, roads are always changing.

Hints on map-reading If you are not an expert map-reader, it is worth acquainting yourself with IGN mapping's conventional symbols by looking at the key on any *Serie Rouge* folded sheet. But above all, when on the road, map-read *actively*, rather than passively.

This comes down to knowing where you are on the map *all* the time. Understanding the implications of scale is, therefore, essential. On 1:250,000 mapping, one centimetre on the map represents two-and-a-half kilometres on the ground. So for every kilometre you travel, you should mentally tick off the appropriate portion of map. To do that, of course, you need a point of reference from which to start. This is generally easy: obvious landmarks present themselves continuously in the form of villages and road junctions.

Don't forget that IGN produces maps at the larger scale of 1:100,000 which can be useful in conjunction with *France on Backroads*; and indeed walking maps at the scale of 1:50,000.

The route directions Printed in italics, these are an aid to trouble-free navigation, *not* a complete set of instructions for getting round the routes. You will find that they are most detailed on tricky backroads stretches, and especially so on the odd occasion where your route follows a road not actually marked on the map. It is of course particularly important to follow the directions carefully on such stretches. The text does not always draw your attention to the fact that a road is not marked.

Food

Our contributors set out not only to make each tour an interesting drive, but to find good restaurants on or near the routes. Some areas are not, however, as well endowed with restaurants as others, and this is reflected in the varying numbers of recommendations.

The restaurants mentioned are not by any means the only ones you will find on or near the routes: but they will be particularly interesting for some or all of the following reasons: value, food and wine, ambience, friendly service and for being representative of the local *cuisine*. They are generally, but not always, in the middle-to-lower price bracket. Although they have been chosen with the lunchtime stop in mind, they are usually excellent places for an evening meal as well.

Recommendations come in two forms: a main recommendation, with essential details such as telephone number and closing times; and a passing mention, intended as a helpful extra, with minimum details, usually just a telephone number. Although the restaurant information was accurate at time of going to press, remember that opening and closing times change. Where no closing time is given, assume the restaurant is always open; assume also that some but not all establishments will be closed on national holidays. **To avoid disappointment, book in advance whenever possible.**

Hotels

Like the restaurant recommendations, these are not exhaustive. They are a selection of interesting accommodation at sound value prices which link in with the routes. No opening and closing times are given.

Recommendations are in two forms: main, and passing.

Fuel

In some parts of France, and particularly on the minor roads used for the tours, filling stations can be scarce. Try to think ahead, therefore, and preferably fill up before starting. (Best prices are to be found at giant supermarket pumps.)

Fuel stops are mentioned specifically on some tours where there is a marked shortage. Once again, the mentions are selective, rather than exhaustive; there will be other filling stations on the routes.

Picnic places

In a country where such a wealth of instant picnic materials is available, no one wants always to eat in restaurants. A selection, rather than an exhaustive survey, of useful picnic stops is given for most tours. You can assume that they are representative of the best, but not the only places to picnic on a route.

National holidays

New Year's Day; Easter Monday; 1 May (Labour Day); 8 May (Victory in Europe Day); Ascension Day (the sixth Thurs. after Easter); Whit Monday (the second Mon after Ascension); 14 July (Bastille Day); 15 Aug (Assumption); 1 Nov (All Saints Day); 11 Nov (Remembrance Day); Christmas Day.

Shopping hours

Food shops are generally open 7-6.30 or 7.30 and do not close for lunch (12-2). Some open on Sun. Other shops open at 9 or 10, close for lunch, and close finally at 6.30 or 7.30. Hypermarkets are open 9 or 10-10.

Virtually all shops close for a whole or half-day on Mon. In small towns, particularly in the south, lunchtime closing may extend to 3 or 4.

Time

France is one hour ahead of Greenwich Mean Time in winter and two hours ahead in summer.

THE PRICE BANDS

To give an indication of cost, four restaurant price bands are quoted. They represent approximate prices for lunch, typically three courses, service but no wine included.

Price band A	Under 100 francs
Price band B	100-200 francs
Price band C	200-300 francs
Price band D	over 300 francs

Price band D necessarily covers the large price differentials found in the top range: it is easy to find yourself with a bill of 350-600 francs a head or more for dinner in a famed restaurant.

The prices quoted were correct at time of printing, but liable, of course, to increase. In most cases, however, increases will remain in proportion, so that the price banding system is likely to remain useful. Note that the price banding system does not apply to accommodation, even when rooms are available at the same establishment.

Eastern Picardy:

SOISSONS, LAON AND COMPIEGNE

Speeding south on the *autoroute* to Paris from the Channel ports, you may catch a glimpse of this region in the distance. Mile upon mile of ancient forest - Compiègne, St-Gobain, Retz - made the country around Soissons the playground of the kings of France: a place to hunt stag and wild boar, to ride, and to romance. The kings are long gone, but the châteaux they built, and the forests, remain.

It is a richly varied land. Royal hunting forests run down to green river valleys, or give way to endless plains of wheat. The Aisne, Ailette and Oise rivers cut deep into limestone plateaus on their way to join the Seine.

Route One explores the countryside between Soissons and Laon, the ancient capital of France, heading north through Coucy and the Fôret de St-Gobain, then down through Laon into the rolling hills of the Côte Laonnois. The second route meanders through the Retz and Compiègne forests before heading back along the Aisne valley.

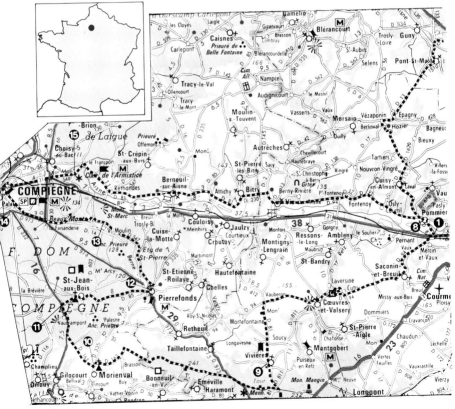

ROUTE ONE: 116 KM

**Soissons -
Coucy-le-
Château**

① *Leave Soissons on the main road to Compiègne - the N31 - and after 2
km turn left on to the D6 to Pommiers. In Vézaponin, turn right on to the
D13 for Coucy. A short climb from the marshy Aisne valley brings you
out on to a wide open plateau.*

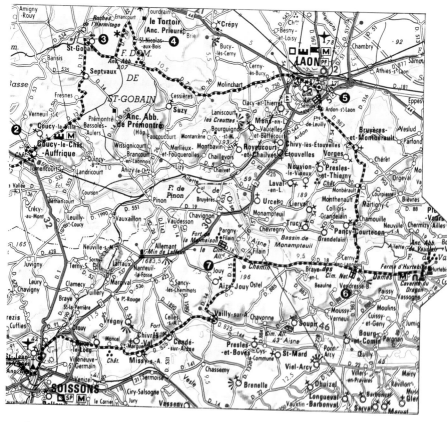

**Coucy-le-
Château**

Straddled right across its commanding hilltop site, the castle of the lords
of Coucy was once the greatest medieval fortress in Europe. There is
not much left except for the ramparts and a vast pile of rubble: the
demolition Cardinal Mazarin failed to complete in 1652 was thoroughly
accomplished by the Germans in 1917. Yet it is still worth paying to
wander around the ruins, and the view from the ramparts is splendid.
Park in the village square by the lions and follow the signs to the
entrance. In her classic history of 14thC France, Barbara Tuchmann gives
a fascinating account of the Coucy dynasty, and in particular of the

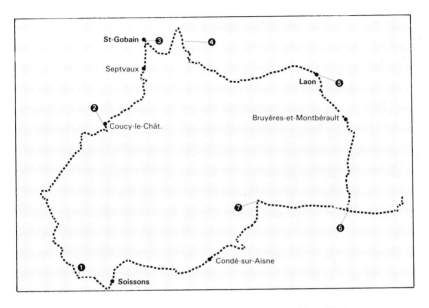

flamboyant Enguerrand VII, last of this powerful line. Their motto proclaimed: *'Roi ne suis, ne prince ne duc ne comte aussi; je suis le sire de Coucy'*. Few argued. *Open am and pm all year; closed Tues, Wed.*

**Hotel
Belle Vue**
*(restaurant,
Coucy)*

You can lunch pleasantly at the Hotel Belle Vue; or sip a beer in the garden opposite. The Belle Vue do particularly fine *ficelles Picardes* - the pancakes with ham in mushroom sauce that are a speciality of Picardy. *Just off the Place du Marché; price band C.*
② *Leave Coucy through the narrow Porte de Laon on the D5; after about one km, bear left along the D13 signposted St-Gobain.*

**Coucy -
Laon**

Wonderful driving through the ancient Forest of St-Gobain, famous for its wild mushrooms, though most are now grown in *champignonnières*.

St-Gobain

St-Gobain's royal glass works, established by Marie de Luxemburg in the 17thC, is a working factory and visitors are not encouraged.
③ *Leave St-Gobain by the D7 for Laon and, after 2.5 km, turn left at the mini roundabout, following the sign to Centre du Recreations. At the crossroads, turn sharp right signposted Anizy and St-Nicolas, and then left on to the D556.*

**Roches
de l'Her-
mitage**

About 0.5 km past the mini-roundabout, a small sign on the left indicates the footpath to the Roches de l'Hermitage of St-Gobain, a 7thC Irish martyr. A fine 20-minute stroll through the trees brings you to the rocks where he had his hideaway - a useful picnic spot.

The abbey. St-Nicolas-aux-Bois.

St-Nicolas-aux-Bois

This Benedictine abbey is set in an enchanting woodland glade and has a mysterious, magical atmosphere. Sadly, the occupants do not welcome visitors; you can only peer through the trees from the road.
④ *Continue on the D55, then the D7 for Laon.*

Laon

Tumbling over a hill that rises steeply from the surrounding plain, the walled medieval town of Laon persuaded Victor Hugo to exclaim, 'In Laon, everything is beautiful - the churches, the houses, the countryside, everything.' Today, chic shops and pedestrian precincts have eroded some of the charm, but the narrow streets and crumbling old houses still give you a tremendous sense of the town's long and chequered history.

The cathedral is not to be missed: it is one of the loveliest in France, especially late in the day when the sun catches the stonework on the west front - the stone oxen peering from the towers are said to commemorate the poor beasts who had to drag the stone for the cathedral all the way up the hill. If the cathedral is crowded, you can escape to the chapel founded by Knights Templar, grateful for their safe return from the Crusades - the garden is a welcome oasis from the bustle of the town (closed Tuesday). From here it is just a step to the ramparts with their superb views over the Laonnois countryside.

Park in the lower town near the station and catch the Poma 2000 monorail up to the old town. As you walk up to the cathedral, you may be tempted by the shops. If you weaken, try the local caramels or the superb *fromagerie* on Rue Châtelaine.

La Bannière de France
(restaurant, Laon)

Superb regional dishes from the best local ingredients in a 17thC coaching inn: the restaurant is famed for its rognons de veau au Bouzy - veal kidneys cooked in Bouzy, the still red wine from nearby Champagne - and its delicious desserts, but the cost will rise steeply unless you stick to the excellent value three-course menu. 11 Rue Franklin Roosevelt (near the town hall); closed 20th Dec-20th Jan; tel 23.23.21.44; price band B/C.

⑤ Descend from Laon near the Porte d'Ardon and head out on the D967 signposted Bruyères-et-Montbérault. Continue on this road through Chamouille to Cerny-en-Laonnois. At Cerny ⑥ turn right on to the D18 signposted Soissons. Or make this recommended detour.

Caverne du Dragon
(detour)

Turn left at ⑥ along the D18 signposted Caverne du Dragon, which is reached in about 4.5 km. Old field guns and armoured cars from both World Wars mark the entrance to this grim underground museum to the Chemin des Dames offensive. Expect to leave angry and depressed: the horror of war is chillingly brought home. In this very cavern 6,000 German troops were holed up during the April 1917 offensive; and many French and German troops died here. Some of the entries in the visitors' book are heart-rending. Open all day, April-Oct.

Ferme d'Hurtebise
(detour)

From the Caverne, continue on the D18 another 0.5 km. The strategically-placed Ferme d'Hurtebise was at stake in the Battle of Craonne in March 1814, a fierce engagement in Napoleon's dazzling but forlorn defensive manoeuvres against the advancing Prussian armies. A hundred years later, the farm was again at stake in September 1914.

Abbaye de Vauclair
(detour)

From the Ferme d'Hurtebise turn left on to the D886. Continue one km. If you are at all interested in medicinal herbs, stop at this ruined Cistercian abbey: it has one of the best herb gardens in France. Open all day until 8 pm. Retrace to ⑥.

Le Chemin des Dames

From Cerny, this road runs straight as an arrow along the Chemin des Dames on the crest of a ridge with superb views either side over the Aisne and Ailette valleys. The road is an old Roman road, but is called le Chemin des Dames after the daughters of Louis XV, who used to hurtle along here on their way to the Château Bove. The peaceful scene gives no reminder of the terrible day in April 1917 when the French tried to break through the German front here. The pointless slaughter precipitated mutiny in the French army.

Hostellerie du Château
(detour to rest., Fère-en-Tardenois)

Turn off the Chemin des Dames on to the D967 in the direction of Bourg and Fismes for what could be the gourmet experience of a lifetime. It is expensive, but the food, lovingly prepared by Patrick Michelon, is unforgettable, and the setting, an old château, is magnificent. Three km from Fère-en-Tardenois on the D967; tel 23.82.21.13; closed Jan and Feb; last bookings 9pm; price band D.

████ **ROUTE TWO: 109 KM**

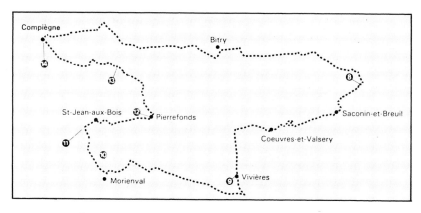

⑦ *Turn left on to the D15, signposted Vailly. In Vailly, turn right along the D925 to return to Soissons.*

Soissons - Vivières
Leave Soissons on the main road to Compiègne - the N31 - and after about 3.5 km, ⑧ *turn left on to the D94, signposted Saconin-et-Breuil. Continue on the D94 through Saconin and Coeuvres and, 4 km beyond Coeuvres, turn left on to the D81 to Vivières.* You now have a leisurely drive across the Soissonais plateau.

Vivières
An unspoiled village of ancient stone cottages in the local style, Vivières deserves at least a brief stop. Park near the crossroads by the Ecole Communale and wander through the quiet lanes up to the right towards the 17thC château (not open to visitors).
⑨ *Continue on the D81 until you pass the D811, then hairpin right on the tiny road to Forêt de Compiègne. Pick up this road again after a short spell on the D973. Once you emerge from the trees turn left and, soon after, left again, signposted Fossemont.*

Vivières - Morienval
This is a ridge-top route through the beautiful Forêt de Retz. The broad swathe through the trees opposite the telecommunications tower is the Allée Royale, which leads to the château in Villars-Cotteret, 4 km away.

Morienval
The original 9thC abbey of Morienval had the dubious distinction of housing both monks and nuns under the same roof; the present abbey, dating from the 11thC, can claim to be the finest Romanesque building in France. Students of architecture will find the place fascinating.
⑩ *Turn left on to the D335, then almost immediately turn sharp right, by the Elf garage, on to the D163 to Compiègne. At the D332, turn right for Vaudrampoint.*

Morienval - *Compiègne*	Here the road runs by the Forèt de Compiègne, less wild than St-Gobain, but equally beautiful. Felled trees and broad clearings show the ancient forest is exploited for its wood as well as its scenery; but careful management ensures the forest will always regenerate.

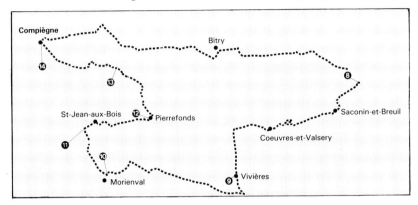

Auberge **du Bon** **Accueil** *(restaurant,* *Vaudram-* *pont)*	Idyllic country inn atmosphere and excellent food make this the place for a long, extravagant lunch; for a cheaper lunch, go on to St-Jean-aux-Bois. You can stay here, too. *On the road from Morienval to Vaudrampont; tel 44.42.84.04; price band C; closed February, Monday evenings, Tuesday.* ⑪ *Soon after the Bon Accueil, turn right for St-Jean-aux-Bois.*
St-Jean- **aux-Bois**	An attractive old hamlet of stone houses clustered around a 12thC abbey, right in the heart of Compiègne forest.
Pierre- **fonds**	Avoid the château tour: the rooms are gloomy, the tour long and costly, and there is no way to escape from the noisy crowds and the guide's rambling monologue - they lock you securely in each room. Much better to park down by the lake, relax with a drink in the garden of the Hôtel l'Etranger, and admire the château from a distance. It was completely rebuilt from a medieval ruin in the 19thC by the famous restorer and architect, Viollet-le-Duc. *Open am and pm all year, Wed-Sun Oct-Mar; closed 1 Jan, 1 May, 1 and 11 Nov, 25 Dec.* ⑫ *Head out of Pierrefonds on the D335 in the direction of Attichy; just after the Fontenoy brasserie, turn sharp left on to the D547 for Compiègne.*
Etang de *St-Pierre -* *Mont St-* *Marc*	This serene lake in the forest is a fine picnic site on weekdays, with pleasant walks in all directions. At weekends, it is overrun with day trippers. The same goes for the charming village of Vieux Moulin just up the road. But you can park by the Auberge du Mont St-Marc and walk up through the trees, away from the crowds. *After the Auberge du Mont St-Marc, bear right ⑬ and, at the next crossroads, turn left (not*

signposted) and then right. Turn left at the next crossroads, and follow signs to Compiègne.

Com-piègne   The grandiose royal palace of Louis XV stands on the eastern edge, its formal gardens merging into the wilderness of Compiègne forest. At weekends, the palace is packed with tourists, and the tour can be a real ordeal - but there are compensations. Some of the rooms are magnificent, and the Musée du Second Empire recalls the glittering days when Napoleon III and his Empress, Eugénie, presided over extravagant house parties here - the *Series de Compiègne* - attended by such celebrities as Verdi, Meyerbeer, Gounod, Flaubert, Dumas, Pasteur and Prosper Merimée. The entry price also includes the Musée de la Voiture; entry to the gardens is free; *open 9.30-5 daily, closed Tues.*

If, however, your visit to Compiègne is brief, give the palace a miss and sample some of the town's less obvious attractions. It was outside the walls of Compiègne that Joan of Arc was finally captured, and in the Place St-Jacques you can see the church where the Maid of Orléans prayed that very day in May 1430; but there is no truth in the story that she was then incarcerated in the (misnamed) Tour Jeanne d'Arc near the river. Near the tower is the Musée de Vivenel (*open am and pm, except Tues*) with a fascinating collection of Greek and Roman pottery, Dürer drawings and local folk art, and just outside the museum is the best picnic spot in town - the atmospheric Parc de Songeons between the River Oise and the old Hotel-Dieu (a 12thC hospital). You can buy delicious food for a picnic in the delicatessen in the little street just off Rue Magenta to the right past the Hotel de Ville.

The Hotel de Ville itself is one of the highlights of the town, a 15thC gothic masterpice with a façade described by R. L. Stevenson as 'all turreted and gargoyled and slashed and bedizened with half a score of architectural fancies.' There is a flower market outside on Saturday.

⑭ *Leave Compiègne on the Soissons road (N31), and turn left just past the traffic lights, signposted Clairière de l'Armistice.*

Clairière   The armistice which ended World War I was signed in a railway carriage in the middle of Compiègne forest on 11 November 1918. Hitler insisted on using the same carriage again when the defeated French came to terms in 1940. The Führer danced a jig beneath the trees outside. An identical carriage is on display, with the original contents. *Open am and pm all year, except Tues. 15 Leaving the Clairière on the road to Choisy, at le Mancport turn right on to the D81 for Rethondes. Continue to Vic-sur-Aisne, where continue on the D91 for Soissons,* a pleasant winding drive, with views, along the Aisne valley.

Auberge au Bord de l'Eau   About 0.5 km off to the right on to the D17 in Port Fontenoy, this bar with a garden on the banks of the Aisne is perfect for a late drink to round off the day.

Normandy:

ROUEN AND THE SEINE VALLEY

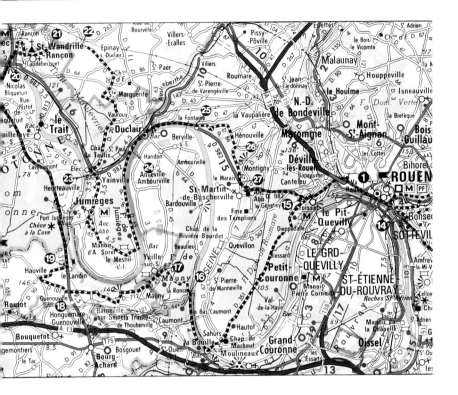

Rouen, the hub of this tour, is a cheerful, busy city, much damaged by bombs in World War II but superbly restored to its former glory. Streets lined with half-timbered houses, the Gothic cathedral (often painted by Monet), and several fine churches and museums all demand attention; but Rouen is only the start.

Route One includes pleasant châteaux, rural churches, a fortress with a view and a peep-show collection. For many, however, the highlight will be the modern art exhibition set in the garden of an enchanting château.

Route Two crosses the River Seine by road and by water, and goes in search of abbeys both ruined and flourishing - solemn legacies of Norman grandees.

Food is simple but plentiful - few signs of *nouvelle cuisine* here - and every menu includes the ubiquitous apple, as well as cream or cheese from Normandy's own breed of cow, whose brown and white colouring is enhanced by the dappled light of the orchards where it is so often seen grazing. The apple trees are in blossom from April to May, and of all seasons spring must be the best for exploring these charming parts.

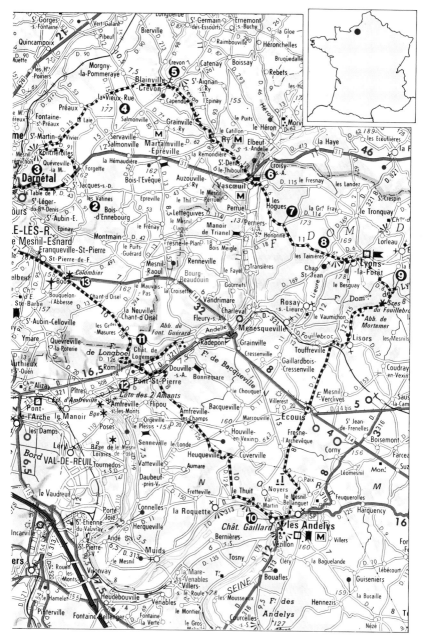

ROUTE ONE 107 KM

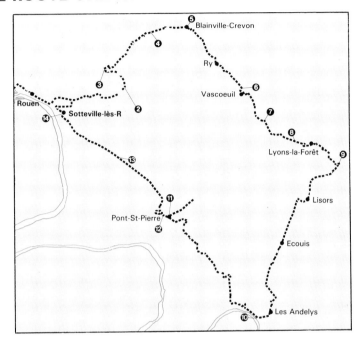

Rouen

Apart from the cathedral, be sure to take in the market place, with its medieval and modern architecture, where St Joan was martyred in 1432. By the side of the Cross of Rehabilitation, where the stake once stood, is the church of Joan of Arc, like a great ship in full sail, with side windows shaped like fishes swimming past, and the curved, green-crested roofs of the market the waves on which it rides. Inside, you must see the 16thC stained-glass windows rising from floor to ceiling.

① *Leave Rouen on the right bank of the river, following Beauvais/Amiens signs on to the N31.*

② *In 10 km (just before Forgette) slow down when you see on the left a large white silo, with a hexagonal tiled roof; immediately before the silo turn left on to a minor unsignposted road.*

Roncher-olles

③ *Follow the D15 to the far end of the village.* At the *Cidre bouché fermier* sign, go down the drive to the farm, where M. Poixblanc will welcome you with a grin, a torrent of French, and copious tastings of his delicious cider, and also *poiré* (perry) grown from 200-year-old trees. Inspect the oak vats where the cider matures, then compare the sweet *cidre doux* with the dry *cidre bouché* before buying at very fair prices.

Continue to La Vieux-Rue, passing several small charming châteaux.

La Vieux-
Rue - Ry
④ *At crossroads go straight ahead on the D61.* Pause to admire the tiny church, with its old wooden porch and new spire topped by an amazingly lifelike red-crested cockerel.

Just beyond Gruchy (not on map) turn right at T-junction on to the D12. ⑤ *In central Blainville-Crevon, at crossroads, turn left on to the D7, then turn right immediately on to the D12, signposted Ry.* Drive along the valley, through which the tiny Crevon meanders peacefully. In 4 km the wide verge, on the right by an uphill path, makes a good picnic spot.

Ry
Turn left at main crossroads to visit the Madame Bovary Museum (*Gallerie d'Automates*). As a tribute to Flaubert's famous novel, which was was set in the village, M. Burgaud has made several hundred miniature automatons, which act out scenes from *Madame Bovary*; other subjects, including cowboys and eskimos, will appeal to children, while Flaubert lovers may prefer the carefully restored Ry pharmacy, also in the museum. *Open Easter to Oct, Sat-Tues.*

Auberge
la
Crevon-
nière
(hotel-
restaurant,
Ry)
Next to the museum, this picturesque but comfortable inn (built in 1634) has four bedrooms and four dining rooms. Choose from the cheapest menu, for good plain cooking - the trout from the stream running through the hotel grounds is particularly recommended; *tel 35.23.60.52; closed Aug, Tues evening and Wed; price band B.* If you have time to spare before your meal, walk to the church to see the rustic carved wooden porch (interior not worth visiting).

Rejoin the D12, signposted Vascoeuil.

⑥ *At the junction with the N31, turn right across bridge, then immediately turn left.* Car park for Château de Vascoeuil on right.

Château
de
Vascoeuil
This little-known château is one of the most charming in France. Lovingly restored to become a modern art collection, the works of art not only fill the château, but overflow into the informal gardens, where sculptures and mosaics (Calder, Leger, Braque and others) grow between trees. Important summer exhibitions, ranging from Dali to Lurçat add to the permanent collection, and overflow into the elegant dovecote usually devoted to tapestries. *Open July to mid-Aug, 2-6.*

Vascoeuil -
Lyons-la-
Forêt
The route now continues through the remains of the great forest of Lyons, where dukes of Normandy once hunted. The tradition continues still. From late autumn until spring, during the season of *la chasse*, sportsmen aim at most things that move, so the numerous and lovely walks are best enjoyed Apr-Oct.

⑦ *Beyond Les Hogues go over crossroads and in about 0.75 km the les Molaises signpost indicates a route forestière.* Turn left and park under the beech trees for a shaded picnic, then return to road.

On entering Les Tainières, stop to admire an unrestored timbered farmhouse on the right.

⑧ *Beyond village take right fork* and in 90 metres park on the verge below statue for panoramic view of Lyons-la-Forêt.

Lyons-la-Forêt
The tourist tradition of dining too well in France may have started with King Henry I of England, who died here of a surfeit of lampreys which he had eaten at Mortemer Abbey. The central 18thC covered marketplace offers a choice of food for picnics. The rest of the village is self-conscious and commercialized. *Turn left on to the D6, signposted Gisors, then after 3.5 km* **⑨** *turn right, signposted Abbaye de Mortemer.* Drive past the sources of Fouillebroc and St Catherine, unless actively seeking a husband (according to local legend).

Abbaye de Mortemer
Ignore guided tour, and stroll through 12thC ruins to lake. Children will enjoy wandering among miniature deer, sheep and hungry ducks. At weekends there are train rides. *Open Easter-Sept, 10-12, 2-6.*

Ecouis
The 16thC twin-towered church is remarkable both for its wealth of carved wooden panels and its superb statuary, of which the most unusual is Sainte Marie l'Egyptien or St Agnes - her identity is uncertain. She is shown swathed in her hair,which ripples to her feet.

Ecouis - Château Gaillard
Approaching Les Andelys, Château Gaillard is silhouetted against the sky. *In the town turn left on to the main road and follow signposts for Château Gaillard Autos (turn right opposite church).*

Château Gaillard
You must stop in the car park as there is a one-way system, but if full there is an overflow car park further down the hill.
   The remains of this important fortress are doubly impressive when one discovers that Richard Coeur-de-Lion, King of England and Duke of Normandy, built it in just one year (1196) to defend Rouen from the King of France. The moat was dug 14 metres deep and was not broached in his lifetime. It was Richard's brother, King John, who lost the castle, and thus Normandy, to France.
   Walk along steep, rough and sometimes muddy paths to the ruins. Not worth paying for a guided tour of the fort, as access to most of the huge battlements is free, with panoramic views of the Seine in both directions. The faint-hearted may prefer the almost equally fine view from the hillside by the car park, which also makes a picnic site.
⑩ *At bottom of hill follow signpost* Autre Directions, *then at T-junction turn left, signposted* Pont-St-Pierre.

Pont-St-Pierre
After crossing the River Andelle in the middle of the village, turn right into avenue immediately before Auberge de l'Andelle for magnificent view of a romantic château, and an ideal picnic spot on the river bank. If it is wet, the Auberge de l'Andelle makes a sound-value lunch stop. It is popular with locals, has a cheerful atmosphere and offers hearty cooking; *tel 32.49.70.18; price band B/C.*

Abbaye de Fontaine-Guérard
(detour)

⑪ For a worthwhile detour, *continue 0.5 km, then at church take tiny road signposted Abbaye de Fontaine-Guérard*. Drive through overhanging beeches and past an ivy-clad 20thC medieval ruin, reminiscent of some horror movie set. The abbey itself, founded by the Earl of Leicester in the 12thC, is a genuine ruin and several rooms in the 13thC chapter house can be visited. *Open every afternoon except Mon Apr-Oct.*
Return to Pont-St-Pierre.
⑫ *Just beyond the village turn right on to the D138, signposted Rouen.*
⑬ *At Boos, turn left on to the N14.*

Hotel St-Léonard
(Le Mesnil-Esnard)

After entering Le Mesnil-Esnard, turn right at third set of traffic lights and follow the hotel's own signposts. Situated next to the church, this is a typical, moderately-priced, family-run hotel in an extremely quiet setting; tel 35.80.16.88; *closed 14-31 July, Nov-Mar, Sun evening.*

Le Mesnil-Esnard - Rouen

⑭ *This next turning is easily missed. Just before the N14 curves to the left to descend to Rouen (6.5 km after entering Le Mesnil-Esnard), take minor road to the right, signposted Corniche. Continue across roundabout*, and soon reach a spectacular viewpoint. Park in lay-by on left, crossing the road carefully to avoid traffic approaching round the blind corner. From here, the whole of Rouen lies below you. The view is best appreciated at sunset, perhaps with a bottle of wine. *Descend Corniche to Rouen.*

▰ ROUTE TWO: 94 KM

The great clock tower gate, Rouen.

Rouen - La Bouille

Leaving Rouen along the right bank of the Seine, following signs to Duclair/Canteleu/Lillebonne. Take care not to enter Autoroute A15. At crest of the steep ascent from Rouen, where there are traffic lights with a church on the left, ⑮ *Turn left into minor road; the Sahurs signpost is only visible after turning.* Delightful wooded drive to Sahurs. *Go straight on at crossroads (signposted Bac de la Bouille).*

The Bac (small car ferry) will take you across the Seine to the romantic village of La Bouille for a small fee, every half hour, 6-10.

Hôtel le   Eccentrically elegant, comfortable hotel with classy cooking (specialities
St-Pierre   are fish and game dishes). The cheaper menu is best value. *Booking*
(La Bouille) *advisable; tel 35.18.01.01; closed Tues evening and Wed, Nov-April;*
                price bands B/C/D.

La Bouille - From La Bouille follow the Seine, with tiny farmsteads nestling between
Hauville   river and cliffs.

> ⑯ *At La Ronce turn on to the D64a signposted Mauny, then immediately*
> *turn right on to the D265 signposted Yville.*
> ⑰ *Turn left at junction with the D45 and in 90 metres pull on to verge*
> for view of the 18thC Yville château and Seine. *Continue to Barneville,*
> *then take the D101 to Hauville.*

Hauville -   ⑱ *After crossing the D313, a 15thC stone windmill soon comes into*
St-Wandrille   view. The car park has excellent information displays (in French only).
                 ⑲ *From the village rejoin the D313,* which continues through the edge
                 of the forest of Brotonne. *At Pont de Brotonne cross the spectacular*
                 suspension bridge (toll).
                 ⑳ *Immediately after the bridge turn right on to the D37, signposted St-*
                 Wandrille. Beneath bridge turn left on to the D982. NB: extremely
                 dangerous crossing of main road - take great care. In 100 metres turn left
                 to St-Wandrille; park against the abbey wall to the left of gate.

St-   The ruins of the abbey, founded by the saint himself in the 7thC, are
Wandrille   worth a visit but not a tour, especially for women, who are banned
                 from the cloisters. The old church has almost disappeared but has been
                 replaced by a medieval barn, transported 50 km and rebuilt by the
                 monks. It is a remarkable experience to attend Mass or Vespers,
                 listening to Gregorian chant as old as the abbey. Mass 9.15 (Sun and
                 Feastdays 9.45); Vespers 5.30 (Sun and Feastdays 5).
> *Leave on the D22, then* ㉑ *take the right fork (D263) through a*
> *wooded valley.* ㉒ *At next crossroads turn sharp right, signposted Duclair.*
> *Follow D20 back to main road,* descending through beech woods where
> grassy verges provide cool picnic places.
> ㉓ *Turn left on to the D982; shortly after turn right on to the D143*
> *signposted Jumièges.*

Jumièges   The towering ruins of the Benedictine abbey are among the finest in
                 France. The church was built by Abbot Robert, later Archbishop of
                 Canterbury, and William the Conqueror attended its consecration in
                 1067. There are no guides to hurry you along. *Open 9-12, 2-6 Apr-*
                 Sept; 10-12, 2-4 Oct-Mar; closed Tues.
                 Most abbey visitors ignore the church up the hill, but if you penetrate
                 the Ministry of Works rubble (and go through the temporary internal
                 partition), you will be well rewarded by the 11th and 12thC stonework
                 and the naive painted wooden statues.

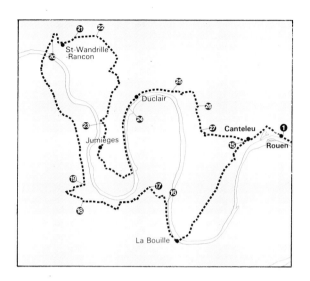

Restau-
rant du
Bac
(Jumièges)

Take road signposted Bac de Jumièges to this old riverside inn. Friendly, informal (goat living in car park) and popular with locals, its amazing value four-course menu gives good Norman cooking in generous quantity. Particularly delicious pheasant pâté, and *escalope de veau vallée d'Auge*. In mid-meal, try the sorbet drenched in Calvados. *Booking advisable; closed Wed and Tues evening (and Mon evening out of season); tel 35.37.24.16; price band A/B.*

Jumièges -
St-Martin-
de-Boscher-
villea

Follow the D65, passing through an archetypal Normandy scene of timbered farmsteads, each surrounded by its orchard, contentedly shared by grazing sheep, cows, hens and ducks. Just before Mesnil-sous-Jumièges, on the left, a farmhouse incorporates the remains of the manor where Agnès Sorel, mistress of Charles VII, died. Beyond the Bac at Mesnil the road runs between the river and orchards, where many of the farmers sell fruit, and possibly Calvados, at their gates. The local speciality is the Benedictine apple, once grown by the monks, which eats well but does not store (avoid M. Sellier who is wholesale only).
㉔ *Turn right on to the D982.* After Duclair, you stay beside the Seine, while on your left the base of the cliff provides cellars and garages.
㉕ *At La Fontaine take the D86 to Henouville, then immediately fork right.*
㉖ *At far end of Henouville turn right at crossroads;* about 300 metres downhill pause opposite a wooden gateway for a superb view across river and plain; in another 200 metres, a picnic site on verge.

St-Martin-
de-
Boscherville

㉗ *Turn left on to the D982 and immediately take right fork (D67).* It is well worth entering this Romanesque church, whose white interior has hardly changed since the 11thC. *Return to D982; continue to Rouen.*

Normandy:

From the tall, slate-fronted buildings around the harbour of Normandy's most picturesque fishing port, Honfleur, and the *planches* and casino of fashionable Deauville, it is only half an hour's drive to the rolling hills, green pastures, gentle valleys and romantic manor houses of this lovely part of Normandy.

The tour steers a careful course around the commercial and industrial city of Lisieux. Auge manors are a feature of the route; they vary considerably - from moated, timber-framed farmhouses, patterned with tiles or ornate brickwork, to minor châteaux built in the classical style. Most can be viewed from the outside only, but a few are open to the public.

The Pays d'Auge is also cider and cheese country. Regimented orchards cover large areas of the countryside, and there are many places where you can watch the cider-making process and buy flagons of liquid apple in various strengths - from juice to cider to the potent Calvados brandy. Normandy cheese is soft and luxurious, just like the scenery; along the route there are plenty of places where you can buy direct from the churn.

Those who require high standards of creature comfort need to search quite hard in the Pays d'Auge. The Hôtel de France in Orbec (see below) is much more than adequate, but for something special try the Auberge de Vieux Puits in Pont-Audemer, about 36 km north-east of Lisieux, *tel 32.41.01.48*. Timber-framed and complete with a cobbled courtyard, its reasonably priced bedrooms (though simple and a touch cramped) have plenty of rustic character, and the food (*price band C*) is among the best in Normandy.

■ ROUTE: 146 KM

Orbec
In contrast to Lisieux, which is big and dull and exploits its pilgrimage factor to the full, the small country town of Orbec seems unconcerned about the tourist potential of its old buildings and its lazy, rustic atmosphere.

Hôtel de France
(hotel-rest-aurant, Orbec)
This may not be the oldest building in Orbec, but it is certainly one of the grandest. Bedrooms are comfortable and not expensive. The food cannot compete with that served at the town's most highly regarded restaurant, but it is good enough, and you can have *escargots* and *Saumon au Sauce Normande* for less than half the price you will pay for the cheapest meal at the quaint Au Caneton down the road.
Tel 31.32.74.02; closed mid-Dec to mid-Jan, Sun evening from mid-Nov to mid-Mar; price band B.

Orbec - Bellou
① *Take the D4, the Livarot road, out of Orbec. After about 8 km, turn left along the D161. Pass through Préaux, then turn right at the crossroads (the road is unsignposted and is not marked on the map). The D4 is far from dull, but the narrow minor road you turn on to is much more*

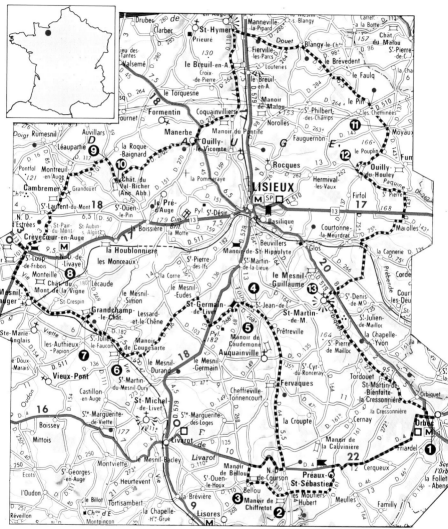

interesting, particularly the last stretch which twists its narrow winding way through woodland down to the Touques valley.

② *At the junction with the D64, at Les Moutiers-Hubert, turn left on to the D110 signposted Bellou.* The road crosses the river then winds up to the flat, tree-covered land at the top of the valley. Past the apple orchards, look out for a huddle of old farm buildings on your right, and pull over to admire the unostentatious, timbered perfection of 16thC Bellou, the first Auge manor on the tour.

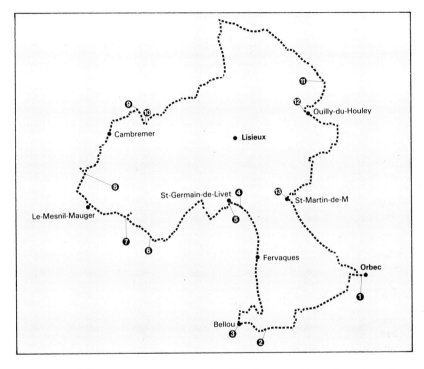

Bellou - St-Germain-de-Livet

③ *Take the next turning to the right, then turn right again at the main road. At the D64, turn left.* The undemanding nature of this road, which follows the meandering course of the wide valley of the Touques, allows drivers plenty of time to enjoy the gentle peace of the scenery. At Fervaques you pass a grand, sprawling château, now a music institution for the handicapped.

④ *At St-Jean-de-Livet, follow the signs - first left, then right - to St-Germain.*

St-Germain-de-Livet

This 15th-16thC château is one of the high points of the tour. Turrets, towers and timbers, and cleverly patterned bricks and stonework are reflected in the waters of the moat, while inside there are Renaissance frescoes, oak furniture and thick, creaking floorboards. The tiny car-park is the first encouraging sign that St-Germain-de-Livet is not on a well-trodden tourist track, but the fact that you have to pull the bell cord to call the *gardien* to gain entrance is what really makes you feel you are entering a privileged and private world. *Open 10-12 and 2-7 (2-5 Oct-Mar); closed Tues and mid-Dec to Jan.*

St-Germain - Coupesarte

⑤ *Return along the road leading to the château, then take the first right.* The narrow road climbs up, providing splendid views over the château and its estate, it continues along a ridge, drops down to a river and then rises up into the hills on its way to the D579. *Go straight across the main road,* and prepare yourself for a short stretch of narrow, bumpy and extremely twisting lanes where grass may poke through the asphalt. You have to drive slowly here, and follow the directions carefully; the road is not marked on the map. *Where the signs indicate a cider farm to your left, bear right; at a T-junction opposite an old farm, turn left; and, at the next T-junction, turn left along the D136.* Beyond the crossroads this becomes a fine drive, past one very grand (and another less imposing but still stylish) stud farm; the views stretch into the distance. *At the junction with the D47 fork right..*

Manoir de Coupe-sarte
A short track leads to the most romantic of all the Auge manors. You cannot go inside the timbered farmhouse and you are not allowed to picnic beside it, but you can stand by the moat and admire this masterpiece of medieval domestic architecture.
⑥ *Continue to St-Julien-le-Faucon and turn left along the D511.*

De la Levrette
(restaurant, St-Julien)
The young owners of this modest, old roadside hotel are enthusiastic and welcoming, and understand the needs of those with young children. The country-style cooking is in the tradition of the area. *Price band A.*
⑦ *Opposite the hotel, take the D269, signposted Grandchamp-le-Château.*

St-Julien - Crève-coeur-en-Auge
When you reach the war memorial, turn right. The sight of the old timbered house here, with its grand, classical-style addition, is well worth this short detour. Fine old gatehouses stand at the corners of the manicured, moated gardens.
Return to the D269E. At Le Mesnil-Mauger, turn right, then right again on to the main road. At Crèvecoeur-en-Auge turn left on to the N13, and then right at the signpost to the Manoir de Crèvecoeur.

Manor, Bellou.

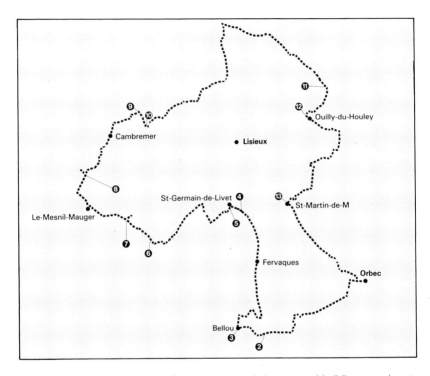

Manoir de Crève-coeur	The main road is a little too near and the restored buildings are almost too perfect, but this is a museum rather than a home - and it does offer you the chance to look inside an Auge manor and to explore its outbuildings. Curiously, much of the museum is devoted to petroleum engineering and research, but there is a collection of old agricultural implements in the gatehouse and an audio-visual presentation on Norman architecture in the chapel. *Open 12-8, daily in July and Aug but closed Tues in June and Sept; closed Dec-Jan; weekends only rest of year.*
Crèvecoeur - La Roque-Baignard	⑧ *Return along the main road to the crossroads and turn left. At the junction with the D50 turn right then immediately left on to the D101, following the signs to La Roque-Baignard.* The drive to Cambremer, and particularly beyond this cheerful village, is one of the most appealing sections of the tour. The road climbs past cider farms to wind its way along lush valleys and up, over and around rolling green hills, passing old farms and smallholdings. The sloping, grassy fields are ideal for picnics.
La Roque-Baignard - Moyaux	⑨ *At the junction with the D59, turn right (or continue straight on for a short detour to a picturesque old cottage where you can buy delicious home-made chèvre).* Slow down to enjoy the isolated leafy setting of

the château of La Roque-Baignard, and not far beyond, look up and to the right for a brief glimpse of a more formal and grand château, the abbey of Val-Richer.

⑩ *Fork left along the D270B. At Manerbe, turn left along the main road, then turn right on to the D270. At the T-junction turn left, then after about 5 km turn right on to the D280A, signposted (but the signpost faces away from you) Blangy-le-Château. From Blangy follow the signs to Moyaux.* There is no shortage of interesting scenery along this section of the route; woodland is followed by the wide Touques valley, then the more intimate valley of the Chaussey and more woodland. At Le Brévedent there are evocative old farmbuildings; and on the final stretch, the leaning spire of Moyaux church provides comic relief.

**Moyaux -
Orbec**

⑪ *Just past the church, turn right for Ouilly-du-Houley.* The thick woodland before Ouilly offers picnic possibilities, and as the road descends to the tiny village, look up and left to the massive château.

⑫ *At the stop sign past the Auberge de la Paquine, turn left along the D262, then turn right at the crossroads, signposted Marolles. Soon after crossing the N13, turn right along the D75B, signposted Courtonne-la-Mac (Courtonne-la-Meurdrac). At the D75 turn left, then first right, signposted La Gare. At the minor crossroads, go straight over, signposted St-Denis-de-Maílloc.* This is the most complicated section of the tour, so follow the directions carefully. Some of the roads are narrow and badly surfaced, but that - given the scenery - is part of the charm.

⑬ *At the main road (D519), turn right. After about 100 metres, turn left along the D149, then left again on to the D272.* Much of this road is single-track and there are several blind corners where you need to sound your horn; but it would be difficult to contrive a more unspoilt sequence of backroads for the closing stretch. *At the junction with the D519, turn right to Orbec.*

Normandy:

LA SUISSE NORMANDE

The area covered in the first loop of this tour is called the Suisse Normande, though there are no Matterhorns or alpine lakes here, not even any particularly high ground.

On its winding north-westerly course the River Orne has cut through the *massif*, creating steep banks and the occasional severe peak. The scenery along the valley is amongst Normandy's prettiest and most interesting, and although in terms of mere metres the heights may not be impressive, they certainly provide some dizzying views. The area is popular for a variety of other reasons. Many come for the canoeing, walking, fishing or rock-climbing; others come simply to throw themselves off the Pain de Sucre - firmly attached to their hang-gliders, of course.

The second loop of the tour takes you into the Parc Naturel Régional Normandie Maine, where bands of thick forest cover high ridges. There are few sights here but no shortage of marvellous views, and there is great scope for getting away from it all - something that is not always easy to do in the Suisse Normande.

If possible, allow two or three days for this tour - to attempt it in a day would mean missing too much. Clécy and Mortain are the best places for overnight stops; if you prefer to have just one base, choose Clécy.

Opposite: the church, Lonlay-l'Abbaye, Route Two.

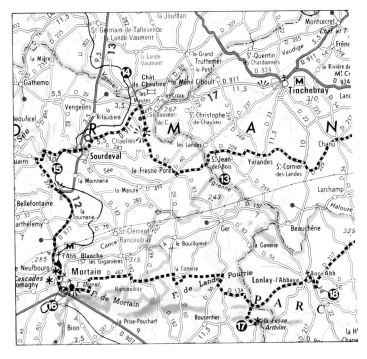

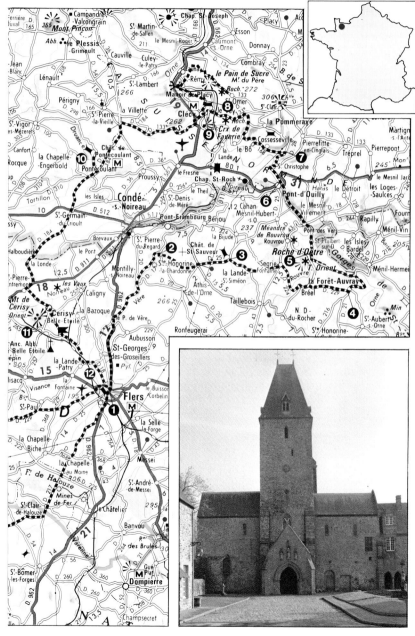

◼◼◼ ROUTE ONE: 90 KM

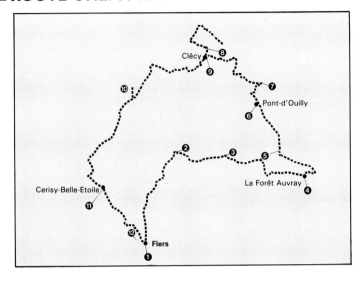

Flers -
Château de
St-Sauveur

There is little to keep you in Flers, so stop at the filling station, stock up with picnic provisions, take a quick look at the château on the east side of town, then head out of town.

① *Take the Caen road for about 4 km, then turn right along the D17, signposted Pont-Erambourg, and follow the river for about 7 km.* This is an evocative drive along a lush, steep-sided valley past a succession of moody, dark old mills which long since ceased turning out textiles.

② *Take the hairpin right turn on to the C10 (not on map) signposted Ste-Honorine.* The almost single-track road winds steeply up through forest to the heights. Just past a crossroads, look out for the château (La Pompelière) to your left. *At the junction with the D15 turn right, then turn left on to the D25, signposted Château de St-Sauveur.*

Château
de St-
Sauveur

The Renaissance was a time for decorative skills, extravagance and flights of fancy. The controlled, classical style of architecture that followed can seem cold in comparison, but this small, moated Louis XIII château retains some fine original panelling and is elegantly furnished. *Open 2.30-4.30; closed Tues, Wed and Feb; Oct-May open weekends and national holidays only.*

Château de
St-Sauveur -
La Forêt-
Auvray

③ *Turn left on to the D25, then turn right along the C3. At La Lande-St-Siméon turn right, signposted Segrie-Fontaine. At Segrie take the D224 to Bréel, then the D229 to La Forêt-Auvray.* These are beautiful, sleepy backroads through unspoilt villages of mellow old houses. Take your time and stop to explore either Bréel or La Forêt.

La Forêt-Auvray - Roche d'Oëtre

④ *From La Forêt take the D21, signposted Ménil* The views over the Orne valley from the road out of the village are a breathtaking taste of the scenery that is to come later on the tour. *At the valley bottom, just before the road crosses the river, turn left, signposted Roche d'Oëtre.* Soon after you turn off to the Roche, just after a double bend, stop at one of the gaps in the wall for a glimpse of an ancient fortified manor.

Roche d'Oëtre

The signs warn you to take care, and so you should at this magnificent viewpoint over the wild and wooded Rouvre Gorges, just a sheet 119-metre drop - the Suisse Normande at its most dramatic. There is a café at the top, with tables outside; unfortunately, but understandably, the notices put up by the *patron* make it clear that these are not for picnickers. There are, however, other places nearby where you can unleash your hamper.

Roche d'Oëtre - Pont-d'Ouilly

⑤ *Follow the D329 through St-Philbert to Pont des Vers.* From the deceptively high ground around the Roche, you wind down to the Orne to pass under the high arches of the 'pont'. *At the D18 turn left, then turn right on to the D167.*

Pont-d'Ouilly

Just before the sign announcing Pont-d'Ouilly, pull into the lay-by on the right and cross the road. A track to your left or steps to your right take you down to the river bank, where you can enjoy the Orne in one of its tranquil moods. There is plenty of space for a picnic; you can even hire a pedal boat to appreciate the river from a different perspective. Pont-d'Ouilly itself is one of the biggest villages (but not the most charming) in the Suisse Normande.
⑥ *Take the Thury-Harcourt road out of the village, then turn left along the D23, to St-Christophe.*

Auberge St-Christophe
(hotel-restaurant)

This creeper-clad restaurant with nine well-equipped and newly decorated rooms is run with great care by M. and Mme Lecoeur. During the day you may have to pick your way through the toys of Lecoeur junior on your way to the dining room, but whether you are looking for a not-too-expensive lunch or a more extravagant evening treat, you are unlikely to be disappointed. *Tel 31.69.81.23; closed 19 Oct-6 Nov, 13 Feb-12 Mar, Sun evening and Mon; price band B/C.*

St-Christophe - Clécy

⑦ *Continue along the D23, then turn left on to the D168 and follow the signs to Clécy.* It is a gentle, wooded and winding route to this village in the heart of the Suisse Normande. At several points (but best from Le Bô) there are views of the steep rocky escarpment of the Pain de Sucre. The drive is easy, but take it slowly, stopping along the way at Le Vey; here you can picnic by the river, relax in a waterside café, or if you are energetic - hire a boat. You might even stay longer, at the comfortable riverside Moulin du Vey, *tel 31.69.71.08,* although rooms are about twice the price of those at Le Site Normand in Clécy.

Clécy

Clécy's tidy charm is appropriate for the main tourist spot of the Suisse Normande. There is not much to see here - just the church and the 16thC Manoir de Placy, which houses a museum *(open 2-6 Sun and daily in July-Aug; closed Nov-Mar)* - but there are hotels and restaurants.

Le Site Normand
(hotel-rest-aurant, Clécy)

Both the accommodation and the food at this half-timbered hotel and restaurant, right in the middle of Clécy, represent good value. Bedrooms are prettily decorated and comfortable, and the meals in the traditionally decorated restaurant are reliable. *Tel 31.69.71.05; closed Jan, Feb; price band B/C.*

Route des Crêtes, Pain de Sucre
(detour)

⑧ *For a detour to the top of the Pain de Sucre, take the D133C from Clécy, past the Auberge de Chalet de Cantepie, and just as you reach St Rémy, take the sharp right turn, signposted Route des Crêtes.* There are many rewarding trips you can take from Clécy, but this is one you should not miss. Follow the road until you reach a large grassy area which has been set aside for parking, and walk across to the edge of the ridge. The views over the meandering Orne are stunning. Less than one km further on, on the edge of the escarpment, is a hang-glider's launching ramp. *Return to Clécy the way you came.*

Clécy - Ponté-coulant

⑨ *Go straight down the hill from the church in Clécy, cross the main road, then follow the D133A and the signs to the château.* You may be leaving the Suisse Normande, but the first 5 km of this drive, along a green valley, are particularly attractive. *The last sign to the château (as you come into the village of Pontécoulant) faces away from you and is difficult to see.*

Château de Ponté-coulant

Sadly, but luckily for us, this is no longer a family home; old and heirless, the owner of this charming lakeside château transferred it into the hands of the local *département*. Long, formal lawns front the 16th-18thC house, and behind there is woodland. The interior is somewhat musty but still very homely, and the ground and first-floor rooms shown on the guided tour contain many fine pieces of furniture from different periods and countries. *Open 10-12 and 2.30-6 (4.30 in winter); closed Tues and Oct.*
⑩ *Return to Pontécoulant village and take the D184, through St-Germaine-du-Crioult to St-Pierre d'Entremont. Turn right along the main D911, then turn left to Cerisy.*

Cerisy

The high, wooded hill of Mont de Cerisy, which overlooks this little village, is a popular spot. A toll road curves up through rhododendrons to the summit, where the surprising array of facilities includes tennis courts and a boating lake. Other attractions are the views across to the Suisse Normande from the rather spooky ruined château, and the chance to stroll or picnic among the woods.
⑪ *From Cerisy, follow the signs back to Flers.*

███████ **ROUTE TWO: 75 KM**

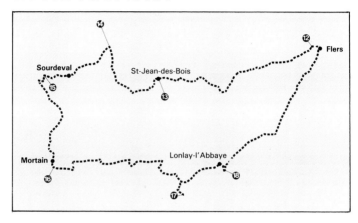

Flers -
Mortain

⑫ *Take the D25 out of Flers for about 1.5 km, then turn right along the D268, signposted St-Paul.* Beyond Chanu, the rural character of this route takes an increasingly firm hold, and once you are across the D22 the views over the Normandy countryside become more and more extensive.

⑬ *At St-Jean-des-Bois turn left along the D237 to Le Fresne-Poret, then turn right along the D83 to Les Maures.* There are some fine views from these minor roads, particularly around St-Martin-de-Chaulieu (not marked on map). *At Les Maures a short detour to the right, along the D911 for 100-200 metres, and then left along a bumpy track, brings you to a derelict château* - a quiet and atmospheric place for a picnic.

⑭ *Return to Les Maures and head west along the D911. At Sourdeval continue on the D911, signposted Vallée de Brouains.* Twisting and turning, the road descends through the fertile valley; steep slopes, dotted with remote farms, open out to more mellow countryside.

⑮ *After about 5 km, and just before a double bend and a tall chimney, turn left on to the D279, then follow the signs to Mortain.* Excitement follows the easy charm of the valley, as you negotiate this steep, narrow backroad up to the security of the D977, at a point which entirely justifies its name of Bellevue.

Mortain

One of the decisive, last battles of the Normandy campaign of World War II took place in the Mortain region, and this small unpretentious town which nestles high up on the edge of the Lower Normandy hills, looking out over the great expanse of the Sélune basin, has been largely rebuilt since that week of fighting and devastation. Mortain is a place to spend some time. Apart from the church of St-Evroult, which has a fine Romanesque doorway, most of the sights lie around the edge of the town. On the D977, to the north, is the Abbaye Blanche, an old monastery which is now a seminary and cultural centre. On the guided tour you are shown the chapter house, chapel and part of the cloister, all of which are 12thC. There is also an exhibition of African art, *open Jun to mid-Sept, 10-11.45 and 2.30-5.30.* Above the town, to the east, there are wide views across the wooded countryside of the Parc Naturel Régional from the Petite Chapelle, and below the town there are two pretty waterfalls. If you find the leafy setting of the Grande Cascade too shaded (or too crowded) for a picnic, walk past the Petite Cascade to the wooded hillocks near the rock chapel of St-Vital.

The Grande Cascade, Mortain.

Cascades *(restaurant, Mortain)* Mortain does not lack hotels, only stylish accommodation. Similarly it is not short of restaurants, only places serving outstanding food. For a good-value lunch, however, the restaurant of this small hotel in the middle of the town is more than adequate. *Tel 33.59.00.03; closed Sun evening and Mon, and 20 Dec-3 Jan; price band B.*

Mortain -
La Fosse
Arthour

⑯ *Take the Domfront road out of Mortain, then turn left along the D487. Follow the Barenton signs (D182) from Rancoudray, pass the left turn back on to the D487, and take the next turning to the left (unsignposted and not marked on map). Turn right on to the D60, then first left, signposted Le Breuil. At the D36 turn right, then turn left along the D134, signposted La Fosse Arthour.* This section of the tour may seem rather complicated but it is about the most direct route to La Fosse and, with the exception of the short stretch along the D36, the countryside you pass through is completely off the beaten track. Even farms and houses are

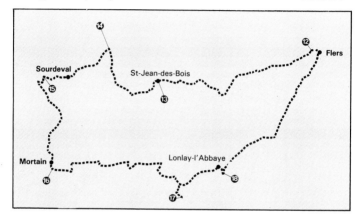

few and far between on these backroads which follow a high ridge, partly forested and partly open, before dropping down to the floor of a valley. Then comes the delectable approach through trees to La Fosse, along the narrow and winding D134.

La Fosse
Arthour

After the totally unspoilt countryside of the drive from Mortain, La Fosse Arthour brings you back to earth. Signs tell you where to park and how to behave, and there is a modern restaurant. From the road past the restaurant there are views of the River Sonce as it cuts its way through steep banks to enter a large pool, and then departs in a succession of little waterfalls. You should not expect anything quite as splendid as the scenery along the Orne valley in the Suisse Normande, but La Fosse offers the chance to picnic among restful scenery.
⑰ *Retrace a short way, then turn right to Lonlay-l'Abbaye.* Enchanting roads led you to La Fosse; enchanting roads take you away.

Lonlay-
l'Abbaye

Dignity, beauty and tranquility - the church at Lonlay-l'Abbaye has all three - from the outside, at least. It was part of an 11thC abbey, and its presence dominates this village which nestles among wooded hills.
⑱ *Fork left by the war memorial in the village; turn left at T-junction, then follow the signs to Flers.*

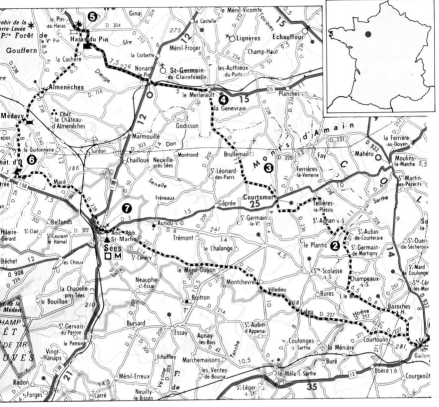

This tour is exceptionally full of interest and variety. The longer, northern loop takes in the equine elegance of the national stud at Haras du Pin, the extremely romantic Château d'O, and the cathedral town of Sées. The southern loop explores the more intimate countryside of the Normandy Perche, an area famous for its powerful Percheron horses (this is one of only three areas in France where the sturdy dray horses are bred) and its manor houses. Perche manors are quite different to the cosy, half-timbered farmhouses of the Pays d'Auge (see the tour in that area); they are much more defensive-looking structures, built of stone and embellished with turrets and towers. Unfortunately, only La Vove opens its doors to the public, but the route also takes you past several of the area's most noble *gentilhommeries*.

The scenery of the Perche is gentle and picturesque rolling hills, in part clothed by dense forest, and lush valleys. Grazing Percherons add an air of serenity; and throughout the region there are numerous seductive villages and small towns. Chief among these are Mortagne, the old capital of the Perche, and Bellême, the present capital, with its fine houses and splendid decorated church.

Mortagne is also the hub of the tour, and makes a convenient base. If you want to make an overnight stop *en route*, Sées would be a sound choice: it has several inexpensive, simple hotels. The driving on both loops presents no problems, and the route is far from complicated. Bear in mind that although the southern circuit is the shorter of the two, you will probably want to linger more along the way.

ROUTE ONE: 104 KM

Mort-agne-au-Perche

Although it is no longer the capital of the region, Mortagne is still the main tourist magnet of the Normandy Perche. The Porte-St-Denis, which houses a small local museum, is the only significant remaining part of the original 15thC fortifications, but numerous fine old houses survive in the streets, alleys and squares of this thriving hilltop town. The church dates from the late 15thC, and contains a huge carved altarpiece which came from a monastery in the nearby Réno Forest. There is an attractive though somewhat shabby arcaded market building, at one end of which is the tourist office, at the other a cinema.

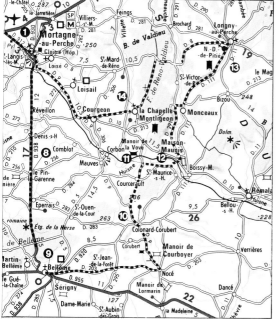

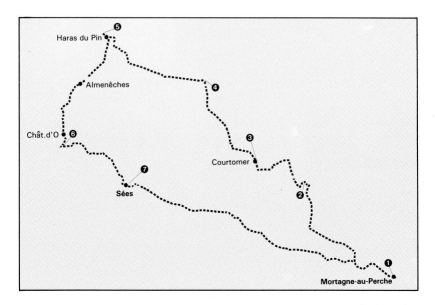

Hôtel Tribunal
(hotel-restaurant, Mortagne)

A quick look at the visitors' book will be reassurance enough: from the British who have made an overnight stop on their way to the beaches of the South of France, to the French, Germans, Dutch and other Europeans who have used it as a base for touring the Normandy Perche, all are generous in their comments about the food and the accommodation. The hotel occupies lovely old buildings on a quiet square near the church. The entrance hall, which is also the breakfast room and sitting room, is homely and welcoming - just as a country *auberge* should be. The restaurant is equally atmospheric, although slightly more formal. Bedrooms are inexpensive and perfectly adequate for a stay of one or two nights. For lunch, you will probably be happy to settle for the basic three-course menu, which includes a dish of the day; for dinner it is worth splashing out on one of the more extravagant menus. *4 Place du Palais; tel 33.25.04.77; closed Christmas-New year; price band A/B.*

Mortagne-au-Perche - Haras du Pin

① *Take the Alençon road out of Mortagne, then turn right along the D8. Beyond Bazoches, and about 10 km from Mortagne, turn right on to the C5, signposted Champeaux-sur-Sartre. At the crossroads, where there is a calvary, bear left along the D271, signposted St-Agnan.* Once you have turned off the fast D8, this becomes an appealing backroads drive. First, you pass an imposing château painted brilliant white; then you wind through sleepy, undulating countryside.

② *At the junction with the D6, turn left, then turn right to rejoin the D271. After about 3 km turn left along the C2, signposted Tellières.* Go *straight on (not right) over the narrow river at the bottom of the hill, then turn right on to the D236 at the T-junction.* The D271 twists its way up a steep hill, through forest, with occasional fine views, while the C2 takes you past a small fortified manor and on through delightful stretches of woodland.

③ *At the D3 turn right, then left immediately along the D4.* On leaving Courtomer, note the large, privately owned château on the right. *Continue along the D4 to Le Merlerault.*

④ *At Le Merlerault turn left on to the N26 and follow the signs to Haras du Pin.* This is a fast main road which becomes increasingly attractive beyond Nonant-le-Pin.

Haras du Pin

Even those who don't love horses will be impressed by the style, indeed the majesty of the national stud. Uniformed stable lads (for no more than a gratuity) blind you with statistics about the size, speed and fecundity of the immaculately groomed stallions; the guided tour also includes a tack room full of finery and a collection of carriages. The stud was founded by Colbert, Louis XIV's minister; the small but imposing château (not open) was designed by Mansart, and the gardens by Le Nôtre, although both men are better known for their contributions to Versailles. From the château you can look out over lush countryside, or back through the main gate up a long and wide woodland ride. Even if you miss the spectacle of the horses setting off for or returning from their daily exercise, don't forgo a stroll along this grand, green avenue - and take your picnic things with you. The stables have most visitors mid-July to mid-Feb; horse races and carriage processions take place *the first Sun in Sept and the second Sun in Oct; guided tours 9-12 and 2-6.*

National stud, Haras du Pin.

Haras du Pin - Chât. d'O	⑤ *Go back a short way along the N26, then turn right along the D26 and follow the signs to Château d'O. At Médavy pull off the road to admire the 18thC château and the domed gate towers in the grounds.*

Château d'O

This place is as enchanting as the family name is curious. Elaborate and moated, its turrets, steeples and steep-sloping roofs are straight from a fairy tale. The original east wing is 15thC, the south wing is 16thC, and the west wing (the living quarters) is 18thC. The guided tour is brief. There are some fine statues in the rooms you are shown. One of the farm buildings has been converted into a restaurant (*de la Fèrme; menus start at band B); open 10-12, 2-6, 2.30-5 out of season, closed Tues.*

Château d'O - Sées

⑥ *Take the lane opposite the main gate of the château. Turn left at the T-junction, then turn right on to the C12. At Macé turn left, then turn right along the D238 to Sées.*

Sées

Sées has been an ecclesiastical centre since it became a bishopric in the 4thC, and its cathedral, whose magnificent spires can be seen from afar, is a fine example of Norman Gothic. The interior contains some fine 13thC stained glass, and is beautifully proportioned. However, the same cannot be said for the exterior, which is marred by the addition of ugly, unwieldy buttresses dating from the 16thC when the building was in danger of falling down due to subsidence. Although this act of constructive vandalism may have saved the cathedral, there is no denying that Sées has declined in importance over the years. More than a lick of paint is needed to restore the town to its former glory, but for all that it is an agreeable, unpretentious place. The numerous monasteries and seminaries combine to create an atmosphere of serenity around the cathedral; and it is worth looking at the former Bishops' Palace, the 18thC abbey and the old market building.

Normandy
(restaurant, Sées)

Its position, just across the road from the cathedral, no doubt brings this modest and popular restaurant a large share of the tourist trade. Marie Antoinette would not have approved (for herself, at least) of the workmanlike surroundings and plain cooking, but for holidaymakers on a budget there is much to be said for easily affordable prices. *Pl Gén-de-Gaulle; tel 33.27.80.67; closed mid-Sept to early Oct; price band A.*

Chéval Blanc
(hotel-restaurant, Sées)

Sées is not the home of sophistication, and the rooms at the Chéval Blanc are unequivocally simple. However, the restaurant is slightly smarter than the Normandy, and the cooking more adventurous. *1 Pl St Pierre; tel 33.27.80.48; closed mid-Oct to mid-Nov, holidays in Feb, Thurs evening and Fri evening and Sat out of season; price band B.*

Sées - Mortagne-au-Perche

⑦ *Take the D3 out of Sées, then turn right along the D227. At the junction with the D31 turn right, then almost immediately turn left to rejoin the D227. Join the D8 and follow the signs to Mortagne.*

▬▬▬▬ ROUTE TWO 82 KM

*Local
farmhouse
architecture.*

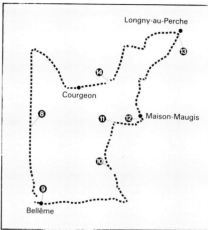

Longny-au-Perche

⑬

⑭

Courgeon

⑧   ⑪ ⑫ Maison-Maugis

⑩

⑨

Bellême

Mortagne-au-Perche - Le Pin-la-Garenne	*From Mortagne take the D938, signposted Bellême.* Typically French (but for the switchbacks), this road leaves Mortagne via an avenue of tall plane trees, and then heads, straight as an arrow, for Le Pin-la-Garenne, with some long views over the gentle scenery of the Perche. At Le Pin, tarmacadam smoothness may give way to ruts and the occasional pothole, as the road winds its way through the village. At the right-angle bend by the Hôtel des Voyageurs (see below) another avenue of trees leads up to a fine château. Although it is not open to the public, there is nothing to stop you driving up to the gates of the château; the avenue makes a pleasant walk, too.
Hôtel des Voyageurs *(restaurant, Le Pin-la-Garenne)*	Close your ears to the noise from the main road, and enjoy the creeper-clad exterior, cosy interior and low prices of this country inn. As the yellow and green sign indicates, it is a member of the generally reliable Logis and Auberges de France. *Tel 33.25.25.46; closed late Dec to early Jan, Sun evening and Mon; price band A.* ⑧ *Continue along the D938.* There are a few bends and bumps before the road recovers its sheen and lunges straight ahead into the distance on its roller-coaster route. Soon you enter the dense woodland of the Forest of Bellême. Look out on your left for a lake (Etang de la Herse); there are plenty of paths and delightful picnic places in the vicinity.
Bellême	The name is apt: Bellême has a turbulent past. It was the fortress of the Counts of Alençon, and was the site of many battles during the Middle Ages. Its position, on a spur, exemplifies its strategic importance, and the remaining fortifications are a powerful reminder of those brutal times.

Bellême is best appreciated if approached as follows. *When you reach the roundabout at the top of the hill (there are a couple of restaurants on your left) go straight over, continuing on the main road. Soon after, just by the war memorial, turn left, following the signs to the car park.* Before you enter the main gate to the town, wander along the narrow Rue Ville-Close to your right; here are some of Bellême's finest houses - stately 17thC and 18thC buildings, somewhat faded and peeling but still elegant. Through the gate is the town's spacious and steeply sloping main square, the focal point of which is the church. St-Saveur is no Gothic masterpiece, merely a squat 17thC local church, but its elaborately carved and richly painted interior is memorable.

**Bellême -
La Vove**

⑨ *Follow the signs towards Rémalard, then turn right on to the D203, through St-Jean-de-la-Fôret. At Nocé, head towards the church and take the D9, signposted Mortagne.* This is a route which gradually seduces you into the charms of the Normandy Perche. Pleasing until you reach St-Jean, undeniably pretty from St-Jean to Nocé, then uplifting (in all senses of the word) along the D9. But don't get carried away; look out on your right for the Manoir de Courboyer, and stop for a glimpse of this prince of Perche manors, with its round turrets and towers - both homely and dignified.

⑩ *At Colonard-Corubert turn left, then turn right along the D9 and follow the signs to Courcerault.* This is a marvellous stretch along twisting roads, through woodland, with views. *At Courcerault, go straight on; just after a mill house* (antiques enthusiasts should stop to browse) *turn left at the T-junction, for a short detour along the D256 to the Manoir de la Vove.*

**Manoir
de la
Vove**

La Vove is unique among Perche manors. It is not a particularly stunning example of local domestic architecture (although you will not be disappointed); but it is the only manor in this area that you can visit. *Open 10-12, 2-7, Sat and Sun 2-6; closed Nov-Mar.*

**Manoir de
la Vove -
Maison-
Maugis**

⑪ *Head east along the D256; at the junction with the D10, turn right. Before you reach Boissy Maugis, turn left along the narrow C2, signposted Maison-Maugis,* and prepare yourself for a manorial feast. Keep looking right along this tree-lined lane so as not to miss first the medieval warmth of the Manoir de Moussetière, across the fields; then, the classical grandeur of the château of Maison-Mougis.

**Maison-
Maugis -
Longny**

⑫ *At the junction with the D291, head straight on, following the signs to Monceaux.* This is a lovely rural backroad, with several farms advertising bed-and-breakfast. *At Monceaux, turn left to Longny-au-Perche.*

**Longny-
au-Perche**

In many ways, Longny is Mortagne's poor relation; it is a less vivacious place, and its accommodation and tourist facilities cannot match Mortagne's. Geography may partly explain this state of affairs; after all, from its hilltop position Mortagne can look down on the countryside of

La Chapelle-Montligeon.

the Perche, whereas Longny is set in a bowl of the wooded Jambée valley. The tourist potential is there but, no doubt, the burghers of Longny have quite sensibly decided that the lazy appeal of the town's spacious main square and surrounding streets should not be spoiled. There is not much to see in the town, but on your way out you should take in the views from the chapel of Notre-Dame-de-Pitié.

Longny-au-Perche - La Chapelle-Montligeon

⑬ *Take the D8 out of Longny, signposted Mortagne. After entering the forest, and beyond the turning to Monceaux, turn left, signposted La Chapelle-Montligeon.* The narrow road cuts a rather eerie corridor through the dense, regimented forest, and is crossed by occasional wide paths which double as fire breaks.

La Chapelle-Montligeon

Pilgrims come in their thousands to this huge elaborate chapel to pray for the disabled. It completely dominates the tiny industrial village, and though awesome and incongruous, it has a grotesque fascination.

La Chapelle-Montligeon - Mortagne au Perche

⑭ *From the chapel go down the hill and cross the D5.* A quick backward glance will enable you to appreciate fully how out of proportion the chapel is, compared to the size of the village. *At the junction with the main road, turn right and follow the signs to Mortagne.*

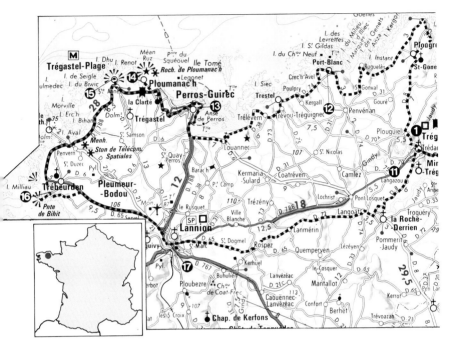

Sweeping sandy bays, rocky headlands, secret inlets and meandering estuaries: the Brittany coast is over 1,500 km long and has many moods. Nature has been more than generous here, for there is yet another dimension to the scenery: the mystery, even magic, of countless offshore islands, islets and rocks.

This tour gives you the chance to see the coast at its most intricate and complicated. The route takes in a few popular resorts along the pink granite coast to the west, but the high spots are in the less commercialized east. Around the Pointe de l'Arcouest, on Route One, the shore is dramatic and the sea a pattern of islands. Along the Côte des Ajoncs, on Route Two, the scenery is gentler, but even more intriguing: it is almost impossible to determine what is mainland and what lies offshore, and at low tide great stretches of sand and rock make wonderful beachcombing.

To give a chance to linger along the Côte des Ajoncs and fit in a trip to the island of Bréhat from the Pointe de l'Arcouest, the tour is best tackled over two or more days. The tour's midpoint is Tréguier, an excellent base if you want to be near the coast but away from the hurly-burly of Brittany's summer tourist trade. If you would prefer to stay outside the town, head 2 km west on the Lannion road, and take advantage of the Breton welcome offered by Kastell Dinec'h, a converted farmhouse (tel 96.92.49.39).

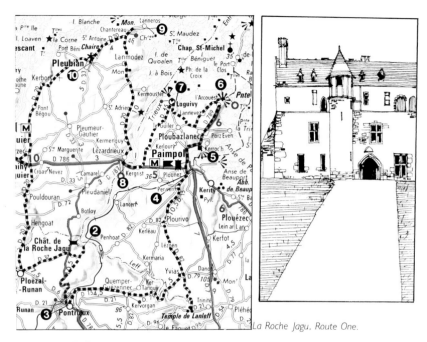

La Roche Jagu, Route One.

ROUTE ONE: 85 KM

Tréguier

This mellow and dignified town was established in the 6thC by one of Brittany's founding fathers, St Tugdual. Legend has it that before he made Tréguier the seat of the diocese, St Tugdual rid the region of a dragon - and that he later went on to become Pope. Tréguier's history may be a subject for scholarly scepticism but its appeal to the present-day tourist is undoubted. Set at the confluence of two rivers, its sheltered, deep waters are a popular anchorage for yachts; the narrow streets are full of half-timbered buildings; and the spacious main square is dominated by one of Brittany's finest cathedrals. To avoid the steep walk from the marina, try to park by this magnificent building. It dates from the 13thC and contains some beautiful stained-glass windows. Make sure you don't leave this 'masterpice of airiness', as the philosopher Ernest Renan (a resident of Tréguier) described it, without visiting the serene Gothic cloisters. Near the cathedral, the 17thC house where Renan lived has been converted into a museum. *Open 10-12, 2-6, and 2-5, Easter to end Sept; closed Tues and Wed.*

Tréguier - La Roche Jagu

① *Head east on the D786 and 1.5 km after crossing the bridge over the river (and just after picnic site) turn right on to the D20. At the junction with the D6 turn left then left again, signposted La Roche Jagu.*

La Roche Jagu Restored about 20 years ago, La Roche Jagu lies buried in woodland above the River Trieux. Behind the homely château there are paths through the forest down to the river, where there are picnic places. *Open 1 April-15 Sept, 10-12.30, 2-7, rest of year Sun and hols only, 2-7.* ② *Turn left out of the castle entrance.*

Pontrieux Once the road starts to wind steeply down, you soon reach this large and animated riverside village - a useful place to stop, wander, relax and enjoy the colour and bustle of Breton rural life. Pontrieux can also be reached by boat from Pointe de l'Arcouest (see below).

Pontrieux - Paimpol ③ *Take the D6, signposted St-Brieuc, then turn left on to the D15. At Quemper-Guézennec turn right along the D79 to Yvias. At Yvias turn right for a detour to Lanleff.* The scenery along the road to Yvias is green and lush. Near the church and behind a tiny cottage in the backwater village of Lanleff are the curious ruins of a small, circular 12thC temple. *Return to Yvias and take the D82 to Plourivo to rejoin the D15.*

Paimpol Paimpol is more a working port than a tourist resort, but the harbour is interesting and active, and there is quite a range of restaurants and modest hotels. *Follow the signs to the port;* park, then walk along the front for the best views of the river making its way out to the bay. ④ *Leave Paimpol on the D789, signposted Pointe de l'Arcouest.*

Château de Coat-guélen
(hotel-rest., Pléhédel) Some way out of Paimpol to the South-east, this beautifully positioned little 19thC château could provide a whole day's relaxation. The food is excellent - light and imaginative; there is a swimming pool, tennis and a nine-hole golf course. The atmosphere is relaxed, and the bedrooms are spacious. *Tel 96.22.31.24; Pléhédel is about 10 km SSE of Paimpol on the D79; closed Nov-Mar; price band B/C/D.*

Kerroc'h Tower *About one km from Paimpol, at a bend in the road, turn right along a signposted track.* It is only a minute's walk up to the squat, three-storeyed tower, and if you find that you have the place to yourself the promontory is fine for a picnic. From here you can see back to Paimpol and the low surrounding countryside, and out to the islands in the bay. The views are no better from the tower, but if you do climb it, don't go beyond the first floor - there is no viewing platform at the top and the balustrade is dangerously low. ⑤ *Continue on the D789.*

Pointe de l'Arcou-est Providing you can tolerate the crowds of other visitors, there is no better place than this to stand and admire the extraordinary island seascape of Brittany's Côtes-du-Nord; quite close by, the island of Bréhat is surrounded by a mass of rocky islets.

Ile-de-Bréhat The hour-long boat trip around the island is not to be missed, and it is well worth while spending a couple of hours actually on Bréhat. A mild

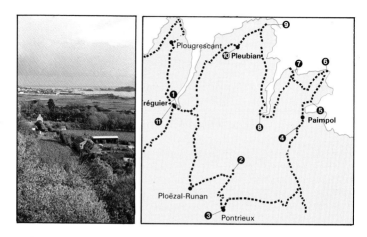

The coast near Paimpol.

climate has given this mass of pink granite a sub-tropical vegetation. There are no cars on Bréhat; it is an ideal place for getting away from it all. *Boat services (9 am-7 pm) depend on the weather; trips also go along the River Trieux to Pontrieux. Tel 96.20.0006 or 96.20.82.30.*
⑥ *Return along the D789 for a short distance, then turn right, following the signs to Loguivy. At the main road - the D15 - turn right (not signposted at time of going to press).*

Loguivy
From the promontory by the harbour mouth you can look across to Bréhat and the other islands. Although the views are less striking than from the Pointe de l'Arcouest, fewer people will be sharing them.

Loguivy - Lézardrieux
⑦ *Leave Loguivy on the D15; go past the turning to Ploubazlanec on left, and take the next turning to the right to Kergoff (not on map) - the signpost faces away from you. Carry straight on over two crossroads and turn left at the T-junction, signposted Lézardrieux. At the main D786 turn right.* This is a thoroughly rural alternative to taking the main road via Paimpol. *Approaching Lézardrieux, just before the graceful suspension bridge, turn right in front of the Bar du Pont.* A short track takes you to a river viewpoint under the bridge, another useful picnic place.

Lézardrieux - Sillon de Talbert
⑧ *Cross the bridge, turn right into Lézardrieux, and follow the D20.* The glimpses of the estuary from this road are encouragement enough to take one of the two or three side roads to the right, signposted 'panorama', which lead to the river bank - and more picnic possibilities. One of these lanes offers the bonus of taking you to the Phare de Bodic, a strange building which looks more like a small castle or folly than a lighthouse.
At Armor de Pleubian (not on map) turn right and then left to Sillon de Talbert.

Sillon de Talbert   The views from here are nowhere near as magnificent as those from Pointe de l'Arcouest, but this low-lying area of mudflats, marsh, sandbanks and seaweed has a charm of its own. The 3-km Talbert sand spit, a curious and unusual feature, makes an interesting walk - provided that the local motorbike boys are not using it for scrambling practice. (9) *From Sillon de Talbert take the D20, signposted Tréguier.*

Pleubian   The ornately carved calvaries - granite monuments depicting religious scenes, found in many of the province's churchyards - are one of the most notable features of Breton art. The Côtes-du-Nord is not in general the best area to see them, but near the church in this village is one of the finest calvary-pulpits in Brittany.

Pleubian - Tréguier   (10) *Follow the signs to Tréguier.* For those who want still more seaside driving, detours along the coast are well signposted.

The sand spit of Sillon de Talbert.

████ ROUTE TWO: 93 KM

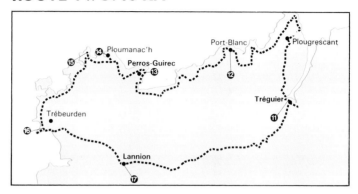

Tréguier -
Plougre-
scant

⑪ *Leave Tréguier on the D8. Ignore signs to the Circuit de la Côte des Ajoncs until you reach Plougrescant, then pick up the signposted route at the right turning just past the church with a wonderfully crooked spire.*

La Côte
des
Ajoncs

The route makes a winding tour of some superbly unspoilt coast, while inland the scenery is hilly, varied and intimate. There are countless picnic places from which to choose; there are coastal paths, some of which are waymarked; and at low tide you can walk out over the vast expanses of sand to clamber over rocks, examine rock pools, and watch the local fishermen collecting seaweed or digging for bait.

The route takes you through several sleepy hamlets but only one fishing village of any size, Buguelès. Make a point of stopping at Pointe du Château and Le Gouffre (not on map). At the Pointe there is a charming cluster of houses set behind a small beach and slipway and by a giant granite outcrop, and the views stretch right across the wide estuary mouth, dotted with rocky islets, many of which are crowned with small lighthouses. And at Le Gouffre there is a much-photographed cottage wedged unbelievably between huge granite boulders. The route is generally well-signposted; when in doubt turn right.

Port-
Blanc

After the simplicity of the previous stretch of coast, where even camping is forbidden, it comes as a surprise to arrive at a village where there are hotels. However, the concessions Port-Blanc has made to tourism are few: at heart it remains an unspoilt, peaceful fishing port. On the front, on top of Sentinel Rock, there is a small granite shrine to the Virgin Mary. Even more unusual is the chapel with a roof that slopes right down to the ground.

Port-Blanc -
Perros-
Guirec

⑫ *Follow the Circuit route through pretty Les Dunes (not on map); at the junction with the D38 turn right (do not follow the Circuit signs straight on). This is a fast road that passes through the resort area of Trévou-*

Tréguignec. *At Trélévern, turn right on to the D73, left on to the D38, then turn right immediately and fork left (passing a* boulangerie *on the left).* Once you are through a short stretch of suburbia, this becomes a fine coastal drive as the road winds down then up through vivid countryside and cool woodland. In the distance, across the bay, the views of the Perros-Guirec headland provide a taste of the rugged scenery to come. *Turn right at the junction with the D6 and follow signs to Perros-Guirec.*

Perros-Guirec

This bustling resort has a large marina and a thriving fishing industry. Grand old houses enjoy secluded settings among the pines that cover the slopes of the north-eastern headland, and at the bottom of the cliffs are two excellent sandy beaches. In summer, boats leave from Trestraou beach for the Sept Iles nature reserve.

Perros-Guirec - Plou-manac'h

⑬ *From the marina follow the road signposted Corniche and Trégastel (D786).* The Corniche is only a short stretch, so make sure you stop at the viewpoint on a bend just past the Plage de Trestignel: it will make up for the few built-up kilometres which now follow. About one km before Ploumanac'h, you suddenly find yourself in exhilarating open countryside. There is a lay-by near a sharp bend, from which you can walk towards the cliffs for yet more views.

Plou-manac'h

The jumbled piles of huge light pink boulders that can be seen all along the Côte de Granite Rose are one of the most bizarre features of the entire coast of Brittany. When you leave the main road to drive into this small and cheerful family resort and working port, *follow signs for the* phare *(lighthouse).* This will bring you to a big expanse of rugged parkland, the best starting point for striding off to explore the rocky shore: turn left for St-Guirec beach, or right to a striking headland. ⑭ *Return to the main road and turn right.* Just after crossing a creek, drive slowly so as not to miss the views of Ploumanac'h harbour. *Turn right into Trégastel-Plage and follow the signs to the Plage de Coz-Pors.*

Tréga-stel-Plage

Trégastel-Plage lacks the vitality and appeal of Ploumanac'h, but the pink granite boulders along the shore of this scattered resort make it worth a visit. The two main areas to explore are the Ile Renot, a long peninsula of rocks and secluded beaches, and the Grève Blanche. Near Coz-Pors beach an aquarium and museum have been built in the caves under a huge pile of rocks, on top of which stands an awful statue. ⑮ *Return to the main road and turn right.*

Tré-beurden

Turn right as soon as you enter Trébeurden and follow the signs to the port. The green beauty of the wooded promontories which separate Trébeurden's sheltered sandy beaches is particularly striking after the rose-tinted strangeness of Ploumanac'h and Trégastel-Plage. Park by the headland on the front and climb up for views.

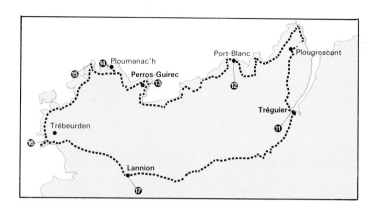

Manoir de Lan Kerrelac *(hotel-rest. Trébeurden)*

If you feel like going for broke, this stylish, comfortable hotel is a good place to do so. Book a table by the window, and take your time over the seafood specialities. *Tel 96.23.50.09; closed mid-Nov to mid-Mar, and Mon (except mid-June to mid-Sept); price band C/D.*

⑯ *From the middle of Trébeurden follow the signs to Pointe de Bihit. The winding road leads to a viewpoint. Return and follow signs to Lannion.*

Lannion

Try to park by the Centre du Communications in Lannion; it is convenient, and is the easiest place from which to pick up the road to Tréguier when you leave. If you cannot park here, carry on following the Tréguier signs, then head for the Hotel de Ville (signposted); this will bring you to the main square where there are more parking places. Lannion is very much a working town, but its compact old quarter, on the left bank of the River Léguer, has character.

Le Kériavily *(restaurant, Lannion)*

This rustic-style first-floor restaurant in a modern building is conveniently sited in the old town. We trust that the recent change of name will not be reflected by a change in its previously high standards. *7 Rue de Kériavily; tel 96.37.14.23; closed 1-10 Sept and Mon; price band A/B.*

Lannion - Tréguier

⑰ *Follow the signs to Tréguier, then turn right on to the D65 to Rospez. From here take the D72. At the junction with the D6 turn right, then left on to the D8. This is a much more rural (and not much slower) alternative to the main road back to Tréguier.*

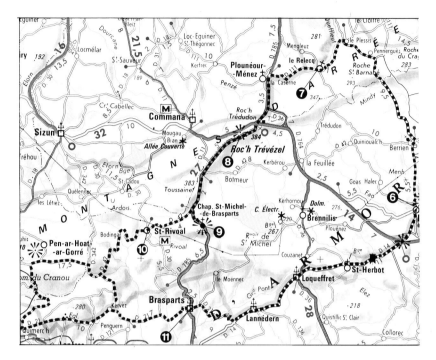

When you drive up into the Montagnes d'Arrée from the surrounding lowland it is hard to believe that their highest peak is not much more than 50 metres higher than the Eiffel Tower in Paris. But these are Brittany's biggest mountains and this area is one of the most beautiful parts of the interior of the province. In the east great swathes of woodland cover the hills, and sparkling rivers and streams cut winding paths through the cool forest. In summer the green is overpowering. But the mountains also have a severe and lonely side to their character; in the west, around Roc'h Trévézel, there are bare, jutting peaks, surrounded by gorse and heather, with hardly a tree in sight.

Since the creation of the Parc Naturel Régional d'Armorique in 1969, this whole area has enjoyed protected status, although one wonders whether things would have changed a great deal even without this act of conservation. Rural life continues much as it has for centuries and tourism seems to be no more than a sideline - accommodation is thin on the ground and modest in style, while restaurants are almost without exception simple.

The Montagnes d'Arrée are for those who enjoy peaceful villages and sweeping views. The tour takes you through the whole range of scenery that the mountains have to offer and includes stops at several interesting

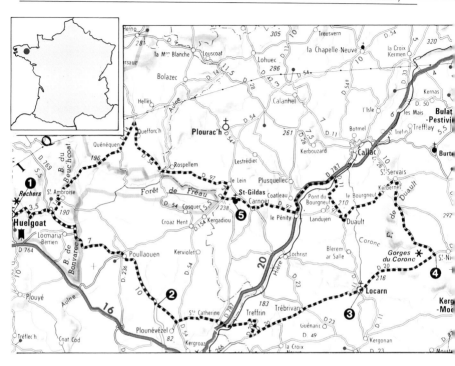

churches and an open-air museum; you might also like to visit one of the craft workshops signposted along the route. Many of the roads are narrow and you need to follow the directions carefully, but driving is not difficult.

ROUTE ONE: 93 KM

Huelgoat Not only is the lakeside village of Huelgoat the best start for exploring the Montagnes d'Arrée, it is also almost the only place in the area that has much in the way of tourist facilities. Around its spacious main square and in the surrounding streets are four small hotels (the An Triskell, *tel 98.99.71.85*, is good value) and several restaurants.

The name Huelgoat means 'high wood', and the great forests surrounding the village offer plenty of opportunities for walks along woodland paths. North of the village, giant granite rocks lie hidden among the trees; one, known as 'la Roche Tremblante', pivots on its base if pushed correctly; other rocks have been weathered into interesting shapes. South and west, the walks include one along the River Argent to a plunging chasm, and another along the canal that was built in the 18thC to serve the silver mining industry. Before leaving, fill your tank - filling stations are scarce on backroads of both loops.

**Huelgoat -
Locmaria-
Berrien**

① *Take the Carhaix-Plouguer road out of Huelgoat.* This is a winding road which cuts a narrow corridor through the forest before entering a wide valley.

**Auberge
de la
Truite**
*(restaurant,
Locmaria)*

This traditionally furnished restaurant on the Huelgoat-Carhaix road is reckoned to serve the best food in the area. Specialities include lobster and, not surprisingly, *truite de l'auberge.* Mme le Guillous's cosy hostelry also has six bedrooms. *Tel 98.99.73.05; closed mid-Jan to Apr, Sun evening and Mon (except July and Aug); price band C.*

**Locmaria-
Berrien -
Locarn**

② *About 4 km beyond Poullaouen, take the left turn signposted Plounévézel; soon turn left and cross the D54, signposted Ste-Catherine. At the junction with the D787 go straight across, signposted Treffrin. At the T-junction turn right along the D20A.* Once you have crossed the D54 there is the first of many long views over the undulating Breton countryside. Because traditional farming methods are still employed here, hedgerows have not been bulldozed, nor trees uprooted or cut down; the patchwork pattern of small fields and clumps of woodland

*Opposite:
Huelgoat's
lake.*

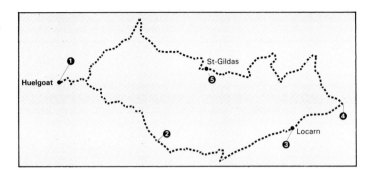

remains more or less as intimate and restful as it has been for hundreds of years. *At the junction with the D20, turn left to Locarn.*

Locarn

A break from driving is in order after the invigorating descent through a leafy valley before the road rises up to reach the quiet hillside village of Locarn. The views over a tributary of the Hière merit more than momentary contemplation; the church contains some fine stained glass; and the silver reliquary of St Hernin, the 16thC cross and 17thC chalice, which are kept in the presbytery, are well worth seeing.

③ *From Locarn take the D20, signposted St-Nicodème, turn left (the signpost to the Gorges faces away from you) then, after about 2 km, turn left once more.*

Gorges du Coronc

From the small parking area, a 15-minute walk through woodland, alongside a narrow river and past big granite outcrops, brings you to the spot where the river passes under a great pile of boulders in a series of small waterfalls. The path continues, but children (and adults, no doubt) will be happy enough to stop here to clamber over the rocks. On a hot day the shade of the forest and the sound of the river are a welcome tonic for those who are starting to feel weary. You need to search around for picnic places; alternatively, the Ty-Pikouz, a small, simple *auberge*, just along from the car park, is an adequate place to stop for a meal or a snack.

Gorges du Coronc - St-Gildas

④ *Return along the short no through road to the Gorges, then turn left and follow the signs to St-Servais (there is one unsignposted T-junction where you should turn left). At St-Servais turn left (not signposted but opposite the church) and as you climb up out of the village take the left turn to Duault.* In contrast to the route from the Gorges to St-Servais, the road follows a high ridge from which you can look out over great expanses of utterly rural countryside. *At Duault bear right on to the D11; drive on for a short while then turn left along the D787.* The D11 winds gently down to the main road and the Hière valley. *Opposite a trout farm, turn right, signposted Carnouët and Chapelle St-Gildas.*

St-Gildas   The chapel, which stands at the end of an unsignposted track lined by an avenue of trees, is visible from the road. Around the roof at the rear of the 16thC building are some fearsome grotesques (one of which is enjoyably crude). Opposite the main door to the chapel and across a stile, a 5-minute walk takes you to the top of a hill from which you can enjoy the most extensive views on this loop of the tour - winds permitting, this is an ideal place to reflect on the charm of the Breton countryside.

St-Gildas -   ⑤ *Return along the tree-lined track and turn left. At the T-junction turn*
Huelgoat   *right, then turn left at the crossroads, signposted Morlaix. At the junction just past Quefforc'h, follow the signs to Huelgoat.* The scenery varies almost as much as the road twists and turns; eventually you rejoin the road which leads through the dark forest back to Huelgoat.

ROUTE TWO: 87 KM or 102 KM

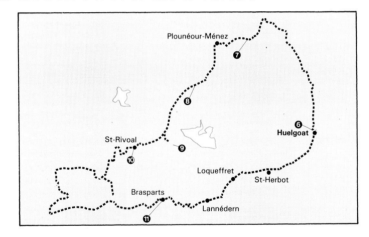

Huelgoat -   ⑥ *Take the D14 north to join the D769 at Berrien. At Le Plessis turn left*
Le Relecq   *along the D111 to Le Relecq.* From Huelgoat the road climbs up to run through high open countryside, part moorland and part grazing land. The D111 is through woodland.

Le Relecq   Time seems to have stood still in this village; the only indication that tourists ever pass is the sign advertising the local potter. Driving between the pillars of an old gateway on the right-hand side of the road, you enter a large rustic square. On your left is a small L-shaped cluster of stone houses. Opposite, a couple of somewhat shabby, more substantial houses stand in delightfully natural gardens, and on your right

View from above the chapel of St-Gildas.

is the church of the old Cistercian abbey. Dating from the 12thC (although the façade is 18thC), the church has a dilapidated charm which is entirely in keeping with the rest of the village.

Le Relecq - Roc'h Trévézel

⑦ *Continue on the D111. At Plounéour-Ménez turn left on to the D785.* For the most part the Montagnes d'Arrée can only be described as impressively hilly; the Roc'h, however, is definitely a mountain. Its jutting peaks, which rise out of a high moorland plateau, can be seen in the distance even before you reach Plounéour, although the nearby communications mast is likely to be the first thing that catches your eye. Not far beyond the D764-D785 crossroads is a signposted footpath to the Roc'h (there is no special car park, just pull in by the roadside). It is only a few minutes' walk to the top, and the views from here are among the most memorable on the tour: to the west you can see as far as Brest; to the north the Baie de Lannion is visible, while to the south you can see the St-Michel mountain (your next stop) and beyond to the Montagnes Noires, Brittany's other principal mountain chain. The view to the south-east, over the St-Michel reservoir, is unfortunately marred by the nuclear power plant buildings. A leisurely picnic will give you time to absorb it all; however, if you prefer not to carry your *baguettes*, cheese and *vin de table* quite so far, the next stop offers another agreeable picnic spot.

Roc'h Trévézel - St-Michel-de-Brasparts

⑧ *Continue on the D785, then either turn right to St-Rivoal along the D42, or, for a short detour to the Montagne St-Michel, keep on the D785, past a small crêperie, then turn right to St-Michel.* A flight of steps from the car park leads to the tiny chapel of St-Michel-de-Brasparts, which crowns this great rounded mountain; the views from here are stunning, although not quite in the same class as those to be seen from Roc'h Trévézel.

St-Michel -   ⑨ *Return to the D785 and turn left. After about 2 km turn left again*
St-Rivoal   *along the D42 to St-Rivoal.*

St-Rivoal   Nowhere else is the conservationist spirit of those who run the Parc
Régional more evident. Here you can see a variety of well-preserved
Breton buildings; other exhibits include agricultural implements and
machinery. *Open daily except Sat, mid-Mar to mid-May, Sept and Oct;
pm only mid-May and June; 11-7, July and Aug.*

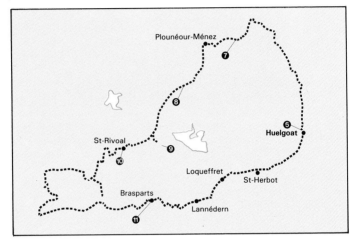

St-Rivoal -   ⑩ *From St-Rivoal, take the D42 in the direction of Le Faou.* This winding
Brasparts   road provides just the right contrast to the bleakness of the peaks
around Roc'h Trévézel, as it makes its way up and down through
woods and farmland. Those who are pressed for time should take the
short route to Brasparts. However, the scenery on the longer route
makes it well worth driving the extra 15 km.
  *Short route: turn left after about 7 km, signposted Lopérec, then after 3
km turn left on to the D21 to Brasparts.*
  *Longer route: continue following the signs to Le Faou until you reach the
turning to the left signposted Quimerc'h; at the junction with the D21 turn
left, signposted Brasparts.* After a stretch of open countryside, the road
descends into Le Forêt du Cranou and the mood of the tour changes
yet again as you pass through a great band of oak and beech woods.
There are several places where you can pull off the road to walk into
the depths of the forest, and almost next to the turning to Quimerc'h
there is a picnic site, with tables. Soon after this the road emerges from
the woods, becoming quite narrow for a while. From the D21, which
follows the line of a high ridge, you can look out over what seems to
be the whole of southern Britanny. Near Kervez the road leaves the
high ground of the ridge.

Brasparts   During the 16th and 17th centuries the parish closes of Brittany became a focus for creative energy, and they are now one of the special features of the villages of the region. Partly as a result of the spiritual vigour of the times and partly because of inter-village rivalry, increasingly elaborate graveyard sculptures (calvaries) were crafted, while in the churches themselves it was woodcarvers who made their mark. Brittany's two most famous parish closes are at St-Thégonnec and Guimiliau, some 20 km north of Roc'h Trévézel (see earlier on this tour), but the one in Brasparts is a good example; the calvary is particularly fine and the church one of the most interesting on the tour.

Brasparts -   ⑪ *Continue along the D21, signposted Huelgoat. At the junction with the*
Lannédern   *D14, turn left to Lennédern.* Both this village and its neighbour,
and   Loqueffret, have small parish closes that are worth pausing to see. The
Loqueffret   church at Lannédern is tucked away on a hillside to the left of the main road, and is easily missed.

Roc'h   After leaving Loqueffret look out on the right for the brown sign to
Bégheor   this *'magnifique pointe de vue'*. A short walk from the tiny area where you can park your car brings you to the edge of an escarpment and a large rock (not marked on map). You are unlikely to disagree with the sign's description of the panorama; it is worth climbing on to the rock to get above the few trees which impede your view.

St-Herbot   The big Gothic church in this tiny village has a finely carved porch beside which is a small charnel house. The interior of the church is dank, dark, but atmospheric and worth a visit for its carved oak screen. Opposite the church there is a café which is also an *épicerie* and bread shop; a *digestif* or a cup of excellent coffee in these friendly surroundings would be a perfect way of rounding off the drive.
Continue along the D14 to Huelgoat.

South-West Brittany:

CORNOUAILLE

The ancient kingdom of Cornouaille, which was given its name by early British settlers from Cornwall, is a region of marked contrasts. The north is majestically hilly; the south-west is flat - except for the rugged Pointe du Raz; and the south is an intricate maze of rivers, inlets and bays. As the landscape has its widely differing moods, so too do the resorts: Audierne is animated, Bénodet sophisticated, Concarneau bustles, while pretty La Forêt Fouesnant goes about its business in a more restrained way.

Not all these places are featured on this tour, which as far as possible steers clear of the most crowded areas, where the summer traffic can be nightmarish; but the route is within easy reach of all the major south-western resorts. The northern loop includes one of Brittany's most picturesque villages, a quiet stretch of coast and some extensive views. The southern loop starts with the restful River Odet, then becomes much more coastal, taking in fishing villages, seaside resorts and some beautiful scenery.

Fishing is such a key industry in this area that you are overwhelmed when it comes to seafood. The same is not quite so true of hotels. If money is no object you could opt for the Manoir du Stang, *tel 98.56.97.37*, a grand mansion set in noble grounds just outside La Forêt Fouesnant. Less formal and considerably cheaper is Le Goyen in Audierne, *tel 98.70.08.88*; the harbour-front building has been attractively renovated and the food is excellent. And there are, in addition, the hotels mentioned *en route*.

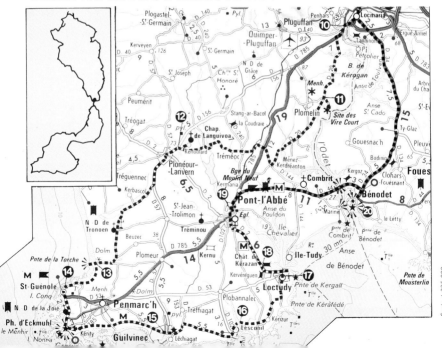

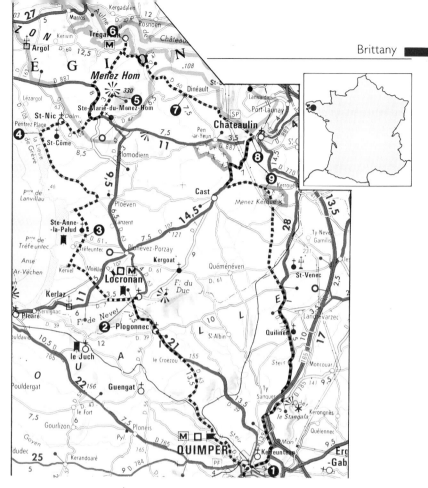

▮ ROUTE ONE: 104 KM

Quimper This big, thriving and stylish town, set in a beautiful wooded valley, was the capital of Cornouaille. If you explore no more than its old quarter of cobbled streets and half-timbered buildings, your visit will have been worthwhile. Within this compact area there are chic shops, a mouth-watering covered market and Quimper's main sights: the imposing Gothic cathedral with its 19thC spires; the Musée des Beaux Arts, which contains works by Rubens, Boucher, Boudin and Fragonard, as well as interesting paintings of old Brittany; and the Musée Départemental Breton (adjacent to the cathedral in the old Bishop's Palace), the perfect place to get a feel for Breton history and culture.

Next door to the Brittany museum is the tourist office; ask here about boat trips along the River Odet.

Quimper is an excellent start for this tour, but a word of warning: be prepared for busy traffic and exasperating one-way systems; it is best

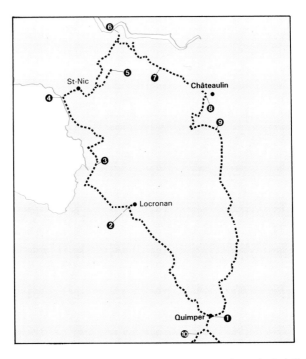

to park on the north bank of the river, near the cathedral; if this proves impossible, follow the signs to the large *centre ville* car park.

Quimper - Locronan

① *Take the Douarnenez road out of Quimper. On the outskirts of the town fork right on to the D63, then follow the signs to Locronan.*

Locronan

A worthy contender for the prize of 'most picturesque village in Brittany', Locronan used to make its money from the manufacture of cloth; today its prosperity comes from the crowds of tourists who come to admire the grey granite beauty of the Renaissance buildings around the main square. In the chapel adjacent to the church, do not miss the magnificent black granite tomb of St-Ronan.

Near the church, a small local museum has exhibits which range from Breton furniture and costumes to contemporary art. Other buildings house antique shops, tea shops and craft *ateliers*.

Overlooking the village is the Mountain of Locronan; from here you can look west to the Baie de Douarnenez, north to Menez Hom (see below) and north-east to the Monts d'Arrée. Every July a pilgrims' procession makes its way to the mountain-top. These *pardons* (but here called *troménies*) are a feature of Breton life, and if you get the chance to see one, you should.

Au Fer à Cheval, Locronan.

Le Fer à Cheval
(restaurant, Locronan)

Conveniently situated on the main square opposite the church, this comfortable restaurant offers sound value. From the lowest-priced menu, the *limande meunière* is recommended, if available. *Tel 98.91.70.74; price band B.*

Manoir le Moëllien
(hotel-restaurant, near Locronan)

If you would prefer to eat (or sleep) in more gracious surroundings, *leave Locronan on the D7, signposted to Douarnenez, then turn right, not far from the village, at the signpost to the Manoir.* A few minutes' drive brings you to this large and lovely 17thC country house set in splendid rural isolation. Beams, antiques and good food await you inside. Bedrooms (all on the ground floor) are comfortable, although fairly expensive; you can eat quite cheaply. *Tel 98.92.50.40; closed mid-Nov to mid-Dec, Jan to mid-Mar, and Wed Oct-Apr; price band B/C.*

Locronan - Ste-Anne-la-Palud

② *Take the Douarnenez road out of Locronan. After about 2 km, turn right on to the V3 (beyond the turning to the Manoir), then follow the signs to Kervel, Tréfuntec and Ste-Anne-la-Palud.*

Ste-Anne-la-Palud

In July and August this rural backwater is forced out of hibernation. Not only do campers, attracted by the sweeping sandy beaches, colonise the empty fields, but great hordes of pilgrims descend on the lonely church to take part in one of Britanny's biggest *pardons.*

Plage
(hotel-rest., Ste-Anne-la-Palud)

The setting is out of this world, but there are other qualities which combine to make Mme La Coz's beachside hotel an absolute gem and an ideal place to recharge your batteries. It is comfortable, well-equipped (there is a heated swimming pool) and the cooking, particularly the seafood, merits superlatives. There is a price to pay for such high standards, but you get value for money. *Tel 98.92.50.12; closed mid-Oct to Mar; price band D.*

Ste-Anne-la-
Palud -
Pentrez

③ *At the crossroads by the church, head for the sea and follow the signs to Ploéven until you reach another crossroads; turn left here, signposted Lestrevet (but signpost difficult to see).* Between Ste-Anne and Ty-Anquer and from Lestrevet to Pentrez, the road hugs the coast, and there are fine views across the Baie de Douarnenez to Cap de la Chèvre. There are plenty of places where you can pull off the road for a picnic, a dip in the sea or a walk along the beach.

Pentrez -
Menez
Hom

④ *From Pentrez follow the signs first to St-Nic, and then towards Châteaulin. At the junction with the D887, turn right, then turn left to Menez Hom.* Once the road begins to climb after St-Nic the views become increasingly better, culminating with the magnificent panorama that is spread out before you when you reach the top of Menez Hom, on the western edge of the Montagnes Noires. From this viewpoint the long peninsulas and huge bays of the complicated west coast are as clear as a map; and the Monts d'Arrée are visible in the distance to the north-east.
⑤ *Return to the D887, turn right and after about 2 km turn right again, following the signs to Trégarvan.*

Trégar-
van

The wooded slopes of the north bank of the meandering Aulne are a delightful contrast to the vast scale of the view from Menez Hom. Down in the valley, this small village is one of only two places on the tour where you can get to the river's edge.

Trégarvan -
Quimper

⑥ *Return to the D60 and turn left.* For a more rustic view of the river than from Trégarvan (and better picnic places) *detour left, signposted L'Aulne, after about 2 km.*
⑦ *At Dinéault follow the signs to the left of the church to Châteaulin de Gare (do not take the D60, signposted Châteaulin).* The route follows a high ridge, affording occasional glimpses of the Aulne.
⑧ *By an industrial building called Ets Kerbrat, just before the suburban approaches to Châteaulin* (a fairly ordinary town with a pleasant riverside setting), *fork right; at the main road turn right, then left along the D7, signposted Douarnenez. After about 3 km, turn left, signposted Chapelle de St-Gildas, then left again at the crossroads (unsignposted).* The short stretch on the pretty, winding D7 is partly through forest; the minor road you turn on to (not marked on map) takes you first through a leafy backwater, then up through open, rugged countryside.
⑨ *At the crossroads before the communications mast, turn right.* The road, as straight as a Roman road, descends from the high ground, providing the last big vistas on this loop of the tour. *At the junction with the D770, turn right for Quimper.*

ROUTE TWO: 96 KM

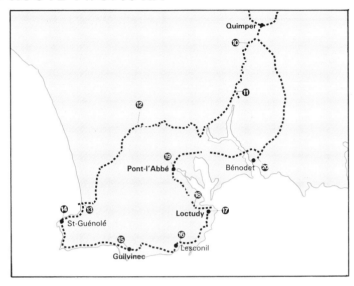

Quimper - *Vire Court*	⑩ *Follow the signs to Pont l'Abbé out of Quimper, then turn left along the D20, signposted Plomelin. After about 4 km turn left to Vire Court.*
Vire **Court**	The approach to Vire Court is irresistible. A tunnel of trees leads to a parking area, from which it is only a short walk, past a ruined house, to the wooded banks of the Odet. By the slipway, take the path above you on your left until you come to a small picnic area (there is at least one table) on a small headland overlooking the river.
Vire Court - *Chapelle de* *Languivoa*	⑪ *Rejoin the D20 and turn left, signposted Ile-Tudy. After about 5 km, turn right along the D144, signposted Quimper; cross the main road and follow the signs first to Tréméoc, and then to Plonéour-Lanvern. Just before you reach Plonéour, turn right to Chapelle de Languivoa.*
Chapelle **de** **Langui-** **voa**	This short detour brings you to an utterly rural backwater of farms, cottages and barns and one very quaint outbuilding with moss-covered thatch. Above the road and dominating the village is a big church with a curiously-shaped tower. East of the village are the ruins of the Chapel of our Lady of Languivoa, where young mothers used to pray to be given enough milk to suckle their children.
	⑫ *At the junction with the D156, turn left into Plonéour, then take the D57, signposted Penmarc'h. After about 2 km turn right, signposted Mejou, then follow the signs to Pointe de la Torche.*

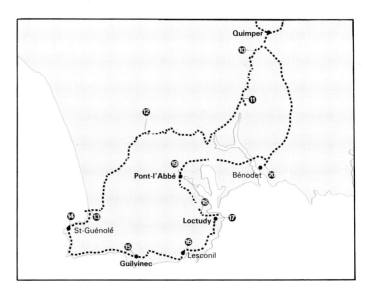

Pointe de la Torche The sign recording the number of people who have drowned off the Pointe makes it abundantly clear that this is not a safe place to swim. However, the island-like promontory, surrounded by rocks, is a pleasant spot for a picnic.
⑬ *A short way from the Pointe, turn right to St-Guénolé* (road not marked on map).

St-Guénolé First impressions of St-Guénolé are not encouraging - grey houses spread about a flat, bleak peninsula. But you soon warm to the salty character of this quiet holiday resort and important fishing port. There is a long sandy beach, a lighthouse and a museum of prehistory, but these are minor attractions compared with the extraordinary rocky plateau that extends from the shore. Rough seas breaking against these fiercesome, jagged rocks are an exhilarating sight.

La Mer
(hotel-restaurant, St-Guénolé) This small hotel and restaurant serves the best seafood in St-Guénolé. *Tel 98.58.62.22; closed mid-Jan to end Feb, Sun evening and Mon out of season; price band B/C.*
⑭ *Leave St-Guénolé via the lighthouse, then take the road signposted Kérity. A ridge of dunes lies between the road and the sea, so pull off the road and find a sheltered, sandy nook from which to view the intricate, rocky seascape. On entering Guilvinec, follow the signs to the port.*

Guilvinec Gaily painted trawlers add vivid dashes of colour to the monochrome granite buildings surrounding Guilvinec's harbour.
⑮ *Drive right round the port and follow the signs to Lesconil.*

Lesconil   Lesconil is another agreeable, small fishing port, prettier and more charming than Guilvinec. As you reach the outskirts of the village, there is a short track which leads to one of the best beaches along this southern coast: golden sand, interesting rocks and big boulders providing shelter from the wind make it an ideal picnic place.
⑯ *From Lesconil follow the signs to Loctudy.*

Loctudy   The views from Loctudy's port are among the prettiest on this tour: across the mouth of the estuary to Ile-Tudy; along the estuary to the thickly wooded island of Garo, and beyond to Ile Chevalier. From the harbour you can take a boat trip up the Odet to Quimper, or out to sea to the Iles de Glénan (a rocky archipelago with interesting birdlife). There is also a passenger ferry service to Ile-Tudy, where there is a lovely long beach. If lack of time rules out a boat trip, do not miss Loctudy's Romanesque church; don't be put off by the 18thC façade.
⑰ *Follow the signs to Pont l'Abbé until the right turn to Ch. de Kérazan.*

Château de Kérazan   Look for the scenes of old Brittany in the art collection housed in this gracious château with lovely gardens. The house was given to the Institut de France in 1929; it dates from the 16thC. *Open 10-12 and 2-6; closed mid-Sept to May, Tue.*
⑱ *Continue to Pont l'Abbé and follow the signs to the middle of town.*

Pont-l'Abbé   *Turn right by the Hôtel de Ville and park by the river, or (except on market day, Thurs) turn left and follow the signs to the car park in the market square.* Pont l'Abbé is the capital of the Bigouden district and its inhabitants stick firmly by their traditions. The museum by the Hôtel de Ville has a large collection, but just wandering the streets you are likely to see people in traditional dress.

Pont-l'Abbé   ⑲ *From Pont-l'Abbé follow the signs to Bénodet. On reaching the Odet,*
- Benodet   *you will have to pay a toll to cross the river; drive slowly over the bridge, taking in the views over the estuary.*

Bénodet   Bénodet may not have architectural panache, but it is slick, smart and very popular, and enjoys a splendid setting among pine trees at the mouth of the Odet. Various boat trips are available (the options are much the same as from Loctudy) and there is also a passenger ferry to Ste-Marine on the opposite bank of the river.

L'Agape   If you decide to cross to Ste-Marine, don't be misled by the outside of
(hotel-rest.,   Le Jeanne d'Arc, a small hotel and restaurant not far from the beach.
Ste-Marine)   Within what appears to be a simple road-house is a fairly smart and highly regarded restaurant which serves delicious seafood. *Tel 98.56.32.70; closed Tues evening and Wed out of season; price band B/C.*
⑳ *From Bénodet take the main road back to Quimper.*

Ile de France:

A thousand years ago, the Ile de France *was* France. Outside a radius of about 80 km from Paris nothing important happened and the French kings exerted no real authority. The Ile was then a land of rich meadows and broad, slow-paced rivers and a good deal of it was taken up by the royal hunting forests of Fontainebleau, Rambouillet and St-Germain-en-Laye. In the middle ages, on the foundations of the hunting lodges, great monumental palaces arose, with satellite châteaux around them.

Today, Paris and its suburbs occupy much of the Ile; industry has made famous abroad the names of places which once consisted only of a manor house and a couple of farms; highways and railways from all corners of France converge on it; and the broad rivers carry many commercial barges. Shops, hotels and restaurants tend to proclaim a Parisian *chic*, and to charge Parisian prices.

The tour sets out to explore the rivers and countryside south of Paris where some flavour of the bygone Ile still lingers. The centre is Nemours, a Roman town, and ancient capital of the Gâtinais, a tract of marshy woodland and wild heath, noted for its honey. On the southern loop you follow Nemours' river, the Loing, and go westward among villages which few strangers seek out and no trains stop at. The northern loop covers well-trodden ground in the forest of Fontainebleau, but tries to avoid the crowds, and also takes a look at the forest's less-frequented outposts.

Church with twisted spire, Puiseaux.

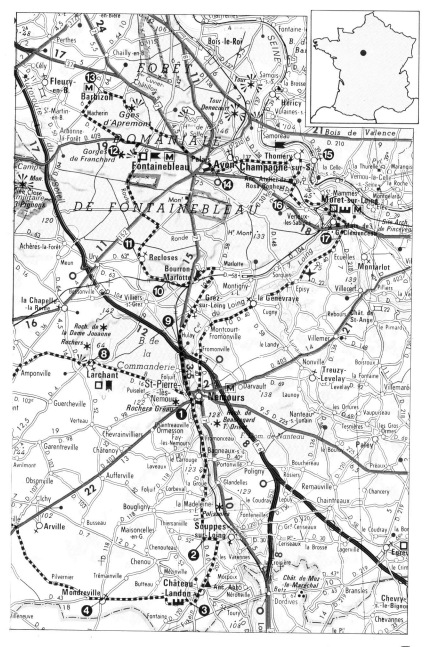

■ ROUTE ONE: 75 KM

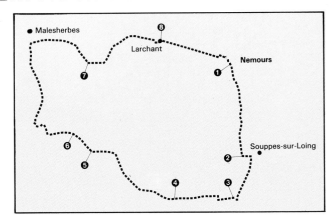

Nemours
For most foreign tourists, Nemours is a town you see from the motorway. The Autoroute du Soleil, Paris to Marseille, which is also the E1 international highway from Le Havre to Palermo, sweeps round it. There is a motel - (Euromotel: *tel 64.28.10.32*) - 2 km along it, going south, but like all European motels it is costly to stay or eat at. As an important river crossing of Roman Gaul, the town was a military station and it preserves the rectilinear Roman layout which was once enclosed in perimeter ramparts. The stern old château on the river bank, just south of the Grand Pont, is steeped in memories of the Agincourt and Joan of Arc era, when it was briefly in English hands. The restored section incorporates the civic museum - a collection overshadowed by the Ile-de-France prehistorical museum across the river in Avenue Stalingrad (where you will find two large car-parks).

On either side of the main thoroughfare, most streets are one-way. This makes town-centre driving confusing, despite the geometrical plan of the 'urban nucleus'. Some fine old buildings survive, and round them are some smart expensive shops, but the farther you go from the centre the less there is to catch the eye. The exception to that is the park on the right of the main exit to Orléans, just beyond the bridges: strange stony pinnacles, the Rochers Gréau, rise from the sandy soil.

Les Roches
(restaurant, Nemours)
It is close to the church of St-Pierre and a short walk from the Rochers Gréau. This is probably the best restaurant in Nemours and by no means the most expensive. Duck, guinea-fowl and beef are cleverly dealt with. *Avenue d'Ormesson; closed Nov, restaurant only Mon and Sun evening (except July, Aug); tel 64.28.01.43; price band C.*

Nemours - Baigneaux-
① *Keeping château and Loing close on left, follow one-way system round Place Victor-Hugo and go straight across at traffic lights, signposted*

sur-Loing *Baigneaux.* If you have come from the rarified atmosphere of the Vosges tour, you may find this route claustrophobic. Factory chimneys obstruct the view, industrial sites have replaced the workshops of humble craftsmen. (The most celebrated local entrepreneur emigrated to Delaware, USA, and started a chemicals factory. It expanded into the multinational which bears his family name: Du Pont.) To this valley the Bohemians of the Latin Quarter brought their mistresses on spring flower-gathering expeditions. Among the river meadows and singing birds Mimi's friend, in *La Bohème,* pouted: "But in the country you never meet anyone." She would make no such complaint today.

Baigneaux - Ch.Landon Smooth and relatively quiet, the road enters rural scenes and cuts through maize plantations and attractive woodland with far-ranging views across the Loing to the Champagne country.
② *Turn left at crossroads, signposted Souppes, right at sugar factory and straight on at crossroads (no signpost).* The sturdy old tower of Château-Landon's parish church is visible ahead - and more factory chimneys.

Château-Landon One of the venerable fortified hill-top towns which ring the Paris basin, Château-Landon exacts a toll from visiting motorists: narrow streets and a labyrinthine one-way system. Park on the outskirts, near the abbey - it is not far to walk. The site indicates a prehistoric settlement; the Romans were here, and so was the wandering monk who brought Christianity to the Gaulish princes - St Gâtian. Foulques le Réchin, born here in 1043, offspring of a local brigand chieftain, was the first of the Plantagenets, England's longest dynasty. Remnants of fortifications from those distant days are best seen as a group from the terrace adjoining the market square. And do not forget to look into Notre-Dame church with its fine open-work belfry - medieval, but quite modern compared with some of the hoary stones around it.
③ *Leave by the D43, signposted Beaumont.*

Château-Landon - Puiseaux The scene is a foretaste of typical Gâtinais landscapes on which a 20thC agriculture, with strips of woodland for windbreaks, has been imposed.
④ *Just after Mondreville turn sharp right, signposted Pilvernier. Near an antiquated church, cross the main road - the D403.* Bromeilles church is seen ahead; around it huddles the small town. These insignificant byways are smooth and straight and a pleasure to drive on. Don't hurry; don't let the variegated flora of the verges become a blur.
⑤ *Follow signs to Puiseaux: narrow road, sharp bend.*

Puiseaux The church's architectural features, including a curiously twisted spire, attract students of ecclesiastical building.
⑥ *Cross the main road and bear left, signposted Pithiviers. After 2 km turn right, signposted Francorville, and cross the Essonne river in two stages.* This is an insignificant little road, but soon you *turn right to a better one (the D25, possibly no signpost) and enter Briarres.*

Briarres-sur-Essonne

If it were a place on one of the *grandes routes,* you would hardly notice it as you hurtled through. Here, in the sleepy Essonne valley, it is one more of those Gâtinais villages which seem to have sprouted naturally and harmoniously out of the roots of their churches. In such places rustic trades once thrived. Their shops are shops such as you can only find in the country and in them you may discover evidence of occupations now forgotten: the gathering of saffron, madder, wild honey, coriander and chicory, fungi and other useful plants.

Malesherbes

The château, uphill beyond the church, not well signposted, is another kind of time-capsule: the world of Marcel Proust. Although his 'Combray' (now Illiers-Combray) is 64 km away near Chartres, the disdainful château suggests the life-style of the landed *noblesse* that Proust describes in *A La Recherche du Temps Perdu.* Malesherbes is on the route of the *Hauts Dignitaires* - historical personages who did the state great service and built mansions in the Ile de France on the proceeds. The first Malesherbes was a courtier of Louis XVI; his descendants have been in possession ever since; worth visiting. *Open daily, 2-5 in winter, 2.30-6.15 in summer except Mon and Tues.*

Males-herbes - Larchant

⑦ *Follow signs to Rumont, there take second left and after 0.75 km turn right, no signpost. Turn left, signposted Amponville. After that hamlet turn right, signposted Larchant.*

Larchant

Larchant has only 500 inhabitants (charmingly known as Liricantois) but the abbey church of St-Mathurin could hold thousands, even though it is obstructed by long-term restoration works. It is sometimes fairly crowded for evening concerts and recitals of sacred music. There are sand-dunes all round the village, which for centuries has exported the sand to glass factories. Numerous walks and picnic spots.
⑧ *Return by the D16 to Nemours.*

The Rochers, a short walk from Larchant, are big outcrops, some forming weird shapes.

◼︎◼︎◼︎ ROUTE TWO: 74 KM

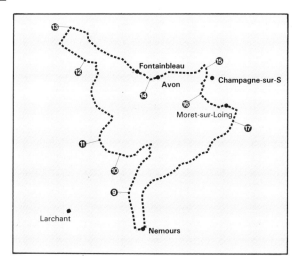

Nemours - Bourron-Marlotte
⑨ *Leave Nemours on main road north and just beyond motorway turn right, signposted Grez-sur-Loing.* Delius, the English composer, lived here for the last 37 years of his life and Robert Louis Stevenson parked his canoe at the jetty when writing *An Inland Voyage. Continue straight on, signposted Bourron-Marlotte.*

Bourron-Marlotte
The château is a mini-Fontainebleau. Moat and canal emphasise its serene formality. The whole makes a superb picture. *Open: gardens only.*
⑩ *Bear left towards railway, then across main road (no signpost).* The road goes in among the aged oaks of the Fontainebleau forest, mercifully shady in summer heat. *Bear right to Recloses.*

Casa del Sol
(restaurant, Recloses)
Parisians beat a path every evening to Mme Courcoul's oak-beamed dining-room. (In warm weather meals are served on the terrace.) You plunge in through a thicket of auto-club, credit-card and Logis de France plaques. Exceptional cishes *à la mode du pays* and wines far from *ordinaires*. Delicious crab. The *patronne*, herself a vegetarian, strikes a neat balance between the wholesome and the fancy cuisines. *63 Rue des Canches, Recloses: tel 64.24.20.35; price band C.*

Recloses - Franchard
⑪ *Turn right from Recloses on to the D63e and after two intersections (not marked on map) turn left into the forest. Follow signposts for Franchard. Be prepared to miss a turning or two: forest roads and trackways are confusing. At monument turn left.*

Franchard The monument commemorates half a million beeches, oaks and pines destroyed in the severe winter of 1878-9. The area is a nature reserve, but picnicking is encouraged. Fine sandy topsoil on eroded rock, a feature of the forest topography, makes walking a pleasure. At the Hermitage, 1.5 km ahead, you are within strolling distance of a famous rocky ravine, the Franchard gorges.

⑫ *Join the major road - the D409 - westbound and in 1.5 km turn right, signposted Macherin. Here turn right again for Barbizon.*

Barbizon The 'cradle of Impressionism', enthusiastically prettified for tourists, ceases to have meaning for those in search of the rustic seclusion and soft light which attracted Millet, Corot, Rousseau, Daubigny and other painters. They came, not intentionally to create a new movement, but to lead a landscape-painting renaissance; and the English artist Constable and the Dutch masters Hobbema and Ruysdael were their inspiration. The early Impressionists met in a great barn at Barbizon to criticise each other's works. Rousseau and Millet became residents and you can visit their houses; also their favourite pub, the Auberge Ganne. The present-day 'studios' of Barbizon do a roaring trade in Impressionist reproductions.

Two restaurants at Barbizon are worth stopping for. One is La Clé d'Or, *tel (1) 60.66.40.96,* quite a charming restaurant-with-rooms on the main street; the other is Le Relais, *tel 60.66.40.28; booking essential at weekends,* a smart country-style place which has a terrace shaded by lime and chestnut trees.

Barbizon- ⑬ *From Barbizon, take the Fontainebleau road and bear right, no*
Fontaine- *signpost.* In 0.75 km park the car and inspect the Apremont gorges on
bleau the left. Along with those of Franchard, they are the outstanding natural curiosity of the forest. You walk on fine crystalline sand and view fantastically contorted sandstone pillars. *Continue on Route du Château to Fontainebleau.*

Fontaine- Perhaps you have seen the palace before; everyone must, at some time
bleau in their lives. You will certainly have seen pictures of its regal frontage with the famous double flight of steps and in front the cobbles of the Cour des Adieux, as it was called after 1814, when Napoleon said farewell to his Old Guard there and everyone broke down and wept. So celebrated is this 'true abode of kings' that one forgets it is attached to a sizeable town which has its own life, history and antiquities.

Here the saintly Louis XI, around 1260, sat under an oak tree and dispensed justice; here the Mona Lisa was first exhibited in France; here the renowned landscape artist Le Nôtre planned his most ambitious gardens; here Napoleon imprisoned a Pope and here he signed away his own imperial powers; here in World War II, at different times, both German and Allied commanders-in-chief were established (soldiers

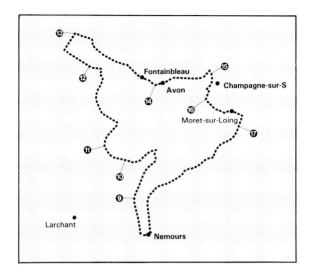

drained the carp pond and ate all the fish, so tales of the longevity of Fontainebleau carp may be treated with scepticism); and here, when NATO set up its first headquarters at the palace, former enemies came together as colleagues.

⑭ *Follow signposts to Avon. Turn left at traffic lights on Rue des Cascades and follow signposts to Thomery, which lies in an arm of the Seine.*

Thomery ⑮ *Turn right, signposted Champagne. Instead of crossing river, turn right and right again into street named for the painter Rosa Bonheur.* Visit the charming Château de By, where Rosa lived, a tremendous celebrity in her 19thC heyday. Part of the building is a museum, a reconstruction of the scenes which inspired her paintings.

⑯ *Under a canopy of trees turn left (no signpost) for Moret-sur-Loing.*

Moret-sur-Loing An old-fashioned town, approached through noble gatehouses. Impressionists Sisley and Pissarro lived and worked here, and those who know and like their work will have a sense of *déjà-vu* in the shimmering riverscape and its weeping willows. Three rivers and a canal converge at Moret, an interchange of long-haul barge traffic.

⑰ *Cross the Loing and turn right, signposted Ecuelles; right again for Nemours.*

Moret-sur-Loing - Nemours The quiet road hugs the canal bank all the way. There are footpaths and parking places all along it and the level countryside gives no hint of imminent factory chimneys.

There is more to the Alsatian provinces than shepherd dogs, white wines and memories of Franco-German confrontations. There are big towns standing guard on the Rhine: Strasbourg, Colmar, Mulhouse. There is a turbulent chaos of highlands, the domed and crinkled peaks of the Vosges. There is plenty of folklore - in places the main occupation seems to be getting into fancy dress and slapping the thighs to a brass band. (Both the *Marseillaise* and the greatest of all march tunes, the *Marche Lorraine*, were composed here.) Alsace was German for 800 years, then given to France, then taken back, then bitterly fought over ... all that is history, but it explains the prevalence of German names and dialects (and German tourists) and a somewhat heavy pork-and-goosefat sort of cuisine.

The loop is based on the mountain resort of Gérardmer and it encircles the high hills, where places prominently marked on the map turn out to be tiny hamlets. At the Grand Ballon (1,426 metres) it touches the summit of the Vosges. There you can trace your circuit without the map, squirming among torrent valleys and forests and small glacial lakes. *Ballon* is a corruption of *bois long*, a reference to the evergreens which once softened the outlines of the high escarpments.

The road touches at many a ski-ing centre and passes under many a chair-lift: this is the winter playground of various Rhine cities. Outside the short winter season, accommodation at hotels, *gîtes* and *fermes auberges* (farm guest houses) is no problem. There are few foreign tourists.

▆▆▆▆ ROUTE: 142 KM

Gérard-mer   Tourism is highly developed here, which is as it should be because the tourist office at the railway station proclaims itself the oldest in France, established 1875. Discos and night-clubs make for a lively night-life. Outdoor activities are centred on the lake which washes Gérardmer's doorsteps only 400 metres from the town centre. Charlemagne was here - if you doubt it you will be shown the rocky outcrop which bears the hoofprint of his horse. Early this century Gérardmer must have been a lovely old town, a scene from Grimms' fairy-tales. It escaped all the medieval wars, all the turmoil of Revolution and Empire, even the Franco-Prussian war of 1870 and the First World War. But it was almost obliterated in the last days of 1944 when the German army withdrew across the Rhine and now there is scarcely a building older than that date. The streets are clean and colourful, with many floral displays and gift shops. Local products include pine honey, Vosges *charcuterie* (smoked hams and sausages, chiefly) and a cheese called Le Gérômé. The wines come from French vineyards on the Rhine and are stronger and less flowery than German Rhine wines.

① *Leave town by the main street, Boulevard d'Alsace, and bear right on to the D147, signposted Col de la Schlucht. Turn right on to the C12, signposted Xonrupt, then left, signposted Lac de Longemer.*

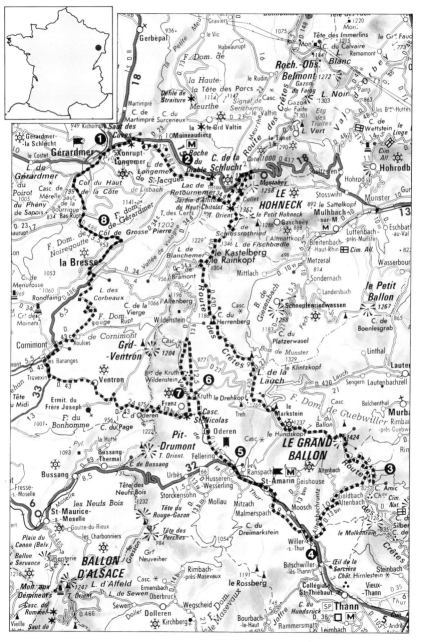

Xonrupt- *Longemer*	Summer pastimes and winter sports occupy adjacent sites in many Vosges resorts; consequently, scenes of activity alternate with scenes of near desolation. At Xonrupt, in summer, you tour a corridor of boarded-up chalets for skiers. Five minutes later you roll past the Longemer lake, which is almost invisible behind tents, caravans and the coloured sails of boats on its surface. In winter, all the action shifts to the chalets and to *aprés-ski* diversions.

The village houses Expo Faune Lorraine, a collection of the wildlife of the Vosges *en tableau* in mini-landscapes of growing vegetation. The exhibition is more educational than entertaining, promoting the ideals of a conservation-conscious community in a serious but quite endearing way. *Open daily, pm only, June-Sept.*

La Moineaudiére, just across the main road, takes all the stock-in-trade of a typically musty provincial museum - butterflies, eggs, wild flowers, minerals - and displays them with imaginative presentation and skilful lighting effects. Well worth a quick tour of inspection. *Open daily, all year round.*

Xonrupt- *Longemer -* *Le Collet*	② *At the end of the lake turn right, signposted Retournemer.* Here the road curves round a smaller lake, another hectic aquatic playground. *Turn left, signposted Le Collet.* Energetic passengers can get out of the car at this point and climb the well-marked short cut to Le Collet, where you will meet them half an hour later after some low-gear work in the car. *Turn right, signposted Le Collet, and right again on to the D430.* More slow climbing and more hairpin bends are in front of you: this is the start of the Route des Crêtes.

Le Collet - *Le* *Markstein*	The Alpine garden of Haut-Chitelet, on the right at 1,228 metres should not be missed. Here, amid kaleidoscopic rockeries, the University of Nancy cultivates species of high-altitude plants, some quite rare, from all over Europe and also from North America, China and Japan. Admission is free. If you want a scientific tour, a resident botanist will conduct you round. Delightful surroundings, but you must not picnic here. *Open daily July-Oct.*

On the left, a stone's throw farther on, you come to a roadside parking area where you may picnic; tables and benches are provided. (Note: the Alsatians are sensitive about litter.) There is a panoramic indicator at which you have wide and spectacular views over a comprehensive tract of the Vosges and the provinces of Haut Rhin and Bas Rhin. This summit is called the Petit Hohneck. The '*petit*' must be ironic - at 1,362 metres it is higher than any other point on the Hohneck massif. Pray for a high cloud base on this section. For many who travel it, swirling mist blots out the true grandeur of the scene.

Route des **Crêtes**	You have now reached the high ground and for the next 35 km will follow the crests from which the Vosges mountains sweep down among jumbled foothills to the west and drop abruptly to the Rhine valley in

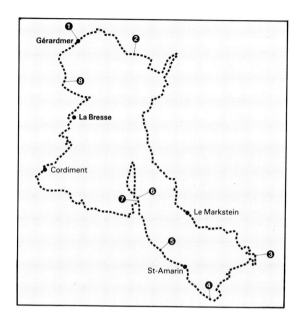

the east. At times you will see the southern chain of the Vosges at the Ballon d'Alsace; then the Belfort Gap, and beyond it the Jura mountains. Eastwards, in clear weather, the Black Forest in Germany is plainly visible. To the south-east you may catch a glimpse of Mont Blanc. These highlands were once remote from the world, known only to shepherds and smugglers (they were the historical frontier between Germany and France). In the First World War the heights marked the extreme right of the Allied line. Your road, the Highway of the Crests, was built by French military engineers towards the end of that war. It could not have been a communications link of any significance, nor was it strategically important; but it makes a wonderful skyline drive.

The kilometre stones give distances and altitudes, the latter ranging from 1,200 to 1,300 metres. The road is mostly unfenced, with near-vertical drops of several hundred metres.

Le Markstein Not a village, merely a ski station. Neighbouring slopes are etched with ski-tows. Just before arriving at Le Markstein you may see people hang-gliding in the direction of Lac de la Lauch, another of the little melt-water lakes which are embedded like precious stones in the forested and heather-clad foothills. Hereabouts the road itself enters pine forests, but they do not obstruct the tremendous panoramas. There are marked nature trails here and there. Chalets and cafés are springing up, and at the latter you may buy bilberry tart, the local speciality, for your picnic at one of the numerous sites.

Gallic flair for exterior decoration, Alsace.

Grand Ballon

Here the Route des Crêtes reaches its greatest altitude, 1,424 metres. The summit is a scattered community of hotels, bars and ski terminals. From it, your descent on the south side is moderately severe in places. The zigzags are well banked, but treat the slippery cobbles on the bends with respect if the surface is wet.

Guebwiller
(detour)

To the left, just beside the Goldbach turning, an enticing but very minor road goes off to Guebwiller, the so-called Pearl of the Florival. (Many small Alsatian towns are 'pearls' of something or other.) Guebwiller's vineyards and wine caves, Friday evening folkloristic spectacles and wide range of leisure opportunities attract many people to the Florival, which in spring and summer is indeed a floral valley. This detour would add about 30 km to the tour.

Alsace
(restaurant, Guebwiller)

This is the restaurant of one of Guebwiller's three hotels. The atmosphere is a trifle bleak but the food is meticulously prepared and served and lavish portions are offered. You are clearly in an establishment which is used to catering for strong hungry people in a bracing climate. The rabbit terrine is a meal in itself. Smoked Strasbourg sausage and smoked leg of pork are among the meats served in the regional *sauerkraut* platter. Memorable baking, including bilberry tart. *140, Rue de la République, tel 89.76.83.02; price band B.*

③ *Turn right, off the Route des Crêtes, signposted Goldbach.*

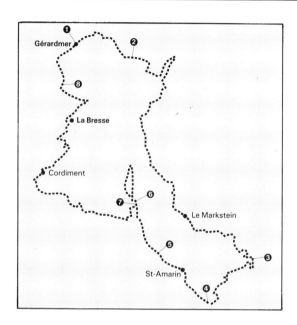

**Goldbach -
Willer-sur-
Thur**

The road drops alarmingly, the hairpins seem to go on for ever ... and all at once you are on the Bâle-Nancy highway.

④ *At Willer-sur-Thur* (observe the attractive church with its eccentrically coiffeured spire) *turn right on to the main road, left across the river and bend sharp right at the station yard.* On this minor road a few hamlets cower away from the thunder of traffic on the N66. *Keep left and turn left again into St-Amarin.*

**St-
Amarin**

Formerly a stopover on the old-time *diligence* routes, St-Amarin is trying hard to become a tourist centre by exploiting its hilly surroundings and the attractions of the Thur valley in which it sits. A gridiron of footpaths is marked with the signs of the Club Vosgien; the most popular route is upstream to Ranspach and Wesserling, notable for wild flowers and spring blossom. Escorted walks to the Vosges highlands, including the Route des Crêtes, along which you have just driven, are organized by the Club. (They take place on *Wed every week, July to mid-Sept, one whole day, not too strenuous*). Another possible guided excursion is to the Sée d'Urbés (actually a peatbog) and the source of the Moselle river about 10 km west on the N66.

⑤ *In 3 km turn off the main road, signposted Kruth.* The road is narrow, and carries local tourist and forestry traffic, but the surface is good.

Kruth

The restaurant Perring often has local river trout on its menu.

⑥ *Turn right in the village and bear left, signposted Barrage.*

Lac de Kruth-Wilden-stein

Above the dam is one of those little smudges of turquoise which you saw far below as you passed along the Route des Crêtes. *Take the serpentine road round it, preferably anti-clockwise.* It turns out to be an impressive sheet of water - artificial, but serene in its setting. At the top end the stream which feeds the lake tumbles headlong in cascades; picnic spots on both sides of the water - consult the information board at the Barrage, which also gives details of short walks.
⑦ *Turn right in Kruth, signposted Ventron.*

St-Nicholas

In 1.5 km you arrive at the toy chapel of St-Nicholas, hexagon-shaped with modern stained-glass windows. Alongside it, more powerful cascades, a whole mile of them, come racing into the Thur. Paths follow the rapids on both sides and you can picnic beside them.

Auberge des Cascades de St-Nicholas
(restaurant, near Kruth)

This *auberge* is not grand, nor is it unpopular with visitors, so booking ahead for a room or a meal is advised. It stands on the right, close to the cascades, a rather fussy-looking chalet-hotel backing on to the pine forest. The plaque on the door, portraying a hand balancing a steaming saucepan on a tray, with the legend *'Plat du Terroir'*, indicates low-budget regional cuisine. The restaurant has a reputation for its typical Alsatian food, including *quiche Lorraine* (the authentic kind, without cheese), smoked ham, sauerkraut and appetizing fruit tarts.

St-Nicholas - Ventron	With many windings and a threat now and again to give it all up and turn back, the road sets itself to surmount the last ridge of the highlands. At the summit, the Col d'Oderen (875 metres) you leave the Haut-Rhin province and return to that of Vosges. A tortuous descent on the west side threads round-topped wooded hills.
Ventron	Inhabitants of this modern village seem to choose to live as far from each other as possible, consistent with the narrow confines of the valley. They would seem to have a lonely life in winter, and here the snow lies late. But of course it is not at all lonely - winter is when Ventron really comes to life. The centre of winter-sports activity is the Hermitage of Frère Joseph overlooking the village. *(Turn left at crossroads just before entering Ventron.)* Besides ski-schools and chair-lifts there are two hotels, one big enough to host conferences. Their restaurants offer a sophisticated Alsatian cuisine - at a price. Summer visitors to Ventron energetically explore the woodland, fish in the trout streams and gather rustic fruits, including the wild raspberries and strawberries from which liqueurs are distilled. The countryside round about offers some strenuous rock-climbing, but nature really designed the whole scene for picnicking and sipping your *vin fin d'Alsace* and dozing in the sunshine.
Travexin	On the left, before you turn right to the main road - the D486 - is a permanent exhibition of wood sculpture, a demonstration of the Vosges craftsman's inherited skills in taking cold timber and breathing life into it again.
Cornimont - Xoulces	Cornimont is a small industrial town, much knocked about in 1944. *Drive through without stopping and bear right, signposted Xoulces, along the torrent valley; at Xoulces turn left.*
La Bresse	To anyone coming from the upland hamlets, La Bresse is like a city, especially when it is humming with winter-sports visitors. Clean and colourful, almost entirely rebuilt since 1944, it attracts summer visitors who like to see a bit of life around them in the streets, bars and cafés.
Auberge du Pecheur *(La Bresse)*	This offers the best of venison, trout in Riesling and other Alsatian delicacies; also a classy wine-list with excellent house wine by the carafe. *On the D34d, 6.5 km north of La Bresse; tel 29.25.43.86; closed two weeks in June and Dec, Tues and Wed out of season; price band B.*
La Bresse - Gérard-mer	Much holiday traffic negotiates the awkward hairpin bends on this road. At wayside houses local produce is sold, including goats' cheese and pottery - but you may find better bargains in Gérardmer. ⑧ *At Bas-Rupt, turn right before the river bridge to a minor road.* On the right, a rock-painting of Notre-Dame de la Cruse draws attention to her rustic shrine. *Re-enter Gérardmer.*

In the geological upheavals of pre-history, water in this locality south of Orléans was trapped on clay beds and settled into stagnant ponds. The resulting lakeland, now known as the Sologne, is a cartographer's nightmare, and to the hurrying motorist on the N20 a featureless land; and to those who explore it a dreamy country of silent pools and heather and abundant wildlife. This route, one continuous circuit, goes through the Sologne; then, by way of the great châteaux of Cheverny and Chambord, it crosses the valley of the Loire to the fertile plain of Beauce. This is not a conventionally beautiful drive; more of a voyage into a mysterious twilit world. Foreigners to France look blank when you mention the Sologne. French tourists have heard of it, but few have been there. In a few years maybe all that will change. There are plans to create wildlife parks and ecological reserves and to offer shooting, fishing and boating expeditions among the jigsaw puzzle of the meres. Meantime, the network of backroads does not spoil the simplicity and soft colours of a countryside which guidebooks too often dismiss as mournful and melancholy. There are no towns apart from the tour centre, Beaugency. It can be a fair distance between filling stations. Hotels are tiny, so do not count on rooms or meals at short notice. In secluded areas like this, touring families should consider accommodation at camping parks, pre-booked through a reliable operator.

ROUTE: 140 KM

Beau-gency

Everything in Beaugency slides downhill to the Loire. Even the lateral streets have a slight tilt. Many travellers have slid through this cosy, genteel little town - it used to have the only bridge on 60 km of river. One who knew the place well was Dunois, Bastard of Orléans, faithful warrior of France and comrade-in-arms of Joan of Arc. His modest château is wedged under the town walls, beside the gate facing the square keep called Caesar's Tower. (You are in a district of Roman memories: the Orléanais is named after Marcus Aurelius.) The château is now the Orléanais museum, not very interesting. Time is better spent roaming the alleyways and, at night, strolling under old-fashioned street-lamps. Hardy walkers should look out for the *Sentier de Grande Randonnée* signs marking a fine long-distance footpath, which starts at Beaugency, goes along the south bank of the Loire and ends at Chinon in Touraine, 140 km away.

(Accommo-dation and eating, Beaugency)

A reasonable, above-average hotel is the Ecu de Bretagne; it has plenty of parking space, always a consideration at Beaugency; *Place Martroi; tel 38.44.67.60.* An acceptable restaurant, if you do not insist on gourmet fireworks, is the Auberge des Trois Cheminées; *Route Blois; tel 38. 44.74.20, price band B; the Auberge also has a car-park and a few rooms.* ① *Leave the town by the Route d'Orléans and turn right at the traffic lights in Baule.*

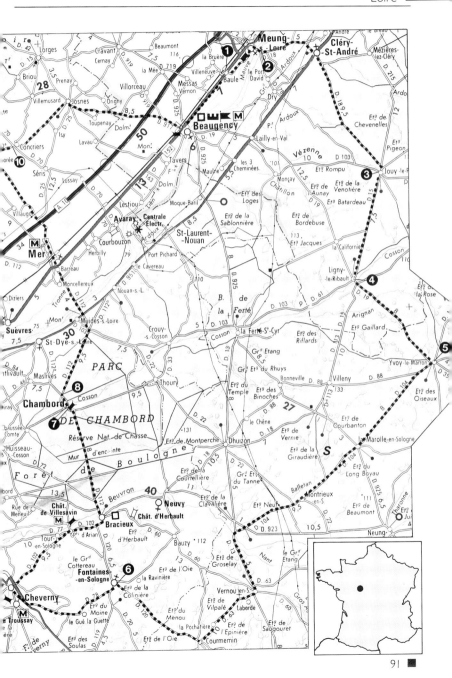

Beaule   A narrow little lane with a fine view of the Loire as you enter Meung.

Meung   Do not be put off by the fact that it lies on a busy highway. Easy to park in, this is a pleasant town of solid houses, semi-subterranean waterways and woodland walks. Its pale château and ruined *donjon* recall the adventures of two French poets, Jean de Meung (responsible for most of the medieval poem-cycle, the *Roman de la Rose*) and François Villon. Villon came to Meung under sentence of death - twice. And twice he benefited from an unexpected general amnesty.

Auberge St-Jacques
(restaurant, Meung)   There are better places than Meung to eat or sleep in, but if you are doing either, an out-of-the-ordinary establishment is the Auberge St-Jacques close to the château. It is mentioned in Dumas' *Three Musketeers* as the hostelry where the prickly d'Artagnan fights a duel and is wounded, all because another guest has smiled at the colour of his horse. M. and Mme Le Gall, chef and proprietress, keep a neat house and serve idiosyncratic fish dishes; *tel 38.44.30.39; closed two weeks Oct, Jan-Feb and Mon; price band C.*
② *Cross the Loire.*

Cléry-St-André   Guidebooks call it dull, but many visitors are charmed by the half-timbering of the gaunt old houses. Centuries ago it was an important stopover on the pilgrim route to Santiago de Compostela in Spain and when farm labourers ploughed up a primitive statue of the Virgin and Child the place attracted pilgrims on its own account, especially when the statue started working miracles. To house it, Charles VII and Dunois began the large church of Nôtre-Dame (1430) and Louis XI completed it - to the satisfaction of generations of martins which peer inquisitively at you from cracks in doorways and arches as you enter. The statue is on the altar, the bodies of Louis XI and his queen are in the crypt. Their skulls are displayed in a glass case.

Cléry - Ligny-le-Ribault   The road is wide with ragged-edged tarmac and an undulating surface, best taken at moderate speed. It is the gateway to the Sologne and for the next 40 km you may expect to see pheasant, hare, deer and possibly wild boar. In the season (late autumn, winter) you will hear shotguns and see sportsmen emerging from the undergrowth.
③ *Turn right, signposted Ligny-le-Ribault.*

Ligny-le-Ribault   Pause for a glance at the illuminated windows of the church, with leaded glass in unconventionally abstract designs.

St-Jacques, Ste-Anne
(restaurants, Ligny)   At Ligny, in the middle of what is generally considered a gastronomic desert, another Auberge St-Jacques rates an entry in Michelin. *Tel 38. 45.41.54; closed throughout Sept; price band B.*
    Freshwater fish and game dishes and snacks, from both homely and *cordon bleu* recipes, are nicely presented at the Auberge Ste-Anne, M.

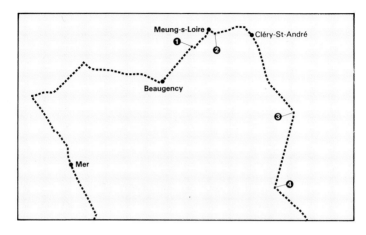

Lelait's bar-restaurant; *opposite the church in Place de l'Eglise; tel 38.45.42.19; closed Mon evening and Tue; price bands A upwards* - the broad price range reflects the cosmopolitan clientèle. This backwater is always thronged; it is a mystery where all the people come from.
④ *Turn left on to the road signposted Lamotte-Beuvron.*

Ligny - Yvoy-le-Marron

Woodland, boggy heath and lonely farmsteads on this road. Some farms sell goats' cheese, a Sologne speciality. Within a few minutes' walk of the road you might discover hidden pools and a rich, strange botany. But in autumn excitable wildfowlers deter you from straying and the most interesting looking meres are protected with chain-link fences and No Entry signs.

Yvoy-le-Marron

This small metropolis has curious houses, some red-bricked and pantiled, others faced with tiles stuck in cement. Such communities support carpenters, coopers and wheelwrights, all the old trades; and you may see a spire of blue smoke rising from the trees, indicating that charcoal-burners are at work somewhere not far off.
⑤ *Turn right, signposted La Marolle.*

Monté-vran
(detour)

Turn left in Yvoy-le-Marron. Both roads going east skirt the zoological park of Montévran. The entrance is on the N20, Orléans-Vierzon road. Rare fauna of the region is Montévran's speciality but, like so many zoos, the place gives the impression of being short of cash.

La Marolle - Vernou

Characteristic Solognais cottages at Montrieux - squat bricks and half-timber, flat tiles or thatch or 'cob' (timber in-filled with a mortar of clay and straw) for the older buildings; an education in rural domestic architecture. Deer may be a hazard on this stretch. Tales are told of fatal collisions between motorists and bucks in the rutting season.

Typical Sologne timber-frame cottage at Courmemin.

Vernou   Visit the dried-flower workshops. You follow signs *Fleurs Séchées* to the farm meadow where everlasting flowers grow in many colours. The workshop turns out decorative items of various kinds, including ceramic heads adorned with dried blossoms. Sounds awful, but the results are sometimes artistic and Gil, Patricia and friends offer a cheerful, not heavily commercial, welcome. A small bouquet at ten francs makes a souvenir of a possibly unique cottage craft.

Cour-memin   It is set in its own little lakeland where duck and water-lilies abound and is among the most venerable of Sologne communities. On the left, as you leave, you have a close-up view of the Etang de l'Oie, an exceptionally pretty pool. Nearby and all along the well-surfaced but corrugated road you will find parking spaces and woodland clearings which make useful picnic places.

Fontaines -en-Sologne   At this rather down-at-heel village (the main-street bar/café totters alarmingly) you make your exit from the Sologne.
⑥ *At the village crossroads turn left, signposted Selles, then bear right, signposted Cheverny.*

Cheverny   Entering the trophy room at the château, confronted by 2,000-odd stags' heads, you understand why the wildlife of the Sologne was not quite as prolific as you had hoped to find it. Cheverny also has its cultural side - the guidebooks rhapsodise over tapestries, paintings and furniture. Such places breed shops and stalls the way the Sologne meres breed tadpoles. Here you can buy local wines, honey, glassware, pottery, wood carvings, leather, jewellery and stuffed animals. Souvenir

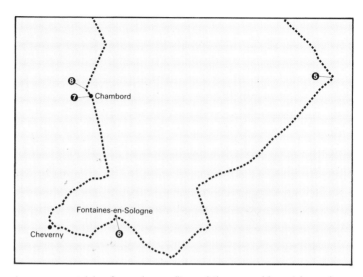

items are certainly of superior quality and the general layout is spacious - the orangery, a separate heated building, is itself capable of accommodating 500 visistors. But the whole operation is geared to mass tourism and one's heart sinks at the sight of all those coaches in the car-park. *Open am and pm all year; hours vary.*

Cour-Cheverny
Centre of 24 wine communes, some in business for 450 years. They grow the white Romorantin, Sauvignon, Pineau and Pinot grapes and the red and rosé Gamay, Pinot Noir and Cabernet. The Syndicat d'Initiative de Cheverny, *tel 54.79.95.63,* will tell you which cellars and vineyards are receiving visitors and selling wine on which day. From here the road to Bracieux is excellent, through open country with wide horizons.

Villesavin
(detour)
On the left, approaching Bracieux, take the minor road to the Château de Villesavin ($\frac{1}{2}$ km), a lovely mellow old building of monastic and manor-house origins. It was never 'improved' by the extravagances of monarchs and their mistresses, but always remained in private hands. A stroll round the exterior is quite enough. Closed Jan-Feb.

Bernard Robin
(restaurant, Bracieux)
Here is a pleasant uncluttered dining-room and much more than genuine local cuisine in the otherwise unremarkable village of Bracieux. You will appreciate the finesse which goes with the unassuming friendliness of M. Robin. A la carte prices for such dishes as quail with cabbage salad and river-fish-and-oyster *blanquette* are out of this world. Note there is no shortage of customers for them, or for the humbler *plats du jour. 1, Avenue Chambard; tel 54.46.41.22; closed end of Dec-Jan, Tues evening and Wed; price band D.*

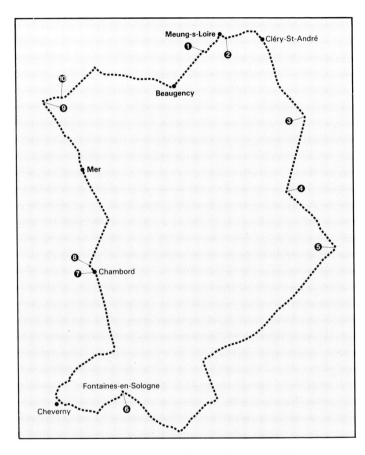

Bracieux - Chambord	Enter the conifer plantations of the Forest of Boulogne. Although straight, wide and well-shod, the road is intersected by ramps which you may find the hard way, by hitting them. There are no warning signs. When you pass through the boundary wall of the Chambord estate you still have 7 km to go to the château - which gives an idea of the scale on which this biggest of Loire residences is conceived. The park's boundary wall, enclosing a sanctuary for deer and wild boar, is 35 km in circumference.
Cham-bord	The strange agglomeration of towers, belfries and chimneys, like a mushroom growth in stone, will be familiar to readers of books about Loire châteaux - it is usually the jacket illustration. Few of the 400 apartments are furnished, but all are redolent of court history and intrigue. Molière presented his plays here. Having bought your parking

ticket and paid your entrance fee you are free to roam unescorted - a rare privilege in Loire châteaux. Ascend the famous double-spiral staircase: those going up are invisible to those coming down. Walk among the chimneys on the roof - it is like walking through a fantastic, Kafka-esque stage set. Includes a museum of hunting. *Closed Tues.*
⑦ *From the car-park follow the signs for Orléans.*

Chambord - Mer For 8 km you are still in the park of Chambord where game is under protection. On your left is the area open to the public, with some rectilinear paths for pedestrians. At the roadside on the right is an observation post, one of three 'hides' for studying the wildlife. But you really need binoculars. There is a helpful interpretative display in words and pictures.
⑧ *At the perimeter pavilion turn left, signposted Mer, then bear right on the D112.* Beyond the crossroads the Loire smiles up like an old friend. For views of an exceptional stretch of the river, park your car close to the bridge and go over and back on foot.

Mer The stained-glass windows in the church are worth more than a glance in passing.

Mer - Talcy These are the fringes of Beauce: the landscape is flat, the sightlines along the roads run straight to the horizon. You feel that if you could climb a tree you would have a view of Chartres cathedral, 80 km away - but there is not a tree in the landscape. An old-fashioned windmill on the right and then the prospect of Talcy château ahead remind you that you have come into another sort of country and that the Loire divides two cultures and two different styles of life and character.

Talcy Modest by Chambord standards, with no river running by, Talcy is impressive in its own way and good value for its relatively homely period furnishings. *Closed Tues out of season.* It has fine Renaissance gardens; laid out by horticulturists who had also to be skilled mathematicians and sergeant-majors too, one suspects, to keep the plants growing to order and preserve the uniform patterns of the gravelled walks and parterres. The shade of the 16thC poet Ronsard hangs over Talcy. He loved the owner's daughter and she inspired him to write the favourite recitation piece: *Mignonne, allons voir si le rose...*
⑨ *Return to the D70 and turn left, signposted Concriers.*

Concriers A well and its bucket and chain are a feature of many churchyards in this region, but have a look at the Concriers well - it must be one of the biggest ever constructed.
⑩ *Turn right and immediately left, signposted Josnes.*

Concriers - Beaugency In 7 km a fine avenue of poplar trees welcomes you back to Beaugency and the Loire.

The Middle Loire

In the Romance languages, many rivers are masculine, but not the Loire. Is this because she is wayward and unpredictable in her course? But *La Loire*, between Blois and Tours, is feminine in a different way. She is graceful and shy, hidden among low cliffs and vineyards in the flattish landscape, scarcely visible until you reach her banks. The tour is entitled the 'Middle Loire' but it is really an expedition to three rivers and three major riverside châteaux. It explores the Loire in the north, the serpentine Indre in the south-west, and, en route, it crosses and re-crosses the Cher, a waterway of modest charm and tranquility. The three principal châteaux - Amboise and Chaumont on the Loire and Chenonceau on the Cher - are among the most historic, photogenic and dramatically-poised in all France.

This is the 'garden of France', a great salad bowl with a timeless and refined air which proclaims the prodigality of nature and the Gallic countryman's genius for co-operating with the natural order of things. Such are among the themes of novels by Balzac, Zola and Alain-Fournier, set in this region.

Nor would a little preliminary reading of court and political history up to the *belle époque* be a bad thing on this tour. Much of that history was written around the châteaux and seigneurial demesnes through which you will pass. From Montrichard on the Cher, our northern loop offers lightly-trafficked alternatives to the main touring highways and achieves new perspectives on some famous sights. Southward you will penetrate the shallow valleys of the Indre and its tributary the Indrois, secret waterways unknown to many tourists.

◼◼◼◼ ROUTE ONE: 88 KM

Mont-richard

This township on the northern bank of the Cher is backed by the woodlands and deer-parks of the Montrichard and Amboise estates. Under a ruined keep like a block of concrete, atmospheric churches and half-timbered houses are crammed into an urban nucleus which has remained virtually intact since the Middle Ages. There are tourist roads through the forests - these forests actually have trees - and numerous picnic areas, cool on a hot day; also attractive riverside paths where the Cher loiters under pale *tuffeau* cliffs honeycombed with mushroom caves and wine cellars, some visitable. A few miles downstream the Cher becomes a canal. Of several small hotels, the Tête Noire in Rue de Tours is the biggest, the Bellevue at Quai du Cher probably the most appealing to the visitor. You will find ample parking close to the principal sights between the Rue de Vierzon and the river bank. At quays on the sleepy river you may hire boats.

① *Following signs 'Autres Directions' from town centre, cross river and crossroads and turn left, signposted Loches. (Ignore the road on the left to the ancient abbey; it is strictly private.) After 5 km turn left on to the unsignposted road through the larchwoods.*

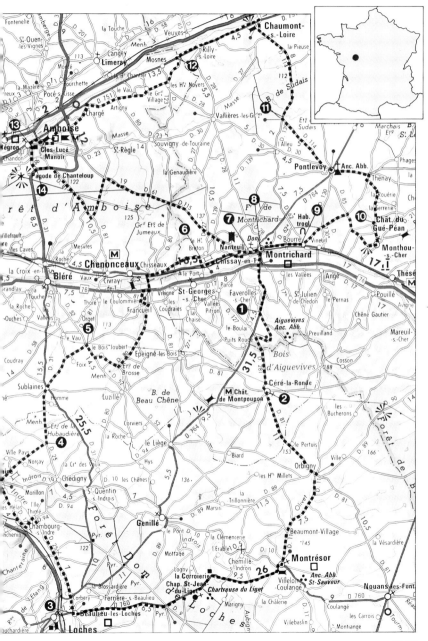

Entrance to the Charter-house of Liget.

Cère-la-Ronde
(detour)

The road on the right leads in 8 km to the château-museum of Montpoupon, via the fringes of a lake. This *gentilhommerie* has a history of 700 years devoted entirely, it seems, to field sports. The multifarious trophies of the chase, the saddlery and so forth will interest riding and hunting enthusiasts, not others. Impressive, with a splendid *châtelet* (gatehouse); you may picnic under its walls. *Open holidays, July, Aug.*
② *From Céré-la-Ronde follow signposts to Orbigny.*

Orbigny

No village in this part of France lacks interest for the ecclesiastical pilgrim, and Orbigny church with its iron-studded doors, pump in yard and colourful abstract stained-glass is particularly noteworthy. High up on an old house opposite the church you can make out a warning to horsemen of times past, *Défense de Trotter.*

Mon-trésor

Very narrow streets, single-file for donkeys in the old days: vertical expansion compensated for lack of horizontal space. From old houses to old church to old ivy-clad château, everything is tall and slim.

Le Liget

Beyond orchards, predominantly pear, the route crosses flat open country. At 8 km, just beyond the turning on the left to the Charterhouse, look out on the left for the 12thC chapel of Liget

standing all alone. It is locked, but you can get the key from the
Charterhouse. *(Open all year, 9-7.)* The medieval frescos inside are a
revelation. This chapel was founded Henry II in remorse for the
murder of Thomas à Becket at Canterbury. You can also visit the
Charterhouse - on foot. The car park is on the right of the road.

Le Liget - Now you are traversing the old hunting forest of Loches, and also a
Loches   section of the tourist circuit called *Route des Dames de Touraine.*
               Beware, therefore: stray deer and also motorists with eyes on maps.

Loches   The poet Alfred de Vigny *('J'aime le son de cor, le soir au fond des bois')*
               was born here. Much earlier, the fortified town and its château were
               the heart and homeland of war-ravaged Touraine. Avoid the lengthy
               official tour of the fortress - it is enough to sit among the willows on
               the Indre bank and reflect on the rough story of those honey-coloured
               walls. King John of England sold them during Richard Coeur-de-Lion's
               absence abroad. Richard was furious. On his return he repossessed
               Loches in three hours - a feat which stupefied the medieval chroniclers.
               In the dungeons Louis XII kept many noble prisoners, confining them for
               greater security in small iron-bound cages. The Duke of Milan survived
               eight years of crippling confinement and on release he stumbled and fell
               dead, dazzled by the sunlight. The Loches skyline is impressively floodlit
               on summer nights. For superior local products - dolls, glassware,
               pottery - visit the art gallery Le Moulin at Flére la Rivière.

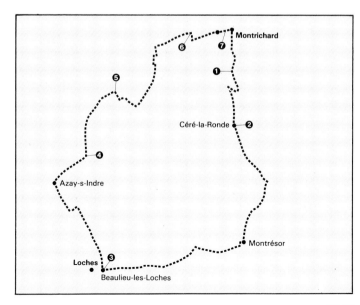

La France
*(restaurant,
Loches)*

The restaurant of the Hotel France at Loches is deservedly popular and prior booking is advisable. The very reasonable fixed-price menu might include soup, river eels in Vouvray wine, a game pie and a creamy pudding. *Rue Piçois: tel 47.59.00.32; closed Jan, two weeks in Feb, Sun evening and Mon lunch July and Aug; price band B/C.*

③ *Take the D25 to Chambourg and continue on road signposted Azay-sur-Indre.*

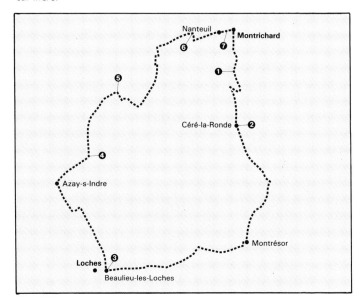

Azay-sur-Indre

The road uses two bridges and an *îlot* to cross the Indre. Before the first bridge, on the left, there is a children's playground; after it, a beautiful shady park with benches, ideal for a picnic. Watch a game of *boules* on the nearby court. You may park safely at the roadside and once you are among the greenery the picnic spot is quite secluded.

Azay - Sublaines

Bid farewell to the pretty Indre where it receives an even prettier tributary, the Indrois, hedged in with willows, alders and fruit gardens. *Turning right, head for Sublaines, rejoining* ④ *the D25*. It is a deceptively quiet little road. But in the harvest season tractors and combines take it over, and you cannot always hear them coming. On rural roads generally, the local farm traffic claims priority over city folk and tourists.

Sublaines - Chenonceaux

⑤ *Bear right after Sublaines, signposted Villaines, right at crossroads signposted Luzille, then left (possibly no signpost). At subsequent crossroads (exercise care) follow the signs for Francueil. At the road junction after Franceuil bear left then right, signposted Epeigné as far as the church; thereafter follow signs for Chenonceaux and glimpse the celebrated château on the left as you cross the bridge on the Cher.*

Chenon- Cottages smothered in ivy and vine, window-boxes and hanging baskets
ceaux full of geraniums... this is an epitome of a 'garden of France' showplace. Proximity to the château, 1.5 km down the road, accounts for the many bars, hotels, antique and souvenir shops.

Bon Knowledgeable locals recommend the restaurant of this medium-sized
Labou- Chenonceaux hotel for a taste of the regional cuisine at its most
reur refined. River fish, including pike, imaginatively presented in *terrines* and
(restaurant, *mousselines*. An exclusive *tournedos* called *'Vendôme'*. Some of the great
Chenon- wines of Touraine are on the list, including Camay and Montlouis. *Tel*
ceaux) *47.23.90.02; closed between mid-Dec and mid-Feb; price band C.*

Chenon- Note that the château of Chenonceau has dropped the 'x' -
ceau carelessness on the part of some old-time lawyer's clerk. Most delicately sited of Loire valley châteaux, most evocative of the loves and jealous rages of the grandest *dames de Touraine*, it has the added advantage of being visitable at one's own pace - none of the cattle-market regimentation which guides impose on visitors to some of the stately homes of France. Sumptuous as the interior is, nothing can surpass the view from the south bank of the Cher, upstream or down. Picnic among the trees, where you can fix in the memory the solemn beauty of Chenonceau and its reflection under seven supporting arches. (Each time you buy the well-known Menier chocolates you are contributing to Chenonceau's upkeep.) *Open all year.*

Chenon- ⑥ *Return through the village on the main road and at Chisseaux take the*
ceaux - *first left into Rue d'Eglise. This road climbs and winds and once again a*
Nameuil panorama of the valley opens out. *At crossroads follow the lane signposted La Touche, go straight on at next crossroads, turn right at the road junction and at the bottom of a steep hill turn left.*

Chissay If you turn right at the bottom of the hill and right again you come in
(detour) one km to the intricately-wrought iron gates and railings of Château de la Menaudière, now an expensive restaurant, but a stylish building, perhaps worth stopping at for a drink. On this road, observe how naturally the cottages appear to grow out of their environment.

Nameuil - ⑦ *At the main road turn right and almost immediately second left at a*
Montrichard *five-way junction.* On the left, note the cluster of antique farm buildings, with an even more antique *donjon* among them. Such buildings, originally the square central towers of châteaux, were safe deposits for family archives. The more ostentatious *donjon* of Montrichard, your destination, is now ahead.

■ ROUTE TWO: 80 KM

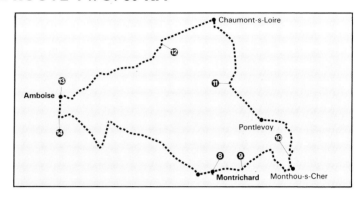

Mont-richard

(8) *Follow 'Autres Directions' signs. Do not cross river bridge but go straight on, signposted Bourré.*

Bourré - Monthou-sur-Cher

(9) *Turn left at Bourré, signposted Pontlevoy, then right at crossroads, signposted Thenay.* Monthou is a quaint little place to stretch one's legs in. Its rather lop-sided château, three towers conical and the other bell-shaped, offers an hour-long tour - a bit too much for what is mostly bric-à-brac. Mercifully there are no ice-cream kiosks or hucksters of trash and you are welcome to picnic in the park.

Le Gué-Péan

The château is a big four-square *gentilhommerie*, authentically furnished and lived in. It has come down in the world. Four centuries ago, as a powerful royal fortress, it helped write a pathetic page of English history. Young Mary Tudor, Henry VIII's sister, came here with her lover Brandon. To reinforce a claim to the French throne she pretended to be pregnant by the deceased French king. But his widow outsmarted Mary and sent her packing. In frustration she married Brandon. A grandchild of the union was Lady Jane Grey, nine-day queen of England - beheaded in her teens by order of her grandmother 'Bloody' Mary. *Open all year.* (10) *Follow signs to Thenay, then Pontlevoy.*

Hôtel de l'Ecole
(restaurant, Pontlevoy)

Elegant, creeper-covered, spotlessly clean, this hotel at Pontlevoy has only a few rooms and they are often booked weeks ahead, the price is so reasonable. Fine panelling indoors, wrought-iron furniture under a vine pergola outside. Families patronise the restaurant because children can eat for a ten-franc supplement on the adults' bill. Inexpensive but limited *à la carte* menu; the cellar contains only the best, so wines are *inevitably pricey. Tel 54.32.50.30; closed pm Mon and lunch Tue in low season; price band B/C.* If you lunch here, allow time for a stroll to the neighbouring 11thC abbey which incongruously houses a Heavyweights Museum - not prizefighters, but vintage commercial vehicles.

Pontlevoy -
Chaumont ⑪ *Turn left to the main road in town centre then right, signposted Chaumont, at crossroads.* Sudais lake is on right. Picnic spots abound. On Sundays you will have company. This is a meandering, but suitably regal approach to the great château ahead.

Chau-
mont Cylindrical towers, battlements, drawbridge...a toy fort come to life-size. The pure Renaissance interior expresses the Valois dynasty's notorious obsession with exotica. The startling coolie-hatted structure in the corner of the stable yard has served in its time as dovecot, art workshop and children's riding school. *Open daily except public holidays. Leave by the road past the church.* Here is the queenly Loire.

Chaumont -
Amboise ⑫ *Approaching Mosnes, take the minor road on left, signposted Les Hauts Novers.* It is a narrow, uneven alternative to the main route, but worth it for quaint hamlets and some neat cameos of the Loire valley.

Amboise This town is famous for fishing-tackle - and tourists. There are nooks and crannies to explore and some delightful ornate brick-and-stone houses, orange and white, among which you should not overlook Clos-Lucé and its rose garden on Rue Victor Hugo, five minutes' walk from the château. (Best to park at the château or on the riverfront tarmac.) Clos-Lucé, a Renaissance manor-house, is where Leonardo da Vinci lived and died, a guest in his old age of François I. A secret passage connects the house with Amboise château, 400 metres away. Now a museum, it has models and blueprints of Leonardo's inventions, including prototype gliders, parachutes and swing-bridges. His specifications are hard to decipher - he was left-handed and wrote backwards. The château, once the biggest in the Loire valley, was cut down in size after the French Revolution, but is still a grand sight on its walled cliff above the river. View it from Amboise bridge or from the Ile d'Or (accessible by road) in midstream. Inside, you may be deterred by the long academic discourse of the guide and the commercialisation. ⑬ *Leaving tourist office on right, take the first left, signposted Bléré, along a tree-lined avenue. Turn right at signpost for Pagode.*

Chante-
loup The Chanteloup park is highly recommended for picnics, walks and a snooze beside the lake, lulled by the humming of dragon-flies and the scuffle of lizards. The château has gone but the Pagoda remains. The view from the top tier (150 steps, no elevator) embraces the Loire valley and the Amboise forest.

Chanteloup -
Montrichard *Take the D31 going east, then the D81 on the right, signposted Chenonceaux. Later turn left, signposted St-Règle, and then right on to the D61.* Another sizeable lake, the Grand Etang de Jumeaux, is on the right, just before you emerge from the forest and descend - with a final panorama of the Cher valley - on the red roofs of Montrichard.

Loire:
TOURAINE

'Fair Touraine' has a magic sound: it calls to mind maids, knights and minstrels, affairs of the heart and indeed of Plantagenet power politics, played out in fairy-tale châteaux. Nowadays they call it more prosaically Indre-et-Loire, from two of the principal rivers. Heading south-west from Paris towards the Biscayan coast of France you must pass through this region. The châteaux are not all frivolous - some are menacing and steeped in blood, for around them, for more than two centuries, from Richard Coeur-de-Lion to Joan of Arc, the French struggled to throw off the English yoke. In riverbank towns and villages an amiable rusticity goes hand-in-hand with stormy memories.

It is a quiet, watered land, mostly agricultural with traces of royal hunting forests, not overburdened with tourists. The Indre, Cher and Vienne rivers make their way through it into France's longest river, the Loire. The first loop of the figure-of-eight explores the country south-west of Tours, the old capital of Touraine; it keeps south of the Vienne river and runs along the frontiers of Anjou, where England's Plantanaget dynasty originated and where some members of it returned to die. The other loop makes for the Loire valley and embraces several important châteaux. Much of the driving is through woodland and past grassy slopes, with no shortage of picnic spots; just as well - restaurants are rather thin on the ground.

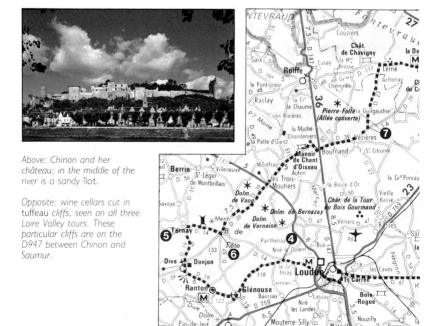

Above: Chinon and her château; in the middle of the river is a sandy îlot.

Opposite: wine cellars cut in tuffeau cliffs, seen on all three Loire Valley tours. These particular cliffs are on the D947 between Chinon and Saumur.

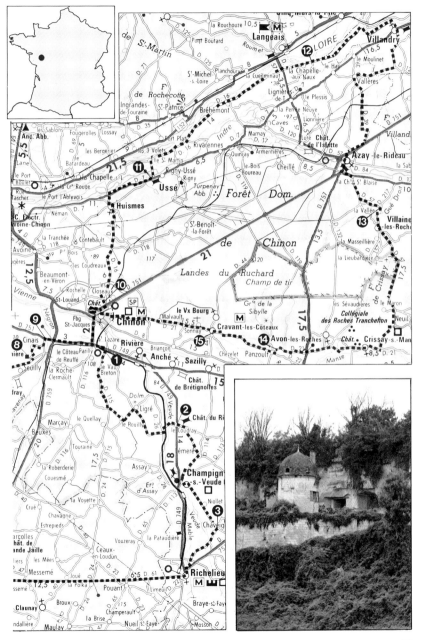

◼ **ROUTE ONE: 96 KM**

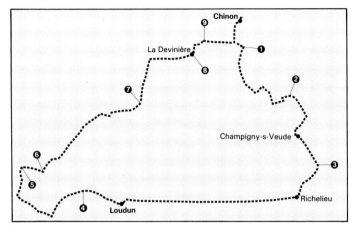

Chinon
A mixture of the quaint and the trendy, the town receives many tourists. The ruined château, more of a château-fort, sprawls over a ridge which stops short above the Vienne river and the town; and it has done so, in one form or another, since Roman times. '*Petite ville, grand renom*', wrote Rabelais - but after it came into the hands of the Plantagenet kings in 1154, Chinon's whole history was the history of its château. The kings' pride in it started the fashion for royal residences in the Loire country.

You can walk round the dilapidated ruins and enter chambers where the Dauphin, afterwards Charles VII of France, toyed with his beautiful but brazen mistress Agnès Sorel, the first woman in France to go topless. You can enter the great hall where in 1429 the Dauphin came under the spell of a very different woman, when one of history's most dramatic scenes was played: the royal prince, disguised among his courtiers, was instantly recognized by the innocent country girl Joan of Arc. *Open am and pm, hours vary (longer in summer); closed Wed out of season, and Dec-Jan.* Park off Rue J. J. Rousseau and walk through the Grand Carroi, the quarter of tight-packed, top-heavy medieval tenements. There, near the ascent to the château, you will find a couple of interesting museums, one devoted to the history of Chinon wines and cooperage, the other evoking the town's daily life in bygone ages.

You can take your pick of restaurants in Chinon. Au Plaisir Gourmand, *tel 47.93.20.48; booking essential,* is classy and expensive. For complete contrast try Jeanne de France, a *pizzeria* that offers steak and jugfuls of local wine; informal, youthful, and popular with families; *tel 47.93.20.12.*
① *Leave Chinon by tree-lined avenue across the Vienne (two bridges) and turn left on to the D751; after 0.75 km turn right, signposted Ligré.*

Chinon - *Le Rivau*	A steady ascent through tunnels of leaves and branches. Note the liana-like creepers on the ancient trees. The upland landscapes are like a tract of central Europe, all vines, sunflowers and maize.
Château **de** **Marçay** *(restaurant,* *Marçay)*	This famous hotel provides the gourmet experience of the region and the fresh-fruit-based desserts can be quite memorable. An atmosphere of restrained aristocratic elegance will suit some, and make others feel slightly uncomfortable. *At Marçay, 6.5 km from Ligré, 13 km from Chinon; tel 47.93.03.47; closed mid-Jan to mid-Mar' price band D.*
	② *Just before entering Ligré, turn right, signposted La Mortière. Cross the railway and the Veude river and at the main road - the D749 - turn right, then immediately left, signposted Lémere.*
Le Rivau	On the left. This Gothic château is mentioned by Rabelais and it has powerful Joan of Arc associations (it is not alone in that). Pierre-Laurent Brenot, owner and painter, exhibits his works.
Champ- **igny-sur-** **Veude**	The florid Sainte-Chapelle, a pious work of Louis de Bourbon (1540), has some beautifully luminous stained glass. Tours are guided with reluctance and there is not much to see. Unfortunately, you have to go round before they will let you walk in the gardens.
	③ *Having followed the Veude river upstream to Chaveignes, turn right signposted Richelieu.* All the villages hereabouts delight students of architecture. For the lay visitor, the charm lies in the harmony of old cottages and farmsteadings and the endless vistas of rolling countryside.
Richelieu	La Fontaine called it "the finest village in the universe." The great Cardinal was not satisfied with that: he decided that Richelieu should become capital of France (this was around 1630) and he pillaged the château of Chinon for masonry to create his 'new town'. It is now a strangely lifeless place, like an Olympic village when the Games are over. Take a stroll in the great park, a mathematical diagram of sycamores and chestnut avenues. The most endearing bit about Richelieu is the resurrected steam train, vintage 1900, which trundles you to Chinon and back on summer weekends. (Be prepared to pay in high season – July to Sept.)
Richelieu - *Loudun*	Tormenting lanes are behind you, but there are more to come, so make the most of this dead-straight and peaceful road.
Loudun	A hilly site: perimeter avenues round its base mark the lines of the old city walls. Inside them it is not easy to find parking space. Thanks to Cardinal Richelieu (he could not bear to see noble buildings in 'his' landscape unless he owned them himself), the former citadel is reduced to one square tower.

(Eating, *Loudun)*	Loudun is a convenient lunch stop. If you feel extravagant, try La Reine Blanche, *price band B*. If merely hungry, eat at the *crêperie* in Place de la Poulaillerie, *price band A*. The local speciality is *tuffeau du Loudunais*, a spicy rock-cake. (*Tuffeaux* are the low chalky cliffs of the Loire region which have been excavated in many places for storerooms, wine caves and even dwellings.) ④ *Leave Loudun by the Angers road, turn left on to the D14, signposted Insay, then left again on to a narrow road signposted Glénouse.*
Loudun - **Ranton**	This is the *Côte Loudunaise*, an attractive drive above the valley of the Dive with a chance of cool breezes on a hot day. There are magnificent views to the south-west just before Ranton and again on leaving it.
Ranton	The thin wooden racks scattered over the fields are for drying the maize-cobs. Note the unusual construction of the farmhouses, done with small irregularly-shaped cobbles. One farmhouse is the Musée Paysanne, exhibiting agricultural life of the past century, *open every afternoon in summer.*
Curçay	The donjon (a maximum security tower) on the right is a landmark from the middle ages, but not of much significance historically. On the left, from the fine viewpoint, a downhill footpath goes through the village and takes you to the bank of the Dive river canal - a pleasant 20-minute stroll, and an ideal spot for a picnic. ⑤ *Continue on the D19 to the right, then left, signposted Ternay.*
Ternay	The manoir de Savoye is on the left as you leave the village. it is a family-owned château and, despite the misleading symbol on your map, it is open at weekends. In fact, the residents seem genuinely pleased to see visitors - rare enough in these parts - at any time. ⑥ *Follow road signposted Loudun, then turn left on to D39 for Chinon.*
Ternay - **Lerné**	⑦ *Continue over two crossroads, Les Trois Moûtiers (an old word for monastery) and Bournand. At Vezières bear left, signposted Lerné.* You will see apricot orchards among the groves and woodlands of this serene and undulating landscape. Tiny picturesque cottages are a feature of all the villages, notably Lerné, where there is also a really elegant church. After Lerné the Château du Coudray on the right is not accessible.
Fonte- **vraud** *(detour)*	*Backtrack on the D17 to Fontevraud (16 km).* The glory of this huge 12thC abbey departed at the French Revolution, when it became a state prison. But it still contains the tombs of two English queens and two English kings (Henry II and Richard Coeur-de-Lion). There is no truth in the myth found in many guide books and travel books that the British royal family continually pleads for the bones to be removed to Westminster Abbey.

■ **ROUTE TWO: 84 KM**

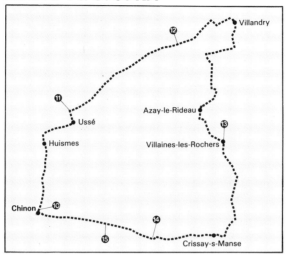

Lerné - La Devinière	⑧ *Bear left at the fork signposted Côteau, and enter Seuilly; then turn left at road junction, signposted Cinais. Rabelais' Gargantua and Pantagruel is set in this countryside.*
La Devinière	The Rabelais museum is best seen from outside; a simple 15thC cottage, steep-pitched with slender stone pillars and an outside staircase, *open daily except Dec, Jan, Wed.* ⑨ *After Cinais, follow D751 to Chinon.*
Chinon - Huismes	⑩ *From Chinon take the Tours road past the château and turn left, signposted Huismes.*
(Eating, Huismes)	They sell apples and pears (*Bon Chrétien*, whose homeland this is) at the farm. A useful lunch stop is La Devinière (not to be confused with the village of Rabelais), close to Huismes church, with agreeable service rendered by *patron* Michel Martin; *price band B.* No embargo on children here, or at the perfectly adequate Auberge du Grillon, almost next door; *price band A.*
Ussé	The château tour is long and costly, the guides are incomprehensible, the leaflet is dull and entry to the formal gardens is prohibited. Best sit opposite, under the catalpa trees at the Café au Bois Dormant, gossip *with the cheerful young proprietors and enjoy the view of this white-stone château, the scene of Perrault's Sleeping Beauty story. Open daily, Easter-Nov.*
Ussé - Villandry	⑪ *Take the first left and, on three narrow bridges, cross the Indre, a river which flirts a long time with the Loire before actually joining it;*

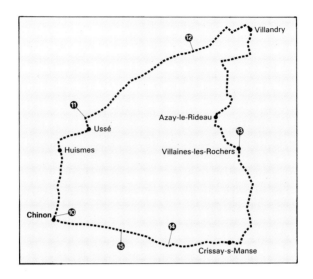

then turn right, signposted Azay. This riverside drive is delightful, partly wooded and offering plenty of shade. The Loire, the longest river in France and the most useless navigationally, rolls over shallows and past end-to-end *îlots* (sandbanks).

In 5 km there is an idyllic picnic spot, with parking and riverbank footpaths in both directions. Close to Bréhémont is another good picnic area on low dunes. After Bréhémont, look over your left shoulder for a view of the graceful *pont suspendu.*

La Chapelle   Here you have access to several sandy *îlots.* On the right is the furniture workshop of M. Moral, who does chests, tables and so on in oak, mahogany and cherrywood with traditional carvings.

⑫ *Bear left, signposted Villandry, then right through a leafy glade (beyond the monument) into Villandry.*

Villandry   You may park under the lime trees beside the main road. The château, pure Renaissance, was built in 1532 on earlier Gothic foundations called Colombiers. The three-tiered gardens (water, ornamental, kitchen), severely geometrical, are one of the mandatory sights of the Loire.

Azay-le-Rideau   The babel of tongues in the queue for admission confirms the worldwide fame of this 'floating' château on a diverted loop of the Indre. Feminine taste inspired the interior décor - the royal treasurer's wife ran riot in 1510, until François I nailed her swindling husband and confiscated the place. *Open all year.* The *ridellois* (inhabitants of Azay) are carpenters and fruit-growers and their white wines, Côteaux de Touraine, have achieved the distinction of an *appellation contrôlée.*

Azay - Villaines

⑬ *Turn left, then right, signposted Villaines les Rochers.* This is a dreamy, winding route through vineyards. From the top of the steep hill you have a broad view of a well-clothed, well-watered landscape.

Villaines - les- Rochers

This is the 'troglodite' village, where cellars and garages are hollowed out of the *tuffeau* rock. The basket-making co-operative, flourishing since 1849, when a parish priest founded it, welcomes visitors and does not harass them.

Chrissay- sur-Manse

A charming, completely unspoiled village, almost wholly pre-16thC, Chrissay merits at least half an hour of your time. Park the car near the first old well and stroll the skein of alleyways. The tourist office, on the street which leads to an abbey (not open to visitors), occupies someone's kitchen, and that someone has developed a nice line in home baking and honey - so picnic ingredients are at hand, and so is the picnic site, down the hill beyond the church and second well, on the path signposted Vieux Moulin.

Chrissay - Cravant- les-Côteaux

⑭ *Continue on the D21, crossing main road and bearing right at Panzoult.* This is a fast, well-surfaced road with little traffic, but do not ignore the pleasant views which now open over the vale of the Vienne river. They are typical of the panoramic prospects of Touraine which have been a feature of this loop.

Cravant's big bottle.

Cravant- les- Côteaux

The gigantic wine bottle on a wall advertises the local vineyard, from whose cavernous cellars you can bring away a bottle or a half-case, together with some understanding of the mystique of the Chinon wine trade.

⑮ *Continue on the D21 to Chinon.*

Rivers of Jura

The Franche-Comté, the historic 'free country' which separates the upper Rhone valley from the Swiss border, is a region of flattish Alps and chalet-style dwellings inhabited by men and women of *montagnard* character, clean and industrious and moderate in all things. The Jura mountains, which form a crescent-shaped barrier to this ancient province, reach heights of around 1,500 metres, but they are not a chain of peaks - more a rippling banner of high pastures and folded hills, coloured dark green (the forests), bright green (the meadows) and grey (the limestone crags). The tinkle of the cow-bell emphasises the serenity of the uplands, traffic is light, and it gives way, morning and evening, to herds of milking cattle in the lanes.

The cuisine is largely based on dairy products and the fish (some species peculiar to the region) from beautiful clear rivers which have forced their way through the broken limestone to create, on a smaller scale, a landscape similar to the Belgian and Luxembourg Ardennes. Among culinary ingredients, the *Gruyère*-type cheese called *Comté* is pre-eminent; the tour touches at some points the so-called *Route du Comté* which connects the principal *fromageries* and the caves where the cheese is matured.

The centre of the figure-of-eight is Pontarlier. One loop follows the Swiss border and takes in stretches of the Doubs, which some consider the most impressive river in France. The second loop embraces the springs of Ain, another limpid torrent, and a variety of Jura scenery.

On backroads in these parts, fuel can be quite a rare commodity, possibly on account of the proximity to Switzerland, where it is cheaper.

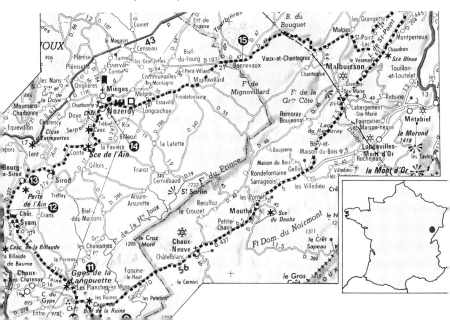

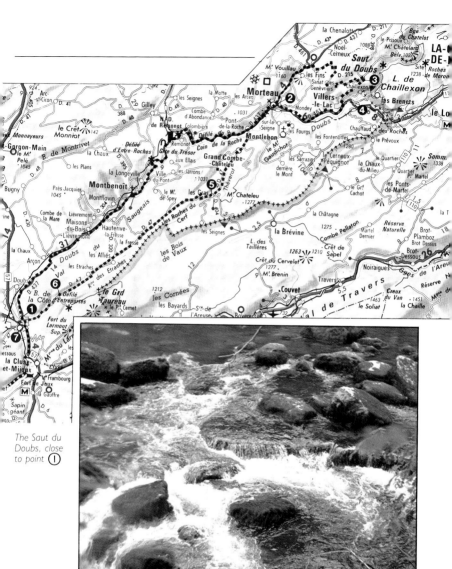

The Saut du Doubs, close to point ①

▰▰▰ ROUTE ONE: 83 KM

Pontarlier

Pontarlier is the town everyone knows and no one stops at - it is the last French town you pass through *en route* from the Channel ports to Switzerland and Italy. There is really not much to stop for, unless you are attracted by the grotesque little spruce-wood bottles in which the local liqueur, an inferior kind of *retsina*, is sold. In the streets on either side of the main street an awkward one-way system is in force.

Grand Hotel de la Poste
(restaurant, Pontarlier)

On Pontarlier's main street, but by no means as grand as its name, this coaching-house of ancient repute offers an excellent introduction to the Jura cuisine. On the fixed-price menu you may be supplied with stuffed pike, crayfish *gratin* or kirsch-flavoured *fondue* as well as veal and poultry dishes. *55, Rue de la République; tel 81.46.47.91; closed Sun and when demand is low; price band A/B/C.*
① *Cross the bridge over the Doubs river and turn left on Rue de Morteau; then follow signposts for Montbéliard, afterwards for Morteau.*

Pontarlier - Montbenoît

On the outskirts of Pontarlier, on the left, note the tall needle-like spire of the little church at Doubs. After you have crossed the river of that name at Arçon, you will perhaps rub your eyes at the first of the natural 'wonders' and *trompe-l'oeil* effects for which the river systems of the Jura are notorious: the Doubs appears to be flowing uphill.

Mont-benoît

The solemn old abbey church has been a beacon of the faith for 700 years and during that time some comical wood-carvings have made their appearance on the pulpit, the pews and the misericords. Observe the two peasant women pulling each other's hair out, and similar naïve examples of wood-sculptors' piety.

Auberge de l'Abbaye
(restaurant, Montbenoît)

Like some other restaurants on this route, the Abbaye at Montbenoît bears the sign *Route de Comté*, which means that it offers not only the famous cheeses of the region but also some local speciality on the fixed-price menu. *Tel 81.38.11.63; closed Wed and Sun evening; price band A/B/C.*

Montbenoît - Morteau

The road squeezes through an impressive canyon called the Défilé d'Entre-Roches. You can park on the left and should really get out and walk a short way to appreciate the grandeur of the ravine. Five km on, with the dark forest fleece on your left growing ever more dense, you come to the statue of St Ferjeux at Remonot. This saint introduced Catholicism to the Franche-Comté. Near it is the grotto of La Chapelle, which has a church tucked inside it. Walk past the altar, if no service is in progress, and cross a bridge. Beyond the bridge a network of caverns runs deep into the rock. After the grotto you have to drive through another awesome defile, the Coin de la Roche, where the crystal-clear Doubs thrusts through high forested cliffs and emerges suddenly on an open plain.

Morteau

It would be a village in more populated parts of France, but here it is a sizeable town spread over green pastures at about 1,000 metres altitude. People come here for their holidays - there are fine walks in the neighbourhood and first-class fishing, bathing and canoeing on the Doubs, which is here a sedate, unhurried river. Local industry seems

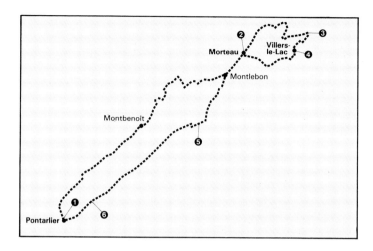

equally designed to attract the tourists; at Morteau they make clocks, bells and chocolate - and of course cheese. The restaurant Paris - *tel 81.67.06.70; price band B/C/D* - specializes in the Jura cuisine, which here comprises *Comté* and Emmental cheeses, mountain butter, smoked ham, fishy *croûtes* and the locally celebrated smoked sausage called *Jésus de Morteau*.

② *Continue through the town, an uphill road signposted Besançon. At Les Fins bear right, then turn sharp right on to the D215, signposted La Suisse. This is a steep road with many hairpin bends and good views of the last ripples of the Jura range in Switzerland. Follow signposts for Villers-le-Lac and after the steep descent to the crossroads go straight on.*

Saut du Doubs

The cascade, 27 metres high, would be impressive on most rivers, but the Doubs proceeds amid so many natural wonders that you take big waterfalls for granted. Ideally, one should take a two-hour walk along this stretch of the river as far as the Chatelot dam and the *Belvédère*. From the car park, where hotels, both Swiss and French, add nothing to the view, a ten-minute walk brings you to the *Saut* (cascade). There are scores of trinket stalls - even though one of them describes itself as the *Loup Solitaire*. The souvenirs are nasty without being particularly cheap. But this should not deter you from viewing the Saut, one of the *Grands Sites Régionaux* - a rare and coveted designation.

③ *Returning, keep left along the river, signposted Villers.*

Villers-le-Lac

It has an amphitheatrical site above the Doubs and from the quay near the bridge you can embark for a voyage downstream, where beech, pine and chestnut climb almost vertically from the glassy water's edge. There are lovely walks around Villers too, along which the local tourist board has provided belvederes. The Swiss frontier is only 8 km down the road - a crossing with minimal formalities. In fact, at times you find the gate open and unattended.

④ *Trace the windings of the Doubs upstream and re-enter Morteau. Follow the one-way system through the town. Turn right on to the D437, signposted Les Gras, and cross railway and river.*

**Grand'
Combe-
Châteleu**

Several venerable occupations are pursued here and in neighbouring hamlets: ham-curing in timber oast-houses called *fermes à tuyé*; taxidermy; and woodworking. On the right, signposted Ferme Atelier, is the 'Ecomuseum' of Beugnon, where rare old implements of blacksmiths, wheelwrights and foresters are displayed. This may sound boring, but the exhibition does give real insight into the harsh life of the *montagnard* people.

**Les Gras -
Pontarlier**

⑤ *Keep right in Les Gras.* Hereabouts the road goes into the forest again, picks up a tributary of the Doubs and comes within inches of the Swiss frontier. Beware the occasional very sharp bend. There are up-and-coming ski centres on this road, notably Les Alliés. Just beyond Les Etraches, on the right and within one km of the road is another slender rocky gorge, the Défilé d'Entreportes. ⑥ *Straight on for Pontarlier.*

■ ROUTE TWO: 109 KM

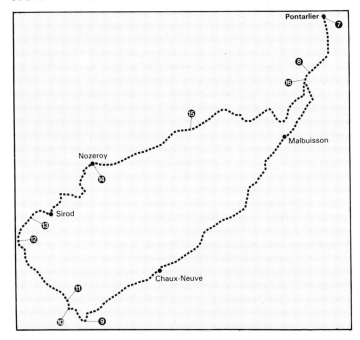

Pontar-
lier
Leave by the main road for Switzerland, signposted Lausanne, and
⑦ turn right, signposted Malbuisson. Almost immediately you are in a
deep and eerie ravine.

Fort de
Joux
The gloomy old fortress high above you seems to have come out of a
Gothic novel, and in its long history it has known some Gothic
moments. The young Mirabeau, some years before the French
Revolution, was imprisoned there at the instigation of his own father.
Another patriot, the Negro Toussaint-Louverture, died here in captivity
in 1803. You cannot reach the fortress from this road and in any case it
is an empty shell.

Oye-et-
Pallet
As you leave this hamlet there is a splendid view of the Lac de St-
Point, whose 7-km length you are about to measure.
⑧ Keep left at head of lake.

Chaudron
On the left, a short footpath climbs to the source of the Bleue river -
not a very dramatic scene, but you could picnic here with the expanse
of the lake in front of you. It is the largest in the Jura.

Mal-
buisson
An important water- and winter-sports area with numerous hotels and
open-air cafés.

Laberge-
ment-Ste-
Marie
If you have not yet inspected a Jura bell foundry, here is an
opportunity. The Obertino establishment has been making bells for
schools, chapels, hotels and especially for cattle since 1834. To some
extent, the casting, firing and stockpiling of the bells are still done
according to methods which were in use when Louis-Philippe was on
the throne. You may walk around freely. You can buy bells and bell-
shaped trinkets - paperweights and suchlike - of different sizes, in
bronze or steel. Closed for holidays throughout Sept.

Mouthe
To the left, a rough walk of about ten minutes takes you to the springs
of the Doubs - humble enough origin for a torrent which, as you saw
on the northern loop of this tour, soon becomes a majestic river.

Chaux-
Neuve - Les
Planches-
en-Mone
After Chaux-Neuve you will pass through rocky canyons with many
acute curves. Most tiny hamlets along the route aspire to become ski
resorts; skiing is very much a growth industry in the Jura. Froncine-le-
Haut has restaurants, bars and a general *après-ski* atmosphere. It also
marks the start of a forest trail (on the right) which leads out to high
pastures and the Bulay viewpoint, with its panoramic indicator at 1,139
metres. At Foncine-le-Bas there is fuel at a price.

⑨ *Turn right, signposted Champagnole, and bear right to the D127.*
Hairpins continue coming thick and fast, and on this section of the route
they are all shrouded in woodland.

Les Planches-en-Mgne

Just before you enter the village you will see on the left a car park for the use of those who walk to the Langoulette gorges 0.75 km away. ⑩ *Bear right at road junction.* The roughish track on the left leads to the smaller Langoulette parking area, close to the precipitous steps which lead along the side of the gorges past a series of spectacular waterfalls. This undisciplined river is the Saine. The Langoulette gorges are a really fine sight, especially after heavy rain. Not the least striking aspect of them is the row of houses close to the village, which teeter on the very brink of the chasm. (They say they chain their toddlers to the railings to prevent them from falling in.) At Les Planches honey is sold, said to be of epicurean quality.

⑪ *Bear right in village, then follow signs for Syam.* The road passes through a corridor of shining rocks.

Syam

The château is Italianate, not very old or distinguished. But it costs little to enter and it is one of the few accessible private houses in the region. *Open pm Sat, Sun and Mon only, July-Sept.* ⑫ *At road fork, bear right.*

Bourg-de-Sirod

On the right is a short footpath to the Pertes de l'Ain. *Pertes* are swallow-holes. The infant Ain river is supposed to disappear through fissures in its limestone bed. Whether this is a 'wonder' or not, it will be one if you actually see it happening. If you pass through Bourg-de-Sirod in dry weather following prolonged rain it may be worth while visiting the *pertes* on the off-chance of seeing the phenomenon.

Fortunately this pretty little river gradually recovers and reappears and becomes an attractive waterway, flowing into the Rhône near Lyon.

Those interested in idiosyncratic craft pottery should not miss the Pertes de l'Ain studio of Régina Le Moigne, opposite the road fork; a rustic creeper-covered building with huge tubs of fuchsias in front. The work is of a high standard, according to experts.

Pertes-de-l'Ain
(restaurant, Bourg-de-Sirod)

This restaurant offers a simple menu from the less adventurous side of the Jura cuisine - a sort of refined peasant diet. House wine is available by the carafe or half-carafe. *Tel 84.52.26.31; closed Mon; price band A/B.*

⑬ *The road bears right and goes through the mountain in a tunnel. From Sirod, follow signposts for Conte.*

Conte

The narrow streets of the hamlet can be hopelessly congested on Sat and Sun. One km onward, bear left for the source of the Ain. For once, this is a source worthy of a big beautiful river. Its emerald pool, astonishingly deep, is lost in woodland - you locate it from the sound of dripping water. A picnic area, admirably set up, is close by.

Nozeroy

Long ago this was the feudal capital of a well-populated district and it still has its old ramparts and fortifications, its medieval castle and important Gothic church, enclosed in decayed city walls.

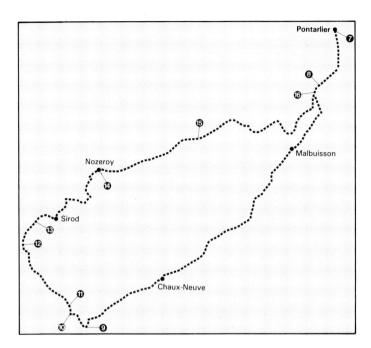

⑭ *Bear right in Nozeroy and within 100 metres turn right again,*
signposted Longcochon. The road looks difficult and there are some
formidable gradients, but it is good enough and it traverses rich
pastureland, flowery in spring and summer. Watch out for sauntering
cattle around milking time. *Follow road signposted Pontarlier.*

Bonne-
vaux

⑮ *Next door to an attractive house fronted with lapped tiles, turn right,*
signposted Lac de St-Point; on arrival at the lake, turn left, signposted St-
Point. On the right, at the bar, small craft are hired out.

Les
Grang-
ettes

The arts-and-crafts gallery Du Mouton Noir on the right is among the
most stylish and interesting in the whole of provincial France. About 25
artists have their studios here and display wrought-iron work, clothing,
jewellery, ceramics, glassware and sculptures of a serious standard.

Le Bon
Repos
(restaurant,
Grangettes)

The restaurant of this two-star hotel is praised for its no-nonsense,
thoroughly satisfying country cuisine. It is privately owned and family-run
by people who clearly enjoy meeting strangers and children. *Tel 81.69.*
62.95; closed Nov, Dec, Tues eve and Wed out of season; price band B.

Grangettes
- Pontarlier

⑯ *At the end of the lake rejoin the route by which you travelled out, and*
at the main road turn left, signposted Pontarlier.

Burgundy:
THE MACON COUNTRY

Outh of Dijon on the Riviera route, or north of Lyon if you are heading
for Paris, the motorway brushes aside a hilly territory of bracken, gorse
and foxglove. It looks rather wild and inhospitable, more like the west of
Ireland than the centre of France. It has been called, from the metallic glint
of its rocky outcrops, the Land of Golden Stones. On the hottest day there
may be a breeze sweeping across the moor and rattling the shutters of
roadside cafés. "Do those windows have to be open?" asks a tourist. "Yes,
madame," says the *patronne* sweetly. "We have arrangements with the
Paris hairdressers."

The unlikely wilderness protects some of the famous vineyards of the
Saône valley. For mile after mile on the main road the small red and white
posts and the rows of stakes along the furrows mark the complicated
classifications and sub-divisions of the Burgundy wine *communes*. They were
the monks of Cluny, long ago, who put these lands under cultivation.
Wherever you climb out of the valley, you find that all roads still lead to
Cluny. It is one of the great names in the history of western civilization.

It is also this tour's centre. The two loops thread the wilderness, which of
course is not a wilderness at all once you have come to grips with it. The
northern loop proceeds by way of the Grosne valley to make a circuit of
the Mont St-Romain ridge (579 m) and returns via the prehistoric caves of
Azé on the slopes of the Mâconnais. The southern loop is short, almost a
rally-driver's route with many zigzags and hairpin bends. It explores the
spectacular uplands which look to the Beaujolais region in the south.

▬▬▬▬ ROUTE ONE: 81 KM

Cluny   No doubt the Mâcon wines helped provide the wealth and influence of
Cluny - like other Burgundian convents and monasteries, Cluny's
Benedictine abbey acquired much sunny alluvial soil and judiciously
developed it. The ruins and restorations of that immensely rich
foundation still overshadow the little town. It has been a major pilgrim
venue for a thousand years - and still they come, as you may gather
from the number of hotels and the latest pilgrim amenities, including
hamburger joints. "We are on the American circuit," says a
restaurateur - as though that explains everything. Cluny is thronged in
summer and parking is not well organized. (Use the roadside parks on
the way to the industrial zone, a ten-minute walk from the centre.) It
lies on the TGV track, so you may see that high-speed train hurtle
through; and an important trans-European highway, the Swiss-Atlantic,
passes close by. For all that, an air of monastic calm pervades the
scene. Twenty minutes suffice if you are merely walking round. If you
are keen on Romanesque architecture you will need the whole day.

Cluny -   ① *Leave town by the Pont de la Levée and D15 road and turn left at rail
Toury   crossing, signposted Varanges. The road, disconcertingly cambered,*

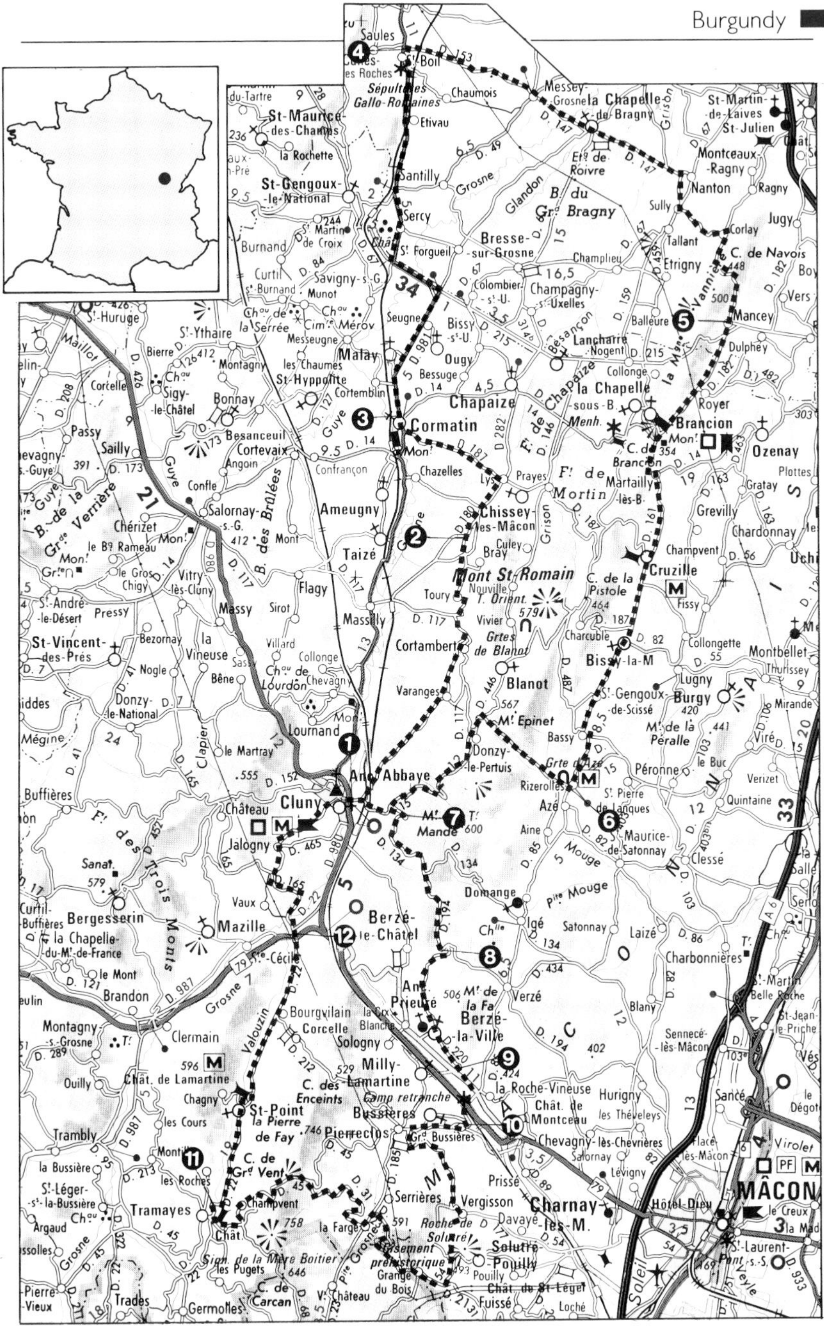
Saules
St-Boil
Sépultures Gallo-Romaines
Chaumois
Messey-Grosne
la Chapelle-de-Bragny
St-Martin-de-Laives
St-Julien
Etivau
St-Maurice-des-Champs
la Rochette
Santilly
Grosne
Ét. de Roivre
B. du Gr. Bragny
Montceaux-Ragny
Nanton
Ragny
St-Gengoux-le-National
Sercy
Sully
Jugy
Corlay
Tallant
Bresse-sur-Grosne
Champlieu
Etrigny
C. de Navois
Burnand
St Forgueil
Colombier-s.-U.
Champagny-s.-Uxelles
St-Huruge
St-Ythaire
Seugne
Bissy-s.-U.
Balleure
Mancey
Lancharre
Nogent
Malay
Ougy
Dulphey
St-Hyppolite
Bessuge
Collonge
la Chapelle-sous-B.
Chapaize
Royer
Cormatin
Brancion
Ozenay
Passy
Sailly
Besanceuil
Cortevaix
Confrançon
C. de Brancion
Chazelles
Prayes
Martailly-lès-B.
Confle
Salornay-s.-G.
Chérizet
Ameugny
Chissey-lès-Mâcon
Grevilly
Chardonnay
Taizé
Bray
Culey
Champvent
Mont St Romain
C. de la Pistole
Cruzille
Flagy
Massy
Toury
Fissy
St-André-le-Désert
Massilly
Vivier
St-Vincent-des-Prés
Cortambert
Grtes de Blanot
Bissy-la-M
Collongette
Montbellet
la Vineuse
Nogle
Blanot
Lugny
St-Gengoux-de-Scissé
Burgy
Bêne
Chevagny
Varanges
Mt Epinet
Bassy
Mt de la Péralle
Donzy-le-National
Lournand
Donzy-le-Pertuis
Péronne
le Martray
Grte d'Azé
Rizerolles
Buffières
Château
Cluny
Anc Abbaye
Mt Mandé
Azé
St Pierre de Lanques
Quintaine
Jalogny
Aine
St-Maurice-de-Satonnay
Clessé
Vaux
Domange
Bergesserin
Mazille
Berzé-le-Châtel
Igé
Satonnay
Laizé
Charbonnières
la Chapelle-du-Mt-de-France
Ste-Cécile
le Mont
Brandon
Verzé
Prieuré
Mt de la Fa
Berzé-la-Ville
Blany
Montagny-s.-Grosne
Clermain
Bourgvilain
Corcelle
Sologny
Sennecé-lès-Mâcon
Milly-Lamartine
Chât. de Lamartine
C. des Enceints
Camp retranché
Chagny
St-Point
la Pierre de Fay
Bussières
la Roche-Vineuse
Chât. de Montceau
Hurigny
les Théveleys
Sancé
Trambly
les Cours
Pierreclos
Gd Bussières
Chevagny-lès-Chevrières
Salornay
Montil
C. de Grd Vent
Place-lès-Mâcon
MÂCON
la Bussière
St-Léger-s.-la-Bussière
les Roches
Champvent
Serrières
Vergisson
Prissé
Charnay-lès-M.
Lévigny
Hôtel-Dieu
Tramayes
Chât
la Farge
Roche de Solutré
Davayé
Argaud
Gisement préhistorique
Solutré-Pouilly
St-Laurent-s.-S.
Sign. de la Mère Boitier
les Pugets
Grange du Bois
Pouilly
Chât. de St-Léger
C. de Carcan
Trades
Germolles
Château
Fuissé
Loché
Veyle
Soleil
F. des Trois Monts
B. des Brûlées
F. de Chapaize
F. de Mortin
B. de la Gr. Verrière
Mont St Romain

enters the parkland of the *forêt dominale*, an old-time game preserve of the monks. *Keep left, signposted Cortambert, turn left at road junction (no signpost) and follow signs to Toury.* In this little maze of forest trails there are roads unmarked on the IGN map and it is easy to go astray - but not far astray.

L'Orée du Bois
(detour to hotel-restaurant, Massily)

Turn left just before Toury and follow signposts for Massily to the hotel at the river bridge, 3 km on. Festooned in flowers (the ubiquitous geranium predominates) and floodlit at night, the place is smart, friendly, cheap and much frequented by local people. Few foreign visitors - though once the B.B.C. descended on the restaurant; they loved the chicken Benedictine with crayfish. Mme Maréchal is the new *patronne. Tel 85.50.00.25; price band A; rooms a very reasonable price, but usually booked up.*
② *From Toury make for the D180 and turn right.*

Lys

This old-fashioned village has a cosy charm all its own. The bar, which doubles as a greengrocer's, is a haven for dedicated beer-drinkers: it sells real ale, something quite uncommon in rural France.

Cormatin

Rooms in the castle are distinguished by their mouldings and carvings. The entrance is on the right as you approach it. Park on the broad pavement. For craftwork and souvenirs, continue up the main street and look out on the left for signs to Galerie Artisanale. The work of about 20 local artists, photographers and woodworkers is on display.

Cormatin - Sercy

The route traverses the broad valley of the Grosnes and its tributaries.
③ *Turn left at the crossroads and continue north on the D981 - a 'red' road on the map, but a very quiet one.* Vineyards abound and some delicate wines are produced, eminently drinkable but lacking the *réclame* of the burgundies of the Sâone valley and Côte d'Or regions. To the rear, you have striking views of the Mont St-Romain ridges, the highest summits of the Mâconnais.

Sercy

Nothing to detain you here. The church is boringly modern and the medieval castle ruins, though picturesque, are fragmentary. The eye-catching château at the end of the lake is *open Apr to Nov on request.*

St-Gengoux

Just beyond Sercy turn sharp left and in 2 km enter St-Gengoux-le-National, a throw-back to the Middle Ages with a well-preserved 12thC church.

St-Boil

Burial chambers of Romans and Gauls, following some great battle unrecorded in history, have been excavated at about 1½ km along the minor road west of the village. To visit them, apply to the *mairie* in St-Boil. There is not much to see, but the site is atmospheric.
④ *At the end of the village turn right, signposted Messey.* A winding

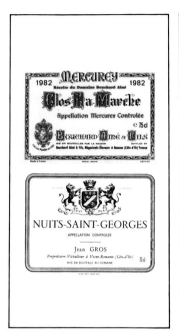

Famous names in Burgundy.

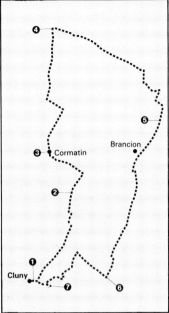

road, but well-surfaced; continue through the long sprawling village of Messey, road now signposted Nanton, and re-cross the Grosne river.

Le Moulin de la Chapelle *(rest., La Chapelle-de-Bragny)* The terrace of this restaurant, delightfully situated among lilyponds and lawns near the river bank before you enter La Chapelle-de-Bragny, is an ideal place for toying with *coq-au-vin* and sipping a glass or two of Mâcon wine. French touring organizations say that both food and drink are cheaper than they ought to be. There are 9 inexpensive rooms. *Tel 85.44.00.58; closed Jan, Feb; price band A/B.*

La Chapelle-de-Bragny It has the usual rustic equipment of a simple little church and a modest château (private, as so many in this region are). If you have come from more tourist-oriented places you will appreciate villages like La Chapelle, which seem to be locked in a time-warp. To sit and study an unpretentious château amid untrampled surroundings where no touring coach has penetrated can be a refreshing change from the dubious pleasures of being herded around some great showplace to the tedious accompaniment of a guide's monologue.

Nanton The first of the hilly places on the route. Note some modification of architectural styles - cottages built of small bricks with red pantiled roofs. To the south you have the first of increasingly dramatic views.

**Nanton -
Brancion**

The road narrows as it climbs. After Sully it enters dense woodland. From Corly onward it is low-gear work, a narrow, tortuous and steeply-graded ascent. Above the tree line, on the rugged shoulders of Vannière, you have fine views to the north. There is a parking area at the summit of the road, Col des Chèvres, and a marked path goes off to the high point of the ridge (500 metres). The walk takes half an hour and not everyone will want to attempt it but, if you do, and always providing there is no mist, the summit panoramas are enough to take away such breath as you have left.

⑤ *Keep left in Mancey and right at next crossroads, signposted Brancion.* Here you are back among vineyards. *Turn sharp right, signposted Château, to Brancion.*

Brancion

It has been a little metropolis of the hills for 1,000 years and has the historic stones to prove it: a château-fort on 8thC foundations, embellished with 12thC towers, dungeon and gatehouses; a 12thC Romanesque church with faded frescoes, hardly discernible; an inn and a covered market of the 15thC and cottages to match. You buy picture postcards at the ancient communal bakehouse, which was in use as recently as 1930. You cannot always drive through Brancion - the closely-knit streets are pedestrianized on Sundays and holidays. For a first-rate picnic spot, go up the hill behind the village, park at the top, (fine views of the Charollais and shaggy Morvan in the north-west) and take the short winding path into a grassy clearing.

Cruzille

As you enter the village, inspect the modern (1982) sundial, which is as inaccurate as most of the old ones. Drive up to the château - it is worth looking at, though you cannot enter despite the map's suggestion that you can. It is now a school for the mentally handicapped.

Romanesque church at Brancion.

Lamp sculpture in the studio, Vignes du Maynes.

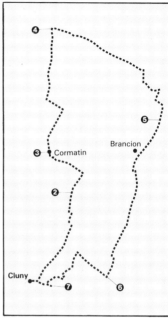

Vignes du Maynes This is the large white house on the outskirts of Cruzille. It claims to be the oldest wine *domaine* in France - *maynes* is dialect for 'monk' and the Maynes labels all bear the cherished crossed-keys symbol of the Cluny abbots. Since 1954 the vineyard has been organically cultivated. No anti-freeze. In fact, the wine is so free from additives that some French customers complain this Mâcon lacks the agreeable tang of insecticide. Three nice people run the business. Mme Guillot, having lived in London, speaks good English. You are not pressured to buy but, if you do, go for a half-case rather than a bottle or two. Part of the house is a museum of old trades.

⑥ *After 8 km turn right to the D15, signposted Cluny.*

Azé On the right, in 2½ km, are some large and exceptionally interesting caves on three levels. A subterranean river runs through and there is no dearth of stalactites. Science, aided perhaps by legend, peoples the caves with sub-humans from half a million years ago. The tour is well conducted, the leaflets are sensible and the admission fee is not extortionate. Near the entrance is a pottery, a restaurant punningly named *La Fortune de la Pot* and a swimming pool for children.

Azé - Cluny The road climbs steeply, then descends to Cluny.

■ ROUTE TWO: 56 KM

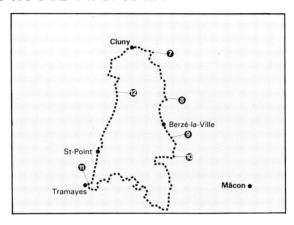

Cluny -
Berzé

⑦ *Leave Cluny by the D15 (on which you returned from the previous loop) and 1½ km beyond the level crossing turn right on to the D134, signposted Mâcon.* It is a well-engineered road, ascending fairly steeply into an evergreen forest. Near the junction is a picnic area.

⑧ *At next junction turn sharp right, signposted Berzé.* This is a single-track road between acres of vineyards.

Berzé-la-
Ville

There are 11th and 12thC Byzantine-style frescos on the walls of the Chapelle des Moins; they merit at least a brief survey. The chapel is open daily between mid-Mar and mid-Nov.

⑨ *Descend to major road; turn left and right, signposted Bussières.*

Bussières

Here they make and sell good goats' cheese. In the adjoining village (a five-minute walk) of Milly-Lamartine, the poet and patriot Alphonse de Lamartine spent his boyhood. The tomb and grottoes of Jocelyn, the subject of one of this poet's best works, can also be seen.

⑩ *Opposite the Milly-Lamartine turning, turn left; then right (possibly no signpost) and left, signposted Vergisson. Entering Vergisson, turn sharp right to a narrow road signposted Solutré-Pouilly.*

Solutré-
Pouilly

Some years ago, under the towering Roche de Solutré, a cave full of bones and pots revealed a settlement of prehistoric horse-tamers. It justified setting up a museum in Solutré-Pouilly, but everything worthwhile was carted off to the Mâcon museum 16 km away. Solutré-Pouilly is a pretty little place with orange-pantiled roofs, huddled under the tremendous rock and successfully resisting the 20thC.

(restaurant,
Solutré)

There is nothing sensational about Pichet de Solutré, a country bar/hotel, but it is a useful halfway house for snacks and drinks.

The Roche de Solutré see the description of Solutré-Pouilly, page 128.

Solutré-
Pouilly -
Tramayes

Here you pass between the Mâcon and Beaujolais regions, close to the hamlets whose combined names, Pouilly and Fuissé, signify renowned white burgundies.

Mère
Boitier
(detour)

On the descent to Tremayes, look for the left turning signposted Signal de la Mère Boitier. It is 2 km to the car-park and picnic area under the 758-metre summit. If the weather is clear, take the steep path to the Signal viewpoint and panoramic indicator, about 20 minutes there and back. The view is wide and magnificently kaleidoscopic. In late afternoon the sun gives a rosy glow to the snows of the French Alps.

Tremayes

The château is not open to the public.
⑪ *Turn right in the village, signposted St-Point.*

St-Point

It is the principal resort and Sunday-afternoon-excursion destination of the inhabitants of this mini-mountainland: what used to be called a 'climatic station'. Here you have an opportunity to reward the children for their patience on the trip by showing them some amusements. There is an artificial lake with swimming, fishing, wind-surfing and pedal-boating amenities; also a dry-land playground and an open-air restaurant and snack bar. Picnic tables are strategically distributed and you will find privacy if that is what you want. On the left, just beyond the village, is the Château de Lamartine, chief of the poet's residences in this district, now the Lamartine museum. You may feel that the *memorabilia* assembled here are rather humdrum; but the official tour is, for a change, pleasantly informal.

St-Point -
Cluny

⑫ *Continue north on the D22, crossing the railway and the Swiss-Atlantic highway. Follow signposts to Cluny.*

To think of summer in the Alps is to think of the clanging of cowbells in bright green meadows, geranium-laden chalets and snow-capped peaks rising above dark forests. Actually, this image has more to do with Austria and Switzerland than with France, but the French Alps can deliver the goods if you know where to look. Without doubt, the place to look first is the area covered by this tour, to the east of the glorious Lac d'Annecy. Throughout an intricate network of valleys, considerable mountains rear up behind pastoral scenes to rival almost anything in the Tirol or the Valais. Even the ski resorts here have mostly been developed with some regard for appearance and for traditional styles.

From fashionable Megève, at the south-east corner of the area, streams flow north to join the Arve and south-west to the Isère, separating the massif slightly from the Alps proper. Its backbone is the Chaîne des Aravis, a range which makes up in drama what it may lack in sheer altitude, and which offers fine views of neighbouring Mont Blanc.

Not surprisingly, the Alps don't offer the choice of roads that you find elsewhere in rural France, and this tour necessarily contains a larger-than-usual proportion of yellow roads, and even some red. The two loops start from close to the major resort of the area, La Clusaz. The northern one takes you through deep gorges and over the highest pass, the Col de la Colombière; the southern one offers less drama but plenty of other interest. The roads are not steep, but they are often narrow, and there are some exciting drops.

NOTE: the Col de la Forclaz (Route One) is cleared of snow, but not as a matter of high priority. If there has been recent snow, the Col will probably be closed. This applies from early October right through to early June. To check its condition ring the tourist office at La Clusaz (tel 50.02.60.92). The Col de la Colombière is not generally cleared of snow and is likely - but not certain - to be closed all winter and indeed through spring. Again, check with the La Clusaz tourist office. The rest of the roads used on both loops are likely to be clear, even in winter, within 24 hours of a heavy fall of snow: but it must again be emphasized that this is a rule of thumb. On-the-spot enquiry is the only way to avoid disappointment.

██████████ ROUTE ONE: 103 KM

St-Jean-de-Sixt   The setting of St-Jean is its most interesting feature: two streams converge on the village from the east, but fail to meet - they come within a km of one another only to be forced apart again by the mass of Mont Lachat. The more northerly stream - the Borne - flows into the Arve at Bonneville, and its waters thus join the mighty Rhône as soon as it has left Lake Geneva. The southerly Nom becomes the Fier, which skirts the Lac d'Annecy before heading for its rendezvous with the Rhône.

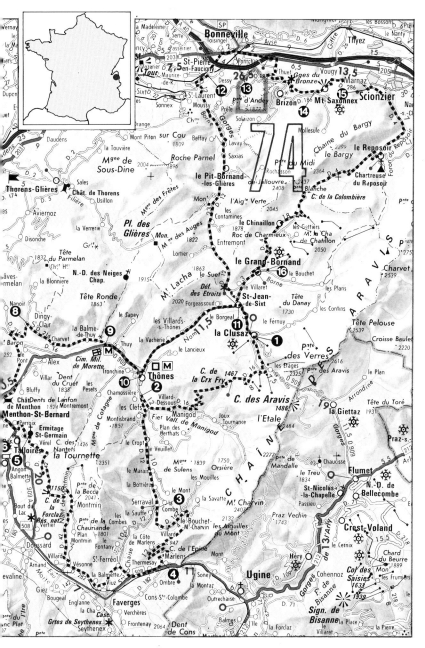

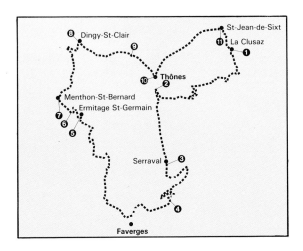

La Clusaz   La Clusaz rates as one of the most attractive of French ski resorts. That is not saying much: with its chalet-style buildings it is not offensive (which many other resorts are in summer), but neither is it particularly charming. It has an elaborate swimming pool perched on a south-facing slope, several tennis courts, and a cable-car to give you a flying start on some of the fine local mountain walks (for example to Thônes). There is a fair range of shops (including perfume and soap makers), and a reasonable choice of good-value, pleasant places in which to stay or eat, though nothing out of the ordinary. The only restaurant in the village with any pretensions to serious cooking is the Ecuelle. *Tel 50.02.42.03; price band B/C.*

Leave the resort ① on the D909, and if not making the detour to Col des Aravis, bear right in 2.5 km on to the D16 (signposted for the Col); at the next fork, keep left, signposted Col de Merdassier.

Col des Aravis *(detour)*   *Go through La Clusaz sticking to the main D909; after 2.5 km keep left, still on the D909, signposted for the Col.* This pass, at 1,486 metres, is the only major break in the Aravis chain. The road up from La Clusaz (unlike the road down the other side) is fairly broad and straightforward, with only a handful of hairpins, the pastures beside it carpeted with crocuses in early summer. What makes this detour worthwhile, especially if you can arrange to do it as the sun is going down, is the view of Mont Blanc. The highest mountain in Europe is not the easiest to appreciate - from many points of view it is simply bulky; but from a little way beyond the Col it is mightily impressive, dwarfing the skiing mountains of Megève in the foreground. Off to the left of the main mountain are the spiky *aiguilles* which range along the Chamonix valley. A footpath leading south from the Col gives energetic walkers even broader views of the high Alps.

Col de la Croix Fry This lower Col is quickly reached through pine forests. It has been turned into a big skiers' car-park and has little to detain you in summer. A little way down beyond the Col is the Chalet Hôtel Croix Fry, where you might consider stopping for a simple but satisfying meal on the sunny and beautifully situated terrace *(price band B/C/D)* or a night in the main chalet or one of the smaller self-contained ones *(tel 50.44.90.16; pool, tennis)*. From here a series of long, gentle hairpins leads down across a broad flank of the pretty, pastoral valley of Manifod.

Manigod - Faverges ② *At the junction with the D12 in the valley bottom, turn sharp left; as you do so, signs to Serraval and Faverges become visible; follow them.* The road climbs gently over the Col du Marais (837 metres).
③ *At Serraval fork left on to the D162 for Le Bouchet and Col de l'Epine.* The road contours around the hillside giving a series of striking mountain views in all directions - the southern end of the Tournette massif (of which this loop is a circumnavigation) is seen to advantage. At the Col de l'Epine, attention switches to the sharp ridge of the Dent de Cons, directly south as the road descends the steep hillside (beware the sharp and unsignposted hairpin).
④ *In the valley bottom, ignore the sign left to Marlens Chef-Lieu; all remaining lanes lead to the major road along the valley (N508), at which turn right; in about 2 km, after crossing a river, turn right for Thônes and St-Ferreol; follow the main road through the edge of St-Ferreol to Le Noyeray; follow signs for Faverges, then take a small road to the right, signposted Viuz; at a fork, go right signposted Vesonne (D282); at the memorial on the edge of Vesonne, fork right; go straight through the village.*

Col de la Forclaz Some maps make this road look terrifying. Do not be deterred; the road is adequate, and the scenery is worth any qualms you may experience. At first you wind up through woods, then across sunny meadows beneath the towering cliffs of La Tournette. At 1,150 metres, the Col is relatively low, but is perfectly placed to give a picture-postcard view of the Lac d'Annecy - an intense milky blue from this height. There is a small car park just beyond the Col itself. Hôtel L'Edelweiss, beside the Col, has a pleasant terrace where you can get simple meals *(price band B)*, though the little chalet La Pricaz, up the opposing hill, enjoys better views. The best views of all are reserved for picnickers who walk up across the meadows beyond the chalet (and the sign forbidding picnics) until the distant mountains south of the lake come into sight. Each establishment has in front of it a wooden ramp built out over the steep hillside facing the lake, and people come from far and wide to run down these ramps and hurl themselves down the mountain - strapped to hang-gliders.

Ermitage-St-Germain ⑤ *Past Verel, watch for a sign on the right; take the little road which it marks, go past the church and park a little way down the hill.* As you walk back up the shady lane, a footpath on the right takes you along a ledge to a cave where St-Germain, the first prior of Talloires, retreated. The accommodation looks a bit cramped, but the outlook is exceptional. *Carry on down the hill and turn left (yes, left).*

(6) *The road descends to lake level some way to the north of Talloires, where the promontory of the Roc de Chère forces the main D909a away from the shore; turn right.* This family resort-village spreads along the road some way from the lake, with pleasant residential lanes running off to the shore, where there are boat jetties and a bathing 'beach'. For walks through woods on the Roc de Chère, follow narrow lanes signposted first for the lake and then for the Roc, and park when you start worrying about the car's suspension. The looming château, dating from the 13thC and 15thC, is worth exploring (*open Sun in summer*).
Follow signs from middle of village away from lake to château.

Annecy
(detour)

Annecy is a busy, confusing town which the dedicated backroadsperson may be inclined to miss. But it has a charming medieval area (cut through by streams flowing out of the lake) at the foot of its imposing château, and boat trips (and boat hire) on the lake. There are car-parks on the way in along the lake shore which are not inconvenient, but for immediate access to the old town (and car-free glossy shopping streets nearby) it is best to aim for the waterfront town-hall car-park.
If you go on up the lake to Annecy, you can regain the tour route by taking the D5 out of town signposted Thorens, and then going off right on the D16 for Thônes.

Menthon - Thônes

(7) *From the bridge leading to the château continue up the little valley; cross the main road down a rough lane; in 2.5 km go over a crossroads, and then take a left turn just after a right-hand bend; at the D16 go left. At the stone bridge over the Fier where the valley narrows, turn right for Dingy-St-Clair, and immediately right again.* Downstream of the bridge you may see canoeists competing at weekends. Ahead of you as you go upstream are the exceedingly molar-like Dents de Lanfon and the flat-topped cliffs of the Dent de Cruet.
(8) *In Dingy turn right for Thônes.* The single-track road goes through a series of peaceful hamlets, their wooden chalets surrounded by orchards and meadows; beware goats and chickens wandering about. Look south as you drive along the sunny shelf (useful for picnics) and you can see distant peaks which are beyond the Lac d'Annecy. As you leave La Balme-de-Thuy, streams cascade down the rock face from the Plateau des Glières, 1,000 metres above you.
(9) *Join the D909; turn left to go directly to Thônes, or make this detour.*

Cimetière de Morette
(detour)

Turn right at (9) *and soon locate cemetery on left.* The Aravis region was a stronghold of the French Resistance in World War II - especially the high Plateau des Glières, just to the north of here. This immaculate little cemetery and small museum tell the story of a stubborn fight.

Thônes A solid, amiable little town with a range of shops under its stone arcades and a busy market on Saturday mornings. Park by the tourist office on the right as you enter the town. Picnic provisions bought here should include the extraordinary variety of breads available from the *boulangerie* in Rue de la Saulne and also *Reblochon*: an unusually creamy soft cheese which is made locally, mild-tasting but strong-smelling. Its name comes from the verb *reblocher*, meaning to milk a cow for a second time. The story goes that in medieval times when landlords called to collect their percentage of the milk, the peasants would stop milking before the cow was exhausted, leaving the creamiest part to be extracted later for their own use. You can try before you buy (and see the cheese being made) at the small co-operative factory beside the road in from Annecy.

Thônes is well-placed for mountain walks (a detailed map is available from the tourist office) and for excursions by car, as three valleys meet here. There are no very wonderful hotels, but the Nouvel Hôtel Commerce is adequate (*tel 50.02.13.66*) and takes its cooking seriously. ⑩ *In mid-town go left for Les Villards and La Clusaz.*

■ ROUTE TWO: 66 KM

Classic Alpine scenery, Aravis region.

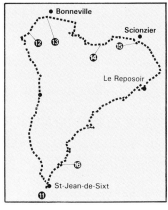

St-Jean-de-Sixt - Bonneville ⑪ *Take the D4 for Le Grand-Bornand, then in one km turn sharp left on to the D12 for Entremont and Bonneville; in another km, go left again at the T-junction.* Looming ahead as you descend towards the Borne are the steep walls of the Défile des Etroits, separating Mont Lachat to the south-west from the Chaîne du Bargy to the north-east. Beyond it, the valley of the Borne opens out on to pleasant meadows around Entremont (where you can acquire a complete log-cabin kit from the timber yard). Some way past the village is a popular picnic area where you may have to rely on the noise of the rushing Borne to give some sense of privacy. After another defile, a prominently signposted road on the left goes up to the Plateau des Glières. A more rewarding detour starts in Le Petit-Bornand; a road winds east up into the high valley of the Jalandre and on to the optimistically named ski station of Paradis, with close-up views of the Pic de Jalouvre.

The several hamlets making up the community of Le Petit-Bornand-les-Glières are strung along a classically beautiful Alpine valley - vivid green meadows dotted with chalets, and apparently enclosed at both ends by mountain walls. At the northern end you escape via another defile, the Gorges des Eveaux; you wind between rocky cliffs to emerge on the gentle southern slopes of the valley of the Arve.

⑫ *As you enter St-Pierre-en-Faucigny, the D6 goes off left (past a hideous small shopping area) for La Roche-sur-Foron; if not making the next detour, go straight on, cross railway then motorway, and at N203 turn right.*

La Roche-sur-Foron *(detour)*
La Roche sits in a slightly elevated position, well to the south of the Arve, in surroundings which are surprisingly rustic considering the proximity of two motorways and the city of Geneva. A round tower is all that remains of its ancient castle (finely set, as you might have guessed, on a rock outcrop, and giving views across the broad valley to the crags of Le Môle). The spacious mid-town area is regularly occupied by markets (and at other times crammed with parked cars), and jolly old streets leading away from it which are being restored. There are tempting food shops for picnic supplies.

Marie Jean *(rest. near La Roche)*
If you are in search of a real meal, head 2.5 km east of La Roche-sur-Foron for this elegant little roadside mansion offering indulgent cuisine and charming service. *Tel 50.03.33.30; closed 28 July-18 Aug, Sun eve and Mon; price band C.*

Bonneville - Mont-Saxonnex
⑬ *From Bonneville, take the N205 south of the river bridge; in 3 km (after crossing the motorway again) take a small road on the right signposted Thuet; go straight through Thuet; as you leave the village, a sign warns of bends for 4 km.* As you drive towards Thuet, your route back into the mountains is not obvious; but there is a tight, wooded cleft away to the left - the Gorges du Bronze - and the road finds its way into it. There are occasional places to stop for views of the Bronze tumbling over rocks way below the road. On a left-hand hairpin with parking space for a couple of cars, a footpath is signposted off into the woods for La Cascade du Dard. It is a short walk, but a precarious scramble, along the banks of the stream to the point where the Bronze spills over a broad rock shelf; a fine spot for a picnic unless crowded.

Mont-Saxonnex
This small, rustic resort-cum-farming-community spreads its chalets and orchards over a shelf on the mountainside 500 metres above the Arve. ⑭ *At the first settlement - Pincru - follow signs left for Marnaz; in the main village, 500 metres further on, go left down a narrow lane for the church.* From the church there are views in all directions - back up to

In the Vallée de Manigod.

the Pointe Blanche, along the valley of the Arve (with the snowy peaks around Chamonix to the east) and steeply down to the flat valley bottom where the Giffre joins the Arve.

Mont-Saxonnex - Le Reposoir

The main road through Mont-Saxonnex takes you gently down towards Marnaz. ⑮ *As soon as you enter the village of Blanzy (unsignposted), take a small road leading off to the right; there are signs for Le Reposoir and Col de la Colombière, but they are not visible as you approach the junction; this is the D4.*

Le Reposoir

The village of Le Reposoir may be unremarkable but it enjoys a lovely setting - an elevated meeting of valleys beneath the northernmost peaks of the Chaîne des Aravis and the Chaîne du Bargy. The Charterhouse, in suitably contemplative surroundings a couple of kms south of the village, has been restored to use as a religious retreat, but is now Carmelite rather than Carthusian; visitors welcome.

Col de la Colomb-i-ère

This is the tamest of Alpine passes, with no serious drops, few hairpins and a gentle gradient. Fine views across the valley as you go up the flank of the Chaîne du Bargy to the Col (1,613 metres), and plenty of picnic spots from which to enjoy them. Once over the Col, the developing ski resort of Le Chinaillon soon comes into view; it is not a pretty sight. But beyond it the road gives views of the Aravis chain.

Le Grand-Bornand

⑯ *As you enter the village, ignore signs advising you to go right; instead go on down to the small central square; turn right for St-Jean (or park).* More than most mountain resorts, Le Grand-Bornand feels like a real community; and never more so than on Wednesday mornings, when the market comes to town. To complete the loop, *keep left for St-Jean one km out of the village.*

The Vercors massif is one of the most attractive areas of the French Alps for the touring motorist. Slightly detached from the body of the northern Alps, its high plateaux were a natural (though ultimately not invulnerable) sanctuary for Resistance fighters in World War II. It has some of the classical charm of the book's other Alpine tour, in the Aravis area, but its main appeal lies in a few grand set pieces - the spectacular chasms and caverns cut in the limestone of the massif by the water flowing off it.

The nature of the landscape means that there is precious little choice of practical route between the principal sights, which is why the southern loop of this tour consists entirely of classified 'yellow' roads. This does not mean that they are major roads; on the contrary they are narrow, slow and hazardous - and definitely not for the nervous. Motor caravans and other van-like vehicles are effectively prohibited from the most interesting roads by low overhangs and tunnels.

The northern loop from Pont-en-Royans starts with splendid distant views of the dramatic Gorges de la Bourne and ends by bringing you back through the gorges themselves; in between there is some lush countryside. Do not attempt this loop before June: the high road between St-Quentin and Autrans is shaded by cliffs, and can be blocked by snow even when every other road in the Vercors is open.

The southern loop tours the rather harsher countryside of the Vercors proper, and links the two other major spectacles - the precipitous Combe Laval and the cavernous gorges of the Grands Goulets.

■■■■■■■ ROUTE ONE: III KM

Pont-en-Royans
At the western extremity of the massif, the rock of the Vercors makes a final futile attempt to prevent the waters of the Bourne joining those of the Isère. River and road squeeze through a narrow cleft to emerge on to the undulating shelf of Royans. There is not the space to accommodate a village around the river bridge, but Pont-en-Royans has nevertheless grown up here. The tiled roofs of its houses, built into the rock and in terraces up the steep hillside opposite, are reminiscent of Provençal villages.

Bonnard
(rest., Pont-en-Royans)
This pleasant little hotel, in the main street leading away from the bridge, is a reliable choice for meals or accommodation. *Tel 76.36.00.54; closed Oct, Dec-Feb and Wed, April-May; price band B.*

Pont-en-Royans - St-Gervais
① *From the river bridge go upstream on the D531; shortly after crossing the river again (about one km from the village) turn left along the D292, signposted Presles.* The narrow road winds steeply up the mountainside, affording increasingly impressive views of the ridges, precipices, gorges and combes to the south and east; the driver, whose eyes should not stray from the single-track road, will have to make the most of the few

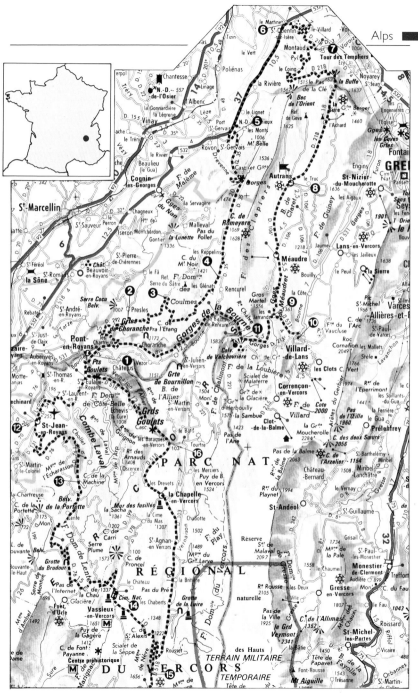

Typical stone house of the Briançon area: the large wooden upper storey is the hay loft.

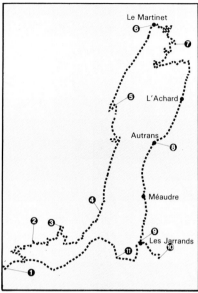

places where it is possible to stop and look around - the two obvious points are at the Col de Toutes Aures, where the road changes direction but continues upward, and the end of the climb where a tunnel leads to the high plateau surrounding the hamlet of Presles.

② *Less than one km across the plateau, take a right turn (poorly signposted) to Rencurel; in about 3 km, at a T-junction, turn left, indistinctly signposted to Rencurel (the signpost pointing in the opposite direction is faintly marked cul de sac).*

③ *In a further 4 km, where a left fork is signposted to the Col du Mont Noir, carry straight on along the Rencurel road, unless you fancy the slightly more adventurous route on forest roads over the Col (1,421 metres).* During this stretch you pass through pleasantly mixed woods - the Forêt Domainale des Coulmes. There are occasional parking areas and picnic tables, and paths leading off into the forest. The narrow road descends gently along the flank of a broad, prosperous valley around the settlement of Rencurel.

④ *On joining the 'main' valley road above Rencurel, go straight on up the valley.* From the Col de Romeyère (1,074 metres), a tiny ski-station, there is a relentless straight descent of some 4 km to the entrance to a gorge. The dark tunnel into which you plunge after only a glimpse of the precipitous sides of the gorge is a little unnerving - not only is it unlit, but there is apparently no end to it. When you finally emerge at the far end, park and go back on foot up the old road - cut in the cliff face of the gorge. It makes you appreciate the tunnel after all. For those with a head for heights, there are stunning views down into the gorge and across to the rolling hills on the far side of the Isère valley. The road you are following can be seen crossing the cascading stream hundreds of metres below. *Continue to St-Gervais.*

St-Gervais -
Autrans

⑤ *At the church, turn right on to the D35C, signposted to St-Quentin and Grenoble; when you reach the main N532, turn right; stay on this road until you reach the traffic lights at St-Quentin.*

⑥ *Turn right at the lights, then bear left immediately following signs for Montaud; at the crossroads in the village, go straight across, following signs for Montaud and Route d'Autrans.* The road zig-zags up the steep side of the Isère valley, then wanders through charming rustic hamlets on the lush little plateau of Montaud. The cliffs above may look impenetrable, but that is where you are heading.

⑦ *At the T-junction, turn right to Montaud.* Beyond Le Coing the road enters a forest of tall pines and starts to climb again under the towering cliffs of the Pas de la Clé. Serious mountain walkers properly equipped can make expeditions from the forest road to the peak of Bec de l'Orient (1,568 metres) for superb views in all directions. Those who stay in the car do not do badly, however. As the road climbs, there are better and better views across the plateau of Montaud (and the steep little valley of the Voroize to the east of it) to the mountains beyond the Isère. The occasional stopping places along this stretch make convenient picnic spots. Eventually, the road turns south at La Buffe, the northernmost crag of the Vercors massif, opening up new views across the Isère to the Chartreuse massif and along the river to Grenoble, before disappearing into a long tunnel into the interior of the massif.

Beyond the tunnel, gentle forested slopes lead into a long, grassy valley; the only indication that you are 1,000 metres above the Isère are the ski runs and lifts scarring the sides of the valley and, straight ahead on the little hill beyond Autrans, the ski-jumps used for the Grenoble Winter Olympics in 1968. Behind, in the distance, the pale swathes through the forest are the ski runs of Méaudre.

Autrans -
Villard-de-
Lans

Autrans and Méaudre are small, plain villages whose houses, with their sloping-step parapets designed to keep water and snow off the porous stone of the gables, are characteristic of the area. Both villages attract Sunday visitors from Grenoble, and each has a handful of simple places in which to stay or eat, and adequate shops for picnic supplies. Autrans is smaller, less affected by ski-ing development, and the more pleasant place in which to pause; the Hôtel de la Buffe just north of the village *(tel 76.95.33.26)* has better amenities than the older, more central Ma Chaumière *(tel 76.95.30.12).*

⑧ *In Autrans, turn right and then shortly left for Méaudre and Villard-de-Lans; just before Méaudre, turn right on to the D106. In Méaudre, veer slightly left, following the main road.* The Gorges du Méaudret, just south of Méaudre, are by local standards not spectacular, but they are more easily appreciated from the road than their famous neighbours downstream - all you have to do is look up. There are organized picnic areas by the stream in the woody defile.

⑨ *On reaching Les Jarrands, turn left at the T-junction for Villard-de-Lans; do not take the first road to the right signposted to the centre of Villard, but stay on the bypass for a further one km before turning right. As you near the middle of Villard there are large car parks on the right; park here to avoid the one-way system.*

Villard-de-Lans

A popular winter and summer resort, Villard is at its liveliest at weekends. Outdoor attractions include a cable-car ride (starting 4 km outside the village) up on to La Côte 2,000 - a shoulder of La Grande Moucherolle (2,284 metres). From the top station (1,720 metres) you can walk to the summit of La Côte 2,000, though for the best views to the east and south you need to cross the summit plateau to the Pas de l'Oeille and the Col des Deux Soeurs (not a trivial undertaking). Hearty walkers who shun mechanical assistance can launch off directly from Villard to follow minor lanes through woods and meadows to the Calvaire de Valchevrière - a memorial to the valiant but unsuccessful defence of the hamlet in 1944. From here, there are views of the Gorges de la Bourne.

Le Dauphin
(hotel-rest., Villard-de-Lans)

There is plenty of accommodation in Villard, and all sorts of places in which to eat. Le Dauphin is a charming and good-value restaurant opposite the information office, with a comfortable small hotel attached. *Tel 76.95.11.43; closed mid April-mid May; price band B, with a half-price menu for children.*

Christiana *(hotel, Villard-de-Lans)*

Slightly to the south of the central area, the Christiania is a smart, chalet-style hotel, with a south-facing grassy garden and its own small pool (not far from the big public pool). *Tel 76.95.12.51; closed May, Oct to mid-Dec, restaurant hours vary out of season; price bands C/D.*

⑩ *Retrace to the D531, then turn left. At Les Jarrands, go straight on, for Pont-en-Royans.*

Gorges de la Bourne

Shortly after leaving Les Jarrands, the road enters the gorges and soon becomes narrow and hazardous; built on a ledge cut into the side of the gorge, it occasionally resorts to tunnels. Although the high cliffs closing in above you are impressive enough, to get the full impact you need to park in one of the few stopping places, from where you can peer down at the roaring stream. The height from which the Bourne drops through the gorges is sufficient to have justified the creation of a small hydro-electric installation, which sadly makes the banks of the river dangerous - when they turn the tap on, the water level rises almost instantly.

⑪ *One km after crossing to the left bank of the Bourne, take a right turn*

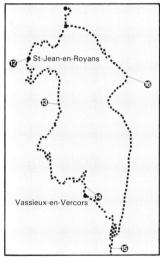

(signposted La Balme) to regain the right bank. The more open area around La Balme offers one of the few opportunities on this part of the tour to have a picnic without risking vertigo. Shortly afterwards the cliffs close in again and the road is once more forced into the rock face before the valley swells to much grander proportions; as you descend, look out for a stream way off across the valley, spilling down the vertical cliffs.

Grottes de Choranche
The caves - reached by a new approach road that forks right along the flank of the valley - are not essential viewing for cave connoisseurs who have sampled the more famous subterranean sights of France, but they do have their own fascination: crystal-clear pools as well as the usual weird and wonderful concretions. And having gained the hillside car park you can always admire the view from the terrace café instead of walking on to the caves, if the picture postcards don't impress you. *Return to the valley road and descend to Pont-en-Royans.*

ROUTE TWO: 87 KM

Late winter afternoon, in the Vercors massif.

St-Jean-en-Royans

Vassieux-en-Vercors

Pont-en-Royans - St-Jean-en-Royans
Leave Pont-en-Royans on the D54, following the left bank of the river. In Ste-Eulalie and St-Laurent, follow signs for St-Jean. As the road climbs gently towards Ste-Eulalie, the conclusion of this loop comes into view on the left - the cleft of the Petits Goulets.

St-Jean-en-Royans
An inoffensive small town, the main settlement of the rustic, rolling Royans; if attempts to find a picnic spot along the way have failed, the shady benches in its little squares may come in handy (market: Sat).

*Spring,
the Vercors
massif.*

 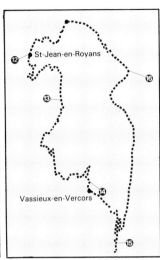

⑫ *Go straight through the town, eventually bearing left on to the D76 for Col de la Machine and Col de Rousset.*

**Combe
Laval -
Foret de
Lente**

As you ascend the western side of the Montagne de l'Echarasson there are fine views - but nothing prepares you for the sheer excitement of the eastern side, which is practically a precipice. The road runs along ledges and through tunnels, and it is perhaps just as well that there are few places where you can stop to appreciate the steepness of the drop beyond the flimsy stone wall. At the head of the valley the road burrows through a tunnel which takes you to the Col de la Machine.
⑬ *Beyond the Col de la Machine, take the turning to the right, signposted Lente.* The Forêt de Lente is famous for the length, straightness and resilience of its timber, which made it ideal for use in ships' masts; it was to speed the delivery of this timber to the valley that the extraordinary road along the lip of the Combe Laval was created. These days the area probably makes more money out of its ski-lifts. In early summer, the little plain of Lente grows masses of wild flowers. As you descend the Col de la Chau, at the eastern edge of the forest, the high point of the Vercors - Le Grand Veymont (2,341 metres) - lies straight ahead.
⑭ *At the junction by the cemetery, take the turning to the right, signposted Col de Rousset.*

**Vassieux-en-
Vercors -
Col de
Rousset**

Rebuilt since the war, the unremarkable-looking village of Vassieux, in its high, dry and rocky valley has become a place of pilgrimage. Vassieux was largely destroyed in 1944, and those who died are interred at the Cimetière National mentioned above.

Continuing along the Col de Rousset road, there is another little col (de St-Alexis) and another change of scenery as you go from the Vassieux valley to the lower, lusher valley of the Vernaison, the long, straight axis of the southern Vercors.

⑮ *Turn right at the hairpin junction halfway down the hill.*

Col de Rousset

Many ski resorts have a curiously Wild West air about them in summer, when they are virtually deserted; the clutch of bars and shops around the entrance to the disused tunnel of the Col de Rousset is an extreme example, and you are unlikely to want to pause here even if the chair-lift is working. Instead, go through the new tunnel on the near side of the 'village'. On the far side of the tunnel there are parking places. They say that the Col represents the meeting of the northern (wet) and southern (dry) Alpine climates, and that the contrast is, under certain conditions, visible.

Col de Rousset - St-Agnan-en-Vercors

The Grotte de la Luire to the right of the road is another focus for memories of the Resistance: it served as a hospital for the wounded until its discovery by the Germans in July 1944. It is also of some interest simply as a cave.

St-Agnan-en-Vercors

This little village retains a more old-established feel than its larger neighbours. The Veymont, in the tiny central square, is a satisfactory simple hote with a cheap menu *(tel 75.48.20.19)*.

La-Chapelle-en-Vercors

Here the cost of the Vercors' resistance movement is made painfully clear by the evident newness of much of this substantial village. There is no particular reason to pause, but there are comfortable rooms and reliable, traditional food at the chalet-style Bellier, in the main street *(tel 75.48.20.03; price band B)*.

Les Grands Goulets

⑯ *Turn right at Les Baraques-en-Vercors in search of a parking space.* Les Baraques is right at the top of the narrowest part of the gorges of the Grands Goulets, and it is well worth parking here and walking a short way down the road to inspect this impressive work of nature - though it means dodging the traffic.

The road from Les Baraques accompanies the torrential River Vernaison through tunnels and clefts which are barely penetrated by the light of day, so high and close are the walls. Soon the the valley widens and deepens, offering grand views that can be admired in comfort from the terrace restaurant of Le Refuge, a useful roadside hotel *(tel 75.48.68.32; price bands A/B/C)*. Try the local cheese ravioli. On the last lap of this tour the road goes through Les Petits Goulets - another dramatic conflict between rock and river. *Turn right in Ste-Eulalie to return to Pont-en-Royans.*

Auvergne:

The imposing presence of the Puy de Sancy, the highest peak in the Massif Central, can be felt throughout this tour, whether it is just peeping over a distant horizon or hanging before you, almost unreal, like a piece of rumpled tapestry. At its northern foot lie the source of the River Dordogne and the spa and ski resort of Le Mont-Dore, which is the starting point for both routes. The rival spa of La Bourboule is located a few km downstream.

The landscape of this region, like much of the Massif Central, is of volcanic origin, as can be guessed from its many dome-like mountains. But another sign is the paradoxical presence of lakes at the *top* of passes or plateaux, as a result of rainwater filling a crater or lava forming a natural dam. There are a couple of these lakes on the tour, as well as the largest artificial lake in the Auvergne, the Lac de Bort, and a delightfully convoluted stretch of water formed by glacial erosion, the Lac de Crégut. All these are ideal for picnics.

As well as thrilling mountain scenery - the driving, incidentally, is always easy and does not require a head for heights - this tour takes in some of the finest architecture the Auvergne has to offer. At the top of the list are two sophisticated Romanesque masterpieces: the churches of Orcival and St-

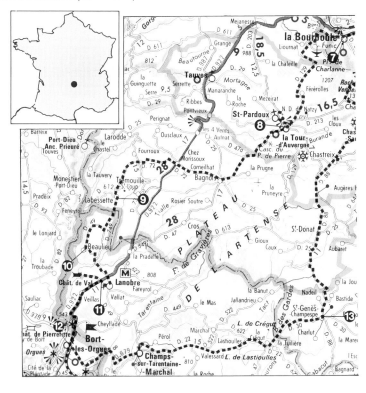

Nectaire. There are also many lesser-known churches, whose engaging craftsmanship deserves attention, and two fine châteaux.

◾◾ ROUTE ONE: 87 KM

Le Mont-Dore
The hot springs of Le Mont-Dore were exploited by the Gauls, the Romans and Louis XIV, but the spa only really took off in the 19thC. Today the main attraction is still the Etablissement Thermal, a fine example of grand turn-of-the-century spa architecture. Le Mont-Dore is an ideal base and has plenty of accommodation. Market day: Fri.

Skieurs
(rest., Le Mont-Dore)
This welcome *auberge* (actually called L'Auberge Des Skieurs) serves hearty regional dishes, such as *chou farci* and *tripous* (sheep's tripe). There are a few simple rooms. *Rue Montlosie; tel 73.65.05.59; price band B.*

Puy de Sancy
(detour)
Le Mont-Dore is only 4 km as the crow flies from the top of the Massif Central's highest peak, the Puy de Sancy (1,885 metres). *For this detour,* ① *leave the town by the D983, then take a cable car, which will deposit you within walking distance (20 minutes) of the top. On a clear day the view in every direction is overwhelming. Return to Le Mont-Dore.*

First World War Memorial in the church at Beaulieu, Route Two.

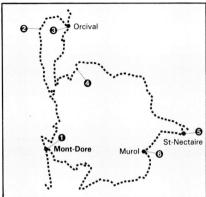

Le Mont-Dore - Rochefort-Montagne	*Take the D983 in the direction of Clermont-Ferrand* and climb the flank of the Puy de la Tache. *Fork left at the junction with the D996,* and continue up through a scree-covered gorge. Suddenly, you emerge at the Col de Guéry with its lake, trapped in a volcanic crater, sitting incongruously at the top of a mountain pass. Just beyond the lake look back at the superb view (the first of many) over the Sancy range, then *turn left along the D80 to Rochefort-Montagne.* This road goes between two spectacular conical outcrops, the Roche Tuilière and the Roche Sanadoire. The valley between them was ground out of the mountain by a glacier during the ice age.
Rochefort-Montagne - Orcival	② *When you reach Rochefort-Montagne,* a busy little town with some interesting old buildings, *veer right in the middle and, just before the junction with the N89, turn right on to the D216. Drive on for about one km, then turn right again on to the D27e to Orcival.* Along the way there is a fine view to the left over the Monts Dômes, a comparatively recent chain of volcanoes (their creation would have been witnessed by earliest man). The tall, thermometer-like object sticking up from the highest of them, the Puy de Dôme, is a broadcasting tower.
Orcival	The village of Orcival is dominated by its impeccably proportioned 12thC Romanesque church, whose interior, thanks to its many windows, is lighter (in both senses of the word) than most comparable buildings in the Auvergne, which tend to be chunky and dimly-lit. The striking 12thC statue of the Virgin and Child attracts many pilgrims.
Château de Cordès *(detour)*	③ The multi-turreted L-shaped Château de Cordès, set among tree-lined avenues and formal gardens designed by Le Nôtre, is definitely worth a detour. *Take the D27 signposted Clermont-Ferrand; 1.5 km beyond Orcival, turn left into the château's drive. Open all year 10-12 and 2-6.*

Orcival -
Lac Servière
Leave Orcival in the direction of Le Mont-Dore along the D27. Drive on for about 4 km then turn sharp left at the junction with the D983, which now sweeps majestically along the mountainside with pinewoods to the right and the Monts Dômes to the left. Shortly after a small road comes in from the left, pull in opposite the only house on the road. Here, a badly signposted track leads up through conifers (5 minutes' walk) to another high crater-lake, Lac Servière - a peaceful spot for a picnic.

Lac Servière
- St-
Nectaire
④ *Continue along the D983, then turn right to Saulzet-le-froid along the D74e.* The distant Monts du Forez and du Livradois can be seen straight ahead. *When you join the D74, keep on it via several crossroads and forks, through Saulzet-le-Froid and on to the T-junction with the D5* (where there is fuel). *Turn right towards Murol, then left along the D74, following the signs to St-Nectaire.* After crossing what feels like a table mountain with vistas in every direction, the road wends its way down an attractively miniature mountain valley. Two right turns later *(on to the D150e and D150)*, you will see St-Nectaire - or rather its two separate halves - down below you.

St-
Nectaire
This small town is famous for three things: its superb Romanesque church, its hot springs, and its delicious nutty-flavoured cheese. The church, which occupies a promontory in the older part, St-Nectaire-le-Haut, contains some vivid capitals depicting scenes from the Bible and the life of St-Nectaire, and several remarkable treasures. *Out of season the church is open 10.30-11.30 and 2.30-4.30; closed Tues and Thurs.*
　　Drive down to the D996 and turn left into St-Nectaire-le-Bas, a curiously elongated spa with a turn-of-the-century atmosphere. The Syndicat d'Initiative will give you details of another, less-known aspect of St-Nectaire: its druidic past. The town itself and the surrounding countryside are dotted with dolmens, menhirs and sacred caves.
　　As for the cheese, try to buy some St-Nectaire *fermier* (as opposed to *laitier*, or dairy-made), either from a cheese shop or direct from a farm: look out for signs on both Route One and Route Two. If buying from a farm, you will be expected to purchase at least half a cheese (750 g). Don't be daunted: its unfatty texture is ideal for picnics.

Marinette
(hotel-rest.,
St-Nectaire)
This simple hostelry in the upper part of St-Nectaire offers copious *cuisine bourgeoise* and, as you would expect, excellent St-Nectaire cheese. *Menu du terroir. Tel 73.88.50.35; price band A.*

St-Nectaire
- Murol
⑤ *From St-Nectaire, take the D996 to Murol,* a pleasant, large village dominated by the massive rounded walls of its 12th-16thC fortress. To see the castle *(open Apr-Sept 9-7; Oct-Mar Sun and national holidays only, 2-7),* turn sharp right just after entering Murol and drive round the back to the car park. *The exit, marked wiht an arrow, is by another road that leads back down to the D996. Turn right and, at the next junction, left up the D5 signposted Besse.*

Murol - Col de la Croix St-Robert

⑥ *Continue on the D5, and just after entering St-Victor-la-Rivière turn right in the direction of Le Breuil. At the next junction, turn right along the D36.* The driving here is exhilarating, as the unusually straight road seems to be heading directly into the side of the Puy de Sancy. *At the next T-junction turn left towards Le Mont-Dore.* The road, which begins to snake up through a landscape of bare grass and crags, is excellent and not at all precipitous; it seems to climb up and up forever - then suddenly you come out on the Col de la Croix St-Robert. This pass, 1,426 metres high, offers breathtaking views on both sides. La Bourboule can be seen in the distance.

After crossing a steppe-like tract with the Puy de Sancy looming to the left, the road dips down through lichen-covered birch trees to Le Mont-Dore.

ROUTE TWO: 113 KM

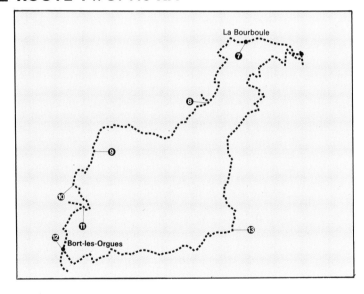

Le Mont-Dore - La Bourboule

Follow the River Dordogne along the D130 to La Bourboule. This spa, which like its neighbour Le Mont-Dore has hot springs, is altogether more congenial in character. It has many tree-lined squares, one with a bandstand, a delightful park, the Parc Fenestre, and a number of attractive art nouveau and art deco buildings and café interiors.

La Bourboule - La Tour d'Auvergne

⑦ *Drive along the left bank of the Dordogne, past the gingerbread casino, and straight on to the D129 to La Tour d'Auvergne.* The road skirts pleasant woodlands and winds its way to the Plateau de Charlanne. If you are doing this tour in July or August you will be rewarded by the sight of fields of great yellow gentian; this plant, which flavours various Auvergne drinks such as Avèze and Salers, is happy only above an altitude of 1,000 metres.

Soon you are confronted, suddenly, with a wide vista over the Plateau de l'Artense ahead. The Puy de Sancy peeps over the horizon to the left. Note that the typical farmhouse design of this area consists of a single long, tall building with living quarters at one end and a cowshed or barn at the other. *On joining the D213, turn right to La Tour d'Auvergne*, a small town whose well-preserved houses cling to a hillock on a mountain plateau.

Notre-Dame de Natzy and St-Pardoux

⑧ *For the short detour to Notre-Dame de Natzy and St-Pardoux turn sharp right in the middle of town (signposted Bagnols and Bort), and at the junction a few hundred metres later keep straight on along the D203. Just beyond the sign saying you are leaving La Tour d'Auvergne, stop at the car park on the right.* Go up the path (follow the Stations of the Cross) past a dilapidated open-air altar to the huge statue of the Virgin and Child at the top of the hill (10 minutes' walk): this is Notre-Dame-de-Natzy, a folly erected by a local notable in 1850 after he was miraculously cured. There is an extensive view in every direction. *Return to the car park and continue along the D203, then take the first turning to the left for St-Pardoux.* Its Gothic church of harmonious proportions contains an unusual 16thC altarpiece that is a riot of gilt and cabled columns. Note the sinister bust of the Virgin in the neighbouring school playground.

La Tour d'Auvergne - Labessette

Leave La Tour d'Auvergne as indicated for the detour, but turn left at the first junction on the edge of town (no warning) along the D47 to Bort. Soon the road offers a fine view back over the town with the Puy de Sancy behind. You are now on the Plateau de l'Artense, which is strewn with boulders and curious rock formations caused by glacial erosion. *As you come into the sleepy village of Bagnols, turn sharp right just before the church, then fork left immediately along the D72*, through attractive park-like country. Continue over the N122, taking great care at a dangerous crossroads about 3 km later (sign may be obscured). *At the minute village of Labessette, turn right* to its correspondingly minute Romanesque church, which has a gable belfry and a touchingly asymmetrical apse.

Labessette - Beaulieu

⑨ *Continue along the D72. About 3 km beyond Labessette in the middle of a very straight stretch of road, turn right along the D49 (no warning) towards Beaulieu. Keep straight on (follow sign to La Plage). In Beaulieu turn right in front of the church and follow signs to Château de Thynières.* Park the car, then walk through a farmyard and up a promontory to the ruins of the castle. This site (an ideal picnic spot) is interesting not so much for the castle itself as for the superb views it offers along the huge Lac de Bort, which is 18 km long.

Château de Val.

Beaulieu -
Lanobre

⑩ *Leave Beaulieu by the picturesque D49 signposted Lanobre. Cross the N122 into Lanobre,* which has a fine 12thC Romanesque church with some interesting capitals and superb 13thC wrought-iron decorations on its door. *Turn right at Lanobre church and right again to the N122.*

Château
de Val
(detour)

⑪ *For this detour, a 5-km return journey, go straight over the N122.* The dam of Port-les-Orgues was designed so that the waters of its artificial lake would (just) spare this picturesque 15thC castle, which is now romantically situated at the end of a narrow peninsula. Well worth a visit, but crowded in high summer. Leave the car at one of the many car parks on the way down to the castle, as you will not be able to park at the bottom. *Open 9-12 and 2.30-6.30; closed Nov to mid-Dec and Tues mid-Sept to mid-Jun, hours vary.*
Return to the N122 and drive on to Veillac.

Beau
Rivage
(hotel-rest.,
Veillac)

Nice garlicky *terrine*, tasty pheasant (when in season), a well-stocked cheese platter and excellent pastries are some of the things on offer at this friendly hotel-restaurant. There is a quiet garden where meals are served in summer. *Tel 71.40.31.11; closed out of season; price bands A/B.*

Bort-les-
Orgues

This straggling town, overlooked by a massive dam and an overrated ridge of basalt columns that are supposed to look like organ pipes (hence 'les Orgues'), need not detain you.

Saut de la
Saule
(detour)

For a short detour to this impressive series of waterfalls, where the River Rhue has sliced its way through massive gneiss boulders, *leave the middle of Bort on the N922. Fork left up a small road signposted C.A.T.*

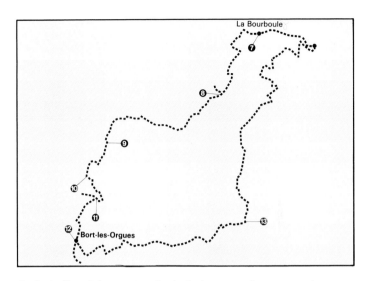

La Saule. Keep following signs for La Saule, eventually crossing railway at level crossing. Soon park by football field. Take the path marked Saut de la Saule over a small suspension bridge, then turn left (follow blue arrows). *Return to Bort the way you came.*

Bort-les Orgues - St-Genès-Champespe

⑫ *Drive from Bort to Champs-sur-Tarentaine on the D979, then turn left along the D22 signposted Marchal.* You are now back on the characteristic terrain of the Plateau de l'Artense. The Puy de Sancy soon reappears to the left, while the distant Puy Mary range can be seen to the right. The lake formed by the dam at La Crégut has a charming Scandinavian quality - and not too many tourists. *Follow signs to St-Genès-Champespe.*

St-Genès-Champespe - Chastreix

⑬ *Turn left in the village and take the D88 to St-Donat. Veer left round its Romanesque church and continue on the D89.* The countryside becomes more rugged as you approach the Puy de Sancy. *Turn left at the junction with the D203, then turn right along the D88 to Chastreix.*

Chastreix

This small village is notable for its outsize Gothic church, which has an interesting porch and wall paintings. Sadly its jewel - a superb 11thC statue of the Virgin and Child - was stolen (but postcard available).

Chastreix - Le Mont-Dore

Continue on the D88 to the left of the church. At the first main T-junction, branch left to Le Mont-Dore (sign hard to see). Extraordinary views open up to the west. *Ignore the turning to the right to a 'télé-ski'. At the junction with the D213 turn right, and later fork right for Le Mont-Dore.* As you drive, there is a view over La Bourboule.

The two loops of this tour, which is centred on the attractive little town of Entraygues-sur-Truyère (normally known just as Entraygues), take in two quite different types of countryside. Route One explores the untamed scenery of the Gorges de la Truyère, whose lack of human habitation, narrowness, and resistant granite sides made them the ideal site for a series of major hydroelectric dams.

Route Two meanders through a little-known area called the Châtaigneraie (as its name suggests, it is full of sweet chestnut trees), whose friendly landscape of gently rounded hills, woods, pastures and tree-lined hedges is bisected by trout streams. Here you will see a profusion of dormer-windowed houses whose steep roofs are covered with the distinctive local form of slate, mica schist; distinctive gable-belfries, often perched on roofs; and pigs roaming loose in the woods, rooting for chestnuts and acorns, hence the excellence of the local *charcuterie* (restaurants, incidentally, offer real value in the Châtaigneraie); but you will see few tourists, even at the height of summer - except possibly at Conques, whose picturesque houses, extraordinary church, and even more extraordinary treasure are the highlight of this tour.

■■■■■■ ROUTE ONE: 95 KM

Typical Auvergnois building: stone construction, simple austere style and, at higher levels, steep-pitched roofs.

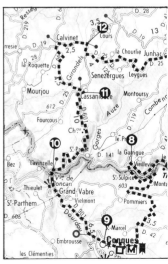

Entraygues   The small town of Entraygues (its name means 'between the waters') is situated at the confluence of the Truyère and the Lot. It has an elegant Gothic bridge, an imposing castle - originally built in the 13thC, then razed and rebuilt in the 17thC - and a fascinating old quarter.

Entraygues - Pons

(1) *Follow the signs out of Entraygues for Mur-de-Barrez, crossing the bridge over the River Truyère, then turning sharp right along the D904.* The road runs straight along the Truyère, which has already taken on its typically fjord-like appearance; you will probably have noticed that the bridge you crossed was in fact a dam. *As you approach Couesque,* which is overlooked by terraces where vines used to be grown, *take the first turning to the left signposted Montsalvy, then bear right in Les Carrières (not on map) for Pons,* which soon comes into view, tucked away cosily at the end of the valley. *Bear right across the bridge, then left into the middle of Pons.*

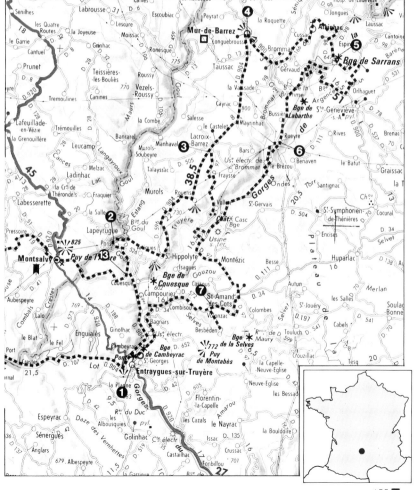

Pons

This charming little village, notable for its idiosyncratic church and well-preserved old houses, marks the eastern edge of the Châtaigneraie.

Pons -
Rouens

② *Leave Pons on the steep St-Hippolyte road (not marked on map),* which offers views first to the left over the conical Puy Haut and Puy de la Pause, then to the right over the Château de Vallon, the Gorges de la Truyère and the vast and windswept Aubrac plateau beyond. *Ignore the sign to Mur-de-Barrez and continue into St-Hippolyte, bearing right past the church* (which like most in these parts, has a gable-belfry). *Shortly after leaving the village,* which affords a fine view back over the Couesque dam, *turn left on to the D904 to Rouens.* As the road comes over the top of the hill, the entire Puy Mary massif appears ahead.

Rouens -
Lacroix-
Barrez

Turn right into this hamlet, which has many fine mica-schist roofs covering barns as well as houses, and follow the signs to the neatly laid out *belvédère.* This is a pleasant place for a picnic if there is not too much wind; views all round. *Return to the D904, which now becomes an exhilarating ridge road, and continue to Lacroix-Barrez.*

Château
de Vallon
(detour)

③ *For this detour, which entails a 9-km round trip, turn right in Lacroix-Barrez on to the D97.* The road runs down an attractive steep valley to Vallon, a totally unspoilt hamlet (no cars), perched on a rocky spur overlooking the Gorges de la Truyère and dominated by a ruined castle (inhabited by wall-creepers, birdwatchers please note). *Return to Lacroix-Barrez and continue on the D904.*

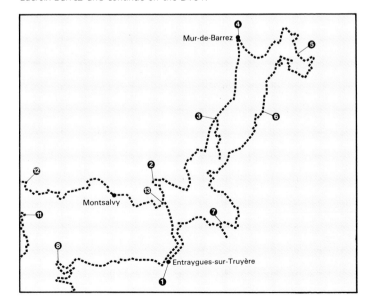

Mur-de-Barrez
An atmospheric little town, taken by the English in 1418 and turned into a Protestant stronghold; later it was given by Louis XIII to the Prince of Monaco. It has a large number of interesting 17thC buildings and a 12th-13thC church (note the unusual keystone representing a recumbent Christ above the organ loft). Sensibly, the oldest part of the town has been made into a pedestrian precinct.

Auberge du Barrez
(hotel-restaurant, Mur-de-Barrez)
Follow the signs to the *gendarmerie* for this easy-to-miss hostelry, a bland new building which its owners, the town council, have obviously been at pains to make as unobtrusive as possible (look for the Logis de France sign). The cuisine, which is excellent value, delicately combines the traditional and the *nouvelle*. The rooms are quiet (except when the *gendarmes* are called out - not often in this part of the world). *Tel 65.66.00.76; closed Mon, Sun eve Nov-Easter, Jan-8 Feb; price bands A/B/C.*

Mur-de-Barrez - Barrage de Sarrans
④ *Take the D900 to Brommat, whose church has an extraordinary asymmetrical clock tower. Cross the bridge and bear left towards the middle of the village, then turn sharp right on to the D98.* This high road, with sweeping views both left and right, goes through the attractive hamlet of Albinhac, which has yet another church with a gable-belfry and a charming little turreted manor.

As the road (now the D98) approaches the Barrage de Sarrans, a portion of the 35-km long lake created by the dam comes into view below. Drive over the dam and up to the car park and *belvédère*. The only sign of human habitation is a group of incongruous (for this area) ochre-coloured chalets, built before the Second World War for the dam engineers.

Barrage de Sarrans - Rueyre
⑤ *Continue on the D98, then turn right on to the D537 to Orlhaguet* (note the quirky church which has a castle turret up one side). *At the T-junction with the D900, turn right towards Brommat.* The road twists and turns through wild and craggy ravines with the Truyère, for once looking like a river rather than a fjord, flowing below: this section gives some idea of what the Gorges must have looked like before man decided to harness the Truyère's waters. *Continue on the D621 across a surprising (in this context) stretch of plain.* Soon the horizon is filled with a forest of pylons and electrical installations - the Rueyre interconnection station. Set in the middle of nowhere, with its cables swooping to their destinations in every direction, this silent non-polluting complex has a powerful science-fiction beauty.

Rueyre - Volonzac
⑥ *Do not drive into Rueyre itself, but fork right towards Le Brezou.* Soon the road reveals a fantastic plunging view ahead over the Truyère and undertakes a series of hairpin bends down past the mysterious underground power station of Brommat - a colossal construction hollowed out of the granite mountainside.

After crossing the Truyère (which by this time has become an elongated lake again, because of the Barrage de Couesque downstream), there is a relaxing drive along a recently built section of the D621 (not marked on map) gouged out of the sides of the gorge. The Château de Vallon (see detour in Route One) can be seen on the right from a new angle - i.e. from below. *At the first crossroads keep straight on along the D97 towards Montézic. In Montézic veer right for St-Amand-des-Cots*, through less spectacular countryside. *Go straight through St-Amand-des-Cots on the Entraygues road, the D34, to Volonzac.*

Besbéden
(detour)

⑦ *For this short detour, bear left in Volonzac along a narrow and at times rather precipitous road up the gorges of the River Selves.* The microscopic hamlet of Besbéden soon appears below, perched on a narrow rocky ridge in the middle of the valley. Drive past its tiny 12thC church (gable-belfry, of course) and down to a 14thC bridge - a delightful spot for a picnic. *Return to Volonzac.*

Volonzac -
Entraygues

Continue on the D34 as it joins and follows the Selves, then crosses the river in the direction of Bagnars (where the church belfry is protected by an eccentric umbrella-like construction) and Entraygues. As you come into Entraygues, keep straight ahead for the town.

Conques, remarkable town in the gorge of the River Duche.

██████ ROUTE TWO: 87 KM

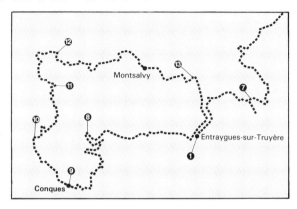

Entraygues - Vieillevie — *Follow the signs to Aurillac over the dam-bridge. When you reach the crossroads by the Gothic bridge, keep straight ahead on the D107, signposted Conques.* This road snakes attractively along the steep side of the Lot valley. Don't swim in the river - it is treacherous.

Vieillevie Once a lively little river port when boats carried oak planks to Bordeaux for barrel-making.

Hôtel-restaurant de la Vallée *(Vieillevie)* A family-run restaurant, which provides simple fare at ludicrously low prices. Regular dishes include a tasty boar stew and *chou farci*, but if you happen to be in the area between November and Easter, make a point of sampling *stofinado*, a unique local speciality found only in the triangle formed by Villefranche-de-Rouergue, Maurs and Entraygues. It is a delicious, subtly flavoured mixture of potatoes, hard-boiled eggs, cream, parsley, garlic and stockfish (unsalted wind-dried cod, which has to be soaked in water for a week before it is soft enough to eat). *Tel 71.49.94.57.*

Vieillevie - Conques ⑧ *Return to the bridge you passed as you entered the village, cross it and veer left for Conques along the C7,* which takes you past the diminutive church of Notre-Dame d'Aynès and its equally diminutive cemetery, then forks right up the hillside, revealing ever more spectacular views. *At various junctions and forks, follow the signs to Conques. At Peyssonet (not on map) bear left (no sign). Later, at a dangerous and unmarked T-junction, turn right along the D42.* Use car park on edge of Conques.

Conques The village - a cluster of perfectly preserved half-timbered houses clinging to the hillside and dominated by the large church of Ste-Foy - is all the more remarkable because of its unexpected location in the wild gorges of the River Duche. Allow time to explore.

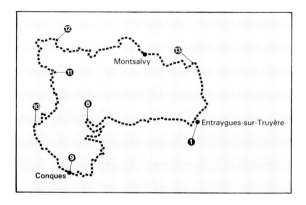

**Eglise
Ste-Foy,
Conques**

This mainly 12thC Romanesque masterpiece is one of the great buildings of France. An informative leaflet is available which recalls its history as a stopping-place for pilgrims on their way to Santiago de Compostela and describes in detail the various things to be admired: its 12thC tympanum, teeming with lively, almost Bosch-like sculpted figures; its 212 capitals, many of them depicting scenes from the Bible; and above all its priceless treasure, the centrepiece of which is the gold-encased reliquary statue of Ste-Foy herself, who was martyred in 303. Over the centuries pilgrims brought the Saint gems, cameos and intaglios, many of them Greek and Roman, which were added to the statue and the throne; to see these properly you need a pocket flashlight. *Treasure open daily 9-12 and 2-6.*

*Conques -
Lavinzelle*

⑨ *Drive straight through Conques and down towards Grand-Vabre, first on the D550, then on the D901.* The craggy, narrow gorges of the River Dourdou open out as you approach Grand-Vabre and the Pont de Coursavy over the Lot. Those who feel like a strenuous walk should make a detour to the hamlet of Lavinzelle.
⑩ *Turn left after the bridge on to the D42 and park about 100 metres later.* You will see varnished wooden signs pointing up a steep path to Lavinzelle (round trip: 1½ hr). One section of the path, once used by pilgrims, consists of a boxwood tunnel. Ignore the turning off to the right, half-way up.

Lavinzelle is a totally unspoilt little village perched precipitously on the side of a steep, south-facing hillside. Because it is completely protected from the north wind, it has an exceptionally warm microclimate that is a boon to market gardeners. There is yet another unusual bell tower, this time separate from its church (except for the bell-ringer's cable), on a rock at the topmost point of the village. From this eyrie (a good picnic spot) you can enjoy a superb view over the Lot valley, and may be lucky enough to spot a peregrine. The village can also be reached by car: *continue along the D42, turning off at signpost to Lavinzelle.*

Lavinzelle - *Return to the D42. Turn right after the Pont de Coursavy (not on map),*
Cassaniouze *then bear left up the D601.* ⑪ *Shortly after the D25 joins the D601*
from the left on the edge of Cassaniouze, turn left along the D66 to
Calvinet, which takes you past the 18thC Château de Lamothe.

Calvinet   Renowned in the past for its cattle market (you can still see the
weighbridge in the central square), the village of Calvinet is known
today for its formidably steep main street - a regular feature of the
Tour de France cycle race.

Hôtel   Louis-Bernard Puech recently took over the family business (hotel,
Beau-   restaurant and *charcuterie* rolled into one) after working with some of
séjour   the best chefs in France. Both influences show: there are
(hotel-   straightforward local specialities such as *pied de porc farci* and *tripous*
restaurant,   (sheep's tripe), but you can also sample more sophisticated, skilfully
Calvinet)   executed dishes such as his imaginative salad of sautéed chicken livers,
curly endive, French beans, and raw cèpe mushroom, *cassolette
d'escargots aux noix, mousseline de brochet aux écrevisses*, and a deep
and richly flavoured *salmis de canard* based on his mother's recipe. The
desserts are delicious. Rooms simple (shower). *Tel 71.49.91.68; closed
1 week Oct, 2 weeks Jan, Sun eve and Mon Oct-Jun; price bands A/B/C.*

Calvinet-   *Leave Calvinet by the D19 signposted Montsalvy.* ⑫ *At the first T-junction,*
Montsalvy   *turn right in the direction of Rodez, then, a little later, left on to the D25*
towards Junhac. This road goes through a particularly attractive stretch
of country, sensuously rounded hills and dips and, on the right, the
compactly turreted Château de Senezergues, which can be seen from
several angles silhouetted against the valley below. *As you come into
Junhac, turn right on to the D19; straight on through the village.*

Mont-   Once a fortified village (the English besieged it unsuccessfully in 1357),
salvy   Montsalvy no longer has its surrounding walls, though several of the
original gates are still standing.

Hôtel du   This cosy establishment offers a menu which includes many Auvergnat
Nord   specialities often neglected by other local chefs - for example, *aligot*
(hotel-   (mashed potatoes with garlic and unmatured Cantal cheese), *pounti* (a
restaurant,   kind of savoury pudding), *tripous* and trout with bacon. *Tel 71.49.20.03;*
Montsalvy)   *closed Jan-Mar; price bands A/B/C.*

Montsalvy - *Take the Pons road down the valley of the Palefer through tall, cool pine*
Entraygues   *forests. At first rather narrow, it quickly widens and becomes a much*
easier drive. ⑬ *At Les Carrières (not on map), turn right to Couesque,*
then right again along the D904 to Entraygues.

Dordogne:
PERIGORD BLANC

Set in the northern part of the Dordogne *département*, this tour more or less covers the area known as the Périgord Blanc because of the local prevalence of limestone. It is based on the city of Périgueux, which has a long and turbulent history going back to Roman times.

The route ranges eastwards along the Auvézère river, whose landscape changes from a majestic broad valley to narrow and densely wooded gorges. (The latter can be sampled by taking the detour at point 4.) Then you turn westwards through more typically Dordogne countryside - gently rolling, but with quite frequent outcrops of whitish limestone that can give a certain grandeur to the scenery.

After the market towns of Excideuil and Thiviers, the route goes through the picturesque village of St-Jean-de-Côle and the magical, water-lapped

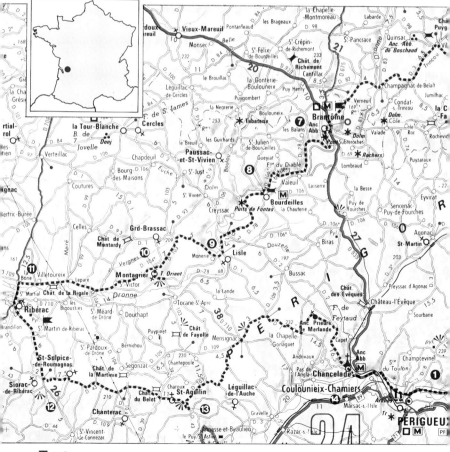

town of Brantôme. This is a relatively long loop to complete in a single day and the most enjoyable way to do it is with a night at Brantôme, where there is a choice of hotels and fine restaurants - as indeed there is elsewhere on the tour, including a Michelin two-star restaurant, the Moulin du Roc, at Champagnac-de-Belair *(tel 53.54.80.36; price bands C/D)*.

From Brantôme you follow a charming course along the valley of the Dronne via Bourdeilles to Ribérac, and then via some untroubled countryside to Périgueux. This makes a restful second day's drive.

Included in the route are three of the finest châteaux in south-west France - Hautefort, Puyguilhem and Les Bories. But just as important in building up a picture of this, the least spoiled part of the Dordogne, are the less obvious charms of many an ordinary Périgord village, manor and farmhouse.

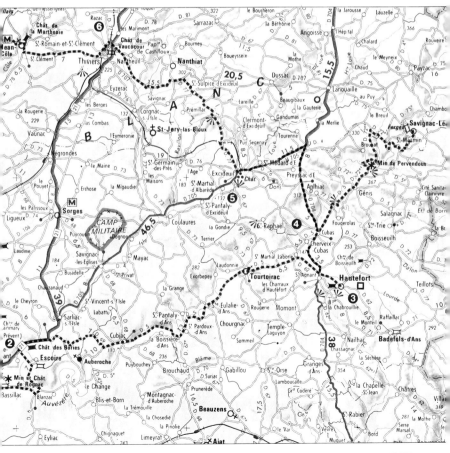

ROUTE: 165 KM

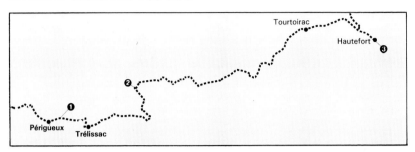

Périgueux   Périgueux is blighted by traffic jams (it is an important road junction), graceless modern buildings (following indiscriminate demolition), and sprawling suburbs. But its considerable charms are immediately revealed once you step into the self-contained and mostly pedestrianized old town, which contains a large number of yellowish (and now attractively worn) stone buildings. If possible, take a stroll here after dark, when the buildings' many decorative details - on doorways, windows and staircases - are theatrically set off by street lighting of exemplary intelligence. There are two pleasant cafés in the tiny Place St-Louis (where the celebrated truffle market is held on *Wed and Sat, Nov-Feb*).

The Cathédrale St-Front, a cavernous Byzantine construction restored almost beyond recognition in the 19thC, has a certain eccentric charm (eg its huge *trompe l'oeil* organ case). But the delicately proportioned Romanesque Eglise St-Etienne-de-la-Cité, although partly demolished in the 16th and 17thC, is a far more interesting building.

Musée du   A little museum containing many different kinds of exhibits, most
Périgord,   interesting of which are the prehistoric and Gallo-Roman collections,
Périgueux   mostly from local sites. *Open 10-12, 2-7; closed Tues.*

L'Oison,   Try this plush restaurant if you feel like treating yourself to some
(restaurant,   superb cuisine that does not confine itself to such Périgord favourites as
Périgueux)   *confits, foie gras* and *pommes sarladaises*. Régis Chiorozas is particularly skilful with fish, often cleverly serving three or four different kinds together in a single sauce; but his meat courses (sweetbreads with an onion purée, *noisettes d'agneau à la glace d'estragon*) and desserts are also imaginative - and generously served. *31, Rue St-Front; tel 53.09.84.02; closed July, mid-Feb to 3 Mar; price bands C/D.*

① *Leave Périgueux on the Limoges road; at the main junction on the edge of town turn right as though for Bergerac, and a little later left on to the D5 signposted Bassillac. When you get there, fork right into the village.*

Bassillac   This little village, not yet engulfed by Périgueux' ribbon development, has a charming domed Romanesque church.

Rejoin the D5 and continue to the junction with the D6. Turn left and follow the signs to Antonne. After bearing left in Escoire, be sure to stop and look back at the elegant and original late 18thC château.

At the T-junction ② *with the N21 in Antonne, turn right.* Just after leaving the village, and on a right-hand bend, there is a drive leading to the Château des Bories.

Château des Bories, Antonne

This stout-turreted 16thC castle has two remarkable features: a staircase which encloses, instead of a stair well, a dark and tiny vaulted room on each floor; and an ornate kitchen. *Open 10-12, 2-7, July-Sept.*

Continue briefly on the N21, taking the first right turn on to the D69 signposted Cubjac. After driving up through woodland, bear left on to the D5 and down to the Auvézère river, bypassing Cubjac and continuing through Ste-Eulalie-d'Ans to Tourtoirac.

Ancienne Abbaye de Tour-toirac

Sadly dilapidated, but to be restored, this early 11thC abbey is worth visiting for its chapter house and its prioral chapel, whose vaulting is most unusual in that it contains small cavities designed to dampen the echo. *Open 9-12, 2-5, Mon-Sat; ask for key at nearby* mairie.

Hôtel des Voyag-eurs
(hotel-restaurant, Tourtoirac)

You will get straightforward local fare, including *omelette de Négrondes* (with pork scratchings), good value, and a friendly welcome from Georgette and Louis Couty at this hotel-restaurant, whose garden backs on to the Auvézère. *Tel 53.51.12.29; closed Jan; price bands A/B.*

Continue on the D5. When it turns left towards Cubas, keep straight on in the direction of Hautefort on the D62 and, after crossing the D704, the D62E1. Soon Hautefort will appear high above you on the right.

Château de Hautefort

This imposing 17thC château is one of the largest in south-west France. Although much of it was burnt down in 1968, it has been lovingly restored by its owner. One turret which escaped destruction contains, beneath its domed roof, a superb example of chestnut timberwork. There is a large shady park, ideal for picnics. *Open 9-12, 2-7, 2-6 Nov-Easter; closed 15 Dec-15 Jan; closes at 5 in Feb.*

③ *Return to the D704 and turn right for Cubas.*

Auvézère Gorges
(detour)

This is a long but attractive detour (round trip, 15 km) through the wooded gorges of the Auvézère to Savignac, where there is an interesting piece of industrial archaeology.

④ *Emerging from Cubas, turn right on to the D5 and make for Génis. Bear right in the middle of that village, then turn immediately left along the D72E4 signposted Payzac.* This true backroad winds its way down through dense woodland into the wild and sparsely inhabited gorges - a landscape untypical of the Dordogne as a whole. *Soon after climbing out of the woods on to a plateau of pasture, take the hidden turning right on to the D72E5 to St-Mesmin, which takes you back into the gorges. Turn*

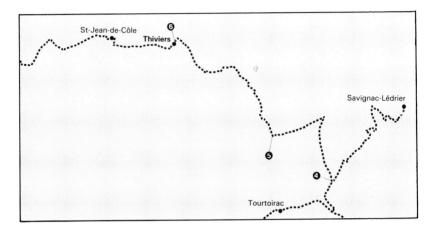

right just after St-Mesmin's naive little Romanesque church (worth a quick glance inside), then left for Savignac-Lédrier. Turn left in Savignac, then left again on to the Lanouaille road. At the bottom of the hill after Savignac, turn left for La Forge, an exceptional example of a 16thC ironworks complete with original charcoal-fired blast furnace, which stopped production only in 1930. Although the interior is not visitable for much of the year, a stroll round the outside is interesting enough. *Open 2-6 in summer, on request in winter. Either retrace via Gorges, or rejoin main route by continuing towards Lanouaille as far as crossroad with the D4. Turn left and follow the signs to Excideuil, crossing D704 and soon joining the D705.*

Excideuil As you approach, extensive views open up to the west. It is a lively little market town (market: Thurs) containing a number of 17thC houses and a curious château that is half medieval keep, half Renaissance manor. It has had a particularly eventful history: it was besieged by Richard Coeur du Lion (unsuccessfully), and changed hands several times during the Hundred Years War and the Wars of Religion. It cannot be visited, but a stroll round the walls reveals a good deal.
⑤ *Turn right at the Monument aux Morts in Excideuil, then immediately left on to the D77 to St-Sulpice-d'Excideuil. There bear left by the church, and on reaching the T-junction with the D707 turn left for Thiviers.*

Thiviers Bustling Thiviers holds weekly markets (Sat) which enjoy a considerable local reputation, especially from Nov to March, when there is a staggering array of geese, ducks, *foie gras* and truffles.
⑥ *Turn right at the church in the middle of Thiviers; continue on D707.*

**St-Jean-
de-Côle** An attractively compact village; the Château de la Marthonie (15th-17thC) overlooks a small square and an old covered market, which nestles against an eccentrically asymmetrical and partly 11thC

church. A broad cobbled street leads down to the Côle river, which is spanned by a narrow Gothic bridge with pier-heads.

Cross the river, then turn left on to the D98. Follow the signs for Château de Puyguilhem.

Château de Puy-guilhem, Villars
On reaching Villars, turn left, then right, for the château, which is just outside the village. The elegant architecture and decoration of this early 16thC building, with its turrets of different shapes, are reminiscent of the best of the Loire valley châteaux. Inside, the main staircase and several fireplaces are notable for their sculpting. *Open 10-12, 2-5 Feb-March; 9.30-12, 2-6 April-June and 8 Sept-15 Oct; 9-12, 2-7 July-7 Sep; 10-12, 2-7 16 Oct-15 Dec; closed 16 Dec-Jan 31 and Tues 8 Sep-June.*

Leave Villars on the D3 and follow the signs to Brantôme via Champagnac-de-Belair.

Brantôme
Brantôme's charm has, of course, a great deal to do with its setting. The former abbey, now occupied by the town hall, school and a museum, tucked away against a cliff and topped by an extraordinary late-11thC bell-tower erected on a rock above the church, is separated from the town itself by an arm of the Dronne. An L-shaped 16thC bridge leads from the abbey to the former monks' gardens, which are dotted with ornamental trees (including giant sequoias) and Renaissance stone *reposoirs* (shelters).

Ancienne Abbaye, Brantôme
The abbey church, massively over-restored in 1846, contains two powerful bas-reliefs. The monastery is chiefly interesting for the caves behind it, where scenes were carved out of the rock by the monks.

Musée Des-moulin, Brantôme
Don't miss this fascinating little museum in the former abbey, which has a collection of prehistoric art as well as the disturbing works of Fernand Desmoulin, a 19thC local painter who executed 'automatic' portraits of the dead (even in pitch darkness) after being put in a trance by a medium. Both abbey and museum *open am and pm all year, hours vary.*

Moulin de l'Abbaye *(hotel-restaurant, Brantôme)*
You can peer from the L-shaped bridge across to the dining room windows of this idyllically positioned restaurant. It is expensive, but, besides the setting, you get imaginative dishes from a wide-ranging menu; the wine list carries some of the best from Cahors and Bergerac. There are ten sumptuous bedrooms. *Tel 53.05.80.22; closed 23 Oct-4 May; price bands C/D.*

Hôtel Chabrol *(hotel-restaurant, Brantôme)*
Also known as the Frères Charbonnel, this place is less glamorous than the Moulin de l'Abbaye, but nonetheless pleasant, with a charm of its own, and some rooms overlooking the river. The welcome is friendly, rooms are comfortable (if, in some cases, small) and the food in the large, sober dining room is excellent without being flashy. *59, Rue*

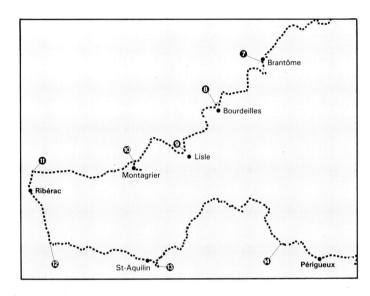

Gambetta; tel 53.05.70.15; closed mid-Nov-mid-Dec, Feb. Sun evening and Mon Oct-June; price bands B/C/D.

Brantôme - Bourdeilles

⑦ *Take the D78 (Bourdeilles) road out of Brantôme, later continuing on the D106 and* enjoy a marvellous drive along the north side of the Dronne (frequent access to picnic places on riverside meadows, shaded by poplars). At points you will be dwarfed by dramatic cliffs. ⑧ *Turn left across the river into Bourdeilles.*

Bourdeilles

Just across the bridge, keep left up the main street, which leads past the great bulk of the château; park at the top. The guided tour is worthwhile, revealing a medieval fortress and a beautifully furnished Renaissance palace. The gold room is a highlight, but perhaps just as rewarding is the view from the terrace. *Open am and pm, hours vary; closed mid-Dec to Mar, Tues except in high season.*

Griffons
(hotel-restaurant, Bourdeilles)

With a prime position on the south side of the Dronne this is a reputable place with ten rooms. *Tel 53.05.75.61; closed mid-Oct to mid-March; price bands B/C/D.*

Leave Bourdeilles on the D78 in the direction of Lisle and ⑨ *turn right on to the D1, re-crossing the Dronne.* Just across the bridge is a pleasant spot with ample parking where you can picnic under weeping willows by a weir, or, if fine, bathe in the river, or watch children leaping into the water from the bridge. *Immediately after the bridge, turn right, keeping on the D1. At the next crossroads* ⑩ *turn left if you wish to visit Montagrier, otherwise go straight on.*

Mon-tagrier

A pretty village with two simple *auberges*, and fuel. Drive through, down the hill, looking for an unsignposted tarmac turning on the left; take it and in 20 metres turn right along an avenue of chestnuts to Montagrier's clumsily restored 12thC church. It stands, however, in a fine isolated position, commanding marvellous views of the Dronne valley. *Retrace through village and turn left on to the D104e; continue, ignoring side turnings, via St-Victor. At La Borie* ⑪ *turn left on to the D708, re-crossing the Dronne for the last time.* Riverside picnicking is virtually impossible between St-Victor and La Borie.

Ribérac

A market and tourist town, with a dignified, mainly 18thC main street, and plenty of bars and cafés. For a proper meal, there is the Hôtel de France *(tel 53.90.00.61; price bands A/B).*
   Continuing straight ahead on Ribérac's main street, leave the town on the D709 and in about 6 km (fast driving through a lush valley) *turn left* ⑫ *at the staggered crossroads on to the D43 signposted St-Aquilin.* Just outside the village (notice the turrets of nearby Château de Belet) you pass the Etang de Garennes, a pleasant, man-made lake where you can bathe and hire pedal boats, or have a drink, or a simple meal.

St-Aquilin - La Chapelle-Gonaguet

St-Aquilin is dominated by its cream-coloured, fortified Gothic church; fuel here. *Continue out of the village on the D43 (views to the right) and in one km from the middle of the village, where the D43 turns right, turn sharp left* ⑬ *then immediately bear right, on the D103. Continue ignoring one minor turning left and two to the right and in 2.5 km, at the crossroads, take the third right in the direction of Mensignac. Follow the D109 through Mensignac, and in 0.5 km go left. In 2.5 km take the second right on to the D1 for La Chapelle-Gonaguet. Go straight through the village, taking the first left just outside it, followed by the first right. In another 1.5 km, you come to the* Ancien Prieuré *on the left.*

Ancien Prieuré de Merlande

In a meadow in the forest, only the restored chapel and the prior's house remain of this priory built by the monks of Chancelade. Inside the gaunt chapel with its rough stone floor a surpise is in store: fearsome, and finely carved monsters and lions embellish the capitals of the chancel's blind arcades - a rather aggressive touch for so peaceful a place. *Continue on the partly single track road (blind corners) leading to the D2, where turn right.*

Chan-celade

The Augustinian abbey founded here in the 12thC was a powerful force and had a chequered history up to the Revolution. Remaining today are the abbey church, with a fine arcaded belfry, and the endearing little Romanesque chapel of St-Jean. Grouped around a courtyard and some pretty gardens are further monastery buildings, including a small museum of religious art. Nearby are the ruins of a fortified abbey mill.
   Leaving Chancelade fork left ⑭ *on to the D710 and soon right on to the D939 to the outskirts of Périgueux.*

Dordogne:

VINEYARDS, RIVERS AND *BASTIDES*

The valley of the Dordogne and its vicinity are among the most popular tourist destinations in France, particularly for those renting *gîtes* or farmhouses. Famed for the gentle beauty of its landscape, it also boasts some spectacular sights, especially along the great river itself - clifftop castles, *villages perchés*, prehistoric caves; and it is the land of *foie gras, confits* and the truffle.

This, the most southerly of the book's two Dordogne tours steers away from the area's most famous - and crowded - attractions and has been devised to include and contrast three distinct features of the region: the river itself, the historic *bastides* and the vineyards of Bergerac.

The first route is a gentle meander through pretty wine country south of Bergerac. There are fine views, some enchanting châteaux, both private and open to the public, and opportunities to taste and to buy the local wines. For those wishing to continue on the second route, there is a pleasant linking stretch of some 15 km between Issigeac and Beaumont.

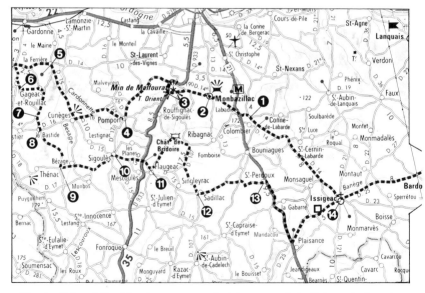

The *bastides* of the Dordogne are walled towns each built to a similar plan with grid pattern streets surrounding an arcaded central square. They were constructed by both the French and English during the 13thC wars. The second route takes in the *bastides* of Beaumont and Monpazier and then turns towards the Dordogne and Vézère rivers and the peaceful hill country between. The route recrosses the Dordogne at one of its most attractive points and returns to Beaumont past the lovely abbey of Cadouin.

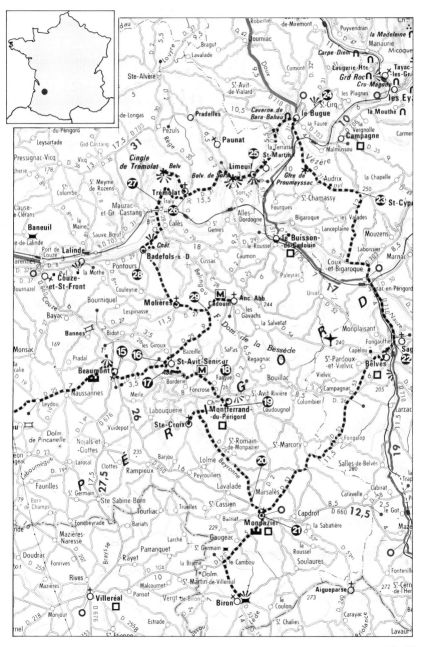

ROUTE ONE: 70 KM

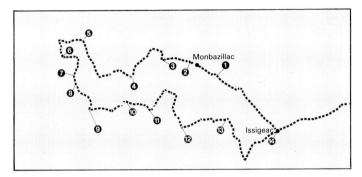

Issigeac

This is a pretty country town on the River Banège. The bishops of Sarlat found it an agreeable place: one built the lovely Gothic church in the early 16thC, and another the huge bishops' palace, now the town hall, in the late 17thC. *Leave Issigeac by the D14 (Bergerac) road and, in 9 km, after joining the RN21* ① *take the next turning left, poorly signposted to Labardie. At T-junction turn right into Labardie (signpost broken). Follow signs to Château de Monbazillac. At junction before Monbazillac turn right into village.*

Château de Monbaz- illac

Like a child's cardboard cut-out, all brown and grey with pointed roofs and four fat towers, this endearing château stands guard over the vast surrounding Monbazillac vineyard. Now owned by the regional wine co-operative, it houses a small museum of Protestantism - Bergerac was the centre of that faith in Périgord - and a collection of wine-making implements. If you don't have time for the guided tour (about 3/4 hour), content yourself with a stroll round the château and the view from the north terrace. You will, though, forfeit the chance to taste Monbazillac, the star of Bergerac's wines, and once considered the equal of Sauternes. Its fame has rather unjustly diminished in recent years: sweet, golden and fragrant, it is perfect with *foie gras* or as an aperitif. *Open daily am and pm May to Sept, hours vary; Oct-Apr 9.30-12, 2-5; restaurant.* ② *After visiting the château. return to the village and carry straight on signposted Moulin de Malfourat.*

Moulin de Malfourat

From this sail-less mill (viewing table on roof terrace of the bar/créperie) there is another panoramic view of the Monbazillac vineyards, Bergerac sprawled out in the Dordogne valley and the hills beyond. From the other side of the road there is a fine and different view to the south.

Moulin de Malfourat - Saussignac

③ *At the D933 turn right. Take the first left signposted Pomport.* The route plunges into the vineyards of Monbazillac, which, typically of the Bergerac region, are mostly small family-owned plots. It is possible to buy wine direct from many of these châteaux, but remember that it is not easy to taste without being obliged to buy. It is generally best to choose your wines from a large selection at a *cave coopérative* or even at a good shop with helpful staff. And resist the temptation to buy gallons of *vin ordinaire* and crow because they only cost a few francs: the real bargains here are among the better local wines which you would have less opportunity of sampling at home.

④ *In Pomport turn right by the war memorial signposted Cunèges. At the T-junction turn left on to the D16. At crossroads just before Cunèges, turn right. This is an attractive road with wide views to the right.*

⑤ *At La Ferrière, turn left on to the D14. Before turning, notice the hilltop château on the left.*

Saus-signac

The nobly proportioned château of Saussignac which stands in the centre of the village has a delightfully tamed and domesticated air. The graceful three-sided facade is a pretty row of terraced houses, with the post office housed in one corner. Washing lines, chicken runs and vegetable plots encircle the never-finished 16th and 17thC building, once inhabited by the beautiful Louise de la Béraudière, who entertained Rabelais and captivated Montaigne here.

Like Monbazillac, Saussignac is another of the wine *appellations* within Bergerac, and the surrounding vineyards produce a pleasant white country wine.

Château de Monbazillac presiding over its vineyards, source of the distinctive white wine known as Monbazillac.

Relais de Saus-signac
(restaurant)

A sound modernized village inn (and a *Logis de France*). The food in the spacious restaurant is not unadventurous and the place is a fair choice for a family lunch. There are 20 inexpensive, peaceful bedrooms. *Tel 53.27.92.08; closed holidays in Feb, Oct-Apr, Sun evening and Mon; price band B.*

⑥ *At the Co-op shop turn left signposted Gageac-Rouillac. This road is not marked on the map. Go through Les Cavailles, and at the unmarked junction with minor road, follow your road round to the left.*

Gageac-
Rouillac
-Sigoulès

You will emerge at a small T-junction directly opposite the portcullis gateway of the enchanting dry-moated château of Gageac-Rouillac. Built as a fortress in the 14thC, it was the seat of Geoffroi de Vivans, Huguenot leader in the Wars of Religion.

Facing the château at the T-junction, turn right. At the electricity pylon turn right again signposted Monestier and after 1.5 km.
⑦ *Turn left at bottom of hill signposted Tourmentine and La Bastide.*

⑧ *At La Bastide turn left opposite the church and then turn right signposted Thénac. Follow the next signpost to Thénac.* Fine views of the gentle countryside open to the left. Notice, further on, the imposing turreted Château Panisseau, also on the left. This produces perhaps the best Bergerac sec, crisp and dry. You have now left the Saussignac vineyards and entered the large Bergerac region, which produces excellent everyday red wines; amongst the whites choose the driest (such as Panisseau), or the sweetest.
⑨ *At the crossroads (poorly signposted), turn left. After Bézage, follow the signs for Sigoulès.*

Sigoulès

If you are feeling hot and want a dip, or the children are becoming restless, *turn left in Sigoulès signposted Base de Loisirs Sigoulès-Pomport. Follow signs to Base de Loisirs on the D17.* This is one of several man-made lakes which dot the region, with sandy beach, picnic tables, bar, fishing and tennis (there is another excellent one with an outdoor restaurant not far away at St-Sernin near Duras).
⑩ *To continue the tour, turn right in Sigoulès signposted Flaugeac.* On the right is the local *cave coopérative* where you can taste and buy.
⑪ *Having crossed the D933 (main road) turn left at the blue Renault repair garage signposted Ribagnac. At the T-junction turn left.* Beware - this road is pot-holed. The towers of Bridoire and Malfourat Mill are visible ahead. *Turn left at T-junction.*

Château
de
Bridoire

It was much restored in the 19thC but today this formidable yet romantic 15thC château is deserted and to date its future is uncertain. After driving round the château, *return to the junction and carry straight on. At the next crossroads turn right for Sadillac.*

Sadillac

In Sadillac turn left uphill into the village proper. Carry on over small crossroads to the village square. Typical of this pocket due south of Bergerac, Sadillac seems almost fast asleep. The fine 12thC church in the square looks neglected, though the adjoining 16thC château has been saved by the de Conti family, local wine producers.
⑫ *Return to the small crossroads in the village and turn right.*
⑬ *At the unmarked crossroads in St-Perdoux, go straight over and follow the single track road through the hamlet, round a left- and then a right hand- bend to emerge on the main RN21. Turn right. In about 5 km turn left signposted Issigeac.*

◼ ROUTE TWO: 100 KM

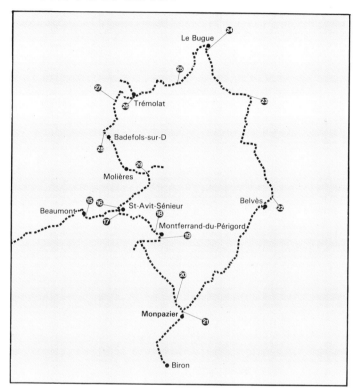

⑭ *To continue on Route Two, leave Issigeac by the D25, signposted Autres Directions and then Beaumont.*

Beaumont The market town of Beaumont is a fortified English *bastide* built in 1272. One of its original gateways, the Porte de Luzier, still survives; from there (signposted from the square) you have a clear idea of a walled town and of how, even today, the open countryside begins immediately beyond. The fortified church is splendid.

Hôtel des Voyageurs Chez Popaul *(restaurant, Beaumont)* Usually crowded with local families, this popular restaurant prides itself on its vast selection of hors d'oeuvres (except Sun). Choose one of the cheaper set menus, dabble with the soup (plonked on the table in a big saucepan) and pile your plate with crayfish, prawns, mussels and endless *salades variées* from the groaning buffet table. There is a children's menu. *Tel 53.22.30.11; closed mid-Nov to mid-Dec, mid-Jan to mid-Feb, Sun evening and Mon except in season; price bands B/C/D.*

⑮ *Leaving Beaumont turn left at the filling station signposted Cadouin.*

⑯ *Turn right signposted St-Avit-Sénieur*, a tiny hilltop village sporting a sleepy café, a couple of fuel pumps and a mammoth fortified church. Next to it are the ruins of an 11thC abbey.

⑰ *Keeping the church on the left follow the road into a pretty wooded valley past a stonemason's yard. At the staggered crossroads go straight on following the sign to Montferrand-du-Périgord.*

⑱ *In 2.5 km, at the T-junction with a grassy island in the middle, turn*

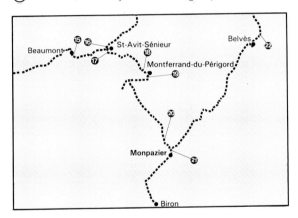

left, then bear right immediately, signposted Montferrand.

Montferrand-du-Périgord   Montferrand begins with a lovely covered market supported by fine squat pillars and continues with a succession of mellow old houses straggling uphill towards the ruins of a medieval château.

⑲ *At the top of the hill turn right down a lane signposted Eglise. This road is marked on the map only by a single line.* It passes a tiny romanesque chapel with an interior covered in peeling frescoes. All around are fields and woods, perfect for picnics. *At the crossroads go straight over to see Ste-Croix; turn left to continue the route.*

Ste-Croix *(detour)*   Here, in an isolated setting, is a 12thC church notable for the purity of its lines; there are also the ruins of an *ancien prieuré* with ornate mullioned windows and a large classically-styled 17thC château.

Montferrand - Monpazier   A long gentle road which follows the Beyronne stream through tranquil countryside. Just past the turning to Marsalès is the peaceful little man-made Lac de Veronne, with sandy beach, picnic tables and bar.

(20) *At the junction with the D660 turn left (signposted Château de Biron).*

Mon-pazier

Leave the car outside the town walls and walk into the perfect arcaded central square. You are among tourists again, but Monpazier is a delight, the best preserved of all the Dordogne *bastides*. The rectangular plan of the streets is still intact, and in the square the usual covered market hall has grain measures still to be seen. Monpazier was founded in 1284 by the English, but suffered at the hands of both English and French during the Wars of Religion. Today it is a useful place to stock up for a picnic, filled as it is with shops selling local *spécialitiés*; there are also plenty of cafés and pizza houses.

Montferrand-du-Périgord, described on page 176.

Château de Biron *(detour)*

Leaving Monpazier follow signs to Château de Biron (8 km). It suddenly appears, towering above the landscape and seeming almost to crush the little village that clusters at its feet. The château was owned by the same eminent family, Biron-Gontaut, from the 12th to the 20thC. Until the 18thC each generation busily added bits on, resulting in an amusing jumble of styles and a visual surprise at every turn. Though essentially a fortress, there are some charmingly light touches of Renaissance architecture, notably the double chapel and inner loggia. *Open am and pm; hours vary, longer in summer.*

(21) *To continue route take the D53 from Monpazier signposted Belvès.*

Belvès

An attractive walled town whose old houses and terraced gardens overlook the Nauze valley. In the covered market notice the pillory chain, still attached to one of the pillars. Walnuts are a major local product.

(22) *From Belvès, follow the ring road (signposted Autres Directions) and at the T-junction turn left signposted Périgeux.*

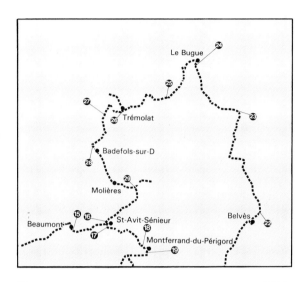

㉓ *Five km beyond Coux-et-Bigaroque turn left off the D703 signposted Audrix and Gouffres de Proumeyssac.*

Audrix   A pretty wooded lane with views on both sides leads to this little visited hilltop village, a delightfully tranquil spot, particularly for those joining the route from nearby Les Eyzies, heaving with tourists. Stand behind the attractive Romanesque church for a view over the Vézère valley and in front of the *mairie* for a view over the Dordogne valley. Pause for a drink or a simple meal at the Auberge Médiéval with its pretty vine-covered terrace, or picnic in the surrounding fields.

Gouffres   A chance to visit one of the many extraordinary caverns for which the
de Prou-   Dordogne is so famous. This is a huge watery domed chasm covered in
meyssac   stalagmites (up) and stalactites (down) and many other strange shapes. Cups, jugs and other objects placed on the cavern floor help to demonstrate the rapidity of calcification. *Open 8.30-11.30, 2-6 daily Easter-Sept; Sun only Oct. Tour leaves every half-hour and lasts three-quarters of an hour.*

㉔ *At the T-junction with the D31 turn right into Le Bugue. After crossing the river take the first turning left signposted St-Alvère on the D703. In 2 km turn left signposted Trémolat.*

Limeuil   Notice on the road to Limeuil the domed 12thC church of St-Martin, ringed by cypress trees. Limeuil stands at the confluence of the Dordogne and Vézère rivers and it makes a picturesque spot at which to stretch your legs, picnic or bathe.

㉕ *Leave Limeuil on the D31, signposted Trémolat.* The road passes a viewpoint (layby) of the river below, known as the Belvédère de Sors.

Trémolat   The route now rejoins the Dordogne at the point where it describes its famous and spectacular loop, known as the Cingle de Trémolat. The attractive old village is worth a look; less charming is its church, a great windowless barrack of a place, though in contrast you will find in the cemetary a charming Romanesque chapel, recently restored.

Vieux   This is a heavenly place: an old creeper clad building full of antiques
Logis   with a dining-room converted from a barn and the most beautiful
(restaurant,   flower-filled garden with a stream where you can sample excellent
Trémolat)   Périgordine cuisine. Despite being part of the prestigious *Relais et Châteaux Hôtels* group, the atmosphere is relaxed and prices are reasonable; lovely bedrooms. *Tel 53.22.80.06; closed Jan to mid-Feb, Tues; price band C.*

Belvédère   *Following the 'Route du Cingle de Trémolat' signpost drive from the village*
de Raca-   *to the belvedere 2 km north.* A platform on top of a water tower gives
madou   a wonderful view of the curling river set in a patchwork landscape.
(detour)   ㉖ *Return to Trémolat and the junction with the D31 where turn right.* At the bridge, tracks to left and right lead to riverside picnic spots.

㉗ *At the Y-junction in Traly bear right signposted Calès. At the junction with the D29 turn right and follow the scenic riverside road to Badefols-sur-Dordogne.*

㉘ *As you enter Badefols turn left at the sign for Lou Cantou* (a genteel small hotel which has had a Red R in Michelin for its food) *and then turn right signposted Molières.*

Molières   A peaceful village which began its existence as an English *bastide* but was never finished. It possesses a plain but eye-catching Gothic church and a grassy square bordered by attractive old houses, with views from the far corner over the *Périgord Noir.*

Cadouin   As in other villages in the area, the yellow stone of the houses gives Cadouin a pleasant mellow quality. In the central square is a pretty covered market and the abbey, once a revered place of pilgrimage owing to its possession of a (bogus) piece of the Holy Shroud. Dispense with the long guided tour, but take time to stroll in the lovely flamboyant gothic cloisters, admiring the four fine corner doors, the highly realistic sculptures, the faded frescoes and the serene atmosphere. Entrance at side of church in the square; *open am and pm, hours vary; closed Dec and Jan, and Tues 8 Sept-May.*
   Retrace on the D25 out of Cadouin and ㉙ *at junction with the D27 keep left on the D25 for St-Avis-Sénieur and Beaumont.*

Avoiding the undeniably spectacular but much visited Gorges de l'Ardèche in the south of the *département*, this tour features the less known, more varied and equally beautiful northern Ardèche.

The tour revolves around Mont Gerbier de Jonc (where the River Loire has its source) and the majestic Mézenc massif, extending to the spa of Vals-les-Bains in the south and the mountain plateau of the Velay in the north (with a brief sally into the Haute-Loire *département*).

To get the best out of this tour, you have to be prepared to do a certain amount of easy hill-walking - though no proposed walk will take you away from the car for more than 50 minutes. However, those unwilling or unable to engage in such energetic activities will still be able to enjoy wonderful views from the roadside. The tour's hub lies on the watershed between the Atlantic and the Mediterranean. This dividing line can be seen almost physically in the marked difference in the landscape that occurs as you cross it. To the north-west there are vast moors and windswept plains at an average altitude of about 1,200 metres, over which tower the numerous *sucs* (cones of extinct volcanoes) of the Mézenc massif; to the south-east, the deeply eroded valleys take on an almost Provençal look with their vineyards and orchards.

Those with a penchant for geology, botany and ornithology will probably enjoy this tour most, although the scenery alone is worth the trip, especially in late October, when autumn colours are at their most vivid. At this time of year, check in advance that hotels and restaurants are open; the food, incidentally, tends to consist of straightforward home cooking (excellent and copious) rather than *haute cuisine*.

◼◼◼◼ ROUTE ONE 72 KM

Gerbier de Jonc

The Gerbier de Jonc, which is 1,551 metres above sea-level, is a massive hunk of rock that rises abruptly out of the bleak moors of the Mézenc massif like a huge marshmallow. It is made of fine-grained rock called phonolite, also known as clinkstone, which as its name suggests emits a sound when struck. The view from the top, particularly towards the south-east, is well worth the effort (40 minutes there and back by the steep path that leaves from the large car park at its foot).

Nearby, several streams emerging from different points in the hillside together form the source of the River Loire, which perversely flows south at the start of its 1,020-km journey north and west to the Atlantic.

Gerbier de Jonc - Les Estables

① *Leave the Gerbier de Jonc westwards (i.e. to the left when facing the mountain) on the D378.* This excellent road becomes the D36 when it crosses from the Ardèche *département* into the Haute-Loire, shortly before swooping down to Les Estables. It offers a majestic view over the broad valley of the Gazeille.

Les Estables

This sprawling, fast-expanding, cross-country skiing resort is a good starting point from which to tackle Mont Mézenc.

Les 3 Monts
(rest., Les Estables)

Although housed in rather a graceless building, this large restaurant offers genuine local fare at reasonable prices. Specialities include several kind of salad; *menu du terroir. Tel 71.08.35.06; closed Nov-20 Dec; price band A.*

Mont Mézenc
(detour)

②) *For this detour, take the D631 out of Les Estables for almost 3 km to the Croix de Boutières.* From there, a 25-minute energetic walk will take you to the top of the mountain (signposted), 1,753 metres above sea-level. The panoramic view from the top is truly flabbergasting: laid out before you is the whole of the Auvergne, with its lakes, valleys, mountain plateaux and extinct volcanoes. On a clear day, the Alps can be seen hovering like a mirage on the horizon. Those who have seen the sun coming up over the Alps from the top of Mont Mézenc say it is an unforgettable experience; but to do this you have to rise early and put on plenty of layers. The mountain is a favourite haunt of botanists. In addition to the expanses of bilberries and wild raspberries, several rare species of Alpine plants are to be found. Bilberries (French, *myrtilles*) are an important local industry: several hundred tons are picked each year in the region, much for export.

Les Estables - Chaud-ayrac

Return to Les Estables and continue on the D36 (fork right as you leave the village) towards Fay-sur-Lignon. After turning right on to the D500, you will drive through a vast tract of almost treeless pastureland with Mont Meygal in the distance: this landscape is typical of the Velay. Note the interesting architecture of many of the farmhouses: the front door is in a kind of porch-cum-penthouse which sticks out from the front wall. The point of this design was to prevent snow from getting into the house and, in the old days, to enable the farmer to use the projecting room as a cowshed in winter, thus avoiding the necessity of going outside at all in cold spells.

Chaudayrac - Fay

③) *At a dangerous crossroads at Chaudayrac (not on map), the D500 makes a 90° right turn to Fay-sur-Lignon (no warning is given).*

Fay-sur-Lignon

Hardy mountain cattle of the kind that you will have seen grazing on the moors are on sale at the big livestock market regularly held in this delightfully unspoilt little town. An ordinary market (ideal for picnic fare) is also held here every Wednesday. Away from the two marketplaces, houses huddle together to resist the fiercely cold winds that come up from the Lignon valley in winter - the town's altitude is almost 1,200 metres. Explore the narrow streets, and don't miss the view over the Lignon valley from the cemetery next to the church. The Hôtel-Restaurant des Négociants (see below) has only one or two rooms. the Hôtel du Lignon is cheap and pleasant. *Tel 71.59.51.44.*

The Ardèche and its gorge - enjoying a respite from the flotillas of canoes.

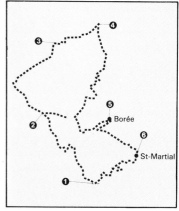

Des Négociants
(rest., Fay)

M. and Mme Ladreyt are expert as such hearty dishes as leek soup and beef *daube*, and everything is served in mountainous quantities. The restaurant's cosy first-floor dining-room overlooks the cattle market. *Tel 71.59.50.61; price band A.*

Fay-sur-Lignon - Borée

④ *Leave Fay-sur-Lignon on the D262, and bear right along the D410 (not on map) at the junction with the D247 to St-Clément.* This marvellous new - though not always perfectly surfaced - stretch of road is flanked by Mont Mézenc on the right and offers plunging vistas to the left. It meanders past clumps of yellow-flowered gentian (the bitter roots of which flavour the local apéritifs, Avèze and Salers), herds of white cattle and long, low farmhouses with distinctive rust-coloured lichen on their walls and stone roofs. The road, although an easy and pleasant drive, zigzags so relentlessly that one is soon disorientated; valleys and peaks heave in and out of view in magically quick succession. *Ignore the turning off to the right to Les Estables, and a little later turn left along the D378 to Borée.*

Borée - St-Martial

⑤ *Turn sharp right along the D215 to St-Martial.* On the right, the uncannily rounded Suc de Touron towers above the road. *Shortly after crossing a small river, beware of an invisible crossroads which may remain unmarked.*

St-Martial - Gerbier de Jonc

An unassuming little village overlooking a small lake that is an ideal picnic spot.
⑥ *Fork right in the middle of the village along the D237.* The road twists and turns through fragrant conifers as it climbs up towards the Gerbier de Jonc. To the right, there is a splendid view of the Suc de Sara with the massive Mont Mézenc looming behind. *On reaching the junction with the D378, turn right to the Gerbier de Jonc.*

■■■ ROUTE TWO 87 KM

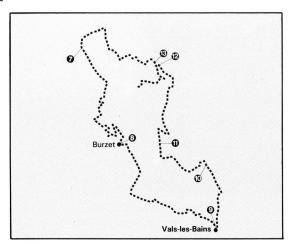

Gerbier de Jonc - Burzet

⑦ Leave the Gerbier de Jonc by the D116, which follows the infant River Loire through moorland as far as Ste-Eulalie and beyond, but turn left on to the D122 before reaching Ste-Eulalie (unless you are interested in medicinal plants and it happens to be the first Sunday after 12 July, when a special herb market, the Foire aux Violettes, is held there). *A little farther on, fork right along the D289 in the direction of Sagnes-et-Goudoulet and Burzet.*

About 3 km beyond Sagnes-et-Goudoulet, stop and look back over the hauntingly beautiful, bleak moors and mountain peaks in the distance. Then drive on for about 1.5 km, to reach one of the points where the watershed between the Atlantic and the Mediterranean is most striking. Suddenly, a whole new landscape will open out before you, a landscape that foreshadows the Midi farther south (vines, walnut trees, poplars). Nestling in the valley bottom 700 metres below, but only 3 km as the crow flies, is the village of Burzet. The road down the mountainside is strictly for those with a head for heights, but it is expertly engineered - as well it might be, for it forms part of the circuit of a motor rally which Burzet holds every year in mid-winter, called the Monte Carlo (sic).

Burzet

If you are in this area around Easter, make a point of visiting Burzet on Good Friday, when a ceremony takes place which dates back to the Middle Ages: the inhabitants, many of them dressed in biblical costume, walk in procession to a calvary perched high above the village. The visit to the Ray Pic waterfall mentioned in a later detour, (see ⑫) can be made from Burzet if it suits you better, but the drive is longer - 22 km there and back: *turn left out of the village along the D215.*

**Burzet -
Vals-les-
Bains**

⑧ *Turn right across the bridge in Burzet along the D26 in the direction of Vals-les-Bains.* After the excitement of the D289, this is an easy, relaxing drive along the verdant valley of the Bourges. *On reaching the T-junction, turn left along the D536. A minute or two later, almost immediately after entering the hamlet of Pont-de-Veyrières (not on map), turn left again on to the D253 to Vals-les-Bains (the signpost is virtually invisible).* This narrow road at times twists completely back on itself and offers superb views over the wild Tanargue Massif on the far side of the River Ardèche.

**Vals-les-
Bains**

Slotted into the narrow valley of the River Volane, the sausage-shaped spa of Vals-les-Bains - 'town of 100 springs' - need not detain you unless you want to take its celebrated waters (especially good for diabetics) or have a fling at the casino.

If you wish to stay overnight in Vals-les-Bains, try the Hôtel Europe *(tel 75.37.43.94; closed mid-Oct-Mar),* which offers old-fashioned food at middling prices. However, for a more pastoral setting it is worth leaving Vals-les-Bains and driving 13 km along the N102, in the direction of Thueyts, to the Hotel du Levant in leafy Neyrace-les-Bains *turn left immediately after the garage in Neyrac; the hotel is signposted).* As well as serving good simple food, the hotel is quiet, unpretentious, and inexpensive *(tel 75.36.41.07; hotel only closed Oct-Easter).* Out of season, you should be able to find a room in one of the many hotels in Aubenas, 6 km south of Vals-les-Bains on the N102.

Local farmhouse, front door in the projecting porch: see entry for Les Estables - Chaudayrac.

Chez
Mireille
(restaurant,
Vals-les-
Bains)

This is the one restaurant in Vals-les-Bains - and, indeed, in the whole of the area explored on this tour - where you can find gourmet food at reasonable prices. M. and Mme Martin are the new *patrons*. Their freshly-prepared food centres around fish and meat. Sound value. Local wines are on offer at ludicrously low prices. *3 Rue Jean-Haurès; tel 75.37.49.06; price bands A/B.*

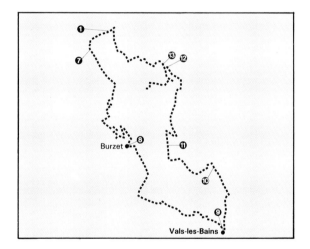

Vals-les-
Bains -
Antraigues

⑨ *Take the D578 out of Vals-les-Bains up the valley of the River Volane*, a narrow gorge lined with vineyards. The road skirts the base of the village of Antraigues. If you have time to visit it, *turn sharp right up the hill (signposted).*

Perched on an outcrop of volcanic rock, this little village has been described as the Saint-Tropez of the Ardèche, with all that that entails: trendy bistros, antique shops, high prices, and so on. The central square with its plane trees has undoubted charm on a balmy summer evening. Antraigues is the adopted home of the well-known singer and iconoclast Jean Ferrat.

Antraigues -
Freyssenet

⑩ *Just before the sharp right turn up into Antraigues, the Route de la Bézorgues branches off the D578 to the left in the direction of Labastide de Juvinas.* This delightful little road winds up from the Volane valley through an Italianate landscape of chestnut groves, Lombardy poplars and houses with flat red-tiled roofs, and eventually leads over a ridge and down into the adjacent valley of the River Bézorgues. *On reaching Labastide turn right along the D254 to Freyssenet.*

Freyssenet -
Lachamp-
Raphaël

⑪ *Follow the road round to the left, then turn sharp right up the D354 in the direction of Lachamp-Raphaël.* This section of road running up the Bézorgues valley is like an action replay, in slow motion and in reverse, of the sudden switch from moor to vineyards just before Burzet: as the road loops gently uphill - passing, incidentally, one of the few surviving farmhouses with a traditional thatched roof - trees gradually thin out and the landscape becomes more inhospitable. Then, after a stretch of pine forest, you suddenly emerge on to something resembling Arctic tundra: you are back on the plateau of the Mézenc massif. *When the D354 joins the D122, keep straight ahead into Lachamp-Raphaël.*

Les Cimes
(restaurant,
Lachamp)

The keynote here is simplicity, quality produce and value for money. There are also a few rather spartan rooms (showers and WC on landing). *Tel 75.38.78.58; closed Nov; price band A.*

Ray Pic
(detour to
waterfall)

⑫ *For a detour to the Ray Pic waterfall, take the D215, a sharp left turn as you drive into Lachamp-Raphaël from Freyssenet.* Although it involves a 15-km return journey along a small and sometimes rather uneven road, this detour is strongly recommended. Park in the large car park and walk to the waterfall along the signposted path (40 minutes there and back). The austerity of the site is reinforced by the booming 'caw' of the ravens that live there. The waters of the River Bourges emerge through two gaps in the rocks and crash down into a surprisingly placid pool below. But more striking than the waterfall itself is the rock formation flanking it - a monstrous overhanging outgrowth of dark-grey columnar basalt pointing down to the pool as though it, too, were still flowing as it did when it was molten. The Ray Pic waterfall is an ideal place for a cool picnic on a hot day, always supposing there are not too many people with the same idea.

Lachamp-
Raphaël -
Gerbier

After you have returned to Lachamp-Raphaël, there is an easy ridge drive along wide roads to the Gerbier de Jonc. *First take the D122 through the village, and a few km later* ⑬ *veer on to the D378 for the final section of the loop.*

Gorges du Tarn:

AND THE CAUSSE MEJEAN

The verdant Gorges du Tarn.

The great attraction of this tour lies in the contrast between the Gorges du Tarn themselves - an immensely deep, verdant valley (strictly speaking a canyon) gouged out by the River Tarn - and the high arid *causses* (limestone plateaux) on either side. The Causse Méjean, which forms the central part of the tour, is a geological oddity. Its limestone crust is so porous that it retains no rainfall, hence the sparseness of trees and vegetation which, in some parts, results in an awesomely empty, moon-like landscape. Streams and rivers are found not on the surface but below ground, flowing through a complex network of subterranean galleries.

There are, however, some pockets of arable land known as *dolines*. These small depressions are caused by the erosion of the limestone crust by rainfall. When erosion goes one stage further, an *aven* (pothole) leading down to a subterranean river is formed.

The plateau is extremely inhospitable in winter. On a hot summer's day however, it is fragrant with wild thyme, savory and an abundance of rare plants. The Causse Méjean has few human inhabitants, but many sheep.

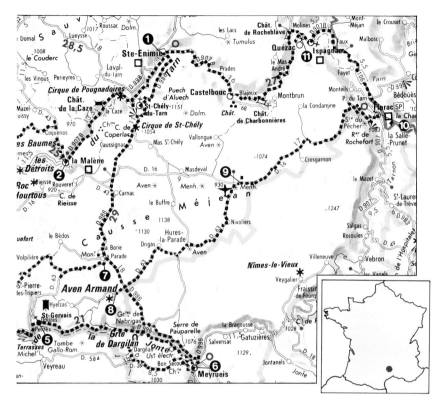

The Gorges du Tarn have a more obvious beauty than the bleak *causses*, so it is hardly surprising that they have become a major tourist attraction. In high summer be prepared for plenty of traffic, at least in the gorges themselves. A visit to the area in October is particularly recommended, when the usual palette of autumn colours that lines the canyon is enhanced by the bright crimson leaves of the local Montpelier maple.

▬▬ ROUTE ONE: 109 KM

Ste-Enimie

Named after a 7thC Merovingian princess who founded a convent here after being miraculously cured of leprosy by the waters of a spring, Ste-Enimie is a small town whose spotless cobbled streets rise in rows up the hillside beneath the cliffs of the Causse de Sauveterre. Be sure to see the Halle au Blé (former cornmarket) and the ancient Place au Beurre nearby. The Vieux Logis, a folk museum *(open daily, am and pm; out of season at Easter and public holiday weekends apply to Mairie)*, is also worthwhile.

Auberge du Moulin (restaurant, Ste-Enimie)

The Auberge is housed in a handsome building just by the D907. Specialities include the *terrine maison*, delicious jugged hare, and the tasty local blue cheese, *Bleu des Causses*. *Tel. 66.48.53.08; closed 15 Nov-20 Mar; price band B.*

Grandeur of the Gorges du Tarn.

Ste-Enimie - La Malène

① *Leave Ste-Enimie by the D907B, past the bridge over the Tarn, in the direction of La Malène.* The road either bends gracefully round the bulging sides of the canyon or goes straight through them via a series of short tunnels. When the beautifully turreted Château de la Caze comes into view to the left, drive on past it, then admire it in safety from the lay-by. This romantic 15thC château is now a luxury hotel.

La Malène

La Malène was laid waste during the Revolution, and marks made by the smoke from one of its burning houses can still be seen on the cliff overhanging the old part of this small village. Downstream from La Malène, the Tarn flows between absolutely vertical cliffs 100 metres high; the total depth of the canyon at this point is about 500 metres. The best way to see this part of the river is to take a punt to the Cirque des Baumes. It is not cheap (you hire a boatman, and a taxi to bring you back), but the experience is unforgettable. *Details from the boatmen's co-operative at La Malène, tel 66.48.51.10.*

La Malène - Point Sublime

② *Turn right in the centre of La Malène up the D43, which climbs a rocky gorge. When nearly at the top, turn sharp left along a small road marked Point Sublime.* The drive along the plateau goes through typical *causse* countryside of the less rugged kind (stone-walled fields enclosing *flocks of sheep, scattered trees, a few isolated farmhouses). At the junction with the D46, turn left towards St-Georges-de-Lévéjac, and just as you reach the village turn left again along a little road signposted to Point Sublime, 1.5 km away. Ample parking space and, in season, a café.*

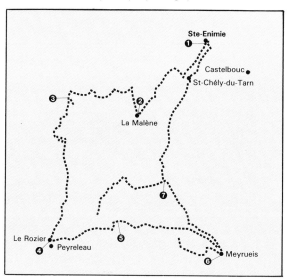

Point Sublime

As its name suggests, this rocky promontory offers a stunning view over the Gorges du Tarn, back along the section you have just driven through, and, to the right, towards the massive jumble of rocks called the Pas de Souci.

Point Sublime - Peyreleau

③ *Drive back to the D46, then turn left in the direction of Les Vignes. At the junction with the D995, bear left again towards Les Vignes.* The road ahead - a succession of hairpin bends leading down to the bottom of the canyon - is not for those who suffer from vertigo, but is perfectly engineered and safe. *In the village of Les Vignes, turn right towards Le Rozier along the D907B.* As you cruise along this easy stretch of road you can admire successively, on the far side of the Tarn, the ruined Château de Blanquefort, the idyllic hamlet of La Bourgarie with its neat kitchen gardens, and the colossal Rocher de Cinglegros, which has broken off the *causse* like an iceberg from a polar icecap. *At the junction with the D996 turn left into Le Rozier, then immediately right across the bridge to Peyreleau.* Drive straight ahead to a large car park.

Peyreleau

You are now (briefly) in the Aveyron *département.* Climb the steps opposite the car park up into Peyreleau's pleasant, if slightly over-restored, labyrinth of streets.

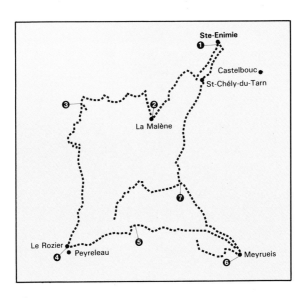

Peyreleau - **Les Douzes**	④ *Drive back into Le Rozier and turn right along the D996 in the* *direction of Meyrueis.*
Hôtel- **Restau-** **rant de la** **Jonte** *(Les* *Douzes)*	Nestling against the cliff, the Hôtel-Restaurant de la Jonte has succeeded in retaining its character (and local clientele) despite the seasonal influx of tourists. Pierre and Jacqueline Vergély, who have run the place for 26 years and radiate friendliness, offer a wide range of excellent local fare (*confit de canard*, lamb from the *causses*, delicious home-made pâté). In summer you can eat outside under trees. This is also an inexpensive place to stay. *Tel 65.62.60.52; price bands A/B.*
Les Douzes **- Meyrueis**	⑤ *Continue up the D996,* having asked the Vergélys to explain how to find the mysterious resurgence of the Jonte - the spot where the river emerges after flowing underground for several kilometres. The character of the Gorges changes: they become more classically canyon- like, with a sheer cliff at the top, followed by a scree-covered slope and then a second cliff plunging down to the river.
Meyrueis	Meyrueis, like Ste-Enimie, is an important tourist attraction but it has kept more of its individuality because it is a bigger and busier town. There is a market on Wed and Fri, part of it in what must be one of the smallest covered marketplaces in France (on main street).
La **Renais-** **sance**	This is a real gem of a hostelry: not only are the Burguet family extremely hospitable, but their 16thC hotel (once their family home) is furnished from top to bottom with perfect taste and lots of personality.

(hôtel-restaurant, Meyrueis) Here one is surrounded by engravings, paintings, antique furniture and harmonious wallpaper. There are even bookshelves in the bedrooms. The restaurant specializes in a wide range of local dishes, such as *poularde au coulis d'écrevisses* and *godiveau de truites*) and offers a choice of around 400 wines (several by the glass). *Rue de la Ville; tel 66.45.60.19; closed mid-Nov to Mar; price band B/C; booking essential.*

Grotte de Dargilan ⑥ *For a detour to the Grotte de Dargilan, 8.5 km from Meyrueis, take the D986 in the direction of Lanuéjols, and on the edge of Meyrueis turn sharp right up the D39. Turn right 7 km later along the D139 to the cave.* The Grotte de Dargilan is in fact a series of caves full of very varied, pinkish stalagmites and stalactites. Their arresting beauty is undeniable, but if you have time for only one cave the Aven Armand is even more spectacular. It features on Route Two, but could just as easily be included on Route One. Grotte de Dargilan *open Easter-Sept 9-7; first two weeks Oct 1-5.*

Meyrueis - La Parade *Leave Meyrueis in the direction of Ste-Enimie, forking left up the D986 shortly after crossing the Jonte.* This excellent road climbs in leisurely fashion up on to the Causse Méjean. Stop at one of the lay-bys for a bird's eye view of the narrow Gorges de la Jonte. Soon you are on the plateau, whose stark landscape is awe-inspiring. At La Parade there is a strategically placed filling station.

Les Arcs de St-Pierre ⑦ *The detour to Les Arcs de St-Pierre is well worth the 20 km round trip across flat terrain. Turn left at La Parade along the D63, and after a kilometre or two turn sharp right along a narrow but perfectly surfaced road signposted to Le Courby. After going through the hamlet of La Volpilière, which contains some superb examples of the domestic architecture of the* causse, *ignore the turning to Le Courby and continue through St-Pierre-des-Tripiers until you reach a crossroads with La Viale to the left and a car park to the right.* Park here and follow the signpost to Les Arcs. The walk (allow about 25 minutes each way) takes you through a sheltered, almost Arcadian landscape of rocky outcrops, dells and stone pines; it is easy to see why the site attracted prehistoric settlers. The various things to see should (*pace* vandals) be signposted. The Arcs themselves - three massive natural arches formed by rock erosion - stand round a small tree-dotted hollow: a magical spot.

La Parade - Ste-Enimie *Return to La Parade, then bear left along the D986 to Ste-Enimie.* When the road leaves the *causse* and begins its easy descent into the canyon, stop at the lay-by on the first sharp right-hand bend: there is an almost vertical view down over the Cirque de St-Chély.

Ste-Enimie - Aven Armand *Leave Ste-Enimie by the D986, over the bridge, in the direction of Meyrueis. If you have not already done Route One, stop when you get to the top of the* causse *to look back down into the canyon. A couple of km after*

■■■■■■■ ROUTE TWO: 76 KM

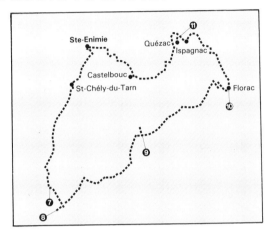

La Parade, there is a well-signposted right turn to the Aven Armand.

Aven Armand
Rightly considered one of France's greatest natural sights, the Aven Armand, a single but immense cavern which could almost accommodate Notre-Dame Cathedral, contains an extraordinary forest of stalagmites. *Open June, July and Aug 9-7; May and Sept 9-12 and 1.30-6.*

No food at cave; but try the delightful Ferme-Auberge Les Herans, Meyrueis - excellent value. Book first, *tel 66.45.64.42; price band A/B.*

Aven Armand - Nivoliers
⑧ *Return to the D986, cross it and go straight ahead along the D63 in the direction of Nivoliers.* The road goes through the small, crouching villages of Drigas and Hures-la-Parade. To the right, there is a hauntingly bare, lunar landscape. A word of warning about driving on the more barren parts of the Causse Méjean: the road can seem deceptively level and straightforward, but the lack of visual reference points (such as trees or hedges) can make it easy to misjudge a slope or bend.

Auberge Le Chanet
(restaurant, Nivoliers)
If you have not planned a picnic, this is a useful stand-by on the otherwise restaurant-bereft *causse.* It offers hearty local specialities served in pleasant surroundings. *Tel 66.45.65.12; price band A.*

Nivoliers - Florac
Beyond Nivoliers, the road opens out on to the strikingly fertile (in this context) plain of Chanet. As you pass the tiny Florac-Chanet Aerodrome (used mainly for gliders) you will see a solitary menhir standing quizzically at the end of the runway on your left. If, by the way, you should see a bird bigger than a golden eagle soaring high in the skies above the *causse,* it is probably a griffon vulture (a species

that has just been reintroduced into the area). *At the junction with the D16, turn right for Florac.*

The causse is peppered with scores of small *avens* (potholes). If you want to see what one of them looks like, take this short detour.

⑨ *Not far along the D16, turn left towards Poujols. Drive for just over one km, then park about 250 metres beyond the point where the conifer plantation on the right gives way to a flat rocky field.* The *aven* is about 75 metres from the road, to the right. It is not fenced, so don't venture too near the edge. *Return to the D16 and turn left for Florac.* When the road reaches the edge of the *causse*, there is a totally unexpected, plunging view over the grey roofs of Florac 500 metres below - the *causse* here seems to have been sliced off with a knife.

Florac
A rather severe little town with a turbulent, bloodstained history of Catholic fighting Protestant, Florac forms a rectangular complex of narrow streets. A market is held every Saturday in the shade of the plane trees on the pleasant central esplanade. If you just want to look round, bear right on entering the town up a small street leading to the church, where there is usually plenty of parking space.

Gd. Hôtel du Parc
(hotel-rest.Florac)
This hotel, set back from the road amidst pleasant gardens, does indeed look very grand. It is in fact a reasonably priced, old-fashioned, well-run hotel-restaurant. *Tel 66.45.03.05; closed Dec to mid-Mar and Mon out of season; price bands B/C.*

Florac - Ispagnac
⑩ *Leave Florac in the direction of Mende along a short stretch of the N106, with the Causse Méjean towering above you to the left, then fork left on to the D907B in the direction of Ispagnac and Ste-Enimie.*

Ispagnac
Ispagnac, cradled in a bend of the Tarn, enjoys a warm microclimate, hence its market gardens, vines, orchards and Lombardy poplars.

Ispagnac - Quézac
(detour)
Shortly after leaving Ispagnac, you will see an elegant five-arched bridge to the left; once it is in sight look out for the turning off to Quézac (the signpost missing). Quézac is a tiny village worth a detour for its houses with their overhanging eaves, and its church, which has an unusual 16thC porch. *Turn left and cross the Tarn by the bridge,* which was built by Pope Urban V in the 14thC, destroyed during the Wars of Religion, and rebuilt to its original design in the early 17thC. If you continue on the little road that goes through Quézac, you will find plenty of bucolic picnic spots along the banks of the river.

Quézac - Ste-Enimie
⑪ *Return to the D907B and continue in the direction of Ste-Enimie.* Don't bother to turn off to Castelbouc: this well-known and much visited little village, built against the cliff with a ruined castle perched on a rock above, is best appreciated from a distance, i.e. the car park on the D907B about one km beyond the signpost.

The Bastides of Gascony

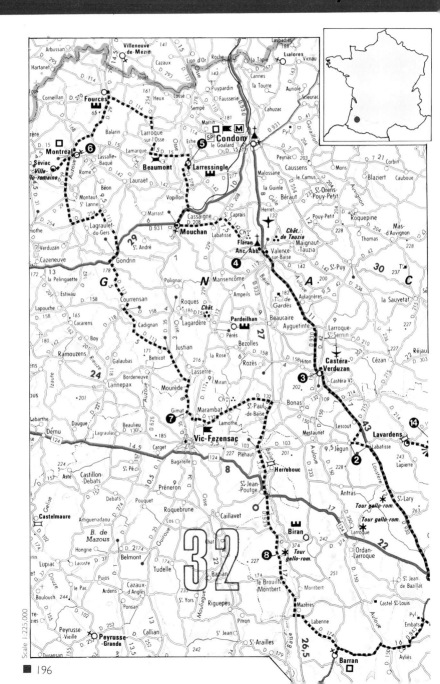

This tour covers the part of Gascony (the old name for the region) that lies in the Gers *département*, a curious, unspoilt and individual area. It is dotted with scores of *bastides* - villages and small towns, often fortified, which were built in the 13th and 14thC according to a strictly geometrical plan, usually with a central arcaded square around a covered market. It boasts no less than 146 castles, and hosts of beautifully proportioned stone manors and farmhouses (some empty and crying out to be restored).

It has been impossible to mention all the architectural treasures to be found on this tour, so do explore for yourself when you see a turret or

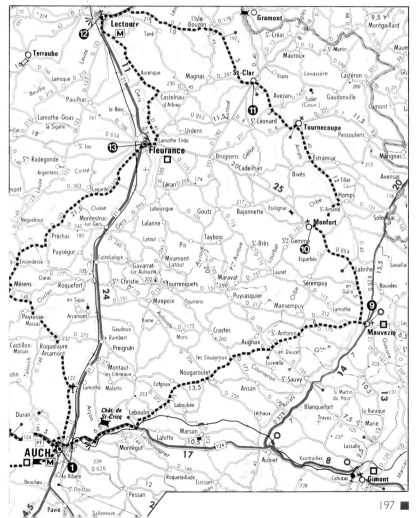

clock tower peeping romantically through the trees. This part of Gascony, incidentally, was the home of the 'real' d'Artagnan, Charles de Batz, on whose memoirs Alexandre Dumas based *The Three Musketeers*.

Just as the *bastides* are a variation on a theme, so the countryside is strikingly uniform - an attractively rolling mixture of fields, hedges, vineyards, copses and little valleys, through which rivers with strangely assonant names flow (e.g. Aulouste, Auloue, Auroue, Auzoue, Lauze, Douze, Ousse, Osse). There are virtually no winding roads and little traffic, so distances are covered easily and pleasantly.

Foie gras and *confits* are the great gastronomic specialities of the area, but fortunately in recent years most local chefs have realized that their customers cannot take such rich food all the time, and have consequently extended their culinary range. There are usually three or four menus to choose from and wine lists give priority to the *appellations* of the south-west. The local brandy, Armagnac, and the Armagnac-based aperitif, *floc*, are worth sampling.

ROUTE ONE: 137 KM

The Romanesque church at Mouchan.

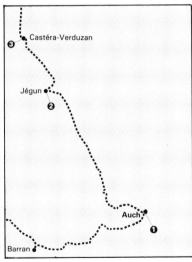

Auch A compact and pleasant little town, Auch is the capital of Gascony and therefore makes an ideal centre for this tour. Its cathedral (15th-17thC) is chiefly remarkable for what it contains within: some vivid stained-glass windows by Arnaut de Moles, a 17thC organ, and more than 1,500 vigorously carved, and occasionally immodest, saints and mythical figures on its oak choir stalls (a coin in the slot will illuminate them a little, but enthusiasts should take a pocket flashlight with them). As befits the capital of a gastronomic province, Auch takes its markets (Thurs and Sat) seriously.

Hôtel de France
(hotel-restaurant, Auch)

This well-appointed hotel, which has been in the Daguin family for almost a century, sets a standard it would be hard to beat anywhere at any price. The soul of the place is its kitchen, where André Daguin devises an astonishing number of variations on a single theme, the culinary traditions of Gascony. Foie gras, *magret* (duck breast served pink like an underdone steak), *confits* (preserved duck or goose), truffles, and the local vegetable *par excellence*, the broad bean, are served in a multitude of often surprising guises. Even if your holiday budget cannot accommodate the prices at Daguin's main restaurant (which are justifiably high), do try the hotel's less expensive bar-restaurant, Le Neuvième, whose *plats du jour* are cooked in the same kitchens. *Place de la Libération; tel 62.05.00.44; closed Jan, Sun evening and Mon in winter; price bands: main restaurant, D; Le Neuvième, C/D; Côt Jardin (a new addition) closed mid-Oct to mid-Apr; B.*

Auch - Jégun

① *Follow the signs for Condom, first on the N124, then on the D930. At Labatisse, turn left to Jégun.* This *bastide* is unusual in that it does not have a central square (though there is a tiny covered market tucked away in the middle). Instead, there is a delightful balustraded esplanade at one end of the village, with pollarded trees and a bandstand. This is where players of *boules* and the mysterious local game of *palettes* congregate.

Le Bastion
(restaurant, Jégun)

Mireille Fauqué has few strings to her culinary bow - but what strings. Vegetable soup containing tasty morsels of duck, gently sautéed oyster mushrooms, juicy charcoal-grilled *magret* and wonderful pastries. *Tel 62. 64.54.57; closed Mon and first three weeks Jan; price bands A/B/C.*
② *Leave Jégun on the road you came in on, turning left on the edge of the village on to the D215, then back on to the D930 to Castéra-Verduzan.*

Castéra-Verduzan

A strung-out little village which has, believe it or not, been a spa since Roman times and has recently come back into vogue (its waters are reputed to be good for gum disorders). Even if your gums are fine, don't be in a hurry to leave Castéra-Verduzan, for it boasts a restaurant and a hotel that offer philanthropically good value.

Le Florida
(restaurant, Castéra-Veduzan)

Bernard Ramounéda, certainly the best *restaurateur* on this tour apart from Daguin, offers set menus and local wines that are absurdly cheap in view of their quality. His pâtés are breathtaking, his *feuilletés* featherlight, his *confits* crisp and succulent, and his desserts tasty and unusual (e.g. *poire aux épices*). In summer there is a congenial terrace, and in chillier weather the comfort of a log fire. *Tel 62.68.13.22; closed Feb, and Sun evening and Mon Oct-Apr; price bands B/C.*

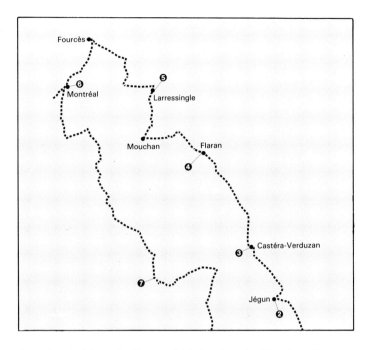

Hôtel Ténarèze
(Castera-Verduzan)

A modern hotel, run by Ramounéda's brother, the Ténarèze offers pleasant, bright rooms with bath and WC. The prices, which include a proper breakfast with home-made jam and real orange juice, should make some other hoteliers in the district blush with shame. *Tel 62.68.10.22; closed Feb, Sun and Mon.*

Castéra-Verduzan - Abbaye de Flaran

③ *Continue on the D930 through Valence-sur-Baïse, a bastide whose* arcades have been disfigured by garish shop signs. *Branch left after a bridge on to the D142 to the Abbaye de Flaran.* Now a cultural centre, this Cistercian abbey is well worth a visit not just for its 12thC church and 14thC cloisters (now disused), but for its quite exemplary permanent exhibition devoted to local architecture. *Open 9.30-12 and 2-7 (2-6 Sat, Sept-May); closed Tues Oct-May.*

Abbaye de Flaran - Larressingle

④ *Continue on the D142, bearing left at Cassaigne on to the D208 to Mouchan,* whose Romanesque church is unusual in having been built around an earlier defensive tower (now its clock tower). *Turn right on to the D931, soon veering left on to the D142. Now follow the signs to Larressingle, and park the car outside its walls.*

Larres-single

This charming and well-preserved fortified village, which was the refuge of the bishops of Condom in the Middle Ages, is the size of a pocket-

The central square, Fourcès.

handkerchief. The Gascons, with typical tongue-in-cheek exaggeration, call it 'the Carcassonne of the Gers'.

⑤ *Follow the sign to the D15, turn left, cross the River Osse and just after reaching the top of the hill turn right along the D254. Shortly after going through Larroque-sur-l'Osse, turn left along the D114 to Fourcès.*

Fourcès   Founded by the English in the 13thC, this engagingly small and self-contained *bastide* is unusual in that its central 'square' is in fact round. It has been well restored.

Drive along the D29, lined with Lombardy poplars, to Montréal.

Montréal   Here the local rugby football team is treated with respect: the *bastide*'s central arcaded square has been called Place-des-Champions-de-France ever since they came top in their division.

La Gare   After the closure of Simone Daubin's excellent restaurant, Chez
(restaurant,   Simone, Montréal has only one place to offer the hungry tourist. La
Montréal)   Gare is housed in a turn-of-the-century railway station. It is decorated to match. *Tel 62.29.43.37; closed Jan, Thurs evening (except July, Aug) and Fri; price band A/B.*

Cross the bridge over the Auzone and turn left along the D29

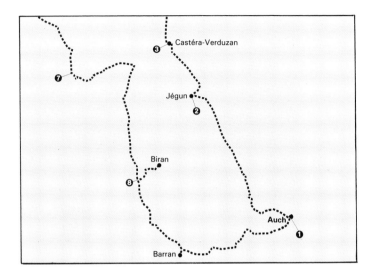

Séviac
(detour)

⑥ *Turn right almost immediately for short detour to Séviac. After one km turn right up a track* to the interesting ruins of a 4thC Gallo-Roman villa (mosaics, etc.). *Open 9.30-12, 2-7, daily July and Aug, and Sun, April-Nov. Return to the D29.*

La Gare
(restaurant, near Montréal)

Turn right just before an overhead bridge 3 km beyond Montréal to reach this amusing restaurant housed in the ticket office of a former railway station. There is much to keep children entertained: old railway lamps, posters, tickets, ticket machines, railway noises (on request) and, in the garden, swings and a see-saw. As you would expect in this area, the food is excellent too. *Tel 62.29.43.37; closed Jan, Thurs evening Sept-June and Fri; price band B.*

Shortly after the overhead bridge, fork left on to the D230. At the first main crossroads turn left on to the D254, signposted Lauraêt, bearing left at forks until you reach the D113. Turn right to Gondrin, a pretty enough *bastide* except for the fact that in a moment of collective lunacy the local council decided to erect a water tower right in the middle of the village. *On leaving Gondrin, fork left along the D113 to Courrensan.*

Cour-rensan

Turn right into the village, a wonderfully unspoilt haven with a carefully restored castle and overhanging half-timbered houses. *Continue on the D113, veering right when it joins the D35.*

Maram-bat

⑦ *After about 5 km, where a majestic avenue of conifers leads off to the right, turn left to Marambat (no sign),* yet another little *bastide* worth exploring. *Turn right on to the D112 on the edge of the village, then almost immediately turn left on to the D132, signposted Bonas.* This pretty road runs through countryside which, by Gers standards, could almost be described as mountainous. *At the crossroads with the D939, turn right.* About 4.5 km after St-Jean-Poutge, you will see to your left a Gallo-Roman *pile*, or stack, of which there are several in the area (their purpose is unknown).

Biran
(detour)

⑧ *Turn left here on to the D374 for a short detour to Biran,* a tiny fortified village. Strikingly positioned on a rock, it contains some fine medieval buildings, many in need of repair. *Return to the D939. Continue up the valley of the Baïse, later turning left to Barran along the D174.* The imposing Château de Mazères can be seen to the left.

Barran

A picturesque *bastide* with moat, covered market, arcades, overhanging houses and an interesting outsized church. The latter contains a Renaissance lectern and some fine 15thC choir stalls, but its most curious feature, as you will see from a distance, is its helicoidal slate-covered spire.

    D943 as far as Embats, then turn right opposite the church for Auch.

▰▰▰▰ ROUTE TWO: 110 KM

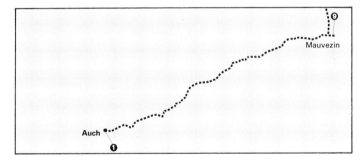

**Auch -
Mauvezin**

Leave Auch on the Toulouse road, the N124, turning left after 6 km on to the D175 in the direction of Mauvezin.

Mauvezin

Once an important Protestant centre, Mauvezin earned itself the nickname of 'Little Geneva'.

**La
Rapière**
(restaurant,
Mauvezin)

Book ahead at Michel and Marie-Thérèse Fourreau's constantly packed restaurant, even out of season: it provides some of the best value in Gascony. The B-price-band menu might consist of the following (all excellent): pumpkin soup, salmon *terrine* with *sauce verte, huîtres chaudes au sabayon,* two duck drumsticks in a Madiran-based sauce, cheese and dessert. *Rue des Justices; tel 62.06.80.08; closed mid-June to 4 July; Tues evening 1-20 Oct and Wed; price bands B/C.*

Mauvezin - *Monfort*	⑨ *Follow the signs for Fleurance out of Mauvezin on to the D654*, which coasts along the valley of the Arrats to Monfort. Yet another nice *bastide*, though sleepier than most, Monfort has an interesting early 14thC church, whose single nave leads to a polygonal choir with little chapels built between the buttresses.

Monfort -
Château
d'Avezan

⑩ *Leave Monfort on the Homps road, the D151. At Homps turn left on to the D40, and left again on the edge of Tournecoupe along the D7 signposted to St-Clar. About 3 km beyond Tournecoupe, follow sign to 13thC Château d'Avezan on the right,* one of Gascony's few visitable privately-owned castles. *Open 10-6, mid-Mar to mid-Oct.*

St-Clar

Founded by the English in 1274, St-Clar has two arcaded squares and a fine covered market, where a garlic fair is held on the second Thursday in Aug (St-Clar is the biggest producer of garlic in the Gers).

A hive of activity in this otherwise pleasantly somnolent village is Art Village, a shop-cum-publisher run by the sprightly Maurice Vidal, who not only writes a witty little annual guide to the restaurants of Gascony (*Le Guide Gascon*) but also sells a wide range of excellent Armagnacs, *flocs* and local wines at growers' prices, *confits*, foie gras, etc. *Open Mon-Sat 10-12.30 and 2.30-7 (6 in winter).*

St-Clar -
Lectoure

⑪ *Leave St-Clar by the D953 in the direction of Lectoure. Drive into the centre of the town and park near the Hôtel de Ville.* There are lots of things to see in this hilltop capital of Lomagne (the north-eastern part of Gascony) and erstwhile fortress of the Comtes d'Armagnac: its Cathédrale St-Gervais; its Promenade du Bastion, which offers a superb view over the Gers and, on a clear day, the Pyrénées; its many old buildings; and its museum in the Hôtel de Ville.

Musée de
Lectoure

The museum contains many relics of Lectoure's pre-Christian history: prehistoric tools, Gallic pottery, Gallo-Roman mosaics, and no less than 20 rare taurobolic altars from the 2nd and 3rdC (well explained by the guide). *Guided tours 10-12 and 2-7.*

Lectoure-
Fleurance

⑫ *Leave Lectoure in the direction of Fleurance; and just after the Agen road comes in from the left, turn left along a small road signposted Lac des Trois Vallées.* Ignore the lake, which is overcrowded and ringed with bungalows, and continue along a picturesque, if at times bumpy road that skulks along the flank of the Gers valley to Aurenque, which has a charming little chapel. If you are looking for a pleasant riverside picnic spot, park near the tiny 15thC bridge a few hundred metres to the right. *Otherwise keep straight on until the junction with the D45; turn right and follow signs to Fleurance.*

Fleurance

From the time of its foundation in the 13thC (it was named after Florence) to the beginning of the 17thC, this large, bustling and

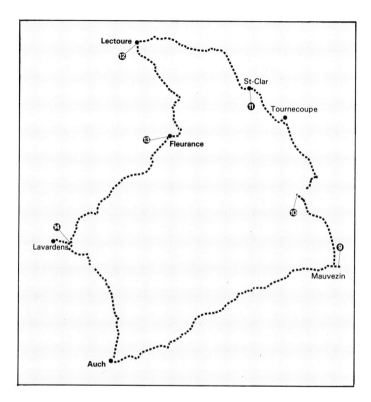

strategically located *bastide* was the scene of many battles, first between English and French, then between Protestants and Catholics.

Fleurance -
Lavardens

⑬ *Leave Fleurance on the D103 in the direction of Préchac and Mérens. Shortly after bearing left on to the D148, you will see a turning to the right signposted Lavardens; ignore this, and continue along the pretty ridge road to Mérens, where you can enjoy a good view over Lavardens.*

Lavardens
(detour)

⑭ *For this short detour to Lavardens, turn right at Mérens on to the D518. The Château de Lavardens, whose asymmetrical architecture cunningly hugs the limestone outcrop it is built on, is one of the most imposing castles in the Gers, a massive top-heavy construction erected in the early 17thC. Open mid-June to mid-Sept, 10-12 and 3-8.*

Lavardens -
Auch

Return to Mérens and continue on the D148, with the Gers valley spread out to your left, then bear left on to the D272 to Roquelaure-Arcamont. After passing some ruined ramparts, turn sharp right at the crossroads and through the village of Roquelaure-Arcamont towards Auch.

Lower Rhône:

The area covered by this tour roughly corresponds to the Comtat Venaissin, the part of France that was under papal rule from 1274 to 1791 (and is now contained mainly within the Vaucluse *département*).

Route One, which skirts the crags of the Dentelles de Montmirail and strikes out across the low-lying plains of the Rhône valley, takes in two historic towns, Vaison-la-Romaine and Carpentras, and offers a detour to a third - Avignon, residence of the popes from 1309 to 1377.

Each of these three towns holds a top-quality summer festival. Perhaps as a result, the Vaucluse has a high concentration of country cottages owned (and often restored) by Parisian intellectuals. The climate could have something to do with it too: hot without being torrid as in lower Provence, it provides ideal conditions for holidaymaking.

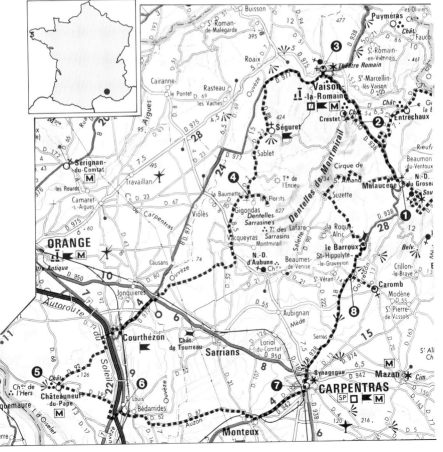

The Vaucluse also includes some of the best of the Rhône wine-growing appellations, such as Châteauneuf-du-Pape, Gigondas and Vacqueyras, as well as the less well-known, less heady Côtes-du-Ventoux. If you buy wine at a cooperative or a vineyard in this area, you will rarely be disappointed.

Route Two, which takes you up to the top of the Mont Ventoux with its staggering views, can only be undertaken in full from June to mid-Nov; the rest of the year the snowbound section of the D974 between Mont Serein and Chalet Reynard is closed.

On both routes many of the villages - in particular Sablet, Gigondas, Vacqueyras, Le Barroux, Aurel, Brantes and Entrechaux - have retained much of their old-world charm and deserve exploration if time permits.

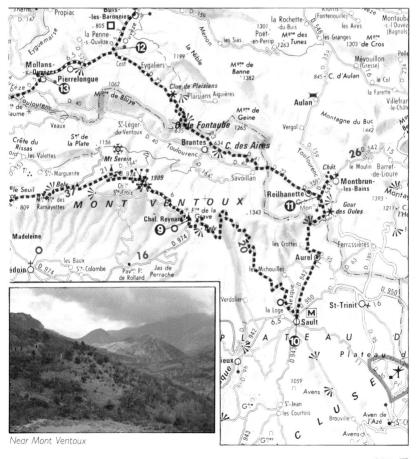

Near Mont Ventoux

ROUTE ONE: 93 KM

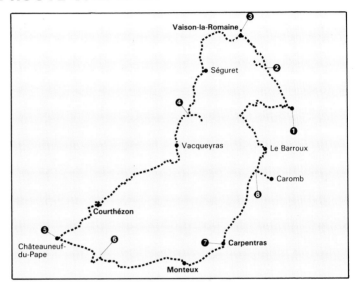

**Malau-
cène**
The tour is based on this little town famed for its cherries. Malaucène
has avenues of age-old plane trees, cool fountains and above all an
interesting 14thC Romanesque church, which used to form part of the
town fortifications (hence its iron-plated door and fortress-like
appearance) and contains a well-known 18thC organ.
① *Take the D938, signposted to Vaison,* which coasts along the lush
valley of the Groseau river.

Crestet
(detour)
② *After about 5 km, you can turn left on to the D76 for a short detour
to Crestet. Drive up through olive groves to the T-junction at the top, turn
right and park by the 12thC castle* (restoration should be complete).
There are no roads to speak of in this tiny village, just a maze of
alleyways and steps to explore. Everywhere the emphasis is on tasteful
restoration. *Retrace to the D938 and continue to Vaison.*

**Vaison-la-
Romaine**
Once one of the most important Roman towns in Gaul, its Roman
bridge still carries traffic (first right turn as you drive in). As well as two
large and fascinating excavated sites, complete with streets, columns
and vestigial walls, there is a Roman theatre scooped out of the hillside
(where many of the events in Vaison's annual drama, ballet and music
festivals are held), and an excellent museum containing the main finds
from the site; also worth visiting are the Cathédrale Notre-Dame and
adjoining cloisters. *The same opening times apply to all these places: 9-7
July-Sept, 9-6 March-June and 9-5 Nov-Feb.*

The quaint and recently restored old town, clinging to a rocky outcrop on the south side of the Ouvèze river, is where the inhabitants of Vaison lived during the troubled Middle Ages. One of the largest and most varied markets in Provence is held every Tues.

(3) *Leave Vaison on the D977, the Avignon road, and after 5.5 km turn left on to the D88, signposted Séguret.*

Séguret By describing itself, on a bill-board, as 'France's most beautiful village', Séguret goes a little overboard, but its old gate, fountain, bell-tower, church, castle and steep streets are undoubtedly picturesque.

Le Mesclun Friendly Jean Vassort, ably assisted by his equally friendly wife Joëlle,
(restaurant, provide expertly cooked, generous seasonal cuisine (e.g. *charlotte*
Séguret) *d'asperges à la crème de ciboulette, rognons d'agneau au cerfeuil,* and excellent fruity desserts). Depending on the weather, there is a choice between an impeccably decorated interior and an airy terrace. Booking is essential. *Tel 90.46.93.43; closed mid-Feb to mid-Mar and Mon, Oct-Apr; price bands B/C.*

Séguret - *Leave Séguret on the D23 and drive through Sablet to Gigondas,* a fortified
Gigondas village as small as its celebrated wine is big.

Les (4) *For a detour that offers the opportunity to have a picnic with a view,*
Dentelles *or visit a popular hotel-restaurant, follow the signs to Les Florets restaurant*
de *and the Col du Cayron. Drive past the restaurant and up to a car-park*
Montmir- *overlooking the Dentelles.* Rock-climbers come from afar to tackle these
ail *(detour)* extraordinarily jagged mini-mountains. There are plenty of picnic spots on the tracks that lead off from the car-park.

Les This large, bustling but friendly restaurant offers classical cuisine with a
Florets rustic touch (eg *civet de porcellet,* which goes well with one of the many
(hotel- Gigondas vintages on the wine list); the sumptuous-looking dessert
restaurant, trolley lives up to expectations. *Tel 90.65.85.01; closed Jan-Feb, and*
Gigondas) *Tues evening and Wed out of season; price band B.*

Gigondas - *Follow the signs to Vacqueyras. Just beyond this fortified village turn right on*
Château- *to the D52, signposted Sarrians. A little later, bear right (on a left-hand*
neuf-du- *bend, no signpost) and keep going until you come to a road signposted*
Pape *Château de Roques. Go along this road for several kms, over a vast plain.*

After crossing a railway bridge, turn right over a river, then turn left immediately on to the D977 to Courthézon. This road takes you through a pretty landscape of tidy vineyards, neat rows of cypresses and trim wine-growers' houses. *At the T-junction, turn into Courthézon, bearing left at roundabout and following Châteauneuf-du-Pape signs across motorway.*

The road now meanders through a tiny enclave of vine-covered hills in the middle of the flat Rhône valley; soon you can see the imposing ruins of the castle of Châteauneuf-du-Pape silhouetted against the sky.

Château-neuf-du-Pape
A strangely dead little town that has grown fat on the fame of its wine; it has more *caveaux de dégustation* than cafés. But don't miss the unusual view of Avignon and the Rhône valley from the castle.
⑤ *Leave Châteauneuf on the Avignon road, then at the crossroads on the edge of town take the D192 for Bédarrides. After converging with the motorway, turn left underneath it towards Orange.*

Avignon
(detour)
This is, of course, one of the most rewarding cities to visit in France, worth at least a day to itself. From ⑥ *it is a 31-km round trip: turn right on to the N7 almost immediately after going under the motorway.*

Bédar-rides
Cross the N7 into this unassuming village, which has two oddities: a triumphal arch and a church with a 17thC Baroque front stuck on a Romanesque nave.

Bédarrides - Carpentras
Go over the old bridge in the direction of Entraigues, and about 1.5 km later turn left on to the D87 to Monteux. The road runs alongside the little Auzon river, which is enclosed within high dykes and hidden by trees. There are plenty of shady places to picnic by the river. *On reaching the D31 bear right into Monteux and follow signs to Carpentras.*

Carpen-tras
A busy, unspoilt town which has a number of interesting old buildings - a Roman arch, France's oldest synagogue (*open 10-12, 3-5 Mon-Fri*) a 17thC Palais de Justice, and the Cathédrale St-Siffrein, known for its fine stained-glass, 17thC organ, and striking portal in the flamboyant style (called the Porte Juive: it was used by converted Jews). Market: Fri.
⑦ *Leave Carpentras on the D938, the Vaison road.*

Caromb
(detour)
⑧ *At a crossroads 9 km beyond Carpentras, turn right on to the D21 for a short detour to Caromb*, a charming village whose large 14thC church contains yet another historic organ. There is a 16thC bell-tower topped by a delicate 18thC wrought-iron 'cage' for the bell.

Le Beffroi,
(hotel-rest., Caromb)
The fare on offer at this establishment is straightforward and classical, the welcome most amiable, and the rooms, many of which have beamed ceilings, cosy. *Tel 90.62.45.63; closed Jan and Mon out of season; price bands B/C/D.*

Caromb - Malaucène
Return to the D938. In a short while turn left to Le Barroux on the D78, then continue to Suzette on the D90A and the V3, a rather poor road. There is a superb view up towards the Dentelles as you climb steeply to Suzette. *On the edge of Suzette bear right on to the D90.*
There follows a particularly exhilarating stretch, first under the sheer cliffs of the Cirque de St-Amand, then past fields of rosemary up to a pass with views to the north over the Ouvèze valley and east towards the Mont Ventoux - scenery whose depth of perspective is reminiscent of Italian Renaissance landscape paintings. *Continue down to Malaucène.*

▬▬▬ ROUTE TWO: 100 KM

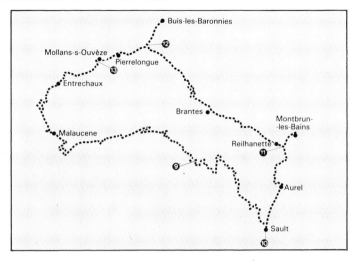

Malaucène - Notre-Dame du Groseau

Leave Malaucène along the excellent D974, signposted to the Mont Ventoux. You soon reach the appealingly tiny, 11thC Romanesque chapel of Notre-Dame du Groseau, which has a sculpted frieze outside and well-preserved capitals within (*open 6-7 Sat in May and Aug*).

A few hundred metres further on, opposite a café, the Source du Groseau issues from the mountainside, forming a little pond beside which are picnic tables. The spring water is drinkable - and delicious.

Continue along the D974, which now begins its relentless climb to the summit of the Mont Ventoux.

Mont Ventoux

Almost immediately the view begins to look pretty good, but by the time you are at the ski resort of Mont Serein, two-thirds of the way up, the panorama has become breathtaking.

After emerging from the forest and entering a lunar landscape of blindingly white rocks, you reach the viewing table at the summit (1,909 metres). By this time, the surrounding countryside has retreated so far into the distance as to appear almost map-like. On an exceptionally clear day it is just possible to make out the Mont Canigou in the Pyrenees some 300 km away.

Winds at the top of the Mont Ventoux can reach 250 km per hour, so the drive should not be attempted in a lightweight car on a gusty day. Some say that the mountain's name comes from '*venteux*', meaning 'windy' - but it is just as likely to derive from the Celtic '*ven top*', meaning 'white mountain'.

The Mont Ventoux forms a nature reserve of great interest to botanists and ornithologists. The former come out in early July in search of rare species of poppy, saxifrage and iris, while birdwatchers hope to see crossbill, rock thrush, Tengmalm's owl or subalpine warbler.

Continue on the D974 to Chalet Reynard, where there is a café.

Chalet Reynard - Sault

⑨ *From Chalet Reynard, take the D164, signposted Sault.* This road takes its time meandering downhill, with yet more wonderful views, in particular over the Montagne de Lure to the east. Pine forest gives way to gnarled and stunted oak, then to acres of wild thyme. The neat rows of mauve lavender bushes can be made out in the valley below.

Sault

If your ears are popping after coming down the mountain, relax for a moment in the medieval streets of Sault.

⑩ *Leave Sault on the D942 signposted Montbrun-les-Bains.*

Montbrun-les-Bains *(detour)*

⑪ *Instead of turning off along the D72, continue along the D542 for a short detour to the tiny spa of Montbrun-les-Bains,* whose once celebrated baths (containing hydrogen sulphide) are again open. Access to the village is through a fortified 14thC clock-tower.

Brantes, with Mont Ventoux in the background.

Montbrun-les-Bains - Buis-les-Baronnies

Return to the junction with the D72 and turn right. The road goes along a flat stretch of the Toulourenc valley up to the Col des Aires, where there is a fine view of the awesome, almost sheer north face of the Mont Ventoux. Continue past the hamlet of Brantes (arts and crafts) on the left, and the Clue de Plaisians on the right (a clue is a deep cleft in a mountain ridge).

Buis-les-Baronnies *(detour)*

⑫ *For this detour, which involves a 4-km round trip, turn right at the junction with the D5.* As you drive towards Buis-les-Baronnies, the knife-edge ridge of the Rocher St-Julien can be seen to the right. The town enjoys an exceptionally sheltered micro-climate that is ideal for growing olives, almonds and apricots. It also holds Europe's biggest lime-blossom

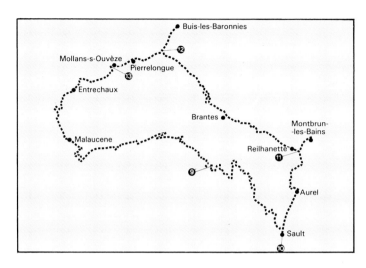

market on the first Wed in July. Its streets are fragrant for two weeks beforehand while the blossom is being dried in lofts and warehouses.

Make a point of dropping into the Moulin à l'Huile du Puits Communal, a marvellous shop-cum-museum in the old quarter near the Place du Marché. At one end there is a display of fossils, rocks and semi-precious stones found in the area, as well as an olive press and other utensils used in the manufacture of olive oil; at the other end a tempting selection of local products are on sale (lime-blossom *eau de toilette*, various soaps, lavender essence, finest olive oil, and Provençal preserves such as *tapnade* and *saussoun*). *Rue de Puits-Communal; closed Sun.*

Sous l'Oliviers (hotel-restaurant, Buis-les-Baronnies)	This hotel-restaurant is one of the few in this small town. The staff are helpful and the prices reasonable. *Tel 75.28.01.04; closed Nov to mid-Mar; price band B.*
Buis-les-Baronnies - Mollans-sur-Ouvèze	*Returning from Buis to the junction with the D72, continue along the D5 to Pierrelongue,* whose church is preposterously perched on a high rock in the middle of the hamlet, *and then on to Mollans.* Pause here to take a look at the fine fountain, arcaded public wash-house, heterogeneous clock-tower and restored 13thC castle.
Mollans - Malaucène	⑬ *Continue on the D5, D13 (through the old village of Entrechaux) and D938, across a smiling landscape of orchards, vines and market gardens, to Malaucène.*

If your idea of paradise involves sipping a *pastis* in the shade of a giant plane tree, watching old men in berets play *boules*, and allowing yourself to be lulled by the grating of cicadas and the hot perfumes of lavender and thyme, then this is the tour for you.

Route One concentrates on the Montagne Ste-Victoire - whose colour varies from bleached white to dull grey or luminous violet depending on the weather - and the elegant town of Aix-en-Provence, with its renowned music festival, large and lively student population, and many old buildings. It also provides glimpses of the extraordinary Canal de Provence network of watercourses, begun in the 16thC and constantly extended ever since; by channelling the unpredictable Durance and Verdon rivers, it provides much of the Rhône basin with irrigation, electricity and drinking water.

Route Two explores a lesser-known, less spectacular part of Provence, where there is a lower concentration of tourists - and some rather second-rate roads. Villages and little towns such as La Verdière, Barjols and Cotignac have a truly authentic Provençal feel and have not yet been invaded by chic boutiques. Similarly, the surrounding countryside, planted largely with vines and olive trees, has on the whole escaped the clutches of property developers, mainly due to water supply problems. Much of Provence is parched in summer - and much of it goes up in smoke every year, so be sure to heed the numerous fire warnings.

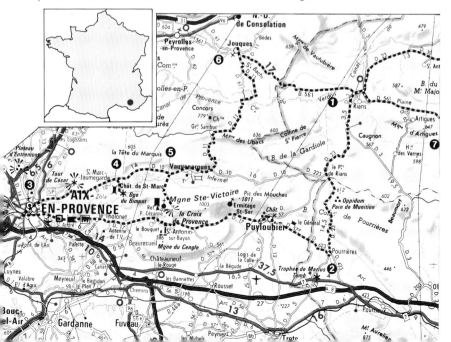

ROUTE ONE: 82 KM

Rians

The tour is based on the sleepy little town of Rians, which has been chosen for its geographical convenience rather than for any specific interests of its own. For good plain fare and accommodation at reasonable prices, L'Esplanade hostelry is a useful standby. *Tel 94.80.31.12; price bands A/B.*

Rians - Pourrières

① *Leave Rians on the St-Maximin-la-Ste-Baume road, turning right shortly on to the D23 signposted Pourrières.* This road takes you through an evocative, uninhabited landscape dotted with that most beautiful of Provençal trees, the parasol-shaped stone pine. Then comes some strenuous driving as you twist and turn down an attractive rocky gorge to Pourrières.

Pourrières - Aix-en-Provence

② *Go through Pourrières, then turn right to Puyloubier*, for your first good view of the Montagne Ste-Victoire. *In Puyloubier, fork right on to the D17.* The road runs through sparse woodland and the occasional meadow, edging closer and closer to the mountain, a curious ghostly presence covered with crinkles and folds, which fascinated Aix-born painter Paul Cézanne to the point of obsession. Beyond St-Antonin-sur-Bayon a series of tight hairpin bends leads through pine forest to Le Tholonet, a plush suburb of Aix. *Drive on into the town.*

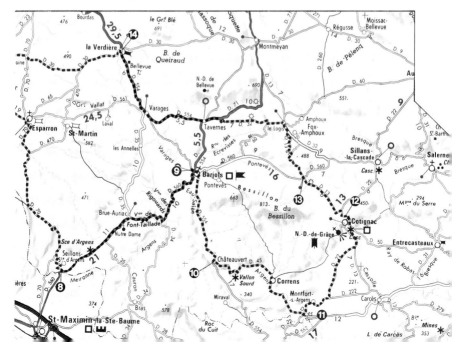

Aix-en-Provence

Parking in Aix can be a nightmare even when the festival is not in progress; the best advice is to drive into town until you get on to its one-way circular boulevard system, then make for the huge open-air car park near the bus station (well signposted). From there it is only a short walk to the old town, which is extremely compact and can easily be explored on foot.

Many of Aix's delights are to be sampled in the open air: its impressive fountains, its plethora of imposing 17thC *hôtels particuliers* (town houses), its Hôtel de Ville, and of course its celebrated Cours Mirabeau, a broad leafy boulevard lined on one side by austere private houses and banks, and on the other by one of the most congenially extrovert series of café terraces in France. This is where all those who matter (or think they matter) in Aix - students, intellectuals, festival-goers, beautiful people - get together.

Indoor attractions are numerous too, but priority should be given to the following:

Cathéd-rale St-Saveur

This remarkable church, built between the 5th and 17th centuries, contains a fascinating multitude of styles; be sure to walk round its marvellously elegant cloisters.

Musée Granet

Works by Hals, Rembrandt and Cezanne (eight paintings) are on show here; the interesting Aix-born artist, Francois Granet, is also well represented. *Open 10-12, 2-6; closed Tues, except July and Aug.*

A harsh, rugged face of Provence.

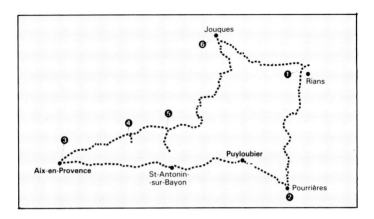

Atelierde Cézanne	The studio of Aix's best-known painter contains moving mementoes of the man and several objects (e.g. apples, changed every day) that feature in his still lifes. *Open 10-12 and 2.30-6 (2-5 Oct-May); closed Tues.*
Restaurants, Aix	There are many restaurants and hotels where you can eat well in Aix, several of them meriting a place in the Red Michelin guide. Even in a town so overrun with tourists, prices for meals are not always extravagant. Try the Bistro Latin - *tel 42.38.22.88* - and the Abbaye des Cordeliers - *tel 42.27.29.47.*
Le Prieuré *(hotel, Aix)*	This quiet, reasonably priced and welcoming hotel can be a lifesaver when Aix is buzzing. Most of the rooms are fairly small (as you would expect in a former priory), but some overlook a garden designed by Le Nôtre. *Route des Alpes (about 2.5 km from Aix's circular boulevard on the Manosque road); tel 42.21.05.23.*
Aix - Barrage de Bimont	③ *Leave Aix on the D10, the St-Marc-Jaumegarde and Vauvenargues road, which climbs easily and quickly into the hills.* ④ *About 8 km from Aix, turn right for the following detour:*

Barrage de Bimont *(detour)*	A 5-km return journey: the dam offers a spectacular view of the Montagne Ste-Victoire across the lake's usually turquoise waters (like the mountain, they tend to vary in hue), and pleasant picnic spots in the woodlands on the far side of the dam.
	    The energetic may wish to continue on foot for 30 minutes down a pretty defile to the Barrage Zola, designed by Emile Zola's father and claimed to be the world's first arched dam.
	    There is ample parking by the Barrage de Bimont, but no café, so bring plenty of liquid refreshment - despite the proximity of the cool waters of the lake, this is a notoriously hot spot.
	    Return from the dam and continue along the recently improved D10.

La Croix-de-Provence
(detour)

⑤ Only attempt this detour, which involves a strenuous three-hour return journey on foot up the Montagne Ste-Victoire, at times of the year or day when temperatures are below scorching. Those who reach the Croix-de-Provence, one of the mountain's highest points, will be well rewarded: the 360° view over the surrounding countryside and mountain ranges is staggering. Park at Les Cabassols, about 4 km beyond the turning to Bimont on the D10, and strike off up the signposted footpath to the right (Grande Randonnée 9).

Vauven-argues - Jouques

The D10 soon sweeps past the fast-expanding little village of Vauvenargues. Pablo Picasso is buried in the grounds of its 14thC château (not open to the public).

Shortly after Vauvenargues, turn left on to the D11, which elbows its way up through a narrow rocky gorge. On the way down to Jouques, on the other side, there are views of the Lubéron mountains in the distance. The road crosses one of the arms of the Canal de Provence. *At the junction with the D561, turn left into Jouques.*

Jouques

This relaxed village, once the residence of the archbishops of Aix, has a ruined castle and an interesting 12thC chapel.

Jouques - Rians

⑥ *Leave Jouques as you came in, continuing this time on the D561 to Rians*. After passing *underneath* the Canal de Provence (which is held aloft in a huge silvery tube by a suspension bridge), the road goes through a pretty landscape of green pastures and brick-red soil.

ROUTE TWO: 112 KM

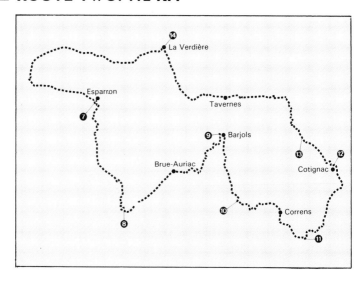

Rians -
Esparron

Leave Rians in the direction of Manosque. Just outside the town bear right
on to the D561, signposted Esparron.
    A word of warning about the road-sign policy in force in the area
around Rians: the local traffic authorities have not yet adopted the
almost universal system of making one set of traffic give way to the
other at major intersections, so great caution is required at all
crossroads within a 15-km radius of the town.
    The D561 runs along the broad flat valley of the aptly named River
Plaine. The Bois du Mont Major and the Montagne d'Artigues rise to
the left and right respectively.

Esparron -
Seillons-
Source
d'Argens

⑦ *On reaching Esparron*, a gently decaying village built on the side of
the hill and overlooked by a large château, *turn right on to the St-*
Maximin-la-Ste-Baume road, which leads up to a deserted plateau. Here
you can observe several different types of Provençal landscape: *garrigue*
(desolate heath), rock-strewn woodland (densely populated by spindly
truffle oaks), and, at times, thick carpets of thyme bushes.
    On reaching the D270, turn left for Seillons, then keep straight ahead as
far as the T-junction with the D560. This downhill drive affords views of
Mont Aurélien to the south-west, and Montagne Ste-Victoire to the
west - i.e. on your right.

Seillons -
Barjols

⑧ *Turn left in the direction of Barjols.* After going through the quiet,
wine-growing village of Brue-Auriac, the road winds its way down the
narrower and more verdant Vallon de Font-Taillade, then up towards
Barjols.

Barjols

If the weather is very hot - as it often is in this part of the world -
there is no greater pleasure than to drive into the little town of Barjols,
turn off the engine and listen to the cool, splashing waters of one of its
25 fountains. Despite the many *boules* players, parking is usually easy on
the tree-lined Place de la Rouguière, which boasts one of the finest
fountains, a large moss-covered, mushroom-shaped structure.
    Nestling in an amphitheatre of limestone cliffs, Barjols is delightfully
unspoiled. Allow time to explore its maze of tiny streets and alleys, as
well as its church, the Collégiale, whose fine organ case and choir-stall
carvings date from the 16thC. If you happen to be around in mid-Jan,
you can enjoy the unusual Fête de St-Marcel (a costumed procession
and, every four years, a spectacular spit-roasted steer). Lively markets
are held in Barjols every Tues, Thurs and Sat. There are a few hotels
and restaurants in the town.
    ⑨ *Leave Barjols on the D554, the Brignoles road, and follow the valley of*
the quirkily named Eau Salée river as far as Châteauvert.

Auberge
de Chât-
eauvert

Delicious trout and crayfish from the open-air fish tank (other dishes
are good, but not quite on a par) served in an idyllic riverside setting.
Tel 94.77.06.60; closed Tues, Sun evening in July and Aug, mid-Oct to
1st Sat in Mar (except Sun, holidays); price band B.

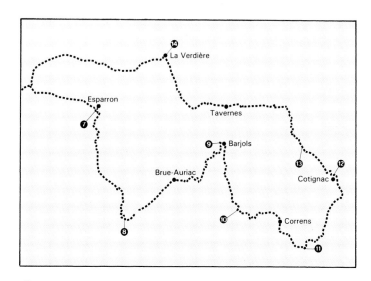

Châteauvert - Cotignac ⑩ *Fork left by the restaurant up the D45 to Correns.* This little road meanders along the enchanting Vallon Sourd, a small-scale gorge with miniature jagged cliffs whose many caves were used as hiding places during the Wars of Religion. There are plenty of shaded picnic spots by the River Argens.

Beyond Correns, the gorges open out into an attractive verdant valley that contrasts with the parched *garrigue* which can be seen rising to the left.

⑪ *At the junction with the D22, turn left to Montfort-sur-Argens and Cotignac.*

Cotignac Like Barjols, Cotignac is a typical Provençal village tucked away in a rocky cleft, but it has more facilities for visitors (as well as a regular programme of open-air ballets and concerts in July and Aug). Through-traffic no longer disturbs the peace of its central esplanade (Cours Gambetta), which is shaded by massive plane trees. Do not miss the charming Place de la Mairie, with its old bell-tower and fountain.

The village wine co-operative, Les Vignerons de Cotignac (*closed Sun*), sells various excellent local wines, from *vin de pays* - suitable for picnics - to the more expensive Côtes-de-Provence.

Lou Calen *(hotel-restaurant, Cotignac)* Book well ahead in season if you want one of the tastefully decorated rooms in this gem of a hostelry. But in any case make a point of sampling the cuisine, which combines classical French dishes with such tasty Provençal specialities as *daube, pieds et paquets* (sheep's tripe and trotters), and *soupe au pistou*. The service, like *patronne* Claudine Mendes's welcome, in spontaneously friendly, and prices, in view of the facilities provided (a private swimming pool and a magical secluded garden with exotic trees), are remarkably reasonable. *Tel 94.04.60.40; closed Wed and Jan-Easter; price bands B/C/D.*

Rest. des
Sports
(Cotignac)

Also on the Cours Gambetta, this is a useful restaurant (with terrace) to fall back on if Lou Calen is closed or full. The fish soup is especially good. *Tel 94.04.60.17; closed mid-Oct to mid-Mar; price band A.*

Cotignac -
La Verdière

⑫ *Leave Cotignac on the D13.* As the road climbs out of the village in the direction of Riez and Barjols, there is an excellent view of the strikingly pock-marked tufa cliff which overhangs the town, and which is itself topped by two 13thC watchtowers. Soon the D13 crosses a plateau of olive groves, vineyards and woodland.
⑬ *At the junction with the D560, turn right then left almost immediately and continue towards Fox-Amphoux. At the next T-junction, turn left towards Riez. At the following crossroads turn left on to the D32, signposted Avignon. On reaching the main D71, turn left,* and drive down to the completely vine-encircled Tavernes, with a view of the Montagne Ste-Victoire in the distance. *Keep straight on to Varages. Turn right in Varages for La Verdière.*

La
Verdière

Park on the main road, which skirts this *village perché*, and walk up through its narrow streets to the promenade and château at the top. This vast, mainly 18thC building (believed to have 365 windows and a hectare of roofing) has been undergoing restoration.

A la
Ferme
(restaurant,
La Verdière)

When the late Wolf Raukamp - a biblical figure with a flowing white beard - and his wife Rolande decided to call their restaurant A la Ferme they meant the words literally; much of the produce that finds its way on to your plate (chicken, goose, kid, goat cheese) comes from their own adjacent farm. The restaurant's décor, and indeed the welcome, have a personal touch more commonly found in a private home. On top of that, the cuisine is very good (with rarities such as scrambled eggs with *grisets,* the local mushroom) and the prices are astoundingly low in view of the mountainous portions. It is better not to try to make friends with the geese, who guard Rolande's car. *The restaurant is 2.5 km north of La Verdière on the Manosque road. Tel 94.04.10.50; price bands A/B.*
⑭ *Take the D30 back to Rians.*

Côte d'Azur:
AND THE HINTERLAND

The overcrowded stretch of Mediterranean coast between Monte Carlo and Marseille known as the Côte d'Azur is still one of Europe's most beautiful: a succession of rocky headlands and wooded coves, strung with palms and cypress trees, cacti and flowers. Despite the overexposure, it has an undeniable draw: sweeping seafront boulevards, little harbours crowded with yachts, magnificent beaches, hotels and restaurants. Nothing in all Provence is more striking than the contrast between this hectic, brilliant coast and its mountainous hinterland, serene and mostly unspoilt.

These two loops are designed primarily to discover those lovely inland hills and mountains, but to highlight the contrast, the route dips down to the

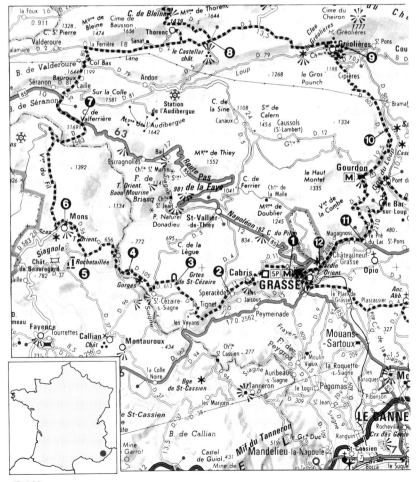

coast at one of its most beautiful parts, Cap d'Antibes, and takes in some of Provence's rich art collections. Picasso, Matisse, Léger and Renoir, whose museums the route passes, are only some of the artists who have been inspired by the clear light and beautiful landscapes of the south of France.

Both loops start at Grasse, an inland town perched above countryside whose greenery and abundance of blossoms partly compensate for the recent mushrooming of villas. From there the route reaches far into the upper hinterland with its breathtaking scenery.

Just as the scenery on this spectacular tour is diverse, so are the restaurants, from the world-famous Colombe d'Or to little-known inns offering real value. Gift shopping in also catered for, with stops at the craft villages of Tourette, Biot and Vallauris.

There is so much to see and do in this area that it is obviously not possible to take in all the suggested sights in a one-day trip. The tour presents a real case for an overnight stop, perhaps at Thorenc, Vence or Grasse (outside Grasse there is a lovely hotel at Pégomas: Le Bosquet, tel 93.42.22.87).

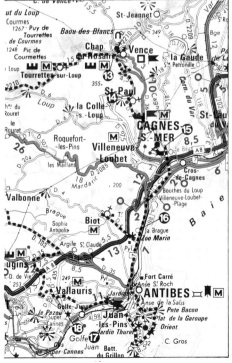

Sunset, Antibes.

ROUTE ONE: 104 KM

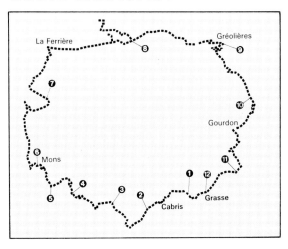

Grasse Grasse, once a well-known winter resort, is not a good place to stay or eat in; but it is worth taking in the old town, the Cathédrale Notre-Dame (three paintings by Rubens and one by Fragonard, who was born in Grasse), and the Place aux Aires (market: Tues and Sat). Grasse is also capital of the French perfume industry, and the Parfumerie Fragonard (*20 Bd. Fragonard*) offers daily conducted tours (dreadful smells) and has a small museum and a shop (delightful smells).

Grasse -
Grottes de
St-Cézaire

① *Leave Grasse on the D4 signposted Cabris*. The D4 winds its way along the hillside, which although increasingly built up still sports more flowers and foliage than brickwork.

Cabris From its position on the spur of a steep hill, the views from this tastefully restored village are superb: to the south the Iles des Lérins, and to the west Lac St-Cassien. *Continue on D11 to Spéracèdes.*

La Soleil-
lade,
(restaurant,
Spéracèdes)

In a charming village, which most tourists overlook, this jolly restaurant relies on straightforward menus and fresh local produce. Service, under the directions of English-speaking, ex-circus artiste M. Forest, is brisk and helpful. *Rue des Orangers; tel 93.66.11.15; closed Wed (except in July, Aug and Oct; price bands A/B.*
② *Follow signs to St-Cézaire, bearing right on to the D613 to the Grottes.*

Grottes
de
St-Céz-
aire

Children particularly will love the guided tour round these fascinating caves, discovered by chance at the end of the last century by the father of the present owner: thousands of stalagmites and stalactites. *Open 10-12, 2-6, June-Sept; 2-5 March, April, May and Oct.*

Grottes de
St-Cézaire -
Mons

③ *After leaving the caves continue on the D613, then turn left at the crossroads on to the D5 and then right on to the D105*, a narrow road which twists and turns its way down the side of the sheer Siagne gorge. ④ *After crossing the bridge over the Siagne, continue on the even narrower D656* (there are passing points) *up past striking rock formations to a wooded plateau.*
⑤ *On reaching the T-junction with the D56, turn right for Mons.*

Mons

A typical Provençal hill village, with its maze of tiny streets, steps, courtyards and jumbled rooftops, all refreshingly unrestored. Park on the Panorama, a large esplanade favoured by *boules* players, with breathtaking views to the south-east (there is a viewing table and a telescope). Mons has no fuel.

Mons - Col
Valferrière

⑥ *From Mons take the D563 signposted Castellane.* Shortly after leaving Mons the valley of the River Fil broadens into tiny meadows, and for a 2-km stretch there are plenty of easily accessible waterside picnic spots.

Col
Valferrière -
Thorenc

⑦ *At the Valferrière pass (altitude 1,169 metres), turn left along the N85, then fork right 3 km later on to the D79 signposted Caille. Bear left as you come into Caille and follow signs to Thorenc, skirting an extraordinarily flat-bottomed valley. Just before reaching the village of La Ferrière, turn right along the D2, which sweeps easily up the Lane valley.* This is a far cry from the hemmed-in feel that is characteristic of the busy roads down on the coast. *Ignore the tiny road with a red-bordered sign indicating Thorenc and turn left into the village a little later up the D502.*

Thorenc

Thorenc (altitude 1,250 metres) has retained much of the charm that used to attract the English. It has a lake and tennis courts.

Hôtel des
Voyag-
eurs
(hotel-
restaurant,
Thorenc)

Claudette and Albert Rouquier offer genuine and carefully cooked local dishes on their two *prixe fixe* menus (no *à la carte*). The light and airy dining room is decorated with stuffed animals and birds. There is also a charming terrace overlooking an orchard. *Tel 93.60.00.18; closed Nov-1 Feb, Thur out of season; price bands A/B; accommodation available if you take full board (or half-board out of season).*
Return to D2; in 3 km turn left to the Quatre Chemins crossroads.

Col de
Bleine
(detour)

⑧ *For this detour, a 9-km round trip, turn left on to the D5.* As you climb to the pass you get a view of Thorenc's gingerbread villas below. The Col de Bleine reveals staggering vistas over the surrounding mountains, with the snow-capped Alps in the distance. There is an even better vantage point - and a fine place to picnic on a windless day - up the road branching off to the right at the pass; it has no passing points and is better tackled on foot (15 minutes).
Returning to the Quatre Chemins crossroads, turn sharp left on to the D2 for Gréolières, a quiet old village.

Gréolières - Gourdon ⑨ *Two hairpin bends after Gréolières, turn sharp right on to the Cipières road. On the edge of Cipières bear left along the D603 to Gourdon. This* enchanting road leads through the dramatic valley of the Loup; at ⑩ *it joins the D3 beneath beetling cliffs at the beginning of the Gorges du Loup proper.*

Gorges du Loup The D3 winds along the Gorges, which plunge away to the left. At one point there is a well-marked parking bay and viewing platform perched almost vertically above the Courmes waterfall. There are many accessible picnic spots away from the road.

Gourdon The grey stone houses here are barely distinguishable from the sheer rocks to which they cling. Gourdon is one of the most dramatic of all the *villages perchés* in this area; views are as spectacular as one might expect. The 13thC château *(open mid-Sept 11-1, 2-7; rest of year 2-6 and closed Tues out of season)* contains interesting naive paintings.

At Gourdon the coast seems suddenly near again: every cranny of the village, which is not much larger than its ample car park, is filled with gift shops selling anything from kitsch to genuine works of art.

Take the D3 to the junction with the D2085, then ⑪ *turn right for Grasse.*

▦ **ROUTE TWO: 88 KM**

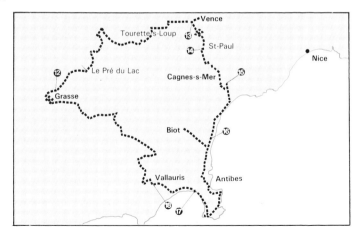

Grasse - Vence ⑫ *Leave Grasse by the D2085 and at the roundabout in Châteauneuf follow signs left and half-right for Le Bar-sur-Loup and Vence on D2210.*

Le Bar-sur-Loup The Gothic church in this weathered village holds an arresting curiosity: an anonymous 15thC painting called the *Danse Macabre*, depicting the fate that befalls sinners when they die.

Tourette-sur-Loup A fortified hill village whose lonely setting, yet in close proximity to the coast, has attracted many artists and craftsmen.

Vence A sizeable resort which, although thronged by tourists much of the year, has a lived-in feel because of its many permanent residents (both French and foreign). Its long history stretches back to pre-Roman times. The attractive *vieille ville* is filled with shops selling antiques and local pottery. See the Place du Peyra and the Romanesque cathedral.

La Farigoule, *(restaurant, Vence)* Success has not gone to Georgette Gastaud's head: on her two set menus she still proposes the same genuine, generously served Provençal specialities - rabbit *à la farigoule* (with thyme), sardines *à l'éscabèche*, and *mesclun* salad (with rocket). In fine weather you can eat on the congenial patio. *15 Av. H. Isnard; tel 93.58.01.27; closed Friday and 15 Nov-15 Dec; price band B.*

Chapelle du Rosaire *(Vence)* This is a little chapel decorated with characteristic flair and simplicity by Matisse in 1950, when he was 80. It was a present from the artist to the adjacent convent of Dominican nuns, who had nursed him through a long illness. *Route St-Jeannet; open Tues, Thurs 10-11.30, 2.30-5.30; or by special arrangement - tel 93.58.03.26.*
⑬ *Take the D2 on the edge of the old town, signposted St-Paul.*

St-Paul-de-Vence Park in one of the car parks on the road signposted Nice outside the village ramparts; expect parking difficulties in high season. Stroll through mosaic-paved alleys and pretty piazzas to the church on the hilltop, and then to the ramparts. Despite its being choc-a-bloc with tourists and gift shops of every description, St-Paul still gives an inkling of the charm that attracted Bonnard and Modigliani here in the 1920s.

Fonda-tion Maeght *(museum, St-Paul-de-Vence)* This famed modern art museum (on the Pass-Prest road opposite the turn-off into St-Paul) is remarkable not only for its contents but for its setting and the building itself. Designed by the Spaniard J.L.Sert, the boldly modern building is crowned by two inverted domes. Most of the major artists and sculptors of the 20thC are represented. *Open 10-7, July and Sept; 10-12.30, 2.30-6 Oct-Apr.*

La Colombe d'Or *(hotel-rest., St-Paul-de-Vence)* If you are touring in a Rolls Royce, then this renowned hotel with its own important art collection is the natural choice for a lunchtime stop; if you are not, consider giving yourself a special treat anyway. Sip *kir* by the lovely pool amid Braque and Calder sculptures, and eat on the terrace with its marvellous Léger mural. The food itself, despite the prices, must be said to be enjoyable rather than superb. *1 Pl. Géneral de Gaulle; tel 93.32.80.02; closed Nov-21 Dec; price band D.*
⑭ *Fork left at the end of the series of car parks on the Nice road on to the D2 signposted Villeneuve-Loubet. After 3 km turn left along the dual carriageway signposted Cagnes-sur-Mer.*

Cagnes-sur-Mer	This is an unremarkable resort except for the old part, Haut-de-Cagnes, which perches on a hill; but see also the former home of Renoir in Cagnes-Ville, Les Collettes, now open to the public. It is an unpretentious villa standing in a large garden. Renoir spent his last years here, from 1907 to 1919. He suffered from rheumatoid arthritis, and so that he could continue to paint his brushes were tied to his stiffened fingers. The artist's peaceful studio has been faithfully reconstructed and recreates, touchingly, even disturbingly, the nature of the man who worked in it. *Les Collettes, Av. des Collettes, Cagnes-Ville; open 10-12, 2-6 June-Oct, 2-5 mid-Nov-May; closed Tues, mid-Oct mid-Nov.*
Cagnes-sur-Mer - Antibes	⑮ *Keep driving towards the sea, through Cagnes' ugly suburbs. Get into the right hand lane to avoid the motorway, and just before the flyover turn right on to the N7 signposted Cannes.* ⑯ *Keep on the N7 to La Brague, turning right on to the D4 if you want to make a detour to Biot (8-km round trip).*
Biot (detour)	This is a lively village with an arcaded square and 16thC gates and ramparts. Pottery and glass-blowing flourish here, and there are many shops where you can browse and buy. Novaro has a particularly fine selection. *The turning to the Léger Museum, on the D4, is opposite.*
Musée Fernand Léger	Léger's artistic development is traced in over 300 pieces on show in this museum made especially for his work. Built by his widow Nadia after his death in 1955, this was the first major museum in France for one artist. *Open 10-12, 2-6 (2-5 in winter); closed Tues.*
Café des Arcades (restaurant, Biot)	André Brothier's interestingly decorated inn has an easygoing atmosphere. A good place to try the Provençal speciality of *aioli (Fri only), Pl. des Arcades; tel 93.65.71.20; closed Sun eve, Mon; price band B.* *Return from Biot and continue along the N7 into Antibes.*
Antibes	The town began life as a Greek trading post and is still busy and commercial, but also has an undeniably charming old quarter.
Musée Picasso	In 1945 Picasso was given temporary use of Château Grimaldi as a studio, and in gratitude he left the whole huge output of that period on permanent loan here. The paintings are mainly exuberant fantasies inspired by the sea and Greek mythology, such as *La Joie de Vivre* and *Ulysse et Les Sirènes. Château Grimaldi, Vieille Ville; open 10-12, 3-7 in summer, 2-6 in winter, closed Tues, Nov-10 Dec.* *Emerging from Antibes, follow the coastal route, well signposted from the town, right round this little pine-forested peninsula.*
Cap d'Antibes	Cap d'Antibes is the haven of the rich *par excellence*, graced with splendid villas in superb sub-tropical gardens. If you have time, visit the strange little Sanctuaire de la Garoupe which stands by a lighthouse in

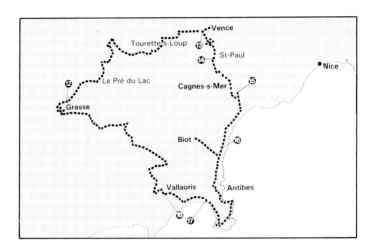

the middle of the peninsula. Its walls are hung with touchingly naïve ex-voto paintings by sailors and others rescued by Our Lady from death or other fates. Next to the chapel is an exceptional viewing point.

La Gardiole,
(hotel-restaurant, Cap d'Antibes)
The route round the Cap leads past the famous Hôtel Cap d'Antibes and its equally illustrious restaurant, the Eden Roc. Those with more modest tastes might like to try the Gardiole, with its sandy beach nearby and family atmosphere. This little hotel is on the way up the Garoupe sanctuary. *Chemin de la Garoupe; tel 93.61.35.03; closed Nov to mid-Mar; price band B.*

Leaving the peace of the Cap, enter garish Juan-les-Pins.
⑰ *Follow the signs to Cannes and continue west on the N7 to Golfe-Juan, then turn right for Vallauris.*

Vallauris
Pottery has been important to Vallauris since ancient times, but only after Picasso himself came to live and work here for six years did it become a world name in ceramics. Pottery on sale at every turn.

Musée Picasso
(Vallauris)
The artist's haunting *War and Peace*, painted on plywood panels in his Vallauris studio, covers the entire walls and ceiling of this little chapel at the top of the main street. Opposite is his bronze of a man holding a struggling sheep. *Open 10-12, 2-6 (2-5 Oct-March), closed Tues.*
⑱ *At Vallauris take the D135 signposted Grasse. Then follow signs to Valbonne, first on the D35, then left on the D103.*

After Vallauris you drive up through Cannes' opulent hinterland. In contrast, 2 km along the D103, note on the right the ambitious Scientific Park of Sophia Antipolis, a modernistic industrial zone which displays the Côte d'Azur's developing role as a location for high-technology companies. Continue following signs for Grasse.

The famous city of Carcassonne attracts thousands of visitors each year; most leave by the same motorway which brought them and few stay to explore the beautiful countryside just a few miles from the city walls. This relatively short tour has been devised to add an extra dimension to an outing to Carcassonne by tempting you to explore two adjacent and little-known areas, the Montagne Noire and the Minervois (you could visit the city in the morning and drive just one loop in the afternoon if time is short).

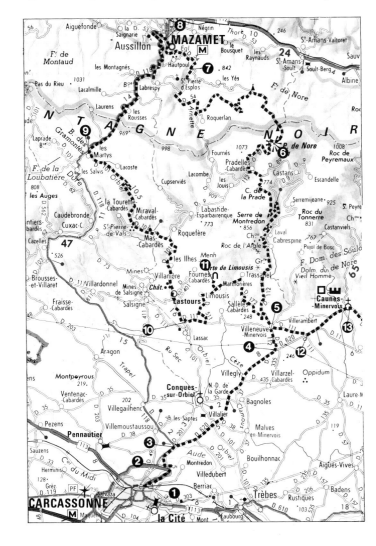

This is indeed a backwater: the landscape has great natural beauty and moments of drama, but beyond that there are few frills and the unassuming people work hard to earn a living from the land. Restaurants, even colourful village cafés, are scarce, and the local shops are unexciting, but for a picnic, who needs more than a fresh *baguette*, some salami and cheese, and a bottle of the ridiculously cheap Minervois?

The two loops contrast the Montagne Noire, far south-western corner of the Massif Central, scored with deep gorges, and the Minervois, a rocky limestone region dedicated to wine growing wherever it may. The routes have frequent reminders of Languedoc's medieval past, particularly of its stubborn religious dissension. In the early 13thC the Pope ordered the Albigensian crusade, led by Simon de Montfort, to ruthlessly eradicate the Cathars, whose religion had taken root in Languedoc; many retreated to inaccessible fortresses, often to be starved to death during long sieges.

██████ ROUTE ONE: 90 KM

Carcas-sonne   The town is in two parts: the historic walled *Cité* on its hill, and the newer bustling town on the banks of the Aude. In the latter you will find good shops and food markets, including a large and colourful open-

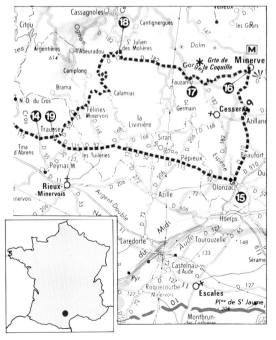

The fortified outer walls of the Cité, Carcassonne.

air fruit and vegetable market in the central Place Carnot. Park on one of the main Boulevards surrounding the maze of inner streets and walk from there.

For the *Cité*, car-parks are situated just outside the ramparts at the entrance, Porte Narbonnaise. If there is a strange feeling of unreality inside the *Cité*, it is because it is not, as it appears, a perfectly preserved medieval walled city, but a brilliant, if somewhat over-enthusiastic restoration. The restorer was the architect Viollet-le-Duc, who rebuilt the crumbling *Cité* in the 1840s.

Carcassonne has a suitably hectic and colourful medieval history, both in legend (you will doubtless be regaled with a fanciful story concerning a certain Lady Carcas and a bloated pig) and in fact. It played its part in the Albigensian crusade, being under the control of the dreadful Simon de Montfort while he pursued his campaign to stamp out the Cathars.

The Porte Narbonnaise, with its double line of ramparts, gives on to narrow, very *touristique* streets which lead up to the Château Comtal. From there visit the *Cité's* architectural *tour de force*, the church of St-Nazaire with its wonderfully graceful Gothic choir and transepts, and superb stained glass and statuary. Then on to the Tour St-Nazaire with a view north of the Montagne Noire, where the route now leads.

① *From the middle of Carcassonne, follow the signs for Mazamet; this can be confusing and difficult in the heavy traffic. There is one rather inconspicuously marked junction soon after leaving the central square, at the end of a short stretch of road flanked by plane trees: be sure to continue straight on, soon turning right.*

Canal du Midi

The road out of Carcassonne follows for a short, rather impressive stretch the banks of the Canal du Midi. Of France's network of inland waterways, this is perhaps the loveliest and certainly the most popular for an idle floating holiday, though it is still very much a working canal. Stretching from the river Garonne near Toulouse to the Mediterranean at Sète, this engineering feat was begun in 1666 and completed a few years later by Paul Riquet, Baron de Bonrepos.

After crossing the canal the road soon ② *turns sharp right. In about one km be ready for* ③ *the right turn on to the D620 signposted Caunes-Minervois.*

④ *Turn left signposted Villeneuve-Minervois on to the D112. If you happen to miss this turning take the next left - the D111.*

⑤ *In Villeneuve-Minervois follow signs for the Pic de Nore.*

Villeneuve-Minervois - Cabrespine

The route climbs into the Montagne Noire, following the Clamoux gorge towards the range's highest point, the Pic de Nore. At first the road runs along the bottom of the gorge, cultivated first by allotments and then vineyards, planted wherever there is space. Then as the gorge deepens, the road climbs upwards high above its rocky sides.

The Canal du Midi, which can be seen at Carcassonne.

Auberge du Roc de L'Aigle
(restaurant, Cabrespine)

One of those out-of-the-way country restaurants which can produce delightful surprises when one is least expecting them. Service is prompt and willing and the *patron*'s food, though simple, shows imagination - *mousselines* of fish, good chicken dishes, fresh crayfish. Eat for preference on the pleasant terrace overlooking the street. *Tel 68.26.16.61; closed Sun evening and Mon; price band B.*

Cabrespine - Pic de Nore

Though the road is comfortable, with little traffic, driving becomes increasingly slow round the many hairpin bends, while the scenery becomes increasingly dramatic. Lining the road are sweet chestnuts (*châtaignier*), magnificent when in summer flower. Towards the top the landscape flattens out and suddenly one is on a country lane among corn fields.

At Pradelles-Cabardès there is a filling station, and splendid views. *Follow signs for Pic de Nore in the village;* they warn that the road can be snowbound in winter.

Pic de Nore

The *Pic* itself is hardly a pretty sight: its huge television aerial looks like a rocket ready for launch, but the views (orientation table) to south, east and west are impressive.

Pic de Nore ⑥ *From the Pic de Nore follow signs for Mazamet. In about 5 km, where*
- Mazamet *the road divides, bear left.* The route now descends the humid northern
slopes of the Montagne Noire which, in marked contrast to the
Mediterranean side, are thickly wooded with spruce, fir, beech and
oak. Towards Mazamet, which has a large textile industry, forest gives
way to factories, making a rather grim and malodorous descent.

⑦ *Turn left signposted Mazamet. Follow the D54 into suburbs and*
⑧ *at the main road turn left (Avenue Georges Guynemer). Staying on the*
main road, which bears round to the left and becomes the D118, follow
signs for Carcassonne.

Mazamet - The suburbs of Mazamet are soon left behind and the scenery
Mas- recovers; soon after leaving the town there is a viewpoint on the left of
Cabardès the road overlooking Hautpoul to the south and Mazamet to the north.
Further on, a turning to the right leads to the Lac des Montagnés, a
reservoir where you can fish and picnic.
⑨ *Just outside Les Martys turn left signposted Miraval-Cabardès on the*
D101. The route now descends through the picturesque Cabardès
region which is dotted with ruined reminders of medieval times. A
sensational road follows the Orbiel river through a narrow gorge;
though the landscape is small scale, it is punctuated by dramatic rocky
outcrops and sharp hairpin bends. At Miraval-Cabardès are the remains
of its château, associated in the 13thC with a famous troubadour,
Ramon de Miraval - Languedoc was the land of the wandering poet
and musician troubadours. After Miraval-Cabardès, notice on the right
the ruins of the 16thC church of St-Pierre-de-Vals.

Mas- You pass a huge 16thC stone crucifix, standing at a vantage point above
Cabardès the road, and a tiny bar/café on the river.
    For an amusing diversion, especially for those with children, and the
wherewithal for a deliciously fresh meal, *turn right 0.9 km outside Mas-*
Cabardès signposted Pisciculture. Here you can fish your own trout from
storage pools (the owner will do it for you if you are short of time,
though with worm and float it does not take long). You pay for those
you take; live crayfish also on sale.

Lastours As the road approaches the village of Lastours, the stark ruins of the
Châteaux de Lastours come into view high above. If you want to visit
them on foot there is parking on the right, and a path which leads up
(allow about three quarters of an hour in all). The four châteaux,
looking barbarous in their wild setting on a huge rock pedestal, made
up Cabaret, a 12thC Cathar fortress which held out against the attacks
of Simon de Montfort until 1211, the year after the fall of Minerve (see
Route Two), but then bloodily capitulated. Pierre-Roger de Cabaret
only surrendered after an agreement on territories had been struck.
⑩ *About 1.75 km beyond Lastours turn left over a bridge, signposted*

Villeneuve-Minervois, and in 1.5 km turn left on to the D511. Follow signs for the Grottes de Limousis.

Grottes de Limoussis
From the first chamber of this deep limestone cave the calcified formations are impressive, and as you penetrate further and further they become increasingly interesting - delicate crystalline structures as well as stalagmites and stalactites. The party is led from chamber to chamber, cleverly lit, via narrow defiles, finally arriving at a darkened cavern. When the lights are thrown on they reveal the cave's *pièce de résistance... By guided tour, daily June-Oct, Sun and national hols Oct-June.*

(11) *To complete the route, retrace to the D511 and return to the D620 (Carcassonne road) via the D172 and Villeneuve-Minervois.*

ROUTE TWO: 50 KM

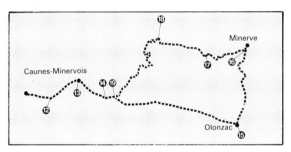

If joining Route Two from Carcassonne, follow directions 1, 2 and 3. Once on the D620 continue straight on for Caunes-Minervois.
If joining Route Two from Route One, leave Villeneuve-Minervois on the D111 and (12) at the D620 turn left.

Caunes-Minervois
Like many villages in these parts, Caunes presents a rather blank face to through traffic, but if you stop and wander around you will find some rather fine 16th and 17thC houses and a Benedictine abbey.

Hotel d'Alibert
(restaurant, Caunes-Minervois
Popular with the few local tourists since there is a dirth of restaurants in the neighbourhood, the Alibert can be relied upon for adequate if unexciting cooking - *pâté maison, charcuterie, pintade* (Guinea-fowl), *côte d'agneau* and so forth. If you visit the restaurant, be sure to step out into the Renaissance courtyard at the rear - like suddenly being transferred to 16thC Italy. *Tel 68.78.00.54; closed 24 Dec-1 Mar, Sun evening and Mon out of season; price bands A/B.*
(13) *Continue straight through Caunes, following signs for Trausse. Outside Caunes, detour if you wish by following the sign on the left to Notre Dame du Cros, a chapel of pilgrimage in a picturesque setting.*

Caunes-
Minervois -
Olonzac

⑭ *At the entrance to the village of Trausse, fork right on to the village bypass road and soon follow signs for Pépieux and Olonzac.* The route now heads into the heart of Minervois wine country. This important wine producing region is a pocket within Languedoc-Roussillon, a prime source of the everyday wines of France, mostly without character or

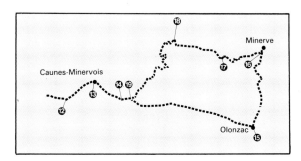

quality. Minervois also produces sound light red wines of VDQS quality, as well as some rosé and white. *Vente direct* factory sales counters abound in these parts; you need to take your own bottles to be filled. The *vente direct* at Peyriac-Minervois, south of Trausse on the D55, is excellent: reds, whites and a good rosé on sale.

The road to Olonzac runs through a broad flat-soled vale which is a sea of vines. To the left, the hills adjacent to the Montagne Noire, to the right, the distant foothills of the Pyrenees.

Olonzac

A pleasant little town, in the midst of the Minervois wine industry and a useful stopping point for the bank or post office, buying film, stocking up for a picnic, or filling the tank. There is a small archaeological museum. The Caves du Minervois (signposted on the right as you approach the middle of the town) offers a cross-section of local wines. ⑮ *From the middle of town retrace to the Caves du Minervois (ie heading west); continue 30 metres and take the right turn signposted Minerve and Azilanet (junction also marked by a conspicuous Auto Ecole sign). Note: the signpost at this junction is difficult to spot if approaching from the east.* Thereafter keep following signs to Minerve through increasingly spectacular scenery with frequent opportunities for picnic stops.

Minerve

Leave your car in the roadside parking area and cross over the bridge to Minerve by foot. This is a remarkable place, built on a spur in the Cesse gorge at the point where it meets the Briant gorge, and just before the Cesse disappears underground for some 20 km. On the far side of the spur, two tunnels have been dug by the Cesse out of the riverbed; in summer, when the riverbed is dry, you can walk to them.

Minerve itself has never forgotten the horrific events of 1210 when Simon de Montfort laid siege for seven weeks to this fortified Cathar

Minerve: mellow stone belying a turbulent history.

stronghold. Using a fearsome catapult sited on the far side of the gorge (there may be a replica there for you to see) he succeeded in destroying the town's only water supply and burned alive more than a hundred '*parfait*' men and women who preferred to die rather than renounce their faith.

As well as a little museum of archaeology, and the ruins of its fortress, Minerve also boasts the oldest altar in Gaul, dating from 456, in its little church.

Relais Chanto-vent
(restaurant, Minerve)

After a stroll round the ramparts and down the narrow Rue des Martyrs you could have a drink and a snack at the bar/café (plenty of seats oustide) where you may also make use of the swimming pool. Alternatively, try a simple but hearty lunch at the Chantovent (may be crowded and noisy in summer). *Tel 68.91.14.18; closes Jan to mid-Mar, Sun evening and Mon except July-Aug; price bands A/B; rooms to let.*

Minerve - Fauzan

⑯ *Returning to the car, head down what looks like a road back into town: it leads off downhill, just by the bridge. At the bottom stay with the main road, ignoring a turning to the right. The road climbs a hill; in about 0.5 km, at a junction, follow the signpost for Fauzan straight ahead. At the junction with the D182, turn right for Fauzan.* A marvellous drive, this, following the Cesse gorge through the rugged landscape.
⑰ *In Fauzan follow signs for St Julien des Molières.* The road now offers distant views over the plain below. Driving it at night, with the lights of villages twinkling beneath, is almost like flying.

⑱ *In St Julien des Molières follow signs for Félines-Minervois, and from Félines follow signs for Trausse.* ⑲ *Turn right for Trausse and continue to Caunes-Minervois returning to Carcassonne on the D620.*

Pottok *pony.*

This single loop is in the lesser-known part of the Basque country, the inland provinces of Basse Navarre and Soule. The coastal province of Labourd, which includes Biarritz, Bayonne and St-Jean-de-Luz, is jam-packed for much of the year.

The drive offers something for everybody. You can trace the route of medieval pilgrims on their way to Santiago de Compostela in Spain - it traverses several villages on the tour. Or, setting aside matters spiritual, you could visit one of France's top restaurants, the Hôtel des Pyrénées, in St-Jean-Pied-de-Port.

Then there is natural beauty: the final section of the drive takes in the amazing Gorges de Kakouetta and the heights of the Forêt d'Iraty. You probably will not encounter one of the 20 or so Pyrenean bears that have survived on the French side of the border with Spain, but you do have a fair chance of spotting one or two uncommon birds, including the water pipit and the griffon vulture. In summer, the mountain slopes resound to the delightful tinkle of bells worn by cows (the handsome Blond d'Aquitaine breed), and are dotted with shaggy black-faced sheep (which produce the tasty *fromage de brebis* available from some farms) and stocky *pottok* ponies (which used to be wild, and are depicted in cave paintings).

The Basqueness of the Basques manifests itself in several ways: in their popular and highly spectacular game of *pelote*, their love of festivity and dancing, their (to outsiders) outlandish language and proper names, and their strong sense of national identity and desire to keep themselves to themselves - reflected in a sometimes infuriating lack of signposts - which of course is remedied in the route directions.

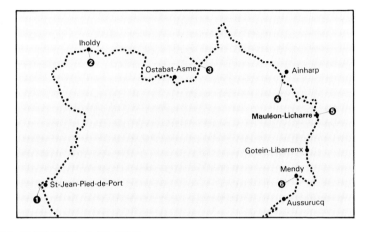

Iholdy ❷

Ostabat-Asme ❸

Ainharp

❹

Mauléon-Licharre ❺

Gotein-Libarrenx

Mendy ❻

St-Jean-Pied-de-Port ❶

Aussurucq

▰ ROUTE: 163 KM

St-Jean-Pied-de-Port

Once an important staging post on the road to Santiago de Compostela, St-Jean-Pied-de-Port is now invaded each summer by a different, less energetic breed of pilgrim. Although a town of only 1,800 inhabitants, it has ample tourist facilities in the form of hotels, restaurants and cafés, and so makes an ideal start for the tour.

Stroll round the tiny old town, or *ville haute*, with its 14thC Gothic church, two gates (Porte Navarre and Porte St-Jacques), and handsome 16-18thC houses built of maroon sandstone (most of these bear the date of construction, plus ornamental details, on the lintel of the front door); climb the 15thC battlements; admire the view from the old bridge over a waterfall and down the backs of the old houses that line the Nive river.

Hôtel des Pyrénées
(hotel-restaurant, St-Jean)

Imagination and simplicity are the hallmarks of Firmin Arrambide's exceptional culinary talents. If you don't take his cheapest menu, which consists of straightforward Basque specialities, you are faced with an *embarras de choix*. Especially good are his jumbo-sized raviolis (which may contain anything from *langoustines* to *cèpe* mushrooms), *pigeon à l'ail confit, rognons de veau aux échalotes confites* (with a touch of orange peel), and superb soufflés and chocolate desserts. Most extraordinary in this class of restaurant is the value for money offered by both the menus and the wine list. *19, Place Général de Gaulle; tel 59.37.01.10; closed 5-28 Jan, 20 Nov-22 Dec, Mon evening Nov-March and Tues 15 Sept-30 June; price bands C/D.*

Pécoïtz,
(hotel-rest., Aincillé)

It is well worth the trouble of driving 7 km out of St-Jean *(on the D933 to St-Jean-le-Vieux, then the D18 and D118 to Aincillé)* in order to enjoy this restaurant's verdant setting, its honest local fare and the friendly welcome of its owners, Jean-Paul and Michèle Pécoïtz. *Tel 59.37.11.88; closed Jan, Feb, and Fri; price band B.*

St-Jean -
Iholdy

① *Take the St-Palais road (D933). As you leave Ispoure, a suburb of St-Jean, turn left on to the D22. Bear left in the first village (no signpost) and continue past the Padera restaurant (signposted) to the junction with the D422. Keep straight on to Irissarry*, a village with typical broad-based Basque houses sporting red-painted shutters and timbers, *then turn right on to the D8 to Iholdy*

Iholdy

The important position of the game of *pelote* in Basque society can be judged from the fact that the *fronton* (the wall against which one version of the game is played) is often located next to a place of worship - as in Iholdy, whose church has an elegant and characteristically Basque open wooden gallery on one side.

Garat
(hotel-rest.,
Iholdy)

This place is an institution: renowned locally for her sharp tongue, deadpan sense of humour and golden heart, Anne-Marie Garat manages single-handedly, and simultaneously, to serve customers both in the bar and in the huge beamed dining room. Each of the five courses on the single menu arrives unannounced eg. excellent soup, *langue sauce piquante*, roast lamb, a mammoth cheese platter including roquefort and *brebis des Pyrénées*, and *katalembroche*, a Basque cake with walnuts that is rarely made nowadays because the process is so long and difficult: it is cooked on a spit in a special wooden contraption. You are expected, by the way, to help yourself to the magnum of *hors d'age* Armagnac that is unceremoniously plonked on your table at the end of the meal. Food is seasonal. *Tel 59.37.61.46; closed Mon and Oct; price band B; rooms available July-Sept.*

Iholdy -
Mauléon-
Licharre

② *Take the St-Palais road out of Iholdy. At the next main junction turn right on to the D508 signposted Ostabat. This road runs between neat drystone walls, then up through heathland to the Col d'Ipharlatze, from which there are great views east and west. Bear right in the next village (Ostabat, no signpost) to the T-junction with the D933. Turn left.*

Haram-
bels
(detour)

About 3.5 km after the left turn on the D933, turn left ③ *for this detour to the tiny hamlet of Harambels which, like St-Jean-Pied-de-Port, lies on one of the main routes to Santiago de Compostela. The present inhabitants of its four houses are direct descendants of the donats who used to offer hospitality to pilgrims.*

Chapelle
St-
Nicolas,
Haram-
bels

An undistinguished building from the outside, it has brightly painted and gilded woodwork and a superb 15thC-16thC reredos within. The chamber above the entrance, reached by a step-ladder, used to be the pilgrims' dormitory. Since the French Revolution, the chapel has belonged to the four families of Harambels, who are responsible for its upkeep; so contributions to the collection box are welcome. *Open 2-5, Mon-Sat; apply to the house with the green shutters.*

Return to the D933 and continue to the junction with the D242 signposted Mauléon. Turn right on to this road, which climbs through pleasant countryside. *About 4 km after Lohitzun-Oyhercq, at the point where good views open up left and right, the D242 seems to continue straight on up the hill; in fact, at a dangerous unmarked crossroads, it turns half right.*

Ainharp
(detour)

④ *This typically Basque village is a 3-km round trip.* It is, like Harambels, on a route to Compostela; its most interesting feature is its church (the pilgrims' dormitory is now occupied by the *mairie*. Both outside, in its well-kept cemetery, and under the shelter of its porch, it has a fine collection of old Basque tombstones, many of them disc-shaped.

Return to the D242, turn left, and wind down to Mauléon-Licharre.

Mauléon-Licharre

Once world capital of the *espadrille* (but now facing severe competition from the Chinese), Mauléon is increasingly turning to tourism: it is conveniently located near the mountains, gorges and fast-flowing rivers of the Haute-Soule area (covered later in the drive). Actually, it is worth exploring parts of Mauléon itself - in particular the old town, with its Chapelle de Nôtre-Dame (note the characteristically Basque three-pronged bell-tower), ruined medieval castle and market place (market: Tues morning). *Pelote basque* is much-played in Mauléon, some of it against the huge *fronton* opposite the Château d'Andurain.

Château d'Andur-ain, Mauléon

Harmoniously proportioned and with several unusual features, over the centuries it has remained in the possession of the De Maytie family, who built it at the end of the 16thC. It is one of the few buildings in France whose roof is covered with wooden tiles (made of chestnut, which resists woodworm); and it is also remarkable for its sculpted doors, fireplaces and *mascarons* - grotesque masks on the walls with a hole in the middle through which a musket could be pointed. *Open 11-12.30, 3-6 July-15 Sept; closed Thur and Sun morning.*

Bidegain
(hotel-restaurant, Mauléon)

Housed in an old building alongside the Château d'Andurain, this cosy hostelry offers, in addition to some charming and tastefully furnished rooms with beamed ceilings, a number of Basque culinary specialities such as *pipérade*, trout in Jurançon wine and *poule au pot*. Other plus points include smiling service and a garden on the Saison river. *13, Rue de la Navarre; tel 59.28.16.05; closed 24-30 Nov, 15 Dec-15 Jan, Fri evening, Sat lunch and Sun evening Sept-June; price bands A/B/C.*

Mauléon - Gotein

⑤ *Leave Mauléon on the Tardets road, the D918.* As you approach Gotein, the massive peaks of the Pyrenees can be seen ahead. *Turn into Gotein.* As at Iholdy, a *fronton* adjoins the church, a recently restored 17thC building with one of the finest three-pronged bell-towers in the

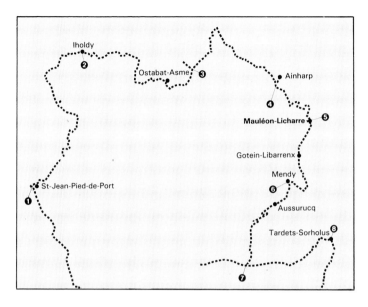

area. As always in the Basque country, the seats in the gallery, which rise in tiers as in a theatre, are reserved for male worshippers. There is a curious statue of the Virgin and Child: the infant Jesus has his index finger stuck in his mouth.

Gotein -
Tardets-
Sorholus

Continue along the D918. Shortly after it converges with the Saison river, turn right on to the V2 and then over the river to Menditte. Here follow the signs to Mendy, forking left near the top of the hill.
⑥ *Turn left at the junction with the D147 for Aussurucq,* which has several old Basque houses. The road (room for improvement) then plunges into the vast Forêt des Arbailles, which consists mainly of beeches interspersed with large boulders and attractive glades. You climb steeply, emerging eventually on to an almost bare hillside near a *cayolar* - a shepherd's hut - the first building since Aussurucq.

Col
Burdin
Olatzé
(detour)

To make this detour, 3.5 km each way, ⑦ *keep straight on up the mountain valley.* The sensuously smooth grassy slopes - and occasionally the road - are dotted with sheep, cows and *pottok* ponies from May to Nov. Park at the next road junction, the Col Burdin Olatzé, and admire the panoramic view over the Pyrenean peaks that run along the border with Spain. The Pic d'Orhy directly to the south is only 12 km away as the crow flies; the Pic d'Anie, to the south-east, rises to 2,504 metres. If you feel energetic you can walk up past the house on the hill to the Fontaine d'Ahusquy, whose waters have medicinal properties.
Returning from the Col, take the road that leads off to the right by the

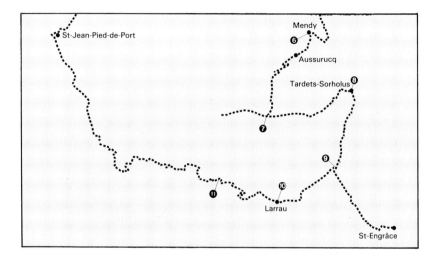

cayolar *and make your way down to Alçay on a sometimes very steep
road, not marked on map. At a fork by a house signposted Tardets both
ways, bear right, then, by a* fronton, *turn right and keep straight on down
to the T-junction with the D247. Turn left for Tardets.*

**Tardets-
Sorholus**

This *bastide* (fortified village) founded in 1280 holds a celebrated festival
of Basque dancing and *pelote* on the *Sat, Sun, Mon and Tues following
the public holiday of 15 Aug.* At this point, check your fuel gauge: there
are no filling stations between Tardets and Chalets d'Iraty.
⑧ *Take the Oloron road out of Tardets, shortly forking right on to the
D26 to Larrau. After an enjoyable 8.5-km stretch beside the Saison, you
reach the turn-off to Ste-Engrâce, which you take if you wish to make
the following highly recommended detour.*

**Uhaytza
Valley**
(detour)

This is quite a long detour - 22 km there and back - but definitely
worth it. ⑨ *Climb the narrow D113 past the sign to Gorges de
Kakouetta (which you can visit on the way back) and continue up the
valley of the Uhaytza. Soon Ste-Engrâce is seen set against the dead end of
the valley. There is a huge cleft in the mountain side to the right - the
beginning of the Gorges d'Ehujarré.*

**Ste-
Engrâce**

Keep straight on through the hamlet to its asymmetrical church,
formerly the chapel of an abbey founded in the 11thC. This is one of
the few Romanesque buildings in the Basque country not to have been
tampered with. In the choir behind the 14thC wrought-iron grille there
is a 17thC reredos depicting the life and martyrdom of Ste-Engrâce in
the 3rdC. But the most interesting feature is the series of lively, and in
one case erotic, painted and sculpted capitals.

Gorges de Kakouetta.

Gorges de Kakouetta

On no account miss these justly celebrated gorges. The river waters have sliced an incredibly thin wedge out of the soft limestone mountain: at some points the defile is only 3 metres across and more than 200 metres deep. As you follow the riverside path into the ever-narrower, darker and gustier cleft, whose walls are covered with rare mosses, ferns and lilies, you feel something like a Rider Haggard hero being led to a lost kingdom. At the end of the negotiable part of the gorges, there is a sinister cave, a waterfall that shoots straight out of the cliff face (it is in fact a resurgence) and some thoughtfully provided picnic tables. Although there are handrails, planking and numerous little bridges over the stream, it is advisable to wear non-slip shoes. *Open 8 until dusk, Easter-Oct; apply for tickets at the café by the entrance. Continue on the D26 to Larrau.*

Etchemaité
(hotel-restaurant, Larrau)

This is a useful place for an overnight stop before tackling the highlands and the Forêt d'Iraty when they are at their best (ie in the morning). The cuisine is simple and relies on local produce such as trout and tasty moutonnet (eight-month-old lamb). *Tel 59.28.61.45; price bands B/C.*
⑩ *Leave Larrau on the D19.* This starts as a leafy road beside a rushing stream, but in just 8 km climbs to 800 metres to the Col Bagarguiac, revealing the Pic d'Orhy in all its splendour.
⑪ *Turn left at the Col,* past a chalet that calls itself a *centre commercial* (you are in part of the Châlets d'Iraty ski resort), and drive down through stately beech forest to a lake. *Turn left on to the D18 signposted St-Jean-Pied-de-Port.* This good, if narrow road tends to be strewn with rock fragments, so take care. It runs along a mountain ridge, with breathtaking views in every direction, before plunging down through Estérençuby to St-Jean-Pied-de-Port.

East Pyrenees

Like many border areas, the part of France covered by this tour has had a troubled history of invasion (by Arabs and Spaniards) and internecine warfare (between the Albigensians and the Roman Catholic church). This is reflected with extraordinary vividness in its architecture: the castles of Peyrepertuse and Quéribus, like the abbey of St-Martin-du-Canigou, are located in almost absurdly inaccessible spots, and churches often resemble fortresses, with arrow slits instead of windows, letting in little light.

Today the only invaders are tourists, which is why July and August are months to be avoided, unless you want to attend the celebrated Pablo Casals Music Festival in Prades. Visitors are drawn to the area by its exceptionally balmy climate, summed up by the local saying: "If it's cloudy here it must be raining elsewhere."

The climate can be explained by the region's geography. The two big valleys included in this tour, which roughly correspond to the areas known as the Haut-Conflent and the Fenouillèdes, run in almost straight lines from east to west, and are thus protected from the north wind. The warm waters of the Mediterranean have more influence on the climate than the Pyrenees.

The startling proximity of those peaks is another major attraction of this tour. On a clear day, the Mont Canigou is visible from almost any viewpoint. Sometimes it just peeps over the horizon, at other times it seems to fill the whole sky - as from the village of Eus which is only 14 km as the crow flies from the mountain's summit.

ROUTE ONE: 87 KM

Sournia

Sournia is a large, sleepy and unspoilt village set among vines and *maquis* in the rocky uplands between the Fenouillèdes and the Haut-Conflent. Although it springs to life in summer when its camp site and *gîtes* are filled, it has hardly been affected by tourism. Sournia has no hotel (though it does have a filling station).

Auberge de Sournia *(restaurant)*

The Auberge is an oasis in an otherwise gastronomic desert. Try their delicious *feuilleté* of goat cheese with a tomato *coulis* and fresh basil, pork in a sauce of almonds, cream and Roquefort, and a not oversweet honey and hazelnut cake. The décor is resolutely rustic. *Tel 68.97.72.82; closed Sun and Mon out of season; price band A.*

Chapelle St-Michel *(detour)*

(1) *For this short detour, take the D2 out of Sournia and turn left on the edge of the village to the 10thC Chapelle St-Michel, forking left soon afterwards away from Le Puch.*

After one km, park by the signpost to the chapel. A three-minute walk up a narrow path through woodland will bring you to the building, whose ruins are in the care of the *Monuments Historiques.*

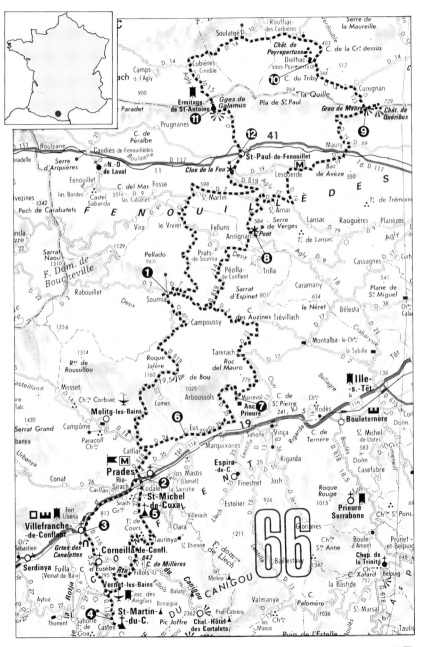

Capitals in the church of St-Jacques, Villefranche-de-Conflent.

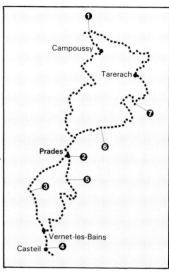

Sournia - Campoussy

Return to Sournia and take the D619 towards Prades. It wends its way up and up an increasingly desolate and chaotic landscape of boulders and scrub. *Turn left shortly on to the D67 to the hamlet of Campoussy,* whose tiny square is dominated by a large central lime tree. From behind the church there is a staggering view to the east over the whiter than white Roc Blanc, the Corbières mountain range and the sea.

Campoussy - Prades

Continue out of Campoussy and rejoin the D619. About 4 km later, there is a well-preserved dolmen a stone's throw from the road (signposted). The incisions on it are thought to represent wild boar. After passing the Roc Cornu (a huge boulder doing a balancing act on another one) and driving through landscape that looks increasingly like that of the Wild West, you will see down below to your left an exceptionally large menhir, about 6 metres tall, known as the Pierre Droite (signposted). Unfortunately it is not very accessible.

At the Col de Roque Jalère, the pass that leads over into the valley of the River Têt and the Haut-Conflent, the colossal Mont Canigou and its sister peaks heave into view with breath-taking suddenness. Prades, below, seems close - but this is an illusion, for the D619 takes its time to zigzag down the mountainside.

Prades

The geography of this part of the Pyrenees means that all traffic from Perpignan to Font-Romeu and Andorra takes the bypass around the little Catalan town of Prades - it used to go through the middle. Its straightforward one-way system is, however, well signposted.

traffic; its pink marble paving stones come from local quarries. On one side is the church of St-Pierre, whose 12thC bell tower is a typical example of the local Romanesque style. Its dark, Spanish interior contains a striking baroque reredos. Prades' main claim to fame is its Pablo Casals Music Festival, started by the renowned cellist in the 1950s. It is held from 24 July to 15 Aug in the nearby abbey of St-Michel-de-Cuxa (see below).

L'Etape
(restaurant, Prades)

The best place to eat in Prades is a *Restaurant Routiers*, L'Etape, near the bus station on the N116, which takes plenty of trouble over local specialities (not easy to find in the area). *Tel 98.96.53.38; closed Wed, 15 days in winter and 15 days in June; price bands A/B.*

Prades - Ville-franche-de-Conflent

② *Leave Prades on the N116 in the direction of Font-Romeu.* Soon you will see what appears to be a large castle ahead of you: this is the fortified 'town' (it is minuscule) of Villefranche-de-Conflent, once the area's capital. Park the car outside the walls.

It is well worth visiting the 11th-17thC ramparts *(open June-Sept 9-7, Oct, May 10-12, 2-6; rest of the year, telephone 68.96.10.78).* Protected by the ramparts is a maze of quiet streets with medieval houses and the church of St-Jacques, which has two remarkable 11thC marble portals (interesting capitals), and a powerful recumbent Christ.

Hôtel Vauban, Villefranche

This peaceful, spotless inn, opposite St-Jacques, offers a tempting alternative to hostelries in the tourist hub of Vernet-les-Bains or Prades. Booking advised; *5 place de l'Eglise; tel 68.96.18.03; price band B.*

Les Grandes Canal-ettes

③ *Take the D116 towards Vernet-les-Bains.* Soon you will see the sign for the Grandes Canalettes (and car park) on the right. The white concretions in these caves are remarkable. *Guided tours hourly 10-6 May-Oct, and 2-5 Sun Nov-Apr.*

Corneilla-de-Conflent

Continuing along the D116, turn left for the church when you arrive in Corneilla-de-Conflent. This fascinating Romanesque church, which is being extensively restored, contains some superb works of art: an entombment (a group of five 15thC painted statues), a vivid sculpted reredos made of Carrara marble, a 13thC Spanish chest of drawers, a fine marble portal with a sculpted tympanum, and some interesting windows bordered both inside and outside by four small columns with capitals. *Guided tour by M. Perez (house adjoining church) 3-6 or at other times by appointment - tel 68.05.60.64.* The tour is free, but a small contribution to the restoration fund is welcome.

Vernet-les-Bains

A small spa town (speciality: ear, nose and throat) with little to offer except its quaint old quarter, and a congenial position.

St-Martin-du-Canigou
(detour)

④ *The detour to this extraordinary abbey involves a return journey of 5 km, plus a strenuous 50-minute walk each way. Take the D116 to Casteil. Parking may be difficult, so keep going right into the village, then turn right up the C2 signposted Col de Jou, where there should be room by the roadside.* Those who relish a really steep walk up a cool valley with a spectacular view of the abbey from below should continue on foot up the C2, bearing left and left again. If you prefer the easier climb, follow signs to the Abbaye from the middle of Casteil.

The original building, started in the 9thC, was perched on its mountain eyrie, 364 metres above Casteil, in order to be invisible to invaders. When it grew into a monastery in the 11thC, its original chapel became a crypt and the present church was built on top of it. Although the abbey was comprehensively restored at the beginning of this century (when it was little more than a ruin), its stark architecture, unusual pagan motifs and unique lofty position give it an undeniable magnetism. *Open daily, 10-12, 2-5.*

Bell tower, St-Martin-du-Canigou.

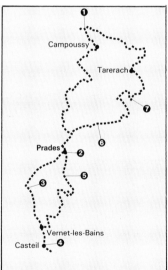

Vernet - St-Michel

Leave Vernet by the D27, which winds its way through a valley of conifers, chestnut trees and alders. Prades can be seen laid out far below.

St-Michel-de-Cuxa

Much of this abbey, too, where the concerts of the Prades music festival are held, had to be rebuilt (half the capitals of its original cloisters found their way to America). The main church is one of the very few extant examples of Mozarabic architecture in France. *Open 9.30-11.30, 2.30-6 in summer; 9.30-11.55, 2.30-5 in winter.*

Eus: labyrinth-ine charm, despite development.

St-Michel-de-Cuxa - Eus

⑤ *Continue on the D27 to Prades, get into the one-way system and follow the signs to Molitg-les-Bains. When you get to Catllar, whose church has a curious wrought-iron bell tower, turn right along the D24, and later bear left along the D35 to the hilltop village of Eus.*

Eus

On the outskirts of Eus, fork left to the car park (you cannot drive into the village itself). Although undergoing an inevitable process of gentrification (quite pricey restaurants and a growing number of arts and crafts shops) its labyrinth of little streets and alleys has great charm, and there is a magnificent view of Mont Canigou.

Eus - Marcevol

⑥ *Return to the D35 and continue in the direction of Marquixanes; the road coasts along the orchard-filled valley of the Têt (take care when crossing the narrow little bridges over streams flowing into the river). Ignore the turning on the right to Marquixanes and keep on the D35 as it climbs the almost vertical-sided Ravin de la Combe Perdrix, passes the village of Arboussols and takes you to Marcevol.*

Marcevol

As you approach this hamlet, whose Lilliputian houses huddle out of sight as though still fearing invaders from the south, you pass a peaceful, ruined 12thC priory with a well-proportioned pink-marble porch.

Marcevol - Sournia

⑦ *Continue on the D35. At the various T-junctions, follow the signs to Tarerach and then to Sournia on the D13, D2 and D619. This last stretch along the Desix valley is a pleasant, easy drive, with fleeting views up side valleys. It offers a delightfully secluded waterside picnic spot by the ruined chapel of Ste-Félicité: about 1½ km after joining the D619, park near a weather-beaten sign to the chapel on the left, and walk down the track to the chapel; just beyond it, the River Desix forms a pool in the shade of the trees.*

■ ROUTE TWO: 91 KM

Vineyards near Ansignan.

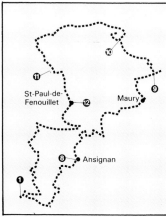

St-Paul-de-Fenouillet

Maury

Ansignan

Sournia - Ansignan

Take the St-Paul-de-Fenouillet road out of Sournia and fork right immediately along the D619. This road will take you all the way to Ansignan along the valley of the Desix.

Société Coopér-ative Agricole d'Ansig-nan

The most important feature of Ansignan, apart from an obtrusive water tower, is its Société Coopérative Agricole *(turn left in the middle of the village),* which sells excellent red and rosé Côtes du Roussillon and an aromatic white Côtes d'Agly at unbeatable prices; there is also a spicy, far from ordinary *vin ordinaire,* suitable for picnics. *Tel 68.59.00.89; open daily 10-12 and 2-5.*

Ansignan - Maury

⑧ *Beyond Ansignan, the D619 goes through a narrow fractured gorge, which shows patches of the pink marble used in so many buildings in the area. Turn right over a bridge on to the D77 to St-Arnac and straight through the village in the direction of Lansac.* There are views of neighbouring peaks in every direction. *Before reaching Lansac turn left on to the D79 signposted Maury. At the junction with the D19, turn right.* The flattish landscape here is subject to fierce winds, hence the dense rows of cypresses acting as windbreaks to the vineyards.

Further on there is a superb view across the Maury valley, which is dotted with curious dome-shaped hillocks and overlooked by the jagged white ridge of the Grau de Maury. At the top of the ridge, the clean-cut outline of Château de Quéribus can be made out against the sky.

Maury - Château de Quéribus

Turn right in Maury (whose only claim to fame is its pleasant eponymous fortified wine), *then shortly turn left along the D19, passing a boule playing area shaded by plane trees. Follow the signs to Cucugnan.* The road climbs straight up the flank of the mountain.

Château de Québirus (detour)

⑨ *At the top of the pass, turn right for a 1½ km detour to the Château de Québirus,* the last of the Albigensians' hilltop castles in the region to fall to the crusaders in 1255. Superb views. *Open daily Apr-Sept, Sun and holidays Oct-Mar, 9.30-12.30 and 2.30-7.*

Château de Québirus - Cucugnan

As you drive down the D123, you can see Cucugnan, the pleasant little village immortalized in Alphonse Daudet's *Lettres de Mon Moulin,* nestling in the valley below, with the vast and rugged forests of the Corbières stretching out behind it. To the left, you will spot another Albigensian stronghold, the Château de Peyrepertuse - if you know what to look for since from this distance it is virtually indistinguishable from a rocky crag. *Turn right into Cucugnan at the junction with the D14.*

Auberge de Cucugnan (restaurant)

This well-known restaurant (not to be confused with a newcomer to Cucugnan, the Auberge du Vigneron) is housed in a former barn that is partly hollowed out of the rock. It serves unchanging menus of straightforward local dishes with local wine at reasonable prices. *Tel 68.45.40.84; closed 1-15 Sept and Wed from Jan to Mar; price band B.*
  On leaving Cucugnan, take the D14 towards Duilhac; as you come into the village turn left ⑩ *up the road signposted to Château de Peyrepertuse.*

Cucugnan - Château de Peyrepertuse (detour)

This 7-km return journey really is worthwhile. The fortress, a colossal construction, strung out along a high mountain ridge, looks like a rocky excrescence rather than the work of man until you are right upon it. *Open at all times.*

Château de Peyrepertuse - Gorges de Galamus

Return to the D14 and continue through the narrow streets of Duilhac, following the arrows on the road, then turn left out of the village. From here there is a view of the Château de Peyrepertuse, which from this side looks much more like a castle. *After driving through Soulatgé and Cubières-sur-Cinoble, turn left on to the D10.*

Gorges de Galamus

⑪ The D10 seems to be going straight into the hillside, but amazingly it follows the River Agly, which has sliced a passage through the rock. The road, which winds its way timidly beneath overhanging cliffs, is so narrow that it is impossible to park. *Drive through to the exit on the far side, where there is a car park,* and explore the gorges on foot.
  Continue down into St-Paul-de-Fenouillet, turning right at the rail crossing. ⑫ *In St-Paul-de-Fenouillet, go straight over the traffic lights in the direction of Sournia.* You soon come to the Clue de la Fou, a perpetually windswept gap cut through the rocky ridge by the Agly. *Turn right over the bridge, then fork right immediately along the D7 in the direction of Prats-de-Sournia.*
  As you continue on the D7, *ignoring the turning to Fosse,* you can briefly glimpse to the right the massive, sinister mountain of Pech de Carabatets. *Turn left at T-junction into Le Vivier, bear left in the village, and keep going on the D7 via unsightly Prats-de-Sournia to Sournia.*

Index

Includes: towns, villages and hamlets given a substantial mention; major, identified châteaux and manors; notable landmarks, viewpoints, cols, defiles, rivers, gorges and valleys.

Acknowledgements

Picture Credits
Stephen Brough 31, 35, 40, 45, 49, 53, 55, 60, 63; **Andrew Duncan** 212; **John Farndon** 1, 15;
Fotobank Cover, 144; **Leslie and Adrian Gardiner** 74, 78, 94, 101, 113, 127, 129; **Chris Gill**
135, 137, 143; **Peter Graham** 148, 152, 183, 185, 188, 190, 198, 201, 248, 250, 251, 252; **Susan
Griggs Photo Library** 26, 106, 233; **Robert Harding Photo Library** 158, 237; **Richard Platt** 107.

Editorial and Design
Copy editing **Gilly Abrahams**; proof reader **Linda Hart**; editorial assistance and index **Rosemary
Dawe**; art editor **Mel Petersen**; designer **Lynn Hector**; illustrations **Mike McGuiness**. Our thanks
also to **Lucinda Cookson** and **MJG**, without whom this book could not have
been written.